Toward a feminist future for our children:

Paul Shih-mien Tong,
John Joseph Tong,
Sonya Kourany Sterba.

Table of Contents

Postmodern Feminism

Ecological Feminism

Toward Multicultural Feminism

Toward Gender-Inclusive Feminism: Men's Responses to Feminism

Preface

This anthology is designed to be a basic text for a first course in feminist philosophy or a first course in women's studies. Part I deals with a broad range of the most significant problems confronting women today. It deals with them from perspectives as diverse as those of the psychologist, sociologist, and economist on the one hand, and those of the philosopher, poet, and children's story writer on the other. Part II presents some of the most promising theoretical frameworks thus far proposed to explain and resolve these problems. No other anthology combines so extensive and detailed a treatment of the problems confronting women today with the most current theoretical and practical means for resolving them.

A number of changes have been made in this second edition. Part I has been updated throughout, with new readings on such topics as date rape, sexual harassment, and the new reproductive technologies. In all, fifteen new or revised readings have been added here. Part II has been revised to make it more accessible and more relevant to today's students. In addition, sections have been added on cultural feminism, ecological feminism, and men's responses to feminism (to move us toward gender-inclusive feminism). In all, eleven new readings have been added here. The result is a more comprehensive, more interesting, more useful text.

Many people have offered helpful suggestions for this second edition. Foremost among them are: Natalie Dandekar, University of Rhode Island; Laura Duhan Kaplan, University of North Carolina at Charlotte; Marilyn Fischer, University of Dayton; Leah R. Jacobs, University of Oregon; David Wisdo, Susquehanna University who served as reviewers for Prentice Hall and my student, Megan Greene. Their suggestions proved invaluable as we worked to select the most appropriate articles for our readers. Particular thanks also go to Karita France, the Philosophy Editor at Prentice Hall, and Elaine Lynch, our Production Editor. Together they offered extraordinary patience and good cheer, meticulous attention to detail, and an uncanny ability to keep us on schedule.

Janet A. Kourany

James P. Sterba

Rosemarie Tong

Introduction
to Feminist Philosophies

Feminism. For many women as well as men this term evokes an image of strident, unattractive women angrily demanding the abandonment of the family, the desertion of husbands, the killing of fetuses, or perhaps just the burning of bras. However, this picture of feminism grossly misrepresents its real nature and significance. To be sure, feminists sometimes have controversial ideas about the family, sexual relations, the mother-child relationship, and the female body, but these controversial ideas are far less "radical" than the public has been led to believe. One of the central aims of this anthology is to provide a vision of feminism that communicates its positions accurately.

In contrast to media misrepresentations of feminists as look-alike women cut from the same ideological cloth, feminists differ, one from the other, in a variety of ways. Feminists come from all types of religious, educational, ethnic, racial, and class backgrounds; they are of different ages, body sizes, and sexual orientations; and they include men as well as women. Yet, although no single profile of the "typical feminist" exists, feminists do have some things in common: a firm commitment to gender equality, a painful awareness that such equality is far from achieved, and a continuing desire to work toward such equality. In the past feminists pressed for such social transformations as the abolition of slavery, the inauguration of universal suffrage, free public education, affordable health care, accessible birth-control clinics, and improved working conditions for women and children. More re-

cently feminists have sought the passage of the Equal Rights Amendment, quality child care facilities, equal pay for equal work (or work of comparable worth), reproductive rights, and an end to sexual violence against women (rape, pornography, sexual harassment, wife beating, and the like).

The fact that feminists have generally pursued such goals does not mean that each individual feminist has pursued them with equal conviction. Feminists disagree about many matters, including the original causes of gender inequality, the factors that continue to perpetuate it, and the actions that should be taken to end it. That feminists should disagree even about these fundamental matters should not surprise us, however. After all, any feminist who seeks to understand the present condition of women requires knowledge from such diverse fields as biology, psychology, anthropology, sociology, political science, economics, history, religion, and philosophy—knowledge that is oftentimes confusing and complex, and sometimes unavailable and unreliable. Small wonder, then, that feminists are greatly challenged by the problems that routinely confront women.

In this anthology we provide several descriptive accounts of problems confronting women together with a variety of feminist theories that address them. Because both the descriptive accounts and the theories are partial and provisional in nature, it is vital that we neither accept nor reject them at face value. Indeed, with respect to each of the descriptive accounts in Part I, we should ask ourselves some serious questions:

1. Does the account portray a pressing and present problem for women, or a pseudo or past problem that no longer exists?
2. What evidence does, or can, the author offer to support her or his account?
3. How are the problems that the author analyzes related to each other, and which seem the most important?
4. Do the authors gloss over or omit problems of equal or greater significance? If so, what are these larger problems?
5. Do the authors pay adequate attention to issues related to racism, classism, homophobia, ageism, and ableism?
6. Do our experiences confirm the authors' accounts, or is there an enormous gap between their thoughts and our experiences?

With respect to each of the theories in Part II, we should also ask some serious questions:

1. How well does each theory explain women's problems? How convincing is it?

2. How sound and complete is the evidence that the theory provides for its claims? (This evidence can be abstract or concrete, general or specific, biological, psychological, anthropological, sociological, political, economic, historical, religious, and/or philosophical.)
3. How useful is the theory? Does it provide concrete strategies for dealing with women's concerns? If these strategies have been tried, have they worked? Why or why not? If they have not been tried, do they seem promising? Why or why not?
4. Does the theory adequately account for women's differences as well as similarities?
5. From whose vantage point or perspective is the theory constructed?

No doubt readers will have some of their own questions about the descriptive accounts and theories we have selected for this anthology. We encourage readers to reflect upon their own questions and to answer them to their satisfaction. Indeed, we view our readers as our co-authors, seeking with us a better understanding of what makes a philosophy truly "feminist."

Part One
BEING A WOMAN: PROBLEMS OF GENDER INEQUALITY

Sex-Role Socialization

In our society men are thought to be independent, aggressive, competitive, rational, and physically strong, while women are thought to be passive, nurturant, cooperative, emotional, and physically weak. These masculine and feminine gender characteristics are distinct from male and female sex characteristics. The fact that masculine and feminine gender characteristics vary not only in different cultures but also in our own culture provides some evidence that biological sex has little, if anything, to do with social gender. Studies of hermaphrodite babies, whose sex is difficult to determine at birth, also provide some evidence that sex and gender are separable phenomena. When hermaphrodite babies are assigned to the "wrong" sex—that is, when they are reared as girls when they are really boys, or vice versa—they cultivate the gender identities, traits, and behaviors associated with this "wrong" sex.

Whether gender is able to keep biological sex at bay permanently remains controversial, however. Nevertheless, very few people deny that the process by which female and male babies are turned into "feminine" and "masculine" adults is heavily social. Numerous studies show that adults teach children their gender identities in subtle as well as blatant ways. For example, parents send specific gender messages to their children—messages that girls are passive and nurturant and that boys are independent and aggressive. Mothers and fathers convey these messages to their sons and daughters through words and gestures; through the toys and clothes they buy them; and by the rights and responsibilities they give or do not give them.

Consider, for example, the astronaut or superman pajamas that boys wear versus the dainty, ruffled nighties that girls wear, or the floral arrangements and pastel bedspreads in girls' rooms versus the military motifs and sports pennants in boys' rooms. These parental messages are reinforced by teachers and peers, who have their own strong ideas about how girls and boys should think, talk, and act. Clearly, society deliberately channels girls and boys in different directions, oftentimes irrespective of their individual needs, abilities, and interests. This channeling process promotes a sex-segregation that denies children of both sexes valuable opportunities to sample one another's interests and activities. As a result, children and adolescents tend to be far more comfortable in same-sex groups than in mixed-sex groups—a feeling that many children and adolescents carry with them, as adults, into the public realm.

That gender socialization psychologically and socially underdevelops boys and girls in certain areas is undeniable, but according to Claire Renzetti and Daniel Curran (authors of "Gender Socialization") these developmental distortions limit girls even more than they do boys. After all, "feminine" characteristics such as passivity and physical weakness do seem objectively inferior to "masculine" characteristics such as activity and physical strength. Moreover, society still tends to regard certain arguably *good* "feminine" characteristics (for example, cooperativeness) as somehow inferior to their arguably *bad* "masculine" counterparts (for example, competitiveness,) and as somehow inappropriate for persons in positions of power to cultivate. As a result, girls tend to have lower career aspirations and expectations for themselves than boys have for themselves.

Would gender-free socialization be better? In "X: A Fabulous Child's Story," novelist Lois Gould relates a tale about a child who is brought up in a gender-free way—as an X. The story describes the ways in which society pressures boys and girls to conform to its gender roles. It also suggests what it would take and what it would mean for individuals to depart from these gender roles. As Gould sees it, such departures would make for happier, more well-adjusted individuals. But what happens to "gender-free" children when they grow up and their biological sex becomes apparent? How does a person confront fundamental differences after he or she has been instructed that everyone is exactly the same? Gender socialization is debilitating and destructive when it is imposed rigorously and without opportunity for variation, but we may ask whether all acknowledgments and appreciation of difference are necessarily wrong.

Gender Socialization

Claire Renzetti
and
Daniel Curran

Imagine that it is ten years from now. You are married and would like to start a family, but you and your spouse have just been told that you can have only one child. Which would you prefer that child to be: a boy or a girl?

From *Women, Men, and Society*, Third Edition, by Claire M. Renzetti and Daniel J. Curran, pp. 77–80, 90–103, 112–113, 116–126. Copyright © 1995 by Allyn & Bacon. Reprinted by permission of Allyn & Bacon.

If you are like most college students in the United States, you would prefer your only child to be a boy. Indeed, since the 1930s, researchers have documented that Americans in general have a "boy preference." Not only do we prefer boys as only children, but also, in larger families, we prefer sons to outnumber daughters, and we have a strong preference for sons as firstborns. There is some evidence to suggest that this may be weakening a bit in the United States; for instance, several recent studies have reported an increasing tendency for people to express no preference rather than an explicit son or daughter preference. There also appears to be a strong desire among most American couples to have at least one child of each sex. Outside the United States, however, boy preference remains so strong that,

as Box 1 on pages 5–6 shows, in some countries, such as India and China, parents are using technology to choose the sex of their offspring, resulting in a disproportionate ratio of boys to girls.

It appears, then, that children are born into a world that largely prefers boys over girls.

Box 1   Sex Selection

Although research indicates that in the United States and Europe both women and men have a slight preference for sons, there remains in these countries strong disapproval of the use of medical technology, such as ultrasound and amniocentesis, for sex selection. However, in some countries, such as China and India, where son preference is exceptionally strong, recent studies show that such technology is increasingly being used not for diagnostic purposes, but solely to identify the sex of a fetus. In India, for example, there are physicians who specialize only in doing ultrasound tests on pregnant women. In India, as well as China and several other countries, if the fetus is the "wrong" sex— that is, if the fetus is female—the parents frequently opt for an abortion. Kristof (1991:C12) quotes from an article in a Chinese publication in which a man from a rural peasant community states, "Ultrasound is really worthwhile, even though my wife had to go through four abortions to get a son."

As Table 1 shows, in China, India, and a number of other countries, the sex ratio is skewed in favor of males. This has been the case historically. In these countries and

TABLE 1   Estimated Deficits in Female Populations Caused by Excess Female Mortality: Selected Areas, Latest Available Data

COUNTRY OR REGION	RATIO OF MALES TO FEMALES		NUMBER OF FEMALES (MILLIONS)	PERCENT OF FEMALES MISSING[b]	NUMBER OF MISSING FEMALES (MILLIONS)
	ACTUAL RATIO	EXPECTED RATIO[a]			
China, 1990	1.066	1.010	548.7	5.3	29.1
India, 1991	1.077	1.020	406.3	5.6	22.8
Pakistan, 1981	1.105	1.025	40.0	7.8	3.1
Bangladesh, 1981	1.064	1.025	42.2	3.8	1.6
Nepal, 1981	1.050	1.025	7.3	2.4	.2
West Asia, 1985	1.060	1.030	55.0	3.0	1.7
Egypt, 1986	1.047	1.020	23.5	2.6	.6

[a]Based on a model stable population incorporating levels of fertility and mortality prevailing some ten years earlier and assuming 1.059 as the sex ratio at birth.

[b]Females missing as a percent of the reported female population shown in column 3.

Source: Reprinted with the permission of the Population Council from Ansley J. Coale, "Excess Female Mortality and the Balance of the Sexes in the Population: An Estimate of the Number of 'Missing Females,'" *Population and Development Review* 17, no. 3 September 1991: 522.

Box 1   *continued*

others, female infants were often killed by being left exposed to the elements, or else they died in early childhood from neglect or from lack of food. It is still not uncommon in many countries for boys to be breastfed longer than girls.

Philosopher Mary Anne Warren refers to this phenomenon as *gendercide*—that is, the deliberate killing of females simply because of their sex. She notes that the suggestion that such a practice occurs on a widespread basis strikes many people as simply false or paranoid. Available statistics, however, indicate that in some areas the practice may actually be increasing. Since the 1970s, for example, the sex imbalance in China and India has widened, and many analysts attribute the growing gap to the wider availability of amniocentesis and ultrasound.

One of the reasons that sex selection with amniocentesis or ultrasound may still be unpopular in the United States and Europe is that in these countries, due to potential hazards the tests pose for the developing fetus, use of the technology has been limited to diagnosis of fetal abnormalities in high-risk pregnancies. The majority of these are wanted pregnancies. In addition, ultrasound, in particular, has a high error rate with regard to sex determination, and both tests are done fairly late in a pregnancy (usually after sixteen weeks), making the decision to abort more difficult, while also increasing the health risks.

At the same time, however, some analysts have argued that as new technology, such as *chorionic villus sampling* (CVS), becomes available, gendercide may become more common in the United States and Europe. CVS, like ultrasound and amniocentesis, is a fetal diagnostic tool that also reveals the sex of the fetus. A catheter is inserted through a pregnant woman's cervix (or, in some cases, through her abdomen) so that pre-placental tissue can be suctioned out for analysis. A major advantage of CVS relative to ultrasound and amniocentesis is that CVS may be done as early as the ninth week of pregnancy, thus possibly making the decision to abort a fetus of the "wrong" sex an easier one to make. Moreover, recent surveys of physicians and genetic counselors indicate a growing willingness on the part of the medical community to use fetal diagnostic tools for the sole purpose of identifying the fetus's sex. According to Kolker and Burke, for instance, in 1972, only 1 percent of U.S. physicians indicated they were willing to use fetal diagnostic technology solely to determine fetal sex; by 1975, 25 percent stated they would do so. Similarly, in an international survey of geneticists conducted in 1988, 24 percent of those in Britain, 47 percent in Canada, and 60 percent in Hungary expressed the belief that sex selection is morally acceptable. In light of such findings, as well as rapid advances in medical technology and the continued preference for male children in most cultures, ethicists' concerns about a potential rise in gendercide seem far less paranoid than they may have seemed just twenty years ago.

Some of the more common reasons that adults give for this preference are that boys carry on the family name (assuming that a daughter will take her husband's name at marriage) and that boys are both easier and cheaper to raise. The small minority that prefers girls seems to value them for their traditionally feminine traits: they are supposedly neater, cuddlier, cuter, and more obedient than boys. Although it is uncertain whether children perceive their parents' sex preferences, it is clear that these attitudes are closely associated with parental expectations of children's behavior and tend to reflect gender stereotypes.

In this chapter, we will discuss how parents transmit these expectations to their children through *socialization*. Socialization is the process by which society's values and norms, including those pertaining to gender, are taught and learned. This is a lifelong process, but in this chapter, we will concentrate on the socialization that occurs mostly in the early childhood years. We will see that gender socialization is often a conscious effort in that expectations are reinforced with explicit rewards and punishments. Boys in particular receive explicit negative sanctions for engaging in what adults consider gender-inappropriate behavior. Gender socialization may also be more subtle, however, with gender messages relayed implicitly through children's clothing, the way their rooms are decorated, and the toys they are given for play. In addition, children may socialize one another through their interactions in peer groups.

GROWING UP FEMININE OR MASCULINE

If you ask parents whether they treat their children differently simply on the basis of sex, most would probably say "no." However, there is considerable evidence that what parents *say* they do and what they *actually* do are often not the same.

It has been argued by some that gender socialization actually may begin *in utero* by those parents who know the sex of their child before it is born. As Kolker and Burke (1992:12–13) explain, "The knowledge of sex implies more than chromosomal or anatomical differences. It implies gender, and with it images of personality and social role expectations." Such a hypothesis is difficult, if not impossible to test, but what currently is known is that gender socialization gets under way almost immediately after a child is born. Research shows, for instance, that the vast majority of comments parents make about their babies immediately

following birth concern the babies' sex. Moreover, although there are few physiological or behavioral differences between males and females at birth, parents tend to respond differently to newborns on the basis of sex. For example, when asked to describe their babies within twenty-four hours of birth, new parents frequently use gender stereotypes. Infant girls are described as tiny, soft, and delicate, but parents of infant boys use adjectives such as strong, alert, and coordinated to describe their babies. Interestingly, fathers provide more stereotyped descriptions than mothers.

It is not unreasonable for us to suspect that parents' initial stereotyped perceptions of their children may lay the foundation for the differential treatment of sons and daughters. Maccoby and Jacklin, for example, found that parents tend to elicit more gross motor activity from their sons than from their daughters, but there appears to be little if any difference in the amount of affectionate contact between mothers and their sons and daughters. Additional research indicates that parents tend to engage in rougher, more physical play with infant sons than with infant daughters. This is especially the case with respect to father-infant interactions. Studies show that fathers play more interactive games with infant and toddler sons and also encourage more visual, fine-motor, and locomotor exploration with them, whereas they promote vocal interaction with their daughters. At the same time, fathers of toddler daughters appear to encourage closer parent-child physical proximity than fathers of toddler sons. Parents are also more likely to believe—and to act on the belief—that daughters need more help than sons. In these ways parents may be providing early training for their sons to be independent and aggressive, while training their daughters to be dependent and helpless.

This pattern continues through the preschool years. For example, Fagot and her colleagues discovered that adults respond differently to boys' and girls' communicative styles. Although thirteen- and fourteen-month-old children showed no sex differences in their attempts to communicate, adults tended to respond to boys when they "forced attention" by being aggressive, or by crying, whining, and screaming. Similar attempts by girls were usually ignored, but adults were responsive to girls when they used gestures or gentle touching, or when they simply talked. Significantly, when Fagot and her colleagues observed these same children just eleven months later, they saw clear sex differences in their styles of communication: boys were more assertive, whereas girls were more talkative.

In studies with a related theme, researchers have found that parents communicate differently with sons and daughters. Gleason reports that parents speak more to their daughters about feelings and emotions than they do to their sons. However, the one emotion that parents discuss extensively with sons, but not with daughters, is anger, thus perhaps sending children the message that anger is an appropriate emotion for boys to express, but not girls. Additional research supports this observation. For instance, when parents tell stories to their children, they tend to use more emotion words with daughters than sons, except that they speak more about anger in stories told to boys. One outcome is that by the age of two, girls typically use more emotion words than boys.

Finally, Weitzman and her colleagues found that mothers tend to speak to their sons more explicitly, teach and question them more, and use more numbers and action verbs in speaking to them. Others have reported similar findings with respect to father-son communication. This indicates that parents provide more of the kind of verbal stimulation thought to foster cognitive development to their sons than to their daughters. What is also interesting with respect to Weitzman's study, however, is that the researchers included mothers who professed not to adhere to traditional gender stereotypes. Although the differential treatment of sons and daughters was less pronounced among these mothers, it was by not means absent.

It is significant to note that the studies discussed so far have been based almost exclusively on samples of white, middle-class, two-parent families, making generalizations with regard to other types of families' socialization practices unreliable at best. Despite the limitations of such studies, they do help to explain why sex differences that are absent in infancy begin to emerge during early childhood. However, as we have already mentioned, gender socialization is accomplished not only through parent-child interaction, but also through the ways parents structure their children's environment. Let's turn, then, to a discussion of this latter aspect of the socialization process, keeping in mind that this research, too, tends to be race- and class-specific. We will examine more carefully the variables of race and social class later in the chapter.

The Gender-Specific Nature of Children's Environments

What is the easiest and most accurate way for a stranger to determine the sex of an infant? According to Madeline Shakin and her associates, a baby's clothing provides the best clues. Ninety percent of the infants they observed in suburban shopping malls were dressed in sex-typed clothes. The color of the clothing alone supplied a reliable clue for sex labeling: the vast majority of the girls wore pink or yellow, while most boys were dressed in blue or red. The style of children's clothing also varies by sex. On special occasions, girls wear dresses trimmed with ruffles and lace; at bedtime, they wear nighties with more of the same; and for leisure activities, their slacks sets may be more practical, but chances are they are pastel in color and decorated with hearts or flowers. In contrast, boys wear three-piece suits on special occasions; at bedtime, they wear astronaut, athlete, or super-hero pajamas; and for leisure activities, their overalls or slacks sets are in primary colors with sports or military decorations. Disposable diapers are even different for girls and boys, not only in the way they are constructed, which arguably might have a rational basis to it, but also in the way they are decorated: girls' diapers often have pink flowers on them; boys' diapers are embellished with sailboats or cars and trucks.

All of this may seem insignificant, even picky, to you. However, what we must emphasize here is that clothing plays a significant part in gender socialization in two ways. First, by informing others about the sex of the child, clothing sends implicit messages about how the child should be treated. "We know ... that when someone interacts with a child and a sex label is available, the label functions to direct behavior along the lines of traditional [gender] roles" (Shakin et al. 1985:956). Second, certain types of clothing encourage or discourage particular behaviors or activities. Girls in frilly dresses, for example, are discouraged from rough-and-tumble play, whereas boys' physical movement is rarely impeded by their clothing. Boys are expected to be more active than girls, and the styles of the clothing designed for them reflect this gender stereotype. Clothing, then, serves as one of the most basic means by which parents organize their children's world along gender-specific lines.

Parents also more directly construct specific environments for their children with the nurseries, bedrooms, and playrooms that they furnish and decorate. The classic study in this area was conducted by Rheingold and Cook (1975), who actually went into middle-class homes and examined the contents of children's rooms. Their comparison of boys' and girls' rooms is a study of contrasts. Girls' rooms reflected traditional conceptions of femininity, especially in terms of domesticity and motherhood. Their rooms were usually decorated with floral designs and ruffled bedspreads, pillows, and curtains. They contained an abundance of baby dolls and related items (e.g., doll houses) as well as miniature appliances (e.g., toy stoves). Few of these items were found in boys' rooms,

where, instead, the decor and contents reflected traditional notions about masculinity. Boys' rooms had more animal motifs and were filled with military toys and athletic equipment. They also had building and vehicular toys (e.g., blocks, trucks, and wagons). Importantly, boys had more toys overall as well as more types of toys, including those considered educational. The only items girls were as likely to have as boys were musical instruments and books (although, as we will see shortly, the content of children's books is rarely gender-neutral). Given that similar findings were obtained more than ten years later, it appears that Rheingold and Cook's conclusion remains applicable, at least with regard to the socialization of middle-class children:

The rooms of children constitute a not inconsiderable part of their environment. Here they go to bed and wake up; here they spend some part of every day. Their rooms determine the things they see and find for amusement and instruction. That their rooms have an effect on their present and subsequent behavior can be assumed; a standard is set that may in part account for some differences in the behavior of girls and boys (1975:463).

The Rheingold and Cook study also highlights the importance of toys in a young child's environment. Toys, too, play a major part in gender socialization. Toys not only entertain children, but they also teach them particular skills and encourage them to explore through play a variety of roles they may one day occupy as adults. Thus, if we provide boys and girls with very different types of toys, we are essentially training them for separate (and unequal) roles as adults. What is more, we are subtly telling them that what they *may* do, as well as what they *can* do, is largely determined (and limited) by their sex.

Are there clear differences in the toys girls and boys are expected to play with and, if so, just what are these differences? Rheingold and Cook's research already answered these questions to some extent, but a quick perusal of most contemporary toy catalogs further addresses the issue. The toys for sale are frequently pictured with models; pay careful attention to which toys are pictured with female models and which are shown with males. In the catalogs we picked up (Best Products 1992–93; Childcraft 1993; F. A. O. Schwartz 1993), most of the toys were obviously gender-linked. We found, for instance, that little girls were most frequently shown with dolls or household appliances. The only "dolls" boys were pictured with were a vinyl six-foot inflatable Godzilla; "Big Frank," a talking Frankenstein construction toy that has a gear box that says "Fix me" if he needs fixing; and the "Totally Awesome Duelin' Dudes," which requires two players, aged three years or older, to use "the multi-action control to knock [their] opponent's head off!" and makes "Exciting sound effects." Costumes for dressing up also were featured in gender-specific ways. An "authentic western outfit" for boys included red chaps decorated with rodeo cowboys, a matching vest, and matching hat. For girls, the costume was a pale pink miniskirt with fringed hem, a pale pink vest decorated with silver ornaments, and a white hat. On other pages, little girls were shown driving a hot pink "beach buggy," while boys drove a yellow and black "sand blaster." Girls were shown dressing up in child-size Barbie "glamour" costumes, making bows for their hair, and applying makeup at a beauty salon (for which you can also buy the "working beauty kit for the world's most unforgettable girls"). Boys drove a crane and trailer, built a house with a plastic construction kit, and played basketball. Only boys were shown with computers.

Toy catalogs are directed primarily to parents. In the United States, parents make over 70 percent of all toy purchases and typically encourage their children to play with gender-stereotyped toys, while discouraging them from playing with toys associated with the opposite sex. However, children themselves spend con-siderable time looking at toy catalogs and often ask their parents to buy specific toys they see advertised. If the catalogs we examined are typical of toy catalogs in general—and we have no reason to doubt that they are—then children are receiving very clear gender messages about the kinds of toys they are supposed to want.[1] These messages are reinforced by their parents, by television commercials, by the pictures on toy packaging, by the way toy stores often arrange their stock in separate sections for boys and girls, and by sales personnel who frequently recommend gender-stereotyped toys to potential customers. It is no wonder that by two years of age, children show a preference for gender-stereotyped toys.

The toys themselves foster different traits and abilities in children, depending on their sex. Toys for boys tend to encourage exploration, manipulation, invention, construction, competition, and aggression. In contrast, girls' toys typically rate high on manipulability, but also creativity, nurturance, and attractiveness. As one researcher concluded, "These data support the hypothesis that playing with girls' vs. boys' toys may be related to the development of differential cognitive and/or social skills in girls and boys" (Miller 1987:485). Certainly the toy manufacturers think so; the director of public relations for Mattel, Inc. (which makes the Barbie doll) stated in a recent interview that, "Girls' play involves dressing and grooming and acting out their future—going on a date, getting married—and boys' play involves competition and conflict, good guys versus bad guys" (quoted in Lawson 1989:C1).

Interestingly, at the 1993 American International Toy Fair, representatives of the $15 billion a year toy industry claimed that manufacturers were making efforts to produce toys that appeal to both sexes and that overcome gender stereotyping. One example, offered by Mattel, was "Earring Magic Ken," an updated version of Barbie's longtime boyfriend. The new Ken has blond streaks in his brown hair and wears an earring in his left ear. Barbie herself has been given a number of nontraditional roles, including astronaut and business executive (the latter carries a portable lap-top computer). However, the best-selling doll is still Totally Hair Barbie, which in 1992 was the fifth-best-selling toy in the United States, and every Barbie continues to have a figure that translates into proportions of 36–20–32 (that is, the bust of an adult woman, the hips of a teenager, and the waist of a child).[2]

As for the new toys that are supposed to cross gender lines, closer examination reveals that they are hardly gender-neutral. In most cases, in fact, the toys are simply produced in male and female versions. Troll dolls are a good example. As the Hasbro television commercial claims, girls like smiling trolls with jeweled belly buttons and cotton-soft hair in bright colors, but boys like Battle Trolls, nasty-looking characters who wear paramilitary clothing, are heavily armed, and have nasty-sounding names. The Battle Trolls burst onto the television screen by breaking down a door that smashes one of the "girls' trolls" when it falls.

Apart from toys, what other items stand out as a central feature of a child's environment? You may recall from the Rheingold and Cook study that books are one of only two items that boys and girls are equally likely to have. Unfortunately, children's literature traditionally ignored females or portrayed males and females in a blatantly stereotyped fashion. For example, Lenore Weitzman and her colleagues found in their now-classic analysis of award-winning picture books for preschoolers that males were usually depicted as active adventurers and leaders, while females were shown as passive followers and helpers. Boys were typically rewarded for their accomplishments and for being smart; girls were rewarded for their good looks. Books that included adult characters showed men doing a wide range of jobs, but women were restricted largely to domestic roles. In about one third of the books they studied, however, there were no female characters at all.

In a replication of the Weitzman research, Williams and colleagues noted significant improvements in the visibility of females. Only 12.5 percent of the books published in the early 1980s that they examined had no females, while a third had females as central characters. Nevertheless, although males and females were about equal in their appearance in children's literature, the ways they were depicted remained largely unchanged. According to Williams et al. (1987: 155), "With respect to role portrayal and characterization, females do not appear to be so much stereotyped as simply colorless. No behavior was shared by a majority of females; while nearly all males were portrayed as independent, persistent, and active. Furthermore, differences in the way males and females are presented is entirely consistent with traditional culture."

To mark the twentieth anniversary of the publication of the Weitzman study, Clark and his colleagues also reconfirmed, using more specific evaluation criteria, Weitzman's findings. In addition, however, Clark and his colleagues analyzed children's picture books that received awards during the years 1987 through 1991 and compared those illustrated by white illustrators with those illustrated by African-American illustrators. Among their findings were that while all the recent children's picture books contained more female central characters who are depicted as more independent, creative, and assertive than those in the past, the books illustrated by African-American artists (and written by African-American authors) gave female characters the greatest visibility and were significantly more likely to depict these females as competitive, persistent, nurturant, aggressive, emotional, and active. Clark and his colleagues argue that the recent books illustrated by white artists reflect the liberal feminist emphasis on more egalitarian depictions of female and male characters, whereas those illustrated by African-American artists reflect the aims of Black feminist theorists who emphasize women's greater involvement in an ethic of care and an ethic of personal accountability.

These researchers' general findings with respect to recent children's literature may also be a byproduct of the considerable attention that has been given to the problem of sexism in children's literature and the resulting efforts to change it. Publishers, for instance, have developed guidelines to help authors avoid sexism in their works, and a number of authors' and writers' collectives have set to work producing egalitarian books for youngsters. Some researchers, though, now claim that the so-called nonsexist picture books frequently advantage female characters at the expense of male characters, thus simply reversing traditional depictions of gender rather than portraying gender equality. However, others praise the nonsexist books for their depictions of females as highly independent and males as nurturant and nonaggressive. Still, regardless of what adults think of these books, the nontraditional gender messages may be lost on children. In an interesting study, Bronwyn Davies (1989) read storybooks with feminist themes to groups of preschool boys and girls from various racial and ethnic and social class backgrounds. She found that the majority of children expressed a dislike for and an inability to identify with storybook characters who were acting in nontraditional roles or engaged in cross-gender activities. By the time the children heard these stories (at the ages of four or five), "[t]he power of the pre-existing structure of the traditional narrative [prevented] a new form of narrative from being heard." There were no differences across racial, ethnic, or social class lines. What did emerge as significant was parents' early efforts to socialize their children in nonsexist, non-gender-polarizing ways. Thus, the two children in the study whose parents did not support polarized gender socialization did not see anything wrong with characters engaged in cross-gendered behaviors and had less difficulty identifying with these characters.

One way that writers and publishers have tried to overcome sexism in children's literature is to depict characters as genderless or gender neutral. However, recent research casts doubt on the potential success of this approach since it has been found that mothers who read these books to their children almost always label the characters in gender-specific ways. In 95 percent of these cases the labeling is masculine. In this study, the only pictures that prompted feminine labels were those showing an adult helping a child, an interpretation consistent with the gender stereotypes that females need more help than males and that females are more attentive to children. Based on this research, then, it appears that "picturing characters in a gender-neutral way is actually counterproductive, since the adult 'reading' the picture book with the child is likely to produce an even more gender-biased presentation than the average children's book does" (DeLoache et al. 1987:176).

To summarize our discussion so far, we have seen that virtually every significant dimension of a child's environment—his or her clothing, bedroom, toys, and, to a lesser extent, books—is structured according to cultural expectations of appropriate gendered behavior. Despite their claims, even parents who see themselves as egalitarian tend to provide their children with different experiences and opportunities and to respond to them differently on the basis of sex. Consequently, the children cannot help but conclude that sex is an important social category. By the time they are ready for school, they have already learned to view the world in terms of a dichotomy: his and hers. Parents are not the only socializers of young children, however; recent research has demonstrated the importance of peers in early childhood socialization. Let's consider, then, the ways in which young children help to socialize one another.

Early Peer Group Socialization

As we noted previously, socialization is not a one-way process from adults to children. Rather, childhood socialization is a collective process in which "children creatively appropriate information from the adult world to produce their own unique peer cultures" (Corsaro and Eder 1990:200). Indeed, according to Beverly Fagot, children's same-sex peers are the most powerful agents of socialization.

Children socialize one another through their everyday interactions in the home and at play. Research indicates, for example, that one of young children's first attempts at social differentiation is through increasing sex segregation. Observations of young children at play indicate that they voluntarily segregate themselves into same-sex groups. This preference for play with same-sex peers emerges between the ages of two and three and grows stronger as children move from early to middle childhood. Moreover, when compared with girls, boys tend to interact in larger groups, be more aggressive and competitive, and engage in more organized sports.

Thorne is critical of much of this research for focusing solely on sex differences and ignoring sex similarities and cross-sex interaction. She gives a number of examples in which young children work cooperatively and amiably in sex-integrated groups. She also points out that children frequently engage in "borderwork"; that is, they attempt to cross over into the world of the other sex and participate in cross-gender activities. There is considerable evidence, however, that children reward gender-appropriate behavior. Boys especially are criticized more by their peers for cross-gender play, but both boys and girls who choose gender-appropriate toys are more likely to have other children play with them.

Unfortunately, the research on peer cultures in early childhood is limited; much more is needed before we can fully appreciate the ways that young children actively participate in the socialization process. However, we may say that available data do indicate that at the very least, young children should be considered partners with parents and other caregivers in socialization, including gender socialization.

The Intervening Variables of Race and Social Class

We must emphasize again that much of the research on early-childhood gender socialization has recruited subjects from white, middle- and upper-middle-class, two-parent families. There are indications that the findings of such studies may not be representative of the socialization practices of families of other races and social classes. The work of Janice Hale-Benson (1986) is instructive on this point.

Hale-Benson has studied the socialization goals and practices of black families. She emphasizes the dual nature of the socialization that takes place in black households. "One of the challenges Black families must face in socializing their children is to understand and assist their children to function within their peer group. In addition, Black parents must also provide them with the skills and abilities they will need to succeed in the outside society" (1986:64). For both male and female children, black parents stress heavily the importance of hard work, ambition, and achievement. Thus, black children of both sexes tend to be more independent and self-reliant than their white peers. They are also imbued at an early age with a sense of financial responsibility to earn income for themselves and to contribute to the support of their families. Finally, black children of both sexes are taught racial pride and strategies for responding to and overcoming racism.

Still, the socialization experiences of young black males and females are not identical. Hale-Benson points out, for example, that among the traits and skills taught to black boys (largely in the context of their peer group) are the ways to move their bodies distinctively, athletic prowess, sexual competence, and street savvy, including how to fight. In contrast, black girls are socialized into "a very strong motherhood orientation," although this does not preclude the general expectation that they will also work outside the home. The development of personal uniqueness or distinctiveness is also emphasized, with special attention given to sexuality, clothing, and body movement.

Black children are often exposed to women and men sharing tasks and assuming collective responsibility. A number of studies indicate that in two-parent black families, women are typically employed outside the home and men participate in child care, although there is also evidence that disputes the finding of role-sharing in black households. Almost 62 percent of black children live with just one parent, usually their mother, compared with 21 percent of white children and 33 percent of Hispanic children. In black single-parent households, the parent may be aided in the care and socialization of the children by an extended kin and friendship network. Segura and Pierce also emphasize the significance of multiple mothering figures in the socialization of Mexican-American children. In addition, Hale-Benson (1986:53) notes that the black church offers "a kind of extended family fellowship that provides other significant adults to relate to the children, and it also provides material and human resources to the family."

In light of these data, it is not surprising that Hale-Benson and others have found that black children are not taught to perceive gender in completely bipolar terms. Instead, both males and females are expected to be nurturant and expressive emotionally as well as independent, confident, and assertive. Reid reports that black girls more than black boys are encouraged to be high achievers, and Carr and Mednick have found that this nontraditional gender socialization leads to high achievement motivation in black female preschoolers. Bardwell and colleagues have also found that black children are less gender stereotyped than white children. Importantly, Isaaks obtained similar results in a comparison of Hispanic and white children. However, there is some research that reports contradictory findings. For instance,

Gonzalez and Price-Bonham and Skeen found at least as much, if not more, gender stereotyping among blacks and Hispanics as among whites. Similarly, in her study of Mexican fathers' interactions with their seven- to twelve-year-old children, Bronstein reports that, similar to white fathers, these men interacted more socially with daughters than with sons, but encouraged their sons' cognitive achievement more than their daughters'.

The picture becomes blurred or more complex when social class is taken into account. For example, there is modest support for the hypothesis that gender stereotyping decreases as one moves up the social class hierarchy. However, if parental educational level may be used as an indicator of a family's social class, it appears that, at least among whites, gender stereotyping may be greater the higher a family's social class position. Most studies of black and Hispanic or Chicano socialization practices, though, still utilize middle-class samples, and there is little research that examines the interaction of social class with race and ethnicity. One study that did address this interaction indicates that the latter is the more important variable; that is, race and ethnicity have a stronger influence on child-rearing practices than does social class, although this research did not examine gender socialization specifically. We can only conclude that much more research is needed to elucidate the rich diversity of gender socialization practices and their outcomes among various races and social classes.

BY THE TIME A CHILD IS FIVE

At the outset of this chapter, we argued that children are born into a world that largely favors males. Throughout much of the remainder of our discussion, we examined research that indicates that this male preference carries over into parents' and other adults' interactions with children. We have seen here that during early childhood, boys and girls—at least those from white, middle-class families—are socialized into separate and unequal genders. Little boys are taught independence, problem-solving abilities, assertiveness, and curiosity about their environment—skills that are highly valued in our society. In contrast, little girls are taught dependence, passivity, and domesticity—traits that our society devalues. Children themselves reinforce and respond to adults' socialization practices by socializing one another in peer groups.

We have seen that gender-typed clothing, room furnishings, toys, and books serve both to organize children's everyday experiences in terms of a gender dichotomy and to reinforce children for stereotypic gender-appropriate behavior. Not surprisingly, children as young as two years old already adhere to gender stereotypes and exhibit preferences for gender-typed toys and activities.

May we conclude, then, that nonsexist socialization is impossible? Certainly not. Considerable research is under way to evaluate a variety of nonsexist socialization techniques. Davies's study indicates that attempts at nonsexist socialization by parents do have a positive impact on children's attitudes and behavior. However, we must keep in mind that parents are not the only ones responsible for gender socialization. Indeed, schools and the media take up where parents leave off, and peers remain active socializers throughout our lives.

EDUCATING GIRLS AND BOYS: THE ELEMENTARY SCHOOLS

When elementary school teachers are asked about the way they treat their students, they respond in the same way that parents do, and state that they treat all their students fairly, regardless of their sex. Research indicates, however, that in practice, teachers typically interact differently (and often inequitably) with their male and female students. The interactions differ in at least two ways: the *frequency* of teacher-student interactions and the *content* of those interactions.

With respect to frequency of teachers' interactions with their students, studies show that regardless of the sex of the teacher, male students interact more with their teachers than female students do. Boys receive more teacher attention and more instructional time than girls do. Of course, this may be due to the fact that boys are more demanding than girls. Boys, for instance, are eight times more likely than girls to call out answers in class, thus directing teachers' attention to them more often.[3] However, research also shows that even when boys do not voluntarily participate in class, teachers are more likely to solicit information from them than from girls.

Apart from the frequency of teacher-student interactions, education specialists Myra and David Sadker report that the content of teacher-student interactions also differs, depending on the sex of the student. By observing teacher-student interaction in the classroom over many years, the Sadkers found that teachers provided boys with more remediation: for instance, they more often helped boys than girls find and correct errors. In addition, they posed more academic challenges to boys, encouraging them to think through their answers to arrive at the best possible academic response.

Other studies support these findings. For example, teachers' comments to boys are more precise than their comments to girls. Boys also get more praise for the intellectual quality of their work, whereas girls are praised more often for the neatness of their work. At the same time, however, while boys generally engage in more positive interactions with teachers, they are also more likely than girls to incur their teachers' wrath. Boys are subject to more disciplinary action in elementary school classrooms, and their punishments are harsher and more public than those handed out to girls. Perhaps boys misbehave more than girls: after all, as we learned [previously], preschool boys are encouraged to be active and aggressive, while preschool girls are rewarded for quiet play and passivity. It may be that the early childhood socialization of girls better prepares them for the behavioral requirements of elementary school. Nevertheless, classroom observations show that when boys and girls are being equally disruptive, it is the boys that teachers most frequently single out for punishment.

The American Association of University Women argues that the sex inequities embedded in teacher-student interactions lower female students' academic self-esteem and confidence. This relationship is complicated, however, by the factors of race and social class. Black boys interact with their teachers less than other students. Black girls interact with their teachers less than white girls, but try to initiate more teacher-student interaction than do white girls and black and white boys; unfortunately, teachers often rebuff these students. The interaction that black students have with their teachers is also less positive than that experienced by white students. Black boys, for example, receive significantly more qualified praise (e.g., "That's good, but . . .") than do other students. Black students, regardless of their sex, are more likely to be reinforced for their social behavior, whereas white students are more likely to receive teacher reinforcement for their academic achievements. In one study, in which the reinforcement practices of sixty female black and white teachers were observed, it was found that teachers tended to reinforce children of their same race less than opposite-race children and to reinforce boys more often than girls. However, the study showed that black girls received the least reinforcement of any group of children. A study by Jensen and Rosenfeld indicated that children's social class mediated this pattern to some extent in that middle-class children, regardless of race, receive more favorable evaluations from teachers than lower-class children. "Interestingly, however, academic ability has the reverse effect

upon teachers' reinforcement of black children. Black girls with high academic ability were ignored even more than those with less ability. The same effect was true to some extent for black boys. It seem as though teachers prefer black children to conform to expectations of low academic ability" (Reid 1982:144). Indeed, the AAUW report states that when black girls perform as well as white boys in school, teachers tend to attribute their success to the black girls' effort, but at the same time assume that the white boys must not be working up to their full potential. Clearly, race and social class prejudices interact with sexism to have an especially pernicious effect on some students' educational experiences. We will return to this point shortly.

It is hardly surprising that teachers respond to their students in these ways given that few teacher preparation programs do anything to prevent it. In one study of teacher-education textbooks, for instance, researchers found that the problem of sexism in the schools is rarely addressed. In fact, the authors of these texts are sometimes guilty of sexism themselves.

The gender messages that teachers send to students are reinforced by the traditional curricular materials available in elementary schools. Students learn not only the academic subjects of their school's formal curriculum, but also a set of values and expectations of a hidden curriculum. We can see the hidden curriculum at work in the selective content of textbooks and other educational materials. Studies conducted during the 1970s showed that, although the United States is a country with citizens of both sexes who share a rich and varied racial and ethnic heritage, racial minorities and women were conspicuously absent from elementary school textbooks and readers. During the 1980s, research revealed some improvements, but according to the AAUW (1992:62), "the problems persist . . . in terms of what is considered important enough to study." Regardless of the subject—English, history, reading, science—women and minorities continue to be underrepresented in textbooks. In history texts, for example, Native Americans and Chicanos are rarely mentioned apart from such events as Custer's last stand or the Alamo, and in both cases, it is made extremely clear who the "bad guys" were. African Americans and women are more likely to be included, but the presentation is usually limited to a few "famous women" or "famous blacks"; or they are mentioned only in traditional historical contexts (slavery, the Civil War, and the civil rights movement for blacks; the suffrage movement for women) or in terms of traditional roles (e.g., women who were married to famous men). That there is a heterosexist bias in the texts goes without saying.

Most publishers today issue guidelines to textbook authors to assist them in avoiding sexist language, but the extent to which the guidelines are actually followed is uneven, and such guidelines do little to increase the representation of women and minorities in the texts nor to expand the content of the texts to include the perspectives of women and minorities on their own terms. For example, there is evidence that children's readers have improved significantly with respect to the use of gender-neutral language and the inclusion of females. However, there continue to be imbalances in favor of males with regard to rate of portrayal and types of roles assigned to males and females in the stories (e.g., girls need to be rescued more than boys; boys are more adventurous than girls).

The AAUW notes that the major curriculum reform projects that have been undertaken in the United States since the early 1980s have not explicitly addressed the issue of gender equity. However, since 1990, several state boards or commissions on education, such as those in New York and Pennsylvania, have begun to reevaluate the formal curriculum of their schools and to consider revisions that would make the curriculum more gender-fair, multicultural, and inclusive of lesbians and gay men. Needless to say, such efforts have generated considerable controversy, and most

changes in schools' curricula regarding sex, race, sexual orientation, and social justice have occurred at the local level in only a handful of school districts. The importance of using non-biased, multicultural curriculum materials, however, is exemplified by evidence that indicates that children learn their lessons quite well. Consider, for instance, the results of a recent survey of almost 7,500 school children in grades one through twelve living in the Minneapolis-St. Paul area. The majority of the youngsters expressed the belief that only men can be president of the United States; some stated that women cannot even try to become president.

The organization of school activities also gives children messages about gender. For example, many teachers continue to use various forms of *sex separation* in their classrooms. They may seat girls on one side of the room and boys on the other; they may ask girls and boys to form separate lines; or they may organize teams for a spelling or math competition according to students' sex. Teachers also sometimes assign girls and boys different classroom chores; for instance, girls may be asked to dust or water the plants, whereas boys are asked to carry books, rearrange desks, or run equipment. Sociologist Barrie Thorne, who has made extensive observations of elementary school classrooms, points out that teachers engage in contradictory practices: sometimes they reinforce sex separation, but other times they challenge or disrupt it. She notes that teachers more often mix boys and girls than separate them, but that separating girls and boys in lines or seating arrangements, as well as pitting them against one another in classroom contests, is not uncommon. Moreover, this physical separation is reinforced by a verbal separation, in that teachers routinely use gender labels as terms of address to the students and invariably put "boys" first in speaking to the children, as in "boys and girls." Thorne observed that girls and boys typically separate themselves in school lunchrooms and on school playgrounds—probably much more than they do in their home neighborhoods—and teachers and aides often ratify this division by seeing certain areas as "girls' territory" and other areas as "boys' territory."

Trivial though they may appear to be, these kinds of sex separations have at least three interrelated consequences. First, sex separation in and of itself prevents boys and girls from working together cooperatively, thus denying children of both sexes valuable opportunities to learn about and sample one another's interests and activities. Second, it makes working in same-sex groups more comfortable than working in mixed-sex groups—a feeling that children may carry with them into adulthood and which may become problematic when they enter the labor force. Third, sex separation reinforces gender stereotypes, especially if it involves differential work assignments.

Thorne found that in a classroom activity with a central focus, such as the collective making of a map or taking turns reading aloud from a book, girls and boys participated together. Similar observations have prompted some educators to advocate that classroom activities be reorganized to facilitate *cooperative learning*. Cooperative learning involves students working together in small, mixed-sex, mixed-race groups on a group project or toward a group goal (e.g., solving a problem, writing a report). The cooperative learning approach is designed to lessen classroom competition, maximize cooperation, foster group solidarity and interdependence, and promote understanding among members of diverse groups of children. Research indicates that cooperative learning does have a number of benefits: it appears to increase interracial friendships, it raises the self-esteem of students of all races, and it is especially helpful in mainstreaming students with disabilities. Unfortunately, it appears to be less successful in fostering positive relationships between boys and girls in school. According to the AAUW (1992:73):

Some research indicates that the infrequent use of small, unstructured work groups is not effective in reducing gender stereotypes, and, in fact, increases stereotyping. Groups often provide boys with leadership opportunities that increase their self-esteem. Females are often seen as followers and are less likely to want to work in mixed-sex groups in the future. Another study indicates a decrease in female achievement when females are placed in mixed-sex groups.

As the AAUW concludes, more fundamental changes than simply providing mixed-group learning activities are necessary to bring gender equity to elementary school classrooms.

Finally, children receive messages about gender simply by the way adult jobs are distributed in their schools. Although approximately 85 percent of elementary school teachers and 83 percent of teachers' aides are women, women are underrepresented in upper management of school administrations. Chief state school officers, for example, are the leaders of a state's public school system: in 1991, only nine of the fifty chief state school officers were women. Just 4.8 percent of school superintendents and 27.7 percent of principals are women. As research indicates, the sex of a school administrator can have a measurable effect on children's gender-role perceptions. According to one study of first graders, for instance, children who attended a school headed by a female principal held fewer gender stereotypes than those who went to a school with a male principal.

In light of our discussion so far, it may be somewhat surprising to learn that girls earn higher grades than boys throughout their school years. However, girls' achievement test scores, as well as their self-confidence, decline as they progress through elementary school and high school. Let's consider now girls' and boys' educational experiences in high school in order to better understand these findings.

EDUCATING TEENAGE GIRLS AND BOYS: THE SECONDARY SCHOOLS

Both parents and teenagers will attest that adolescence is one of the more stressful periods of the life cycle. As one's body changes and matures, so do one's interests, and the opinions of friends take on greater significance in the formation of one's self-concept. Young men and women both feel the need to be popular with their peers, but the means and measures of their success at this are somewhat different.

For teenage boys, the single most important source of prestige and popularity is athletic achievement. The teenage boy tends to measure "himself by what he can do physically compared to others his age, and how he stacks up determines to a great extent his social acceptance by others and his own self-esteem" (Richardson 1981:69). The "non-jock" is at an obvious disadvantage, socially and psychologically. It is the athlete who is looked to as a leader, not only by his peers, but also by teachers and parents. Moreover, on the court or on the playing field, boys are taught a variety of stereotypically masculine skills and values: aggression, endurance, competitiveness, self-confidence, and teamwork.

It is also in high school that young men are expected to formulate their career goals. For those not planning to attend college, there are vocational training programs that provide the educational background needed for jobs in the skilled trades or in preparation for technical school. Most boys, though, study an academic or college prep curriculum, which may seem a bit surprising given their greater likelihood for academic difficulties in the lower grades. However, as we will discuss shortly, boys' academic performance usually improves during high school.

What about girls? How does their high school experience differ from that of boys? For one thing, physical prowess and athletic ability are not their chief sources of prestige and popularity. Indeed, most teenage girls learn that to be athletic is to be unfeminine, and schools reinforce this message with inadequate funding for girls' sports programs. Instead, what contributes most to a teenage girl's prestige and popularity is having a boyfriend. "A girl may be bright, friendly, competent, and attractive, but without a boyfriend she lacks social validation of these positive attributes. It is as though being selected by a boy tells others that a girl is worthwhile" (Lott 1987:71). Obviously, teenagers, both female and male, who are not heterosexual face tremendous difficulties in high school and, as Box 2 shows, frequently experience isolation and ostracism from their peers as well as from adults.

During high school, young women also begin to plan for their futures. Until the late 1960s, studies showed that high school boys had higher career aspirations than high school girls. However, more recent research has found no sex differences in either the educational or occupational aspirations of young women and men, and some studies show girls as having higher aspirations than boys. Despite their raised aspirations, though, teenage girls still tend to underestimate their academic abilities and to express greater pessimism about their ability to achieve their goals. In their recent study of adolescents at a private girls school in New York, for example, Carol Gilligan and her colleagues found that by age fifteen or sixteen, girls who had earlier exuded confidence became less outspoken and more doubtful about their abilities.

This decline in females' self-confidence and self-efficacy during adolescence is a phenomenon that researchers have observed for a number of years. Why does it occur? One explanation that gained considerable popularity during the 1970s was offered by psychologist Matina Horner, who argued that women fear success. In her research, Horner asked female and male subjects to write stories based on information she provided them; in some cases, the story theme was success. She found that 62 percent of the women, but only 9 percent of the men, wrote stories containing negative imagery in response to success-related cues. She subsequently discovered that these women tended to perform better on word-game tasks when they worked alone rather than in mixed-sex groups. This led her to conclude that women's fear of success was related to a discomfort they experienced when competing with men. Horner argued that women may deliberately, though perhaps unconsciously, underachieve because they fear the consequences that success in high achievement situations might bring—specifically, that they will appear unfeminine and, therefore, be rejected socially.

Box 2   The High School Experience for Lesbian and Gay Youth

Adolescence is a period of tremendous physical and emotional change. It is a time when most young women and men begin to actively explore their sexuality and sexual identities. Indeed, research indicates that more than a quarter of the adolescent population is sexually active by the age of fourteen. Historically, our schools have been woefully remiss in educating young people about sex, but they have been most neglectful with respect to lesbian and gay youth. Although recent surveys indicate a willingness on the part of teachers and school administrators to treat homosexual students in a nonjudgmental way and to attend school-sponsored workshops related to homosexual students, there remains an unwillingness to proactively address the special needs of homosexual students or to openly affirm their sexual identities. Most school personnel, in fact, continue to assume the heterosexuality of their students and never raise the issue of sexual orientation. Except for responding to especially blatant or heinous forms of harassment against homosexual students, the majority of school personnel do not seriously confront the problem of *homophobia*—an unreasonable fear of or hostility toward homosexuals—in their classrooms or on school grounds. "The absence of visible support from educators conveys to *all* students the legitimacy and desirability of the heterosexual standard" (Sears 1992:74).

What are the consequences of this neglect for lesbian and gay high school students? Uribe and Harbeck report that lesbian and gay adolescents have a disproportionately high rate of substance abuse, sexual abuse, parental rejection, homelessness, and conflict with the law. Although the participants in their study were very intelligent, few were achieving their full academic potential. Lesbian and gay adolescents, in fact, are at an especially high risk of dropping out of school. The social rejection and violence that these students often receive from their nonhomosexual peers and, not infrequently, from their parents, lead to low self-esteem, alienation, feelings of isolation, and a sense of inadequacy. Those who hide their sexual orientation may escape some of the physical and verbal harassment, but their secretiveness is likely to increase their feelings of loneliness and alienation. "By developing elaborate concealment strategies these young people are often able to 'pass as straight,' but at some significant, unmeasurable cost to their developmental process, self-esteem, and sense of connection" (Uribe and Harbeck 1992:11). According to recent estimates, more than 30 percent of the 5,000 suicides committed each year by young women and men between the ages of fifteen and twenty-four are related to emotional trauma resulting from sexual orientation issues and from societal prejudices about same-sex relationships.

Box 2   *continued*

In response to these disturbing statistics, about 170 organizations nationwide have been established to specifically meet the special needs of lesbian and gay youth. The Harvey Milk High School in New York is a secondary school designated specifically for lesbian and gay students and staffed primarily by lesbian and gay teachers and administrators. Agencies, such as the Hetrick-Martin Institute in New York, the Gay and Lesbian Community Services Center in Los Angeles, and the Sexual Minority Youth Assistance League in Washington, D.C., offer a variety of services, including counseling, tutoring, meals and, sometimes, shelter for homosexual youth who have been kicked out of their homes after coming out to (or being found out by) their parents. A central goal of all of these organizations is to affirm the identities of homosexual teenagers and thereby raise their self-esteem. Some of the organizations also do programs, such as peer trainings, at local schools to help foster acceptance of homosexual youth and to help prevent harassment and violence. A number of them also engage in political lobbying with school boards and state departments of education to make the school activities and curriculum more inclusive of gay and lesbian youth.

There is evidence that such organizations are successful in raising the self-esteem and, consequently, the academic achievement of the youth they serve, while also lowering rates of suicide attempts, substance abuse, and other destructive behavior. But they have been less successful in getting school boards and education departments to respond. As the AAUW (1992:80) concludes, until the mainstream education system effectively addresses homophobia among its staff, students, and students' parents, it is abdicating its "responsibility not only to adolescents who are questioning their individual sexual orientation but to all students."

Empirical research on the "fear of success" theory, however, has yielded inconsistent findings. There is evidence that girls tend to feel uneasy and embarrassed about academic success, and that they often avoid subjects defined as masculine because they think boys will not like them. There is also evidence that their concerns are not unfounded. Pfost and Fiore report that females described as masculine and seeking traditionally masculine jobs were considered by research subjects as undesirable heterosexual partners and friends, although subjects' responses to males described in gender-incongruent ways were not consistently negative. It is certainly the case, too, that girls do excel in many areas; the fact that our male-centered culture devalues what it defines as feminine accomplishments

should not detract from their successes. In addition, replications of Horner's research have produced no significant differences between females and males in their use of negative imagery in response to success-related cues. In other words, male subjects in subsequent experiments were just as likely as female subjects to exhibit fear of success.

By focusing on the psychology of the adolescent girl, the fear of success argument also ignores the *invisible ceiling* that others frequently impose on young women's ambitions. This invisible ceiling takes a variety of forms. First, there is the widespread belief that girls are not as intellectually gifted as boys and, therefore, cannot be expected to do as well in school. Research reveals, for example, that both parents and teachers tend to attribute boys' academic failures to achieve to "bad luck." They do just the opposite for girls; if they are successful, they were lucky or the task itself was easy; if they do poorly, it is because they are not smart. Consequently, high school teachers, like their elementary school counterparts, appear to offer male students more encouragement, to publicly praise their scholastic abilities, and to be friendlier toward them than they are toward female students. As Bush (1987:15) notes, "These findings are analogous to those for teacher expectations linked to class and/or race" in which teachers respond more positively to middle- and upper-class students than to working class and poor students or to white students relative to minority students. We can only speculate on the impact that the intersection of teachers' sexism, racism, and classism may have on students, but there is evidence that students internalize these beliefs which, if one is female, could reasonably lead to lowered self-confidence and self-efficacy—not for fear of success, but for fear of failure.

Curriculum materials may also send girls the message that they are unlikely to realize their ambitions. Recent reviews of high school textbooks, for instance, have found both subtle and blatant gender biases, including language bias and gender stereotypes, omission of women and a focus on "great men," and neglect of scholarship by women. As in elementary school, research indicates that the type of curriculum materials used in the schools clearly has an impact on students' attitudes and behaviors. According to the authors of a recent review of more than 100 studies of gender-fair curriculum materials, "Pupils who are exposed to sex-equitable materials are more likely than others to 1) have gender-balanced knowledge of people in society, 2) develop more flexible attitudes and more accurate sex-role knowledge, and 3) *imitate role behaviors contained in the material*" (Scott and Schau 1985:228; em-

phasis added). The gender bias common in high school curriculum materials is compounded by the lack of attention to racial and ethnic diversity. As one young African-American woman noted, "In twelve years of school. I never studied anything about myself" (quoted in AAUW 1992:61).

School personnel often contribute to making girls feel that they will be unable to fulfill their own aspirations. There is evidence that gender stereotyping is common among high school guidance counselors. Counselors may channel male and female students into different (i.e., gender stereotyped) fields and activities, especially in vocational education programs. There is also evidence that counselors sometimes steer female students away from certain college prep courses, particularly in mathematics and the sciences. For example, in one study of girls who went on to study engineering after high school, the women who participated reported that although their teachers tended to encourage them to pursue an engineering degree, their counselors tended to discourage them from that pursuit (see Box 3).

Finally, although elementary school girls can identify with their teachers, who are almost always women, it becomes more difficult to do so in high school, where about 46 percent of the teachers are men. In vocational courses, female teachers are concentrated in subjects traditionally considered feminine: occupational home economics (92 percent), health (90 percent), and office occupations (69 percent). They are rarely found in industrial arts (4 percent), agriculture (6 percent), and trade and industry (9 percent). High school students are especially likely to have a male teacher for their math courses (57.7 percent) and science courses (65.4 percent). Teachers of these subjects also are usually white: only 11 percent of math teachers, 10 percent of biology teachers, and 7 percent of chemistry teachers in grades nine through twelve are minority group members.

Although there is no research that shows a clear cause and effect relationship, it is not unlikely that the rather discouraging nature of girls' high school experience, more than their fear of success, is what weakens their self-confidence and self-efficacy. Nevertheless, a high number of female high school graduates goes on to college. In fact, they now constitute a slight majority of college students. Unfortunately, the education they receive continues to differ from that of their male peers in many important respects.

Box 3   Sex Differences in Mathematics and Science

For many years, much has been made of the fact that boys score higher than girls do on the Scholastic Assessment Test (S.A.T., formerly the Scholastic Aptitude Test) and that the differences between boys' and girls' scores are especially large on the math portion of the exam. Some observers have argued that this gap is biologically or genetically caused—that males, for example, have a genetic predisposition to excel at math or that the organization of their brains favors math achievement. Despite the widespread attention such claims receive in the popular media, there is little, if any, scientific data to support them. There is considerable evidence, however, of gender bias in the S.A.T. and other standardized exams that may give male test takers an advantage over female test takers. If we consider, instead, achievement in math and science courses as well as scientific investigations of math and science ability, we find that sex differences are small and have been decreasing since the mid-1970s. The differences that remain appear to be due to a number of *social* factors: (1) the extent to which these subjects are oriented to males, (2) teacher-student interaction, and (3) parental encouragement.

With regard to the first factor, observers have noted an absence of women from science curricula. For instance, Marie Curie is typically the only female scientist individuals ever recall being mentioned in their science classes. In addition, several observers have noted that math word problems are often oriented toward traditionally masculine-typed areas and interests. Other research has pointed to the masculine orientation of much computer software, particularly computer games. Hess and Muira found that the educational software programs most likely found in math and science classes center around male themes of violence and adventure. Consequently, girls may come to see math, science, and computer-related activities as masculine—a perception that may affect not only their performance, but also their career aspirations. In addition, research indicates that girls may pay a heavy social cost for computer proficiency. When interviewing adolescents, for example, Crawford (1990:25) heard many stories from female achievers in computer studies "of the boys being 'jealous' of [the girls'] knowledge of electronics and of 'hassling' the girls in class. The boys confirmed their view." Not surprisingly, then, as one young woman reported about girls who pursue computer science, "It's usually the brave that do it" (quoted in Crawford 1990:25).

Box 3   *continued*

Fennema and Sherman discovered that the major difference between males and females with regard to mathematics is not math ability per se, but rather extent of exposure to mathematics. Girls and boys with identical math backgrounds show little difference in performance on math tests. Yet girls are less likely than boys to pursue math training beyond their schools' requirements for graduation, and two critical factors influencing their decisions appear to be their interactions with teachers and the encouragement of their parents. Sherman, for example, reports that girls (33 percent) are much more likely than boys (10 percent) to cite a teacher as the factor that most discouraged them from studying math. Research on teacher-student interaction indicates that there are various ways that teachers differentially reinforce math achievement in male and female students: by perceiving and conveying the belief that math is more important for boys than for girls, by encouraging girls to become proficient at computational math and boys at problem solving, and by calling on boys more than girls to solve problems in class.

Girls who pursue math training tend to be closer to their parents and more influenced by them. Although few parents openly discourage their daughters from studying math or math-related fields, the message may be communicated indirectly. For instance, recent research indicates that parents are much less likely to enroll daughters than sons in computer camps, especially when the cost of the camps is high. Importantly, although girls and boys both recognize that computers will have a significant impact on their personal futures, boys are more likely to report having access to computers at home.

In summary, the weight of the evidence points to a variety of social factors as being responsible for observed differences in math achievement between males and females. In one sense, this is encouraging since socially induced conditions are more easily changed than those that are biologically caused. Indeed, the solution seems obvious: educators and parents must consciously commit themselves to providing a more supportive and less sex-segregated learning environment for both boys and girls. Until steps are taken, math will probably remain a "critical filter" that blocks females' advancement into the lucrative and prestigious scientific professions

NOTES

1. We did find that, compared with our examination of toy catalogs in 1989, there were some minor improvements in the 1993 catalogs in terms of the gender images depicted. For example, in 1993, it was common to see a little girl playing with a doctor's kit and a little boy playing in a toy kitchen. The biggest improvement, however, has been that minority children are shown more frequently than in the past. Unfortunately, children with physical disabilities are still missing from toy catalogs, although they are sometimes shown in children's clothing catalogs.

2. In late 1991, a small woman-owned company, High Self-Esteem Toys Corporation, began marketing a new doll called "Happy to Be Me." The doll was created by Cathy Meredig out of concern for women's and girls' commonly expressed dissatisfaction with their bodies and their chronic (and often harmful) dieting. Consequently, the Happy to Be Me doll is proportioned more like an average woman (36–27–38) and has larger feet which, unlike Barbie's, are not molded into a shape to wear

only high heels (*New York Times* 15 August 1991:C11).

3. Interestingly, research also shows that when boys call out comments in class without raising their hands, teachers usually accept their answers. When girls call out, however, teachers typically reprimand them for this "inappropriate" behavior by responding with comments such as, "In this class we don't shout out answers, we raise our hands" (Sadker and Sadker 1994).

REFERENCES

American Association of University Women (AAUW) 1992 *How Schools Shortchange Girls*. Washington, DC: American Association of University Women Educational Foundation and National Education Association.

Bush, D. M. 1987 "The Impact of Family and School on Adolescent Girls' Aspirations and Expectations: The Public-Private Split and the Reproduction of Gender Inequality," Paper presented at the Annual meeting of the American Sociological Association, Chicago, IL.

Corsaro, W. A., and D. Eder 1990 "Children's Peer Cultures," Pp. 197–220 in W. R. Scott (Ed.), *Annual Review of Sociology, Volume 16*, Palo Alto, CA: Annual Reviews, Inc.

Crawford, K. 1990 "Girls and Computers," *Refractory Girl* May:21–26.

Davies, B. 1989 *Frogs and Snails and Feminist Tales*. Sydney: Allen and Unwin.

DeLoache, J. S., D. J. Cassidy, and C. J. Carpenter 1987 "The Three Bears Are All Boys: Mothers' Gender Labeling of Neutral Picture Book Characters." *Sex Roles* 17:163–178.

Hale-Benson, Janice E. 1986 *Black Children: Their Roots, Culture and Learning Styles* (Revised Edition). Provo, UT: Brigham Young University Press.

Kolker, A., and B. M. Burke 1992 "Sex Preference and Sex Selection: Attitudes of Prenatal Diagnosis Clients," Paper presented at the Annual Meeting of the American Sociological Association, Pittsburgh, PA.

Kristof, N. D. 1991 "Stark Data on Women: 100 Million are Missing," *New York Times* 5 November: C1, C12.

Lawson, C. 1989 "Toys: Girls Still Apply Makeup, Boys Fight Wars," *New York Times* 15 June:C1, C10.

Lott, B. 1987 *Women's Lives: Themes and Variations in Gender Learning*. Monterey, CA: Brooks/Cole Publishing Company.

Miller, C. L. 1987 "Qualitative Differences Among Gender-Stereotyped Toys: Implications for Cognitive and Social Development in Girls and Boys," *Sex Roles* 16:473–488.

Reid, P. T. 1982 "Socialization of Black Female Children," Pp. 137–155 in P. Berman (Ed.), *Women: A Developmental Perspective*. Bethesda, MD: National Institutes of Health.

Rheingold, H. L., and K. V. Cook 1975 "The Content of Boys' and Girls' Rooms as an Index of Parents' Behavior" *Child Development* 46:459–463.

Richardson, L. W. 1981 *The Dynamics of Sex and Gender*. Boston: Houghton Mifflin.

Sadker, M., and D. Sadker 1994 *Failing at Fairness*. New York: Charles Scribner's Sons.

Scott, K., and C. Schau 1985 "Sex Equity and Sex Bias in Instructional Materials," Pp. 218–260 in S. Klein (Ed.), *Handbook for Achieving Sex Equity Through Education*. Baltimore, MD: Johns Hopkins University Press.

Sears, J. T. 1992 "Educators, Homosexuality, and Homosexual Students: Are Personal Feelings Related to Professional Beliefs?" Pp. 29–79 in K. M. Harbeck (Ed.), *Coming Out of the Classroom Closet: Gay and Lesbian Students, Teachers, and Curricula*. New York: Haworth Press.

Shakin, M., D. Shakin, and S. H. Sternglanz 1985 "Infant Clothing: Sex Labeling for Strangers," *Sex Roles* 12:955–964.

Uribe, V., and K. M. Harbeck 1992 "Addressing the Needs of Lesbian, Gay and Bisexual Youth: The Origins of PROJECT 10 and School-Based Intervention." Pp. 9–28 in K. M. Harbeck (Ed.), *Coming Out of the Classroom Closet: Gay and Lesbian Students, Teachers, and Curricula*. New York: Haworth Press.

Williams, J. A., Jr., J. A. Vernon, M. C. Williams, and K. Malecha 1987 "Sex Role Socialization in Picture Books: An Update," *Social Science Quarterly* 68:148–156.

X: A Fabulous Child's Story

Lois Gould

Once upon a time, a Baby named X was born. It was named X so that nobody could tell whether it was a boy or a girl.

Its parents could tell, of course, but they couldn't tell anybody else. They couldn't even tell Baby X—at least not until much, much later.

You see, it was all part of a very important Secret Scientific Xperiment, known officially as Project Baby X.

This Xperiment was going to cost Xactly 23 billion dollars and 72 cents. Which might seem like a lot for one Baby, even if it was an important Secret Scientific Xperimental Baby.

But when you remember the cost of strained carrots, stuffed bunnies, booster shots, 28 shiny quarters from the tooth fairy . . . you begin to see how it adds up.

Long before Baby X was born, the smartest scientists had to work out the secret details of the Xperiment, and to write the *Official Instruction Manual*, in secret code, for Baby X's parents, whoever they were.

These parents had to be selected very carefully. Thousands of people volunteered to take thousands of tests, with thousands of tricky questions.

Almost everybody failed because, it turned out, almost everybody wanted a boy or a girl, and not a Baby X at all.

Also, almost everybody thought a Baby X would be more trouble than a boy or a girl. (They were right, too.)

There were families with grandparents named Milton and Agatha, who wanted the baby named Milton or Agatha instead of X, even if it *was* an X.

There were aunts who wanted to knit tiny dresses and uncles who wanted to send tiny baseball mitts.

Worst of all, there were families with other children who couldn't be trusted to keep a Secret. Not if they knew the Secret was worth 23 billion dollars and 72 cents—and all you had to do was take one little peek at Baby X in the bathtub to know what it was.

Finally, the scientists found the Joneses, who really wanted to raise an X more than any other kind of baby—no matter how much trouble it was.

The Joneses promised to take turns holding X, feeding X, and singing X to sleep.

And they promised never to hire any babysitters. The scientists knew that a babysitter would probably peek at X in the bathtub, too.

The day the Joneses brought their baby home, lots of friends and relatives came to see it. And the first thing they asked was what kind of a baby X was.

When the Joneses said "It's an X!" nobody knew what to say.

They couldn't say, "Look at her cute little dimples!"

On the other hand, they couldn't say "Look at his husky little biceps!"

And they didn't feel right about saying just plain "kitchy-coo."

The relatives all felt embarrassed about having an X in the family.

"People will think there's something wrong with it!" they whispered.

"Nonsense!" the Joneses said cheerfully. "What could possibly be wrong with this perfectly adorable X?"

Clearly, nothing at all was wrong. Nevertheless, the cousins who had sent a tiny football helmet would not come and visit anymore. And the neighbors who sent a pink-flowered romper suit pulled their shades down when the Joneses passed their house.

The *Official Instruction Manual* had warned the new parents that this would happen, so they didn't fret about it. Besides, they were too busy learning how to bring up Baby X.

Ms. and Mr. Jones had to be Xtra careful. If they kept bouncing it up in the air and saying how *strong* and *active* it was, they'd be treating it more like a boy than an X. But if all they did was cuddle it and kiss it and tell it how *sweet* and *dainty* it was, they'd be treating it more like a girl than an X.

On page 1654 of the *Official Instruction Manual*, the scientists prescribed: "plenty of bouncing and plenty of cuddling, *both*. X ought to be strong and sweet and active. Forget about *dainty* altogether."

There were other problems, too. Toys, for instance. And clothes. On his first shopping trip, Mr. Jones told the store clerk, "I need some things for a new baby." The clerk smiled and said, "Well, now, is it a boy or a girl?" "It's an X," Mr. Jones said, smiling back. But the clerk got all red in the face and said huffily, "In *that* case, I'm afraid I can't help you sir."

Mr. Jones wandered the aisles trying to find what X needed. But everything was in sections marked BOYS or GIRLS: "Boys' Pajamas" and "Girls' Underwear" and "Boys' Fire Engines" and "Girls' Housekeeping Sets." Mr. Jones went home without buying anything for X.

That night he and Ms. Jones consulted page 2326 of the *Official Instruction Manual*. It said firmly: "Buy plenty of everything!"

So they bought all kinds of toys. A boy doll that made pee-pee and cried "Pa-Pa." And a girl doll that talked in three languages and said, "I am the Pres-i-dent of Gen-er-al Mo-tors."

They bought a storybook about a brave princess who rescued a handsome prince from his tower, and another one about a sister and brother who grew up to be a baseball star and a ballet star, and you had to guess which.

The head scientists of Project Baby X checked all their purchases and told them to keep up the good work. They also reminded the Joneses to see page 4629 of the *Manual*, where it said, "Never make Baby X feel *embarrassed* or *ashamed* about what it wants to play with. And if X gets dirty climbing rocks, never say, 'Nice little Xes don't get dirty climbing rocks.'"

Likewise, it said, "If X falls down and cries, never say, 'Brave little Xes don't cry.' Because, of course, nice little Xes *do* get dirty, and brave little Xes *do* cry. No matter how dirty X gets, or how hard it cries, don't worry. It's all part of the Xperiment."

Whenever the Joneses pushed Baby X's stroller in the park, smiling strangers would come over and coo: "Is that a boy or a girl?" The Joneses would smile back and say, "It's an X." The strangers would stop smiling then and often snarl something nasty—as if the Joneses had said something nasty to *them*.

Once a little girl grabbed X's shovel in the sandbox, and zonked X on the head with it. "Now, now, Tracy," the mother began to scold, "little girls mustn't hit little—" and she turned to ask X, "Are you a little boy or a little girl, dear?"

Mr. Jones, who was sitting near the sandbox, held his breath and crossed his fingers.

X smiled politely, even though X's head had never been zonked so hard in its life. "I'm a little X," said X.

"You're a *what*?" the lady exclaimed angrily. "You're a little b-r-a-t, you mean!"

"But little girls mustn't hit little Xes, either!" said X, retrieving the shovel with another polite smile. "What good's hitting, anyway?"

X's father finally X-haled, uncrossed his fingers, and grinned.

And at their next secret Project Baby X meeting, the scientists grinned, too. Baby X was doing fine.

But then it was time for X to start school. The Joneses were really worried about this, because school was even more full of rules for boys and girls, and there were no rules for Xes.

Teachers would tell boys to form a line, and girls to form another line.

There would be boys' games and girls' games, and boys' secrets and girls' secrets.

The school library would have a list of recommended books for girls, and a different list for boys.

There would even be a bathroom marked BOYS and another one marked GIRLS.

Pretty soon boys and girls would hardly talk to each other. What would happen to poor little X?

The Joneses spent weeks consulting their *Instruction Manual.*

There were 249 and one-half pages of advice under "First Day of School." Then they were all summoned to an Urgent Xtra Special Conference with the smart scientists of Project Baby X.

The scientists had to make sure that X's mother had taught X how to throw and catch a ball properly, and that X's father had been sure to teach X what to serve at a doll's tea party.

X had to know how to shoot marbles and jump rope and, most of all, what to say when the Other Children asked whether X was a Boy or a Girl.

Finally, X was ready.

X's teacher had promised that the class could line up alphabetically, instead of forming separate lines for boys and girls. And X had permission to use the principal's bathroom, because it wasn't marked anything except BATH-ROOM. But nobody could help X with the biggest problem of all—Other Children.

Nobody in X's class had ever known an X. Nobody had even heard grown-ups say, "Some of my best friends are Xes."

What would other children think? Would they make Xist jokes? Or would they make friends?

You couldn't tell what X was by its clothes. Overalls don't even button right to left, like girls' clothes, or left to right, like boys' clothes.

And did X have a girl's short haircut or a boy's long haircut?

As for the games X liked, either X played ball very well for a girl, or else played house very well for a boy.

The children tried to find out by asking X tricky questions, like, "Who's your favorite sports star?" X had two favorite sports stars: a girl jockey named Robyn Smith and a boy archery champion named Robin Hood.

Then they asked, "What's your favorite TV show?" And X said: "Lassie," which stars a girl dog played by a boy dog.

When X said its favorite toy was a doll, everyone decided that X must be a girl. But then X said the doll was really a robot, and that X had computerized it, and that it was programmed to bake fudge and then clean up the kitchen.

After X told them that, they gave up guessing what X was. All they knew was they'd sure like to see X's doll.

After school, X wanted to play with the other children. "How about shooting baskets in the gym?" X asked the girls. But all they did was make faces and giggle behind X's back.

"Boy, is *he* weird," whispered Jim to Joe.

"How about weaving some baskets in the arts and crafts room?" X asked the boys. But they all made faces and giggled behind X's back, too.

"Boy, is *she* weird," whispered Susie to Peggy.

That night, Ms. and Mr. Jones asked X how things had gone at school. X tried to smile, but there were two big tears in its eyes. "The lessons are okay," X began, "but . . ."

"But?" said Ms. Jones.

"The Other Children hate me," X whispered.

"Hate you?" said Mr. Jones.

X nodded, which made the two big tears roll down and splash on its overalls.

Once more, the Joneses reached for their *Instruction Manual.* Under "Other Children," it said:

"What did you Xpect? Other Children have to obey silly boy-girl rules, because their parents taught them to. Lucky X—you don't have rules at all! All you have to do is be yourself.

"P.S. We're not saying it'll be easy."

X liked being itself. But X cried a lot that night. So X's father held X tight, and cried a little, too. X's mother cheered them up with an Xciting story about an enchanted prince called Sleeping Handsome, who woke up when Princess Charming kissed him.

The next morning, they all felt much better, and little X went back to school with a brave smile and a clean pair of red and white checked overalls.

There was a seven-letter-word spelling bee in class that day. And a seven-lap boys' relay race in the gym. And a seven-layer-cake baking contest in the girls' kitchen corner.

X won the spelling bee. X also won the relay race.

And X almost won the baking contest, Xcept it forgot to light the oven. (Remember, nobody's perfect.)

One of the Other Children noticed something else, too. He said: "X doesn't care about winning. X just thinks it's fun playing boys' stuff *and* girls' stuff."

"Come to think of it," said another one of the Other Children, "X is having twice as much fun as we are!"

After school that day, the girl who beat X in the baking contest gave X a big slice of her winning cake.

And the boy X beat in the relay race asked X to race him home.

From then on, some really funny things began to happen.

Susie, who sat next to X, refused to wear pink dresses to school any more. She wanted red and white checked overalls-just like X's.

Overalls, she told her parents, were better for climbing monkey bars.

Then Jim, the class football nut, started wheeling his little sister's doll carriage around the football field.

He'd put on his entire football uniform, except for the helmet.

Then he'd put the helmet *in* the carriage, lovingly tucked under an old set of shoulder pads.

Then he'd jog around the field, pushing the carriage and singing "Rockabye Baby" to his helmet.

He said X did the same thing, so it must be okay. After all, X was now the team's star quarterback.

Susie's parents were horrified by her behavior, and Jim's parents were worried sick about his.

But the worst came when the twins, Joe and Peggy, decided to share everything with each other.

Peggy used Joe's hockey skates, and his microscope, and took half his newspaper route.

Joe used Peggy's needlepoint kit, and her cookbooks, and took two of her three babysitting jobs.

Peggy ran the lawn mower, and Joe ran the vacuum cleaner.

Their parents weren't one bit pleased with Peggy's science experiments, or with Joe's terrific needlepoint pillows.

They didn't care that Peggy mowed the lawn better, and that Joe vacuumed the carpet better.

In fact, they were furious. It's all that little X's fault, they agreed. X doesn't know what it is, or what it's supposed to be! So X wants to mix everybody *else* up, too!

Peggy and Joe were forbidden to play with X any more. So was Susie, and then Jim, and then *all* the Other Children.

But it was too late: the Other Children stayed mixed-up and happy and free, and refused to go back to the way they'd been before X.

Finally, the parents held an emergency meeting to discuss "The X Problem."

They sent a report to the principal stating that X was a "bad influence," and demanding immediate action.

The Joneses, they said, should be *forced* to tell whether X was a boy or a girl. And X should be *forced* to behave like whichever it was.

If the Joneses refused to tell, the parents said, then X must take an Xamination. An Impartial Team of Xperts would Xtract the secret. Then X would start obeying all the old rules. Or else.

And if X turned out to be some kind of mixed-up misfit, then X must be Xpelled from school. Immediately! So that no little Xes would ever come to school again.

The principal was very upset. X, a bad influence? A mixed-up misfit? But X was a Xcellent student! X set a fine Xample! X was Xtraordinary!

X was president of the student council. X had won first prize in the art show, honorable mention in the science fair, and six events on field day, including the potato race.

Nevertheless, insisted the parents, X is a Problem Child. X is the Biggest Problem Child we have ever seen!

So the principal reluctantly notified X's parents and the Joneses reported this to the Project X scientists, who referred them to page 85769 of the *Instruction Manual*. "Sooner or later," it said "X will have to be Xamined by an Impartial Team of Xperts.

"This may be the only way any of us will know for sure whether X is mixed up—or everyone else is."

At Xactly 9 o'clock the next day, X reported to the school health office. The principal, along with a committee from the Parents' Association, X's teacher, X's classmates, and Ms. and Mr. Jones, waited in the hall outside.

Inside, the Xperts had set up their famous testing machine: the Superpsychiamedicosocioculturometer.

Nobody knew Xactly how the machine worked, but everybody knew that this examination would reveal Xactly what everyone wanted to know about X, but were afraid to ask.

It was terribly quiet in the hall. Almost spooky. They could hear very strange noises from the room.

There were buzzes.

And a beep or two.

And several bells.

An occasional light flashed under the door. Was it an X ray?

Through it all, you could hear the Xperts' voices, asking questions, and X's voice, answering answers.

I wouldn't like to be in X's overalls right now, the children thought.

At last, the door opened. Everyone crowded around to hear the results. X didn't look any different, in fact, X was smiling. But the Impartial Team of Xperts looked terrible. They looked as if they were crying!

"What happened?" everyone began shouting.

"*Sssh*," ssshed the principal. "The Xperts are trying to speak."

Wiping his eyes and clearing his throat, one Xpert began: "In our opinion," he whispered—you could tell he must be very upset— "in our opinion, young X here—"

"Yes? Yes?" shouted a parent.

"Young X," said the other Xpert, frowning, "is just about the *least* mixed-up child we've ever Xamined?" Xclaimed the two Xperts, together. Behind the closed door, the Superpsychiamedicosocioculturometer made a noise like a contented hum.

"Yay for X!" yelled one of the children. And then the others began yelling, too. Clapping and cheering and jumping up and down.

"*SSSH*!" SSShed the principal, but nobody did.

The Parents' Committee was angry and bewildered. How *could* X have passed the whole Xamination?

Didn't X have an *identity* problem? Wasn't X mixed up at *all*? Wasn't X *any* kind of a misfit?

How could it *not* be, when it didn't even *know* what it was?

"Don't you see?" asked the Xperts. "X isn't one bit mixed up! As for being a misfit—ridiculous! X knows perfectly well what it is! Don't you, X?" The Xperts winked. X winked back.

"But what *is* X?" shrieked Peggy and Joe's parents. "*We* still want to know what it is!"

"Ah, yes," said the Xperts, winking again. "Well, don't worry. You'll all know one of these days. And you won't need us to tell you."

"What? What do they mean?" Jim's parents grumbled suspiciously.

Susie and Peggy and Joe all answered at once. "They mean that by the time it matters which sex X is, it won't be a secret any more!"

With that, the Xperts reached out to hug Ms. and Mr. Jones. "If we ever have an X of our own," they whispered, "we sure hope you'll lend us your instruction manual."

Needless to say, the Joneses were very happy. The Project Baby X scientists were rather pleased, too. So were Susie, Jim, Peggy, Joe, and all the Other Children. Even the parents promised not to make any trouble.

Later that day, all X's friends put on their red and white checked overalls and went over to see X.

They found X in the backyard, playing with a very tiny baby that none of them had ever seen before.

The baby was wearing very tiny red and white checked overalls.

"How do you like our new baby?" X asked the Other Children proudly.

"It's got cute dimples," said Jim. "It's got husky biceps, too," said Susie.

"What kind of baby is it?" asked Joe and Peggy.

X frowned at them. "Can't you tell?" Then X broke into a big, mischievous grin. "*It's a Y!*"

Sexuality and Violence

The process of gender socialization obviously includes learning, using, and attending to language. In " 'Pricks' and 'Chicks': A Plea for 'Persons'," Robert Baker argues that our language does not serve women well. First, it regards man as "essentially human, while woman is only accidentally so." Thus, " 'humanity' is synonymous with 'mankind' but not with 'womankind' " (p. 37). Second, women are linguistically related, at least in men's speech, to certain types of animals (chick, fox), playthings (babe, doll), items of clothing (skirt), and anatomical parts associated with sexual intercourse (snatch, cunt). Third, our language embeds a conception of sexual intercourse in which men play the role of active victimizers and women play the role of passive victims (men "screw" women and not vice versa). In sum, says Baker, our language teaches us something very distressing: namely, that what makes men "fully human" is, paradoxically, the fact that they use sex to make women less than fully human. But, continues Baker, since speech not only reflects the way we think but also guides the way we act, if we want better (more equal) sexual relations between men and women, we must revise our conception of heterosexuality and the words we use to articulate it. This revision and others like it, however, will require us to eliminate pernicious gender valences from our conceptual-linguistic schema.

To be sure, concedes Baker, this is no easy task since gender is probably the central feature of our language. When a baby is born, the first thing everyone wants to know is whether it is a "he" or a "she." Baker's call for gender-free language seems, then, far more radical than Lois Gould's plea for gender-free child rearing. But is it possible to change our thoughts and words before we change our practices, or must we change our thoughts, words, and practices simultaneously?

These last questions are urgent ones with implications for the world in which we live. If Baker is correct, for example, about the disturbing conception of heterosexuality that is revealed in our speech and thought, then we can understand the pervasiveness of sexual violence against women in our society. This sexual violence takes many forms—rape, woman-battering, and sexual harassment, among others—and is so prevalent that Carole Sheffield terms it and the fear it evokes "sexual terrorism":

The word *terrorism* invokes images of furtive organizations of the far right or left, whose members blow up buildings and cars, hijack airplanes, and murder innocent people in some country other than ours. But there is a different kind of terrorism, one that so pervades our culture that we have learned to live with it as though it were the natural order of things. Its target is females—of all ages, races, and classes. It is the common characteristic of rape, wife battery, incest, pornography, harassment, and all forms of sexual violence. I call it *sexual terrorism* because it is a system by which males frighten and, by frightening, control and dominate females. ("Sexual Terrorism," pp. 45–46).

Sexual terrorism transcends all boundaries. It is committed by men of all ages, races,

32

and religions, from all socioeconomic classes and educational levels, and whether these men are married, single, separated, or divorced. Most of this violence goes unreported, and when it is reported, unpunished (rape, for example, has the lowest conviction rate of all violent crimes). When society does take sexual violence against girls and women at all seriously, it still tends to blame the victims and to excuse the offenders. Even worse than its "blame-the-victim" attitude, however, is that society usually jokes about, outrightly denies, or misunderstands the nature and function of sexual violence. Underlying all manifestations of sexual violence, claims Sheffield, is misogyny, the hatred of women, and the function of all this violence is the domination of women. Sexual violence against women "is power expressed sexually. It is violence eroticized" (p. 59).

A form of sexual violence especially misunderstood by society and mishandled by our legal system is "date rape," the subject of Lois Pineau's essay ("Date Rape: A Feminist Analysis"). In criminal law, a defendant must display the appropriate mental state (*mens rea*, or "guilty mind"), as well as the appropriate physical action (*actus reas*), in order to be guilty of a crime. Thus, in the case of date rape (or "nonaggravated sexual assault") the defendant must do more than have "sex" with his victim; he must believe (know) that she did not consent to have sexual intercourse with him—that she said a more or less clear "no" to him. Interestingly, despite the fact that date rape occurs far more frequently than so-called stranger rape, date rape has a far lower rate of arrest and conviction than stranger rape, and this because it is so difficult to establish *mens rea* in date rape. Pineau claims that all sorts of myths about women clog our thinking about women's consent (non-consent) to sex—for example, that women are coy about their sexual desires and hence are not to be believed when they protest "no"; that women are naturally reluctant in sexual matters and hence either require or welcome masterful advances; that women "ask for it" (i.e., consent) when they engage in sexually provocative behavior; and that men's sexual response is uncontrollable once aroused. Dispelling each of these myths in turn, Pineau argues for a new norm for sexual encounters which she terms "communicative sexuality." Women have to learn how to voice their sexual wishes and men have to learn how to hear them.

If any man who wants to be "masculine" is a potential perpetrator of sexual violence against women, and if society currently does little to protect women from this violence or even to acknowledge it, we can understand why some women eschew sexual relationships with men, preferring instead to form lesbian relationships with women. But not even women who choose to love women can free themselves from the trap of "masculine" sex. The language women—including lesbian women—use to explore their sexuality is a language dominated by male metaphors and images. Indeed, as Marilyn Frye points out in "Lesbian 'Sex,' " ". . . the concept of 'having sex' is a phallic concept; . . . it pertains to heterosexual intercourse, in fact, primarily to heterosex*ist* intercourse, i.e., male-dominant-female-subordinate-copulation-whose-completion-and-purpose-is-the-male's-ejaculation" (p. 73). Thus, when a scientific study of the sex lives of heterosexual, lesbian, and gay couples concludes that lesbians "have sex" far less frequently than heterosexual and gay couples, the reference point of the scientists conducting the study are unclear. If only acts of "penetration" count as sex, then it is no wonder that lesbians have less sex than heterosexuals and gays. Lesbian sex is not so much about penetration as it is about a rhythmic, pulsating union. Clearly, women need a sexual language that expresses *women's* sexuality in all its sensuous, emotional, intellectual, and aesthetic detail.

"Pricks" and "Chicks": A Plea for "Persons"

Robert Baker

There is a school of philosophers who believe that one starts philosophizing not by examining whatever it is one is philosophizing about but by examining the words we use to designate the subject to be examined. I must confess my allegiance to this school. The import of my confession is that this is an essay on women's liberation.

There seems to be a curious malady that affects those philosophers who in order to analyze anything must examine the way we talk about it; they seem incapable of talking about anything without talking about their talk about it—and, once again, I must confess to being typical. Thus I shall argue, first, that the way in which we identify something reflects our conception of it; second, that the conception of women embedded in our language is male chauvinistic; third, that the conceptual revisions proposed by the feminist movement are confused; and finally, that at the root of the problem are both our conception of sex and the very structure of sexual identification.

IDENTIFICATION AND CONCEPTION

I am not going to defend the position that the terms we utilize to identify something reflect our conception of it; I shall simply explain and

From *Philosophy and Sex,* new revised edition, edited by Robert Baker and Frederick Elliston. Copyright © 1984 by Robert Baker and Frederick Elliston. Reprinted by permission of Prometheus Books.

illustrate a simplified version of this thesis. Let us assume that any term that can be (meaningfully) substituted for x in the following statements is a term used to identify something: "Where is the x?" "Who is the x?" Some of the terms that can be substituted for x in the above expressions are metaphors; I shall refer to such metaphors as metaphorical identifications. For example, southerners frequently say such things as "Where did that girl get to?" and "Who is the new boy that Lou hired to help out at the filling station?" If the persons the terms apply to are adult Afro-Americans, then "girl" and "boy" are metaphorical identifications. The fact that the metaphorical identifications in question are standard in the language reflects the fact that certain characteristics of the objects properly classified as boys and girls (for example, immaturity, inability to take care of themselves, need for guidance) are generally held by those who use identifications to be properly attributable to Afro-Americans. One might say that the whole theory of southern white paternalism is implicit in the metaphorical identification "boy" (just as the rejection of paternalism is implicit in the standardized Afro-American forms of address, "man" and "woman," as in, for example, "Hey, man, how are you?").

Most of what I am going to say in this essay is significant only if the way we metaphorically identify something is not a superficial bit of conceptually irrelevant happpenstance but rather a reflection of our conceptual structure. Thus if one is to accept my analysis he must understand the significance of metaphorical identifications. He must see that, even though the southerner who identifies adult

Afro-American males as "boys" feels that this identification is "just the way people talk"; but for a group to talk that way it must think that way. In the next few paragraphs I shall adduce what I hope is a persuasive example of how, in one clear case, the change in the way we identified something reflected a change in the way we thought about it.

Until the 1960s, Afro-Americans were identified by such terms as "Negro" and "colored" (the respectable terms) and by the more disreputable "nigger," "spook," "kink," and so on. Recently there has been an unsuccessful attempt to replace the respectable identifications with such terms as "African," and "Afro-American," and a more successful attempt to replace them with "black." The most outspoken champions of this linguistic reform were those who argued that nonviolence must be abandoned for Black Power (Stokely Carmichael, H. Rap Brown), that integration must be abandoned in favor of separation (the Black Muslims: Malcolm X, Muhammad Ali), and that Afro-Americans were an internal colony in the alien world of Babylon who must arm themselves against the possibility of extermination (the Black Panthers: Eldridge Cleaver, Huey Newton). All of these movements and their partisans wished to stress that Afro-Americans were different from other Americans and could not be merged with them because the differences between the two was as great as that between black and white. Linguistically, of course, "black" and "white" are antonyms; and it is precisely this sense of oppositeness that those who see the Afro-American as alienated, separated, and nonintegratable wish to capture with the term "black." Moreover, as any good dictionary makes clear, in some contexts "black" is synonymous with "deadly," "sinister," "wicked," "evil," and so forth. The new militants were trying to create just this picture of the black man—civil rights and Uncle Tomism are dead, the ghost of Nat Turner is to be resurrected, Freedom Now or pay the price, the ballot or the bullet, "Vio-

lence is as American as cherry pie." The new strategy was that the white man would either give the black man his due or pay the price in violence. Since conceptually a "black man" was an object to be feared ("black" can be synonymous with "deadly," and so on), while a "colored man" or a "Negro" was not, the new strategy required that the "Negro" be supplanted by the "black man." White America resisted the proposed linguistic reform quite vehemently, until hundreds of riots forced the admission that the Afro-American was indeed black.

Now to the point: I have suggested that the word "black" replaced the word "Negro" because there was a change in our conceptual structure. One is likely to reply that while all that I have said above is well and good, one had, after all, no choice about the matter. White people are identified in terms of their skin color as whites; clearly, if we are to recognize what is in reality nothing but the truth, that in this society people are conscious of skin color, to treat blacks as equals is merely to identify them by their skin color, which is black. That is, one might argue that while there was a change in words, we have no reason to think that there was a parallel conceptual change. If the term "black" has all the associations mentioned above, that is unfortunate; but in the context the use of the term "black" to identify the people formerly identified as "Negroes" is natural, inevitable, and, in and of itself, neutral; black is, after all, the skin color of the people in question. (Notice that this defense of the natural-inevitable-and-neutral conception of identification quite nicely circumvents the possible use of such seemingly innocuous terms as "Afro-American" and "African" by suggesting that in this society it is *skin color* that is the relevant variable.)

The great flaw in this analysis is that the actual skin color of virtually all of the people whom we call "black" is not black at all. The color tones range from light yellow to a deep umber that occasionally is literally black. The skin color of most Afro-Americans is best designated by the word "brown." Yet "brown" is not a term that is standard for identifying Afro-Americans. For example, if someone asked, "Who was the brown who was the architect for Washington, D.C.?" we would not know how to construe the question. We might attempt to read "brown" as a proper name ("Do you mean Arthur Brown, the designer?"). We would have no trouble understanding the sentence "Who was the black (Negro, colored guy, and so forth) who designed Washington, D.C.?" ("Oh, you mean Benjamin Banneker"). Clearly, "brown" is not a standard form of identification for Afro-Americans. I hope that it is equally clear that "black" has become the standard way of identifying Afro-Americans not because the term was natural, inevitable, and, in the context, neutral, but because of its occasional synonymy with "sinister" and because as an antonym to "white" it best fitted the conceptual needs of those who saw race relations in terms of intensifying and insurmountable antonymies. If one accepts this point, then one must admit that there is a close connection between the way in which we identify things and the way in which we conceive them—and thus it should be also clear why I wish to talk about the way in which women are identified in English. (Thus, for example, one would expect Black Muslims, who continually use the term "black *man*"—as in "the black *man's* rights"—to be more male chauvinistic than Afro-Americans who use the term "black *people*" or "black *folk*.")

WAYS OF IDENTIFYING WOMEN

It may at first seem trivial to note that women (and men) are identified sexually; but conceptually this is extremely significant. To appreciate the significance of this fact it is helpful to imagine a language in which proper names and personal pronouns do not reflect the sex of the person designated by them (as they do in our language). I have been told that in some orien-

tal languages pronouns and proper names reflect social status rather than sex, but whether or not there actually exists such a language is irrelevant, for it is easy enough to imagine what one would be like. Let us then imagine a language where the proper names are sexually neutral (for example, "Xanthe"), so that one cannot tell from hearing a name whether the person so named is male or female, and where the personal pronouns in the language are "under" and "over." "Under" is the personal pronoun appropriate for all those who are younger than thirty, while "over" is appropriate to persons older than thirty. In such a language, instead of saying such things as "Where do you think *he* is living now?" one would say such things as "Where do you think *under* is living now?"

What would one say about a cultural community that employed such a language? Clearly, one would say that they thought that for purposes of intelligible communication it was more important to know a person's age grouping than the person's height, sex, race, hair color, or parentage. (There are many actual cultures, of course, in which people are identified by names that reflect their parentage; for example, Abu ben Adam means Abu son of Adam.) I think that one would also claim that this people would not have reflected these differences in the pronominal structure of their language if they did not believe that the differences between unders and overs was such that a statement would frequently have one meaning if it were about an under and a different meaning if it were about an over. For example, in feudal times if a serf said, "My lord said to do this," that assertion was radically different from "Freeman John said to do this," since (presumably) the former had the status of a command while the latter did not. Hence the conventions of Middle English required that one refer to people in such a way as to indicate their social status. Analogously, one would not distinguish between pronominal references according to the age differences in the persons referred to were there no shift in meaning involved.

If we apply the lesson illustrated by this imaginary language to our own, I think that it should be clear that since in our language proper nouns and pronouns reflect sex rather than age, race, parentage, social status, or religion, we believe one of the most important things one can know about a person is that person's sex. (And, indeed, this is the first thing one seeks to determine about a newborn babe—our first question is almost invariably "Is it a boy or a girl?") Moreover, we would not reflect this important difference pronominally did we not also believe that statements frequently mean one thing when applied to males and something else when applied to females. Perhaps the most striking aspect of the conceptual discrimination reflected in our language is that man is, as it were, essentially human, while woman is only accidentally so.

This charge may seem rather extreme, but consider the following synonyms (which are readily confirmed by any dictionary). "Humanity" is synonymous with "mankind" but not with "womankind." "Man" can be substituted for "humanity" or "mankind" in any sentence in which the terms "mankind" or "humanity" occur without changing the meaning of the sentence, but significantly, "woman" cannot. Thus, the following expressions are all synonymous with each other: "humanity's great achievements," "mankind's great achievements," and "man's great achievements." "Woman's great achievements" is not synonymous with any of these. To highlight the degree to which women are excluded from humanity, let me point out that it is something of a truism to say that "man is a rational animal," while "woman is a rational animal" is quite debatable. Clearly, if "man" in the first assertion embraced both men and women, the second assertion would be just as much a truism as the first. Humanity, it would seem, is a male prerogative. (And hence, one of the goals of

women's liberation is to alter our conceptual structure so that someday "mankind" will be regarded as an improper and vestigial ellipsis for "humankind," and "man" will have no special privileges in relation to "human being" that "woman" does not have.)

The major question before us is, How are women conceived of in our culture? I have been trying to answer this question by talking about how they are identified. I first considered pronominal identification; now I wish to turn to identification through other types of noun phrases. Methods of nonpronominal identification can be discovered by determining which terms can be substituted for "woman" in such sentences as "Who is that woman over there?" without changing the meaning of the sentence. Virtually no term is interchangeable with "woman" in that sentence for all speakers on all occasions. Even "lady," which most speakers would accept as synonymous with "woman" in that sentence, will not do for a speaker who applies the term "lady" only to those women who display manners, poise, and sensitivity. In most contexts, a large number of students in one or more of my classes will accept the following types of terms as more or less interchangeable with "woman." (An asterisk indicates interchanges acceptable to both males and females; a plus sign indicates terms restricted to black students only. Terms with neither an asterisk nor a plus sign are accepted by all males but are not normally used by females.)

A. NEUTRAL TERMS: *lady, *gal, *girl (especially with regard to a coworker in an office or factory), * + sister, *broad (originally in the animal category, but most people do not think of the term as now meaning pregnant cow)

B. ANIMAL: *chick, bird, fox, vixen, filly, bitch (Many do not know the literal meaning of the term. Some men and most women construe this use as pejorative; they think of "bitch" in the context of "bitchy," that is, snappy, nasty, and so forth. But a large group of men claim that it is a standard nonpejorative term of identification—which may perhaps indicate that women have come to be thought of as shrews by a large subclass of men.)

C.   PLAYTHING: babe, doll, cuddly

D.   GENDER: (association with articles of clothing typically worn by those in the female gender role): skirt, hem

E.   SEXUAL: snatch, cunt, ass, twat, piece (of ass, and so forth), lay, pussy (could be put in the animal category, but most users associated it with slang expression indicating the female pubic region), + hammer (related to anatomical analogy between a hammer and breasts). There are many other usages, for example, "bunny," "sweat hog," but these were not recognized as standard by as many as 10 percent of any given class.

The students in my classes reported that the most frequently used terms of identification are in the neutral and animal classifications (although men in their forties claim to use the gender classifications quite a bit) and that the least frequently used terms of identification are sexual. Fortunately, however, I am not interested in the frequency of usage but only in whether the use is standard enough to be recognized as an identification among some group or other. (Recall that "brown" was not a standardized term of identification and hence we could not make sense out of "Who was the brown who planned Washington, D.C.?" Similarly, one has trouble with "Who was the breasts who planned Washington, D.C.?" but not with "Who was the babe (doll, chick, skirt, and so forth) who planned Washington, D.C.?")

Except for two of the animal terms, "chick" and "broad"—but note that "broad" is probably neutral today—women do not typically identify themselves in sexual terms, in gender terms, as playthings, or as animals; *only males use non-neutral terms to identify women.* Hence, it would seem that there is a male conception of women and a female conception. Only males

identify women as "foxes," "babes," "skirts," or "cunts" (and since all the other nonneutral identifications are male, it is reasonable to assume that the identification of a woman as a "chick" is primarily a male conception that some women have adopted).

What kind of conception do men have of women? Clearly they think that women share certain properties with certain types of animals, toys, and playthings; they conceive of them in terms of the clothes associated with the female gender role; and, last (and, if my classes are any indication, least frequently), they conceive of women in terms of those parts of their anatomy associated with sexual intercourse, that is, as the identification "lay" indicates quite clearly, as sexual partners.

The first two nonneutral male classifications, animal and plaything, are prima facie denigrating (and I mean this in the literal sense of making one like a "nigger"). Consider the animal classification. All of the terms listed, with the possible exception of "bird," refer to animals that are either domesticated for servitude (to *man*) or hunted for sport. First, let us consider the term "bird." When I asked my students what sort of birds might be indicated, they suggested chick, canary (one member, in his forties, had suggested "canary" as a term of identification), chicken, pigeon, dove, parakeet, and hummingbird (one member). With the exception of the hummingbird, which like all the birds suggested is generally thought to be diminutive and pretty, all of the birds are domesticated, usually as pets (which reminds one that "my pet" is an expression of endearment). None of the birds were predators or symbols of intelligence or nobility (as are the owl, eagle, hawk, and falcon); nor did large but beautiful birds seem appropriate (for example, pheasants, peacocks, and swans). If one construes the bird terms (and for that matter, "filly") as applicable to women because they are thought of as beautiful, or at least pretty, *then there is nothing denigrating about them.* If, on the other hand, the common properties that underlie the metaphorical identification are domesticity and servitude, then they are indeed denigrating (as for myself, I think that both domesticity and prettiness underlie the identification). "Broad," of course, is, or at least was, clearly denigrating, since nothing renders more service to a farmer than does a pregnant cow, and cows are not commonly thought of as paradigms of beauty.

With one exception all of the animal terms reflect a male conception of women either as domesticated servants or as pets, or as both. Indeed, some of the terms reflect a conception of women first as pets and then as servants. Thus, when a pretty, cuddly little chick grows older, she becomes a very useful servant—the egg-laying hen.

"Vixen" and "fox," variants of the same term, are the one clear exception. None of the other animals with whom women are metaphorically identified are generally thought to be intelligent, aggressive, or independent—but the fox is. A chick is a soft, cuddly, entertaining, pretty, diminutive, domesticated, and dumb animal. A fox too is soft, cuddly, entertaining, pretty, and diminutive, but it is neither dependent nor dumb. It is aggressive, intelligent, and a minor predator—indeed, it preys on chicks—and frequently outsmarts ("outfoxes") men.

Thus the term "fox" or "vixen" is generally taken to be a compliment by both men and women, and compared to any of the animal or plaything terms it is indeed a compliment. Yet, considered in and of itself, the conception of a woman as a fox is not really complimentary at all, for the major connection between *man* and fox is that of predator and prey. The fox is an animal that men chase, and hunt, and kill for sport. If women are conceived of as foxes, then they are conceived of as prey that it is fun to hunt.

In considering plaything identifications, only one sentence is necessary. *All the plaything identifications are clearly denigrating since they assimilate women to the status of mindless or dependent objects.* "Doll" is to male paternalism what "boy" is to white paternalism.

Up to this point in our survey of male conceptions of women, every male identification, without exception, has been clearly antithetical to the conception of women as human beings (recall that "man" was synonymous with "human," while "woman" was not). Since the way we talk of things, and especially the way we identify them, is the way in which we conceive of them, any movement dedicated to breaking the bonds of female servitude must destroy these ways of identifying and hence of conceiving of women. Only when both sexes find the terms "babe," "doll," "chick," "broad," and so forth, as objectionable as "boy" and "nigger" will women come to be conceived of as independent *human beings*.

The two remaining unexamined male identifications are gender and sex. There seems to be nothing objectionable about gender identifications per se. That is, women are metaphorically identified as skirts because in this culture, skirts, like women, are peculiarly female. Indeed, if one accepts the view that the slogan "female and proud" should play the same role for the women's liberation movement that the slogan "Black is beautiful" plays for the black-liberation movement, then female clothes should be worn with the same pride as Afro clothes. (Of course, one can argue that the skirt, like the cropped-down Afro, is a sign of bondage, and hence both the item of clothing and the identification with it are to be rejected—that is, cropped-down Afros are to Uncle Tom what skirts are to Uncle Mom.)

The terms in the last category are obviously sexual, and frequently vulgar. For a variety of reasons I shall consider the import and nature of these identifications in the next section.

MEN OUGHT NOT TO THINK OF WOMEN AS SEX OBJECTS

Feminists have proposed many reforms, and most of them are clearly desirable, for example, equal opportunity for self-development, equal pay for equal work, and free day-care centers. One feminist proposal, however, is peculiarly conceptual and deeply perplexing. I call this proposal peculiarly conceptual because unlike the other reforms it is directed at getting people to think differently. The proposal is that *men should not think of women (and women should not think of themselves) as sex objects.* In the rest of this essay I shall explore this nostrum. I do so for two reasons: first, because the process of exploration should reveal the depth of the problem confronting the feminists; and second, because the feminists themselves seem to be entangled in the very concepts that obstruct their liberation.

To see why I find this proposal puzzling, one has to ask what it is to think of something as a sex object.

If a known object is an object that we know, an unidentified object is an object that we have not identified, and a desired object is an object that we desire, what then is a sex object? Clearly, a sex object is an object we have sex with. Hence, to think of a woman as a sex object is to think of her as someone to have sexual relations with, and when the feminist proposes that men refrain from thinking of women in this way, *she is proposing that men not think of women as persons with whom one has sexual relations.*

What are we to make of this proposal? Is the feminist suggesting that women should not be conceived of in this way because such a conception is "dirty"? To conceive of sex and sex organs as dirty is simply to be a prude. "Shit" is the paradigm case of a dirty word. It is a dirty word because the item it designates is taboo; it is literally unclean and untouchable (as opposed to something designated by what I call a curse word, which is not untouchable but rather something to be feared—"damn" and "hell" are curse words; "piss" is a dirty word). If one claims that "cunt" (or "fuck") is a dirty word, then one holds that what this term designates is unclean and taboo; thus one holds

that the terms for sexual intercourse or sexual organs are dirty, one has accepted puritanism. If one is a puritan and a feminist, then indeed one ought to subscribe to the slogan *men should not conceive of women as sexual objects.* What is hard to understand is why anyone but a puritan (or, perhaps, a homosexual) would promulgate this slogan; yet most feminists, who are neither lesbians nor puritans, accept this slogan. Why?

A word about slogans: Philosophical slogans have been the subject of considerable analysis. They have the peculiar property (given a certain seemingly sound background story) of being obviously true, yet obviously false. "Men should not conceive of women as sex objects" is, I suggest, like a philosophical slogan in this respect. The immediate reaction of any humanistically oriented person upon first hearing the slogan is to agree with it—yet the more one probes the meaning of the slogan, the less likely one is to give one's assent. Philosophical analysts attempt to separate out the various elements involved in such slogans—to render the true-false slogan into a series of statements, some of which are true, some of which are false, and others of which are, perhaps, only probable. This is what I am trying to do with the slogan in question. I have argued so far that one of the elements that seems to be implicit in the slogan is a rejection of women as sexual partners for men and that although this position might be proper for a homosexual or puritanical movement, it seems inappropriate to feminism. I shall proceed to show that at least two other interpretations of the slogan lead to inappropriate results; but I shall argue that there are at least two respects in which the slogan is profoundly correct—even if misleadingly stated.

One plausible, but inappropriate, interpretation of "men ought not to conceive of women as sex objects" is that men ought not to conceive of women *exclusively* as sexual partners. The problem with this interpretation is that everyone can agree with it. Women are conceived of as companions, toys, servants, and even sisters, wives, and mothers—and hence not exclusively as sexual partners. Thus this slogan loses its revisionary impact, since even a male chauvinist could accept the slogan without changing his conceptual structure in any way—which is only to say that men do not usually identify or conceive of woman as sexual partners (recall that the sexual method of identification is the least frequently used).

Yet another interpretation is suggested by the term "object" in "sex object," and this interpretation too has a certain amount of plausibility. Men should not treat women as animate machines designed to masturbate men or as conquests that allow men to "score" for purposes of building their egos. Both of these variations rest on the view that to be treated as an object is to be treated as less than human (that is, to be treated as a machine or a score). Such relations between men and women are indeed immoral, and there are, no doubt, men who believe in "scoring." Unfortunately, however, this interpretation—although it would render the slogan quite apt—also fails because of its restricted scope. When feminists argue that men should not treat women as sex objects they are not *only* talking about fraternity boys and members of the Playboy Club; they are talking about all males in our society. The charge is that in our society men treat women as sex objects rather than as persons; it is this universality of scope that is lacking from the present interpretation. *Nonetheless, one of the reasons that we are prone to assent to the unrestricted charge that men treat women as sex objects is that the restricted charge is entirely correct.*

One might be tempted to argue that the charge that men treat women as sex objects is correct since such a conception underlies the most frequently used identifications, as animal and plaything; that is, these identifications indicate a sexual context in which the female is used as an object. Thus, it might be argued that the female fox is chased and slayed if she is four-legged, but chased and layed if she is two. Even if one admits the sexual context *implicit* in *some* animal and plaything identifications, one will not have the generality required; because, for the most part, the plaything and animal identifications themselves are nonsexual—most of them do not involve a sexual context. A pregnant cow, a toy doll, or a filly are hardly what one would call erotic objects. Babies do not normally excite sexual passion; and anyone whose erotic interests are directed toward chicks, canaries, parakeets, or other birds is clearly perverse. The animals and playthings to whom women are assimilated in the standard metaphorical identifications are not symbols of desire, eroticism, or passion (as, for example, a bull might be).

What is objectionable in the animal and plaything identifications is not the fact that some of these identifications reflect a sexual context but rather that—regardless of the context—these identifications reflect a conception of women as mindless servants (whether animate or inanimate is irrelevant). The point is not that men ought not to think of women in sexual terms but that they ought to think of them as human beings; and the slogan *men should not think of women as sex objects* is only appropriate when a man thinking of a woman as a sexual partner automatically conceives of her as something less than human. It is precisely this antihumanism implicit in the male concept of sex that we have as yet failed to uncover—but then, of course, we have not yet examined the language we use to identify sexual acts.

OUR CONCEPTION OF SEXUAL INTERCOURSE

There are two profound insights that underlie the slogan "men ought not conceive of women as sexual objects"; both have the generality of scope that justifies the universality with which the feminists apply the slogan; neither can be put as simply as the slogan. The first is that the conception of sexual intercourse that we have in this culture is antithetical to the conception of women as human beings—as persons rather than objects. (Recall that this is congruent with the fact we noted earlier that "man" can be substituted for "humanity," while "woman" cannot.)

Many feminists have attempted to argue just this point. Perhaps the most famous defender of this view is Kate Millett,[1] who unfortunately faces the problem of trying to make a point about our conceptual structure without having adequate tools for analyzing conceptual structures.

The question Millett was dealing with was conceptual—Millett, in effect, asking about the nature of our conception of sexual roles. She tried to answer this question by analyzing novels; I shall attempt to answer this question by analyzing the terms we use to identify coitus, or more technically, in terms that function synonymously with "had sexual intercourse with" in a sentence of the form "A had sexual intercourse with B." The following is a list of some commonly used synonyms (numerous others that are not as widely used have been omitted, for example, "diddled," "laid pipe with"):

> screwed
> laid
> fucked
> had
> did it with (to)
> banged
> balled
> humped
> slept with
> made love to

Now, for a select group of these verbs, names for males are the subjects of sentences with active constructions (that is, where the subjects are said to be doing the activity); and names for females require passive constructions (that is, they are the recipients of the activity—whatever is done is done to them). Thus, we would not say "Jane did it to Dick," although we would say "Dick did it to Jane." Again, Dick bangs Jane, Jane does not bang Dick. Dick humps Jane, Jane does not hump Dick. In contrast, verbs like "did it with" do not require an active role for the male; thus, "Dick did it with Jane, and Jane with Dick." Again, Jane may make love to Dick, just as Dick makes love to Jane; and Jane sleeps with Dick as easily as Dick sleeps with Jane. (My students were undecided about "laid." Most thought that it would be unusual indeed for Jane to lay Dick, unless she played the masculine role of seducer-aggressor.)

*   *   *

It should be clear, therefore, that our language reflects a difference between the male and female sexual roles, and hence that we conceive of the male and female roles in different ways. The question that now arises is, What difference in our conception of the male and female sexual roles requires active constructions for males and passive for females?

One explanation for the use of the active construction for males and the passive construction for females is that this grammatical asymmetry merely reflects the natural physiological asymmetry between men and women: the asymmetry of "to screw" and "to be screwed," "to insert into" and "to be inserted into." That is, it might be argued that the difference between masculine and feminine grammatical roles merely reflects a difference naturally required by the anatomy of males and females. This explanation is inadequate. Anatomical differences do not determine how we are to conceptualize the relation between penis and vagina during intercourse. Thus one can easily imagine a society in which the female normally played the active role during intercourse, where female subjects required active constructions with verbs indicating copulation, and where the standard metaphors were terms like "engulfing"—that is, instead of saying "he screwed her," one would say "she engulfed him." It follows that the use of passive constructions for female subjects of verbs indicating copulation does not reflect differences determined by human anatomy but rather reflects those generated by human customs.

What I am going to argue next is that the passive construction of verbs indicating coitus (that is, indicating the female position) can *also* be used to indicate that a person is being harmed. I am then going to argue that the metaphor involved would only make sense if we conceive of the female role in intercourse as that of a person being harmed (or being taken advantage of).

Passive constructions of "fucked," "screwed," and "had" indicate the female role. They also can be used to indicate being harmed. Thus, in all of the following sentences, Marion plays the female role: "Bobbie fucked Marion"; "Bobbie screwed Marion"; "Bobbie had Marion"; "Marion was fucked"; "Marion was screwed"; and "Marion was had." All of the statements are equivocal. They might literally mean that someone had sexual intercourse with Marion (who played the female role); or they might mean, metaphorically, that Marion was deceived, hurt, or taken advantage of. Thus, we say such things as "I've been screwed" ("fucked," "had," "taken," and so on) when we have been treated unfairly, been sold shoddy merchandise, or conned out of valuables. Throughout this essay I have been arguing that metaphors are applied to things only if what the term *actually* applies to shares one or more properties with what the term *metaphorically* applies to. Thus, the female sexual role must have something in common with being conned or being sold shoddy merchandise. The only common property is that of being harmed, deceived, or taken advantage of. *Hence we conceive of a person who plays the female sexual role as someone who is being harmed* (that is, "screwed," "fucked," and so on).

It might be objected that this is clearly wrong, since the unsignated terms do not indicate someone's being harmed, and hence we do

not conceive of having intercourse as being harmed. The point about the unsignated terms, however, is that they can take both females and males as subjects (in active constructions) and thus *do not pick out the female role*. This demonstrates that we conceive of sexual roles in such a way that only females are thought to be taken advantage of in intercourse.

The best part of solving a puzzle is when all the pieces fall into place. If the subjects of the passive construction are being harmed, presumably the subjects of the active constructions are doing harm, and indeed, we do conceive of these subjects in precisely this way. Suppose one is angry at someone and wishes to express malevolence as forcefully as possible without actually committing an act of physical violence. If one is inclined to be vulgar one can make the sign of the erect male cock by clenching one's fist while raising one's middle finger, or by clenching one's fist and raising one's arm and shouting such things as "screw you," and "up yours" or "fuck you." In other words, one of the strongest possible ways of telling someone that you wish to harm him is to tell him to assume the female sexual role relative to you. Again, to say to someone "go fuck yourself" is to order him to harm himself, while to call someone a "mother fucker" is not so much a play on his Oedipal fears as to accuse him of being so low that he would inflict the greatest imaginable harm (fucking) upon that person who is most dear to him (his mother).

Clearly, we conceive of the male sexual role as that of hurting the person in the female role—but lest the reader have any doubts, let me provide two further bits of confirming evidence: one linguistic, one nonlinguistic. One of the English terms for a person who hurts (and takes advantage of) others is the term "prick." This metaphorical identification would not make sense unless the bastard in question (that is, the person outside the bonds of legitimacy) was thought to share some characteristics attributed to things that are literally pricks. As a verb, "prick" literally means "to hurt," as in "I pricked myself with a needle"; but the usage in question is as a noun. As a noun, "prick" is a colloquial term for "penis." Thus, the question before us is what characteristic is shared by a penis and a person who harms others (or, alternatively, by a penis and by being stuck by a needle). Clearly, no physical characteristic is relevant (physical characteristics might underlie the Yiddish metaphorical attribution "schmuck," but one would have to analyze Yiddish usage to determine this); hence the shared characteristic is nonphysical; the only relevant shared nonphysical characteristic is that both a literal prick and a figurative prick are agents that harm people.

Now for the nonlinguistic evidence. Imagine two doors: in front of each door is a line of people; behind each door is a room; in each room is a bed; on each bed is a person. The line in front of one room consists of beautiful women, and on the bed in that room is a man having intercourse with each of these women in turn. One may think any number of things about this scene. One may say that the man is in heaven, or enjoying himself at a bordello; or perhaps one might only wonder at the oddness of it all. One does not think that the man is being hurt or violated or degraded—or at least the possibility does not immediately suggest itself, although one could conceive of situations where this was what was happening (especially, for example, if the man was impotent). Now, consider the other line. Imagine that the figure on the bed is a woman and that the line consists of handsome, smiling men. The woman is having intercourse with each of these men in turn. It immediately strikes one that the woman is being degraded, violated, and so forth—"that poor woman."

When one man fucks many women he is a playboy and gains status; when a woman is fucked by many men she degrades herself and loses stature.

Our conceptual inventory is now complete enough for us to return to the task of analyzing the slogan that men ought not to think of women as sex objects.

I think that it is now plausible to argue that the appeal of the slogan "men ought not to think of women as sex objects," and the thrust of much of the literature produced by contemporary feminists, turns on something much deeper than a rejection of "scoring" (that is, the utilization of sexual "conquests" to gain esteem) and yet is a call neither for homosexuality nor for puritanism.

The slogan is best understood as a call for a new conception of the male and female sexual roles. If the analysis developed above is correct, our present conception of sexuality is such that to be a man is to be a person capable of brutalizing women (witness the slogans "The marines will make a man out of you!" and "The army builds *men!*" which are widely accepted and which simply state that learning how to kill people will make a person more manly). Such a conception of manhood not only bodes ill for a society led by such men, but also is clearly inimical to the best interests of women. It is only natural for women to reject such a sexual role, and it would seem to be the duty of any moral person to support their efforts—to redefine our conceptions not only of fucking, but of the fucker (man) and the fucked (woman).

This brings me to my final point. We are a society preoccupied with sex. As I noted previously, the nature of proper nouns and pronouns in our language makes it difficult to talk about someone without indicating that person's sex. This convention would not be part of the grammar of our language if we did not believe that knowledge of a person's sex was crucial to understanding what is said about that person. Another way of putting this point is that sexual discrimination permeates our conceptual structure. Such discrimination is clearly inimical to any movement toward sexual egalitarianism and virtually defeats its purpose at the outset. (Imagine, for example, that black people were always referred to as "them" and whites as "us" and that proper names for blacks always had an "x" suffix at the end. Clearly any movement for integration as equals would require the removal of these discriminatory indicators. Thus at the height of the melting-pot era, immigrants Americanized their names: "Bellinsky" became "Bell," "Burnstein" became "Burns," and "Lubitch" became "Baker.")

I should therefore like to close this essay by proposing that contemporary feminists should advocate the utilization of neutral proper names and the elimination of gender from our language (as I have done in this essay); and

they should vigorously protest any utilization of the third-person pronouns "he" and "she" as examples of sexist discrimination (perhaps "person" would be a good third-person pronoun)—for, as a parent of linguistic analysis once said, "The limits of our language are the limits of our world."

NOTE

1. *Sexual Politics* (New York: Doubleday, 1971); but see also *Sisterhood Is Powerful*, ed. Robin Morgan (New York: Vintage Books, 1970).

Sexual Terrorism

Carole J. Sheffield

No two of us think alike about it, and yet it is clear to me, that question underlies the whole movement, and our little skirmishing for better laws, and the right to vote, will yet be swallowed up in the real question, viz: Has a woman a right to herself? It is very little to me to have the right to vote, to own property, etc., if I may not keep my body, and its uses, in my absolute right. Not one wife in a thousand can do that now.

—Lucy Stone, in a letter to Antoinette Brown, July 11, 1855

The right of men to control the female body is a cornerstone of patriarchy. It is expressed by their efforts to control pregnancy and childbirth and to define female health care in general. Male opposition to abortion is rooted in opposition to female autonomy. Violence and the threat of violence against females represent the need of patriarchy to deny that a woman's

body is her own property and that no one should have access to it without her consent. Violence and its corollary, fear, serve to terrorize females and to maintain the patriarchal definition of woman's place.

The word *terrorism* invokes images of furtive organizations of the far right or left, whose members blow up buildings and cars, hijack airplanes, and murder innocent people in some country other than ours. But there is a different kind of terrorism, one that so pervades our culture that we have learned to live with it as though it were the natural order of things. Its target is females—of all ages, races, and classes. It is the common characteristic of rape, wife battery, incest, pornography, harassment, and all forms of sexual violence. I call it *sexual terrorism* because it is a system by which males frighten and, by frightening, control and dominate females.

The concept of terrorism captured my attention in an "ordinary" event. One afternoon I collected my laundry and went to a nearby laundromat. The place is located in a small shopping center on a very busy highway. After I had loaded and started the machines, I became acutely aware of my environment. It was just after 6:00 P.M. and dark, the other stores were closed, the laundromat was brightly lit, and my car was the only one in the lot. Anyone passing by could readily see that I was alone and isolated. Knowing that rape is often a crime of opportunity, I became terrified. I wanted to leave and find a laundromat that was busier, but my clothes were well into the wash cycle, and, besides, I felt I was being "silly," "paranoid." The feeling of terror persisted, so I sat in my car, windows up and doors locked. When the wash was completed, I dashed in, threw the clothes into the dryer, and ran back out to my car. When the clothes were dry, I tossed them recklessly into the basket and hurriedly drove away to fold them in the security of my home.

Although I was not victimized in a direct, physical way or by objective or measurable standards, I felt victimized. It was, for me, a terrifying experience. I felt controlled by an invisible force. I was angry that something as commonplace as doing laundry after a day's work jeopardized my well-being. Mostly I was angry at being unfree: a hostage of a culture that, for the most part, encourages violence against females, instructs men in the methodology of sexual violence, and provides them with ready justification for their violence. I was angry that I could be victimized by being "in the wrong place at the wrong time." The essence of

terrorism is that one never knows when is the wrong time and where is the wrong place.

Following my experience at the laundromat, I talked with my students about terrorization. Women students began to open up and reveal terrors that they had kept secret because of embarrassment: fears of jogging alone, shopping alone, going to the movies alone. One woman recalled feelings of terror in her adolescence when she did child care for extra money. Nothing had ever happened, and she had not been afraid of anyone in particular, but she had felt a vague terror when being driven home late at night by the man of the house.

The male students listened incredulously and then demanded equal time. The harder they tried, the more they realized how very different—qualitatively, quantitatively, and contextually—their fears were. All agreed that, while they experienced fear in a violent society, they did not experience terror, nor did they experience fear of rape or sexual mutilation. They felt more in control, either from a psychophysical sense of security that they could defend themselves or from a confidence in being able to determine wrong places and times. All the women admitted feeling fear and anxiety when walking to their cars on the campus, especially after an evening class or activity. None of the men experienced fear on campus at any time. The men could be rather specific in describing where they were afraid: in Harlem, for example, or in certain parts of downtown Newark, New Jersey—places that have a reputation for violence. But either they could avoid these places or they felt capable of self-protective action. Above all, male students said that they *never* feared being attacked simply because they were male. They *never* feared going to a movie or to a mall alone. Their daily activities were not characterized by a concern for their physical integrity.

The differences between men's and women's experiences of fear underscore the meaning of sexual terrorism: that women's lives are bounded by both the reality of pervasive sexual danger and the fear that reality engenders. In her study of rape, Susan Brownmiller argues that rape is "nothing more or less than a conscious process of intimidation by which all men keep all women in a state of fear."[1] In their study *The Female Fear*, Margaret T. Gordon and Stephanie Riger found that one-third of women said they worry at least once a month about being raped. Many said they worry daily about the possibility of being raped. When they think about rape, they feel terrified and somewhat paralyzed. A third of women indicated that the fear of rape is "part of the background" of their lives and "one of those things that's always there." Another third claimed they never worried about rape but reported taking precautions, "sometimes elaborate ones," to try to avoid being raped: Indeed, women's attempts to avoid sexual intrusion take many forms. To varying degrees, women change and restrict their behavior, life-styles, and physical appearances. They will pay higher costs for housing and transportation and even make educational and career choices to attempt to minimize sexual victimization.

Sexual terrorism includes nonviolent sexual intimidation and the threat of violence as well as overt sexual violence. For example, although an act of rape, an unnecessary hysterectomy, and the publishing of *Playboy* magazine appear to be quite different, they are in fact more similar than dissimilar. Each is based on fear, hostility, and a need to dominate women. Rape is an act of aggression and possession. Unnecessary hysterectomies are extraordinary abuses of power rooted in men's concept of women as primarily reproductive beings and in their need to assert power over that reproduction. *Playboy*, like all forms of pornography, attempts to control women through the power of definition. Male pornographers define women's sexuality for their male customers. The basis of pornography is men's fantasies about women's sexuality.

COMPONENTS OF SEXUAL TERRORISM

The literature on terrorism does not provide a precise definition. Mine is taken from Hacker, who says that "terrorism aims to frighten, and by frightening, to dominate and control."[2] Writers agree more readily on the characteristics and functions of terrorism than on a definition. This analysis will focus on five components to illuminate the similarities and distinctions between sexual terrorism and political terrorism. The five components are ideology, propaganda, indiscriminate and amoral violence, voluntary compliance, and society's perception of the terrorist and the terrorized.

An *ideology* is an integrated set of beliefs about the world that explains the way things are and provides a vision of how they ought to be. Patriarchy, meaning the "rule of the fathers," is the ideological foundation of sexism in our society. It asserts the superiority of males and the inferiority of females. It also provides the rationale for sexual terrorism. The taproot of patriarchy is the masculine/warrior ideal. Masculinity must include not only a proclivity for violence but also all those characteristics claimed by warriors: aggression, control, emotional reserve, rationality, sexual potency, etc. Marc Feigen Fasteau, in *The Male Machine*, argues that "men are brought up with the idea that there ought to be some part of them, under control until released by necessity, that thrives on violence. This capacity, even affinity, for violence, lurking beneath the surface of every real man, is supposed to represent the primal untamed base of masculinity."[3]

Propaganda is the methodical dissemination of information for the purpose of promoting a particular ideology. Propaganda, by definition, is biased or even false information. Its purpose is to present one point of view on a subject and to discredit opposing points of view. Propaganda is essential to the conduct of terrorism. According to Francis Watson, in

Political Terrorism: The Threat and the Response, "Terrorism must not be defined only in terms of violence, but also in terms of propaganda. The two are in operation together. Violence of terrorism is a coercive means for attempting to influence the thinking and actions of people. Propaganda is a persuasive means for doing the same thing."[4] The propaganda of sexual terrorism is found in all expressions of the popular culture: films, television, music, literature, advertising, pornography. The propaganda of sexual terrorism is also found in the ideas of patriarchy expressed in science, medicine, and psychology.

The third component, which is common to all forms of political terrorism, consists of "indiscriminateness, unpredictability, arbitrariness, ruthless destructiveness and amorality."[5] Indiscriminate violence and amorality are also at the heart of sexual terrorism. Every female is a potential target of violence—at any age, at any time, in any place. Further, as we shall see, amorality pervades sexual violence. Child molesters, incestuous fathers, wife beaters, and rapists often do not understand that they have done anything wrong. Their views are routinely shared by police officers, lawyers, and judges, and crimes of sexual violence are rarely punished in American society.

The fourth component of the theory of terrorism is voluntary compliance. The institutionalization of a system of terror requires the development of mechanisms other than sustained violence to achieve its goals. Violence must be employed to maintain terrorism, but sustained violence can be costly and debilitating. Therefore, strategies for ensuring a significant degree of voluntary compliance must be developed. Sexual terrorism is maintained to a great extent by an elaborate system of sex-role socialization that in effect instructs men to be terrorists in the name of masculinity and women to be victims in the name of femininity.

Sexual and political terrorism differ in the final component, perceptions of the terrorist and the victim. In political terrorism we know who is the terrorist and who is the victim. We may condemn or condone the terrorist, depending on our political views, but we sympathize with the victim. In sexual terrorism, however, we blame the victim and excuse the offender. We believe that the offender either is "sick" and therefore in need of our compassion or is acting out normal male impulses.

TYPES OF SEXUAL TERRORISM

While the discussion that follows focuses on four types of sexual terrorism—rape, wife abuse, sexual abuse of children, and sexual harassment—recent feminist research has documented other forms of sexual terrorism, including threats of violence, flashing, street hassling, obscene phone calls, stalking, coercive sex, pornography, prostitution, sexual slavery, and femicide. What women experience as sexually intrusive and violent is not necessarily reflected in our legal codes, and those acts that are recognized as criminal are often not understood specifically as crimes against women—as acts of sexual violence.

Acts of sexual terrorism include many forms of intrusion that society accepts as common and are therefore trivialized. For example, a recent study of women's experiences of obscene phone calls found that women respondents overwhelmingly found these calls to be a form of sexual intimidation and harassment. While obscene phone calls are illegal, only in rare cases do women report them and the police take them seriously. In contrast, some forms of sexual terrorism are so extraordinary that they are regarded not only as aberrant but also as incomprehensible. The execution of fourteen women students at the University of Montreal on December 6, 1989, is one example of this. Separating the men from the women in a classroom and shouting, "You're all fucking feminists," twenty-five-year-old Marc Lepine systematically murdered fourteen women. In his suicide letter, claiming that "the feminists have always enraged me," Lepine recognized his crime as a political act. For many women, this one act of sexual terrorism galvanized attention to the phenomenon of the murder of women because they are women. "Femicide," according to Jane Caputi and Diane E. H. Russell, describes "the murders of women by men motivated by hatred, contempt, pleasure, or a sense of ownership of women."[6] Most femicide, unlike the Montreal massacre, is committed by a male acquaintance, friend, or relative. In *Surviving Sexual Violence*, Liz Kelly argues that sexual violence must be understood as a continuum—that is, "a continuous series of events that pass into one another" united by a "basic common character." Viewing sexual violence in this way furthers an understanding of both the "ordinary" and "extraordinary" forms of sexual terrorism and the range of abuse that women experience in their lifetimes.

Many types of sexual terrorism are crimes, yet when we look at the history of these acts, we see that they came to be considered criminal not so much to protect women as to adjust power relationships among men. Rape was originally a violation of a father's or husband's property rights; consequently, a husband by definition could not rape his wife. Wife beating was condoned by the law and still is condemned in name only. Although proscriptions against incest exist, society assumes a more serious posture toward men who sexually abuse other men's daughters. Sexual harassment is not a crime, and only recently has it been declared an actionable civil offense. Crimes of sexual violence are characterized by ambiguity and diversity in definition and interpretation. Because each state and territory has a separate system of law in addition to the federal system, crimes and punishments are assessed differently throughout the country.

Rape

Rape statutes have been reformed in the past decade, largely to remove the exemption for wife rape and to use gender-neutral language. The essence of the definition of rape, however, remains the same: sexual penetration (typically defined as penile-vaginal, but may include oral and anal sodomy or penetration by fingers or other objects) of a female by force or threat of force, against her will and without her consent.

Traditional views of rape are shaped by male views of sexuality and by men's fear of being unjustly accused. Deborah Rhode argues, in *Justice and Gender*, that this reflects a "sexual schizophrenia." That is, forced sexual intercourse by a stranger against a chaste woman is unquestionably regarded as a heinous crime, whereas coercive sex that does not fit this model is largely denied. Since most women are raped by men they know, this construction excludes many forms of rape.

Because rape is considered a sexual act, evidence of force and resistance is often necessary to establish the nonconsent needed to convict rapists. Such proof is not demanded of a victim of any other crime. If females do not resist rape as much as possible, "consent" is assumed.

By 1990, forty-two states had adopted laws criminalizing rape in marriage: sixteen states recognize that wife rape is a crime and provide no exemptions; twenty-six states penalize wife rape but allow for some exemptions under which husbands cannot be prosecuted for raping their wives. Eight states do not recognize wife rape as a crime. In spite of statutory reform, wife rape remains a greatly misunderstood phenomenon, and the magnitude of sexual abuse by husbands is not known. In Diana E. H. Russell's pioneering study on rape in marriage [*Rape in Marriage*], 14 percent of the female respondents reported having been raped by their husbands. The prevalence of wife rape, however, is believed to be much higher; approximately 40 percent of women in battered women's shelters also report having been raped by their husbands. Victims of wife rape, according to one study, are at a greater risk of being murdered by their husbands, or of murdering them, than women who are physically but not sexually assaulted.

Wife Abuse

For centuries it has been assumed that a husband had the right to punish or discipline his wife with physical force. The popular expression "rule of thumb" originated from English common law, which allowed a husband to beat his wife with a whip or stick no bigger in diameter than his thumb. The husband's prerogative was incorporated into American law. Several states once had statutes that essentially allowed a man to beat his wife without interference from the courts.

In 1871, in the landmark case of *Fulgham v. State*, an Alabama court ruled that "the privilege, ancient though it be, to beat her with a stick, to pull her hair, choke her, spit in her face or kick her about the floor or to inflict upon her other like indignities, is not now acknowledged by our law."[7] The law, however, has been ambiguous and often contradictory on the issue of wife abuse. While the courts established that a man had no right to beat his wife, it also held that a woman could not press charges against her abusive husband. In 1910, the U.S. Supreme Court ruled that a wife could not charge her husband with assault and battery because it "would open the doors of the court to accusations of all sorts of one spouse against the other and bring into public notice complaints for assaults, slander and libel."[8] The courts virtually condoned violence for the purpose of maintaining peace.

Laws and public attitudes about the illegality of wife abuse and the rights of the victim have been slowly evolving. During the 1980s, there was a proliferation of new laws designed to address the needs of victims of domestic violence and to reform police and judicial responses to wife abuse. These measures include temporary or permanent protection orders, state-funded or state-assisted shelters, state-mandated data collection, and proarrest or mandatory arrest policies. Most states, however, continue to define domestic violence as a misdemeanor crime, carrying jail sentences of less than one year. Felony crimes are punishable by more than one year in jail, and police officers tend to arrest more often for felony offenses. The distinction between misdemeanor and felony crimes is also based on the use of weapons and the infliction of serious injuries. While wife abuse is still considered a misdemeanor crime, a National Crime Survey revealed that at least 50 percent of the domestic "simple assaults" involved bodily injury as serious as or more serious than 90 percent of all rapes, robberies, and aggravated assaults.

Sexual Abuse of Children

Defining sexual abuse of children is very difficult. The laws are complex and often contradictory. Generally, sexual abuse of children includes statutory rape, molestation, carnal knowledge, indecent liberties, impairing the morals of a minor, child abuse, child neglect, and incest. Each of these is defined, interpreted, and punished differently in each state.

The philosophy underlying statutory-rape laws is that a child below a certain age—arbitrarily fixed by law—is not able to give meaningful consent. Therefore, sexual intercourse with a female below a certain age, even with consent, is rape. Punishment for statutory rape, although rarely imposed, can be as high as life imprisonment. Coexistent with laws on statutory rape are laws on criminal incest. Incest is generally interpreted as sexual activity, most often intercourse, with a blood relative. The difference, then, between statutory rape and incest is the relation of the offender to the child. Statutory rape is committed by someone outside the family; incest, by a member of the family. The penalty for incest, also rarely imposed, is usually no more than ten years in prison. This contrast suggests that sexual abuse of children is tolerated when it occurs within the family and that unqualified protection of children from sexual assault is not the intent of the law.

Sexual Harassment

Sexual harassment is a new term for an old phenomenon. The research on sexual harassment, as well as the legal interpretation, centers on acts of sexual coercion or intimidation on the job and at school. Lin Farley, in *Sexual Shakedown: The Sexual Harassment of Women on the Job*, describes sexual harassment as "unsolicited nonreciprocal male behavior that asserts a woman's sex role over her function as a worker. It can be any or all of the following: staring at, commenting upon, or touching a woman's body; requests for acquiescence in sexual behavior; repeated nonreciprocated propositions for dates; demands for sexual intercourse; and rape."[9]

In 1980 the Equal Employment Opportunity Commission issued federal guidelines that defined sexual harassment as any behavior that "has the purpose or effect of unreasonably interfering with an individual's work performance or creating an intimidating or hostile or offensive environment." Such behavior can include "unwelcome sexual advances, requests for sexual favors, and other verbal or physical conduct of a sexual nature."[10] It was not until six years later, however, that the Supreme Court, in *Meritor Savings Bank FSB v. Vinson*, ruled that sexual harassment was a form of sex discrimination under Title VII of the Civil Rights Act of 1964.

In October 1991 national attention was focused on the issue of sexual harassment as a result of allegations made against Supreme Court Justice nominee Clarence Thomas by Professor Anita Hill. (Thomas was subsequently confirmed as a Supreme Court justice by a vote of fifty-two to forty-eight.) While there was a blizzard of media attention about sexual harassment, what emerged most clearly from the confirmation hearings was that the chasm between women's experiences of sexual harassment and an understanding of the phenomenon by society in general had not been bridged. Perhaps most misunderstood was the fact that Professor Hill's experience and

her reaction to it were typical of sexually harassed women.

CHARACTERISTICS OF SEXUAL TERRORISM

Those forms of sexual terrorism that are crimes share several common characteristics. Each will be addressed separately, but in the real world these characteristics are linked together and form a vicious circle, which functions to mask the reality of sexual terrorism and thus to perpetuate the system of oppression of females. Crimes of violence against females (1) cut across socioeconomic lines; (2) are the crimes least likely to be reported; (3) when reported, are the crimes least likely to be brought to trial or to result in conviction; (4) are often blamed on the victim; (5) are generally not taken seriously; and (6) fuse dominance and sexuality.

Violence Against Females Cuts Across Socioeconomic Lines

The question "Who is the typical rapist, wife beater, incest offender, etc.?" is raised constantly. The answer is simple: men. Female sexual offenders are exceedingly rare. The men who commit acts of sexual terrorism are of all ages, races, and religions; they come from all communities, income levels, and educational levels; they are married, single, separated, and divorced. The "typical" sexually abusive male does not exist.

One of the most common assumptions about sexual violence is that it occurs primarily among the poor, uneducated, and predominantly nonwhite populations. Actually, violence committed by the poor and nonwhite is simply more visible because of their lack of resources to secure the privacy that the middle and upper classes can purchase. Most rapes, indeed, most incidents of sexual assault, are not reported, and therefore the picture drawn from police records must be viewed as very sketchy.

The data on sexual harassment in work situations indicates that it occurs among all job categories and pay ranges. Sexual harassment is committed by academic men, who are among the most highly educated members of society. In a 1991 *New York Times* poll, five out of ten men said they had said or done something that "could have been construed by a female colleague as harassment."

All the studies on wife abuse testify to the fact that wife beating crosses socioeconomic lines. Wife beaters include high government officials, members of the armed forces, businessmen, policemen, physicians, lawyers, clergy, blue-collar workers, and the unemployed. According to Maria Roy, founder and director of New York's Abused Women's Aid in Crisis, "We see abuse of women on all levels of income, age, occupation, and social standing. I've had four women come in recently whose husbands are Ph.D.s—two of them professors at top universities. Another abused woman is married to a very prominent attorney. We counseled battered wives whose husbands are doctors, psychiatrists, even clergymen."[11]

Similarly, in Vincent De Francis's classic study of 250 cases of sexual crimes committed against children, a major finding was that incidents of sexual assault against children cut across class lines. Since sexual violence is not "nice," we prefer to believe that nice men do not commit these acts and that nice girls and women are not victims. Our refusal to accept the fact that violence against females is widespread throughout society strongly inhibits our ability to develop meaningful strategies to eliminate it. Moreover, because of underreporting, it is difficult to ascertain exactly how widespread it is.

Crimes of Sexual Violence are the Least Likely to be Reported

Underreporting is common for all crimes against females. There are two national sources for data on crime in the United States: the annual Uniform Crime Reports (UCR) of the Federal Bureau of Investigation, which collects information from police departments, and the National Crime Survey (NCS), conducted by the U.S. Department of Justice, which collects data on personal and household criminal victimizations from a nationally representative sample of households.

The FBI recognizes that rape is seriously underreported by as much as 80 to 90 percent. According to FBI data for 1990, 102,555 rapes were reported. The FBI Uniform Crime Report for 1990 estimates that a forcible rape occurs every five minutes. This estimate is based on reported rapes; accounting for the high rate of underreporting, the FBI estimates that a rape occurs every two minutes. The number of forcible rapes reported to the police has been increasing every year. Since 1986, the rape rate has risen 10 percent.

The National Crime Survey (renamed in 1991 as the National Crime Victimization Survey) data for 1990 reports 130,260 rapes. This data is only slightly higher than FBI data; researchers argue that NCS data has serious drawbacks as well. Just as victims are reluctant to report a rape to the police, many are also reluctant to reveal their victimization to an NCS interviewer. In fact, the NCS does not ask directly about rape (although it will in the future). A respondent may volunteer the information when asked questions about bodily harm. The NCS also excludes children under twelve, thus providing no data on childhood sexual assault.

In April 1992 the National Victim Center and the Crime Victims Research and Treatment Center released a report entitled "Rape in America," which summarized two nationwide studies: the National Women's Study, a three-year longitudinal survey of a national probability sample of 4,008 adult women, and the State of Services for Victims of Rape, which surveyed 370 agencies that provide rape crisis assistance. The National Women's Study sought information about the incidence of rape and information about a number of health issues related to rape, including depression, posttraumatic stress disorder, suicide attempts, and alcohol- and drug-related problems.

The results of the National Women's Study confirm a belief held by many experts that the UCR and NCS data seriously underrepresents the occurrence of rape. According to the National Women's Study, 683,000 adult women were raped during a twelve-month period from the fall of 1989 to the fall of 1990. This data is significantly higher than UCR and NCS data for approximately the same period. Moreover, since rapes of female children and adolescents under the age of eighteen and rapes of boys or men were not included in the study, the 683,000 rapes of adult women do not reflect an accurate picture of all rapes that occurred during that period. The data in this study also confirms the claim that acquaintance rape is far more pervasive than stranger rape. While 22 percent of victims were raped by someone unknown to them, 36 percent were raped by family members: 9 percent by husbands or ex-husbands, 11 percent by fathers or stepfathers, 16 percent by other relatives. Ten percent were raped by a boyfriend or ex-boyfriend and 29 percent by nonrelatives such as friends or neighbors (3 percent were not sure or refused to answer).

Perhaps the most significant finding of the National Women's Study is that rape in the United States is "a tragedy of youth." The study found that 29 percent of rapes occurred to female victims under the age of eleven, 32 percent occurred to females between the ages of eleven and seventeen, and 22 percent occurred to females between the ages of eighteen and twenty-four. Other research suggests that one in four women will be the victim of rape or an attempted rape by the time they are in their midtwenties, and at least three-quarters of those assaults will be committed by men known to the victims. Lifetime probability for rape victimization is as high as 50 percent; that is, one out of two women will be sexually assaulted at least once in her lifetime.

The FBI's Uniform Crime Report indexes 10 million reported crimes a year but does not collect statistics on wife abuse. Since statutes in most states do not identify wife beating as a distinct crime, incidents of wife abuse are usually classified under "assault and battery" and "disputes." Estimates that 50 percent of American wives are battered every year are not uncommon in the literature. Recent evidence shows that violence against wives becomes greatest at and after separation. Divorced and separated women account for 75 percent of all battered women and report being battered fourteen times as often as women still living with their partners. These women are also at the highest risk of being murdered by their former husbands. Thirty-three percent of all women murdered in the United States between 1976 and 1987 were murdered by their husbands.

"The problem of sexual abuse of children is of unknown national dimensions," according to Vincent De Francis, "but findings strongly point to the probability of an enormous national incidence many times larger than the reported incidence of the physical abuse of children."[12] He discussed the existence of a wide gap between the reported incidence and the actual occurrence of sexual assaults against children and suggested that "the reported incidence represents the top edge of the moon as it rises over the mountain."[13] Research definitions as to what constitutes sexual abuse and research methodologies vary widely, resulting in reported rates ranging from 6 percent to 62 percent for female children and 3 percent to 31 percent for male children. David Finkelhor suggests that the lowest figures support the claim that child sexual abuse is far from a rare occurrence and that the higher reported rates suggest a "problem of epidemic proportions."

In a study of 126 African-American women and 122 white women in Los Angeles County,

62 percent reported at least one experience of sexual abuse before the age of eighteen. The same men who beat their wives often abuse their children. Researchers have found that "the worse the wife-beating, the worse the child abuse."[14] It is estimated that fathers may sexually abuse children in 25 percent to 33 percent of all domestic abuse cases. There is also a strong correlation between child abuse and the frequency of marital rape, particularly where weapons are involved.

Incest, according to author and researcher Florence Rush, is the *Best Kept Secret*. The estimates, however speculative, are frightening. In a representative sample of 930 women in San Francisco, Diana E. H. Russell found that 16 percent of the women had been sexually abused by a relative before the age of eighteen and 4.5 percent had been sexually abused by their fathers (also before the age of eighteen). Extrapolating to the general population, this research suggests that 160,000 women per million may have been sexually abused before the age of eighteen, and 45,000 women per million may have been sexually abused by their fathers.

Accurate data on the incidence of sexual harassment is impossible to obtain. Women have traditionally accepted sexual innuendo as a fact of life and only recently have begun to report and analyze the dimensions of sexual coercion in the workplace. Research indicates that sexual harassment is pervasive. In 1978 Lin Farley found that accounts of sexual harassment within the federal government, the country's largest single employer, were extensive. In 1988 the U.S. Merit Systems Protection Board released an updated study that showed that 85 percent of working women experience harassing behavior at some point in their lives.

In 1976 over nine thousand women responded to a survey on sexual harassment conducted by *Redbook* magazine. More than 92 percent reported sexual harassment as a problem, a majority of the respondents described it as serious, and nine out of ten reported that they had personally experienced one or more forms of unwanted sexual attentions on the job. The Ad Hoc Group on Equal Rights for Women attempted to gather data on sexual harassment at the United Nations. Their questionnaire was confiscated by UN officials, but 875 staff members had already responded; 73 percent were women, and more than half of them said that they had personally experienced or were aware of incidents of sexual harassment at the UN. In May 1975, the Women's Section of the Human Affairs Program at Cornell University in Ithaca, New York, distributed the first questionnaire on sexual harassment. Of the 155 respondents, 92 percent identified sexual harassment as a serious problem, 70 percent had personally experienced some form of sexual harassment, and 56 percent reported incidents of physical harassment. A 1991 *New York Times*/CBS poll found that four out of ten women experienced sexual harassment at work, yet only 4 percent reported it.

In *The Lecherous Professor*, Billie Wright Dziech and Linda Weiner note that the low reportage of sexual harassment in higher education is due to the victims' deliberate avoidance of institutional processes and remedies. A pilot study conducted by the National Advisory Council on Women's Educational Programs on Sexual Harassment in Academia concluded:

The sexual harassment of postsecondary students is an increasingly visible problem of great, but as yet unascertained, dimensions. Once regarded as an isolated, purely personal problem, it has gained civil rights credibility as its scale and consequences have become known, and is correctly viewed as a form of illegal sex-based discrimination.[15]

Crimes of Violence Against Females Have the Lowest Conviction Rates

The common denominator in the underreporting of all sexual assaults is fear. Females have been well trained in silence and passivity. Early and sustained sex-role socialization teaches that women are responsible for the sexual behavior of men and that women cannot be trusted. These beliefs operate together. They function to keep women silent about their victimization and to keep other people from believing women when they do come forward. The victim's fear that she will not be believed and, as a consequence, that the offender will not be punished is not unrealistic. Sex offenders are rarely punished in our society.

Rape has the lowest conviction rate of all violent crimes. The likelihood of a rape complaint ending in conviction is 2 to 5 percent. While the intent of rape reform legislation was to shift the emphasis from the victim's experiences to the perpetrator's acts, prosecutions are less likely to be pursued if the victim and perpetrator are acquainted, and juries are less likely to return a conviction in cases where the victim's behavior or *alleged behavior* (emphasis mine) departed from traditional sex-role expectations.

Data on prosecution and conviction of wife beaters is practically nonexistent. This is despite the fact that battery is, according to the U.S. Surgeon General, the "single largest cause of injury to women in the U.S." and accounts for one-fifth of all emergency room visits by women. Police departments have generally tried to conciliate rather than arrest. Guided by the "stitch rule," arrests were made only when the victim's injuries required stitches. Police routinely instructed the parties to "break it up" or "talk it out" or asked the abuser to "take a walk and cool off." Male police officers, often identifying with the male abuser, routinely failed to advise women of their rights to file a complaint.

As a result of sustained political activism on behalf of abused women, many states have revised their police training and have instituted pro- or even mandatory arrest policies. In 1984 the Attorney General's Task Force on Family Violence argued that the legal response to such violence be predicated on the abusive act and not on the relationship between the victim and the abuser. A key issue, however, is the implementation of such reform. The record shows that the criminal justice system has responded inconsistently.

Studies in the late 1970s and 1980s showed that batterers receive minimal fines and suspended sentences. In one study of 350 abused wives, none of the husbands served time in jail. And while the result of pro- and mandatory arrest policies is a larger number of domestic violence cases entering the judicial system, "there is considerable evidence that judges have yet to abandon the historical view of wife abuse."[16] In 1981 a Kansas judge suspended the fine of a convicted assailant on the condition that he buy his wife a box of candy. In 1984 a Colorado judge sentenced a man to two years on work release for fatally shooting his wife five times in the face. Although the sentence was less than the minimum required by law, the judge found that the wife had "provoked" her husband by leaving him. Recent task force reports on gender bias in the courts reveal a pattern of nonenforcement of protective orders, trivialization of complaints, and disbelief of females when there is no visible evidence of severe injuries. In 1987 a Massachusetts trial judge scolded a battered women for wasting his time with her request for a protective order. If she and her husband wanted to "gnaw" on each other, "fine," but they "shouldn't do it at taxpayers' expense." The husband later killed his wife, and taxpayers paid for a murder trial.

The lack of support and protection from the criminal justice system intensifies the double bind of battered women. Leaving the batterer significantly increases the risk of serious injury or death, while staying significantly increases the psychological terrorism and frequency of abuse. According to former Detroit Police Commander James Bannon, "You can readily understand why the women ultimately take the law into their own hands or despair of finding relief at all. Or *why the male feels protected by the system in his use of violence*" (emphasis mine).[17]

In his study of child sexual abuse, Vincent De Francis found that plea bargaining and dismissal of cases were the norm. The study sample consisted of 173 cases brought to prosecution. Of these, 44 percent (seventy-six cases) were dismissed, 22 percent (thirty-eight cases) voluntarily accepted a lesser plea, 11 percent (six cases) were found guilty of a lesser charge, and 2 percent (four cases) were found guilty as charged. Of the remaining thirty-five cases, either they were pending (fifteen) or terminated because the offender was committed to a mental institution (five) or because the offender absconded (seven), or no information was available (eight). Of the fifty-three offenders who were convicted or pleaded guilty, thirty offenders escaped a jail sentence. Twenty-one received suspended sentences and were placed on probation, seven received suspended sentences without probation, and two were fined a sum of money. The other 45 percent (twenty-three offenders) received prison terms from under six months to three years; five were given indeterminate sentences—that is, a minimum term of one year and a maximum term subject to the discretion of the state board of parole.

In Diana E. H. Russell's study of 930 women, 648 cases of child sexual abuse were disclosed. Thirty cases—5 percent—were reported to the police; four were cases of incestuous abuse, and twenty-six were extrafamilial child sexual abuse. Only seven cases resulted in conviction.

Most of the victims of sexual harassment in the Cornell University study were unwilling to use available procedures, such as grievances, to remedy their complaints, because they believed that nothing would be done. Their perception is based on reality; of the 12 percent who did complain, over half found that nothing was done in their cases. The low adjudication and punishment rates of sexual-harassment cases are particularly revealing in light of the fact that the offender is known and identifiable and that there is no fear of "mistaken identity," as there is in rape cases. While offenders accused of familial violence—incest and wife abuse—are also known, concern with keeping the family intact affects prosecution rates.

Blaming the Victim of Sexual Violence is Pervasive

The data on conviction rates of men who have committed acts of violence against females must be understood in the context of attitudes about women. Our male-dominated society evokes powerful myths to justify male violence against females and to ensure that these acts will rarely be punished. Victims of sexual violence are almost always suspect. We have developed an intricate network of beliefs and attitudes that perpetuate the idea that "victims of sex crimes have a hidden psychological need to be victimized."[18] We tend to believe either that the female willingly participated in her victimization or that she outright lied about it. Either way, we blame the victim and excuse or condone the offender.

Consider, for example, the operative myths about rape, wife battery, incest, and sexual harassment.

Rape

> All women want to be raped.
> No woman can be raped if she doesn't want it (you-can't-thread-a-moving-needle argument).
> She asked for it.
> She changed her mind afterward.
> When she says no, she means yes.
> If you are going to be raped, you might as well relax and enjoy it.

Wife Abuse

> Some women need to be beaten.
> A good kick in the ass will straighten her out.
> She needs a punch in the mouth every so often to keep her in line.
> She must have done something to provoke him.

Incest

> The child was the seducer.
> The child imagined it.

Sexual Harassment

> She was seductive.
> She misunderstood. I was just being friendly.

Underlying all the myths about victims of sexual violence is the belief that the victim causes and is responsible for her own victimization. In the National Women's Study, 69 percent of the rape victims were afraid that they would be blamed for their rape, 71 percent did not want their family to know they had been sexually abused, and 68 percent did not want people outside of their family knowing of their victimization. Diana Scully studied convicted rapists and found that these men both believed in the rape myths and used them to justify their own behavior. Underlying the attitudes about the male offender is the belief that he could not help himself: that is, he was ruled by his biology and/or he was seduced. The victim becomes the offender, and the offender becomes the victim. These two processes, blaming the victim and absolving the offender, protect the patriarchal view of the world by rationalizing sexual violence. Sexual violence by a normal male against an innocent female is unthinkable; therefore, she must have done something wrong or it would not have happened. This view was expressed by a Wisconsin judge who sentenced a twenty-four-year-old man to ninety days' work release for sexually assaulting a five-year-old girl. The judge, claiming that the child was an "unusually promiscuous young lady," stated that "no way do I believe that [the defendant] initiated sexual contact." Making a victim believe she is at fault erases not only the individual offender's culpability but also the responsibility of the society as a whole. Sexual violence remains an individual problem, not a sociopolitical one.

One need only read the testimony of victims of sexual violence to see the powerful effects of blaming the victim. From the National Advisory Council on Women's Educational Programs Report on Sexual Harassment of Students:

> I was ashamed, thought it was my fault, and was worried that the school would take action against me (for "unearned" grades) if they found out about it.
>
> This happened seventeen years ago, and you are the first person I've been able to discuss it with in all that time. He's still at _____ , and probably still doing it.
>
> I'm afraid to tell anyone here about it, and I'm just hoping to get through the year so I can leave.[19]

From *Wife-Beating: The Silent Crisis*, Judge Stewart Oneglia comments,

> Many women find it shameful to admit they don't have a good marriage. The battered wife wraps her bloody head in a towel, goes to the hospital, and explains to the doctor she fell down the stairs. After a few years of the husband telling her he beats her because she is ugly, stupid, or incompetent, she is so psychologically destroyed that she believes it.

A battered woman from Boston relates,

> I actually thought if I only learned to cook better or keep a cleaner house, everything would be okay. I put up with the beatings for five years before I got desperate enough to get help.[20]

Another battered woman said,

> When I came to, I wanted to die, the guilt and depression were so bad. Your whole sense of worth is tied up with being a successful wife and having a happy marriage. If your husband beats you, then your marriage is a failure, and you're a failure. It's so horribly the opposite of how it is supposed to be.[21]

Katherine Brady shared her experience as an incest survivor in *Father's Days: A True Story of Incest*. She concluded her story with the following:

> I've learned a great deal by telling my story. I hope other incest victims may experience a similar journey of discovery by reading it. If nothing else, I would wish them to hear in this tale the two things

I needed most, but had to wait years to hear: "You are not alone and you are not to blame."[22]

Sexual Violence is Not Taken Seriously

Another characteristic of sexual violence is that these crimes are not taken seriously. Society manifests this attitude by simply denying the existence of sexual violence, denying the gravity of these acts, joking about them, and attempting to legitimate them.

Many offenders echo the societal norm by expressing genuine surprise when they are confronted by authorities. This seems to be particularly true in cases of sexual abuse of children, wife beating, and sexual harassment. In her study of incest, Florence Rush found that child molesters very often do not understand that they have done anything wrong. Many men still believe that they have an inalienable right to rule "their women." Batterers, for example, often cite their right to discipline their wives; incestuous fathers cite their right to instruct their daughters in sexuality. These men are acting on the belief that women are the property of men.

The concept of females as the property of men extends beyond the family unit, as the evidence on sexual harassment indicates. "Are you telling me that this kind of horsing around may constitute an actionable offense?" queried a character on a television special on sexual harassment. This represents the typical response of a man accused of sexual harassment. Men have been taught that they are the hunters, and women—all women—are fair game. The mythology about the workaday world abounds with sexual innuendo. Concepts of "sleazy" (i.e., sexually accessible) nurses and dumb, big-breasted, blond secretaries are standard fare for comedy routines. When the existence of sexual violence can no longer be denied, a common response is to joke about it in order to belittle it. "If you are going to be raped, you might as

well enjoy it" clearly belittles the violence of rape. The public still laughs when Ralph threatens Alice with "One of these days, POW—right in the kisser." Recently, a television talk-show host remarked that "incest is a game the whole family can play." The audience laughed uproariously.

Sexual Violence is About Violence, Power, and Sex

The final characteristic common to all forms of violence against females is perhaps the most difficult to comprehend. During the past decade, many researchers argued (as I did in earlier versions of this article) that sexual violence is not about sex but about violence. I now believe, however, that the "either-or" dichotomy—either sexual violence is about sex or it's about violence—is false and misleading. Male supremacy identifies females as having a basic "flaw"—a trait that distinguishes males and females and legitimates women's inferior status. This "flaw" is female sexuality: it is tempting and seductive and therefore disruptive, capable of reproducing life itself and therefore powerful. Through sexual terrorism men seek to bring this force under control. The site of the struggle is the female body and female sexuality.

Timothy Beneke, in *Men on Rape*, argues that "not every man is a rapist but every man who grows up in America and learns American English learns all too much to think like a rapist" and that "for a man, rape has plenty to do with sex."[23] Twenty years of research and activism have documented that women largely experience rape, battery, incest, and sexual harassment as violence. That women and men often have vastly different experiences is not surprising. Under patriarchy men are entitled to sex; it is a primary vehicle by which they establish and signal their masculinity. From the male perspective, female sexuality is a commodity, something they must take, dominate, or own. Our popular culture routinely celebrates this particular notion of masculinity.

Women are permitted to have sex, but only in marriage (the patriarchal ideal), or at least in love relationships. Women earn their femininity by managing their sexuality and keeping it in trust for a potential husband. The double standard of sexuality leads inevitably to coercion and sexual violence.

Many believe that re-visioning rape as violence not only accurately reflects many women's experiences but also is a more productive strategy for reforming legislation and transforming public attitudes. While arguing that "theoretically and strategically" the "rape as violence" position is the better one, attorney and author Susan Estrich points out that such an approach obscures the reality that the majority of rapes are coerced or forced but unaccompanied by conventional violence. In fact, one consequence of this approach is that it precludes protest from women who experience sexual intrusions in ways not typically seen as violent.

It is argued that in sexual harassment the motive is power, not sex. There is a wide consensus that sexual harassment is intended to "keep women in their place." Yet, the means by which this is attempted or accomplished are sexual: rude comments about sex or about a woman's body, pornographic gestures or posters, demands for sexual favors, rape, etc. Clearly, to the harassers, a woman's place is a largely sexual one; her very presence in the workplace sexualizes it. In the accounts of women's experiences with sexual harassment in *Sexual Harassment: Women Speak Out*, themes of sexual power and sexual humiliation resonate in each essay.

In wife battery the acts of violence are intended to inflict harm on the woman and ultimately to control her, but the message of the violence is explicitly sexual. For example, the most common parts of a woman's body attacked during battering are her face and her breasts—both symbols of her sexuality and her attractiveness to men. During pregnancy, the focus of the attack often shifts to the abdomen—a symbol of her reproductive power. In addressing the "either-or" debate in the sexual abuse of children, David Finkelhor points out "sex is always in the service of other needs. Just because it is infused with nonsexual motives does not make child sexual abuse different from other kinds of behavior that we readily call 'sexual'."[24]

CONCLUSION

The dynamic that underscores all manifestations of sexual terrorism is misogyny—the hatred of women. Violence against women is power expressed sexually. It is violence eroticized. Diana E. H. Russell argues that "we are socialized to sexualize power, intimacy, and affection, and sometimes hatred and contempt as well."[25] For women in the United States, sexual violence and its threat are central issues in their daily lives. Both violence and fear are functional. Without the power to intimidate and punish women sexually, the domination of women in all spheres of society—political, social, and economic—could not exist.

NOTES

1. Susan Brownmiller, *Against Our Will: Men, Women and Rape* (New York: Simon and Schuster, 1975), 5.

2. Frederick F. Hacker, *Crusaders, Criminals and Crazies: Terrorism in Our Time* (New York: W. W. Norton and Co., 1976), xi.

3. Marc Feigen Fasteau, *The Male Machine* (New York: McGraw-Hill Book Co., 1974), 144.

4. Francis M. Watson, *Political Terrorism: The Threat and The Response* (Washington, DC: R. B. Luce, 1976), 15.

5. Paul Wilkinson, *Political Terrorism* (New York: John Wiley and Sons, 1974), 17.

6. Jane Caputi and Diana E. H. Russell. "Femicide: Speaking the Unspeakable," in "Everyday Violence Against Women. Special Report." *Ms*, 1, no. 2 (1990).

7. *Fulgham v. State*, 46 Ala. 143 (1871).

8. *Thompson v. Thompson*, 218 U.S. 611 (1910).

9. Lin Farley, *Sexual Shakedown: The Sexual Harassment of Women on the Job* (New York: McGraw-Hill Book Co., 1978), 14–15.

10. U.S. House of Representatives. Hearings on Sexual Harassment in the Federal Government, Committee on the Post Office and Civil Service, Subcommittee on Investigations. Washington, DC: U.S. Government Printing Office, 1980.

11. Roger Langley and Richard C. Levy, *Wife-Beating: The Silent Crisis* (New York: E. P. Dutton, 1977), 44.

12. Vincent De Francis, *Protecting the Child Victim of Sex Crimes Committed by Adults* (Denver: American Humane Society, 1969), vii.

13. Ibid.

14. Lee H. Bowker, Michelle Arbitell, and J. Richard McFerron. "On the Relationship Between Wife Beating and Child Abuse," in Kersti Yllo and Michele Bograd (eds.), *Feminist Perspectives on Wife Abuse*. Newbury Park, CA: Sage Publications, Inc., 1988, 164.

15. Frank J. Till, *Sexual Harassment: A Report on the Sexual Harassment of Students* (Washington, DC: National Advisory Council on Women's Educational Programs, 1980), 3.

16. Laura L. Crites. "Wife Abuse: The Judicial Record," in Laura L. Crites and Winifred L. Hepperle, *Women, the Courts and Equality*. Beverly Hills, CA: Sage Publications, Inc., 1987, 41.

17. James Bannon, as quoted in Del Martin, *Battered Wives* (New York: Pocket Books, 1977), 115.

18. Georgia Dullea, "Child Prostitution: Causes Are Sought" (*New York Times*, Sept. 4, 1979), p. C11.

19. Till, 28.

20. Ibid., 115.

21. Ibid., 116.

22. Katherine Brady, *Father's Days: A True Story of Incest* (New York: Dell Publishing Co., 1981), 253.

23. Timothy Beneke, *Men on Rape: What They Have to Say About Sexual Violence* (New York: St. Martin's Press, 1982), 16.

24. David Finkelhor (ed.). *Child Sexual Abuse: New Theory and Research.* New York: The Free Press, 1984, 34.

25. Diana E. H. Russell. *The Secret Trauma: Incest in the Lives of Girls and Women.* New York: Basic Books, Inc., 1986, 393.

Date Rape:
A Feminist Analysis

Lois Pineau

Date rape is nonaggravated sexual assault, nonconsensual sex that does not involve physical injury or the explicit threat of physical injury.

However, if a man is to be convicted, it does not suffice to establish that the *actus reas* was nonconsensual. In order to be guilty of sexual assault, a man must have the requisite *mens rea*, i.e., he must have believed either that his victim did not consent or that she was probably not consenting. In many common law jurisdictions, a man who sincerely believes that a woman consented to a sexual encounter is deemed to lack the required *mens rea*, even though the woman did not consent and even though his belief is not reasonable.[1]

Law and Philosophy 8 (1989) 217–43, Copyright © 1989 by Kluwer Academic Publishers. Reprinted with kind permission of Kluwer Academic Publishers.

Recently, strong dissenting voices have been raised against the sincerity condition, and the argument made that *mens rea* be defeated only if the defendant has a reasonable belief that the plaintiff consented.[2] The introduction of legislation which excludes "honest belief" (unreasonable sincere belief) as a defense will certainly help to provide women with greater protection against violence. But while this will be an important step forward, the question of what constitutes a reasonable belief, the problem of evidence when rapists lie, and the problem of the entrenched attitudes of the predominantly male police, judges, lawyers, and jurists who handle sexual assault cases remains.

The criteria for *mens rea*, for the reasonableness of belief, and for consent are closely related. For although a man's sincere belief in the consent of his victim may be sufficient to defeat *mens rea*, the court is less likely to believe his belief is sincere if his belief is unreasonable. If his belief is reasonable, they are more likely to believe in the sincerity of his belief. But evidence of the reasonableness of his belief is also evidence that consent really did take place. For the very things that make it reasonable for *him* to believe that the defendant consented are often the very things that incline the court to believe that she consented. What is often missing is the voice of the woman herself, an account of what it would be reasonable for *her* to agree to—that is to say, an account of what is reasonable from *her* standpoint.

Thus, what is presented as reasonable has repercussions for four separate but related concerns: (1) the question of whether a man's belief in a woman's consent was reasonable; (2) the problem of whether it is reasonable to attribute *mens rea* to him; (3) the question of what could count as reasonable from the woman's point of view; and (4) the question of what is reasonable from the court's point of view. These repercussions are of the utmost practical concern. In a culture which contains an incidence of sexual assault verging on epidemic, a criterion of reasonableness which regards mere submission as consent fails to offer persons vulnerable to those assaults adequate protection.

The following statements by self-confessed date rapists reveal how our lack of a solution for dealing with date rape protects rapists by failing to provide their victims with legal recourse:

All of my rapes have been involved in a dating situation where I've been out with a woman I know. . . . I wouldn't take no for an answer. I think it had something to do with my acceptance of rejection. I had low self-esteem and not much self-confidence and when I was rejected for something which I considered to be rightly mine, I became angry and I went ahead anyway. And this was the same in any situation, whether it was rape or it was something else.[3]

When I did date, when I was younger, I would pick up a girl and if she didn't come across I would threaten her or slap her face then tell her she was going to fuck—that was it. But that's because I didn't want to waste time with any come-ons. It took too much time. I wasn't interested because I didn't like them as people anyway, and I just went with them just to get laid. Just to say that I laid them.[4]

There is, at this time, nothing to protect women from this kind of unscrupulous victimization. A woman on a casual date with a virtual stranger has almost no chance of bringing a complaint of sexual assault before the courts. One reason for this is the prevailing criterion for consent. According to this criterion, consent is implied unless some emphatic episodic sign of resistance occurred and its occurrence can be established. But if no episodic act occurred, or if it did occur and the defendant claims that it didn't, or if the defendant threatened the plaintiff but won't admit it in court, it is almost impossible to find any evidence that would support the plaintiff's word against the defendant. This difficulty is exacerbated by suspicion on the part of the courts, police, and legal educators that even where an act of resistance occurs this act should not be interpreted as a withholding of consent, and this suspicion is especially upheld where the accused is a man who is known to the female plaintiff.

In Glanville Williams's classic textbook on criminal law we are warned that where a man is unknown to a woman she does not consent if she expresses her rejection in the form of an episodic and vigorous act at the "vital moment." But if the man is known to the woman she must, according to Williams, make use of "all means available to her to repel the man."[5] Williams warns that women often welcome a "mastery advance" and present a token resistance. He quotes Byron's couplet:

A little still she strove, and much repented
And whispering "I will ne'er consent"—consented

by way of alerting law students to the difficulty of distinguishing real protest from pretense.[6] Thus, while in principle a firm unambiguous stand or a healthy show of temper ought to be sufficient, if established, to show nonconsent, in practice the forceful overriding of such a stance is apt to be taken as an indication that the resistance was not seriously intended and that the seduction had succeeded. The consequence of this is that it is almost impossible to establish the defendant's guilt beyond a reasonable doubt.

Thus, on the one hand, we have a situation in which women are vulnerable to the most exploitive tactics at the hands of men who are known to them. On the other hand, almost nothing will count as evidence of their being assaulted, including their having taken an emphatic stance in withholding their consent. The new laws have done almost nothing to change this situation. Yet some solution must be sought. Moreover, the road to that solution presents itself clearly enough as a need for a reformulation of the criterion of consent.

THE PROBLEM OF THE CRITERION

The reasoning that underlies the present criterion of consent is entangled in a number of mutually supportive mythologies which see sexual assault as masterful seduction, and silent submission as sexual enjoyment. Because the prevailing ideology has so much informed our conceptualization of sexual interaction, it is extraordinarily difficult for us to distinguish between assault and seduction, submission and enjoyment, or so we imagine. At the same time, this failure to distinguish has given rise to a network of rationalizations that support the conflation of assault with seduction, submission with enjoyment. I therefore want to begin my argument by providing an example which shows both why it is so difficult to make this distinction and that it exists. Later, I will identify and attempt to unravel the lines of reasoning that reinforce this difficulty.

The woman I have in mind agrees to see someone because she feels an initial attraction to him and believes that he feels that same way about her. She goes out with him in the hope that there will be mutual enjoyment and in the course of the day or evening an increase of mutual interest. Unfortunately, these hopes of *mutual* and *reciprocal* interest are not realized. We do not know how much interest she has in him by the end of their time together, but whatever her feelings she comes under pressure to have sex with him, and she does not want to have the kind of sex he wants. She may desire to hold hands and kiss, to engage in more intense caresses or in some form of foreplay, or she may not want to be touched. She may have reasons unrelated to desire for not wanting to engage in the kind of sex he is demanding. She may have religious reservations, concerns about pregnancy or disease, a disinclination to be just another conquest. She may be engaged in a seduction program of her own which sees abstaining from sexual activity as a means of building an important emotional bond. She feels she is desirable to him, and she knows and he knows that he will have sex with her if he can. And while she feels she doesn't owe him anything and that it is her prerogative to refuse him, this feeling is partly a defensive reaction against a deeply held belief that if he is in need she should provide. If she buys into the myth of insistent male sexuality, she may feel he is suffering from sexual frustration and that she is largely to blame.

We do not know how much he desires her, but we do know that his desire for erotic satisfaction can hardly be separated from his desire for conquest. He feels no dating obligation, but has a strong commitment to scoring. He uses the myth of "so hard to control" male desire as a rhetorical tactic, telling her how frustrated she will leave him. He becomes overbearing. She resists, voicing her disinclination. He alternates between telling her how desirable she is and taking a hostile stance, charging her with misleading him, accusing her of wanting him, and being coy—in short, of being deceitful, all the time engaging in rather aggressive body contact. It is late at night, she is tired and a bit queasy from too many drinks, and he is reaffirming her suspicion that perhaps she has misled him. She is having trouble disengaging his body from hers, and wishes he would just go away. She does not adopt a strident angry stance, partly because she thinks he is acting normally and does not deserve it, partly because she feels she is partly to blame, and partly because there is always the danger that her anger will make him angry, possibly violent. It seems that the only thing to do, given his aggression and her queasy fatigue, is to go along with him and get it over with, but this decision is so entangled with the events in process it is hard to know if it is not simply a recognition of what is actually happening. She finds the whole encounter a thoroughly disagreeable experience, but he does not take any notice and wouldn't have changed course if he had. He congratulates himself on his sexual prowess and is confirmed in his opinion that aggressive tactics pay off. Later she feels that she has been raped but, paradoxically, tells herself that she let herself be raped.

The paradoxical feelings of the woman in our example indicate her awareness that what she feels about the incident stands in contradiction to the prevailing cultural assessment of it. She knows that she did not want to have sex with her date. She is not so sure, however, about how much her own desires count, and she is uncertain that she has made her desires clear. Her uncertainty is reinforced by the cultural reading of this incident as an ordinary seduction.

As for us, we assume that the woman did not want to have sex, but just like her, we are unsure whether her mere reluctance, in the presence of high-pressure tactics, constitutes nonconsent. We suspect that submission to an overbearing and insensitive lout is no way to go about attaining sexual enjoyment, and we further suspect that he felt no compunction about providing it, so that on the face of it, from the outside looking in, it looks like a pretty unreasonable proposition for her.

Let us look at this reasoning more closely. Assume that she was not attracted to the kind of sex offered by the sort of person offering it. Then it would be *prima facie* unreasonable for her to agree to have sex—unreasonable, that is, unless she were offered some pay-off for her stoic endurance, money perhaps, or tickets to the opera. The reason is that in sexual matters agreement is closely connected to attraction. Thus, where the presumption is that she was not attracted, we should at the same time presume that she did not consent. Hence, the burden of proof should be on her alleged assailant to show that she had good reasons for consenting to an unattractive proposition.

This is not, however, the way such situations are interpreted. In the unlikely event that the example I have described should come before the courts, there is little doubt that the law would interpret the woman's eventual acquiescence or "going along with" the sexual encounter as consent. But along with this interpretation would go the implicit understanding that she had consented because when all was said and done, when the "token" resistances to the "masterful advances" had been made, she had wanted to after all. Once the courts have constructed this interpretation, they are then forced to conjure up some horror story of feminine revenge in order to explain why she should bring charges against her "seducer."

In the even more unlikely event that the courts agreed that the woman had not consented to the above encounter, there is little chance that her assailant would be convicted of sexual assault.[7] The belief that the man's aggressive tactics are a normal part of seduction means that *mens rea* cannot be established. Her eventual "going along" with his advances constitutes reasonable grounds for his believing in her consent. These "reasonable" grounds attest to the sincerity of his belief in her consent. This reasonableness means that *mens rea* would be defeated even in jurisdictions which make *mens rea* a function of objective standards of reasonableness. Moreover, the sympathy of the court is more likely to lie with the rapist than with his victim, since, if the court is typical, it will be strongly inclined to believe that the victim had in some way "asked for it."

The position of the courts is supported by the widespread belief that male aggression and female reluctance are normal parts of seduction. Given their acceptance of this model, the logic of their response must be respected. For if sexual aggression is a part of ordinary seduction, then it cannot be inconsistent with the legitimate consent of the person allegedly seduced by this means. And if it is normal for a woman to be reluctant, then this reluctance must be consistent with her consent as well. The position of the courts is not inconsistent just so long as they allow that some sort of protest on the part of a woman counts as a refusal. As we have seen, however, it frequently happens that no sort of protest would count as a refusal. Moreover, if no sort of protest counts, or at least if precious few count, then the failure to register these protests will amount to "asking for it," will amount, in other words, to agreeing.

The court's belief in "natural" male aggression and "natural" female reluctance has increasingly come under attack by feminist critics who see quite correctly that the entire legal position would collapse if, for example, it were

shown empirically that men were not aggressive and that women, at least when they wanted sex, were. This strategy is of little help, however, so long as aggressive men can still be found and relics of reluctant women continue to surface. Fortunately, there is another strategy. The position collapses through the weakness of its internal logic. The next section traces the several lines of this logic.

RAPE MYTHS

The belief that the natural aggression of men and the natural reluctance of women somehow make date rape understandable underlies a number of prevalent myths about rape and human sexuality. These beliefs maintain their force partly on account of a logical compulsion exercised by them at an unconscious level. The only way of refuting them effectively is to excavate the logical propositions involved and to expose their misapplication to the situations to which they have been applied. In what follows, I propose to excavate the logical support for popular attitudes that are tolerant of date rape. These myths are not just popular, however, but often emerge in the arguments of judges who acquit date rapists, and of policemen who refuse to lay charges.

The claim that the victim provoked a sexual incident, that "she asked for it," is by far the most common defense given by men who are accused of sexual assault.[8] Feminists, rightly incensed by this response, often treat it as beneath contempt, singling out the defense as an argument against it. On other fronts, sociologists have identified the response as part of an overall tendency of people to see the world as just, a tendency which disposes them to conclude that people for the most part deserve what they get.[9] However, an inclination to see the world as just requires us to construct an account which yields this outcome, and it is just such an account that I wish to examine with regard to date rape.

The least sophisticated of the "she asked for it" rationales—and in a sense, the easiest to deal with—appeals to an injunction against sexually provocative behavior on the part of women. If women should not be sexually provocative, then, from this standpoint, a woman who is sexually provocative deserves to suffer the consequences. Now it will not do to respond that women get raped even when they are not sexually provocative, or that it is men who get to interpret (unfairly) what counts as sexually provocative.[10] The question should be: Why shouldn't a woman be sexually provocative? Why should this behavior warrant any kind of aggressive response whatsoever?

Attempts to explain that women have a right to behave in sexually provocative ways without suffering dire consequences still meet with surprisingly tough resistance. Even people who find nothing wrong or sinful with sex itself, in any of its forms, tend to suppose that women must not behave sexually unless they are prepared to carry through on some fuller course of sexual interaction. The logic of this response seems to be that at some point a woman's behavior commits her to following through on the full course of a sexual encounter as it is defined by her assailant. At some point she has made an agreement, or formed a contract, and once that is done, her contractor is entitled to demand that she satisfy the terms of that contract. Thus, this view about sexual responsibility and desert is supported by other assumptions about contracts and agreements. But we do not normally suppose that casual nonverbal behavior generates agreements. Nor do we normally grant private persons the right to enforce contracts. What rationale would support our conclusion in this case?

The rationale, I believe, comes in the form of a belief in the especially insistent nature of male sexuality, an insistence which lies at the root of natural male aggression and which is extremely difficult, perhaps impossible, to contain. At a certain point in the arousal process, it is thought, a man's rational will gives way to the prerogatives of nature. His sexual need can and does reach a point where it is uncontrollable, and his natural masculine aggression kicks in to ensure that this need is met. Women, however, are naturally more contained, and so it is their responsibility not to provoke the irrational in the male. If they do go so far as that, they have both failed in their responsibilities and subjected themselves to the inevitable. One does not go into the lion's cage and expect not to be eaten. Natural feminine reluctance, it is thought, is no protection against a sexually aroused male.

This belief about the normal aggressiveness of male sexuality is complemented by common knowledge about female gender development. Once, women were taught to deny their sexuality and to aspire to ideals of chastity. Things have not changed so much. Women still tend to eschew conquest mentalities in favor of a combination of sex and affection. Insofar as this is thought to be merely a cultural requirement, however, there is an expectation that women will be coy about their sexual desire. The assumption that women both want to indulge sexually and are inclined to sacrifice this desire for higher ends, gives rise to the myth that they want to be raped. After all, doesn't rape give them the sexual enjoyment they *really* want, at the same time that it relieves them of the responsibility for admitting to and acting upon what they want? And how then can we blame men, who have been socialized to be aggressively seductive precisely for the purpose of overriding female reserve? If we find fault at all, we are inclined to cast our suspicions on the motives of the woman. For it is on her that the contradictory roles of sexual desirer and sexual denier have been placed. Our awareness of the contradiction expected of her makes us suspect her honesty. In the past, she was expected to deny her complicity because of the shame and guilt she felt at having submitted.[11] This expectation persists in many quarters today and is carried over into a general suspicion about her character, and the fear that she might make a false accusation out of revenge or some other low motive.[12]

But if women really want sexual pleasure, what inclines us to think that they will get it through rape? This conclusion logically requires a theory about the dynamics of sexual pleasure that sees that pleasure as an emergent property of overwhelming male insistence. For the assumption that a raped female experiences sexual pleasure implies that the person who rapes her knows how to cause that pleasure independently of any information she might convey on that point. Since her ongoing protest is inconsistent with requests to be touched in particular ways in particular places, to have more of this and less of that, then we must believe that the person who touches her knows these particular ways and places instinctively, without any directives from her.

Thus we find, underlying and reinforcing this belief in incommunicative male prowess, a conception of sexual pleasure that springs from wordless interchanges and of sexual success that occurs in a place of meaningful silence. The language of seduction is accepted as a tacit language: eye contact, smiles, blushes, and faintly discernible gestures. It is, accordingly, imprecise and ambiguous. It would be easy for a man to make mistakes about the message conveyed, understandable that he should mistakenly think that a sexual invitation has been made and a bargain struck. But honest mistakes, we think, must be excused.

In sum, the belief that women should not be sexually provocative is logically linked to several other beliefs, some normative, some empirical. The normative beliefs are (1) that people should keep the agreements they make; (2) that sexually provocative behavior, taken beyond a certain point, generates agreements; (3) that the peculiar nature of male and female sexuality places such agreements in a special category, one in which the possibility of retracting an agreement is ruled out or at least made highly unlikely; (4) that women are not to be trusted, in sexual matters at least. The empirical belief, which turns out to be false, is that male sexuality is not subject to rational and moral control.

DISPELLING THE MYTHS

The "she asked for it" justification of sexual assault incorporates a conception of a contract that would be difficult to defend in any other context, and the presumptions about human sexuality which function to reinforce sympathies rooted in the contractual notion of just deserts are not supported by empirical research.

The belief that a woman generates some sort of contractual obligation whenever her behavior is interpreted as seductive is the most indefensible part of the mythology of rape. In law, contracts are not legitimate just because a promise has been made. In particular, the use of pressure tactics to extract agreement is frowned upon. Normally, an agreement is upheld only if the contractors were clear on what they were getting into and had sufficient time to reflect on the wisdom of their doing so. Either there must be a clear tradition in which the expectations involved in the contract are fairly well known (marriage), or there must be an explicit written agreement concerning the exact terms of the contract and the expectations of the persons involved. But whatever the terms of a contract, there is no private right to enforce it. So, if I make a contract with you on which I renege, the only permissible recourse for you is through due legal process.

Now, it is not clear whether sexual contracts can be made to begin with or, if so, what sort of sexual contracts would be legitimate. But assuming that they could be made, the terms of those contracts would not be enforceable. To allow public enforcement would be to grant the state the overt right to force people to have sex, and this would clearly be unacceptable. Granting that sexual contracts are legitimate, state enforcement of such contracts would have to be limited to ordering nonsexual compensation for breaches of contract. So it makes no difference whether a sexual contract is tacit or explicit. There are no grounds whatsoever that would justify enforcement of its terms.

Thus, even if we assume that a woman has initially agreed to an encounter, her agreement does not automatically make all subsequent sexual activity to which she submits legitimate. If during coitus a woman should experience pain, be suddenly overcome with guilt or fear of pregnancy, or simply lose her initial desire, those are good reasons for her to change her mind. Having changed her mind, neither her partner nor the state has any right to force her to continue. But then if she is forced to continue she is assaulted. Thus, establishing that consent occurred at a particular point during a sexual encounter should not conclusively establish the legitimacy of the encounter.[13] What is needed is a reading of whether she agreed throughout the encounter.

If the "she asked for it" contractual view of sexual interchange has any validity, it is because there is a point at which there is no stopping a sexual encounter, a point at which that encounter becomes the inexorable outcome of the unfolding of natural events. If a sexual encounter is like a slide on which I cannot stop halfway down, it will be relevant whether I enter the slide of my own free will or am pushed.

But there is no evidence that the entire sexual act is like a slide. While there may be a few seconds in the "plateau" period just prior to orgasm in which people are "swept" away by sexual feelings to the point where we could justifiably understand their lack of heed for the comfort of their partner, the greater part of a sexual encounter comes well within the bounds of morally responsible control of our own actions. Indeed, the available evidence shows that most of the activity involved in sex has to do with building the requisite level of desire, a task that involves the proper use of foreplay, the possibility of which implies control over the form that foreplay will take. Modern sexual therapy assumes that such control is universally accessible, and so far there has been no reason to question that assumption. Sexologists are unanimous, moreover, in holding that mutual sexual enjoyment requires an atmosphere of comfort and communication, a minimum of pressure, and an ongoing checkup on one's partner's state. They maintain that different people have different predilections and that what is pleasurable for one person is very often anathema to another. These findings show that the way to achieve sexual pleasure, at any time at all, let alone with a casual acquaintance, decidedly does not involve overriding the other person's express reservations and providing them with just any kind of sexual stimulus.[14] And while we do not want to allow science and technology a voice in which the voices of particular women are drowned, in this case science seems to concur with women's perception that aggressive incommunicative sex is not what they want. But if science and the voice of women concur, if aggressive seduction does not lead to good sex, if women do not like it or want it, then it is not rational to think that they would agree to it. Where such sex takes place, it is therefore rational to presume that the sex was not consensual.

The myth that women like to be raped is closely connected, as we have seen, to doubt about their honesty in sexual matters, and this suspicion is exploited by defense lawyers when sexual assault cases make it to the courtroom. It is an unfortunate consequence of the presumption of innocence that rape victims who end up in court frequently find that it is they who are on trial. For if the defendant is innocent, then either he did not intend to do what he was accused of, or the plaintiff is mistaken about his identity, or she is lying. Often the last alternative is the only plausible defense, and as a result the plaintiff's word seldom goes unquestioned. Women are frequently accused of having made a false accusation, either as a defensive mechanism for dealing with guilt and shame or out of a desire for revenge.

Now, there is no point in denying the possibility of false accusation, though there are probably better ways of seeking revenge on a man than accusing him of rape. However, we can now establish a logical connection between the evidence that a woman was subjected to high-pressure aggressive "seduction" tactics and her claim that she did not consent to that encounter. Where the kind of encounter is not the sort to which it would be reasonable to consent, there is a logical presumption that a woman who claims she did not consent is telling the truth. Where the kind of sex involved is not the sort of sex we would expect a woman to like, the burden of proof should be not on the woman to show that she did not consent but on the defendant to show that, contrary to every reasonable expectation, she did consent. The defendant should be required to convince the court that the plaintiff persuaded him to have sex with her even though there are no visible reasons why she should.

In conclusion, there are no grounds for the "she asked for it" defense. Sexually provocative behavior does not generate sexual contracts. Even where there are sexual agreements, they cannot be legitimately enforced by the state or by private right or by natural prerogative. Second, all the evidence suggests that neither women nor men find sexual enjoyment in rape or in any form of noncommunicative sexuality. Third, male sexual desire is containable and can be subjected to moral and rational control. Fourth, since there is no reason why women

should not be sexually provocative, they do not "deserve" any sex they do not want. This last is a welcome discovery. The taboo on sexual provocativeness in women is a taboo both on sensuality and on teasing. But sensuality is a source of delight, and teasing is playful and inspires wit. What a relief to learn that it is not sexual provocativeness, but its enemies, that constitutes a danger to the world.

In thinking about sex we must keep in mind its sensual ends, and the facts show that aggressive high-pressure sex contradicts those ends. Consensual sex in dating situations is presumed to aim at mutual enjoyment. It may not always do this, and when it does, it might not always succeed. There is no logical incompatibility between wanting to continue a sexual encounter and failing to derive sexual pleasure from it.

But it seems to me that there is a presumption in favor of the connection between sex and sexual enjoyment, and that if a man wants to be sure he is not forcing himself on a woman he has an obligation either to ensure that the encounter really is mutually enjoyable or to know the reasons why she would want to continue the encounter in spite of her lack of enjoyment. A closer investigation of the nature of this obligation will enable us to construct a more rational and a more plausible norm of sexual conduct.

Onora O'Neill has argued that in intimate situations we have an obligation to take the ends of others as our own and to promote those ends in a nonmanipulative and nonpaternalistic manner.[15] Now, it seems that in honest sexual encounters just this is required. Assuming that each person enters the encounter in order to seek sexual satisfaction, each person engaging in the encounter has an obligation to help the other seek his or her ends. To do otherwise is to risk acting in opposition to what the other desires, and hence to risk acting without the other's consent.

But the obligation to promote the sexual ends of one's partner implies the obligation to know what those ends are, and also the obligation to know how those ends are attained. Thus, the problem comes down to a problem of epistemic responsibility, the responsibility to know. The solution, in my view, lies in the practice of a communicative sexuality, one which combines the appropriate knowledge of the other with respect for the dialectics of desire.

CULTURAL PRESUMPTIONS

Now it may well be that we have no obligation to care for strangers, and I do not wish to claim that we do. Nonetheless, it seems that O'Neill's point about the special moral duties we have in certain intimate situations is supported by a conceptual relation between certain kinds of personal relationships and the expectation that it should be a communicative relation. Friendship is a case in point. It is a relation that is greatly underdetermined by what we usually include in our sets of rights and obligations. For the most part, rights and obligations disappear as terms by which friendship is guided. They are still there, to be called upon, in case the relationship breaks down, but insofar as the friendship is a friendship it is concerned with fostering the quality of the interaction and not with standing on rights. Thus, because we are friends we share our property, and property rights between us are not invoked. Because we are friends, privacy is not an issue. Because we are friends we may see to each other's needs as often as we see to our own. The same can be said for relations between lovers, parents and dependent children, and even between spouses, at least when interaction is functioning at an optimal level. When such relations break down to the point that people must stand on their rights, we can often say that the actors ought to make more of an effort, and in many instances fault them for their lack of charity, tolerance, or benevolence. Thus, although we have a right to end

friendships, it may be a reflection on our lack of virtue that we do so, and while we cannot be criticized for violating other people's rights, we can be rightfully deprecated for lacking the virtue to sustain a friendship.

But is there a similar conceptual relation between the kind of activity that a date is and the sort of moral practice that it requires? My claim is that there is and that this connection is easily established once we recognize the cultural presumption that dating is a gesture of friendship and regard. Traditionally, the decision to date indicates that two people have an initial attraction to each other, that they are disposed to like each other and look forward to enjoying each other's company. Dating derives its implicit meaning from this tradition. It retains this meaning unless other aims are explicitly stated, and even then it may not be possible to alienate this meaning. It is a rare woman who will not spurn a man who states explicitly, right at the onset, that he wants to go out with her solely on the condition that he have sexual intercourse with her at the end of the evening, and that he has no interest in her company apart from gaining that end, and no concern for mutual satisfaction.

Explicit protest to the contrary aside, the conventions of dating confer on it its social meaning, and this social meaning implies a relationship which is more like friendship than the cutthroat competition of opposing teams. As such, it requires that we do more than stand on our rights with regard to each other. As long as we are operating under the auspices of a dating relationship, it requires that we behave in the mode of friendship and trust. But if a date is more like a friendship than a business contract, then clearly respect for the dialectics of desire is incompatible with the sort of sexual pressure that is inclined to end in date rape. And clearly, also, a conquest mentality which exploits a situation of trust and respect for purely selfish ends is morally pernicious. Failure to respect the dialectics of desire when operating under the auspices of friendship and trust is to act in flagrant disregard of the moral requirement to avoid manipulative, coercive, and exploitive behavior. Respect for the dialectics of desire is *prima facie* inconsistent with the satisfaction of one person at the expense of the other. The proper end of friendship relations is mutual satisfaction. But the requirement of mutuality means that we must take a communicative approach to discovering the ends of the other, and this entails that we respect the dialectics of desire.

But now that we know what communicative sexuality is, and that it is morally required, and that it is the only feasible means to mutual sexual enjoyment, why not take this model as the norm of what is reasonable in sexual interaction? The evidence of sexologists strongly indicates that women whose partners are aggressively uncommunicative have little chance of experiencing sexual pleasure. But it is not reasonable for women to consent to what they have little chance of enjoying. Hence, it is not reasonable for women to consent to aggressive noncommunicative sex. Nor can we reasonably suppose that women have consented to sexual encounters which we know and they know they do not find enjoyable. With the communicative model as the norm, the aggressive contractual model should strike us as a model of deviant sexuality, and sexual encounters patterned on that model should strike us as encounters to which *prima facie* no one would reasonably agree. But if acquiescence to an encounter counts as consent only if the acquiescence is reasonable, something to which a reasonable person, in full possession of knowledge relevant to the encounter, would agree, then acquiescence to aggressive noncommunicative sex is not reasonable. Hence, acquiescence under such conditions should not count as consent.

Thus, where communicative sexuality does not occur, we lack the main ground for believing that the sex involved was consensual. Moreover, where a man does not engage in communicative sexuality, he acts either out of reckless disregard or out of willful ignorance, for he cannot know, except through the practice of communicative sexuality, whether his partner has any sexual reason for continuing the encounter. And where she does not, he runs the risk of imposing on her what she is not willing to have. All that is needed, then, in order to provide women with legal protection from "date rape" is to make both reckless indifference and willful ignorance a sufficient condition of *mens rea* and to make communicative sexuality the accepted norm of sex to which a reasonable woman would agree.[16] Thus, the appeal to communicative sexuality as a norm for sexual encounters accomplishes two things. It brings the aggressive sex involved in "date rape" well within the realm of sexual assault, and it locates the guilt of date-rapists in the failure to approach sexual relations on a communicative basis.

NOTES

1. This is true, at present, in jurisdictions which follow the precedent set by *Morgan v. Morgan*. In this case, four men were acquitted of rape because they sincerely thought that their victim had consented, despite their admitting that she had protested vigorously. See Mark Thornton's "Rape and *Mens Rea*," *Canadian Journal of Philosophy*, supp. vol. 8:119–46.

2. Ibid.

3. *Why Men Rape*, ed. Sylvia Levine and Joseph Koenig (Toronto: Macmillan, 1980), 83.

4. Ibid., 77.

5. Williams, *Textbook of Criminal Law* (1983), 238.

6. Ibid.

7. See Jeanne C. Marsh, Allison Geist, and Nathan Caplan, *Rape and the Limits of Law Reform* (Boston: Auburn House, 1982), 32. According to Marsh's study on the impact of the Michigan reform of rape laws, convictions were increased for traditional conceptions of rape, i.e., aggravated assault. However,

date rape, which has a much higher incidence than aggravated assault, has a very low rate of arrest and an even lower one of conviction.

8. See ibid., 61, for a particularly good example of this response. Also see John M. MacDonald, "Victim-Precipitated Rape," in *Rape Offenders and Their Victims* (Springfield, Ill.: Charles C. Thomas, 1971), 78–89, for a good example of this response in academic thinking. Also see Menachem Amir, *Patterns in Forcible Rape* (Chicago: University of Chicago Press, 1972), 259.

9. See Eugene Borgida and Nancy Brekke, "Psycho-legal Research on Rape Trials," in *Rape and Sexual Assault*, ed. Ann Wobert Burgess (New York: Garland Press, 1985), 314. Also see M. J. Lerner, "The Desire for Justice and Reactions to Victims," in *Altruism and Helping Behaviour*, ed. J. Macaulay and L. Berkowitz (New York: Academic Press, 1970).

10. As, for example, Lorenne Clark and Debra Lewis do in *Rape: The Price of Coercive Sexuality* (Toronto: Women's Press, 1977), 152–53.

11. See Sue Bessner, *The Laws of Rape* (New York: Praeger Publications, 1984), 111–21, for a discussion of the legal forms in which this suspicion is expressed.

12. Ibid.

13. A speech-act like "OK, let's get it over with" is taken as consent, even though it is extracted under high pressure, the sex that ensues lacks mutuality, and there are no ulterior reasons for such an agreement. See Davis, "Setting Penalties," 103. Also see Carolyn Schafer and Marilyn Frye. "Rape and Re-spect," in *Readings in Recent Feminist Philosophy*, ed. Marilyn Pearsall (Belmont, Calif.: Wadsworth, 1986), 189, for a characterization of the common notion of consent as a formal speech-act.

14. It is not just women who fail to find satisfaction in the "swept away" approach to sexual interaction. Studies of convicted rapists, and of conquest-oriented men, indicate that men are frequently disappointed when they use this approach as well. In over half of aggravated sexual assaults, penetration fails because the man loses his erection. Those who do succeed invariably report that the sex experienced was not enjoyable. This supports the prevailing view of sexologists that men depend on the positive response of their partners in order to fuel their own responsive mechanisms. See A. N. Groth, in *Rape and Sexual Assault*. Also see *Why Men Rape*, ed. Levine and Koenig, or consult any recent manual on male sexuality.

15. O'Neill, "Between Consenting Adults," *Philosophy and Public Affairs* 14:252–77.

16. As now seems to be the case in Australian law. In a recent Australian case a man was convicted of being an accomplice to a rape because he was reckless in determining whether the woman raped by his friend was consenting. The judge ruled that his "reckless indifference" sufficed to establish *mens rea*. This ruling was possible, however, only because unreasonable belief is not a rape defense in Australia. See *Australian Law Review* 71:120.

Lesbian "Sex"[1]

Marilyn Frye

The reasons the word "sex" is in quotation marks in my title are two: one is that the term "sex" is an inappropriate term for what lesbians do, and the other is that whatever it is that lesbians do that (for a lack of a better word) might be called "sex" we apparently do damned little of it. For a great many lesbians, the gap between the high hopes we had some time ago for lesbian sex and the way things have worked out has turned the phrase "lesbian sex" into something of a bitter joke. I don't want to exaggerate this: things aren't so bad for all lesbians, or all of the time. But in our communities as a whole, there is much grumbling on the subject. It seems worthwhile to explore some of the meanings of the relative dearth of what (for lack of a better word) we call lesbian "sex."

Recent discussions of lesbian "sex" frequently cite the finding of a study on couples by Blumstein and Schwartz,[2] which is perceived by most of those who discuss it as having been done well, with a good sample of couples— lesbian, male homosexual, heterosexual non-married and heterosexual married couples. These people apparently found that lesbian couples "have sex" far less frequently than any other type of couple, that lesbian couples are less "sexual" as couples and as individuals than anyone else. In their sample, only about one-third of lesbians in relationships of two years or longer "had sex" once a week or more; 47% of lesbians in long-term relationships "had sex" once a month or less, while among heterosexual married couples only 15% had sex once a month or less. And they report that lesbians

seem to be more limited in the range of their "sexual" techniques than are other couples.

When this sort of information first came into my circle of lesbian friends, we tended to see it as conforming to what we know from our own experience. But on reflection, looking again at what has been going on with us in our long-term relationship, the nice fit between this report and our experience seemed not so perfect after all.

It was brought to our attention during our ruminations on this that what 85% of long-term heterosexual married couples do more than once a month takes on the average 8 minutes to do.[3]

Although in my experience lesbians discuss their "sex" lives with each other relatively little (a point to which I will return), I know from my own experience and from the reports of a few other lesbians in long-term relationships, that what we do that, on average, we do considerably less frequently, takes, on average, considerably more than 8 minutes to do. It takes about 30 minutes, at the least. Sometimes maybe an hour. And it is not uncommon that among these relatively uncommon occurrences, an entire afternoon or evening is given over to activities organized around doing it. The suspicion arises that what 85% of heterosexual married couples are doing more than once a month and what 47% of lesbian couples are doing less than once a month is not the same thing.

I remember that one of my first delicious tastes of old gay lesbian culture occurred in a bar where I was getting acquainted with some new friends. One was talking about being busted out of the Marines for being gay. She had been put under suspicion somehow, and was sent off to the base psychiatrist to be questioned, her perverted tendencies to be assessed.

He wanted to convince her she had only been engaged in a little youthful experimentation and wasn't really gay. To this end, he questioned her about the extent of her experience. What he asked was, "How many times have you had sex with a woman?" At this, we all laughed and giggled: what an ignorant fool. What does he think he means, "times?" What will we count? What's to *count*?

Another of my friends, years later, discussing the same conundrum, said that she thought maybe every time you got up to go to the bathroom, that marked a "time." The joke about "how many times" is still good for a chuckle from time to time in my life with my lover. I have no memory of any such topic providing any such merriment in my years of sexual encounters and relationships with men. It would have been very rare indeed that we would not have known how to answer the question "How many times did you do it?"

If what heterosexual married couples do that the individuals report under the rubric "sex" or "have sex" or "have sexual relations" is something that in most instances can easily be individuated into countable instances, this is more evidence that it is not what long-term lesbian couples do . . . or, for that matter, what short-term lesbian couples do.[4]

What violence did the lesbians do their experience by answering the same question the heterosexuals answered, as though it had the same meaning for them? How did the lesbians figure out how to answer the questions "How frequently?" or "How many times?" My guess is that different individuals figured it out differently. Some might have counted a two- or three-cycle evening as one "time" they "had sex"; some might have counted it as two or three "times." Some may have counted as "times" only the times both partners had orgasms; some may have counted as "times" occasions on which at least one had an orgasm; those who do not have orgasms or have them far more rarely than they "have sex" may not have

figured orgasms into the calculations; perhaps some counted as a "time" every episode in which both touched the other's vulva more than fleetingly and not for something like a health examination. For some, to count every reciprocal touch of the vulva would have made them count as "having sex" more than most people with a job or a work would dream of having time for; how do we suppose those individuals counted "times"? Is there any good reason why they should *not* count all those as "times"? Does it depend on how fulfilling it was? Was anybody else counting by occasions of fulfillment?

We have no idea how the individual lesbians surveyed were counting their "sexual acts." But this also raises the questions of how heterosexuals counted *their* sexual acts. By orgasms? By *whose* orgasms? If the havings of sex by heterosexual married couples did take on the average 8 minutes, my guess is that in a very large number of those cases the women did not experience orgasms. My guess is that neither the women's pleasure nor the women's orgasms were pertinent in most of the individuals' counting and reporting the frequency with which they "had sex."

So, do lesbian couples really "have sex" any less frequently than heterosexual couples? I'd say that lesbian couples "have sex" a great deal less frequently than heterosexual couples: by the criteria that I'm betting most of the heterosexual people used to count "times," lesbians don't have sex at all. No male orgasms, no "times." (I'm willing to draw the conclusion that heterosexual women don't have sex either; that what they report is the frequency with which their partners had sex.)

It has been said before by feminists that the concept of "having sex" is a phallic concept; that it pertains to heterosexual intercourse, in fact, primarily to heterosex*ist* intercourse, i.e., male-dominant-female-subordinate-copulation-whose-completion-and-purpose-is-the-male's-ejaculation. I have thought this was true since the first time the idea was put to me, some 12 years ago.[5] But I have been finding lately that I have to go back over some of the ground I covered a decade ago because some of what I knew then I knew too superficially. For some of us, myself included, the move from heterosexual relating to lesbian relating was occasioned or speeded up or brought to closure by our knowledge that what we had done under the heading "having sex" was indeed male-dominant-female-subordination-copulation-whose-completion . . . etc. and it was not worthy of doing. Yet now, years later, we are willing to answer questionnaires that ask us how frequently we "have sex," and are dissatisfied with ourselves and with our relationships because we don't "have sex" enough. We are so dissatisfied that we keep a small army of therapists in business trying to help us "have sex" more.

We quit having sex years ago, and for excellent and compelling reasons. What exactly is our complaint now?

In all these years I've been doing and writing feminist theory, I have not until very recently written, much less published, a word about sex. I did not write, though it was suggested to me that I do so, anything in the SM debates; I left entirely unanswered an invitation to be the keynote speaker at a feminist conference about women's sexuality (which by all reports turned out to be an excellent conference). I was quite unable to think of anything but vague truisms to say, and very few of those. Feminist theory is grounded in experience; I have always written feminist political and philosophical analysis from the bottom up, starting with my own encounters and adventures, frustrations, pain, anger, delight, etc. Sometimes this has no doubt made it a little provincial; but it has at least had the virtue of firm connection with *someone's* real, live experience (which is more than you can say for a lot of theory). When I put to myself the task of theorizing about sex and sexuality, it was as though I *had* no experience, as though there

was no ground on which and from which to generate theory. But (if I understand the terminology rightly), I have in fact been what they call "sexually active" for close to a quarter of a century, about half my life, almost all of what they call one's "adult life," heterosexually, lesbianly and autoerotically. Surely I have experience. But I seem not to have *experiential knowledge* of the sort I need.

Reflecting on all that history, I realize that in many of its passages this experience has been a muddle. Acting, being acted on, choosing, desiring, pleasure and displeasure all akimbo: not coherently determining and connecting with each other. Even in its greatest intensity it has for the most part been somehow rather opaque to me, not fully in my grasp. My "experience" has in general the character more of a buzzing blooming confusion than of *experience*. And it has occurred in the midst of almost total silence on the part of others about their experience. The experience of others has for the most part also been opaque to me; they do not discuss or describe it *in detail* at all.

I recall an hours-long and heated argument among some eight or ten lesbians at a party a couple of years ago about SM, whether it is okay, or not. When Carolyn and I left, we realized that in the whole time not one woman had said one concrete, explicit, physiologically specific thing about what she actually *did*. The one arguing in favor of bondage: did she have her hands tied gently with ribbons or scarves, or harshly with handcuffs or chains? What other parts of her body were or weren't restrained, and by what means? And what parts of her body were touched, and how, while she was bound? And what liberty did she still have to touch in return? And if she had no such liberty, was it part of her experience to want that liberty and tension or frustration, or was it her experience that she felt pleased or satisfied not to have that liberty? Who knows? She never said a single word at this level of specificity. Nor did anyone else, pro or con.

I once perused a large and extensively illustrated book on sexual activity by and for homosexual men. It was astounding to me for one thing in particular, namely, that its pages constituted a huge lexicon of *words*: words for acts and activities, their sub-acts, preludes and denouements, their stylistic variation, their sequences. Gay male sex, I realized then, is *articulate*. It is articulate to a degree that, in my world, lesbian "sex" does not remotely approach. Lesbian "sex" as I have known it, most of the time I have known it, is utterly *in*articulate. Most of my lifetime, most of my experience in the realms commonly designated as "sexual" has been pre-linguistic, non-cognitive. I have, in effect, no linguistic community, no language, and therefore in one important sense, no knowledge.

In situations of male dominance, women are for the most part excluded from the formulation and validation of meaning and thereby denied the means to express themselves. Men's meanings, and no women's meanings, are encoded in what is presumed to be the whole population's language. (In many cases, both the men and the women assume it is everyone's language.) The meanings one's life and experience might generate cannot come fully into operation if they are not woven into language: they are fleeting, or they hover, vague, not fully coalesced, not connected, and hence not *useful* for explaining or grounding interpretations, desires, complaints, theories. In response to our understanding that there is something going on in patriarchy that is more or less well described by saying women's meanings are not encoded in the dominant languages and that this keeps our experience from being fully formed and articulate, we have undertaken quite deliberately to discover, complete and encode our meanings. Such simple things as naming chivalrous gestures "insulting," naming Virginia Woolf a great writer, naming ourselves women instead of girls or ladies. Coining terms like "sexism" "sexual harassment" and "incestor." Mary Daly's

book, *Websters' First New Intergalactic Wickedary of the English Language*, is a whole project of "encoding" meanings, and we can all find examples of our own more local encodings.[6]

Meanings should arise from our bodily self-knowledge, bodily play, tactile communication, the ebb and flow of intense excitement, arousal, tension, release, comfort, discomfort, pain and pleasure (and I make no distinctions here among bodily, emotional, intellectual, aesthetic). But such potential meanings are more amorphous, less coalesced into discrete elements of a coherent pattern of meanings, of an *experience*, than any other dimensions of our lives. In fact, there are for many of us *virtually no meanings* in this realm because nothing of it is crystallized in a linguistic matrix.

What we have for generic words to cover this terrain are the words "sex," "sexual" and "sexuality." In our efforts to liberate ourselves from the stifling women-hating Victorian denial that women even *have* bodily awareness, arousal, excitement, orgasms and so on, many of us actively took these words for ourselves, and claimed that we *do* "do sex" and we *are* sexual and we *have* sexuality. This has been particularly important to lesbians because the very fact of "sex" being a phallocentric term has made it especially difficult to get across the idea that lesbians are not, for lack of a penis between us, making do with feeble and partial and pathetic half-satisfactions. But it seems to me that the attempt to encode our lustiness and lustfulness, our passion and our vigorous carnality in the words "sex," "sexual" and "sexuality" has backfired. Instead of losing their phallocentricity, these words have imported the phallocentric meanings into and onto experience which is not in any way phallocentric. A web of meanings which maps emotional intensity, excitement, arousal, bodily play, orgasm, passion and relational adventure back onto a semantic center in male-dominant-female-subordinate-copulation-whose-completion-and-purpose-is-the-male's-ejaculation has been so utterly inadequate as to leave us speechless, meaningless, and ironically, according to the Blumstein and Schwartz report, "not as sexual" as couples or as individuals of any other group.

Our lives, the character of our embodiment, *cannot* be mapped back onto that semantic center. When we try to synthesize and articulate it by the rules of that mapping, we end up trying to mold our loving and our passionate carnal intercourse into explosive 8-minute events. That is not the timing and ontology of the lesbian body. When the only things that count as "doing it" are those passages of our interactions which most closely approximate a paradigm that arose from the meanings of the rising and falling penis, no wonder we discover ourselves to "do it" rather less often than do pairs with one or more penises present.

There are many cultural and social-psychological reasons why women (in white Euro-American groups, but also in many other configurations of patriarchy) would generally be somewhat less clear and less assertive about their desires and about getting their satisfactions than men would generally be. And when we pair up two women in a couple, it stands to reason that those reasons would double up and tend to make relationships in which there is a lowish frequency of clearly delineated desires and direct initiations of satisfactions. But for all the help it might be to lesbian bodies to work past the psychological and behavioral habits of femininity that inhibit our passions and pleasures, my suggestion is that what we have never taken seriously enough is the *language* which forecloses our meanings.

My positive recommendation is this: Instead of starting with a point (a point in the life of a body unlike our own) and trying to make meanings along vectors from that point, we would do better to start with a wide field of our passions and bodily pleasures and make meanings that weave a web across it. To begin creating a vocabulary that elaborates and expands

our meanings, we should adopt a very wide and general concept of "doing it." Let it be an open, generous, commodious concept encompassing all the acts and activities by which we generate with each other pleasures and thrills, tenderness and ecstasy, passages of passionate carnality of whatever duration or profundity. Everything from vanilla to licorice, from puce to chartreuse, from velvet to ice, from cuddles to cunts, from chortles to tears. Starting from there, we can let our experiences generate a finer-tuned descriptive vocabulary that maps and expresses the differences and distinctions among the things we do, the kinds of pleasures we get, the stages and styles of our acts and activities, the parts of our bodies centrally engaged in the different kinds of "doing it," and so on. I would not, at the outset, assume that all of "doing it" is good or wholesome, nor that everyone would like or even tolerate everything this concept includes; I would not assume that "doing it" either has or should have a particular connection with love, or that it hasn't or shouldn't have such a connection. As we explain and explore and define our pleasures and our preferences across this expansive and heterogeneous field, teaching each other what the possibilities are and how to navigate them, a vocabulary will arise among us and by our collective creativity.

The vocabulary will arise among us, of course, only if we talk with each other about what we're doing and why, and what it feels like. Language is social. So is "doing it."

I'm hoping it will be a lot easier to talk about what we do, and how and when and why, and in carnal sensual detail, once we've learned to laugh at foolish studies that show that lesbians don't have sex as often as, aren't as sexual as, and use fewer sexual techniques than other folks.

NOTES

1. When I speak of "we" and "our communities," I actually don't know exactly who that is. I know only that I and my lover are not the only ones whose con-

cerns I address, and that similar issues are being discussed in friendship circles and communities other than ours (as witness, e.g., discussion in the pages of the *Lesbian Connection*). If what I say here resonates for you, so be it. If not, at least you can know it resonates for some range of lesbians and some of them probably are your friends or acquaintances.

2. Philip Blumstein and Pepper Schwartz, *American Couples*, (NY: William and Morrow Company, 1983).

3. Dotty Calabrese gave this information in her workshop on long-term lesbian relationships at the Michigan Womyn's Music Festival, 1987.

4. This is the term used in the Blumstein and Schwartz questionnaire. In the text of their book, they use "have sex."

5. By Carolyn Shafer. See pp. 156–7 of my book *The Politics of Reality* (The Crossing Press, 1983).

6. I picked up the word "encoding" as it is used here from the novel *Native Tongue*, by Suzette Haden Elgin (NY: Daw Books, Inc., 1984). She envisages women identifying concepts, feelings, types of situations, etc., for which there are no words in English, and giving them intuitively appropriate names in a women-made language called Laadan.

Reproduction

According to Angela Davis, birth control is a "fundamental prerequisite for the emancipation of women" (p. 81). But this prerequisite has been very slow in coming. Only in 1965, in *Griswold v. Connecticut*, did the Supreme Court recognize a constitutional right to privacy, covering personal procreative decisions. In recognizing this right, it ruled that married adults may not be barred from purchasing contraceptives. This right was later extended to unmarried adults (*Eisenstadt v. Baird*, 1972) and to unmarried minors (*Carey v. Population Services International*, 1977). In 1973, eight years after *Griswold*, the Supreme Court finally ruled in *Roe v. Wade* and *Doe v. Bolton*, that the right to privacy also implied the right to terminate a pregnancy through abortion. The fact that these landmark decisions were made so late in U. S. history often causes us to forget that throughout the nineteenth century and the early part of the twentieth, many individuals and groups in the United States fought strenuously for so-called voluntary motherhood. Yet despite all their efforts, and even though a large number of U.S. women used contraceptives and had few scruples about early abortion, antibirth-control legislation became increasingly restrictive. One of the more notorious examples of such legislation was the Comstock laws of the 1870s, which defined practicing, advertising, or even owning, lending, or giving away literature on contraception or abortion as pornography, punishable by six months to five years imprisonment at hard labor, or a fine of between $100 and $2,000.

Birth control has come not only slowly but also unevenly to U. S. women. For many white, relatively privileged U. S. women it has been emancipation indeed, but for many women of color, it has proved to be a mixed blessing. Many black women and Latina women, for example, have resorted to abortion not to be free of pregnancy and, therefore, in a better position to pursue higher education or a challenging career, but simply to prevent the birth of a child destined to live in miserable social conditions—indeed, the same conditions through which its mother (and father) have struggled and suffered. In addition, these women, as well as immigrant women, native American women, and poor women in general, have been provided with and encouraged to use contraception for eugenic purposes—as a means of preventing the proliferation of the "lower classes." Far from being freely chosen, this type of contraception has frequently included "elective sterilization," but without informed consent, or even forced sterilization, paid for and sanctioned by the Department of Health, Education and Welfare. In "Racism, Birth Control and Reproductive Rights," Angela Davis traces some of the history of the birth control movement in the United States, showing the different effects it has had on different groups of women. The upshot is that the actual emancipatory value of any kind of birth control needs to be determined in its concrete social and historical context, with regard to all the various groups of women affected by it.

When it comes to abortion in contemporary society, however, Kay Castonguay suggests that its actual emancipatory value can be specified quite generally for *all* women: None. "Liberalized abortion has created an environment in which the unborn child is considered disposable and of little worth" ("Pro-Life Feminism," p. 93), and hence, motherhood as well is considered disposable and of little worth. As a consequence, efforts are not really made to integrate mothers into the work world—to provide them with such basics as adequate health benefits and parental leaves of absence, affordable daycare facilities in or near their places of employment, and reduced hours and flexible schedules. In addition, reliance on abortion has diverted attention away from developing safer, more effective contraceptive methods, and on developing more responsible attitudes in men toward sexuality and childbirth. Finally, reliance on abortion perpetuates the unfortunate mind-set of the past in which people—whether women and children, or blacks, or now even unborn children—are conceived of as the property of other people—men, or whites, or, now, women—to do with as they wish. Small wonder that a significant number of feminists today, as well as such leading feminists of the past as Susan B. Anthony, Elizabeth Cady Stanton, Lucretia Mott, and Fanny Wright, have been strongly *opposed* to abortion.

On the other hand, when we consider that the typical American woman spends 90 percent of her reproductive life trying to avoid pregnancy, that no method of contraception (except surgical sterilization) is foolproof, and that the more reliable methods are also more expensive (e.g., Norplant costs more than $500 to implant even at the cheapest clinics) and hence not truly accessible to many women, we begin to see why so many other feminists see abortion, at least at present, as a necessary component of birth control in the United States. Unfortunately, unsympathetic political forces have done everything in their power to chip away at women's abortion rights. While these forces have met with significant success, especially in the case of poor women who can neither afford an abortion nor make use of federal or other public funds and public hospitals to get one

(but who can be surgically sterilized using public funds and public hospitals!) we must ask whether their antiabortion activities are just ones.

In "Mother/Foetus/State Conflicts," Christine Overall suggests that the antiabortion position is morally flawed. She reminds us that the cornerstone of this position is the belief that the fetus has a "right to life," but in her estimation this belief has never been rationally justified: "Fetal-rights advocates appear to assume that the fact that the fetus is human and living makes it morally equivalent to a two-year-old child or a twenty-five-year-old woman, and gives it a right to life. Yet many of our other practices—practices that seem eminently reasonable—suggest that there is no such equivalence" (p. 96). For example, IUDs—intrauterine devices that prevent the fertilized ovum from implanting in the wall of the uterus—are not treated as murder weapons that deprive the ovum of its "right to life," and lab technicians who dispose of surplus embryos after *in vitro* fertilization are not treated as murderers. What is more, even if the fetus did have a "right to life," it would not follow that it also had a right to the *use* of the pregnant woman's body. "If we are not willing to authorize compulsory 'donations' of blood or organs to save the lives of dying persons, then we should not be willing to tolerate compulsory fetal surgery or Caesarean sections, or to deny abortions" (p. 97). The activities and allegiances of right-to-life advocates move dangerously toward denying the autonomy not only of pregnant women, but also of any persons who regard their bodies as inviolable territory—not to be invaded against their will.

We have concentrated thus far on the emancipatory potential of such reproduction-controlling technologies as contraception, sterilization, and abortion, lamenting the fact that not all women have been equally free to use or not use these methods of birth control. The reproduction-assisting or enhancing technologies—genetic diagnosis, screening, and fetal therapy, for example, or *in vitro* fertilization or other medical remedies for infertility would seem to offer women further reproductive options. In "The New Procreative Technologies," however, Ruth Hubbard suggests that these new technologies, which so far have been extended primarily to the relatively wealthy women who can afford their high cost, are not really increasing women's procreative freedom. For one thing, the increasing medicalization of pregnancy and birth that these technologies entail make women dependent on "experts," thereby robbing women of meaningful control over their own reproductive processes. For another, the very availability of these new technologies serves as a social and even legal pressure for women to use them, so much so that in some cases women have been forced to use diagnostic or therapeutic procedures intended to improve the health of their fetuses. Disturbed by these impositions on women, Hubbard stresses that, for all we know, some of these new technologies might turn out to be more harmful than beneficial: "Most therapies become established on the basis of custom and professional consensus and are not preceded by rigorous, scientific evaluation of their outcomes" (p. 104). Thus,

the current, sometimes indiscriminate use of ultrasound or *in utero* fetal surgery might prove to have the kind of unfortunate outcomes that the indiscriminate use of X-rays, forceps, and artificially induced labor had in the past. Finally, concludes Hubbard, the highest price some women might have to pay for the uncertain benefits of the new reproductive technologies might be their own emotional well-being. Encouraging women to use every conceivable prenatal diagnostic procedure available may, for example, cause many pregnant women to

. . . look on every fetus as potentially disabled and in need of ongoing medical surveillance. But the reality is that only the rare fetus is at risk for serious genetic or developmental problems as long as pregnant women have access to adequate nutrition and the necessary economic and social supports, and can live in a relatively healthful environment. Poverty, malnutrition, and urban decay place a fetus at far greater risk than do the inherited disabilities for which prenatal tests are being developed. (*The Politics of Woman's Biology,* pp. 144–45)

But it is precisely with these conditions that poor women have still to deal; for them, the new reproductive technologies are a luxury item.

Racism, Birth Control and Reproductive Rights

Angela Y. Davis

When nineteenth-century feminists raised the demand for "voluntary motherhood," the campaign for birth control was born. Its proponents were called radicals and they were subjected to the same mockery as had befallen the initial advocates of woman suffrage. "Voluntary motherhood" was considered audacious, outrageous and outlandish by those who insisted that wives had no right to refuse to satisfy their husbands' sexual urges. Eventually, of course, the right to birth control, like women's right to vote, would be more or less taken for granted by U.S. public opinion. Yet in 1970, a full century later, the call for legal and easily accessible abortions was no less controversial than the issue of "voluntary motherhood" which had originally launched the birth control movement in the United States.

Birth control—individual choice, safe contraceptive methods, as well as abortions when necessary, is a fundamental prerequisite for the emancipation of women. Since the right of birth control is obviously advantageous to women of all classes and races, it would appear that even vastly dissimilar women's groups would have attempted to unite around this issue. In reality, however, the birth control movement has seldom succeeded in uniting women of different social backgrounds, and rarely have the movement's leaders popularized the genuine concerns of working-class women. Moreover, arguments advanced by birth control advocates have sometimes been based on bla-

tantly racist premises. The progressive potential of birth control remains indisputable. But in actuality, the historical record of this movement leaves much to be desired in the realm of challenges to racism and class exploitation.

The most important victory of the contemporary birth control movement was won during the early 1970s when abortions were at last declared legal. Having emerged during the infancy of the new Women's Liberation Movement, the struggle to legalize abortions incorporated all the enthusiasm and the militancy of the young movement. By January, 1973, the abortion rights campaign had reached a triumphant culmination. In *Roe* v. *Wade* (410 U.S.) and *Doe* v. *Bolton* (410 U.S.), the U.S. Supreme Court ruled that a woman's right to personal privacy implied her right to decide whether or not to have an abortion.

The ranks of the abortion rights campaign did not include substantial numbers of women of color. Given the racial composition of the larger Women's Liberation Movement, this was not at all surprising. When questions were raised about the absence of racially oppressed women in both the larger movement and in the abortion rights campaign, two explanations were commonly proposed in the discussions and literature of the period: women of color were overburdened by their people's fight against racism; and/or they had not yet become conscious of the centrality of sexism. But the real meaning of the almost lily-white complexion of the abortion rights campaign was not to be found in an ostensibly myopic or underdeveloped consciousness among women of color. The truth lay buried in the ideological underpinnings of the birth control movement itself.

The failure of the abortion rights campaign to conduct a historical self-evaluation led to a dangerously superficial appraisal of Black people's suspicious attitudes toward birth control in general. Granted, when some Black people unhesitatingly equated birth control with genocide, it did appear to be an exaggerated—even paranoiac—reaction. Yet white abortion rights activists missed a profound message, for underlying these cries of genocide were important clues about the history of the birth control movement. This movement, for example, had been known to advocate involuntary sterilization—a racist form of mass "birth control." If ever women would enjoy the right to plan their pregnancies, legal and easily accessible birth control measures and abortions would have to be complemented by an end to sterilization abuse.

As for the abortion rights campaign itself, how could women of color fail to grasp its urgency? They were far more familiar than their white sisters with the murderously clumsy scalpels of inept abortionists seeking profit in illegality. In New York, for instance, during the several years preceding the decriminalization of abortions in that state, some 80 percent of the deaths caused by illegal abortions involved Black and Puerto Rican women.[1] Immediately afterward, women of color received close to half of all the legal abortions. If the abortion rights campaign of the early 1970s needed to be reminded that women of color wanted desperately to escape the back-room quack abortionists, they should have also realized that these same women were not about to express pro-abortion sentiments. They were in favor of *abortion rights*, which did not mean that they were proponents of abortion. When Black and Latina women resort to abortions in such large numbers, the stories they tell are not so much about their desire to be free of their pregnancy, but rather about the miserable social conditions which dissuade them from bringing new lives into the world.

Black women have been aborting themselves since the earliest days of slavery. Many slave women refused to bring children into a world of interminable forced labor, where chains and floggings and sexual abuse for women were the everyday conditions of life. A doctor practicing in Georgia around the middle of the last century noticed that abortions and miscarriages were far more common among his slave patients than among the white women he treated. According to the physician, either Black women worked too hard or

. . . as the planters believe, the blacks are possessed of a secret by which they destroy the fetus at an early stage of gestation . . . All country practitioners are aware of the frequent complaints of planters (about the) . . . unnatural tendency in the African female to destroy her offspring.[2]

Expressing shock that ". . . whole families of women fail to have any children,"[3] this doctor never considered how "unnatural" it was to raise children under the slave system. The episode of Margaret Garner, a fugitive slave who killed her own daughter and attempted suicide herself when she was captured by slave-catchers, is a case in point.

She rejoiced that the girl was dead—"now she would never know what a woman suffers as a slave"—and pleaded to be tried for murder. "I will go singing to the gallows rather than be returned to slavery!"[4]

Why were self-imposed abortions and reluctant acts of infanticide such common occurrences during slavery? Not because Black women had discovered solutions to their predicament, but rather because they were desperate. Abortions and infanticides were acts of desperation, motivated not by the biological birth process but by the oppressive conditions of slavery. Most of these women, no doubt, would have expressed their deepest resentment had someone hailed their abortions as a stepping stone toward freedom.

During the early abortion rights campaign it was too frequently assumed that legal abortions provided a viable alternative to the myriad problems posed by poverty. As if having fewer children could create more jobs, higher wages, better schools, etc., etc. This assumption reflected the tendency to blur the distinction between *abortion rights* and the general advocacy of *abortions*. The campaign often failed to provide a voice for women who wanted the *right* to legal abortions while deploring the social conditions that prohibited them from bearing more children.

The renewed offensive against abortion rights that erupted during the latter half of the 1970s has made it absolutely necessary to focus more sharply on the needs of poor and racially oppressed women. By 1977 the passage of the Hyde Amendment in Congress had mandated the withdrawal of federal funding for abortions, causing many state legislatures to follow suit. Black, Puerto Rican, Chicana and Native American Indian women, together with their impoverished white sisters, were thus effectively divested of the right to legal abortions. Since surgical sterilizations, funded by the Department of Health, Education and Welfare, remained free on demand, more and more poor women have been forced to opt for permanent infertility. What is urgently required is a broad campaign to defend the reproductive rights of all women—and especially those women whose economic circumstances often compel them to relinquish the right to reproduction itself.

Women's desire to control their reproductive system is probably as old as human history itself. As early as 1844 the *United States Practical Receipt Book* contained, among its many recipes for food, household chemicals and medicines, "receipts" for "birth preventive lotions." To make "Hannay's Preventive Lotion," for example,

[t]ake pearlash, 1 part; water, 6 parts. Mix and filter. Keep it in closed bottles, and use it, with or without soap, immediately after connexion.[5]

For "Abernethy's Preventive Lotion,"

[t]ake bichloride of mercury, 25 parts; milk of almonds, 400 parts; alcohol, 100 parts; rosewater, 1000 parts. Immerse the glands in a little of the mixture.... Infallible, if used in proper time.[6]

While women have probably always dreamed of infallible methods of birth control, it was not until the issue of women's rights in general became the focus of an organized movement that reproductive rights could emerge as a legitimate demand. In an essay entitled "Marriage," written during the 1850s, Sarah Grimke argued for a "... right on the part of woman to decide *when* she shall become a mother, how often and under what circumstances."[7] Alluding to one physician's humorous observation, Grimke agreed that if wives and husbands alternatively gave birth to their children, "... no family would ever have more than three, the husband bearing one and the wife two."[8] But, as she insists, "... the *right* to decide this matter has been almost wholly denied to woman."[9]

Sarah Grimke advocated women's right to sexual abstinence. Around the same time the well-known "emancipated marriage" of Lucy Stone and Henry Blackwell took place. These abolitionists and women's rights activists were married in a ceremony that protested women's traditional relinquishment of their rights to their persons, names and property. In agreeing that as husband, he had no right to the "custody of the wife's person,"[10] Henry Blackwell promised that he would not attempt to impose the dictates of his sexual desires upon his wife.

The notion that women could refuse to submit to their husbands' sexual demands eventually became the central idea of the call for "voluntary motherhood." By the 1870s, when the woman suffrage movement had reached its peak, feminists were publicly advocating voluntary motherhood. In a speech delivered in 1873, Victoria Woodhull claimed that (t)he wife who submits to sexual intercourse against her wishes or desires, virtually commits suicide; while the husband who compels it, commits murder, and ought just as much to be punished for it, as though he strangled her to death for refusing him.[11]

Woodhull, of course, was quite notorious as a proponent of "free love." Her defense of a woman's right to abstain from sexual intercourse within marriage as a means of controlling her pregnancies was associated with Woodhull's overall attack on the institution of marriage.

It was not a coincidence that women's consciousness of their reproductive rights was born within the organized movement for women's political equality. Indeed, if women remained forever burdened by incessant childbirths and frequent miscarriages, they would hardly be able to exercise the political rights they might win. Moreover, women's new dreams of pursuing careers and other paths of self-development outside marriage and motherhood could only be realized if they could limit and plan their pregnancies. In this sense, the slogan "voluntary motherhood" contained a new and genuinely progressive vision of womanhood. At the same time, however, this vision was rigidly bound to the lifestyle enjoyed by the middle classes and the bourgeoisie. The aspirations underlying the demand for "voluntary motherhood" did not reflect the conditions of working-class women, engaged as they were in a far more fundamental fight for economic survival. Since this first call for birth control was associated with goals which could only be achieved by women possessing material wealth, vast numbers of poor and working-class women would find it rather difficult to identify with the embryonic birth control movement.

Toward the end of the nineteenth century the white birth rate in the United States suffered a significant decline. Since no contraceptive innovations had been publicly introduced, the drop in the birth rate implied that women were substantially curtailing their sexual activity. By 1890 the typical native-born white woman was bearing no more than four children.[12] Since U.S. society was becoming increasingly urban, this new birth pattern should not have been a surprise. While farm life demanded large families, they became dysfunctional within the context of city life. Yet this phenomenon was publicly interpreted in a racist and anti-working-class fashion by the ideologues of rising monopoly capitalism. Since native-born white women were bearing fewer children, the specter of "race suicide" was raised in official circles.

In 1905 President Theodore Roosevelt concluded his Lincoln Day Dinner speech with the proclamation that "race purity must be maintained."[13] By 1906 he blatantly equated the falling birth rate among native-born whites with the impending threat of "race suicide." In his State of the Union message that year Roosevelt admonished the well-born white women who engaged in "willful sterility—the one sin for which the penalty is national death, race suicide."[14] These comments were made during a period of accelerating racist ideology and of great waves of race riots and lynchings on the domestic scene. Moreover, President Roosevelt himself was attempting to muster support for the U.S. seizure of the Philippines, the country's most recent imperialist venture.

How did the birth control movement respond to Roosevelt's accusation that their cause was promoting race suicide? The President's propagandistic ploy was a failure, according to a leading historian of the birth control movement, for, ironically, it led to greater support for its advocates. Yet, as Linda Gordon maintains, this controversy ". . . also brought to the forefront those issues that most separated feminists from the working class and the poor."[15]

This happened in two ways. First, the feminists were increasingly emphasizing birth control as a route to careers and higher education—goals out of reach of the poor with or without birth control. In the context of the whole feminist movement, the race-suicide episode was an additional factor identifying feminism almost exclusively with the aspirations of the more privileged women of the society. Second, the pro-birth control feminists began to popularize the idea that poor people had a moral obligation to restrict the size of their families, because large families create a drain on the taxes and charity expenditures of the wealthy and because poor children were less likely to be "superior."[16]

The acceptance of the race-suicide thesis, to a greater or lesser extent, by women such as Julia Ward Howe and Ida Husted Harper reflected the suffrage movement's capitulation to the racist posture of Southern women. If the suffragists acquiesced to arguments invoking the extension of the ballot to women as the saving grace of white supremacy, then birth control advocates either acquiesced to or supported the new arguments invoking birth control as a means of preventing the proliferation of the "lower classes" and as an antidote to race suicide. Race suicide could be prevented by the introduction of birth control among Black people, immigrants and the poor in general. In this way, the prosperous whites of solid Yankee stock could maintain their superior numbers within the population. Thus class-bias and racism crept into the birth control movement when it was still in its infancy. More and more, it was assumed within birth control circles that poor women, Black and immigrant alike, had a "moral obligation to restrict the size of their families."[17] What was demanded as a "right" for the privileged came to be interpreted as a "duty" for the poor.

When Margaret Sanger embarked upon her lifelong crusade for birth control—a term she coined and popularized—it appeared as though the racist and anti-working-class overtones of the previous period might possibly be overcome. For Margaret Higgens Sanger came from a working-class background herself and was well acquainted with the devastating pressures of poverty. When her mother died, at the age of forty-eight, she had borne no less than eleven children. Sanger's later memories of her own family's troubles would confirm her belief that working-class women had a special need for the right to plan and space their pregnancies autonomously. Her affiliation, as an adult, with the Socialist movement was a further cause for hope that the birth control campaign would move in a more progressive direction.

When Margaret Sanger joined the Socialist party in 1912, she assumed the responsibility of recruiting women from New York's working women's clubs into the party.[18] *The Call*—the party's paper—carried her articles on the women's page. She wrote a series entitled "What Every Mother Should Know," another called "What Every Girl Should Know," and she did on-the-spot coverage of strikes involving women. Sanger's familiarity with New York's working-class districts was a result of her numerous visits as a trained nurse to the poor sections of the city. During these visits, she points out in her autobiography, she met countless numbers of women who desperately desired knowledge about birth control.

According to Sanger's autobiographical reflections, one of the many visits she made as a nurse to New York's Lower East Side convinced her to undertake a personal crusade for birth control. Answering one of her routine calls, she discovered that twenty-eight-year-old Sadie Sachs had attempted to abort herself. Once the crisis had passed, the young woman asked the attending physician to give her advice on birth prevention. As Sanger relates the story, the doctor recommended that she "... tell (her husband) Jake to sleep on the roof."[19]

I glanced quickly to Mrs. Sachs. Even through my sudden tears I could see stamped on her face an expression of absolute despair. We simply looked at each other, saying no word until the door had closed behind the doctor. Then she lifted her thin, blue-veined hands and clasped them beseechingly. "He can't understand. He's only a man. But you do, don't you? Please tell me the secret, and I'll never breathe it to a soul. Please!"[20]

Three months later Sadie Sachs died from another self-induced abortion. That night, Margaret Sanger says, she vowed to devote all her energy toward the acquisition and dissemination of contraceptive measures.

I went to bed, knowing that no matter what it might cost, I was finished with palliatives and superficial cures; I resolved to seek out the root of evil, to do something to change the destiny of mothers whose miseries were as vast as the sky.[21]

During the first phase of Sanger's birth control crusade, she maintained her affiliation with the Socialist party—and the campaign itself was closely associated with the rising militancy of the working class. Her staunch supporters included Eugene Debs, Elizabeth Gurley Flynn and Emma Goldman, who respectively represented the Socialist party, the International Workers of the World and the anarchist movement. Margaret Sanger, in turn, expressed the anti-capitalist commitment of her own movement within the pages of its journal, *Woman Rebel*, which was "dedicated to the interests of working women."[22] Personally, she continued to march on picket lines with striking workers and publicly condemned the outrageous assaults on striking workers. In 1914, for example, when the National Guard massacred scores of Chicano miners in Ludlow, Colorado, Sanger joined the labor movement in exposing John D. Rockefeller's role in this attack.[23]

Unfortunately, the alliance between the birth control campaign and the radical labor movement did not enjoy a long life. While Socialists and other working-class activists continued to support the demand for birth control, it did not occupy a central place in their overall strategy. And Sanger herself began to underestimate the centrality of capitalist exploitation in her analysis of poverty, arguing that too many

children caused workers to fall into their miserable predicament. Moreover, ". . . women were inadvertently perpetuating the exploitation of the working class," she believed, "by continually flooding the labor market with new workers."[24] Ironically, Sanger may have been encouraged to adopt this position by the neo-Malthusian ideas embraced in some socialist circles. Such outstanding figures of the European socialist movement as Anatole France and Rosa Luxemburg had proposed a "birth strike" to prevent the continued flow of labor into the capitalist market.[25]

When Margaret Sanger severed her ties with the Socialist party for the purpose of building an independent birth control campaign, she and her followers became more susceptible than ever before to the anti-Black and anti-immigrant propaganda of the times. Like their predecessors, who had been deceived by the "race suicide" propaganda, the advocates of birth control began to embrace the prevailing racist ideology. The fatal influence of the eugenics movement would soon destroy the progressive potential of the birth control campaign.

During the first decades of the twentieth century the rising popularity of the eugenics movement was hardly a fortuitous development. Eugenic ideas were perfectly suited to the ideological needs of the young monopoly capitalists. Imperialist incursions in Latin America and in the Pacific needed to be justified, as did the intensified exploitation of Black workers in the South and immigrant workers in the North and West. The pseudoscientific racial theories associated with the eugenics campaign furnished dramatic apologies for the conduct of the young monopolies. As a result, this movement won the unhesitating support of such leading capitalists as the Carnegies, the Harrimans and the Kelloggs.[26]

By 1919 the eugenic influence on the birth control movement was unmistakably clear. In an article published by Margaret Sanger in the American Birth Control League's journal, she defined "the chief issue of birth control" as "more children from the fit, less from the unfit."[27] Around this time the ABCL heartily welcomed the author of *The Rising Tide of Color Against White World Supremacy* into its inner sanctum.[28] Lothrop Stoddard, Harvard professor and theoretician of the eugenics movement, was offered a seat on the board of directors. In the pages of the ABCL's journal, articles by Guy Irving Birch, director of the American Eugenics Society, began to appear. Birch advocated birth control as a weapon to

... prevent the American people from being replaced by alien or Negro stock, whether it be by immigration or by overly high birth rates among others in this country.[29]

By 1932 the Eugenics Society could boast that at least twenty-six states had passed compulsory sterilization laws and that thousands of "unfit" persons had already been surgically prevented from reproducing.[30] Margaret Sanger offered her public approval of this development. "Morons, mental defectives, epileptics, illiterates, paupers, unemployables, criminals, prostitutes and dope fiends" ought to be surgically sterilized, she argued in a radio talk.[31] She did not wish to be so intransigent as to leave them with no choice in the matter; if they wished, she said, they should be able to choose a lifelong segregated existence in labor camps.

Within the American Birth Control League, the call for birth control among Black people acquired the same racist edge as the call for compulsory sterilization. In 1939 its successor, the Birth Control Federation of America, planned a "Negro Project." In the Federation's words,

(t)he mass of Negroes, particularly in the South, still breed carelessly and disastrously, with the result that the increase among Negroes, even more than among whites, is from that portion of the population least fit, and least able to rear children properly.[32]

Calling for the recruitment of Black ministers to lead local birth control committees, the Federation's proposal suggested that Black people should be rendered as vulnerable as possible to their birth control propaganda. "We do not want word to get out," wrote Margaret Sanger in a letter to a colleague,

... that we want to exterminate the Negro population and the minister is the man who can straighten out that idea if it ever occurs to any of their more rebellious members.[33]

This episode in the birth control movement confirmed the ideological victory of the racism associated with eugenic ideas. It had been robbed of its progressive potential, advocating for people of color not the individual right to *birth control*, but rather the racist strategy of *population control*. The birth control campaign would be called upon to serve in an essential capacity in the execution of the U.S. government's imperialist and racist population policy.

The abortion rights activists of the early 1970s should have examined the history of their movement. Had they done so, they might have understood why so many of their Black sisters adopted a posture of suspicion toward their cause. They might have understood how important it was to undo the racist deeds of their predecessors, who had advocated birth control as well as compulsory sterilization as a means of eliminating the "unfit" sectors of the population. Consequently, the young white feminists might have been more receptive to the suggestion that their campaign for abortion rights include a vigorous condemnation of sterilization abuse, which had become more widespread than ever.

It was not until the media decided that the casual sterilization of two Black girls in Montgomery, Alabama, was a scandal worth reporting that the Pandora's box of sterilization abuse was finally flung open. But by the time the case of the Relf sisters broke, it was practically too late to influence the politics of the abortion rights movement. It was the summer of 1973 and the Supreme Court decision legalizing abortions had already been announced in January. Nevertheless, the urgent need for mass opposition to sterilization abuse became tragically clear. The facts surrounding the Relf sisters' story were horrifyingly simple. Minnie Lee, who was twelve years old, and Mary Alice, who was fourteen, had been unsuspectingly carted into an operating room, where surgeons irrevocably robbed them of their capacity to bear children.[34] The surgery had been ordered by the HEW-funded Montgomery Community Action Committee after it was discovered that Depo-Provera, a drug previously administered to the girls as a birth prevention measure, caused cancer in test animals.[35]

After the Southern Poverty Law Center filed suit on behalf of the Relf sisters, the girls' mother revealed that she had unknowingly "consented" to the operation, having been deceived by the social workers who handled her daughters' case. They had asked Mrs. Relf, who was unable to read, to put her "X" on a document, the contents of which were not described to her. She assumed, she said, that it authorized the continued Depo-Provera injections. As she subsequently learned, she had authorized the surgical sterilization of her daughters.[36]

In the aftermath of the publicity exposing the Relf sisters' case, similar episodes were brought to light. In Montgomery alone, eleven girls, also in their teens, had been similarly sterilized. HEW-funded birth control clinics in other states, as it turned out, had also subjected young girls to sterilization abuse. Moreover, individual women came forth with equally outrageous stories. Nial Ruth Cox, for example, filed suit against the state of North Carolina. At the age of eighteen—eight years before the suit—officials had threatened to discontinue her family's welfare payments if she refused to submit to surgical sterilization. Before she assented to the operation, she was assured that her infertility would be temporary.[37]

Nial Ruth Cox's lawsuit was aimed at a state which had diligently practiced the theory of eugenics. Under the auspices of the Eugenics Commission of North Carolina, so it was learned, 7,686 sterilizations had been carried out since 1933. Although the operations were justified as measures to prevent the reproduction of "mentally deficient persons," about 5,000 of the sterilized persons had been Black.[38] According to Brenda Feigen Fasteau, the ACLU attorney representing Nial Ruth Cox, North Carolina's recent record was not much better.

As far as I can determine, the statistics reveal that since 1964, approximately 65% of the women sterilized in North Carolina were Black and approximately 35% were white.[39]

As the flurry of publicity exposing sterilization abuse revealed, the neighboring state of South Carolina had been the site of further atrocities. Eighteen women from Aiken, South Carolina, charged that they had been sterilized by a Dr. Clovis Pierce during the early 1970s. The sole obstetrician in that small town, Pierce had consistently sterilized Medicaid recipients with two or more children. According to a nurse in his office, Dr. Pierce insisted that pregnant welfare women "will have to submit (sic!) to voluntary sterilization" if they wanted him to deliver their babies.[40] While he was ". . . tired of people running around and having babies and paying for them with my taxes,"[41] Dr. Pierce received some $60,000 in taxpayers' money for the sterilizations he performed. During his trial he was supported by the South Carolina Medical Association, whose members declared that doctors ". . . have a moral and legal right to insist on sterilization permission before accepting a patient, if it is done on the initial visit."[42]

Revelations of sterilization abuse during that time exposed the complicity of the federal government. At first the Department of Health, Education and Welfare claimed that approximately 16,000 women and 8,000 men had been sterilized in 1972 under the auspices of federal programs.[43] Later, however, these figures underwent a drastic revision. Carl Shultz, director of HEW's Population Affairs Office, estimated that between 100,000 and 200,000 sterilizations had actually been funded that year by the federal government.[44] During Hitler's Germany, incidentally, 250,000 sterilizations were carried out under the Nazis' Hereditary Health Law.[45] Is it possible that the record of the Nazis, throughout the years of their reign, may have been almost equaled by U.S. government-funded sterilizations in the space of a single year?

Given the historical genocide inflicted on the native population of the United States, one would assume that Native American Indians would be exempted from the government's sterilization campaign. But according to Dr. Connie Uri's testimony in a Senate committee hearing, by 1976 some 24 percent of all Indian women of childbearing age had been sterilized.[46] "Our blood lines are being stopped," the Choctaw physician told the Senate committee, "Our unborn will not be born . . . This is genocidal to our people."[47] According to Dr. Uri, the Indian Health Services Hospital in Claremore, Oklahoma, had been sterilizing one out of every four women giving birth in that federal facility.[48]

Native American Indians are special targets of government propaganda on sterilization. In one of the HEW pamphlets aimed at Indian people, there is a sketch of a family with *ten children* and *one horse* and another sketch of a family with *one child* and *ten horses*. The drawings are supposed to imply that more children mean more poverty and fewer children mean wealth. As if the ten horses owned by the one-child family had been magically conjured up by birth control and sterilization surgery.

The domestic population policy of the U.S. government has an undeniably racist edge. Native American, Chicana, Puerto Rican and Black women continue to be sterilized in disproportionate numbers. According to a National Fertility Study conducted in 1970 by Princeton University's Office of Population Control, 20 percent of all married Black women have been permanently sterilized.[49] Approximately the same percentage of Chicana women had been rendered surgically infertile.[50] Moreover, 43 percent of the women sterilized through federally subsidized programs were Black.[51]

The astonishing number of Puerto Rican women who have been sterilized reflects a special government policy that can be traced back to 1939. In that year President Roosevelt's Interdepartmental Committee on Puerto Rico issued a statement attributing the island's economic problems to the phenomenon of overpopulation.[52] This committee proposed that efforts be undertaken to reduce the birth rate to no more than the level of the death rate.[53] Soon afterward an experimental sterilization campaign was undertaken in Puerto Rico. Although the Catholic Church initially opposed this experiment and forced the cessation of the program in 1946, it was converted during the early 1950s to the teachings and practice of population control.[54] In this period over 150 birth control clinics were opened, resulting in a 20 percent decline in population growth by the mid-1960s.[55] By the 1970s over 35 percent of all Puerto Rican women of childbearing age had been surgically sterilized.[56] According to Bonnie Mass, a serious critic of the U.S. government's population policy,

. . . if purely mathematical projections are to be taken seriously, if the present rate of sterilization of 19,000 monthly were to continue, then the island's population of workers and peasants could be extinguished within the next 10 or 20 years . . . (establishing) for the first time in world history a systematic use of population control capable of eliminating an entire generation of people.[57]

During the 1970s the devastating implications of the Puerto Rican experiment began to emerge with unmistakable clarity. In Puerto Rico the presence of corporations in the highly automated metallurgical and pharmaceutical industries had exacerbated the problem of unemployment. The prospect of an ever-larger army of unemployed workers was one of the main incentives for the mass sterilization program. Inside the United States today, enormous numbers of people of color—and especially racially oppressed youth—have become part of a pool of permanently unemployed workers. It is hardly coincidental, considering the Puerto Rican example, that the increasing incidence of sterilization has kept pace with the high rates of unemployment. As growing numbers of white people suffer the brutal consequences of unemployment, they can also expect to become targets of the official sterilization propaganda.

The prevalence of sterilization abuse during the latter 1970s may be greater than ever before. Although the Department of Health, Education and Welfare issued guidelines in 1974, which were ostensibly designed to prevent involuntary sterilizations, the situation has nonetheless deteriorated. When the American Civil Liberties Union's Reproductive Freedom Project conducted a survey of teaching hospitals in 1975, they discovered that 40 percent of those institutions were not even aware of the regulations issued by HEW.[58] Only 30 percent of the hospitals examined by the ACLU were even attempting to comply with the guidelines.[59]

The 1977 Hyde Amendment has added yet another dimension to coercive sterilization practices. As a result of this law passed by Congress, federal funds for abortions were eliminated in all cases but those involving rape and the risk of death or severe illness. According to Sandra Salazar of the California Department of Public Health, the first victim of the Hyde Amendment was a twenty-seven-year-old Chicana woman from Texas. She died as a result of an illegal abortion in Mexico shortly after Texas discontinued government-funded abortions. There have been many more victims—women for whom sterilization has become the only alternative to the abortions, which are currently beyond their reach. Sterilizations continue to be federally funded and free, to poor women, on demand.

Over the last decade the struggle against sterilization abuse has been waged primarily by Puerto Rican, Black, Chicana and Native American women. Their cause has not yet been embraced by the women's movement as a whole. Within organizations representing the interests of middle-class white women, there has been a certain reluctance to support the demands of the campaign against sterilization abuse, for these women are often denied their individual rights to be sterilized when they desire to take this step. While women of color are urged, at every turn, to become permanently infertile, white women enjoying prosperous economic conditions are urged, by the same forces, to reproduce themselves. They therefore sometimes consider the "waiting period" and other details of the demand for "informed consent" to sterilization as further inconveniences for women like themselves. Yet whatever the inconveniences for white middle-class women, a fundamental reproductive right of racially oppressed and poor women is at stake. Sterilization abuse must be ended.

NOTES

1. Edwin M. Gold *et al.*, "Therapeutic Abortions in New York City: A Twenty-Year Review" in *American Journal of Public Health*, Vol. LV (July, 1965), pp. 964–972.

2. Herbert Gutman, *The Black Family in Slavery and Freedom, 1750–1925* (New York: Pantheon Books, 1976), pp. 80–81 (note).

3. *Ibid.*

4. Herbert Aptheker "The Negro Woman" in *Masses and Mainstream*, Vol. 11, No. 2, p. 12.

5. Quoted in Rosalyn Baxandall, Linda Gordon, Susan Reverby, editors, *America's Working Women: A Documentary History—1600 to the Present* (New York: Random House, 1976), p. 17.

6. *Ibid.*

7. Gerda Lerner, *The Female Experience: An American Documentary* (Indianapolis: Bobbs-Merrill, 1977), p. 91.

8. *Ibid.*

9. *Ibid.*

10. "Marriage of Lucy Stone under Protest" appeared in *History of Woman Suffrage*, Vol. 1. Quoted in Miriam Schneir, *Feminism: The Essential Historical Writings* (New York: Vintage Books, 1972), p. 104.

11. Speech by Victoria Woodhull, "The Elixir of Life." Quoted in Schneir, *ibid.*, p. 153.

12. Mary P. Ryan, *Womanhood in America from Colonial Times to the Present* (New York: Franklin Watts, Inc., 1975), p. 162.

13. Melvin Steinfeld, *Our Racist Presidents* (San Ramon, California: Consensus Publishers, 1972), p. 212.

14. Bonnie Mass, *Population Target: The Political Economy of Population Control in Latin America* (Toronto, Canada: Women's Educational Press, 1977), p. 20.

15. Linda Gordon, *Woman's Body, Woman's Right: Birth Control in America* (New York: Penguin Books, 1976), p. 157.

16. *Ibid.*, p. 158.

17. *Ibid.*

18. Margaret Sanger, *An Autobiography* (New York: Dover Press, 1971), p. 75.

19. *Ibid.*, p. 90.

20. *Ibid.*, p. 91.

21. *Ibid.*, p. 92.

22. *Ibid.*, p. 106.

23. Mass, *op. cit.*, p. 27.

24. Bruce Dancis, "Socialism and Women in the United States, 1900–1912," *Socialist Revolution*, No. 27, Vol. VI, No. 1 (January-March, 1976), p. 96.

25. David M. Kennedy, *Birth Control in America: The Career of Margaret Sanger* (New Haven and London: Yale University Press, 1976), pp. 21–22.

26. Mass, *op. cit.*, p. 20.

27. Gordon, *op. cit.*, p. 281.

28. Mass, *op. cit.*, p. 20.

29. Gordon, *op. cit.*, p. 283.

30. Herbert Aptheker, "Sterilization, Experimentation and Imperialism," *Political Affairs*, Vol. LIII, No. 1 (January, 1974), p. 44.

31. Gena Corea, *The Hidden Malpractice* (New York: A Jove/HBJ Book, 1977), p. 149.

32. Gordon, *op. cit.*, p. 332.

33. *Ibid.*, pp. 332–333.

34. Aptheker, "Sterilization," p. 38. See also Anne Braden, "Forced Sterilization: Now Women Can Fight Back," *Southern Patriot*, September, 1973.

35. *Ibid.*

36. Jack Slater, "Sterilization, Newest Threat to the Poor," *Ebony*, Vol. XXVIII, No. 12 (October, 1973), p. 150.

37. Les Payne, "Forced Sterilization for the Poor?" *San Francisco Chronicle*, February 26, 1974.

38. Harold X., "Forced Sterilization Pervades South," *Muhammed Speaks*, October 10, 1975.

39. Slater, *op. cit.*

40. Payne, *op. cit.*

41. *Ibid.*

42. *Ibid.*

43. Aptheker, "Sterilization," p. 40.

44. Payne, *op. cit.*

45. Aptheker, "Sterilization," p. 48.

46. Arlene Eisen, "They're Trying to Take Our Future—Native American Women and Sterilization," *The Guardian*, March 23, 1972.

47. *Ibid.*

48. *Ibid.*

49. Quoted in a pamphlet issued by the Committee to End Sterilization Abuse, Box A244, Cooper Station, New York 10003.

50. *Ibid.*

51. *Ibid.*

52. Gordon, *op. cit.*, p. 338.

53. *Ibid.*

54. Mass, *op. cit.*, p. 92.

55. *Ibid.*, p. 91.

56. Gordon, *op. cit.*, p. 401. See also pamphlet issued by CESA.

57. Mass, *op. cit.*, p. 108.

58. Rahemah Aman, "Forced Sterilization," *Union Wage*, March 4, 1978.

59. *Ibid.*

Pro-Life Feminism

Kay Castonguay

Although "pro-life feminism" sounds like a contradiction in terms to many people, a closer examination of the underlying philosophies of the feminist and the pro-life movements reveals a striking similarity. The basic foundations of both consist of justice; fairness; equality; non-violence and respect for life.

To establish the legitimacy and purpose of pro-life feminism, it is helpful to take a look at the early feminist movement and the conditions that have existed throughout history which precipitated its growth.

The culture considered women both mentally and physically inferior to men. Women had few real rights; society regarded them as property. Both women and children were at the mercy of a society operated by and for men. Women had little value in and of themselves, but acquired value for the services they performed as wives and mothers. Consider, for example, the terms used to describe an unmarried woman: "old maid" and "spinster." A woman unable to have children merited the label "barren." Women were not allowed to vote or actively participate in the world in which they lived.

Realizing that these conditions were unfair, large numbers of women began to band together and speak out against the injustices they perceived. These early feminists defended not only the rights of women; they defended the rights of Blacks, American Indians, children and the poor—groups which also suffered from oppression, and who were also denied a voice with which to defend their rights. These brave women saw a world filled with violence and cruelty—where the strong controlled the weak. They were determined to bring about a new order, where each and every human being received the respect and dignity to which she or he was entitled—a world of peace and justice, where neither one's race, gender, physical size or economic status would be a deterrent to basic human rights.

How did these early feminists feel about abortion? Many of the leading figures in the women's movement, including Susan B. Anthony, Elizabeth Cady Stanton, Lucretia Mott and Fanny Wright were very much *opposed* to abortion. One early feminist referred to it as "an atrocity, forced upon women by a male-dominated society." Her assessment was true then and is still largely true today. These women saw a very real connection between denying personhood and basic human rights to women and others and denying these same rights to unborn children. They saw in abortion an acceptance of the old paternalistic system in which one "owned" one's dependents. Finally, the concept of having the power of life or death over their progeny reminded them a great deal of their own precarious position in relation to their husbands and fathers, on whom their fates still rested. To accept abortion, they felt, would be to continue the tragic and unjust cycle of violence that has plagued the world since the beginning of history: "Right, not might" should be the code of future generations.

And what about today? If the "right" to abortion was not on yesterday's feminist agenda, should it be included now? Except in life-threatening situations, we feel the answer is "No" for a number of reasons:

• Reliance on abortion diverts attention and effort away from seeking real, positive changes in women's lives. Society's answer to the woman trapped in a hopeless cycle of poverty is "Get an abortion." But is this what she really needs and wants? Abortion will not

From Kay Castonguay, *Political Woman*, Summer 1986, pp. 11, 13, 15. Reprinted by permission.

help her feed and clothe her children. It will not help her find a decent place to live, or obtain the education she needs to find employment and break out of her poverty. In short, abortion does nothing to relieve the cause and effect of injustice, poverty and oppression. It will not bring the victim of poverty what she treasures most: respect and dignity.

• What about women's rights in the workplace? Society must recognize our right to equal opportunity and compensation. We need adequate parental leaves of absence, allowing plenty of time for post partum recovery and bonding with the newly arrived child. We need good quality, affordable daycare facilities, located in or near a parent's place of employment. We need a work environment free of sexual discrimination and harrassment. For those of us who need more time with our families, the workplace must provide more types of employment offering reduced hours, flexible schedules and adequate health benefits. Unfortunately, progress has been slow in achieving these goals. Part of the reason, we believe, is the easy availability of abortion. Society's acceptance of it, coupled with a prevailing attitude toward pregnancy as a totally voluntary condition for which a woman is solely responsible, create precious little incentive for employers to make the workplace more comfortable for mothers and fathers who are career parents. After all, these things cost money and time; it becomes more tempting to encourage women to relinquish their unborn children than to improve working conditions to better accommodate parents.

• Women who stay in the home as full-time mothers and homemakers deserve respect; for the work they do is extremely important. They, too, need their rights protected. This has not been easy, since our society tends to value only salaried occupations. Because of that, homemakers are often treated as second-class citizens. Maintaining self-esteem for the role of motherhood is difficult, since liberalized abor-

tion has created an environment in which the unborn child is considered disposable and of little worth. Allowing demeaning attitudes toward motherhood and homemaking is ultimately counterproductive to equality. After all, if these occupations and those who choose them are looked down upon, what hope is there for inducing men to take more active roles in the home and share parenting duties?

• How has abortion affected reproductive issues and attitudes toward women? A recent article in our local papers expressed surprise that so little real progress has been made in the development of safe, effective methods of fertility control. It does not surprise us: Like the abortion industry, the contraceptive industry is primarily run by males. They do not have to undergo the abortion procedure nor do they use the vast array of birth control methods currently available. Add to that a society which for the most part, considers abortion a panacea for almost every ill that plagues woman and mankind, and one begins to realize why there is so little incentive to improve on what is currently available to control fertility. Thus it is that we have contraceptives such as the intrauterine device (IUD), Depo-Provera and the vastly touted Norplant System (six rubber sticks implanted into a woman's arm). All of the foregoing are either unappealing, uncomfortable or risky—or a combination of all these factors. There is hope however. The old not-too-reliable "rhythm method" has been replaced by the vastly improved ovulation and sympto-thermal methods of natural family planning. Both methods are safe, non-sexist (responsibility is shared by both partners) and best of all, over 98 percent effective. We also believe that our technology is sufficiently well advanced to afford us far better forms of artificial family planning. While we do not wish to lay all the blame on men in the contraceptive industry, or accuse them of being uncaring, nature being what it is, the woman is the one who gets pregnant, and it is the woman for whom most family planning methods are designed. Because of this, it is only right that more women should be involved actively in contraceptive research and development.

• Closely related to fertility control is the issue of male responsibility and attitudes, both toward their partners and their offspring. At first, it may seem to be an advantage for women to be the sole determinants of the choice to continue or not continue the pregnancy. One should, however, keep in mind that feminists have long tried to encourage males to take a more active role in the parenting process, and to contribute their fair share to the support and upbringing of their progeny. Placing the abortion decision squarely on the mother's shoulders has adverse effects on these goals. Several men's rights advocates have stated that pregnancy is now a purely optional state. If men are not to have a legal voice in deciding the fate of their unborn child, even though married to the mother, then men should not be held financially responsible for the expense of carrying the pregnancy to term and seeing the child to adulthood. Some men feel that their obligation to the pregnant woman is satisfied if they offer to pay for the abortion. In other words, it's her body, her decision and ultimately, her responsibility. In making the choice hers alone, everyone else involved can avoid their responsibilities to the mother and child.

• The pornography industry has also been an avid and generous supporter of abortion rights organizations. It should come as no surprise; after all, both are extremely lucrative, and both promote the image of woman as a reusable sex object.

• The battle for legalized abortion has rested heavily on the claim that only illegal abortions are unsafe. But is this true? Not really. Abortions in early pregnancy are done by suction or dilatation and curettage (D & C) procedures. In the suction method, the cervix is forced open, a tube is inserted, and the developing child and placenta are torn to pieces by a machine that produces a suction twenty-nine times more powerful than a home vacuum cleaner. In the D & C procedure, the uterine contents are scraped from the uterus with a loop shaped steel knife. The dilatation and evacuation (D & E) method done on more advanced pregnancies is similar, except that a pliers-like instrument must be used to crush the now hardened bones of the unborn child. Abortions used in later pregnancy are saline and prostaglandin procedures. Both require injections into the amniotic sac. In the former procedure, a salt solution is used, which acts as a poison to the unborn child causing hemorrhage, shock and death. The entire process can take from one to several hours. Prostaglandins force the woman's body into early labor and delivery. Both procedures can be traumatic to the woman, since she is often left alone during the process. Occasionally, the saline and prostaglandin methods are ineffective, resulting in a live birth. A more rarely used procedure for late abortions is the hysterotomy, performed like a Caesarian section. The child is usually too weak and immature to survive on its own.

The argument is often made that abortion is safer than childbirth. This is highly debatable, and in fact, many medical experts would disagree with this statement. The problem is that not all states are required to report abortion complications. In addition, women who are having physical and or psychological problems are not likely to return to the facility where the abortion was done. Statistics comparing childbirth and abortion related complications should be viewed with caution.

Another factor is a seeming reluctance by abortion providers and advocates to admit any risks to legal abortion. Unlike other types of surgery, the laws do not require full disclosure to the patient of the procedures, risks and the physical process going on inside her. Attempts to require abortion providers to give the same detailed information commonly given in other types of surgical procedures have met determined resistance.

Here are some facts and figures: ectopic or tubal pregnancies have increased dramatically since abortion was legalized—more than 300 percent since 1973. The abortion procedure sometimes damages the entrance to the fallopian tubes. When the next pregnancy occurs, the fertilized egg cannot pass into the uterus. The post-abortion woman is approximately ten times more likely to suffer this potentially fatal complication than her never-aborted sister (437 deaths reported from 1974 to 1983).[1] Other complications are perforation of the uterus and perforation or laceration of the cervix (combined incidence 1 percent); hemorrhage (incidence 0.03 to 0.34 percent), retained parts of either placenta or fetus (incidence 0.56 percent); significant infection of reproductive organs (incidence 0.5 to 1.5 percent); fever, an early indication of infection (incidence 89 percent), infertility (incidence 8 to 10 percent after one abortion, up to 20 percent after three or more abortions.[2] Miscarriage occurs twice as often in women who have abortions. Additionally, medical experts have noted a 7 to 15 percent increase in cases of placenta previa—a condition potentially dangerous to both mother and child—in women who have had induced abortions. Moderate to severe psychological complications are experienced by approximately 20 percent of post-abortion women.

If abortion is as safe as supporters claim, why the reluctance to give patients full and complete disclosure of the procedures and risks as required in other types of surgery? Women have a right to know what is going on inside their bodies and what is being done to their bodies. We do not want or need a patronizing "Don't worry your pretty little head" attitude.

Some people feel that women and their unborn children must be placed in an adversarial position in order to insure women's rights. We disagree. Society has willingly conformed itself to the needs of men since the beginning of history. Women are told, in actions and words, that they must deny the very facts that make them female, to become unpregnant at will, so they can be accepted in a world run by and for men. We call upon society to grant our complete equality as women, and to accept and accommodate our bodily functions—without making abortion a condition for acceptance. We intend to build a world like that envisioned by our early feminist sisters. A world where all our sisters and brothers can live free of violence and oppression; where women can reach their great potential; and where all lives and rights are treasured and respected.

Abortion will not fulfill this dream, but we can.

NOTES

1. Dr. J. C. and Barbara Willke, R.N., *Abortion: Questions and Answers.*

2. Lauren Welch, M.D., *Complications of Legal Abortion.*

Mother/Foetus/State Conflicts

Christine Overall

Another title for this chapter might be 'Whose Body Is It Anyway?' Whenever the topic of abortion and foetal rights is examined, there is a tendency to lose sight of the fact that what is at stake is the bodily integrity and autonomy of women. A woman's body does not belong to the state; it does not belong to physicians; it does not belong to the woman's husband or partner, or to the father of her children; and, most important, it does not belong to the foetus.

Nevertheless, many people who attempt to defend foetal rights seem to assume that the pregnant woman's body belongs to some or all of these entities. This chapter will examine the underlying assumptions made by defenders of foetal rights—assumptions that, I believe, lack evidence to support them and in some cases are false. Most of what follows is in no way original,[1] but it clarifies some basic distinctions that I think are worth repeating, and is intended to provide an overview of some of the crucial controversies in discussions of foetal rights.

The cornerstone of the foetal-rights advocates' position is the belief that the foetus has the right to life. They seldom defend this claim, perhaps because they do not think it needs defending. However, we need to see whether there is any evidence for it. Foetal-rights advocates usually rely on the dual claim that the foetus is alive and that it is a human being.[2] It is indeed

From *Human Reproduction: Principles, Practices, Policies,* by Christine Overall, pp. 37–43. (Toronto: Oxford University Press Canada, 1993). Copyright © 1993 by Christine Overall. Reprinted by permission of the author and publisher.

true that the foetus is alive; it is not inert matter and it is not dead. It is also unquestionable that the foetus is human; it is not canine, feline, equine, or bovine. But what is not uncontroversial is what follows from these minimal facts.

Foetal-rights advocates appear to assume that the fact that the foetus is human and living makes it morally equivalent to a two-year-old child or a twenty-five-year-old woman, and gives it a right to life. Yet many of our other practices—practices that seem eminently reasonable—suggest that there is no such equivalence. For example, the intrauterine device (IUD) operates, in part, by preventing the fertilized ovum from implanting in the wall of the uterus and continuing its development. Yet most people do not regard the IUD as a murder weapon that deprives the fertilized egg of its "right to life." In addition, many women suffer unforeseen miscarriages early in their pregnancies. Most people would not advocate a legal investigation to determine whether these women have done something to deprive their foetus of its "right to life," no one regards women who have miscarried as possible murderers. Finally, the process of *in vitro* fertilization, by which sperm and ova are combined in a petri dish rather than inside a woman's body, often produces surplus embryos. Most people do not worry that the right to life of these embryos must be protected from potential murderers. If there were a fire in a laboratory, and the technicians failed to save some embryos produced through IVF, most people would not regard that failure as morally serious in the way that a failure to save babies or children would be.

These moral intuitions about the effects of the IUD on embryos, about women who miscarry, and about IVF embryos do not seem unreasonable: eight-cell embryos and three-month-old foetuses do not warrant extraordinary efforts to preserve their lives, and indeed may justifiably be sacrificed when other goals, such as the preservation of reproductive autonomy, are sought. They suggest that the fact that the foetus is living and is human is not in itself sufficient to establish that it has a right to life. In order to establish that a living, human foetus has a right to life, it would be necessary to show that it is a person, in the same way that the two-year-old child or the twenty-five-year-old woman are persons.[3] In light of our other moral intuitions about foetuses, the burden of proof must rest on those who would claim that the foetus is a person with the same moral status as women, men, and children; it cannot simply be taken for granted, or inferred from the fact that the foetus is living and human.

Although foetal-rights advocates stress the alleged right to life of the foetus, they say virtually nothing about what I believe is another, but more covert, set of assumptions: that the foetus has the right to the use of the pregnant woman's body, that that right should be legally protected, and hence that the pregnant woman has an obligation not to abort, and to permit any intervention in her body that is thought medically necessary for the sake of the foetus.

But in a landmark paper originally published in 1971,[4] philosopher Judith Jarvis Thomson pointed out that *even* if we grant the foetus the right to life, it does not follow that the foetus has the right to the use of the pregnant woman's body. For example, imagine that I have a life-threatening disease that can somehow only be alleviated or cured by my making use of your body. Perhaps I need one of your kidneys, or an injection of your bone marrow. Or perhaps I need to be hooked up to your body for weeks or months or years so that I can receive ongoing transfusions of your blood. I

have a right to life, we would all agree. But my right to life in no way gives me the right to the use of your body, even if I need it for the continuance of my own life, and even if I am related to you.

The reason for this is simple: for me to claim the right to the use of your body would be an assertion of ownership, and we know that slavery is wrong. Hence, even if the foetus does have a right to life (and, as we have seen, that assumption is not proven) it does not follow that the foetus has the right to the use and occupancy of the pregnant woman's body. Nor does it follow, as some have claimed,[5] that the foetus is legally entitled to treatments, such as surgery, that the pregnant woman rejects. Although the foetus is not the property of the pregnant woman, neither is the pregnant woman the property of the foetus.

Whenever our culture limits access to abortion on the grounds of alleged foetal rights, it is saying that pregnant women must sacrifice their independence and accept limits on their autonomy and bodily integrity that are required of no other group of citizens, and that are not even required of women themselves after they have given birth.[6] It is this latter point that must be emphasized: foetuses are the only group of entities that have been given legal entitlement to the medical use of the bodies of adult persons. If we are not willing to authorize compulsory "donations" of blood or organs to save the lives of dying persons, then we should not be willing to tolerate compulsory foetal surgery or Caesarean sections, or to deny abortions.

In discussions of abortion, some defenders of foetal rights suggest that there are no crucial moral differences between the foetus inside the mother's body and the baby born prematurely. It is just a matter of location, they claim, and why should a few inches of travel down the birth canal make any difference to how we treat that being?

In fact, those inches are centrally important when the location is the body of a human person, and when that body is being occupied and used by another entity. No entity has an entitlement to the use of a woman's body, even if that entity is a foetus or embryo at any stage of its development. When extra embryos are produced through *in vitro* fertilization, it would be implausible to claim that they have a right to be reimplanted in the body of the woman from whom the ova were taken. And if a woman candidate for IVF were to die before the implantation of the embryos, no one would argue that the embryos had the right to the occupancy of some other woman's body.[7] Only when the foetus is already occupying a woman's uterus do foetal-rights advocates claim a sort of squatter's rights for it: once the foetus is there, it must be permitted to stay.

There are several reasons why foetal-rights advocates believe that the foetus has squatter's rights to the pregnant woman's body. As a number of feminists have pointed out, discussion of abortion and foetal rights is becoming dominated by metaphors implying that a pregnant woman is like a container or a house inhabited by the foetus. The woman is seen as the "route to the foetus,"[8] or even as a kind of impediment that prevents scientists from seeing the foetus clearly. Ultrasound images and photographic representations of the foetus seem to depict it as independent and self-sufficient; the woman whose body sustains it is nowhere in view.[9] These metaphors reinforce the tendency to see the foetus as having a right to the use of the pregnant woman's body; if that body is just a house or a container,[10] then it is simply a piece of property, with various utilities, that the foetus happens to need for approximately nine months.

In response to these metaphorical depictions of the foetus, it is important to become aware of the ways in which the debates about abortion and alleged foetal rights construct the foetus as a being entirely separate from the pregnant woman. With the development of new forms of reproductive technology, the foetus is seen from a eugenic perspective as an opportunity for actively improving human beings.[11] The possibility of foetal surgery and other forms of intervention seems to transform the foetus into a patient, but a patient with a difference; one to whom access is blocked by the body of the woman, who is often seen as posing a danger to the foetus, whether inadvertently or deliberately.[12]

The foetus is also believed to have interests and needs that are not consistent with the interests and needs of the pregnant woman. Then, because the foetus is small and helpless, it is assumed that it needs an advocate, a more powerful, grown-up human being who will represent its interests and act on its behalf. Some physicians see themselves as the advocates of the foetus; some biological fathers have attempted to assume that role;[13] and those who propose laws to enforce foetal rights and to require foetal treatments would make the state the foetus's advocate.

Once again, some unsupported assumptions are at work here. Why assume that the foetus needs an advocate at all? Such a move is a large and dangerous step towards denying the autonomy of the pregnant woman. To give a physician or spouse or partner the right, as the foetus's representative, to insist on foetal surgery or block an abortion is to hand over control of the woman's body to that physician or spouse. Because pregnancy is an event in a woman's body, the moral relationship of the pregnant woman and the man who impregnated her to the foetus cannot be regarded as symmetrical. Provided the pregnant woman is competent, the responsibility for deciding what happens in and to her body rests with her. This is not to say that she is infallible and cannot make mistakes; it is merely to accord her the same freedom from ownership by others—i.e., slavery—that we accord every member of our culture. Neither the physician nor the spouse has any rights over the woman's body, and that fact should take priority over any claims about the alleged rights of the foetus.

Some people, unsatisfied with these arguments, will be left with the intuition that it is urgent to do something to protect the foetus. That intuition is not entirely unfounded. But I would suggest that we re-evaluate the adversarial and individualistic perspective that pits the foetus against the pregnant woman and makes the physician or sperm provider or state the foetus's advocate. We need to move beyond the isolationist point of view that fails to consider the social context in which women gestate and deliver their babies. We need to understand that protecting and caring for the foetus means protecting and caring for the pregnant woman—through adequate housing, nutrition, education, and medical care, and freedom from physical and emotional abuse. Genuine respect for foetal life would require genuine respect for women. Whenever we reach a stage where interventions in a pregnant woman's body, against her will, allegedly for the sake of the foetus, appear to be necessary, then we should step back and look at the larger picture; in what ways have we failed to support, educate, care for, and appreciate the pregnant woman?

NOTES

1. See, for example, Sanda Rodgers, "Fetal Rights and Maternal Rights: Is There a Conflict?" *Canadian Journal of Women and the Law/Revue juridique la femme et le droit* 1 (1986): 456–69; Barbara Katz Rothman, "Commentary: When a Pregnant Woman Endangers Her Fetus," *Hastings Center Report* 16 (February 1986): 25; and Dawn Johnson, "A New Threat to Pregnant Women's Autonomy," *Hastings Center Report* 17 (August/September 1987): 33–40.

2. "The unborn child is no less a human being whilst residing in his mother's body than he is when he emerges from her body," according to Morris Schumiatcher, lawyer for Joseph Borowski. Schumiatcher is quoted in Sheilah L. Martin, "Canada's Abortion Law and the Canadian Charter of Rights and Freedoms," *Canadian Journal of Women and the Law/ Revue juridique la femme et le droit* 1 (1986): 348.

3. See John Woods, *Engineered Death: Abortion, Suicide, Euthanasia and Senecide* (Ottawa: University of Ottawa Press, 1978), 17–61; and Rosalind Hursthouse, *Beginning Lives* (Oxford: Basil Blackwell, 1987): 91–7.

4. Judith Jarvis Thomson, "A Defense of Abortion," reprinted in James Rachels, ed., *Moral Problems: A Collection of Philosophical Essays*, second ed. (New York: Harper and Row, 1975), 89–106.

5. See John A. Robertson and Joseph D. Schulman, "Pregnancy and Prenatal Harm to Offspring: The Case of Mothers with PKU," *Hastings Center Report* 17 (August/September 1987): 28 and 29; Thomas B. Mackenzie and Theodore C. Nagel, "Commentary: When a Pregnant Woman Endangers her Foetus," *Hastings Center Report* 16 (February 1986): 24–5; and Julius Landwirth, "Fetal Abuse and Neglect: An Emerging Controversy," *Pediatrics* 79 (April 1987): 508–14.

6. Caroline L. Kaufmann, "Perfect Mothers, Perfect Babies: An Examination of the Ethics of Fetal Treatments," *Reproductive and Genetic Engineering* 1 (1988): 139.

7. See Christine Overall, *Ethics and Human Reproduction: A Feminist Analysis* (Boston: Allen and Unwin, 1987), 76–9.

8. Ontario Medical Association Committee on Perinatal Care, "Ontario Medical Association Discussion Paper on Directions in Health Care Issues Relating to Childbirth" (Toronto, 1984): 12.

9. Rosalind Pollack Petchesky, "Foetal Images: The Power of Visual Culture in the Politics of Reproduction," Michelle Stanworth, ed., *Reproductive Technologies: Gender, Motherhood and Medicine* (Minneapolis: University of Minnesota Press, 1987), 57–80.

10. See George J. Annas, "Pregnant Women as Fetal Containers," *Hastings Center Report* 16 (December 1986): 14.

11. See, for example, Ruth Hubbard, "Eugenics: New Tools, Old Ideas," in Elaine Hoffman Baruch, Amadeo F. D'Adamo, Jr, and Joni Seager, eds. *Embryos, Ethics, and Women's Rights: Exploring the New Reproductive Technologies* (New York: Haworth Press, 1988), 225–35.

12. See Robertson and Schulman. "Pregnancy and Prenatal Harm," 23–33.

13. See the favourable discussion by Donald DeMarco, in *In My Mother's Womb: The Catholic Church's Defense of Natural Life* (Manassas, VA: Trinity Communications, 1987), 57–60.

The New Procreative Technologies

Ruth Hubbard

Some of the most recent research in biology is being applied in the new procreative technologies. Prenatal diagnosis and screening are becoming part of routine prenatal care, and new technical interventions can help people who are unable to beget or conceive children or to carry pregnancies to term to have children who are biologically related to at least one of the future social parents. Some of the techniques can also help people without partners of the other sex to have biological children. Why the new, or surely increased, impulse to proceed into these areas? It would be a mistake to assume that this impulse is driven mainly by the availability of new biotechnologies. Technologies can open new possibilities, but we usually do not pursue them unless there are interest groups who want, and have the power to explore and implement, them. So what are the interests?

The Meaning of Procreative Choice

The ideology of procreative choice has become important in our society. In the course of the last hundred years, we in the middle and upper-middle class, who are used to being able to plan other aspects of our lives, have come to expect that we can plan our families. We decide how many children we want and when we are ready to have them. We practice contraception and, if it fails, abortion in order to implement these decisions. Throughout we tend to assume that

we will be able to have a child when we are ready. If we try and nothing happens, we feel not only distressed but wronged—and not by God or fate, as we might have in previous times, but by our bodies. In a time of artificial hearts and kidneys, we expect medical technology to be able to solve such problems. What is more, we do not want to have just any child. We want a healthy one because a child who needs more than the usual care or needs it for longer than usual will be hard to fit into our plans. Thus, prenatal diagnosis and the new technologies that let people have biological children have become part of planning our families.

Yet this kind of family planning is not a possibility for everyone. Owing largely to the work of women of color, the women's movement has begun to acknowledge that women are not a homogeneous group. Not only do we differ as individuals, but we fall into groups with common interests that may be different from those of other groups of women. We have finally realized that people who use the word *women* without qualifiers tend to focus their attention mainly on the young, white, fairly affluent women who became identified with the women's movement in the 1960s. These women have produced major changes; but if the women's movement is to continue to be a force for progressive change, it is essential that we acknowledge the differences in women's needs and interests.

It is not enough to address the issue of diversity without speaking explicitly about racism and class discrimination. And this need is nowhere more apparent than in our concerns about procreation, some of which I will discuss in the sections that follow. The way feminists have framed the important issues in this area betrays the individualistic bias of the affluent, white, American upper-middle class. Our watchwords have been "reproductive freedom" and "choice," but we have not emphasized sufficiently that access to economic and social resources is essential to freedom of choice. In the United States poor women, who because of racism are disproportionately women of color, cannot count on having adequate housing, food, healthcare, jobs, and childcare. Yet all these necessities are basic to procreative freedom and choice. The most recent report of the Washington-based Children's Defense Fund documents the dismal economic situation in which large numbers of women and children in this country are living after many years of inflation, privatization, and cuts in government expenditures for human services.

Most people take the phrase *procreative choice* to mean the choice not to have children, surely an important concern for all women who have sex with men. But procreative choice also needs to mean the choice to have children in the confidence that we will be able to care for them. And that choice is not available to many poor women and usually is not even acknowledged as part of procreative choice.

In the late nineteenth and first half of the twentieth century, a scientific and social movement developed with the aim of denying procreative choice to certain kinds of people. This eugenics movement had as its aim furthering procreation among affluent, native-born, white Americans, while discouraging poor people, immigrants, and other "undesirables" from having children by persuasion and sometimes by forcible sterilization. The birth-control movement, under the leadership of feminists like Margaret Sanger, incorporated considerable portions of this ideology.

In the sections that follow I discuss some of the ramifications of prenatal diagnosis, fetal therapy, and in vitro fertilization. But we must acknowledge from the start that these technologies are not intended for all people who might feel they need them. They are expensive and often require that clients be sophisticated in the ways they relate to the medical system. Also, the techniques designed to enable people to have children are clearly intended for those who fit the stereotypic image of "the family"— bread-winning dad, homemaking mom, and their children. They are not meant for poor people, hence not for the disproportionate number of people of color who are poor. They are not meant for lesbians or gay men. They certainly are not meant for people with disabilities. In fact, these people are high on the list of folks expected to use prenatal testing. They are supposed to avoid having children, and if they are so improvident as to want children, surely to do all they can to avoid having children who have disabilities.

MEDICAL IMPLICATIONS OF PRENATAL TECHNOLOGIES

In the early 1950s it became possible to identify fetuses who are at risk for serious disabilities because they are Rh positive while their mothers are Rh negative. Such women produce antibodies against the Rh antigen in the fetus's blood, and, during successive pregnancies, the antibody concentration can increase sufficiently to endanger the health, or even the life, of the fetus they are carrying. This was the first instance of prenatal diagnosis. The rationale for performing the diagnosis before birth was to enable physicians to be ready to give the baby massive blood transfusions immediately after birth so as to minimize the damage. More recently, physicians have become able to transfuse such a fetus in utero. A few other prenatal diagnostic procedures were developed in the late 1960s and early 1970s.

Since 1972, when *Roe* v. *Wade* made abortion legal at least until the twenty-fourth week of pregnancy, an early diagnosis of fetal health problems has given women the option to abort a fetus that is expected to be born with a disease or disability with which they feel unable to cope. And the availability of prenatal tests has made it possible for women who have reason to believe their prospective children are at risk for a particular, serious health problem to go ahead and become pregnant knowing that they can find out whether the fetus they are carrying is affected with the disease in question. They then have the chance to decide whether to carry the pregnancy to term. Needless to say, the tests cannot guarantee that the fetus does not have some other, unanticipated, health problem. But that is true for any of us and the chance of its happening is small.

By now, quite a number of prenatal tests can be performed, and many more will become available as the project to identify and sequence the human genome gets under way. Some of them involve simply testing samples of the pregnant woman's blood; others are more invasive. Amniocentesis, one of the more usual procedures, requires that a sample of the amniotic fluid that surrounds the fetus in the womb be withdrawn by means of a hypodermic syringe and needle inserted near the pregnant woman's navel. The amniotic fluid can then be tested directly, or the fetal cells that are suspended in it can be cultured under sterile conditions and tested biochemically or examined under the microscope when a sufficient number of cells have accumulated. Amniocentesis cannot be performed until there is sufficient amniotic fluid, which usually requires waiting until about the sixteenth to eighteenth week of pregnancy.

A still experimental procedure, called chorionic villus sampling (CVS), enables physicians to collect fetal cells considerably earlier in a pregnancy than amniocentesis does. The cells are obtained by inserting a probe through the cervix into the uterus and snipping a small sample from the chorion, which is one of the membranes that surrounds the fetus. CVS must

be performed during the first trimester, between the eighth and tenth weeks or pregnancy. Another procedure, called fetoscopy, is used rarely. It involves withdrawing samples of blood or other body fluids or tissues from the fetus itself.

Health Risks of Medicalizing Pregnancy and Birth

Feminist scholars have been documenting the transformation of birth and the ways this change has affected our concepts of motherhood. Birth used to be a social event, experienced at home, in which the birthing woman could get advice and support from female relatives and friends who had borne children. If a midwife was present, she usually was from the birthing woman's class and ethnic and racial group and might know her socially and have attended births by her friends and neighbors. Now childbirth takes place in a hospital, where it is made to conform to medical and hospital routines. Judith Walzer Leavitt (1987) has shown that as long as women gave birth at home, they retained considerable control, even when they were attended by male physicians. And given the risks of childbirth during the nineteenth century, many women who could afford it felt more secure in the care of physicians than they did without them. The real change, Leavitt argues, came with the move from the home, which was the birthing woman's turf, to the hospital, where physicians were in charge.

In 1900, about half of U.S. births were attended by midwives; in 1935, only about one-sixth, mostly in the rural South; and by 1972, 99 percent of births were attended by physicians. Fewer than 5 percent of women had their babies in hospitals in 1900; about half the births took place there in 1940; and essentially all of them did by 1960.

During the same period, many other changes occurred in American society and in medical knowledge and practices. New scientific ideas were formulated about the causes and proper treatment of disease. Industrialization changed patterns of transportation and urbanization, which affected the availability of food and produced changes in diet. People's ways of working and living were transformed. Maternal and infant mortality rates decreased, and life expectancies increased.

The lower rates of maternal and infant deaths and diseases cannot be attributed to any one of these changes and certainly not to the changes in birth practices. Quite the contrary. The shifts from midwives to physicians and from home to hospital births were detrimental to the health of many women and babies, particularly the poorer ones who often ended up with less individualized and expert care than before or with no care at all.

Since the beginning of medical interventions in birth, these have held some risks for women and their babies. From the eighteenth century until the discovery of antibiotics in the late 1930s, childbed fever (also called puerperal fever) took an enormous toll on women's lives and health. It was brought on by physicians with insufficient understanding of their role in spreading bacterial infections.

Similarly, artificial induction and excessive use of forceps damaged infants and their mothers. In 1920, in the first issue of the *American Journal of Obstetrics and Gynecology,* Dr. Charles B. Reed described several methods to induce birth artificially, which, he claimed, were safer than normal birth. In the same issue, Dr. Joseph DeLee advocated the prophylactic (that is, preventive) use of forceps and episiotomy (enlarging the vaginal opening by making a deep cut in the vaginal muscle). He wrote that with proper management and repair, episiotomies produced healthier babies and less debilitated women with "virginal" vaginas, which leads me to conclude that he was primarily concerned with the advantages a woman's husband would derive from the procedure. Dr.

DeLee also advocated using morphine and scopolamine. He wrote that women were so frequently injured during childbirth that he "often wondered whether Nature did not deliberately intend women to be used up in the process of reproduction, in a manner analogous to that of the salmon which dies after spawning," a poetic metaphor that may have been rendered more apt by his forceps and scalpel.

By the 1940s and 1950s, hospitals were routinely using hormones to initiate and speed labor, and barbiturates and scopolamine to erase all memory of the birthing experience. Because these drugs impede the higher brain functions, they were said to induce twilight sleep, a condition in which women could "take orders" from their physicians but not "know" what was happening to them or "remember" it. Because the drugs suspended women's capacities to think rationally, they were tied down to keep them from injuring themselves as they thrashed about during labor. A labor room of the period was a superb confirmation of the cultural stereotype of women as irrational creatures who needed knowledgeable and rational men to protect them against their own unreason. There is no better place to go for a description of what this kind of birthing felt like than to Adrienne Rich's (1976) account of giving birth in Boston during the 1950s.

Twilight sleep throughout labor and birth was in wide use until the 1960s. It was discontinued partly because of the opposition of women's health advocates to the unnecessary medicalization of birth, partly because of mounting evidence that it was bad for babies. Fetuses inevitably got their share of the medication given to birthing women, so that the babies were born half-asleep, limp, and often in need of resuscitation. In the 1950s some hospitals began to depend on spinal anaesthesia, which allowed birthing women to remain conscious without feeling pain because it deprived them of all sensations below the waist. As a result, they could not push the baby out, so birthing required the use of forceps, another potential source of damage to newborns and their mothers.

The early 1960s witnessed the thalidomide disaster. Physicians prescribed this drug to allay nausea and other discomforts some women experience early in pregnancy. Before thalidomide was recalled, its use had resulted in the birth of thousands of limbless infants in Great Britain, Germany and other countries of Western Europe, and Canada. In the United States, we were spared only by the thoroughness and foresight of Dr. Frances E. Kelsey of the federal Food and Drug Administration, who refused to clear this new drug for sale because of insufficient proof of its safety.

During the 1950s and 1960s physicians prescribed the hormones progestin and diethyl stilbestrol (D.E.S.), sometimes routinely, in the mistaken belief that they prevented miscarriages early in pregnancy. Both can harm a fetus. However, because progestin induces excessive growth of the infant's clitoris so that it resembles a penis, the damage was obvious at birth and the use in pregnancy was stopped before long. Unfortunately, physicians did not realize until the late 1970s that D.E.S. could induce a rare form of vaginal cancer and perhaps also testicular cancer and reproductive deficiencies among the daughters and sons pregnant women were carrying at the time they received the drug.

It would be a mistake to believe that all, or perhaps even most, women were unwilling victims of these medical interventions. Many women welcomed the relief offered by drugs, much as they welcomed contraception and baby bottles as respites from the stresses of motherhood. They accepted the reasons physicians gave why drugs and other interventions were necessary as well as physicians' assurances that the interventions were safe and likely to improve birth outcomes. Yet with the best will in the world, physicians cannot foresee the risks of their interventions in pregnancy and birth—

risks for women and for our children. At present, physicians seem to feel that it is all right to use the new diagnostic tools and therapies as long as prospective parents have the opportunity to give their informed consent. But what does "informed" mean when applied to new procedures whose benefits and risks cannot be assessed accurately?

Most therapies become established on the basis of custom and professional consensus and are not preceded by rigorous, scientific evaluations of their outcomes. Usually, by the time therapies are tested in scientifically controlled clinical trials, they have been in use for years. Even after the trials are completed, the results are often contested. For this reason many clinicians trust their intuition and experience more than they trust scientific experiments.

Most of the information prospective parents get about the relative merits of different ways to proceed during pregnancy and birth depends on their physician's ideas about the appropriate course. Particularly with new interventions, prospective parents have access to few, if any, other sources of information. Therefore "informed consent" is better than nothing because it at least obliges physicians to try to explain what they plan to do and their reasons, but it serves mainly to provide legal protection for practitioners and hospitals. There is no way people who do not have access to a range of sources of information can make independent judgments and give truly informed consent.

That is a problem "lay" people always confront when they must make choices about technical matters, be it nuclear energy or prenatal interventions. If there is disagreement among the experts—and there often is—it usually boils down to deciding, on the basis of various criteria, which experts to trust. In the case of nuclear energy, we can gain at least some reassurance from the fact that the experts must live with the outcome. When it comes to interventions in pregnancy, only we and our families have to live with the results, not our physicians.

All tests must be as specific and accurate as possible. That means that there must be a high degree of probability that the condition one intends to test for is the only one being tested, and that the test will not indicate that the condition is present when it is not (false positives), or that it is not present when it is (false negatives). No test satisfies these criteria perfectly, but the better the test, the closer it must come to doing so.

What other risks need women consider? Tests that can be done on samples of blood drawn from the pregnant woman are not likely to impose physical risks because drawing blood is fairly routine. At present, blood samples can be used to measure the level of alpha-feto-protein (AFP), a protein secreted by the fetus at certain stages of development that enters the bloodstream of the pregnant woman. Maternal serum alpha-feto-protein (MSAFP) levels are used to indicate whether the baby is likely to have spina bifida (a malformation of the neural tube) or anencephaly (no brain), both quite rare conditions. MSAFP levels are also now being used as preliminary indications that the baby may have Down syndrome.

Because amniocentesis involves inserting a needle through a pregnant woman's abdominal wall into her uterus, it is more invasive and riskier than blood tests. This is so even when the amniocentesis is done while monitoring the position of the fetus and placenta by means of ultrasound so as not to damage them. If sufficient amniotic fluid has been collected, its AFP content and other chemical properties can be checked. The fetal cells that float in the amniotic fluid can be biochemically tested for specific diseases such as cystic fibrosis, sickle-cell anemia, or Tay-Sachs disease if there is some reason to think the baby might inherit one of them. In order to detect chromosomal abnormalities, such as are present in people who have Down syndrome, it is necessary to culture the fetal cells, which can take two weeks or more. Ultrasound by itself can reveal anatomical mal-formations of the fetal skeleton, nervous system, kidneys, and other organs.

Ultrasound is said to be safe because no ill effects are seen in newborns and children, but it is not clear how to evaluate this claim. There is no question that at higher levels than those ordinarily used for diagnosis ultrasound damages chromosomes and other intracellular structures and breaks up cells. And, as with other radiation, it is questionable whether there is a threshold level below which ultrasound is absolutely safe and to what extent the effects of successive exposures may be cumulative. Symposia that have reviewed the available evidence have usually ended by warning against the indiscriminate use of ultrasound, and some physicians continue to urge caution.

By now, ultrasound is used so routinely to monitor pregnancy and birth and its effects could be so varied that it will take extremely careful studies, involving large numbers of children over long periods of time, to determine whether there are risks and what they are. While such studies are in progress, prospective parents must rely on physicians' assurances not to worry. Unfortunately we were also told not to worry about x-rays, which eventually were shown to provoke an increase in the incidence of childhood cancers and leukemias. It is always a question of balancing possible risks and benefits. In some situations, the immediate benefits of ultrasound imaging clearly outweigh its possible long-term risks. At other times, the balance of benefits and risks is not so clear, and it is often hard to know where to draw the line. Unfortunately, at present many obstetricians believe that using ultrasound involves no risks.

If it is done by an experienced practitioner, amniocentesis carries a small risk of mechanical injury to the fetus or placenta and a somewhat greater risk of infection. In about one case in three or four hundred, for unknown reasons, amniocentesis results in a spontaneous abortion. CVS may involve less risk of infection than does amniocentesis but a somewhat greater risk of spontaneous abortion. There is also a greater chance of wrong diagnoses with CVS because the cells that are removed from the fetal membranes do not always have the same chromosomal constitution as the fetus itself. However, CVS has the advantage of being performed sufficiently early to permit a first-trimester abortion if the results lead the woman to decide to have one. Amniocentesis, however, necessarily involves a second-trimester abortion, which is more dangerous and psychologically stressful. Risk of spontaneous abortion from fetoscopy is much greater than from amniocentesis or CVS and so are the risks of infection and mechanical damage.

If the only alternative to prenatal testing is not to have children because one or both partners consider the risk of having a child with a particular health problem to be too high, they may be prepared to accept considerable risks from prenatal diagnosis, hoping that they will learn that the fetus does not have the disability in question. Even so, they may have difficulty accepting the possibility of injuring or losing a fetus that would have been healthy.

Because of the fear and costs of malpractice suits, physicians increasingly feel that they need to perform tests so as to be legally covered in case a baby is born with a health problem they could have detected. And because of the responsibilities and costs of raising a child with a serious disability, prospective parents also feel pressure to use the tests. Therefore, as the number of conditions that can be diagnosed before birth increases, more women will have to decide whether to undergo testing. If they do, they will experience the uncertainty of waiting for results, which is often the most difficult part of the procedure. Reports can be slow to come, and the decision whether to abort becomes increasingly difficult as the pregnancy advances. There is no reason to doubt that this kind of stress on a pregnant woman gets communicated to her fetus. Yet threats of legal action against

pregnant women as well as physicians increase the pressure to test.

If it is too soon reliably to evaluate the medical risks of prenatal diagnosis, this is even more true for fetal therapy, which is newer. At this point, fetuses are being treated mostly for hydrocephalus ("water on the brain") and for malformations or malfunctioning of the urinary tracts. These are reasonable conditions to try to remedy during pregnancy because the fetus has a better chance to develop normally if the problem is repaired. However, the risk exists that the problem will be repaired but that the baby will be born with life-threatening disabilities. To date, several fetuses who were treated in utero have been born with serious disabilities; a few have been normal; still others have died before or shortly after birth. And, of course, all the interventions are hazardous for the pregnant woman.

PRENATAL TECHNOLOGIES AND THE EXPERIENCE OF CHILDBEARING

I now want to explore some implications of the prenatal technologies for the experience of childbearing. Obviously, I do not mean to imply that there is just one kind of childbearing experience. I assume there are as many experiences as there are women bearing children, and that they range from bliss to agony because they depend on the social and personal circumstances of our lives. However, the new technologies raise issues that can affect all these experiences, although they may affect different ones differently.

Childbearing: A Social Construct

Before going further, I want to clear up one point: I am not trying to distinguish between "natural" and "technological" childbearing practices (and by childbearing I mean the entire range of women's activities from conception through birth and lactation). No human pregnancy is simply "natural." Societies define, order, circumscribe, and interpret all our activities and experiences. Just as our sexual practices are socially constructed and not a natural unfolding of inborn instincts, so our ways of structuring and experiencing pregnancy and birth are shaped by society.

Whether a woman goes off to give birth by herself (as !Kung women do in the Kalahari desert), calls in neighboring women and perhaps a midwife (as my grandmother did in her small town in eastern Europe), goes to a lying-in hospital (as I did in Boston around 1960), or has a lay midwife be with her and her partner at home (as several of my friends have done recently), all these are socially devised ways, approved by one's community, even if sometimes not by the medical profession or the state.

The question we feminists must ask is not which is more "natural" but to what extent different ways of giving birth empower women or, alternatively, decrease our power to structure childbearing around our own needs and those of the people with whom we live.

By now, periodic visualization of the fetus by means of ultrasound is considered routine prenatal care by many physicians in the United States and much of Europe. Indeed, in some places ultrasound visualization is mandatory at least once or twice during pregnancy. Real-time ultrasound recording allows women and their attendants to view the fetus, so to speak, in action. It also tends to reveal its sex. Most prospective parents agree that ultrasound visualization makes the fetus more real, more their baby. However, as we saw in the last section, for some women (although for which ones in the United States may depend more on their social and economic circumstances than on their health needs), ultrasound visualization is followed by amniocentesis and the possibility of a second-trimester abortion, so no baby.

These interventions, and indeed the mere fact that they may occur, affect the way we look on our pregnancies. At the very least, we must decide whether to accept the interventions and how far to take them—something we can still usually do. So you see that pregnancy has become very different from what it was as recently as the 1970s, when once women decided to become pregnant (or to accept an accidental pregnancy), they did not face further decisions about whether to carry the pregnancy to term.

Let me be clear: I completely support every woman's right to decide whether and when to bear a child. She must, therefore, have the right to abort a fetus, whatever her reasons. What is more, on the basis of my own and other people's experiences as pregnancy counselors, I know that the decision to abort need not be traumatic. Whether it is depends on the social context in which it is made and implemented. But it is one thing to terminate a pregnancy when we don't want to be pregnant and quite another to want a baby but to decide to abort the particular fetus we are carrying in the hope of coming up with a "better" one next time.

Research studies and personal accounts are beginning to document women's mixed responses to prenatal diagnosis and the necessity to decide whether to terminate a wanted pregnancy because the baby may be abnormal. The abortion itself may not be so bad once the decision is made, but some of my friends have told me how much they have hated the two or three weeks of waiting while the fetal cells were being cultured and tested, knowing that they might end up deciding not to continue the pregnancy. This state of uncertainty can last until the twentieth week—halfway through the pregnancy and several weeks after most women begin to feel the fetus move. By that time, many women look on it very much as their baby.

Ultrasound and amniocentesis confront women with a contradiction: Ultrasound makes the fetus more real and more our baby, while the possibility of following it with an abortion makes us want to keep our emotional distance in case we will not end up with a baby after all.

The specific problems are somewhat different with CVS, which is still considered experimental but is likely to be generally available soon. As we saw in the last section, CVS results somewhat more frequently in wrong diagnoses (both positive and negative) than does amniocentesis and in a slightly higher rate of spontaneous abortions. However, it lets women who have reason to fear for the health of their fetus have tests early enough to allow for a first-trimester abortion if they decide to terminate the pregnancy.

When even easier methods than we now have become available to examine a fetus early in pregnancy, the pressure to screen fetuses will increase. Once scientists develop a way to identify cells of fetal origin in the bloodstream of pregnant women, which is likely to happen before long, fetal screening could become a routine part of prenatal care.

The Question of Choice

The means to "choose" the kind of baby a parent will accept bring their own problems no matter at what point in the pregnancy they can be used. To sort these problems out, we need to put this new kind of decision into historical perspective.

In most cultures women have exercised a measure of choice about procreation by practicing some form of birth control—from contraceptive and abortifacient herbs and barrier methods to infanticide. But, until recent times, unwanted pregnancies, hazards of childbearing, and high rates of infant and early childhood mortality have made women's reproductive lives largely a matter of chance. Only during the last century have contraception and abortion gradually become sufficiently available, accepted, and reliable that socially and economically privileged women expect to be able to choose whether and when to become pregnant. At the same time, in the technologically developed, affluent countries, maternal and child health have improved sufficiently for us to be able to assume that the children we bear will become adults.

Full of this new confidence, the more privileged of us seem to have glided over into the illusion that we can control not only whether and when to have children, but the kind and quality of children we will "choose" to have. Barbara Katz Rothman (1984, 1989) points out that in this consumer society people tend to look on children as products that they can or cannot "afford." And, by that way of reckoning, it is realistic to look on the prospect of raising a child with a serious disability as beyond our means. In our economy, raising children is expensive. And in the United States, which is the only industrialized country besides South Africa without universal health insurance, the expense of bringing up a child with a disability can be overwhelming. Indeed, Americans often meet the challenge of disability with litigation as a way to increase their financial resources.

Recent medical and social practices have made it possible to commodify procreation all along the line, with eggs, sperm, embryos, "surrogate mothers," and babies available for a price. Some babies who are up for adoption are for sale outright, although this is illegal. Legal adoption agencies prohibit cash payments, but because they are at pains to establish the financial "soundness" of prospective parents, economic status is clearly important for being considered a fit adoptive parent. Once procreation is a form of commodity production, it is an easy step to require quality control. And at this point genetic screening, ultrasound visualization, and the other prenatal tests come in.

Yet all these tests carry a price tag, and many of them are scarce resources. They are not, and indeed cannot be, available to everyone. While affluent women come to view the new tests and other techniques as liberating advances that improve our lives, economically less privileged and socially more defenseless women continue to be deprived of the ability to procreate. Forced sterilizations still happen, often by means of hysterectomy. Less extreme measures also deny choice. For example, legal and financial restrictions that limit access to abortion force pregnant women who want an abortion but cannot afford it to "choose" a hysterectomy, which is covered by social insurance in all states except Arizona, which has never had Medicaid.

The consumerist way of looking at procreation creates the illusion that at least those of us who can afford prenatal tests have the choice to have healthy babies. But that choice is a mirage because it exists only in a few circumscribed situations. Each test can provide information only about a specific disability. Therefore tests help parents who have reason to worry that their child will be born with a particular disability. They cannot guarantee a healthy baby. But before I say more about the limits of our ability to predict the health of our future children, I want to raise another issue.

Trade-Offs of Scientific Progress

Feminists have often portrayed medical interventions in pregnancy as part of an attempt by men to control women's capacity to bear children. And although I agree with much in this analysis, I am bothered by the way it downgrades, and sometimes romanticizes, the pain and travail childbearing has meant for many women. Bearing and rearing children is difficult under the conditions in which most women live. Judith Walzer Leavitt (1987) amply illustrates this in her book *Brought to Bed*, in which she describes the history of childbearing in America. The literary historian Ruth Perry (1979) has calculated that in eighteenth-century England a married woman who "delivered six children (a not unusual number) . . . had at least a ten percent chance of dying, and probably a much higher one." It is small wonder that women have welcomed anesthetics and the other interventions physicians introduced,

hoping that these would lessen the danger and pain of pregnancy and birth.

True, the medical "improvements" took their toll. As we have seen, they brought their own dangers and gave physicians altogether too much authority and control over the ways women experience pregnancy and birth as well as over child rearing. Yet, given the limited choices most women have had and the very real risks of childbearing, it is not surprising that upper-class women in the nineteenth century opted for the benefits their physicians promised them.

Now once again we are at a point where many women believe that the new interventions in pregnancy are increasing procreative choice and improving our lives as well as those of our families. As the new technologies become part of routine pregnancy management, the experiences of past generations of women are erased, and contemporary women find it impossible to imagine how they could live without technologies that women in the past did not miss and often were better off doing without.

Take the pill as an example. Many women who became heterosexually active in the early 1960s seem to think that birth control was rare, if not unknown, for women earlier in the century. Yet in the pre-pill era, many women planned their pregnancies as successfully as women who use the newer products do now. True, condoms and diaphragms involve problems and inconveniences, but from a health viewpoint they are safer than the newer methods. And these days, when protection against AIDS should be on all our minds, a shift back to condoms, used together with spermicides, is widely recommended.

Another example is pregnancies of older women. In this context "older" denotes younger and younger women as time goes on. It used to be over forty; in this country, it is now over thirty-five; I suppose thirty-two and thirty are next. This change seems strange to me, who had my children when I was between thirty-five and forty. I did not think there was anything to worry about because my partner and I were in good health, and when I mentioned my age to the obstetrician, he agreed with this assessment.

Now women that age tell me that if it were not for prenatal diagnosis, they would not dare to have a child. Indeed, because it has been hammered into the present generation of "older" women that the risk of bearing a child with a chromosomal abnormality, such as Down syndrome, increases dramatically after the early thirties, few will just hope for the best when a test can reassure them while they are pregnant. And because all abnormalities are rare, it usually does just that. This reassuring feature is what makes for the popularity of the tests: More often than not they show that there is no problem.

But most of us would not need that reassurance if it were not for the prevalent emphasis on risks. The reasons why chromosomal abnormalities occur when they do are far from clear, and there has not been a great deal of epidemiological research on them. What are the environmental, occupational, and socioeconomic influences? How relevant are the health histories of both partners? And so forth. In the midst of such uncertainties, the prospective mother's age is the only factor we are urged to consider, even though either prospective parent can contribute the extra chromosome responsible for Down syndrome.

I have a not so sci-fi fantasy in which a woman ten years hence will tell me that she could not possibly risk having a child by "in-body fertilization." She will say that only the availability of in vitro fertilization makes childbearing possible. In my fantasy, it will by then be standard practice to fertilize eggs in vitro and allow the embryo to go through the first few cell divisions until it contains six or eight cells. At this point two of its cells will be removed, cultured, and put through a battery of tests, while the rest of the embryo will be frozen and placed in cold storage. Only if the

tests are satisfactory will the embryo be thawed and implanted in the prospective mother's, or some other carrier's womb. Otherwise, it will be discarded or used for research.

How will I explain to this woman why I am troubled by this, by then routine, way of producing babies? We will live in different worlds. I in one in which I continue to look upon childbearing as a healthy, normal function that can sometimes go wrong but usually doesn't. Therefore I will want to interfere as little as possible with the delicate, complicated processes of fertilization and embryonic development. She will live in a world in which the ability to plan procreation means using all available medical techniques to try to avoid the possibility of biological malfunctioning. I will tell her that the manipulations entail unknown and unpredictable risks and that they cannot assure her of having a healthy baby. She will tell me that I am opting for ignorance and stemming progress. But what worries me most is that at that point "in-body fertilization" will not only be considered old-fashioned and quaint, but foolhardy, unhealthful, and unsafe. It will seem that way to the scientists and physicians who pioneer the "improvements" and to the women who "choose" to have their babies the new way.

Nowadays, some women over thirty-five refuse prenatal diagnosis and other, usually poor or Third World women, do not even know it exists. In reality, in this country only a minority of women are being screened. But this is because access to costly resources is uneven, not because physicians are cautious about exposing women to these techniques. In fact, to most physicians being cautious means using all available technology, however little they can yet know about its long-term consequences. By using every test they can avoid the potential legal ramifications of failing to alert future parents to the possibility of an inborn "defect."

I do not want to portray physicians as callous technocrats who think only about possible malpractice suits. Nor do I want to portray women as unwilling victims of scientists and physicians, quite a number of whom, incidentally, by now are women. When women contemplate childbearing, they try to strike the best bargain they can in a society that offers little support for this important social activity. And sometimes technological interventions seem to offer a measure of security from unexpected mishaps. The problem is not the technology itself but the fact that it generates the expectation that it is up to prospective parents, and especially mothers, to do away with disabilities by not bearing children who might have one.

Disabilities: A Social Problem

What shall be called a defect or disability and for how many and what kind shall a fetus be aborted or treated in the womb? Down syndrome? Spina bifida? Wrong sex? These questions are complicated by the fact that, for most inborn disabilities, no one can predict how serious the "defect" will be and just how it will express itself—in other words, how much of a health or social problem it will be.

To some people, and in some circumstances, the prospect of having a child with Down syndrome, no matter how mild, seems intolerable. Before there were tests, women like myself just hoped for the best when we decided to have children after thirty-five. But now that tests exist, many women who have access to them have them as a matter of course. At the same time, many people in the United States reject prenatal testing for purposes of sex selection, although it is done widely in India and China. Many feminists argue against sex selection because they expect it will most often be used to choose boys; but some feminists are for it because it makes it possible for women to choose to have only daughters if that is what they want.

I have problems with such so-called choices. Bearing and raising children is intrin-

sically unpredictable and knowing a person's sex tells us little about them. With all the prenatal tests in the world, we cannot know what our children will be like, whether they will be healthy and able-bodied and remain so, and what sorts of people they will be when they grow up. We have the best chance of successful parenthood if we are prepared to accept our children, whoever they are, and do the best we can to help them accept themselves and, hopefully, us too. People with disabilities have begun to speak about these issues. I agree with them when they say that all children should be welcome and that we are being short-sighted to think that we can circumvent the uncertainties of procreation by aborting "defective" or "wrong" fetuses. Sparing no expense to develop techniques for diagnosing disabilities prenatally, so as to prevent the birth of children who have them, accentuates the stigma to which people with disabilities, as well as their families, are exposed.

Another, rather different, issue we must be aware of is that the increasing emphasis on prenatal testing reinforces this society's unfortunate tendency to individualize people's problems. Yet disability cannot be dealt with properly as long as it is considered a personal problem. Parents cannot possibly provide on their own for a child who may outlive them by decades. The logical solution: Don't have one! Logical, maybe, but neither humane nor realistic. Disability-rights advocates point out that usually the disability is not the main problem. What makes it burdensome is how people are treated because they have it. And as I have said before, many (probably most) disabilities cannot be predicted unless we were to test every embryo or fetus for all conceivable disabilities—an exceedingly cumbersome and expensive process with little benefit to show for it. What is more, the incidence of disabilities resulting from accidents or exposure to chemicals or radiation is considerable and likely to increase, rather than decrease, in the future. It would be better to regard mental and physical disabilities as social, not personal, issues. Many disabilities—whether inborn or acquired later in life—are the result of social circumstances: accidents, inadequate living conditions, chronic poisoning by heavy metals or drugs, and so forth. They cannot be dealt with by victim-blaming individualizations; to prevent them requires social measures.

As the world around us becomes increasingly hazardous and threatens us and our children with social disintegration, pollution, accidents, and nuclear catastrophe, it seems as though we seek shelter among the hazards we are told lurk within us, in the illusion that we may have at least some control over them. And so we applaud the scientists and physicians who tell us that our problems lie in our genes or our womb and who propose technological solutions for them.

I remember a news story that ran in the *Boston Globe* under the headline "Some Schizophrenia Linked to Prenatal Changes in Brain Cells" (Nelson, 1983). It started with the portentous words: "The devastating mental disorder of paranoid schizophrenia seems to have roots in the womb." The rest of the story showed nothing of the sort. Rather, on the basis of the flimsiest evidence gathered by examining the brains of "10 deceased schizophrenics ages 25 to 67" and "eight nonpsychotic subjects used as controls," two researchers decided that schizophrenia has its beginnings in "the first few months of pregnancy" and suggested that visible "abnormalities [in the brain] some day may allow doctors to identify children who have a high risk of becoming paranoid schizophrenics." This is but one of many false messages women get that our children's troubles originate in our womb if not in our genes.

As I have said before, prenatal diagnosis can help the relatively small number of women who have reason to think their future children are at risk for a specific disease, but most disabilities are unexpected. Yet now that some

disabilities can be detected and the fetus aborted or, in rare instances, treated in the womb, people are beginning to feel that if parents bear a child with a disability, it is because they or their physicians were not sufficiently foresightful.

Parents are suing physicians, arguing they should have been forcefully warned about possible risks or disability and told about all available means of prenatal diagnosis. And a child who is born with a health problem that might have been detected and improved prenatally may be able to sue the mother if she refuses to be tested while pregnant. Not only that. Some attorneys have even suggested that the state should be able to mandate prenatal screening "with criminal penalties for the woman who fails to obtain it" (Robertson, 1983).

Fetal Rights

In 1971, Bentley Glass, the retiring president of the American Association for the Advancement of Science, wrote: "In a world where each pair must be limited, on the average, to two offspring and no more, the right that must become paramount is . . . the right of every child to be born with a sound physical and mental constitution, based on a sound genotype. No parents will in that future time have a right to burden society with a malformed or a mentally incompetent child."

More recently, the theologian Joseph Fletcher (1980) has written that "we ought to recognize that children are often abused preconceptively and prenatally—not only by their mothers drinking alcohol, smoking, and using drugs nonmedicinally but also by their *knowingly* passing on or risking passing on genetic diseases" (original emphasis). This language of "rights" of the unborn immediately translates into obligations of the born, and especially of women.

These obligations become explicit in the writings of Margery Shaw, an attorney and physician. Reviewing what she calls "prenatal torts," Shaw (1980) argues as follows:

Once a pregnant woman has abandoned her right to abort and has decided to carry her fetus to term, she incurs a "conditional prospective liability" for negligent acts toward her fetus if it should be born alive. These acts could be considered negligent fetal abuse resulting in an injured child. A decision to carry a genetically defective fetus to term would be an example. Abuse of alcohol or drugs during pregnancy could lead to fetal alcohol syndrome or drug addiction in the infant, resulting in an assertion that he [*sic*] had been harmed by his mother's acts. Withholding of necessary prenatal care, improper nutrition, exposure to mutagens and teratogens, or even exposure to the mother's defective intrauterine environment caused by her genotype . . . could all result in an injured infant who might claim that his right to be born physically and mentally sound had been invaded.

What *right* to be born physically and mentally sound? Who has that kind of right and who guarantees it? Shaw goes on to urge that "courts and legislatures . . . should . . . take all reasonable steps to insure that fetuses destined to be born alive are not handicapped mentally and physically by the negligent acts or omissions of others."

In this argument, Shaw assumes not only that a fetus has rights (a hotly debated assumption) but that its rights are different, and indeed opposed to, those of the woman whose body keeps it alive and who will most likely be the person who cares for it once it is born. What is more, she places the burden of implementing these so-called rights of fetuses squarely on the shoulders of individual women. Nowhere does Shaw suggest that the "reasonable steps" courts and legislatures should take include making sure that women have access to good nutrition, housing, education, and employment so that they are able to secure a fetus its "right" to proper nutrition and avoid its being exposed to mutagens and teratogens. Her language of "rights" does not advocate the

kinds of improvements that would benefit women, children, and everyone. It is a language of social control.

Such control is advocated explicitly by John Robertson (1983), professor of law at the University of Texas (the same faculty on which Shaw teaches). His basic proposition is this:

The mother has, if she conceives and chooses not to abort, a legal and moral duty to bring the child into the world as healthy as is reasonably possible. She has a duty to avoid actions or omissions that will damage the fetus. . . . In terms of fetal rights, a fetus has no right to be conceived-or, once conceived, to be carried to viability. But once the mother decides not to terminate the pregnancy, the viable fetus acquires rights to have the mother conduct her life in ways that will not injure it.

Because the fetus has such rights, "laws that prohibited pregnant women from obtaining or using alcohol, tobacco, or drugs likely to damage the fetus would be constitutional," and "statutes excluding pregnant women from workplaces inimical to fetal health . . . would be valid." This argument leads Robertson even further:

The behavioral restrictions on pregnant women and the arguments for mandating fetal therapy and prenatal screening illustrate an important limit on a woman's freedom to control her body during pregnancy. She is free not to conceive, and free to abort after conception and before viability. But once she chooses to carry the child to term, she acquires obligations to assure its wellbeing. These obligations may require her to avoid work, recreation, and medical care choices that are hazardous to the fetus. They also obligate her to preserve her health for the fetus' sake or even allow established therapies to be performed on an affected fetus. Finally, they require that she undergo prenatal screening where there is reason to believe that this screening may identify congenital defects correctable with available therapies.

This analysis gets women into an awkward predicament, although one with a long history. While he was enunciating these legal principles,

Professor Robertson was a member of a panel that proposed a model statute to guarantee a person's right to refuse treatment. The statute begins with the following proposition: "A competent person has the right to refuse any medical procedure or treatment" (Legal Advisors Committee, Concern for Dying, 1983). Yet we have just seen that Robertson argues that a woman does not have this right if she becomes pregnant and decides to carry the fetus to term. In that case, she comes entirely under the control of physicians and judges, suggesting that a willingly (or enthusiastically) pregnant woman is not a "competent person."

By defining pregnancy as a conflict of rights between a woman and her fetus, attorneys and judges have injected themselves into the experience of pregnancy, where they see themselves as advocates for the fetus. Judging by other precedents, we can see how this new mechanism of social control could be used against women not only when we are pregnant. It could be expanded to cover every woman of childbearing age by invoking "rights" not just of the fetus she is carrying but of a "potential" fetus—one she may carry at some future date. This expansion shades over into the concept of "potential" pregnancy, which has been used to bar women from more prestigious and better-paid jobs than they now have in some male-dominated industries.

To present pregnancy as a conflict of rights is even more inappropriate than to regard it as a disease. The disease metaphor is wrong because it turns the special needs of some of us into the norm for us all. The rights metaphor misrepresents most women's experience of a wanted or accepted pregnancy even more than defining pregnancy as a disability does. Yet both Shaw's and Robertson's arguments refer specifically to women who expect to carry their pregnancies to term. A wanted or accepted fetus is part of a pregnant woman's body. For this reason, contrary to Robertson's statement, her decision to carry it to term is not binding. As long as the 1973 Supreme Court decision in

Roe v. *Wade* stands, she can change her mind and terminate the pregnancy at any point until viability and in some states until birth.

It is in the interest of the well-being of women and children that physicians' judgments not acquire the force of law. Informed consent laws mean that a physician can suggest, advise, and urge treatment, but he or she must not be able to force treatment on unconsenting people. Fetuses cannot consent to tests or treatments. So who speaks for the fetus? Is a judge of the juvenile court, who is called in for the occasion, more appropriate than the woman whose body sustains the fetus and who will be physically, emotionally, and economically affected by whatever is done? If a mother refuses to save her child's life by donating one of her kidneys, no one can force her to do it. What warped logic enables a physician, supported by a judge, to cut her open or penetrate her body with a needle or force her to take medication for the presumed benefit of the fetus she carries inside her?

Fetal Therapy

As we saw in the preceding section, the present status of fetal therapy is equivocal. After an initial rush of operations on fetuses that were hailed as breakthroughs in news and feature articles, some of the physicians who pioneered fetal interventions warned to go slow. Read cynically, the warning can be taken to mean: "We have begun to gain experience using these procedures at a few of the most prestigious teaching hospitals. Let us do them and don't get into the act!" These same physicians are far from restrained in their other writings about "the fetus." They wax eloquent, and even poetic, over the prospect of treating fetuses. For example, Michael Harrison (1982) writes in a review entitled "Unborn: Historical Perspective of the Fetus as Patient":

The fetus could not be taken seriously as long as he [*sic*] remained a medical recluse in an opaque womb; and it was not until the last half of this century that the prying eye of the ultrasonogram [that is, ultrasound visualization] rendered the once opaque womb transparent, stripping the veil of mystery from the dark inner sanctum, and letting the light of scientific observation fall on the shy and secretive fetus. . . . Sonography can accurately delineate normal and abnormal fetal anatomy with astounding detail. It can produce not only static images of intact fetuses, but real-time "live" moving pictures. And, unlike all previous techniques, ultrasonic imaging appears to have no harmful effects on mother or fetus. The sonographic voyeur, spying on the unwary fetus, finds him or her a surprisingly active little creature, and not at all the passive parasite we had imagined.

Who is "we"? Surely not women who have been awakened by the painful kicks of a fetus! Harrison concludes:

The fetus has come a long way—from biblical "seed" and mystical "homunculus" to an individual with medical problems that can be diagnosed and treated, that is, a patient. Although he [*sic*] cannot make an appointment and seldom even complains, this patient will at all times need a physician. . . . Treatment of the unborn has had a long and painstaking gestation; the date of confinement is still questionable and viability uncertain. But there is promise that the fetus may become a "born again" patient.

Frederic Frigoletto, chief of what used to be obstetrics but is now called "maternal and fetal medicine" at Boston's Brigham and Women's Hospital and another pioneer in fetal therapy, is quoted as follows in *Patient Care*, a magazine for physicians (Labson, 1983):

Real-time ultrasound—which is now widely available—allows us to develop a composite picture of [the] fetal state; it's almost like going to a nursery school to watch [the] behavior of 3-year-olds. Eventually we may be able to establish normative behavior for the fetus at various gestational stages. That will help us identify abnormal fetal development, perhaps early enough to be able to correct the environment to treat the fetus in utero.

Considering the personal anb social problems that have been created when scientists have

tried to establish norms, such as the IQ, for children and grownups, I shudder at the prospect of physicians coming up with norms for "fetal behavior." And remember that the "environment" to which Dr. Frigoletto refers happens to be the body of a woman.

So the fetus is on its way to being a person by virtue of becoming a patient with its own legal rights to medical treatment. As we have seen, once the fetus is considered a person, pregnant women may lose *their* right to refuse treatment by becoming no more than the maternal environment that must be manipulated for the fetus's benefit. The same Dr. Harrison, in a medical article he wrote with colleagues, described moving a pregnant woman as "transporting the fetus in situ" (Harrison, Golbus, and Filly, 1981), *in situ* being scientific parlance for "in place." It is not unusual to find pregnant women referred to as the "maternal environment," but now even that term directs too much attention to them. They are becoming "the fetus in situ," the vessel that holds the fetus, that ideal patient who does not protest or talk back.

And What About Women?

Much as this way of viewing pregnancy insults women, the issue to which I want to come back is that many—perhaps most—pregnant women will feel obligated to accept these intrusions and may even do so gratefully. As long as disability is regarded as a personal failure and parents (especially mothers) feel in some sense responsible, as well as ashamed, if their child is born with a disability, pregnant women will hail medical interventions that promise to lessen the likelihood of its happening to them. The very availability of the new techniques, however untested they may be, increases women's isolation by playing on our sense of personal responsibility to produce healthy children and on our fears and guilt if we should fail to do so.

But who is to say what "healthy" means in the face of an ever-lengthening list of diagnosable "defects" and, lately, even of "predispositions" or "tendencies" to develop them? The Human Genome Initiative will produce a raft of new diagnostic tests long before there will be relevant therapies. Add to that the fact that pharmaceutical companies always find it more profitable to market ways to diagnose and screen healthy people than to develop therapeutic measures because relatively few people need therapy. So how should we relate to the ever-increasing number of genetic and metabolic tests that will be done prenatally?

Compare the rare and almost surreal genetic threats the genome project will uncover with the starkly real threats to health reported daily in the press. For example, in July 1988 the Agency for Toxic Substances and the Disease Registry of the Department of Health and Human Services announced that in the United States an estimated four hundred thousand fetuses a year are exposed to harm because of the lead poisoning of their mothers. This is only one of many preventable risks pregnant women and fetuses run by reason of economic and social neglect.

Women are likely to accept untested (or insufficiently tested) technological interventions in their pregnancies because it is becoming more and more difficult to be a responsible childbearer and mother. We get lots of "expert" advice, but little comradely support. Unless our social supports improve, women who can afford it will feel driven to follow every new will-o'-the-wisp that promises to lessen our sense that any problems we encounter in our childbearing are our fault. Meanwhile, women who do not have the economic or social support that make it possible for them to experience a healthful pregnancy will be blamed for "their failures."

REFERENCES

Fletcher, Joseph F. 1980. "Knowledge, Risk, and the Right to Reproduce: A Limiting Principle." In Aubrey Milunsky and George J. Annas, eds., *Genetics and the Law II*. New York: Plenum.

Harrison, Michael R. 1982. "Unborn: Historical Perspective of the Fetus as Patient." *Pharos*, Winter: 19–24.

Harrison, Michael R., Mitchell S. Golbus, and Roy A. Filly. 1981. "Management of the Fetus with a Correctable Congenital Defect." *Journal of the American Medical Association* 246: 744–747.

Labson, Lucy H. 1983. "Today's View in Maternal and Fetal Medicine." *Patient Care* 15 (January): 105–121.

Leavitt, Judith Walzer. 1987. *Brought to Bed: Childbearing in America, 1750–1950*. New York: Oxford University Press.

Legal Advisors Committee, Concern for Dying. 1983. "The Right to Refuse Treatment: A Model Act." *American Journal of Public Health* 73: 918–921.

Nelson, Harry. 1983. "Some Schizophrenia Linked to Prenatal Changes in Brain Cells." *Boston Globe*, June 7: 8.

Perry, Ruth. 1979. "The Veil of Chastity: Mary Astell's Feminism." *Studies in Eighteenth-Century Culture* 9: 25–45.

Rich, Adrienne. 1976. *Of Woman Born*. New York: Norton.

Robertson, John A. 1983. "Procreative Liberty and the Control of Conception, Pregnancy, and Childbirth." *Virginia Law Review* 69: 405–464.

Rothman, Barbara Katz. 1984. "The Meanings of Choice in Reproductive Technology." In Rita Arditti, Renate Duelli Klein, and Shelley Minden, eds., *Test-Tube Women*. London: Pandora Press.

Rothman, Barbara Katz. 1989. *Recreating Motherhood: Ideology and Technology in a Patriarchal Society*. New York: Norton.

Shaw, Margery W. 1980. "The Potential Plaintiff: Preconception and Prenatal Torts." In Aubrey Milunsky and George J. Annas, eds., *Genetics and the Law II*. New York: Plenum.

Self-Images

When we discussed gender socialization, we noted that females are thought to be passive, nurturant, cooperative, emotional, and physically weak. By no means do these gender characteristics totally exhaust society's notion of "femininity." In "Foucault, Femininity, and the Modernization of Patriarchal Power," Sandra Bartky sketches out in more detail our current understanding of femininity, touching on body size and configuration, gestures, facial expressions, postures, styles of movement, and styles of ornamentation. She also describes the "disciplinary practices," or forms of subjection (dieting, exercise, skin care, hair care, makeup, etc.) that women accept to achieve the ideal feminine form—all for the sake of being attractive to men. Because the ideal feminine form is virtually impossible for a typical woman to ever achieve, or to achieve for very long, she may reject her body as grossly inadequate: "The disciplinary project of femininity is a 'setup': it requires such radical and extensive measures of bodily transformation that virtually every woman who gives herself to it is destined in some degree to fail. Thus, a measure of shame is added to a woman's sense that the body she inhabits is deficient . . ." (pp. 125–126). Sadly, even when a woman manages to achieve near physical perfection, all she will gain is some attention and admiration. What she will not gain is real respect and social power. Nevertheless, because she fears the loneliness that comes with rejection, such a woman may swallow her pride and continue to do whatever she has to do to earn the male gaze. Comments Bartky:

. . . Insofar as the disciplinary practices of femininity produce a "subjected and practiced," an inferiorized, body, they must be understood as aspects of a far larger discipline, an oppressive and inegalitarian system of sexual subordination. This system aims at turning women into the docile and compliant companions of men just as surely as the army aims to turn its raw recruits into soldiers. (p. 128)

If Bartky is correct, we must ask ourselves what it will take to motivate women to rebel, or at least to conscientiously object, to "beauty" service.

Underlying this ideal of femininity, of course, is an unquestioned acceptance of heterosexuality. As Julia Penelope points out in "The Lesbian Perspective,"

From the day a girl child is born, everyone who exercises control and authority in her life assumes that she will grow up to "fall in love" with a male, as though that were an "accidental" misstep, and that she will inevitably marry one. All the messages she hears about WHO she is and WHO she's expected to become assume that there's only one kind of love and one kind of sexuality, and that's HETEROSEXUAL. (pp. 134–135)

And all the disciplinary practices Bartky describes that she is expected to engage in are premised on that same outcome. But what if she chooses a different outcome—what if she chooses to love women instead of men? What will society do to her? Penelope observes that society will penalize her severely for her choice; it will force her to live on the margins of society as a "deviant" with little political or personal support. In order to overcome this unjust state of affairs, says Penelope, we need to create a new social order in which lesbians live and love as openly and as happily as heterosexuals do. Society must see to it that lesbians are not "rejected, ridiculed, committed to psychiatric hospitals, jailed, and tortured" (p. 136); or worse, driven to suicide for daring to love women more than men.

In the same way that heterosexual society's image of lesbians has created problems for lesbians, white society's images of African-American women have created problems for them. In "Mammies, Matriarchs, and Other Controlling Images," Patricia Hill Collins describes four images of African-American women prevalent in society: (1) the *Mammy*, who typifies the faithful, obedient, self-sacrificial black mother-figure in a white home; (2) the *Matriarch*, who typifies the unfeminine, castrating, hard-working black mother-figure in a black home; (3) the *Welfare Mother*, an updated version of the breeder woman who is lazy, prolific, and a totally irresponsible mother; and (4) the *Jezebel*, the whore, or hypersexed black temptress. Collins maintains that to the extent African-American women (and men) internalize these images, they function to oppress all African-Americans, but especially African-American women. For example, the Mammy image causes black children to behave deferentially toward whites, even when such deference is not warranted; the Matriarch and Welfare Mother images cause black women to be blamed for the problems black children experience in society; and the Jezebel image causes black women to be blamed for the rapes and beatings men inflict upon them. Furthermore, says Collins:

. . . these controlling images remain powerful influences on our relationships with whites, Black men, and one another. Dealing with issues of beauty—particularly skin color, facial features, and hair texture—is one concrete example of how controlling images denigrate African-American women. . . . Blue eyed, blond, thin white women could not be considered beautiful without the Other—Black women with classical African features of dark skin, broad noses, full lips and kinky hair texture. (p. 149)

If what Collins says is correct, we need to spell out in detail the relationship between the "femininity" of African-American women and that of white women. As hard as it is for a white woman to be a perfect woman in this society, it seems virtually impossible for an African-American woman to achieve this imposed goal.

Cynthia Rich discusses yet another set of problematic self-images in "The Women in the Tower." She analyzes a 1982 *Boston Globe* article about a group of black women, aged 66 to 81, who demanded a meeting with the Boston Housing Authority to complain about the intolerably unsafe conditions in the "housing tower for the elderly" where they lived. Throughout the newspaper article, these old women are portrayed variously as ugly (crow's feet, liver spots), unnatural, powerless, touchy, excitable, quarrelsome, quirky, quaint, annoying, endearing but not to be taken seriously, unkempt, senile, meek, pitiful, and having nothing in common with either young or middle-aged women. But are *all* old women really this awful? Is being an old woman that "bad"? Is life no longer worth living after menopause? Are young, abled, white women the only women worth knowing and loving?

Foucault, Femininity, and the Modernization of Patriarchal Power

Sandra Lee Bartky

I

In a striking critique of modern society, Michel Foucault has argued that the rise of parliamentary institutions and of new conceptions of political liberty was accompanied by a darker countermovement, by the emergence of a new and unprecedented discipline directed against the body. More is required of the body now than mere political allegiance or the appropriation of the products of its labor: the new discipline invades the body and seeks to regulate its very forces and operations, the economy and efficiency of its movements.

The disciplinary practices Foucault describes are tied to peculiarly modern forms of the army, the school, the hospital, the prison, and the manufactory; the aim of these disciplines is to increase the utility of the body, to augment its forces:

What was then being formed was a policy of coercions that act upon the body, a calculated manipulation of its elements, its gestures, its behaviour. The human body was entering a machinery of power that explores it, breaks it down and rearranges it. A "political anatomy," which was also a "mechanics of power," was being born; it defined how one may have a hold over others' bodies, not only so that they may do what one wishes, but so that they may oper-

ate as one wishes, with the techniques, the speed and the efficiency that one determines. Thus, discipline produces subjected and practiced bodies, "docile" bodies.[1]

The production of "docile bodies" requires that an uninterrupted coercion be directed to the very processes of bodily activity, not just their result; this "micro-physics of power" fragments and partitions the body's time, its space, and its movements.

The student, then, is enclosed within a classroom and assigned to a desk he cannot leave; his ranking in the class can be read off the position of his desk in the serially ordered and segmented space of the classroom itself. Foucault tells us that "Jean-Baptiste de la Salle dreamt of a classroom in which the spatial distribution might provide a whole series of distinctions at once, according to the pupil's progress, worth, character, application, cleanliness and parents' fortune."[2] The student must sit upright, feet upon the floor, head erect; he may not slouch or fidget; his animate body is brought into a fixed correlation with the inanimate desk.

The minute breakdown of gestures and movements required of soldiers at drill is far more relentless:

Bring the weapon forward. In three stages. Raise the rifle with the right hand, bringing it close to the body so as to hold it perpendicular with the right knee, the end of the barrel at eye level, grasping it by striking it with the right hand, the arm held close to the body at waist height. At the second stage, bring the rifle in front of you with the left hand, the barrel in the middle between the two eyes, vertical, the right hand grasping it at the small of the butt, the arm outstretched, the triggerguard resting on the first finger, the left hand at the height of the notch, the thumb lying along the barrel against the moulding. At the third stage . . .[3]

These "body-object articulations" of the soldier and his weapon, the student and his desk effect a "coercive link with the apparatus of production." We are far indeed from older forms of control that "demanded of the body only signs or products, forms of expression or the result of labour."[4]

The body's time, in these regimes of power, is as rigidly controlled as its space: the factory whistle and the school bell mark a division of time into discrete and segmented units that regulate the various activities of the day. The following timetable, similar in spirit to the ordering of my grammar school classroom, is suggested for French "écoles mutuelles" of the early nineteenth century:

8:45 entrance of the monitor, 8:52 the monitor's summons, 8:56 entrance of the children and prayer, 9:00 the children go to their benches, 9:04 first slate, 9:08 end of dictation, 9:12 second slate, etc.[5]

Control this rigid and precise cannot be maintained without a minute and relentless surveillance.

Jeremy Bentham's design for the Panopticon, a model prison, captures for Foucault the essence of the disciplinary society. At the periphery of the Panopticon, a circular structure; at the center, a tower with wide windows that opens onto the inner side of the ring. The structure on the periphery is divided into cells, each with two windows, one facing the windows of the tower, the other facing the outside, allowing an effect of backlighting to make any figure visible within the cell. "All that is needed, then, is to place a supervisor in a central tower and to shut up in each cell a madman, a pa-

tient, a condemned man, a worker or a schoolboy."[6] Each inmate is alone, shut off from effective communication with his fellows, but constantly visible from the tower. The effect of this is "to induce in the inmate a state of conscious and permanent visibility that assures the automatic functioning of power"; each becomes to himself his own jailer.[7] This "state of conscious and permanent visibility" is a sign that the tight, disciplinary control of the body has gotten a hold on the mind as well. In the perpetual self-surveillance of the inmate lies the genesis of the celebrated "individualism" and heightened self-consciousness that are hallmarks of modern times. For Foucault, the structure and effects of the Panopticon resonate throughout society: Is it surprising that "prisons resemble factories, schools, barracks, hospitals, which all resemble prisons"?[8]

Foucault's account in *Discipline and Punish* of the disciplinary practices that produce the "docile bodies" of modernity is a genuine *tour de force*, incorporating a rich theoretical account of the ways in which instrumental reason takes hold of the body with a mass of historical detail. But Foucault treats the body throughout as if it were one, as if the bodily experiences of men and women did not differ and as if men and women bore the same relationship to the characteristic institutions of modern life. Where is the account of the disciplinary practices that engender the "docile bodies" of women, bodies more docile than the bodies of men? Women, like men, are subject to many of the same disciplinary practices Foucault describes. But he is blind to those disciplines that produce a modality of embodiment that is peculiarly feminine. To overlook the forms of subjection that engender the feminine body is to perpetuate the silence and powerlessness of those upon whom these disciplines have been imposed. Hence, even though a liberatory note is sounded in Foucault's critique of power, his analysis as a whole reproduces that sexism which is endemic throughout Western political theory.

We are born male or female, but not masculine or feminine. Femininity is an artifice, an achievement, "a mode of enacting and reenacting received gender norms which surface as so many styles of the flesh."[9] In what follows, I shall examine those disciplinary practices that produce a body which in gesture and appearance is recognizably feminine. I consider three categories of such practices: those that aim to produce a body of a certain size and general configuration; those that bring forth from this body a specific repertoire of gestures, postures, and movements; and those that are directed toward the display of this body as an ornamented surface. I shall examine the nature of these disciplines, how they are imposed and by whom. I shall probe the effects of the imposition of such discipline on female identity and subjectivity. In the final section I shall argue that these disciplinary practices must be understood in the light of the modernization of patriarchal domination, a modernization that unfolds historically according to the general pattern described by Foucault.

II

Styles of the female figure vary over time and across cultures: they reflect cultural obsessions and preoccupations in ways that are still poorly understood. Today, massiveness, power, or abundance in a woman's body is met with distaste. The current body of fashion is taut, small-breasted, narrow-hipped, and of a slimness bordering on emaciation; it is a silhouette that seems more appropriate to an adolescent boy or a newly pubescent girl than to an adult woman. Since ordinary women have normally quite different dimensions, they must of course diet.

Mass-circulation women's magazines run articles on dieting in virtually every issue. The *Ladies' Home Journal* of February 1986 carries a "Fat Burning Exercise Guide," while *Mademoiselle* offers to "Help Stamp Out Cellulite" with "Six Sleek-Down Strategies." After the diet-busting Christmas holidays and, later, before summer bikini season, the titles of these features become shriller and more arresting. The reader is now addressed in the imperative mode: Jump into shape for summer! Shed ugly winter fat with the all-new Grapefruit Diet! More women than men visit diet doctors, while women greatly outnumber men in such self-help groups as Weight Watchers and Overeaters Anonymous-in the case of the latter, by well over 90 percent.

Dieting disciplines the body's hungers: appetite must be monitored at all times and governed by an iron will. Since the innocent need of the organism for food will not be denied, the body becomes one's enemy, an alien being bent on thwarting the disciplinary project. Anorexia nervosa, which has now assumed epidemic proportions, is to women of the late twentieth century what hysteria was to women of an earlier day: the crystallization in a pathological mode of a widespread cultural obsession. A survey taken recently at UCLA is astounding: of 260 students interviewed, 27.3 percent of women but only 5.8 percent of men said they were "terrified" of getting fat; 28.7 percent of women but only 7.5 percent of men said they were obsessed or "totally preoccupied" with food. The body images of women and men are strikingly different as well: 35 percent of women but only 12.5 percent of men said they felt fat though other people told them they were thin. Women in the survey wanted to weigh ten pounds less than their average weight; men felt they were within a pound of their ideal weight. A total of 5.9 percent of women and no men met the psychiatric criteria for anorexia or bulimia.

Dieting is one discipline imposed upon a body subject to the "tyranny of slenderness"; exercise is another. Since men as well as women exercise, it is not always easy in the case of women to distinguish what is done for the sake of physical fitness from what is done in obedience to the requirements of femininity. Men as well as women lift weights and do yoga, calisthenics, and aerobics, though "jazzercise" is a largely female pursuit. Men and women alike engage themselves with a variety of machines, each designed to call forth from the body a different exertion: there are Nautilus machines, rowing machines, ordinary and motorized exercycles, portable hip and leg cycles, belt massagers, trampolines, treadmills, and arm and leg pulleys. However, given the widespread female obsession with weight, one suspects that many women are working out with these apparatuses in the health club or at the gym with an aim in mind and in a spirit quite different from men's.

But there are classes of exercises meant for women alone, these designed not to firm or to reduce the body's size overall, but to resculpture its various parts on the current model. M. J. Saffon, "international beauty expert," assures us that his twelve basic facial exercises can erase frown lines, smooth the forehead, raise hollow cheeks, banish crow's feet, and tighten the muscles under the chin. There are exercises to build the breasts and exercises to banish "cellulite," said by "figure consultants" to be a special type of female fat. There is "spot-reducing," an umbrella term that covers dozens of punishing exercises designed to reduce "problem areas" like thick ankles or "saddlebag" thighs. The very idea of "spot-reducing" is both scientifically unsound and cruel, for it raises expectations in women that can never be realized—the pattern in which fat is deposited or removed is known to be genetically determined.

It is not only her natural appetite or unreconstructed contours that pose a danger to woman: the very expressions of her face can subvert the disciplinary project of bodily perfection. An expressive face lines and creases more readily than an inexpressive one. Hence, if women are unable to suppress strong emotions, they can at least learn to inhibit the tendency of the face to register them. Sophia Loren recommends a unique solution to this problem: a piece of tape applied to the forehead or between the brows will tug at the skin when one frowns and act as a reminder to relax the face. The tape is to be worn whenever a woman is home alone.

III

There are significant gender differences in gesture, posture, movement, and general bodily comportment: women are far more restricted than men in their manner of movement and in their spatiality. In her classic paper on the subject, Iris Young observes that a space seems to surround women in imagination that they are hesitant to move beyond: this manifests itself both in a reluctance to reach, stretch, and extend the body to meet resistances of matter in motion—as in sport or in the performance of physical tasks—and in a typically constricted posture and general style of movement. Woman's space is not a field in which her bodily intentionality can be freely realized but an enclosure in which she feels herself positioned and by which she is confined.[10] The "loose woman" violates these norms: her looseness is manifest not only in her morals, but in her manner of speech and quite literally in the free and easy way she moves.

In an extraordinary series of over two thousand photographs, many candid shots taken in the street, the German photographer Marianne Wex has documented differences in typical masculine and feminine body posture. Women sit waiting for trains with arms close to the body, hands folded together in their laps, toes pointing straight ahead or turned inward, and legs pressed together. The women in these photographs make themselves small and narrow, harmless; they seem tense; they take up little space. Men, on the other hand, expand into the available space; they sit with legs far apart and arms flung out at some distance from the body. Most common in these sitting male figures is what Wex calls the "proffering position": the men sit with legs thrown wide apart, crotch visible, feet pointing outward, often with an arm and a casually dangling hand resting comfortably on an open, spread thigh.

In proportion to total body size, a man's stride is longer than a woman's. The man has more spring and rhythm to his step; he walks with toes pointed outward, holds his arms at a greater distance from his body and swings them farther; he tends to point the whole hand in the direction he is moving. The woman holds her arms closer to her body, palms against her sides; her walk is circumspect. If she has subjected herself to the additional constraint of high-heeled shoes, her body is thrown forward and off balance: the struggle to walk under these conditions shortens her stride still more.

But women's movement is subjected to a still finer discipline. Feminine faces, as well as bodies, are trained to the expression of deference. Under male scrutiny, women will avert their eyes or cast them downward; the female gaze is trained to abandon its claim to the sovereign status of seer. The "nice" girl learns to avoid the bold and unfettered staring of the "loose" woman who looks at whatever and whomever she pleases. Women are trained to smile more than men, too. In the economy of smiles, as elsewhere, there is evidence that women are exploited, for they give more than they receive in return; in a smile elicitation study, one researcher found that the rate of smile return by women was 93 percent, by men only 67 percent. In many typical women's jobs, graciousness, deference, and the readiness to serve are part of the work; this requires the worker to fix a smile on her face for a good part of the working day, whatever her inner state. The economy of touching is out of balance, too: men touch women more often and on more parts of the body than women touch men: female secretaries, factory workers, and waitresses report that such liberties are taken routinely with their bodies.

Feminine movement, gesture, and posture must exhibit not only constriction, but grace and a certain eroticism restrained by modesty: all three. Here is field for the operation for a whole new training: a woman must stand with stomach pulled in, shoulders thrown slightly back and chest out, this to display her bosom to maximum advantage. While she must walk in the confined fashion appropriate to women, her movements must, at the same time, be combined with a subtle but provocative hip-roll. But too much display is taboo: women in short, low-cut dresses are told to avoid bending over at all, but if they must, great care must be taken to avoid an unseemly display of breast or rump. From time to time, fashion magazines offer quite precise instructions on the proper way of getting in and out of cars. These instructions combine all three imperatives of women's movement: a woman must not allow her arms and legs to flail about in all directions; she must try to manage her movements with the appearance of grace—no small accomplishment when one is climbing out of the back seat of a Fiat—and she is well-advised to use the opportunity for a certain display of leg.

All the movements we have described so far are self-movements; they arise from within the woman's own body. But in a way that normally goes unnoticed, males in couples may literally steer a woman everywhere she goes: down the street, around corners, into elevators, through doorways, into her chair at the dinner table, around the dance floor. The man's movement "is not necessarily heavy and pushy or physical in an ugly way; it is light and gentle but firm in the way of the most confident equestrians with the best trained horses."[11]

IV

We have examined some of the disciplinary practices a woman must master in pursuit of a body of the right size and shape that also displays the proper styles of feminine motility. But woman's body is an ornamented surface too, and there is much discipline involved in this production as well. Here, especially in the application of makeup and the selection of clothes, art and discipline converge, though, as I shall argue, there is less art involved than one might suppose.

A woman's skin must be soft, supple, hairless, and smooth; ideally, it should betray no sign of wear, experience, age, or deep thought. Hair must be removed not only from the face but from large surfaces of the body as well, from legs and thighs, an operation accomplished by shaving, buffing with fine sandpaper, or applying foul-smelling depilatories. With the new high-leg bathing suits and leotards, a substantial amount of pubic hair must be removed too. The removal of facial hair can be more specialized. Eyebrows are plucked out by the roots with a tweezer. Hot wax is sometimes poured onto the mustache and cheeks and then ripped away when it cools. The woman who wants a more permanent result may try electrolysis: this involves the killing of a hair root by the passage of an electric current down a needle that has been inserted into its base. The procedure is painful and expensive.

The development of what one "beauty expert" calls "good skincare habits" requires not only attention to health, the avoidance of strong facial expressions, and the performance of facial exercises, but the regular use of skincare preparations, many to be applied more often than once a day: cleansing lotions (ordinary soap and water "upsets the skin's acid and alkaline balance"), wash-off cleansers (milder than cleansing lotions), astringents, toners, makeup removers, night creams, nourishing creams, eye creams, moisturizers, skin balancers, body lotions, hand creams, lip pomades, suntan lotions, sunscreens, and facial masks. Provision of the proper facial mask is complex: there are sulfur masks for pimples; oil or hot masks for dry areas; if these fail, then tightening masks; conditioning masks; peeling masks; cleansing masks made of herbs, cornmeal, or

almonds; and mudpacks. Black women may wish to use "fade creams" to "even skin tone." Skincare preparations are never just sloshed onto the skin, but applied according to precise rules: eye cream is dabbed on gently in movements toward, never away from, the nose; cleansing cream is applied in outward directions only, straight across the forehead, the upper lip, and the chin, never up but straight down the nose and up and out on the cheeks.

The normalizing discourse of modern medicine is enlisted by the cosmetics industry to gain credibility for its claims. Dr. Christiaan Barnard lends his enormous prestige to the Glycel line of "cellular treatment activators"; these contain "glycosphingolipids" that can "make older skin behave and look like younger skin." The Clinique computer at any Clinique counter will select a combination of preparations just right for you. Ultima II contains "procollagen" in its anti-aging eye cream that "provides hydration" to "demoralizing lines." "Biotherm" eye cream dramatically improves the "biomechanical properties of the skin." The Park Avenue clinic of Dr. Zizmor, "chief of dermatology at one of New York's leading hospitals," offers not only such medical treatment as dermabrasion and chemical peeling, but "total deep skin cleansing" as well.

Really good skincare habits require the use of a variety of aids and devices: facial steamers, faucet filters to collect impurities in the water, borax to soften it, a humidifier for the bedroom, electric massagers, backbrushes, complexion brushes, loofahs, pumice stones, and blackhead removers. I will not detail the implements or techniques involved in the manicure or pedicure.

The ordinary circumstances of life as well as a wide variety of activities cause a crisis in skincare and require a stepping-up of the regimen as well as an additional laying-on of preparations. Skincare discipline requires a specialized knowledge: a woman must know what to do if she has been skiing, taking medication, doing vigorous exercise, boating, or swimming in chlorinated pools; or if she has been exposed to pollution, heated rooms, cold, sun, harsh weather, the pressurized cabins on airplanes, saunas or steam rooms, fatigue, or stress. Like the schoolchild or prisoner, the woman mastering good skincare habits is put on a time-table: Georgette Klinger requires that a shorter or longer period of attention be paid to the complexion at least four times a day. Haircare, like skincare, requires a similar investment of time, the use of a wide variety of preparations, the mastery of a set of techniques, and, again, the acquisition of a specialized knowledge.

The crown and pinnacle of good haircare and skincare is, of course, the arrangement of the hair and the application of cosmetics. Here the regimen of haircare, skincare, manicure, and pedicure is recapitulated in another mode. A woman must learn the proper manipulation of a large number of devices—the blow dryer, styling brush, curling iron, hot curlers, wire curlers, eye-liner, lipliner, lipstick brush, eyelash curler, and mascara brush. And she must learn to apply a wide variety of products—foundation, toner, covering stick, mascara, eyeshadow, eyegloss, blusher, lipstick, rouge, lip gloss, hair dye, hair rinse, hair lightener, hair "relaxer," and so on.

In the language of fashion magazines and cosmetic ads, making-up is typically portrayed as an aesthetic activity in which a woman can express her individuality. In reality, while cosmetic styles change every decade or so, and while some variation in makeup is permitted depending on the occasion, making-up the face is, in fact, a highly stylized activity that gives little rein to self-expression. Painting the face is not like painting a picture; at best, it might be described as painting the same picture over and over again with minor variations. Little latitude is permitted in what is considered appropriate makeup for the office and for most social occasions; indeed, the woman who uses cosmetics in a genuinely novel and imaginative way is li-

able to be seen not as an artist but as an eccentric. Furthermore, since a properly made-up face is, if not a card of entree, at least a badge of acceptability in most social and professional contexts, the woman who chooses not to wear cosmetics at all faces sanctions of a sort that will never be applied to someone who chooses not to paint a watercolor.

V

Are we dealing in all this merely with sexual *difference*? Scarcely. The disciplinary practices I have described are part of the process by which the ideal body of femininity—and hence the feminine body-subject—is constructed; in doing this, they produce a "practiced and subjected" body, that is, a body on which an inferior status has been inscribed. A woman's face must be made-up, that is to say, made-over, and so must her body: she is ten pounds overweight; her lips must be made more kissable, her complexion dewier, her eyes more mysterious. The "art" of makeup is the art of disguise, but this presupposes that a woman's face, unpainted, is defective. Soap and water, a shave, and routine attention to hygiene may be enough for *him*; for *her* they are not. The strategy of much beauty-related advertising is to suggest to women that their bodies are deficient; but even without such more or less explicit teaching, the media images of perfect female beauty that bombard us daily leave no doubt in the minds of most women that they fail to measure up. The technologies of femininity are taken up and practiced by women against the background of a pervasive sense of bodily deficiency: this accounts for what is often their compulsive or even ritualistic character.

The disciplinary project of femininity is a "setup": it requires such radical and extensive measures of bodily transformation that virtually every woman who gives herself to it is destined in some degree to fail. Thus, a measure of shame is added to a woman's sense that the body she inhabits is deficient: she ought to take better care of herself; she might after all have jogged that last mile. Many women are without the time or resources to provide themselves with even the minimum of what such a regimen requires, for example, a decent diet. Here is an additional source of shame for poor women, who must bear what our society regards as the more general shame of poverty. The burdens poor women bear in this regard are not merely psychological, since conformity to the prevailing standards of bodily acceptability is a known factor in economic mobility.

The larger disciplines that construct a "feminine" body out of a female one are by no means race- or class-specific. There is little evidence that women of color or working-class women are in general less committed to the incarnation of an ideal femininity than their more privileged sisters: this is not to deny the many ways in which factors of race, class, locality, ethnicity, or personal taste can be expressed within the kinds of practices I have described. The rising young corporate executive may buy her cosmetics at Bergdorf-Goodman, while the counter-server at McDonald's gets hers at the K-Mart; the one may join an expensive "upscale" health club, while the other may have to make do with the $9.49 GFX Body-Flex II Home-Gym advertised in the *National Enquirer*: both are aiming at the same general result.

In the regime of institutionalized heterosexuality, woman must make herself "object and prey" for the man: it is for him that these eyes are limpid pools, this cheek baby-smooth. In contemporary patriarchal culture, a panoptical male connoisseur resides within the consciousness of most women: they stand perpetually before his gaze and under his judgment. Woman lives her body as seen by another, by an anonymous patriarchal Other. We are often told that "women dress for other women." There is some truth in this: who but someone engaged in a project similar to my own can appreciate the panache with which I bring it off? But women know for whom this game is

played: they know that a pretty young woman is likelier to become a flight attendant than a plain one, and that a well-preserved older woman has a better chance of holding onto her husband than one who has "let herself go."

Here it might be objected that performance for another in no way signals the inferiority of the performer to the one for whom the performance is intended: the actor, for example, depends on his audience but is in no way inferior to it; he is not demeaned by his dependency. While femininity is surely something enacted, the analogy to theater breaks down in a number of ways. First, as I argued earlier, the self-determination we think of as requisite to an artistic career is lacking here: femininity as spectacle is something in which virtually every woman is required to participate. Second, the precise nature of the criteria by which women are judged, not only the inescapability of judgment itself, reflects gross imbalances in the social power of the sexes that do not mark the relationship of artists and their audiences. An aesthetic of femininity, for example, that mandates fragility and a lack of muscular strength produces female bodies that can offer little resistance to physical abuse, and the physical abuse of women by men, as we know, is widespread. It is true that the current fitness movement has permitted women to develop more muscular strength and endurance than was heretofore allowed; indeed, images of women have begun to appear in the mass media that seem to eroticize this new muscularity. But a woman may by no means develop more muscular strength than her partner; the bride who would tenderly carry her groom across the threshold is a figure of comedy, not romance.

Under the current "tyranny of slenderness" women are forbidden to become large or massive; they must take up as little space as possible. The very contours a woman's body takes on as she matures—the fuller breasts and rounded hips—have become distasteful. The body by which a woman feels herself judged and which by rigorous discipline she must try to assume is the body of early adolescence, slight and un-formed, a body lacking flesh or substance, a body in whose very contours the image of im-maturity has been inscribed. The requirement that a woman maintain a smooth and hairless skin carries further the theme of inexperience, for an infantilized face must accompany her in-fantilized body, a face that never ages or fur-rows its brow in thought. The face of the ideally feminine woman must never display the marks of character, wisdom, and experience that we so admire in men.

To succeed in the provision of a beautiful or sexy body gains a woman attention and some admiration but little real respect and rarely any social power. A woman's effort to master femi-nine body discipline will lack importance just because she does it: her activity partakes of the general depreciation of everything female. In spite of unrelenting pressure to "make the most of what she has," women are ridiculed and dis-missed for their interest in such "trivial" things as clothes and makeup. Further, the narrow identification of woman with sexuality and the body in a society that has for centuries dis-played profound suspicion toward both does little to raise her status. Even the most adored female bodies complain routinely of their situ-ation in ways that reveal an implicit under-standing that there is something demeaning in the kind of attention they receive. Marilyn Mon-roe, Elizabeth Taylor, and Farrah Fawcett have all wanted passionately to become actresses-artists—and not just "sex objects."

But it is perhaps in their more restricted motility and comportment that the inferior-ization of women's bodies is most evident: women's typical body-language, a language of relative tension and constriction, is understood to be a language of subordination when it is enacted by men in male status hierarchies. In groups of men, those with higher status typi-cally assume looser and more relaxed postures: the boss lounges comfortably behind the desk, while the applicant sits tense and rigid on the edge of his seat. Higher status individuals may

touch their subordinates more than they them-selves get touched; they initiate more eye con-tact and are smiled at by their inferiors more than they are observed to smile in return. What is announced in the comportment of su-periors is confidence and ease, especially ease of access to the Other. Female constraint in posture and movement is no doubt overdeter-mined: the fact that women tend to sit and stand with legs, feet, and knees close or touch-ing may well be a coded declaration of sexual circumspection in a society that still maintains a double standard, or an effort, albeit uncon-scious, to guard the genital area. In the latter case, a woman's tight and constricted posture must be seen as the expression of her need to ward off real or symbolic sexual attack. What-ever proportions must be assigned in the final display to fear or deference, one thing is clear: woman's body language speaks eloquently, though silently, of her subordinate status in a hierarchy of gender.

VI

If what we have described is a genuine disci-pline—a system of "micropower" that is "essen-tially non-egalitarian and asymmetrical"—who then are the disciplinarians?[12] Who is the top sergeant in the disciplinary regime of feminin-ity? Historically, the law has had some respon-sibility for enforcement: in times gone by, for example, individuals who appeared in public in the clothes of the other sex could be arrested. While cross-dressers are still liable to some harassment, the kind of discipline we are con-sidering is not the business of the police or the courts. Parents and teachers, of course, have ex-tensive influence, admonishing girls to be de-mure and ladylike, to "smile pretty," to sit with their legs together. The influence of the media is pervasive, too, constructing as it does an image of the female body as spectacle, nor can we ignore the role played by "beauty experts" or by emblematic public personages such as Jane Fonda and Lynn Redgrave.

But none of these individuals—the skincare consultant, the parent, the policeman—does in fact wield the kind of authority that is typically invested in those who manage more straightforward disciplinary institutions. The disciplinary power that inscribes femininity in the female body is everywhere and it is nowhere; the disciplinarian is everyone and yet no one in particular. Women regarded as overweight, for example, report that they are regularly admonished to diet, sometimes by people they scarcely know. These intrusions are often softened by reference to the natural prettiness just waiting to emerge: "People have always said that I had a beautiful face and 'if you'd only lose weight you'd be really beautiful.'" Here, "people"—friends and casual acquaintances alike—act to enforce prevailing standards of body size.

Foucault tends to identify the imposition of discipline upon the body with the operation of specific institutions, for example, the school, the factory, the prison. To do this, however, is to overlook the extent to which discipline can be institutionally *unbound* as well as institutionally bound. The anonymity of disciplinary power and its wide dispersion have consequences that are crucial to a proper understanding of the subordination of women. The absence of a formal institutional structure and of authorities invested with the power to carry out institutional directives creates the impression that the production of femininity is either entirely voluntary or natural. The several senses of "discipline" are instructive here. On the one hand, discipline is something imposed on subjects of an "essentially non-egalitarian and asymmetrical" system of authority. Schoolchildren, convicts, and draftees are subject to discipline in this sense. But discipline can be sought voluntarily as well—for example, when an individual seeks initiation into the spiritual discipline of Zen Buddhism. Discipline can, of course, be both at once: the volunteer may seek the physical and occupational training offered by the army without the army's ceasing in any way to

be the instrument by which he and other members of his class are kept in disciplined subjection. Feminine bodily discipline has this dual character: on the one hand, no one is marched off for electrolysis at gunpoint, nor can we fail to appreciate the initiative and ingenuity displayed by countless women in an attempt to master the rituals of beauty. Nevertheless, insofar as the disciplinary practices of femininity produce a "subjected and practiced," an inferiorized, body, they must be understood as aspects of a far larger discipline, an oppressive and inegalitarian system of sexual subordination. This system aims at turning women into the docile and compliant companions of men just as surely as the army aims to turn its raw recruits into soldiers.

Now the transformation of oneself into a properly feminine body may be any or all of the following: a rite of passage into adulthood, the adoption and celebration of a particular aesthetic, a way of announcing one's economic level and social status, a way to triumph over other women in the competition for men or jobs, or an opportunity for massive narcissistic indulgence. The social construction of the feminine body is all these things, but at its base it is discipline, too, and discipline of the inegalitarian sort. The absence of formally identifiable disciplinarians and of a public schedule of sanctions only disguises the extent to which the imperative to be "feminine" serves the interest of domination. This is a lie in which all concur: making-up is merely artful play; one's first pair of high-heeled shoes is an innocent part of growing up, not the modern equivalent of foot-binding.

Why aren't all women feminists? In modern industrial societies, women are not kept in line by fear of retaliatory male violence; their victimization is not that of the South African black. Nor will it suffice to say that a false consciousness engendered in women by patriarchal ideology is at the basis of female subordination. This is not to deny that women are often subject to gross male violence or that women and men alike are ideologically mystified by the dominant gender arrangements. What I wish to suggest instead is that an adequate understanding of women's oppression will require an appreciation of the extent to which not only women's lives but their very subjectivities are structured within an ensemble of systematically duplicitous practices. The feminine discipline of the body is a case in point: the practices that construct this body have an overt aim and character far removed, indeed, radically distinct, from their covert function. In this regard, the system of gender subordination, like the wage-bargain under capitalism, illustrates in its own way the ancient tension between what-is and what-appears: the phenomenal forms in which it is manifested are often quite different from the real relations that form its deeper structure.

VII

The lack of formal public sanctions does not mean that a woman who is unable or unwilling to submit herself to the appropriate body discipline will face no sanctions at all. On the contrary, she faces a very severe sanction indeed in a world dominated by men: the refusal of male patronage. For the heterosexual woman, this may mean the loss of a badly needed intimacy; for both heterosexual women and lesbians, it may well mean the refusal of a decent livelihood.

As noted earlier, women punish themselves too for the failure to conform. The growing literature on women's body size is filled with wrenching confessions of shame from the overweight:

I felt clumsy and huge. I felt that I would knock over furniture, bump into things, tip over chairs, not fit into VW's, especially when people were trying to crowd into the back seat. I felt like I was taking over the whole room. . . . I felt disgusting and like a slob. In the summer I felt hot and sweaty and I knew people saw my sweat as evidence that I was too fat.

I feel so terrible about the way I look that I cut off connection with my body. I operate from the neck up. I do not look in mirrors. I do not want to spend time buying clothes. I do not want to spend time with make-up because it's painful for me to look at myself.[13]

I can no longer bear to look at myself. . . . Whenever I have to stand in front of a mirror to comb my hair I tie a large towel around my neck. Even at night I slip my nightgown on before I take off my blouse and pants. But all this has only made it worse and worse. It's been so long since I've really looked at my body.[14]

The depth of these women's shame is a measure of the extent to which all women have internalized patriarchal standards of bodily acceptability. A fuller examination of what is meant here by "internalization" may shed light on a question posed earlier: Why isn't every woman a feminist?

Something is "internalized" when it gets incorporated into the structure of the self. By "structure of the self" I refer to those modes of perception and of self-perception that allow a self to distinguish itself both from other selves and from things that are not selves. I have described elsewhere how a generalized male witness comes to structure woman's consciousness of herself as a bodily being. This, then, is one meaning of "internalization." The sense of oneself as a distinct and valuable individual is tied not only to the sense of how one is perceived, but also to what one knows, especially to what one knows how to do; this is a second sense of "internalization." Whatever its ultimate effect, discipline can provide the individual upon whom it is imposed with a sense of mastery as well as a secure sense of identity. There is a certain contradiction here: while its imposition may promote a larger disempowerment, discipline may bring with it a certain development of a person's powers. Women, then, like other skilled individuals, have a stake in the perpetuation of their skills, whatever it may have cost to acquire them and quite apart from the question whether, as a gender, they would have been better off had they never had to acquire them in the first place. Hence, feminism, especially a genuinely radical feminism that questions the patriarchal construction of the female body, threatens women with a certain de-skilling, something people normally resist: beyond this, it calls into question that aspect of personal identity that is tied to the development of a sense of competence.

Resistance from this source may be joined by a reluctance to part with the rewards of compliance; further, many women will resist the abandonment of an aesthetic that defines what they take to be beautiful. But there is still another source of resistance, one more subtle, perhaps, but tied once again to questions of identity and internalization. To have a body felt to be "feminine"—a body socially constructed through the appropriate practices—is in most cases crucial to a woman's sense of herself as female and, since persons currently can *be* only as male or female, to her sense of herself as an existing individual. To possess such a body may also be essential to her sense of herself as a sexually desiring and desirable subject. Hence, any political project that aims to dismantle the machinery that turns a female body into a feminine one may well be apprehended by a woman as something that threatens her with desexualization, if not outright annihilation.

The categories of masculinity and femininity do more than assist in the construction of personal identities; they are critical elements in our informal social ontology. This may account to some degree for the otherwise puzzling phenomenon of homophobia and for the revulsion felt by many at the sight of female bodybuilders; neither the homosexual nor the muscular woman can be assimilated easily into the categories that structure everyday life. The radical feminist critique of femininity, then, may pose a threat not only to a woman's sense of her own identity and desirability but to the very structure of her social universe.

Of course, many women *are* feminists, favoring a program of political and economic reform in the struggle to gain equality with men.

But many "reform," or liberal, feminists (indeed, many orthodox Marxists) are committed to the idea that the preservation of a woman's femininity is quite compatible with her struggle for liberation. These thinkers have rejected a normative femininity based upon the notion of "separate spheres" and the traditional sexual division of labor, while accepting at the same time conventional standards of feminine body display. If my analysis is correct, such a feminism is incoherent. Foucault has argued that modern bourgeois democracy is deeply flawed in that it seeks political rights for individuals constituted as unfree by a variety of disciplinary micropowers that lie beyond the realm of what is ordinarily defined as the "political." "The man described for us whom we are invited to free," he says, "is already in himself the effect of a subjection much more profound than himself."[15] If, as I have argued, female subjectivity is constituted in any significant measure in and through the disciplinary practices that construct the feminine body, what Foucault says here of "man" is perhaps even truer of "woman." Marxists have maintained from the first the inadequacy of a purely liberal feminism: we have reached the same conclusion through a different route, casting doubt at the same time on the adequacy of traditional Marxist prescriptions for women's liberation as well. Liberals call for equal rights for women, traditional Marxists for the entry of women into production on an equal footing with men, the socialization of housework, and proletarian revolution; neither calls for the deconstruction of the categories of masculinity and femininity. Femininity as a certain "style of the flesh" will have to be surpassed in the direction of something quite different—not masculinity, which is in many ways only its mirror opposite, but a radical and as yet unimagined transformation of the female body.

VIII

Foucault has argued that the transition from traditional to modern societies has been characterized by a profound transformation in the exercise of power, by what he calls "a reversal of the political axis of individualization."[16] In older authoritarian systems, power was embodied in the person of the monarch and exercised upon a largely anonymous body of subjects; violation of the law was seen as an insult to the royal individual. While the methods employed to enforce compliance in the past were often quite brutal, involving gross assaults against the body, power in such a system operated in a haphazard and discontinuous fashion; much in the social totality lay beyond its reach.

By contrast, modern society has seen the emergence of increasingly invasive apparatuses of power: these exercise a far more restrictive social and psychological control than was heretofore possible. In modern societies, effects of power "circulate through progressively finer channels, gaining access to individuals themselves, to their bodies, their gestures and all their daily actions."[17] Power now seeks to transform the minds of those individuals who might be tempted to resist it, not merely to punish or imprison their bodies. This requires two things: a finer control of the body's time and of its movements—a control that cannot be achieved without ceaseless surveillance and a better understanding of the specific person, of the genesis and nature of his "case." The power these new apparatuses seek to exercise requires a new knowledge of the individual: modern psychology and sociology are born. Whether the new modes of control have charge of correction, production, education, or the provision of welfare, they resemble one another; they exercise power in a bureaucratic mode—faceless, centralized, and pervasive. A reversal has occurred: power has now become anonymous, while the project of control has brought into being a new individuality. In fact, Foucault believes that the operation of power constitutes the very subjectivity of the subject. Here, the image of the Panopticon returns: knowing that he may be observed from the tower at any time, the inmate takes over the job of policing himself. The gaze

that is inscribed in the very structure of the disciplinary institution is internalized by the inmate: modern technologies of behavior are thus oriented toward the production of isolated and self-policing subjects.

Women have their own experience of the modernization of power, one that begins later but follows in many respects the course outlined by Foucault. In important ways, a woman's behavior is less regulated now than it was in the past. She has more mobility and is less confined to domestic space. She enjoys what to previous generations would have been an unimaginable sexual liberty. Divorce, access to paid work outside the home, and the increasing secularization of modern life have loosened the hold over her of the traditional family and, in spite of the current fundamentalist revival, of the church. Power in these institutions was wielded by individuals known to her. Husbands and fathers enforced patriarchal authority in the family. As in the ancien régime, a woman's body was subject to sanctions if she disobeyed. Not Foucault's royal individual but the Divine Individual decreed that her desire be always "unto her husband," while the person of the priest made known to her God's more specific intentions concerning her place and duties. In the days when civil and ecclesiastical authority were still conjoined, individuals formally invested with power were charged with the correction of recalcitrant women whom the family had somehow failed to constrain.

By contrast, the disciplinary power that is increasingly charged with the production of a properly embodied femininity is dispersed and anonymous; there are no individuals formally empowered to wield it; it is, as we have seen, invested in everyone and in no one in particular. This disciplinary power is peculiarly modern: it does not rely upon violent or public sanctions, nor does it seek to restrain the freedom of the female body to move from place to place. For all that, its invasion of the body is well-nigh total: the female body enters "a machinery of power that explores it, breaks it down and rearranges it."[18] The disciplinary techniques through which the "docile bodies" of women are constructed aim at a regulation that is perpetual and exhaustive—a regulation of the body's size and contours, its appetite, posture, gestures and general comportment in space, and the appearance of each of its visible parts.

As modern industrial societies change and as women themselves offer resistance to patriarchy, older forms of domination are eroded. But new forms arise, spread, and become consolidated. Women are no longer required to be chaste or modest, to restrict their sphere of activity to the home, or even to realize their properly feminine destiny in maternity: normative femininity is coming more and more to be centered on woman's body—not its duties and obligations or even its capacity to bear children, but its sexuality, more precisely, its presumed heterosexuality and its appearance. There is, of course, nothing new in women's preoccupation with youth and beauty. What is new is the growing power of the image in a society increasingly oriented toward the visual media. Images of normative femininity, it might be ventured, have replaced the religiously oriented tracts of the past. New too is the spread of this discipline to all classes of women and its deployment throughout the life cycle. What was formerly the specialty of the aristocrat or courtesan is now the routine obligation of every woman, be she a grandmother or a barely pubescent girl.

To subject oneself to the new disciplinary power is to be up-to-date, to be "with-it"; as I have argued, it is presented to us in ways that are regularly disguised. It is fully compatible with the current need for women's wage labor, the cult of youth and fitness, and the need of advanced capitalism to maintain high levels of consumption. Further, it represents a saving in the economy of enforcement: since it is women themselves who practice this discipline on and against their own bodies, men get off scot-free.

The woman who checks her makeup half a dozen times a day to see if her foundation has caked or her mascara has run, who worries that the wind or the rain may spoil her hairdo, who looks frequently to see if her stockings have bagged at the ankle or who, feeling fat, monitors everything she eats, has become, just as surely as the inmate of the Panopticon, a self-policing subject, a self committed to a relentless self-surveillance. This self-surveillance is a form of obedience to patriarchy. It is also the reflection in woman's consciousness of the fact that *she* is under surveillance in ways that *he* is not, that whatever else she may become, she is importantly a body designed to please or to excite. There has been induced in many women, then, in Foucault's words, "a state of conscious and permanent visibility that assures the automatic functioning of power."[19] Since the standards of female bodily acceptability are impossible fully to realize, requiring as they do a virtual transcendence of nature, a woman may live much of her life with a pervasive feeling of bodily deficiency. Hence a tighter control of the body has gained a new kind of hold over the mind.

Foucault often writes as if power constitutes the very individuals upon whom it operates:

The individual is not to be conceived as a sort of elementary nucleus, a primitive atom, a multiple and inert material on which power comes to fasten or against which it happens to strike. . . . In fact, it is already one of the prime effects of power that certain bodies, certain gestures, certain discourses, certain desires, come to be identified and constituted as individuals.[20]

Nevertheless, if individuals were wholly constituted by the power-knowledge regime Foucault describes, it would make no sense to speak of resistance to discipline at all. Foucault seems sometimes on the verge of depriving us of a vocabulary in which to conceptualize the nature and meaning of those periodic refusals of control that, just as much as the imposition of control, mark the course of human history.

Peter Dews accuses Foucault of lacking a theory of the "libidinal body," that is, the body upon which discipline is imposed and whose bedrock impulse toward spontaneity and pleasure might perhaps become the locus of resistance. Do women's "libidinal" bodies, then, not rebel against the pain, constriction, tedium, semistarvation, and constant self-surveillance to which they are currently condemned? Certainly they do, but the rebellion is put down every time a woman picks up her eyebrow tweezers or embarks upon a new diet. The harshness of a regimen alone does not guarantee its rejection, for hardships can be endured if they are thought to be necessary or inevitable.

While "nature," in the form of a "libidinal" body, may not be the origin of a revolt against "culture," domination (and the discipline it requires) are never imposed without some cost. Historically, the forms and occasions of resistance are manifold. Sometimes, instances of resistance appear to spring from the introduction of new and conflicting factors into the lives of the dominated: the juxtaposition of old and new and the resulting incoherence or "contradiction" may make submission to the old ways seem increasingly unnecessary. In the present instance, what may be a major factor in the relentless and escalating objectification of women's bodies—namely, women's growing independence—produces in many women a sense of incoherence that calls into question the meaning and necessity of the current discipline. As women (albeit a small minority of women) begin to realize an unprecedented political, economic, and sexual self-determination, they fall ever more completely under the dominating gaze of patriarchy. It is this paradox, not the "libidinal body," that produces, here and there, pockets of resistance.

In the current political climate, there is no reason to anticipate either widespread resistance to currently fashionable modes of feminine embodiment or joyous experimentation with new "styles of the flesh"; moreover, such novelties would face profound opposition from material and psychological sources identified earlier in this essay (see section VII). In spite of this, a number of oppositional discourses and practices have appeared in recent years. An increasing number of women are "pumping iron," a few with little concern for the limits of body development imposed by current canons of femininity. Women in radical lesbian communities have also rejected hegemonic images of femininity and are struggling to develop a new female aesthetic. A striking feature of such communities is the extent to which they have overcome the oppressive identification of female beauty and desirability with youth: here, the physical features of aging—"character" lines and graying hair—not only do not diminish a woman's attractiveness, they may even enhance it. A popular literature of resistance is growing, some of it analytical and reflective, like Kim Chernin's *The Obsession*, some oriented toward practical self-help, like Marcia Hutchinson's *Transforming Body Image, Learning to Love the Body You Have*. This literature reflects a mood akin in some ways to that other and earlier mood of quiet desperation to which Betty Friedan gave voice in *The Feminine Mystique*. Nor should we forget that a mass-based women's movement is in place in this country that has begun a critical questioning of the meaning of femininity, if not yet in the corporeal presentation of self, then in other domains of life. We women cannot begin the re-vision of our own bodies until we learn to read the cultural messages we inscribe upon them daily and until we come to see that even when the mastery of the disciplines of femininity produces a triumphant result, we are still only women.

NOTES

1. Michel Foucault, *Discipline and Punish: The Birth of the Prison*, trans. Alan Sheridan (New York: Vintage Books, 1979), p. 138.

2. Ibid., p. 147.

3. Ibid., p. 153. Foucault is citing an eighteenth-century military manual, "Ordonnance du Ier janvier 1766 . . . , titre XI, article 2."

4. Ibid., p. 153.

5. Ibid., p. 150.

6. Ibid., p. 200.

7. Ibid., p. 201.

8. Ibid., p. 228.

9. Judith Butler, "Embodied Identity in de Beauvoir's *The Second Sex*" (unpublished manuscript presented to American Philosophical Association, Pacific Division, March 22, 1985), p. 11.

10. Iris Young, "Throwing Like a Girl: A Phenomenology of Feminine Body Comportment, Motility and Spatiality," *Human Studies* 3 (1980): 137–56.

11. Nancy Henley, *Body Politics* (Englewood Cliffs, N.J.: Prentice-Hall, 1977), p. 149.

12. Foucault, *Discipline and Punish*, p. 222: "The general, juridical form that guaranteed a system of rights that were egalitarian in principle was supported by these tiny, everyday, physical mechanisms, by all those systems of micro-power that are essentially non-egalitarian and asymmetrical that we call disciplines."

13. Marcia Millman, *Such a Pretty Face: Being Fat in America* (New York: W. W. Norton, 1980). pp. 80, 195.

14. Kim Chernin, *The Obsession: Reflections on the Tyranny of Slenderness* (New York: Harper and Row, 1981), p. 53.

15. Foucault, *Discipline and Punish*, p. 30.

16. Ibid.

17. Michel Foucault, *Power/Knowledge: Selected Interviews and Other Writings, 1972–1977*, ed. Colin Gordon (Brighton, U.K.: 1980), p. 151. Quoted in Peter Dews, "Power and Subjectivity in Foucault," *New Left Review*, no. 144 (March-April 1984): 17.

18. Foucault, *Discipline and Punish*, p. 138.

19. Ibid., p. 201.

20. Foucault, *Power/Knowledge*, p. 98. In fact, Foucault is not entirely consistent on this point. For an excellent discussion of contending Foucault interpretations and for the difficulty of deriving a consistent set of claims from Foucault's work generally, see Nancy Fraser, "Michel Foucault: A 'Young Conservative'?" *Ethics* 96 (October 1985): 165–84.

The Lesbian Perspective

Julia Penelope

WHAT'S WRONG WITH THIS PICTURE?

Where do we begin to define our Selves? How are Lesbians unique? In spite of our occasional craving to be "like everybody else," we know that we **aren't**. If we were, we wouldn't be Lesbians. Some deep-seated consciousness knows that the world presented to us as "real" is false. There's something wrong with the picture. The Lesbian Perspective originates in our sense of

"difference," however vague the feeling may be, however much we resist that knowledge, and in our certainty that what others seem happy to accept as "real" is seriously flawed. In order to conceive and define ourselves as Lesbians, we have to defy the "wisdom of the ages." Nobody held up a picture of a wonderful dyke for us and said, "You could grow up to be strong and defiant like her." From the day a girl child is born, everyone who exercises control and authority in her life assumes that she will grow up to "fall in love" with a male, as though that were an "accidental" misstep, and that she will inevitably marry one. All the messages she hears about WHO she is and WHO she's ex-

From *Lesbian Philosophies and Cultures*, edited by Jeffner Allen, pp. 90–96, 100–108. Copyright © 1990 by Julia Penelope. Reprinted by permission.

pected to become assume that there's only one kind of love and one kind of sexuality, and that's HETEROSEXUAL. One of those messages informs us that we possess a biologically-determined "maternal instinct"; another croons at us, "Every woman needs a man." Imagine how many Lesbians there would be in the world if we got the kind of air-time and publicity that heterosexuality gets. In spite of liberal feminist proclamations to the contrary, we're a long, long way from Marlo Thomas's world of "Free to be You and Me." What we're "free to be" is heterosexual. That, and that only.

If we must speak of choice, it is the Lesbian who **chooses** to accept the terms of the heterosexual imperative, not the heterosexual. Heterosexuals don't choose their sexuality, because they believe it's "natural," the only way there is to be. Only Lesbians can choose to define ourselves. Being a Lesbian or a heterosexual isn't a matter of "choosing" a lifestyle or a "sexual preference" from the table spread before us by parents, teachers, and other authority figures. There's only one dish on the social menu—heterosexuality—and we are given to understand that we swallow it or go without. The only options we have are those we create for ourselves because we must do so. Who we decide we are isn't a matter of "taste," although some Lesbians do try to acquire a "taste" for heterosexuality.

There's a large difference between "being heterosexual" and "being" a Lesbian. "Being" heterosexual means conforming, living safely, if uncomfortably, within the limits established by men. "Being" a Lesbian means living marginally, often in secrecy, often shamefully, but always as different, as the "deviant." Some Lesbians have sex with men, often marry one, two, three, or four men, have numerous children, and may even live as heterosexuals for some portion of their lives. Lesbians are coming out at every age, and, regardless of how old we are when we decide to act on our self-knowledge, we say, "I've always been a Lesbian." Some Lesbians die without once acting on their deep feelings for other

wimmin. Some Lesbians live someone else's life. Deciding to act on our emotional and sexual attractions to other wimmin is usually a long-drawn-out process of introspection and self-examination that can take years, because the social and emotional pressure surrounding us is so powerful and inescapable. There's no visible, easily accessible support in our society for being Lesbians, which explains why we have so much trouble imagining what "being Lesbian" means. In many ways, we remain opaque even to our Selves because we haven't yet developed a language that describes our experiences.

The differences among us have to do with our level of tolerance for discomfort, how thoroughly we have learned to mistrust and deny our Lesbian selves. Lesbians can deny ourselves endlessly because we are told that we "should." Being heterosexual is the only identity offered, coerced, supported and validated by male society. Male society makes it easy to deny our inner selves, to disbelieve the integrity of our feelings, to discount the necessity of our love for each other, at the same time making it difficult for us to act on our own behalf. Ask a Lesbian who has lived as a heterosexual if she knew she was a Lesbian early in her life, and most will say "yes." Maybe some didn't know the world *Lesbian*, but they'll talk about their childhood love for teachers and girlfriends. Most will say, after they've named themselves Lesbians, "I've always been a Lesbian." Most will say, "I didn't believe there were others like me. I thought I was the only one." This is reinterpretation of experience from a new perspective, *not* revision. Once a Lesbian identifies herself as *lesbian*, she brings all of her earlier experiences with and feelings for other women into focus; she crosses the conceptual line that separates the known (the "safe") of the social validation awarded to heterosexuals and the tabooed unknown of deviance. Crossing into this territory, she begins to remember experiences she had "forgotten," recalling women and her feelings for them that she had analyzed or named differently; she examines memories of her past from a new perspective. Events and experiences that once "made no sense" to her are now full of meanings she had ignored, denied, or discarded. Reconceiving herself as Lesbian, she doesn't change or revise women, events, and experiences in her past, she reinterprets them, understanding them anew from her Lesbian Perspective in the present.

When we fail to be visible to each other, we invalidate the Lesbian Perspective and the meanings it attaches to our experiences. Each of us pays a price for Lesbian invisibility, in our self-esteem, in years of our lives, in energy spent trying to deny our Selves. But it is a fact that millions of us name ourselves "Lesbian" even when we have no sense of a community, when we know no one else who is like us, when we believe we will live as outcasts and alone for the remainder of our lives. How do we become that which is nameless, or, named shameful, sinful, despised? The Lesbian stands against the world created by the male imagination. What **willfulness** we possess when we claim our lives!

The Lesbian Perspective develops directly out of our experiences in the world: How other people treat us as Lesbians, the negative and positive reactions we get in specific situations, what we're told (and believe) we "ought" to feel about ourselves as Lesbians, and the degree of honesty we come to feel we can exercise in our various relationships. What appear to be important differences among Lesbians are survival skills that enable us to survive in hostile territory. Some of us, for example, have had mostly positive or less damaging reactions to our Lesbianism from others who "count" in our estimation. Some Lesbians have experienced varying degrees of acceptance, tolerance, and open-heartedness from their heterosexual families and friends. Some Lesbians say they've had "no problems" in their lives connected with their Lesbianism. Not every Lesbian has had portions of her mind destroyed by drugs and repeated shock treatments, or been disowned by her genetic family, or had to survive on her

own in the streets, but lots of Lesbians have suffered greatly, have been abused, rejected, ridiculed, committed to psychiatric hospitals, jailed, and tortured. For some, the pain of loving as a Lesbian made death a reasonable choice, and many Lesbians have killed themselves rather than endure an existence that seemed to have no hope. Suicide is a valid choice. Whatever our personal experience is, we are always at risk in this society.

CHOOSING OUR SELVES

Being a Lesbian isn't a "choice." We **choose** whether or not we'll live as **who we are.** Naming ourselves *Lesbian* is a decision to ACT on our truest feelings. The Lesbian who decides to live as a heterosexual does so at great cost to her self-esteem. Heterosexuals don't have to question the assumptions on which they construct their lives and then defend them to a hostile society. I can't estimate the damage done to our emotional lives by the dishonesty forced on us by male dogma, but I know how much of my own life has been lies, lies, and more lies.

We live in a society where dishonesty is prized far above honesty, and Lesbians learn the necessity of lying early on. Parents may tell us to "be ourselves," but we find out quickly, after only one or two "experiments," that honesty is punished, that "being ourselves" really means "Be who we want you to be." I know how much of myself I've tried to cover up, deny, and lie about in order to escape the most violent, lethal methods of suppression. The people who represent "society" for us when we're growing up teach us all we need to know about what being an "adult" means. "Growing up" for females in male societies means *choosing men*, and then lying about how "happy" they are. Naming ourselves Lesbian is one of the most significant steps we take to affirm our integrity, to choose honesty over deception, and to become real to ourselves.

This is why the consensus reality of heteropatriarchy describes Lesbianism as "a phase," as something we're supposed to "grow out of." Adopting the protective coloration of heterosexuality is thus equated with "maturity." "Growing up" is a code phrase signalling one's willingness to perform in specific ways: compromise principles, deny feelings, provide **and** accept descriptions one knows to be false, and read along from the heteropatriarchal script. Some are more adept and credible at acting "mature," but adults lie, and they lie all the time—to their children, loved ones, friends, bosses—but mostly to themselves.

Even after we've begun to explore and expand the meanings of our Lesbian Perspective, we bring that learned dishonesty, and our painful experiences about the cost of being honest, into our Lesbian lives. Unlearning years of heterosexual training isn't something we can expect to accomplish quickly or easily. Staying honest about ourselves takes lots of practice. We bring our lessons about the necessity of disguising ourselves, of lying about our innermost feelings, and a sincere reluctance to self-disclose with us when we become members of Lesbian society. The results can be far more damaging to our attempts to communicate and create a community than they are in male society.

On the one hand, lying, not being honest about who we are or how we feel, is a **survival skill** we have developed. We have to lie to get by in most heterosexual contexts. I realize there are some exceptions to this—there are always exceptions to any generalization. But a majority of Lesbians—today, in 1990—are **afraid** to be honest about their Lesbian identity, and with good reason. As an outfront Lesbian, one of the exceptions, I want to validate their fear. It's real, it's based on real or likely experiences, and no Lesbian should feel she's expected to apologize for protecting herself in the only way she knows.

On the other hand, we've internalized the ethic of fear and secrecy so thoroughly that we discover we can't simply shed it when we're in Lesbian contexts. Again, though, previous experiences suggest that self-disclosure and honesty aren't entirely wise even among Lesbians. Too many Lesbians simply don't feel "safe" among other Lesbians on an emotional level, because of previous experiences, and so we're constantly on guard, prepared to protect ourselves. If we're committed to creating Lesbian communities in which we can work together, we have to deal up front with the fact that Lesbians hurt other Lesbians, not just sometimes, but frequently. We can only stop it when we recognize it, name it for what it is, resolve not to do it, and eliminate it as a behavior.

THE BIG PICTURE

It's been a scary ten or eleven years for Lesbians, and many of us have slipped into an uneasy silence or slammed shut the doors of the closets behind us for a second or third time. We need to keep reminding each other that, *as far as we know,* **nothing like us has ever happened before**. *As far as we know,* there has never been a Lesbian Movement, and we are *global* in our connectedness. Too many Lesbians have learned, again, to think of themselves as "small," "tiny," insignificant. We've heard so much about "broader issues" and "the big picture" that some may think that the Lesbian Perspective is a "narrow" one, restricted to an "insignificant" minority.

"Narrow," when applied to concrete, physical dimensions, is used positively, because it means 'slender' in width, and being 'slender' in our society has become a moral imperative for those born female. But "narrow," used abstractly to describe ideas, implies a primarily negative evaluation of whatever concepts it's used of. We speak, for example, of "narrow opinions," "narrow perspectives," "narrow concerns," and we're much taken by points of view that advertise themselves as part of "the broader picture," as affording us "a broader perspective," a "wider scope," or an opportunity to join the "larger revolution." The word "narrow" is used to trivialize, diminish, and discredit a point of view that some people, usually those with socially-validated power, find threatening, repugnant, and downright outrageous. It is my intention to be outrageous. The "Lesbian Perspective" is certainly no less "real" or compelling than the dominant perspective of the white, heterosexual majority, and it is by no means as "narrow" in the negative sense of that word. We rightly avoid the "straight and narrow path."

Our unacknowledged allegiance to male thought patterns can hypnotize us into passivity, and men frequently succeed in paralyzing us with that word (and others). There is nothing "narrow" about being and thinking **Lesbian**. What I'm warming up to here is a discussion of "category width" in English and where we think we might "fit" into the categories of the man-made framework. The language most Lesbians in the U.S. speak, by choice or coercion, is English (Native American, Black, and Hispanic Lesbians know first-hand about the cultural imperialism of imposed language), and it's the semantic structure of English that binds our minds, squishing our ideas into tidy, binary codes: this/not-this, female/male, big/small, Black/white, poor/rich, fat/thin, seeing/unseeing, powerless/powerful, wide/narrow, guilty/innocent. These are narrow concepts in the most negative sense of the word, but they are the semantic basis of the pale male perspective, and we need to understand the conceptual territory those semantic categories map before we can set about the task of creating a new map that charts the territory of the Lesbian Perspective.

Learning a first language socializes us, and we're dependent creatures when our minds are guided into the conceptual grooves created by the map of the territory men want us to follow. The language forces us to perceive the world as men present it to us. If we describe some behaviors as "feminine" and others as "masculine," we're perceiving ourselves in male terms. Or, we fail to perceive what is not described for us and fall back on male constructs,

such as "butch" and "femme," as inherently explanatory labels for our self-conceptions.

Those of us raised speaking English weren't offered any choice in the matter. While we were passive in the indoctrination process for the first few years, however, there comes a time when we have to put aside the fact that we began as innocent victims and undertake the active process of self-reclamation that starts with understanding what happened to us and questioning the conceptual premises on which male societies are based. Learning to think around categorial givens is hard, but it's something we have to do in order to think well of ourselves. If we refuse to do this, we abandon our Selves.

What is called "consensus reality" is the male-defined, male-described version of "what is," and we are obliged to live around, under, and sometimes within what men say is "reality," even as we strive to conceive and define a Lesbian "consensus reality." The duality of our position as Lesbians, simultaneously oppressed by a society in which we are unwanted and marginal and envisioning for ourselves a culture defined by our values, with Lesbian identity at its core, is, I maintain, a position of strength if we take advantage of it.

First, we must undertake the tedious process of examining and re-examining **every** aspect of how we've been taught to "think," including the process of thinking itself. Every one of us raised in an English-speaking household was programmed to perceive the world, and ourselves in the world, according to the special map of the pale male perspective. Any map is always, and only, a **partial description** of the territory it claims to chart. Each map draws attention only to those topographical features that the map creator thinks are "relevant" or "significant"; each map creator perceives only some of the aspects of the territory while other, perhaps equally important features, remain invisible, unperceived. Some things are left out on purpose, others are distorted. Black and dark, for example, are given negative values in the pale male conceptual structure, while white and light are assigned positive values; being able to see is a "good thing"; not being able to see is a "bad thing." These descriptions, and the values attached to them, are not "the nature of the world," and that is not a coincidence. Whatever conceptual changes are eventually condoned by male culture can occur only by enlarging existing category widths, in particular the referential scope of words like *people* and *gay*. The semantic categories themselves don't change; they aren't allowed to change. They expand and contract, but the essential thought structures remain the same.

One of our difficulties with describing a Lesbian consensus reality is a language problem, the contradictory labels we use to name ourselves, a terminology that's sometimes useful, and often divisive. The way we name ourselves reflects how we understand what we mean in the world. We call ourselves, for example, "people," "human beings," "women," "gays," "Lesbians," "Dykes." Because we're biologically categorized as female, it seems meaningful to say that, by inclusion with heterosexual women, we're oppressed as "women," and our experience of socialization confirms this category overlap. Likewise, because we aren't hetero, we're also oppressed as "homosexuals," so some Lesbians identify with gay men, in which case they call themselves "gay women," as I did for many years. Our invisibility, even to ourselves, is at least partially due to the fact that our identity is subsumed by two groups: women and gays. As a result, Lesbian issues seem to find their way, by neglect or elimination, to the bottom of both liberation agendas. The liberation of Lesbians is supposed to wait for the liberation of all women, or be absorbed and evaporate into the agenda compiled by gay men. Instead of creating free space for ourselves, we allow men to oppress us invisibly in both categories, as "women" or as "gays," without even the token dignity of being named "Lesbians." How we name ourselves determines how visible we are, even to each other.

If we allow ourselves to imagine ourselves as something other than "woman" or "gay," if we try to conceive of our Selves beyond those labels, what comes into our minds? Is it nothing, or is it some-thing? Even if it is hazy, vague, without clear definition, isn't it something we know but haven't yet been able to articulate? The issue here is making explicit the basis of our prioritizing, which is the idea that we are "sub-" somebody else. I think we are much, much more if we choose our Selves. The problem, as I identify it, is calling ourselves *women*. Monique Wittig (1988), and others, have argued that the category *woman* is a man-made category that serves men's purposes. In this case, the label *woman* diffuses Lesbian movement toward our Selves, to divert our attention from Lesbian issues and Lesbian needs. The label shifts our focus, directing our attention away form Lesbian community. As soon as we name ourselves Lesbians, we step outside of the category 'woman'. What we experience as Lesbians and identify as "women's oppression" is the socialization process that tried to coerce us into 'womanhood'. As a result of this tailoring of our identities, when we change categories from 'woman' to 'lesbian', we're still oppressed as 'female' and oppressed for daring to be 'non-woman'. While both Lesbians and hetero women experience misogyny as biological females, our experience of that oppression is very different.

The L-word continually disappears into the labels "gay" and "woman," along with our energy, our money, and our hope. So much Lesbian creativity and activity is called "women's this" or "gay that," making Lesbians invisible and giving heterosexual women or gay men credit for what they can't imagine and haven't accomplished. We need to think LESBIAN. We need to think DYKE. We need to stop being complacent about our self-erasure.

The male map cannot be trusted because the territory it describes isn't a healthy place for us to live in. Accepting male descriptions of the world endangers Lesbians. We can fight for inclusion within already sanctioned categories, such as *people, human being,* or *woman,* thereby forcing other speakers to enlarge them, or we can remain outside of patriarchally given categories and endeavor to construct a different, more accurate map of the Lesbian conceptual territory. We have internalized a description of the world that erodes our self-esteem, damages our self-image, and poisons our capacity for self-love. If the children we were lacked options for the process of self-creation, the Lesbians we've become have the potential, as well as the responsibility, for redefining ourselves, learning to perceive the world in new and different ways from what we were taught, and setting about making maps that accurately describe the territory of our envisioning.

We can choose whether or not we will conform to heterosexual values, and even the degree to which we'll conform to the map men have imposed on reality. How we choose to deal with the defining categories of male culture places us within its boundaries or at its periphery. (See my essay, "Heteropatriarchal Semantics: 'Just Two Kinds of People in the World'," for an analysis of these defining categories.) We are never "outside" the reach of society, because even the negative evaluation of who we are can limit and control our lives. How we describe for ourselves that first wary step into an uncharted world determines how we think of ourselves as Lesbians. The Lesbian situation is essentially **ambiguous**, and that ambiguity provides the foundation of the Lesbian perspective. We must start from where we are.

TERRA INCOGNITA

Deciding to act on our Lesbian perceptions requires each of us to conceive ourselves as someone other than what male society has said we are. The Lesbian process of self-definition, however long it takes, begins with the recogni-

tion and certainty that our perceptions are fundamentally accurate, regardless of what male societies say. This is a STRONG place in us. In order to trust ourselves, we have to be able to push through the lies and contradictions presented to us as "truths," cast them aside, and stand, for that moment, in our own clarity. Every Lesbian takes that step into *terra incognita,* the undescribed or falsely described, the "unknown," beyond the limits posted by the pale male map of reality. Picture for yourself the map of the "known" world presented to us every moment, every day of our lives. Label that map HETEROPATRIARCHY out to the very neatly trimmed edges. Now read the warning signs along the edge: "Dangerous," "monstrous," "sick," "sinful," "illegal," "unsafe," "Keep Out! Trespassers will be violated!" Remember how long you deliberated with yourself before stepping across that boundary, before you decided you had to ignore the warning signs and take your chances in an ill-defined geography.

It's the clarity of that moment, the confidence of self-creation, that creates the "euphoria" so many Lesbians experience when we first come out. We do not forget that moment of clarity, ever. Lesbians think and behave differently because we've had to fight constantly to establish and maintain our identity in spite of covert and overt attempts, some of them violent, all of them degrading, to coerce us into heterosexuality. The Lesbian Self must stand alone, sometimes for years, against the force of the heterosexual imperative, until she can find other Lesbians who will support and affirm her. The out Lesbian has denied the validity of what men call "reality" in order to be Her Self. We do think differently. We perceive the world as aliens, as outcasts. No matter how hard some Lesbians try to "fit in," pale male societies define us as outside the boundary of the categories that maintain its coherence. We are made outcasts, but we can empower our Selves on that ground.

Although we may look back at times with yearning toward the heterosexual land of make-believe, we know that delusion for what it is: a man-made smog that pollutes and poisons all life. We must choose our own clarity, our willfulness, and reject the orthodoxy, "right-thinking," of men. Being Lesbian is nonconforming. The Lesbian perspective demands heterodoxy, deviant and unpopular thinking, requires us to love ourselves for being outcasts, not in spite of it, to create for ourselves the grounds of our being. The Lesbian Perspective isn't something we acquire as soon as we step out of our closets. It's as much a process of unlearning as it is learning. It's something we have to work at, nurture, encourage, and develop. The Lesbian Perspective is furious self-creation.

If we can imagine ourselves into being, if we can refuse to accept the labels and descriptions of men, the "possibilities **are** endless." We **are** outcasts from male society. We have no choice in that. What we can choose is how we define ourselves with respect to our outcast status. The Lesbian Perspective always asks "unpopular" questions. They're not popular because they threatened the interior structure of societies erected by men. What, exactly, does the Lesbian Perspective look like? Because we're already living in a way that men say is impossible, we gradually shed the dichotomies and distinctions we learned as children. The labels, names, and compartmentalizations that accompany those ways come to have less and less relevance in our thought processes, and we find new ways of interpreting our experience in the world because we perceive it differently. What we once memorized and accepted as "facts" no longer accurately describes our perceptions of reality. We realize that what we were taught to think was "real" or "natural" are only man-made constructs imposed on acts and events,

ready-made representations of thoughts and feelings that we can, and must, reject. This is a difficult, gradual, uncertain process only because male societies don't want us to enjoy being outcasts. It's definitely **not** in the interests of men for us to like ourselves. Although it's men who established the boundaries that made us outcasts, what counts is how we organize that information in our minds and act on it in our lives.

The Lesbian Perspective challenges what heterosexuals choose to believe is "fact." As our joy in being outcasts expands, so does our ability to ask dangerous questions and discover magical answers. We have no "givens" beyond that which is "other than": "deviant," "abnormal," "unnatural," "queer," false descriptions we begin with and cannot afford to forget. Indeed, we should wear them proudly. But our major endeavor must be self-definition. We have much to learn yet about ourselves, *our* culture, and we have new maps to draw that show the significant features of our worlds. The Lesbian Perspective makes it possible to challenge the accuracy of male consensus reality, and to create a reality that is Lesbian-defined and Lesbian-sustaining. Once we learn to perceive the world from our own perspective, outside the edges of the pale male map, we'll find it not only recognizable, but familiar.

REFERENCES

Penelope, Julia. "Heteropatriarchal Semantics: 'Just Two Kinds of People in the World,'" *Lesbian Ethics* 2, 2 (Fall, 1986) 58–80.

Wittig, Monique. "One is Not Born a Woman," in *For Lesbians Only*, eds. Sarah Lucia Hoagland and Julia Penelope. London: Onlywomen Press, 1988, 439–48.

Mammies, Matriarchs, and Other Controlling Images

Patricia Hill Collins

Called Matriarch, Emasculator and Hot Momma. Sometimes Sister, Pretty Baby, Auntie, Mammy and Girl. Called Unwed Mother, Welfare Recipient and Inner City Consumer. The Black American Woman has had to admit that while nobody knew the troubles she saw, everybody, his brother and his dog, felt qualified to explain her, even to herself.

TRUDIER HARRIS, *From Mammies to Militants* (1982), 4

Race, class, and gender oppression could not continue without powerful ideological justifications for their existence. As Cheryl Gilkes contends, "Black women's assertiveness and their use of every expression of racism to launch multiple assaults against the entire fabric of inequality have been a consistent, multifaceted threat to the status quo. As punishment, Black women have been assaulted with a variety of negative images" (1983, 294). Portraying African-American women as stereotypical mammies, matriarchs, welfare recipients, and hot mommas has been essential to the political economy of domination fostering Black women's oppression. Challenging these controlling images has long been a core theme in Black feminist thought.

As part of a generalized ideology of domination, these controlling images of Black womanhood take on special meaning because the authority to define these symbols is a major instrument of power. In order to exercise power, elite white men and their representatives must be in a position to manipulate appropriate symbols concerning Black women. They may do so by exploiting already existing symbols, or they may create new ones relevant to their needs. Hazel Carby suggests that the objective of stereotypes is "not to reflect or represent a reality but to function as a disguise, or mystification, of objective social relations" (1987, 22). These controlling images are designed to make racism, sexism, and poverty appear to be natural, normal, and an inevitable part of everyday life.

CONTROLLING IMAGES AND BLACK WOMEN'S OPPRESSION

"Black women emerged from slavery firmly enshrined in the consciousness of white America as 'Mammy' and the 'bad black woman,'" contends Cheryl Gilkes (1983, 294). The dominant ideology of the slave era fostered the creation of four interrelated, socially constructed controlling images of Black womanhood, each reflecting the dominant group's interest in maintaining Black women's subordination. Given that both Black and white women were important to slavery's continuation, the prevailing ideology functioned to mask contradictions in social relations affecting all women. According to the cult of true womanhood, "true" women possessed four cardinal virtues: piety, purity, submissiveness, and domesticity. Elite white women and those of the emerging middle class were encouraged to aspire to these virtues. African-American women encountered a different set of controlling images. The sexual ideology of the period as is the case today "confirmed the differing material circumstances of these two groups of women . . . by balancing opposing definitions of womanhood and motherhood, each dependent on the other for its existence" (Carby 1987, 25).

The first controlling image applied to African-American women is that of the mammy—the faithful, obedient domestic servant. Created to justify the economic exploitation of house slaves and sustained to explain Black women's long-standing restriction to domestic service, the mammy image represents the normative yardstick used to evaluate all Black women's behavior. By loving, nurturing, and caring for her white children and "family" better than her own, the mammy symbolizes the dominant group's perceptions of the ideal Black female relationship to elite white male power. Even though she may be well loved and may wield considerable authority in her white "family," the mammy still knows her "place" as obedient servant. She has accepted her subordination.

Black women intellectuals have aggressively deconstructed the image of African-American women as contented mammies by challenging traditional views of Black women domestics. Literary critic Trudier Harris's volume *From Mammies to Militants: Domestics in Black American Literature* investigates prominent differences in how Black women have been portrayed by others in literature and how they portray themselves. In her work on the difficulties faced by Black women leaders, Rhetaugh Dumas describes how Black women

executives are hampered by being treated as mammies and penalized if they do not appear warm and nurturing. But despite these works, the mammy image lives on in scholarly and popular culture. Audre Lorde's account of a shopping trip offers a powerful example of its tenacity: "I wheel my two-year-old daughter in a shopping cart through a supermarket in . . . 1967, and a little white girl riding past in her mother's cart calls out excitedly, 'Oh look, Mommy, a baby maid!' "[1]

The mammy image is central to interlocking systems of race, gender, and class oppression. Since efforts to control African-American family life require perpetuating the symbolic structures of racial oppression, the mammy image is important because it aims to shape Black women's behavior as mothers. As the members of African-American families who are most familiar with the skills needed for Black accommodation, Black women are encouraged to transmit to their own children the deference behavior many are forced to exhibit in mammy roles. By teaching Black children their assigned place in white power structures, Black women who internalize the mammy image potentially become effective conduits for perpetuating racial oppression. In addition, employing mammies buttresses the racial superiority of white women employers and weds them more closely to their fathers, husbands, and sons as sources of elite white male power.

The mammy image also serves a symbolic function in maintaining gender oppression. Black feminist critic Barbara Christian argues that images of Black womanhood serve as a reservoir for the fears of Western culture, "a dumping ground for those female functions a basically Puritan society could not confront" (1985, 2). Juxtaposed against the image of white women promulgated through the cult of true womanhood, the mammy image as the Other symbolizes the oppositional difference of mind/body and culture/nature thought to distinguish Black women from everyone else.

Christian comments on the mammy's gender significance: "All the functions of mammy are magnificently physical. They involve the body as sensuous, as funky, the part of woman that white southern America was profoundly afraid of. Mammy, then, harmless in her position of slave, unable because of her all-giving nature to do harm, is needed as an image, a surrogate to contain all those fears of the physical female" (1985, 2). The mammy image buttresses the ideology of the cult of true womanhood, one in which sexuality and fertility are severed. "Good" white mothers are expected to deny their female sexuality and devote their attention to the moral development of their offspring. In contrast, the mammy image is one of an asexual woman, a surrogate mother in blackface devoted to the development of a white family.

No matter how loved they were by their white "families," Black women domestic workers remained poor because they were economically exploited. The restructured post-World War II economy in which African-American women moved from service in private homes to jobs in the low-paid service sector has produced comparable economic exploitation. Removing Black women's labor from African-American families and exploiting it denies Black extended family units the benefits of either decent wages or Black women's unpaid labor in their homes. Moreover, many white families in both the middle class and working class are able to maintain their class position because they have long used Black women as a source of cheap labor. The mammy image is designed to mask this economic exploitation of social class.

For reasons of economic survival, African-American women may play the mammy role in paid work settings. But within African-American communities these same women often teach their own children something quite different. Bonnie Thornton Dill's work on child-rearing patterns among Black domestics shows that while the participants in her study showed def-

erence behavior at work, they discouraged their children from believing that they should be deferent to whites and encouraged their children to avoid domestic work. Barbara Christian's analysis of the mammy in Black slave narratives reveals that, "unlike the white southern image of mammy, she is cunning, prone to poisoning her master, and not at all content with her lot" (1985, 5).

The fact that the mammy image cannot control Black women's behavior as mothers is tied to the creation of the second controlling image of Black womanhood. Though a more recent phenomenon, the image of the Black matriarch fulfills similar functions in explaining Black women's placement in interlocking systems of race, gender, and class oppression. Ironically, Black scholars such as William E. B. DuBois and E. Franklin Frazier described the connections among higher rates of female-headed households in African-American communities, the importance that women assume in Black family networks, and the persistence of Black poverty. However, neither scholar interpreted Black women's centrality in Black families as a *cause* of African-American social class status. Both saw so-called matriarchal families as an *outcome* of racial oppression and poverty. During the eras when Dubois and Frazier wrote, the oppression of African-Americans was so total that control was maintained without the controlling image of matriarch. But what began as a muted theme in the works of these earlier Black scholars grew into a full-blown racialized image in the 1960s, a time of significant political and economic mobility for African-Americans. Racialization involves attaching racial meaning to a previously racially unclassified relationship, social practice, or group. Prior to the 1960s, female-headed households were certainly higher in African-American communities, but an ideology racializing female-headedness as a causal feature of Black poverty had not emerged. Moreover, "the public depiction of Black women as unfeminine, castrating matriarchs came at precisely the same moment that the feminist movement was advancing its public critique of American patriarchy" (Gilkes 1983, 296).

While the mammy typifies the Black mother figure in white homes, the matriarch symbolizes the mother figure in Black homes. Just as the mammy represents the "good" Black mother, the matriarch symbolizes the "bad" Black mother. The modern Black matriarchy thesis contends that African-American women fail to fulfill their traditional "womanly" duties. Spending too much time away from home, these working mothers ostensibly cannot properly supervise their children and are a major contributing factor to their children's school failure. As overly aggressive, unfeminine women, Black matriarchs allegedly emasculate their lovers and husbands. These men, understandably, either desert their partners or refuse to marry the mothers of their children. From an elite white male standpoint, the matriarch is essentially a failed mammy, a negative stigma applied to those African-American women who dared to violate the image of the submissive, hard-working servant.

Black women intellectuals examining the role of women in African-American families discover few matriarchs and even fewer mammies. Instead they portray African-American mothers as complex individuals who often show tremendous strength under adverse conditions. In *A Raisin in the Sun*, the first play presented on Broadway written by a Black woman, Lorraine Hansberry examines the struggles of widow Lena Younger to actualize her dream of purchasing a home for her family. In *Brown Girl, Brownstones*, novelist Paule Marshall presents Mrs. Boyce, a Black mother negotiating a series of relationships with her husband, her daughters, the women in her community, and the work she must perform outside her home. Ann Allen Shockley's *Loving Her* depicts the struggle of a lesbian mother trying to balance her needs for self-actualization with the

pressures of child-rearing in a homophobic community. Like these fictional analyses, Black women's scholarship on Black single mothers also challenges the matriarchy thesis.

Like the mammy, the image of the matriarch is central to interlocking systems of race, gender, and class oppression. Portraying African-American women as matriarchs allows the dominant group to blame Black women for the success or failure of Black children. Assuming that Black poverty is passed on intergenerationally via value transmission in families, an elite white male standpoint suggests that Black children lack the attention and care allegedly lavished on white, middle-class children and that this deficiency seriously retards Black children's achievement. Such a view diverts attention from the political and economic inequality affecting Black mothers and children and suggests that anyone can rise from poverty if he or she only received good values at home. Those African-Americans who remain poor are blamed for their own victimization. Using Black women's performance as mothers to explain Black economic subordination links gender ideology to explanations of class subordination.

The source of the matriarch's failure is her inability to model appropriate gender behavior. In the post-World War II era, increasing numbers of white women entered the labor market, limited their fertility, and generally challenged their proscribed roles in white patriarchal institutions. The image of the Black matriarch emerged at that time as a powerful symbol for both Black and white women of what can go wrong if white patriarchal power is challenged. Aggressive, assertive women are penalized—they are abandoned by their men, end up impoverished, and are stigmatized as being unfeminine.

The image of the matriarch also supports racial oppression. Much social science research implicitly uses gender relations in African-American communities as one putative measure of Black cultural disadvantage. For example, the Moynihan Report contends that slavery destroyed

Black families by creating reversed roles for men and women. Black family structures are seen as being deviant because they challenge the patriarchal assumptions underpinning the construct of the ideal "family." Moreover, the absence of Black patriarchy is used as evidence for Black cultural inferiority. Black women's failure to conform to the cult of true womanhood can then be identified as one fundamental source of Black cultural deficiency. Cheryl Gilkes posits that the emergence of the matriarchal image occurred as a counter-ideology to efforts by African-Americans and women who were confronting interlocking systems of race, gender, and class oppression: "The image of dangerous Black women who were also deviant castrating mothers divided the Black community at a critical period in the Black liberation struggle and created a wider gap between the worlds of Black and white women at a critical period in women's history" (1983, 297).

Taken together, images of the mammy and the matriarch place African-American women in an untenable position. For Black women workers in domestic work and other occupations requiring long hours and/or substantial emotional labor, becoming the ideal mammy means precious time and energy spent away from husbands and children. But being employed when Black men have difficulty finding steady work exposes African-American women to the charge that Black women emasculate Black men by failing to be submissive, dependent, "feminine" women. Moreover, Black women's financial contributions to Black family well-being have also been cited as evidence supporting the matriarchy thesis. Many Black women are the sole support of their families, and labeling these women "matriarchs" erodes their self-confidence and ability to confront oppression. In essence, African-American women who must work are labeled mammies, then are stigmatized again as matriarchs for being strong figures in their own homes.

A third, externally defined, controlling image of Black womanhood—that of the welfare mother—appears tied to Black women's increasing dependence on the post-World War II welfare state. Essentially an updated version of the breeder woman image created during slavery, this image provides an ideological justification for efforts to harness Black women's fertility to the needs of a changing political economy.

During slavery the breeder woman image portrayed Black women as more suitable for having children than white women. By claiming that Black women were able to produce children as easily as animals, this objectification of Black women as the Other provided justification for interference in the reproductive rights of enslaved Africans. Slaveowners wanted enslaved Africans to "breed" because every slave child born represented a valuable unit of property, another unit of labor, and, if female, the prospects for more slaves. The externally defined, controlling image of the breeder woman served to justify slaveowner intrusion into Black women's decisions about fertility.

The post-World War II political economy has offered African-Americans rights not available in former historical periods. African-Americans have successfully acquired basic political and economic protections from a greatly expanded welfare state, particularly Social Security, Aid to Families with Dependent Children, unemployment compensation, affirmative action, voting rights, antidiscrimination legislation, and the minimum wage. In spite of sustained opposition by Republican administrations in the 1980s, these programs allow many African-Americans to reject the subsistence-level, exploitative jobs held by their parents and grandparents. Job export, deskilling, and increased use of illegal immigrants have all been used to replace the loss of cheap, docile Black labor. The large numbers of undereducated, unemployed African-Americans, most of whom are women and children, who inhabit inner cities cannot be forced to work. From the standpoint of the dominant group, they no longer represent cheap labor but instead signify a costly threat to political and economic stability.

Controlling Black women's fertility in such a political economy becomes important. The image of the welfare mother fulfills this function by labeling as unnecessary and even dangerous to the values of the country the fertility of women who are not white and middle class. A closer look at this controlling image reveals that it shares some important features with its mammy and matriarch counterparts. Like the matriarch, the welfare mother is labeled a bad mother. But unlike the matriarch, she is not too aggressive—on the contrary, she is not aggressive enough. While the matriarch's unavailability contributed to her children's poor socialization, the welfare mother's accessibility is deemed the problem. She is portrayed as being content to sit around and collect welfare, shunning work and passing on her bad values to her offspring. The image of the welfare mother represents another failed mammy, one who is unwilling to become "de mule uh de world."

The image of the welfare mother provides ideological justifications for interlocking systems of race, gender, and class oppression. African-Americans can be racially stereotyped as being lazy by blaming Black welfare mothers for failing to pass on the work ethic. Moreover, the welfare mother has no male authority figure to assist her. Typically portrayed as an unwed mother, she violates one cardinal tenet of Eurocentric masculinist thought: she is a woman alone. As a result, her treatment reinforces the dominant gender ideology positing that a woman's true worth and financial security should occur through heterosexual marriage. Finally, in the post-World War II political economy, one of every three African-American families is officially classified as poor. With such high levels of Black poverty, welfare state policies supporting poor Black mothers and their children have become increasingly expensive. Creating the controlling image of the welfare mother and stigmatizing her as the cause of her own poverty and that of African-American communities shifts the angle of vision away from structural sources of poverty and blames the victims themselves. The image of the welfare mother thus provides ideological justification for the dominant group's interest in limiting the fertility of Black mothers who are seen as producing too many economically unproductive children.

The fourth controlling image—the Jezebel, whore, or sexually aggressive woman—is central in this nexus of elite white male images of Black womanhood because efforts to control Black women's sexuality lie at the heart of Black women's oppression. The image of Jezebel originated under slavery when Black women were portrayed as being, to use Jewelle Gomez's words, "sexually aggressive wet nurses." Jezebel's function was to relegate all Black women to the category of sexually aggressive women, thus providing a powerful rationale for the widespread sexual assaults by white men typically reported by Black slave women. Yet Jezebel served another function. If Black slave women could be portrayed as having excessive sexual appetites, then increased fertility should be the expected outcome. By suppressing the nurturing that African-American women might give their own children which would strengthen Black family networks, and by forcing Black women to work in the field or "wet nurse" white children, slaveowners effectively tied the controlling images of Jezebel and Mammy to the economic exploitation inherent in the institution of slavery.

The fourth image of the sexually denigrated Black woman is the foundation underlying elite white male conceptualizations of the mammy, matriarch, and welfare mother. Connecting all three is the common theme of Black women's sexuality. Each image transmits clear messages about the proper links among female sexuality, fertility, and Black women's roles in the political economy. For example, the mammy, the only somewhat positive figure, is a desexed individual. The mammy is typically portrayed as overweight, dark, and with characteristically African features—in brief, as an unsuitable sexual partner for white men. She is asexual and therefore is free to become a surrogate mother to the children she acquired not through her own sexuality. The mammy represents the clearest example of the split between sexuality and motherhood present in Eurocentric masculinist thought. In contrast, both the matriarch and the welfare mother are sexual beings. But their sexuality is linked to their fertility, and this link forms one fundamental reason they are negative images. The matriarch represents the sexually aggressive woman, one who emasculates Black men because she will not permit them to assume roles as Black patriarchs. She refuses to be passive and thus is stigmatized. Similarly, the welfare mother represents a woman of low morals and uncontrolled sexuality, factors identified as the cause of her impoverished state. In both cases Black female control over sexuality and fertility is conceptualized as antithetical to elite white male interests.

Taken together, these four prevailing interpretations of Black womanhood form a nexus of elite white male interpretations of Black female sexuality and fertility. Moreover, by meshing smoothly with systems of race, class, and gender oppression, they provide effective ideological justifications for racial oppression, the politics of gender subordination, and the economic exploitation inherent in capitalist economies.

CONTROLLING IMAGES IN EVERYDAY LIFE: COLOR, HAIR TEXTURE, AND STANDARDS OF BEAUTY

Like everyone else, African-American women learn the meaning of race, gender, and social class without obvious teaching or conscious learning. The controlling images of Black women are not simply grafted onto existing social institutions but are so pervasive that even though the images themselves change in the popular imagination, Black women's portrayal as the Other persists. Particular meanings, stereotypes, and myths can change, but the overall ideology of domination itself seems to be an enduring feature of interlocking systems of race, gender, and class oppression.

African-American women encounter this ideology through a range of unquestioned, daily experiences. But when the contradictions between Black women's self-definitions and everyday treatment are heightened, controlling images become increasingly visible. Karen Russell, the daughter of basketball great Bill Russell, describes how racial stereotypes affect her:

How am I supposed to react to well-meaning, good, liberal white people who say things like: "You know, Karen, I don't understand what all the fuss is about. You're one of my good friends, and I never think of you as black." Implicit in such a remark is, "I think of you as white," or perhaps just, "I don't think of your race at all." (Russell 1987, 22).

Ms. Russell was perceptive enough to see that remarks intended to compliment her actually insulted African-Americans. As the Others, African-Americans are assigned all of the negative characteristics opposite and inferior to those reserved for whites. By claiming that Ms. Russell is not really "black," her friends unintentionally validate this system of racial meanings and encourage her to internalize those images.

Although Black women typically resist being objectified as the Other, these controlling images remain powerful influences on our relationships with whites, Black men, and one another. Dealing with issues of beauty—particularly skin color, facial features, and hair texture—is one concrete example of how controlling images denigrate African-American women. A children's rhyme often sung in Black communities proclaims:

Now, if you're white you're all right,
If you're brown, stick around,
But if you're black, Git back! Git back! Git back!

Externally defined standards of beauty long applied to African-American women claim that no matter how intelligent, educated, or "beautiful" a Black woman may be, those Black women whose features and skin color are most African must "git back." Blue-eyed, blond, thin white women could not be considered beautiful without the Other—Black women with classical African features of dark skin, broad noses, full lips, and kinky hair.

Race, gender, and sexuality converge on this issue of evaluating beauty. Judging white women by their physical appearance and attractiveness to men objectifies them. But their white skin and straight hair privilege them in a system in which part of the basic definition of whiteness is its superiority to blackness. Black men's blackness penalizes them. But because they are men, their self-definitions are not as heavily dependent on their physical attractiveness as those of all women. But African-American women experience the pain of never being able to live up to externally defined standards of beauty—standards applied to us by white men, white women, Black men, and, most painfully, one another.

Exploring how externally defined standards of beauty affect Black women's self-images, our relationships with one another, and our relationships with Black men has been one recurring theme in Black feminist thought. The long-standing attention of musicians, writers, and artists to this theme reveals African-American women's deep feelings concerning skin color, hair texture, and standards of beauty. In her autobiography, Maya Angelou records her painful realization that the only way she could become truly beautiful was to become white:

Wouldn't they be surprised when one day I woke out of my black ugly dream, and my real hair, which was long and blond, would take the place of the kinky mass that Momma wouldn't let me straighten? . . . Then they would understand why I had never picked up a Southern accent, or spoke the common slang, and why I had to be forced to eat pigs' tails and snouts. Because I was really white and because a cruel fairy stepmother . . . had turned me into a too-big Negro girl, with nappy black hair. (Angelou 1969, 2).

Gwendolyn Brooks also explores the meaning of skin color and hair texture for Black women. During Brooks's childhood, having African features was so universally denigrated that she writes, "when I was a child, it did not occur to me even once, that the black in which I was encased . . . would be considered, one day, beautiful" (Brooks 1972, 37). Early on Brooks learned that a clear pecking order existed among African-Americans, one based on one's closeness to whiteness. As a member of the "Lesser Blacks," those farthest from white, Brooks saw first-hand the difference in treatment of her group and the "Brights":

One of the first "world"-truths revealed to me when I at last became a member of SCHOOL was that, to be socially successful, a little girl must be Bright (of skin). It was better if your hair was curly, too—or at least Good Grade (Good Grade implied, usually, no involvement with the Hot Comb)—but Bright you marvelously *needed* to be. (1972, 37)

This division of African-Americans into two categories—the "Brights" and the "Lesser Blacks"—affects dark-skinned and light-skinned women differently. Darker women face being judged inferior and receiving the treatment afforded "too-big Negro girls with nappy hair." Institutions controlled by whites clearly show a preference for lighter-skinned Blacks, discriminating against darker ones or against any African-Americans who appear to reject white images of beauty. Sonia Sanchez reports, "sisters tell me today that when they go out for jobs they straighten their hair because if they go in with their hair natural or braided, they probably won't get the job."

Sometimes the pain most deeply felt is the pain that Black women inflict on one another. Marita Golden's mother told her not to play in the sun because "you gonna have to get a light husband anyway, for the sake of your children" (1983, 24). In *Color*, a short film exploring the impact of skin color on Black women's lives, the dark-skinned character's mother tries to get her to sit still for the hot comb, asking "don't you want your hair flowing like your friend Rebecca's?" We see the sadness of a young Black girl sitting in a kitchen, holding her ears so they won't get burned by the hot comb that will straighten her hair. Her mother cannot make her beautiful, only "presentable" for church. Marita Golden's description of a Black beauty salon depicts the internalized oppression that some African-American women feel about African features:

Between customers, twirling in her chair, white-stockinged legs crossed, my beautician lamented to the hairdresser in the next stall, "I sure hope that Gloria Johnson don't come in here asking for me today. I swear 'fore God her hair is this long." She snapped her fingers to indicate the length. Contempt riding her words, she lit a cigarette and finished, "Barely enough to wash, let alone press and curl." (Golden 1983, 25)

African-American women who are members of the "Brights" fare little better, for they too receive special treatment because of their skin color and hair texture. Harriet Jacobs, an enslaved light-skinned woman, was sexually harassed because she was "beautiful," for a Black woman. Her straight hair and fair skin, her appearance as a dusky white woman, made her physically attractive to white men. But the fact that she was Black, and thus part of a group of sexually denigrated women, made her available to white men as no group of white women had been. In describing her situation, Jacobs notes, "if God has bestowed beauty upon her, it will prove her greatest curse. That which commands admiration in the white woman only hastens the degradation of the female slave" (Washington 1987, 17).

This difference in treatment of dark-skinned and light-skinned Black women creates issues in relationships among African-American women. Toni Morrison's novel *The Bluest Eye* explores this theme of the tension that can exist among Black women grappling with the meaning of externally defined standards of beauty. Frieda, a dark-skinned, "ordinary" Black girl, struggles with the meaning of these standards. She wonders why adults always got so upset when she rejected the white dolls they gave her and why light-skinned Maureen Peal, a child her own age whose two braids hung like "lynch-ropes down her back," got the love and attention of teachers, adults, and Black boys alike. Morrison explores Frieda's attempt not to blame Maureen for the benefits her light skin and long hair afforded her as part of Frieda's growing realization that the "Thing" to fear was not Maureen herself but the "Thing" that made Maureen beautiful.

Gwendolyn Brooks captures the anger and frustration experienced by dark-skinned women in dealing with the differential treatment they and their lighter-skinned sisters receive. In her novel *Maud Martha*, the dark-skinned heroine ponders actions she could take against a red-headed Black woman whom her husband found so attractive. "I could," considered Maud Martha, "go over there and scratch her upsweep down. I could spit on her back. I could scream. 'Listen,' I could scream, 'I'm making a baby for this man and I mean to do it in peace.'" (Washington 1987, 422). But Maud Martha rejects these actions, reasoning "if the root was sour what business did she have up there hacking at a leaf?"

This "sour root" also creates issues in relationships between African-American women and men. Maude Martha explains:

It's my color that makes him mad. I try to shut my eyes to that, but it's no good. What I am inside, what is really me, he likes okay. But he keeps looking at my color, which is like a wall. He has to jump over it in order to meet and touch what I've got for him. He has to jump away up high in order to see it. He gets awful tired of all that jumping. (Washington 1987, 421)

Her husband's attraction to light-skinned women hurt Maude Martha because his inability to "jump away up high" over the wall of color limited his ability to see her for who she truly was.

Constructing an Afrocentric Feminist Aesthetic for Beauty

Developing much-needed redefinitions of beauty must involve the critical first step of learning to see African-American women who have classical African features as being capable of beauty. Lorraine Hansberry describes this need for a changed consciousness about African-American women's beauty:

Sometimes in this country maybe just walking down a Southside street . . . Or maybe suddenly up in a Harlem window . . . Or maybe in a flash turning the page of one of those picture books from the South you will see it—*Beauty* . . . stark and full. . . . No *part* of this—but rather Africa, simply Africa. These thighs and arms and flying winged cheekbones, these hallowed eyes—without negation or apology. *A classical people demand a classical art.* (Hansberry 1969, 106)

But proclaiming Black women "beautiful" and white women "ugly" merely replaces one set of controlling images with another and fails to challenge how Eurocentric masculinist aesthetics foster an ideology of domination. Current standards require either/or dichoto-mous thinking: in order for one individual to be judged beautiful, another individual—the Other—must be deemed ugly. Accepting this underlying assumption avoids a more basic question concerning the connections among controlling images, either/or dichotomous thinking, and unequal power relationships among groups. Creating an alternative feminist aesthetic involves deconstructing and rejecting existing standards or ornamental beauty that objectify women and judge us by our physical appearance. Such an aesthetic would also reject standards of beauty that commodify women by measuring various quantities of beauty that women broker in the marital marketplace.

African-American women can draw on traditional Afrocentric aesthetics that potentially free women from standards of ornamental beauty. Though such aesthetics are present in music, dance, and language, quiltmaking offers a suggestive model for an Afrocentric feminist aesthetic. African-American women quiltmakers do not seem interested in a uniform color scheme but use several methods of playing with colors to create unpredictability and movement. For example, a strong color may be juxtaposed with another strong color, or with a weak one. Contrast is used to structure or organize. Overall, the symmetry in African-American quilts does not come from uniformity as it does in Euro-American quilts. Rather, symmetry comes through diversity. Nikki Giovanni points out that quilts are traditionally formed from scraps. "Quilters teach there is no such thing as waste," she observes, "only that for which we currently see no purpose." In describing Alice Walker's reaction to a quilt done by an anonymous Black woman, Barbara Christian notes that Walker "brings together . . . the theme of the black woman's creativity, her transformation, despite opposition, of the bits and pieces allowed to her by society into a work of functional beauty" (Christian 1985, 86).

This dual emphasis on beauty occurring via individual uniqueness juxtaposed in a community setting and on the importance of creating functional beauty from the scraps of everyday life offers a powerful alternative to Eurocentric aesthetics. The Afrocentric notions of diversity in community and functional beauty potentially heal many of the oppositional dichotomies inherent in Western social thought. From an Afrocentric perspective, women's beauty is not based solely on physical criteria because mind, spirit, and body are not conceptualized as separate, oppositional spheres. Instead, all are central in aesthetic assessments of individuals and their creations. Beauty is functional in that it has no meaning independent of the group. Deviating from the group "norm" is not rewarded as "beauty." Instead, participating in the group and being a functioning individual who strives for harmony is key to assessing an individual's beauty. Moreover, participation is not based on conformity but instead is seen as individual uniqueness that enhances the overall "beauty" of the group. Using such criteria, no individual is inherently beautiful because beauty is not a state of being. Instead beauty is always defined in a context as a state of becoming. All African-American women as well as all humans become capable of beauty.

NOTE

1. Brittan and Maynard (1984) note that ideology (1) is common sense and obvious; (2) appears natural, inevitable, and universal; (3) shapes lived experience and behavior; (4) is sedimented in people's consciousness; and (5) consists of a system of ideas em-

bedded in the social system as a whole. This example captures all dimensions of how racism and sexism function ideologically. The status of Black woman as servant is so "common sense" that even a child knows it. That the child saw a Black female child as a baby maid speaks to the naturalization dimension and to the persistence of controlling images in individual consciousness and the social system overall.

REFERENCES

Angelou, Maya. 1969. *I Know Why the Caged Bird Sings.* New York: Bantam.

Brittan, Arthur, and Mary Maynard. 1984. *Sexism, Racism and Oppression.* New York: Basil Blackwell.

Brooks, Gwendolyn. 1972. *Report from Part One: The Autobiography of Gwendolyn Brooks.* Detroit: Broadside Press.

Carby, Hazel. 1987. *Reconstructing Womanhood: The Emergence of the Afro-American Woman Novelist.* New York: Oxford.

Christian, Barbara. 1985. *Black Feminist Criticism, Perspectives on Black Women Writers.* New York: Pergamon.

Gilkes, Cheryl Townsend. 1983. "From Slavery to Social Welfare: Racism and the Control of Black Women." In *Class, Race, and Sex: The Dynamics of Control,* edited by Amy Swerdlow and Hanna Lessinger, 288–300. Boston: G. K. Hall.

Golden, Marita. 1983. *Migrations of the Heart.* New York: Ballantine.

Hansberry, Lorraine. 1969. *To Be Young, Gifted and Black.* New York: Signet.

Russell, Karen K. 1987. "Growing up with Privilege and Prejudice." *New York Times Magazine,* June 14: 22–28.

Washington, Mary Helen, ed. 1987. *Invented Lives: Narratives of Black Women 1860–1960.* Garden City, NY: Anchor.

The Women in the Tower

Cynthia Rich

In April, 1982 a group of Black women demand a meeting with the Boston Housing Authority. They are women between the ages of sixty-six and eighty-one. Their lives, in the "housing tower for the elderly" where they live, are in continual danger. "You're afraid to get on the elevator and you're afraid to get off," says Mamie Buggs, sixty-six. Odella Keenan, sixty-nine, is wakened in the nights by men pounding on her apartment door. Katherine Jefferson, eighty-one, put three locks on her door, but "I've come back to my apartment and found a group of men there eating my food."

The menace, the violence, is nothing new, they say. They have reported it before, but lately it has become intolerable. There are pictures in the *Boston Globe* of three of the women, and their eyes flash with anger. "We pay our rent, and we're entitled to some security," says Mamie Buggs. Two weeks ago, a man attacked and beat up Ida Burres, seventy-five, in the recreation room. Her head wound required forty stitches.

"I understand your desire for permanent security," says Lewis Spence, the BHA representative. "But I can't figure out any way that the BHA is going to be offering 24-hour security in an elderly development." He is a white man, probably in his thirties. His picture is much larger than the pictures of the women.

The headline in the *Boston Globe* reads, "Elderly in Roxbury building plead with BHA

for 24-hour security." Ida Burres is described in the story as "a feisty, sparrow-like woman with well-cared-for gray hair, cafe au lait skin and a lilting voice." The byline reads "Viola Osgood." The story appears on page 19.

I feel that in my lifetime I will not get to the bottom of this story, of these pictures, of these words.

Feisty, sparrow-like, well-cared-for gray hair, cafe au lait skin, lilting voice.

Feisty. Touchy, excitable, quarrelsome; like a mongrel dog.[1] "Feisty" is the standard word in newspaperspeak for an old person who says what she thinks. As you grow older, the younger person sees your strongly felt convictions or your protest against an intolerable life situation as an amusing over-reaction, a defect of personality common to mongrels and old people. To insist that you are a person deepens the stigma of your Otherness. Your protest is not a specific, legitimate response to an outside threat. It is a generic and arbitrary quirkiness, coming from the queer stuff within yourself—sometimes annoying, sometimes quaint or even endearing, never, never to be responded to seriously.

Sparrow-like. Imagine for a moment that you have confronted those who have power over you, demanding that they do something to end the terror of your days and nights. You and other women have organized a meeting of protest. You have called the press. Imagine then opening the newspaper and seeing yourself described as "sparrow-like." That is no simple indignity, no mere humiliation. The fact that you can be described as "sparrow-like" is in part why you live in the tower, why nobody attends. Because you do not look like a natural person—that is, a young or middle-aged person—you look like a sparrow. The real sparrow is, after all, a sparrow and is seen merely as

From *Look Me in the Eye: Old Women, Aging and Ageism*, Expanded Edition, by Barbara Macdonald with Cynthia Rich, 76–89. Minneapolis: Spinsters Ink, 1983. Available from: Spinsters Ink, 32 E. 1st. Street, Suite 330, Duluth, MN 55802. $8.95.

homely, but a woman who is sparrow-like is unnatural and ugly.

A white widow tells of smiling at a group of small children on the street and one of them saying, "You're ugly, ugly, ugly." It is what society has imprinted on that child's mind: to be old, and to look old, is to be ugly, so ugly that you do not deserve to live. Crow's feet. Liver spots. The media: "I'm going to wash that gray right out of my hair and wash in my 'natural' color." "Get rid of those unsightly spots." And if you were raised to believe that old is ugly, you play strange tricks in your own head. An upper middle class white woman, a woman with courage and zest for life, writes in 1982: "When we love we do not see our mates as the young view us—wrinkled, misshapen, unattractive." But then she continues: "We still retain, somewhere, the *memory* of one another as beautiful and lustful, and we see each other at our *once-best*."[2]

Old is ugly and unnatural in a society where power is male-defined, powerlessness disgraceful. A society where natural death is dreaded and concealed, while unnatural death is courted and glorified. But old is ugliest for women. A white woman newscaster in her forties remarks to a sportscaster who is celebrating his sixtieth birthday: "What women really resent about men is that *you* get more attractive as you get older." A man is as old as he feels, a woman as old as she looks. You're ugly, ugly, ugly.

Aging has a special stigma for women. When our wombs are no longer ready for procreation, when our vaginas are no longer tight, when we no longer serve men, we are unnatural and ugly. In medical school terminology, we are a "crock"; in the language of the street, we are an "old bag." The Sanskrit word for widow is "empty." But there is more than that.

Sparrow-like. The association of the old woman with a bird runs deep in the male unconscious. Apparently, it flows back to a time when men acknowledged their awe of what they were outsiders to—the interconnected, inseparable mysteries of life and death, self and other, darkness and light. Life begins in genital darkness, comes into light, and returns to darkness as death. The child in the woman's body is both self and other. The power to offer the breast is the power to withhold it. The Yes and the No are inextricable. In the beginning was the Great Mother, mysteriously, powerfully connected to the wholeness of Nature and her indivisible Yeses and Nos. But for those outside the process, the oneness was baffling and intolerable, and the Great Mother was split. Men attempted to divide what they could not control—nature and women's relationship to it. The Great Mother was polarized into separate goddesses or into diametrically opposed aspects of a single goddess. The Good Mother and the Terrible Mother. The Good Mother created life, spread her bounty outward, fertilized the crops, nourished and protected, created healing potions. The Terrible Mother, the original old Witch, dealt in danger and destruction, devoured children as food for herself, concocted poisons. Womb ≠ tomb, light ≠ darkness, other ≠ self. A world of connectedness was split down the middle.

The Terrible Mother was identified with the winged creatures that feed on mammals: vultures, ravens, owls, crows, bats. Her images in the earliest known culture of India show her as old, birdlike, hideous: "Hooded with a coif or shawl, they have high, smooth foreheads above their staring circular eye holes, their owl-beak nose and grim slit mouth. The result is terrifying . . . the face is a grinning skull."[3]

Unable to partake of the mystery of wholeness represented by the Great Mother, men first divided her, then wrested more and more control of her divided powers. The powerful Good Mother—bounteous life-giver, creator and nurturer of others—became the custodian of children who "belong" to the man or the male state. She can no longer even bear "his" child without the guiding forceps or scalpel of a man. She is the quotidian cook (men are the great chefs) who eats only after she has served others. She is the passive dispenser—as nurse, mother, wife—of the "miracles" of modern medicine created by the brilliance of man.

The Terrible Mother—the "old Woman of the West," guardian of the dead—represented men's fear of the powerful aspect of woman as intimate not only with the mysteries of birth but also of death. Today men are the specialists of death—despite a recent study that suggests that men face natural death with much more anxiety than women do.[4] Today male doctors oversee dying, male priests and rabbis perform the rituals of death, and even the active role of laying out the dead no longer belongs to woman (now the work of male undertakers). Woman is only the passive mourner, the helpless griever. And it is men who vie with each other to invent technologies that can bring about total death and destruction.

The Terrible Mother—the vulture or owl feeding on others—represented the fear of death, but also the fear of woman as existing not only to create and nurture others but to create and nurture her Self. Indeed, the aging woman's body is a clear reminder that women have a self that exists not only for others; it descends into her pelvis as if to claim the womb-space for its own. Woman's Self—her meeting of her own needs, seen by men as destructive and threatening has been punished and repressed, branded "unnatural" and "unwomanly."

In this century, in rural China, they had a practice called "sunning the jinx." If a child died, or there was some similar misfortune, it was seen as the work of a jinx. The jinx was always an old, poor woman, and she was exposed to the searing heat of the summer sun until she confessed. Like the witches burned throughout Europe in the fifteenth to seventeenth centuries, she was tortured by doublethink. If she died without confessing, they had eliminated the jinx. If she confessed her evil powers, she was left in the sun for three more days to "cure her."[5] In Bali today, the Terrible Mother lingers on in magic plays, as Ranga, the witch who eats

children, "a huge old woman with drooping breasts and a mat of white hair that comes down to her feet." It is a man who plays her part, and he must be old since only an old man can avoid the evil spirit of the Terrible Mother.[6]

In present-day white culture, men's fear of the Terrible Mother is managed by denial: by insisting on the powerlessness of the old woman, her harmless absurdity and irrelevance. The dread of her power lingers, reduced to farce—as in the Hansel and Gretel story of the old witch about to devour the children until the boy destroys her, or in the comic juxtaposition of Arsenic and Old Lace. The image of her winged power persists, totally trivialized, in the silly witch flying on her broomstick, and in "old bat," "old biddy," "old hen," "old crow," "crow's feet," "old harpy." Until, in April of 1982, an old woman's self-affirmation, her rage at her disempowerment, her determination to die naturally and not at the hands of men, can be diminished to feistiness, and she can be perceived as sparrow-like.

Sparrow-like. Writing for white men, did Viola Osgood unconsciously wish to say, "Ida Burres is not a selfish vulture—even though she is doing what old women are not meant to do, speak for their own interests (not their children's or grandchildren's but their own). She is an innocent sparrow, frail and helpless"? Or had she herself so incorporated that demeaning image—sparrow-like—that she saw Ida Burres through those eyes? Or both?

Well-cared-for gray hair. Is that about race? About class? An attempt to dispel the notion that a poor Black woman is unkempt? Would Viola Osgood describe a Black welfare mother in terms of her "well-groomed afro"? Or does she mean to dispel the notion that this *old* woman is unkempt? Only the young can afford to be careless about their hair, their dress. The care that the old woman takes with her appearance is not merely to reduce the stigma of ugly; often it is her most essential tactic for survival: it signals to the person who sees her, I am old, but I am not senile. My hair is gray but it is well-cared for. Because to be old is to be guilty of craziness and incapacity unless proven otherwise.

Cafe au lait skin. Race? Class? Age? Not dark black like Katherine Jefferson, but blackness mitigated. White male reader, who has the power to save these women's lives, you can't dismiss her as Black, poor, old. She is almost all right, she is almost white. She is Black and old, but she has something in common with the young mulatto woman whose skin you have sometimes found exotic and sensual. And she is not the power of darkness that you fear in the Terrible Mother.

A lilting voice. I try to read these words in a lilting voice: "I almost got my eyes knocked out. A crazy guy just came in here and knocked me down and hit me in the face. We need security." These words do not lilt to me. A woman is making a demand, speaking truth to power, affirming her right to live—Black, Old, Poor, Woman. Is the "lilting" to say, "Although her words are strong, although she is bonding with other women, she is not tough and dykey"? Is the "lilting" to say, "Although she is sparrow-like, although she is gray-haired, something of the mannerisms you find pleasing in young women remain, so do not ignore her as you routinely do old women"?

I write this not knowing whether Viola Osgood is Black or white. I know that she is a woman. And I know that it matters whether she is Black or white, that this is not a case of one size fits all. But I know that Black or white, any woman who writes news articles for the *Globe*, or for any mainstream newspaper, is mandated to write to white men, in white men's language. That any messages to women, Black or white, which challenge white men's thinking can at best only be conveyed covertly, subversively. That any messages of appeal to those white men must be phrased in ways that do not seriously threaten their assumptions,

and that such language itself perpetuates the power men have assumed for themselves. And I know that Black or white, ageism blows in the wind around us and certainly through the offices of the *Globe*. I write this guessing that Viola Osgood is Black, because she has known that the story is important, cared enough to make sure the photographer was there. I write this guessing that the story might never have found its way into the *Globe* unless through a Black reporter. Later, I find out that she is Black, thirty-five.

And I think that Viola Osgood has her own story to tell. I think that I, white Jewish woman of fifty, still sorting through to find the realities beneath the lies, denials and ignorance of my lifetime of segregations, cannot write this essay. I think that even when we try to cross the lines meant to separate us as women—old and young, Black and white, Jew and non-Jew—the seeds of division cling to our clothes. And I think this must be true of what I write now. But we cannot stop crossing, we cannot stop writing.

Elderly in Roxbury building plead with BHA for 24-hour security. Doubtless, Viola Osgood did not write the headline. Ten words and it contains two lies—lies that routinely obscure the struggles of old women. *Elderly.* This is not a story of elderly people, it is the story of old women, Black old women. Three-fifths of the "elderly" are women; almost all of the residents of this tower are women. An old woman has half the income of an old man. One out of three widows—women without the immediate presence of a man—lives below the official poverty line, and most women live one third of their lives as widows. In the United States, as throughout the world, old women are the poorest of the poor. Seven percent of old white men live in poverty, forty-seven percent of old Black women. "The Elderly," "Old People," "Senior Citizens," are inclusive words that blot out these differences. Old women are twice unseen—unseen because they are old, unseen because they are women. Black old women are thrice unseen. "Elderly" conveniently clouds the realities of power and economics. It clouds the convergence of racial hatred and fear, hatred and fear of the aged, hatred and fear of women. It also clouds the power of female bonding, of these women in the tower who are acting together as women for women.[7]

Plead. Nothing that these women say, nothing in their photographs, suggests pleading. These women are angry, and if one can demand where there is no leverage—and one can—they are demanding. They are demanding their lives, to which they know full well they have a right. Their anger is clear, direct, unwavering. "Pleading" erases the force of their confrontation. It allows us to continue to think of old women, if we think of them at all, as meek, cowed, to be pitied, occasionally as amusingly "feisty," but not as outraged, outrageous women. Old women's anger is denied, tamed, drugged, infantilized, trivialized. And yet anger in an old woman is a remarkable act of bravery, so dangerous is her world, and her status in that world so marginal, precarious. Her anger is an act of insubordination—the refusal to accept her subordinate status even when everyone, children, men, younger women, and often other older women, assumes it. "We pay our rent, and we're entitled to some security." When will a headline tell the truth: Old, Black, poor women confront the BHA demanding 24-hour security?

The housing tower for the elderly. A tall building filled with women, courageous women who bond together, but who with every year are less able to defend themselves against male attack. A tower of women under seige. A ghetto within a ghetto. The white male solution to the "problem of the elderly" is to isolate the Terrible Mother.

That tower, however, is not simply architectural. Nor is the male violence an "inner city problem." Ten days later, in nearby Stoughton, a man will have beaten to death an eighty-seven-year-old white woman, leaving her body with "multiple blunt injuries around her face, head,

and shoulders."[8] This woman was not living in a housing tower for the elderly. She lived in the house where she was born. "She was very, very spry. She worked in her garden a lot and she drove her own car," reports a neighbor. She had the advantages of race, class, a small home of her own, a car of her own. Nor did she turn away from a world that rejects and demeans old women ("spry," like "feisty," is a segregating and demeaning word). At the time of her murder, she was involved in planning the anniversary celebration at her parish.

Yet she was dead for a week before anyone found her body. Why? The reporter finds it perfectly natural. "She outlived her contemporaries and her circle of immediate relatives." Of course. How natural. Unless we remember de Beauvoir: "One of the ruses of oppression is to camouflage itself behind a natural situation since, after all, one cannot revolt against nature."[9] How natural that young people, or even the middle aged, should have nothing in common with an old woman. Unthinkable that she should have formed friendships with anyone who was not in her or his seventies or eighties or nineties. It is natural that without family, who must tolerate the stigma, or other old people who share the stigma, she would have no close ties. And it is natural that no woman, old or young, anywhere in the world, should be safe from male violence.

But it is not natural. It is not natural, and it is dangerous, for younger women to be divided as by a taboo from old women—to live in our own shaky towers of youth. It is intended, but it is not natural that we be ashamed of, dissociated from, our future selves, sharing men's loathing for the women we are daily becoming. It is intended, but it is not natural that we be kept ignorant of our deep bonds with old women. And it is not natural that today, as we re-connect with each other, old women are still an absence for younger women.

As a child—a golden-haired Jew in the segregated South while the barbed wire was going up around the Warsaw ghetto—I was given fairy tales to read. Among them, the story of Rapunzel, the golden-haired young woman confined to a tower by an old witch until she was rescued by a young prince. My hair darkened and now it is light again with gray. I know that I have been made to live unnaturally in a tower for most of my fifty years. My knowledge of my history—as a woman, as a lesbian, as a light-skinned woman in a world of dark-skinned women, as the Other in a Jew-hating world—shut out. My knowledge of my future—as an old woman—shut out.

Today I reject those mythic opposites: young/old, light/darkness, life/death, other/self, Rapunzel/Witch, Good Mother/Terrible Mother. As I listen to the voices of the old women of Warren Tower, and of my aging self, I know that I have always been aging, always been dying. Those voices speak of wholeness: To nurture Self = to defy those who endanger that Self. To declare the I of my unique existence = to assert the We of my connections with other women. To accept the absolute rightness of my natural death = to defend the absolute value of my life. To affirm the mystery of my daily dying and the mystery of my daily living = to challenge men's violent cheapening of both.

But I cannot hear these voices clearly if I am still afraid of the old witch, the Terrible Mother in myself, or if I am estranged from the real old women of this world. For it is not the wicked witch who keeps Rapunzel in her tower. It is the prince and our divided selves.

Note: There was no follow-up article on the women of the tower, but Ida Burres, Mamie Buggs, Mary Gordon, Katherine Jefferson, Odella Keenan, and the other women of Warren Tower, did win what they consider to be adequate security—"of course, it is never all that you could wish," said Vallie Burton, President of the Warren Tower Association. They won because of their own bonding, their demands, and also, no doubt, because of Viola Osgood.

NOTES

The article from the *Boston Globe* on which this essay is based appeared on April 16, 1980, p. 19.

1. William Morris, ed., *American Heritage Dictionary* (Boston: Houghton Mifflin, 1975).

2. Harriet Robey, *There's a Dance in the Old Dame Yet* (New York: Atlantic-Little Brown, 1982), p. 170. Italics mine.

3. Eric Neumann, *The Great Mother* (New York: Bollingen, 1972), p. 150. Neumann has collected the most wide-ranging evidence of the Good and Terrible Mothers in cultures as distant from each other as Peru, Egypt, and India.

4. See Carol M. Schulz, "Age, Sex and Death Anxiety in a Middle-Class American Community," in *Aging in Culture and Society*, ed. Christine L. Fry (New York: J.F. Bergin, 1980), p. 246. According to her findings, old women's attitudes toward dying become increasingly positive and accepting, while "males become emotionally more negative toward approaching death."

5. Annie Dillard, "For the Love of China" (*Harvard Magazine*, July–August, 1983, p. 41). Dillard describes reading about this custom of "sunning the jinx" in Shen Conquen's *Recollections of West Hunan*, translated by Gladys Yeng. Note the brutal use of a source of light—as in the fires built to consume European witches—to destroy the dark powers of the Terrible Mother.

6. Simone de Beauvoir, *The Coming of Age* (New York: Putnam, 1972), p. 78.

7. Several studies of public housing projects for the elderly reveal creative, fluid networks of practical and emotional support among the women. The men, on the other hand, tend to "emphasize impersonal and businesslike, including monetary, aspects" in their occasional assistance as handymen or chauffeurs. (Karen Jones and Edward Wellin, "Dependency and Reciprocity: Home Health Aid in an Elderly Population," in Fry, *op.cit.*, p. 32). Middy Thomas, of the Mayor's Commission on the Elderly in Boston said of Warren Tower, "It's the women who do everything."

8. *Boston Globe*, April 26, 1982, p. 13.

9. Simone de Beauvoir, *The Ethics of Ambiguity* (New Jersey: Citadel, 1948), p. 83.

The World of Work

Ever since World War II, American women have increasingly moved into the paid labor force owing to factors such as relaxed attitudes about proper gender roles, expanded job opportunities, decreased family size, the need for a second income, and higher divorce rates. In spite of legislative initiatives, court rulings, and affirmative-action programs, however, women's salaries still lag behind those of men. Indeed, full-time women workers earn approximately 76 percent of what full-time male workers earn; they enjoy fewer benefits, such as the chance to train for better jobs; and they are more subject to layoffs and firings.

In "Women Wage Earners," Marie Richmond-Abbott analyzes the various explanations that have been offered for the differences in wages and benefits between women and men. According to one explanation, these differences are due to inequalities in "human capital." Because men have accumulated more than women in the way of education, on-the-job training, and work experience, they can produce more for their employers than can women. Therefore, it is only fair that employers pay their male employees more than their female employees. According to another explanation, these differences are due to occupational segregation by sex. Women are clustered in a narrow range of low-paying jobs, whereas men are spread across a broader range of more highly-paid occupations. Still another explanation for these differences stresses women's difficulties in combining work and family responsibilities. Family women usually cannot work long hours, choose jobs involving travel, or accept promotions with added responsibilities since these factors conflict with their role as child rearers and homemakers. A final explanation for these differences is conscious or unconscious discrimination against women. Employers' attitudes toward women are unduly influenced by the stereotypes that women are less committed to and less serious about their work than men are; that women's wages are second incomes and not really needed; and that women cannot handle job-related stresses and strains. So powerful are these stereotypes that one-third of the total wage differences between women and men has been attributed to discrimination.

African-American women and women in blue-collar jobs are particularly hard hit by gender discrimination in the workplace. Many of these women are forced to work because they are the primary or sole support of one or more children. Not only are these women in need of parental leaves, adequate health care, affordable child care, and decent wages, but they are also in need of protection from sexual harassment on the job. Regrettably, an employer or manager may force himself upon a female worker precisely because he knows he can threaten to fire her if she does not comply with his wishes. Whereas a woman with some degree of economic security may be able to bluntly rebuff such advances, a woman who is poor, relatively unskilled, and in fear of winding up on welfare may feel that she has to acquiesce to his demands.

In "Inside the Work Worlds of Chicana and Mexican Immigrant Women," Denise Segura takes a more detailed look at the situation of women in blue-collar jobs and women of color—this time Mexican-American women and immigrant women from Mexico. She finds much in the way of occupational segregation by race/ethnicity and class as well as sex. As we have already noted, male-dominated occupations pay higher wages and have more opportunities for advancement and better working conditions than white-female-dominated occupations. But as we have *not* previously noted, minority-female-dominated occupations have higher turnovers of workers, less stability, lower wages, and fewer avenues for advancement than white-female-dominated occupations. Through in-depth interviews with forty Chicana and Mexicana workers, Segura sheds light on some of the factors that perpetuate minority women's work woes.

To begin with, Segura's interviews disclose that Chicana and Mexicana workers are channeled into female-dominated occupations by biased secondary school counselors or employment programs, the limited information of family and friends (who were employed in or tended to have information about such occupations), and family preferences (husbands, for example, who did not want their wives working in male-dominated occupations). When the Chicana and Mexicana women were placed in white-female-dominated occupations, they found themselves socially isolated from their coworkers, unsupported by their supervisors, and out of the information loops that serve to professionally advance workers. Class differences as well as racial and ethnic differences contributed to this unfair state of affairs, which caused many of these minority women to quit their "white" jobs as soon as their finances permitted them to. Segura stresses that when these Chicana and Mexicana women later joined other minority women in minority-female-dominated occupations, they found themselves assisted by coworkers and fairly treated by supervisors, thereby feeling a part of the workplace. These factors encouraged them to stay in these jobs, despite the fact that these jobs were unstable and offered low pay and no real prospects for advancement. Concludes Segura: "As we become more knowledgeable of the ways

in which structural forces and micro dynamics uphold class, racial-ethnic, and gender segregation in the labor market, we will be that much closer to developing strategies to promote intergroup relations and erode labor market inequality" (p. 188).

In contrast to Richmond-Abbot and Segura, Debra Renee Kaufman focuses on the situation of white-collar women in "Professional Women: How Real Are the Recent Gains?" She observes that nearly ten million women, one out of every five employed, hold white-collar jobs and that their number has increased significantly over the last decade. Even so, "what women are allowed to do remains limited, and barriers still restrict their mobility in the professional world" (p. 189). The professions, says Kaufman, are divided into the lower-paying, less prestigious female-dominated professions—for example, elementary school teaching, nursing, social work, and library science—and the higher-paying, more prestigious male-dominated professions—medicine, law, science, college teaching, and business administration. Female-dominated professions depend on skilled but abundant labor; they are structured for the lives that women lead (for example, career continuity is not essential); they tend to reserve their most respected positions for men; and they typically lack the kind of authoritarian and monopolistic controls that characterize the male-dominated professions.

In contrast, male-dominated professions reserve their lowest-paying, lowest-prestige subspecialties for women; they are structured for the lives that men lead (they demand great investments of time, energy, and commitment away from family life); and they require the exhibition of the more aggressive masculine gender traits. Comments Kaufman:

The high status professions and the prestige specialties in our society are identified with the instrumental, rigorous, "hard-nosed" qualities identified as masculine, not with the "softer," more expressive, nurturing modes of behavior identified as feminine. Since the characteristics associated with the most valued professions are also those associated with men, women fail to meet one of the most important professional criteria: They are not men." (p. 194)

Interestingly, even if a woman exhibits masculine gender traits, she will not be readily accepted in a male-dominated profession. She will tend to be excluded altogether, or at least left out of the power networks that make the difference when decisions for promotion, partnership, tenure, research grants, and co-editorships are under consideration. The woman who manages to break through these barriers will probably do so only because she has paid some extremely high dues. Professional women often give up personal relationships, delay having children, and/or add on major domestic responsibilities to their already demanding workday. Small wonder that Kaufman wonders whether women's professional gains are worth the personal price.

Of course, there is one occupation that women are welcome in and that they excel in, and that is the occupation of housewife. Even though the proportion of adult women engaging exclusively in housework has been dwindling in recent years, it is still the largest single occupation for American women. That this should be the case should not surprise us. After all, the family that includes a housewife devoted full time to child care, food preparation, housecleaning, laundry, grocery shopping, and the like generally benefits from high-quality and timely services. Nevertheless, as Barbara Bergmann points out in "The Job of Housewife," "housewifery" is a very peculiar occupation: "The nature of the duties to be performed, the method of payment, the form of supervision, the tenure system, the 'market' in which the 'workers' find 'jobs,' and the physical hazards are all very different from the way things are in other occupations" (p. 202). So great are these differences that people frequently say that housewives "don't work." Bergmann assures us, however, that housewives *do* work, performing servant-

like tasks seven days a week and potentially twenty-four hours a day.

Unlike servants, however, housewives are usually expected to add sexual and other emotional services to their list of chores. In return for her labor, the housewife receives food, clothing, shelter, and even a share in whatever luxuries her husband's salary provides. What she does not receive, however, is any monetary reward designated as her own to be used as she sees fit. With his monopoly on the household's money, the husband of a housewife is in a position of power over her. He gives her as much or as little money as he chooses to; and if she protests in any way, he may react harshly toward her, reminding her that without him she will be poor indeed. For these and other reasons, Bergmann suggests that "the housewife occupation is one of the most problem-ridden in the economy" (p. 203).

Despite all these problems, however, present laws favor families with full-time housewives in several ways. For example, a man married to a woman with no income pays considerably less in taxes than he would as a single person, and also less, on a percentage basis, than if his wife worked for a wage. Moreover, many women who have worked outside the home and made substantial contributions to Social Security receive the same Social Security benefits they would have received had they stayed at home. Bergmann discusses some of the proposals that have been made to rectify such shortcomings in our laws, as well as such related issues as paid maternity and child-rearing leaves. She also discusses the possibility of paying housewives wages for their work, an idea that we must consider carefully. Who would pay these wages? Would it not be preferable to require men to work as hard around the house as women do, thereby permitting both husbands and wives to work outside the home without either of them having to hold down a second, full-time job within the home? Is all the time that a woman spends with her spouse and children "work"?

Women Wage Earners

Marie Richmond-Abbott

In this century in the United States, women have moved in ever increasing numbers into the labor force. Between 1900 and 1980, female labor force participation grew from 18 percent to 50 percent. (The number of women who work for pay or who are trying to find a job almost doubled between 1950 and 1974 alone.), By 1996, 58 percent of all women were in the workforce. These labor force participation rates are projected to continue to rise to the year 2005, but at a slower pace than in the last 20 years. This movement into paid market activity has had profound consequences for women's lives and for the economics of our society. The reasons for the movement are varied and are closely connected with world events as well as with the economic scene in our own country.

HISTORICAL PERSPECTIVES ON WOMEN'S WORK IN THIS COUNTRY

The historical pattern of women's market work in the United States shows that women were heavily involved in economic production in our early history. In the agrarian society of early America, women had to plant and harvest crops, tend animals, and do other things that produced a money income, as well as work within the household to produce cloth, make clothes, make butter and cheese, preserve food, and the like. In addition, with the short life expectancy, many women became widows and ran businesses or farms; other women were mid-

wives, nurses, teachers, printers, laundresses, and innkeepers. Many middle-class women also worked invisibly by taking in boarders or sewing at home. In the early 1830s and 1840s, women worked in textile mills and tobacco factories. By 1890, estimates are that at least 1 million women were employed in factories, with others working in agricultural and domestic service. Many of these were immigrants. An 1887 Bureau of Labor study found that of 17,000 factory workers surveyed, 75 percent were of immigrant stock. Black women were also more likely to work; the 1900 census showed that 41 percent of all nonwhite women worked outside the home, while only 17 percent of white women were employed. The great majority of white women did not work outside the home: their proper work was considered to be that of homemaker and mother.

Most of those who worked before the 1940s were young, single, or poor. They were segregated into occupations that were defined as "work for women." Thirty percent were clerical workers, and many of the rest were in textile or food-processing factories. Of the few women who were professionals, three out of four worked in elementary-school teaching or in nursing. As one of the well-known historians of this era, William Chafe, points out, there was a "woman's place" in the paid work force as well as at home.[1] Not only was certain work considered women's work, but it was presumed that women should not be paid as much as men and that women should never be placed in a position competitive with or superior to that of men. There was almost no support for the employment of middle-class homemakers.

It was World War II that marked the real turning point in women's employment in the United States. In 1940, 25.6 percent of all women worked; by 1945, that figure had risen to 36 percent, as 6 million women entered the job market to take the place of men who had been called into military service. These women did not fit the stereotype of young, single, or poor. Women who entered the labor market at this time were married and over thirty-five. By the end of the war, it was just as likely for a wife over forty to be employed as for a single woman under twenty-five. At the end of the war, quite a few of these working women returned home to make room for the returning soldiers, but the boom in the economy enabled some in service and clerical work to keep their jobs. In spite of the "feminine mystique," which insisted that women should gain their greatest fulfillment as homemakers and mothers, many women—single and married—continued to work for pay outside the home. During the 1950s, the employment of women increased four times faster than that of men. By 1960, 37 percent of the women in the country were in the labor force, and 30 percent of these were married. By 1996, 58 percent of all women worked outside the home including almost 56 percent of all married women, 61 percent of separated women and 75 percent of those who were divorced.

One of the striking trends of female employment during the 1960s and 1970s was the increasing number of mothers who were working. The fastest rise of all took place in the employment of mothers with preschool children. From 1959 to 1974, the employment rate for mothers with children under three more than doubled, from 15 to 31 percent. By 1995, 65 percent of the mothers of children under six were in the labor force. While some of this rise was due to the need for greater family income, these young women also had more education and thus had greater job opportunities and changing sex-role attitudes to support their employment

Although they were in conflict with the actual economic behavior of women, traditional attitudes about "women's place" persisted. Chafe has stated that this gap between traditional attitudes and actual behavior ironically facilitated expansion of the female labor force. As traditional values were given lip-service, women could enter the labor force "to help out" and were not resisted as crusaders who would change the status quo.[2]

REASONS WHY WOMEN ENTERED THE PAID LABOR FORCE

There were many reasons that women continued to enter the labor force after World War II. Real wages rose and job opportunities in the service sector expanded as the economy boomed. Women were also getting more education, which made the type of working opportunities available more attractive. There was a slow change in gender-role attitudes as well, and by the mid-1960s, the revival of feminism made it difficult to maintain the traditional view of women's place as being in the home. These changing attitudes influenced and combined with several demographic changes. Women began to marry later and were thus more likely to be in the labor force longer in their early single years. They also had fewer children, so that their last child was born sooner in their lives and they were freed from child care earlier to reenter the paid economy. As divorce rates rose, many more women had to rely on themselves for support.

Other demographic and technical changes also helped women enter the labor market. The move from rural areas to the cities made it easier for many women to find jobs. The development of labor-saving devices such as like washing machines and frozen foods also meant that they could, at least theoretically, spend less time in housework and food preparation. In addition, the 1970s were a period of economic inflation in the United States. Families had gotten used to a higher standard of living, frequently maintaining a large home and two cars, sending children to college, and enjoying expensive leisure-time activities. It was difficult to maintain this standard of living with inflation and, as a result, there was more pressure for married women to enter the work force to provide a second income.

THE PRESENT PICTURE: PROBLEMS OF WORKING WOMEN

Salary Problems

By 1996, 59 percent of white women, 59.5 percent of black women and 52.6 percent of Hispanic women were in the labor force. In the 25–44 year-old age group, 75 percent of the women were employed. However, in spite of their increased employment, Supreme Court rulings and affirmative action programs, women's salaries today still lag far behind those of men. Among full-time, year-around workers, women still earn on the average approximately 76 percent of what men earn. White females earn approximately 67 percent of what white males earn; black females earn approximately 82 percent of what a black male earns and Hispanic women earn 60 percent of a Hispanic male's salary. Women are also more likely to work part time so their earnings are even lower than the figures above. In addition, women are more subject to layoffs during bad economic times and they get fewer benefits such as health insurance.

These salary figures are also skewed by the fact that most of the improvement in women's salaries has come in professional and managerial occupations. Women have greatly increased their numbers in law, medicine and a few other professional fields and the pay that these women receive makes the picture look far rosier than it is. Women who are college graduates but have no professional training get less pay than men who have the same credentials, and while women managers make 70 percent of what male managers receive, women in sales average only 58 percent of the salary of men in sales. The great majority of women are still

clustered in clerical and service occupations where they receive low wages.

While differences in pay between black and white men have declined and differences in wages between black and white women have been virtually eliminated, there remains a large gap between the earnings of all women and white men.

Other Inequities

In addition to low pay, women in the labor force have other problems. The National Commission on Working Women, a Washington-based arm of the National Manpower Institute, surveyed 150,000 women and discovered that although wages were a major difficulty for many, other problems were also severe. The women complained of differentials in fringe benefits, the lack of a chance to train for better jobs, increasing pay differentials as men were promoted, sexual harassment on the job, inadequate child care facilities, the stress of the multiple roles of wife-worker-mother, and extremely limited leisure time. (Fifty-five percent of the professional women surveyed and 50 percent of the clerical, sales, and blue-collar workers said they had *no* leisure time!) These women wanted additional education, but lacked the time and money to get it; they wanted job counseling, but could not find it. Their husbands did not object to their work, but provided almost no help with household chores. The women described themselves as frustrated, working in dead-end jobs with no chance in sight for advancement or training. They felt underpaid, underutilized, and afforded little or no respect for the work contributed.

The National Research Council of the Academy of Sciences completed an assessment of job discrimination for the Equal Employment Opportunity Commission in 1983. In this assessment, they tried to pinpoint the reasons for the differential between men's and women's wages. The factors they found that affect wage rates and other benefits can be divided into measurable parts: human capital inequalities, institutional barriers, and discrimination.

Human Capital Inequities

According to human capital theory, some differences in earnings are due to inequalities in human capital, or characteristics of workers that enable them to produce more for a firm. Such characteristics include education, experience, training, and commitment to work. Believers in this theory say that men usually have more human capital than women do, and thus command higher wages.

There are many difficulties with this theory, including the fact that productivity is almost impossible to measure in some jobs, that wages may not reflect the entire reward paid for a job, and that we do not have an open, competitive market for all jobs (remember the "old boy" network). Beyond the basic difficulties, however, the statistics show that women get less return on investments in their own human capital than men do. For example, women with a college education only get on the average 70 percent of the salary of a male college graduate.

In this theory, the major difference in the amount of wages accounted for under human capital is attributed to differences in work experience: overall work experience, on-the-job training, and the like. Women are less likely to get on-the-job training than men are, as employers may believe that women are less committed workers and will not stay with the company. One study showed that a significant amount of the male/female wage differential is explained by less female acquisition of training although the amount of training that women get is greater than what it was in the 1970s. Women are also less likely to have continuous work experience. They may enter their careers after child bearing or interrupt them to raise children. Women are the losers when they drop out of market. One study that documented the

gains from continuous work experience found that women who worked continuously had real wage gains of about 20 percent, while those who entered and left employment were no better off ten years later. Even the women with continuous experience got less of a return on their experience than men did. However, most current research indicates that human capital factors account for less than half the gap in earnings between men and women. We must look elsewhere to find out why women earn so much less than men.

Occupational Segregation and the Dual Labor Market

Other factors such as institutional barriers and job segregation seem to be more important than work experience in explaining the wage gap. One of the major reasons that women's earnings tend to be so low is that women are clustered in a narrow range of jobs. One-third work in clerical occupations. Another quarter work in the fields of health care (not including physicians), education, domestic service, and food service. Many of these jobs require higher than average educational levels (teacher, social worker, nurse) but pay low salaries. Few women have until recently entered male-dominated professions, which are more highly paid. As of 1996, women were only 26 percent of physicians, 14 percent of dentists, 32 percent of lawyers, 29 percent of judges, and 6 percent of engineers.

Job segregation by sex seems to be an important factor in wage differentials. If we look at the twelve major occupational categories—professional and technical, managerial, sales, clerical, and so on—we do not see much difference in male and female salaries, because the categories are so broad and job classifications differ markedly. When 479 job categories are used, however, studies show job segregation accounts for a substantial amount of the gap in earnings. In a study that used both human capital and job segregation variables, every additional percentage of females in an occupation meant that workers in that job got an average of about $42 less in annual income.

Fifty percent of employed women work in only twenty occupations, and 24 percent of the women in the labor force in 1990 were employed in just six occupational categories. Wage differentials occur with job segregation because, by concentrating in only certain fields, women increase the supply of workers for these jobs and thus, decrease their own wages. Economic theorists call this the crowding theory and a 1995 study estimates that it is the primary determinant of the pay gap. In contrast, the short supply of workers in occupations such as engineering elevates wages in this male-dominated profession. Some of the jobs that have been designated for women are also contracting as a result of population trends and changes in our technology. Low-level clerks and secretaries may be replaced as word processing becomes more automatic. Elementary-school teachers are less needed as people have fewer children. Yet women continue to enter the jobs traditionally designated as female. Are women restricted to these jobs? Socialization, training, and custom have made it difficult for women to enter male-dominated fields although more are doing so. While there are some indications of change (women entering law and medicine, for example), occupational segregation by sex is likely to continue. It has hardly decreased at all among whites for several decades, although it has decreased substantially among minorities. Women seldom have the full information or mobility needed to choose jobs. Employers seldom have access to all possible employees and are also constrained by other factors, such as union agreements and agreements to promote from within.

Women are willing to take low pay and to enter occupations with low status because most of these jobs blend well with the stereotype of being "feminine." Many of the jobs with the highest percentage of female workers are nurturing in nature (teacher, social worker, nurse). In addition, some of these jobs have fairly flexible hours, which may aid a woman in combining them with domestic responsibilities. The professions traditionally designated for men, such as engineering, business management, and medicine, may also require proficiency in mathematics or science, and women have been discouraged from taking courses in those areas. Thus, many women do not have the necessary prerequisites to enter those professions.

The Dual Burden Theory of Job Inequities

The concept of the "dual burden" proposes that whatever job women pick, their family duties will make it difficult for them to do the same work and reap the same rewards as men. A woman may have to choose between career and family responsibilities in a way that a man does not have to do. Women may be reluctant to work long hours or choose jobs that mean travel because these things conflict with what they perceive as their responsibility to be the primary child rearer. Women may refuse promotions because of the added burdens that conflict with home responsibilities or because of the fear of equaling or exceeding their husbands' salaries. Women who try to integrate their work lives with their family lives may find that employers are reluctant to grant maternity leaves, resent time taken off to be with sick children and generally believe that a woman's commitment to work is lessened if she becomes a mother. This employer perception may mean fewer promotions and lower salaries.

Arlene Hochschild in *The Second Shift* estimates that men were doing only about 5 percent more household work in the 1980s than they did in the 1970s for a total of 20 percent. Women decreased the amount they did by about 5 percent, but women still did from 70–80 percent of all household work, including most of the repetitive chores. Most research finds that the more housework women do, the lower their wages; however, some studies disagree. Women in these unequal relationships also pay significant costs in terms of career advancement, loss of leisure and impaired wellbeing. One study shows that the work week of American women is 21 hours longer than the work week of American men.

The whole idea of the dual burden has been formalized by Felicia Schwartz. She discusses the problems that women executives have in combining work and family responsibilities and suggests that corporations officially recognize these difficulties with flexible, slower paced jobs for women. Women without children could still be on the fast track career path with men. Feminists are horrified at the idea of a formalized "mommy track" and singling out women with child-care responsibilities for less favorable treatment in the business world. Yet Schwartz has been willing to discuss a very real problem shared by many aspiring career women.[3]

Sylvia Hewlett in *A Lesser Life* shows that never-married women have complete wage parity with never-married men while the wage gap between married men and women is extremely large. For women to move up in the managerial ranks, they must frequently cut their family responsibilities, perhaps by deciding not to have children or even not to get married. More than fifty percent of managerial jobs are held by women who are childless and have continuous work histories. Even for the superwomen who try to do it all, there is just not enough time and energy to equal the effort of male colleagues who are unencumbered with such tasks.

Hewlett points out that there is a catch-22 in the "dual burden" hypothesis. One of the reasons that men are unwilling to help more with the housework is that their wives tend to make less money than they do. (Resources often determine the power you have to decide to do work or have other people do it.) Obviously, if women continue to do the lion's share

of housework and raising children, they will not be able to work in a way that will give them good salaries and related family power.

The Residual Category of Discrimination

When men and women work in the same fields, men still make more money than women do. It is not just the nature of the job, but the nature (sex) of the person that accounts for the difference in the amount of pay. Thus, men who work in "women's" fields still earn $1,200 more annually than women do on the average, and in male-dominated occupations, men's salaries exceed those of women by an average of $2,400.

Segregation within professions may also mean different pay scales. Male computer specialists get $3,714 more than their female counterparts do. In retail sales, women and men are often in sub-categories that pay differently. Men are more likely to sell the big-ticket items such as appliances or furniture, which consequently carry higher commissions.

In addition, certain firms in the same occupational category are more likely to hire male workers, and others are more likely to hire a greater percentage of female workers. Without exception, the firms that are larger and more prestigious are more likely to hire men and to pay them more money. This can be seen in law firms, accounting firms, and even in restaurants, where the more prestigious restaurants (where bills and tips are larger) hire only male table servers. More segregation occurs in this fashion than would be the case in a random hiring process. This difference among firms is believed to account for more of the wage gap than does the difference within any particular firm in the jobs that men and women will take.

Even within the same firm in an occupational category, men and women are still likely to have different jobs. If they do not start in different categories, promotions may soon separate them. For example, women are less likely to make partner in large legal firms. One good example of sex differences in promotion occurred in an insurance company that was sued for sex discrimination. In this company, men were given "claims adjuster" jobs, whereas recruited women got jobs entitled "claims representative." Each job required a college degree, yet not only were "claims adjusters" paid $2,500 more in wages than the "claims representatives" who did the same work, but only the adjusters could obtain promotions.

Thus, a differential exists between men's and women's wages that cannot be accounted for by the human capital or job segregation explanations. Reasons for this gap probably comprise various factors that we can combine under the category of discrimination. The pay differential attributed to discrimination is estimated to be approximately one-third of the gap between female and male earnings. When we talk about discrimination in this sense, we are not necessarily talking about an overt attempt to discriminate against women. We are also talking about the complex of customs, traditions, and understandings that lead to stereotyping and beliefs about who should do what work.

MYTHS THAT JUSTIFY DISCRIMINATION

Why would women in the labor force face such discrimination? To answer this question, we need to look at some of the stereotypes about women workers. One of the first stereotypes is that a woman is a secondary worker, that her income is a second income for the household, and that she does not really need the money. This myth persists in spite of facts that contradict it. The truth is that most of the women who work need money badly. (While all people who work need money as a basis of independence, a large percentage of working women need the money they earn as basic self-support.) Twenty-three percent of working women are

single, and an additional 19 percent are widowed, divorced, or separated and are their families' main support. An additional 26 percent have husbands earning less than $10,000. Of course, whether or not women really need the money should not be an issue: if they do equal work, they should get equal pay. We do not usually ask whether a man needs the money when it is time to adjust his salary or to assess his qualifications for promotion.

Women are also seen as workers who are not serious about their work and are less committed and reliable than men. Employers expect them to be absent more than men and are reluctant to invest in them because they may quit. There seems to be no time when a woman worker is freed from this stigma. When she is single, employers are afraid she will quit to get married. When she is married, they are afraid she will quit to have children or will follow her husband to a better job. If she already has children, employers are afraid she will be absent a great deal because of child care demands; and if she is older and her children have left home, she may be considered too old and unattractive for the job. The actual facts are that women are not absent from work any more than men, which is rather remarkable considering that many of them do have primary child care responsibilities. Women and men are both absent an average of five and a half days a year. While the overall quit rates of women are higher than those of men, when one looks at men and women in the same jobs, women do not quit more than men. The job attachment of anyone in a dead-end job is less than someone in a career that offers opportunity for advancement. Men who are bank tellers quit as often as women who are bank tellers; men who are physicians are no more or less committed to their work than women who are physicians.

Employers also say that they do not promote women because people don't want to work for a woman boss, that women don't want the top jobs, can't handle responsibility, and are too emotional to be in management. The first two statements are probably true in many cases. Traditional gender-role stereotypes have dictated that women be dominated by men and not vice versa. Many people are uncomfortable when these stereotypes are reversed. Even women workers may accept the stereotypes and not want to be supervised by another woman. Sometimes they are accurate in their perception that "Queen Bees" who have reached the top are not eager to help other women up the ladder. In addition, women may not admit to wanting higher-echelon jobs because they know that the probability of their getting such a job is low and that to accept such a position may be to accept job responsibility that may conflict with home and family commitments.

Rosabeth Kanter has pointed out in *Men and Women and the Corporation* that women managers may also be put in positions where it is difficult for them to help their subordinates advance. Some women may fear the difficulties that may come in exercising authority if co-workers resent them. Kanter also points out that a great deal of the interchange in higher-echelon business positions depends on common understandings and values. Men often prefer to work with a *homosocial* group (a group of people who are alike in race, sex, approximate age and socio-economic status) because they believe such a group will share their values. Men may fear that someone of a different status who does not share their background will make working situations more difficult. In addition, many men are used to dealing with women only as secretaries or wives and may have a difficult time adjusting to dealing with a woman on a parallel level. Thus, for many reasons, women may not want to be managers and others may not want them in managerial positions.

SEX AS A STATUS CHARACTERISTIC

As we examine the facts about women workers, we begin to see that sex is a status characteristic. It is used as a category to discriminate at

work and elsewhere in much the same way that other statuses such as race, religion, and age are used. The status of being female influences a woman's career aspirations, hiring possibilities, promotion chances, and salary as much as the personal qualifications she possesses or gains through her education.

When we think of sex as status, we can see that some of the discrimination against women is a matter of the upper-status group (men) retaining power and privilege. As the work of men has always been more prestigious than that of women, men may consciously or unconsciously fear the dilution of their power and privilege if women join their ranks. Because of this difficulty of status, organizations consciously or unconsciously use various techniques to keep women out of the mainstream of advancement and decision making. Women's jobs may be reclassified to a lower category or women may not be trained on the job as men are to be eligible for promotion. Women may also be shifted into fields such as personnel that do not lead to higher positions.

In the blue-collar areas, unions have blatantly discriminated against women. Women were barred from craft unions for many years, and even today requirements for membership may be difficult for women to meet. Union meetings may be held in halls or clubs where women feel uncomfortable going or at hours after work or in the evening when women have primary responsibilities at home. Harassment on blue-collar jobs may be overt and sexual; on white-collar jobs it may take the form of isolation, but the intent is the same: to show the woman that she should stay in her place.

In a more radical perspective on the relationship between job segregation and discrimination, Heidi Hartmann suggests that as industrial society developed, men could not as easily maintain the control over women's work that they had in the more personal preindustrial economic system. As jobs were more impersonal, control had to be more institutionalized. She postulates that such control was continued by segregating industrial jobs by sex, with women making less money or unable to get any work at all. Because of this segregation, women were and are partially or totally dependent on men for support, and must perform domestic chores for their husbands. Thus men maintain control at home and are aided in their jobs by having domestic support. They also get higher wages because the labor supply is limited by women remaining home. Capitalism benefits because men are defined as the primary breadwinners and must work long hours to support their "idle" or partially-employed wives. Hartmann concludes that one cannot change women's position in the economic system without changing their household roles and cannot change household roles without changing job segregation in the economic system. As it is not to the benefit of those in power to change the system, it is unlikely that the system will be changed without conflict.[4]

Hartmann's inference that segregation of jobs by sex and discrimination against women are deliberate devices to enforce women's dependence may not be accepted by everyone. Yet at the same time it is clear that occupational segregation by sex as well as conscious and unconscious discrimination account for a great deal of the discrepancy between women's and men's wages and perpetuate women's secondary status as workers.

WOMEN IN BLUE-COLLAR JOBS

We want to look separately at women in blue-collar jobs because, while they share certain kinds of discrimination with female white-collar workers, they also have unique problems of their own. By the early 1990s, women manual laborers employed in blue-collar industrial and service occupations comprised 25.5 percent of all employed women. Most of these women were white, though three out of five black women work in blue-collar jobs.

While women have gone from 4 percent to 26 percent of the physicians and from .8 per-

cent to 9.1 percent of the engineers between 1960 and 1996, in the same period the proportion of women carpenters rose only from .03 percent to 1.7 percent and the percentage of women welders and machinists topped out at 4 percent. There are several reasons that women have not moved more quickly into non-traditional blue-collar jobs. While there has been an expansion in the number of professional jobs, the number of craft jobs has not grown substantially. Access to skilled craft jobs is provided by union apprenticeship and entry is difficult because of union discrimination. Masculinity and work are interwoven in these blue-collar jobs, and women trying to enter them often face a great deal of resistance from employers and organizational barriers in high schools and vocational schools. Threats of lawsuits have opened some doors, but women in vocational schools and federal job-training programs continue to be tracked into traditionally female blue-collar work. Women entering the non-traditional jobs are more likely to be white and high-school graduates as well as having some family connection to the kind of work they choose. Those who stay in them report being satisfied with the pay and work content. However, they tend to suffer more harassment from supervisors as well as co-workers than women in traditionally feminine blue-collar jobs. While a small number of women have moved into the non-traditional jobs, becoming plumbers, machinists, auto workers and laborers, the majority continue to work in traditional jobs as operators and fabricators. In 1993, for example, 89 percent of sewing machine operators were women. In all, 4.1 million women worked as operators, fabricators and laborers with more women of color entering these jobs as white women moved into higher-paying work.

As in white-collar organizations, blue-collar jobs are often sex segregated. Certain industries have traditionally hired women: garment factories, laundry establishments, small electrical equipment assemblers, communications industries, beauty salons, restaurants, hospitals, and domestic agencies. When both sexes are employed in the same industry, men hold the more prestigious and higher-paying jobs. In the apparel industry, for example, men are the skilled cutters, pressers, and tailors, while women are the mass-production sewing machine operators.

The usual consequence of this segregation is lower pay for women. The women in industrial and service jobs earn about 60 percent of men's wages. While they are more likely to have benefits such as pension plans and health care than their white-collar sisters, they have lower benefits than union men. In addition, many of the industries in which they work have unstable employment and exploitative part-time work. Many of the industries in which women work are not unionized at all. Historically, the women in these female-dominated jobs have been from immigrant families, but recently more women of color have moved into these areas.

While union membership as a whole is down, there are more union members among blue-collar workers. Twenty-five percent of the craft workers and 26 percent of the operators are unionized in comparison to 10 percent of the technical workers and 14 percent of the service workers. Women are now one-third of all union members. However, many are in unions like the ILGWU (International Ladies Garment Workers Union), which are predominately female.

Most unions have not supported wage equality for their female employees and during periods of high unemployment, seniority demands and the desire to keep men on the job have taken precedence over any union demands for affirmative action. There are few women in leadership positions who could change this situation.

Even the union women who get good wages may face difficult situations. They often cope with male workers' hostility and undesired sexual advances. The men seldom help them learn their job, although they readily help an-

other man. Yet it is estimated that as much as 80 percent of some kinds of work is learned informally from others on the job. Manual jobs may also mean changing shifts and forced overtime, which wreak havoc with a working mother's childcare arrangements and family obligations.

BLACK WOMEN IN THE LABOR FORCE

Fifty-nine percent of all black women work and they have traditionally been in the labor force in large numbers. However, striking changes have occurred in the jobs and earnings of black women in the last two decades. Traditionally, the median income among employed black women was very low, with a large proportion of these women working in domestic service and the less-skilled manual trades. The early textile jobs were usually closed to black women, as were clerical and secretarial positions. During the 1980s, however, nearly one-fourth of black women changed jobs, moving into clerical occupations and the female-dominated professions. The shift in occupation caused a marked improvement in their occupational prestige and earnings as they became nurses, teachers and librarians, among other things. Black women thus increased their earnings, and after 1987, they earned an average of 98 percent of what white women were making. They had to work harder and longer for the same pay, however. They were often still in jobs with lower occupational prestige and wages, though they compensated by working longer hours and remaining in the labor force rather than interrupting employment for long periods while children are small.

There are many variations among black women workers. This fact is clearly seen in differences between age groups: older black females are more likely to be in domestic work and other services, while the younger ones are more likely to be in the professions. As 66 percent of black women workers are also likely to be single heads of families or to have husbands who earn lower incomes, it is particularly necessary for them to work.

Differences also exist between black women and black men workers. Although in 1996 black women had slightly higher educational attainment than black men, black women were earning only 82 percent of a black man's annual salary. Sex segregation in occupations again tells the story. Black women, like their white counterparts, are in the "feminine" and low-paid occupations.

There is a disturbing trend toward the possible loss of jobs for many black women. Clerical work is the dominant occupation for young black women, who have been concentrated in routine jobs such as typing and filing. But many of these jobs are being eliminated because of automation. Black clerical workers are also more likely to work for the government than private employers and may lose jobs as a result of recent governmental budget cuts. However, sex discrimination rather than racial discrimination now seems to be the labor-force problem for black women workers. They approximate white women in labor-force participation, occupational prestige, education and earnings.

ISSUES OF EQUALITY FOR MEN AND WOMEN WORKERS

Legislation

The revival of the feminist movement and the increased numbers of working women have interacted to generate concern about the differential between women's and men's wages and about sex discrimination in the marketplace. A spate of laws and court interpretations have resulted from women's attempt to gain legal protection.

There are four basic measures that prohibit discrimination on the basis of sex. The Equal Pay Act of 1963 (Section 6d of the Fair Labor Standards Act of 1938, as amended) requires that employees receive equal wages for "equal work on jobs which are performed under similar working conditions." This act does not prohibit discrimination in hiring or promotions, however. It was designed to aid women who were doing work equal to that done by men but were being paid less. In 1974, the Supreme Court interpreted this act to mean equal pay in all remuneration from the employer, including fringe benefits such as medical insurance and pension plans. However, bona fide (proved to be legitimate) seniority and merit systems were exempted.

Title VII of the Civil Rights Act of 1964 prohibits discrimination by race, color, religion, sex or national origin in hiring, firing, promotion, training, seniority, retirement and all other aspects of employment. The act also prohibits classification of employees in a way that will deprive an individual of employment opportunities. It applies to employment agencies and unions as well as to business. Feminists lobbied strongly for inclusion of sex as one of the categories against which one could not discriminate. While there was opposition to doing this, those opposed finally allowed sex to be included as a category because they wanted to defeat the entire bill and thought that including sex would cause that defeat. However, Title VII passed, and for the first time women were given a legal basis for insisting that they be allowed to compete with men for jobs and promotions. Even then, the Equal Employment Opportunity Commission (EEOC) refused for some time to enforce the sex provision and allowed employers to advertise "male jobs" and "female Jobs."

By 1966, pressure from feminist groups resulted in stricter enforcement of sex discrimination rules, and a 1972 amendment to Title VII (Title IX) expanded the law to include educational institutions and state and local governments as well as employers with fifteen or more employees. Since 1972, the EEOC can bring suits against all those (except government agencies) who violate the act. Two executive orders in 1965 and 1969 extended prohibitions against sex discrimination to federal contractors and to the federal government itself.

Another important piece of legislation was the Age Discrimination Employment Act of 1967, which prohibited government, private employers, employment agencies, and unions from discriminating against persons between forty and sixty-five years of age. As many women were not being hired or were being fired for being "too old" or "old and unattractive," this was an important protection for older women.

There have been major tests of all these laws. Various groups and agencies have gone to court to see if the laws would be judged to be in line with the intent of the Constitution. The court which hears such a case uses a variety of legal "tests" to see if the law is, indeed, constitutional. For example, there is a provision in Title VII that sex can be used to discriminate in jobs when sex is a "bona fide occupational qualification reasonably necessary to the normal operation of that particular business or enterprise." The courts have narrowly interpreted this provision, however, and in most cases have held that being a certain sex was not a "bona fide occupational requirement" for hiring. An example was the decision that men as well as women have to be hired as flight attendants. Pregnancy insurance and pension benefits have been other areas legally tested under the law. For a time the courts ruled that pregnancy and childbirth disabilities should be covered by health insurance, but recently they have ruled that normal pregnancy expenses are not covered. The issue of pension benefits has never been legally resolved.

A final area of concern has been the problem of seniority. The last-hired and first-fired policies that operate under seniority mean that those usually laid off would disproportionately be minorities and women. Despite disagreement in the court system, an appellate court ruled that under due process "if present hiring practices were nondiscriminatory, an employer's use of a long-established seniority system to establish the order of layoff and recall of employees was not a violation of Title VII."

The 1980s and Affirmative Action

During the 1980s, the Reagan administration deemphasized affirmative action. In fact, it followed the premise that affirmative action amounts to unlawful reverse discrimination against white males. Federal funds were cut, Women's Bureau programs for displaced homemakers and new immigrants had to rely upon the private sector, and federal job creation programs were decimated. Cutbacks in the Labor Department reduced staff available for implementation of affirmative action and wage and hour regulations. Any contract violations by business were simply ignored.

It is noteworthy that the Supreme Court did not uphold the Reagan administration's affirmative action philosophy. The Court upheld affirmative action decisions of the lower courts provided they did not unduly harm innocent white males. It did, however, prohibit preferential treatment for blacks during layoffs, preserving seniority rules in such cases. It also forbade rigid, permanent quotas as a mechanism to achieve affirmative action. In one Supreme Court decision which was hailed as a major victory for women and blacks, the court stated that affirmative action violated neither the Constitution nor Title VII of the Civil Rights Act of 1964.

The path pursued by George Bush was not very different from that of the Reagan administration. While he was not as active in attempting to dismantle affirmative action machinery, he did not push for enforcement. By contrast, President Clinton has actively pursued affirmative action goals. He has appointed more women and more minorities to high government office and the judiciary than any preceding President.

COMPARABLE WORTH

Recently there has been an attempt to combat the segregation of women into low-paying jobs by applying the principle of *Comparable Worth*, that is, the idea of paying equally for jobs that demand the same level of skill, effort, responsibility and working conditions even if they are not exactly the same jobs. Many believe that men and women are unlikely to have exactly the same jobs, and without this technique it will be difficult for women to ever have equal pay. The idea of paying on the basis of job evaluation is not a new concept. Many jobs in our society, such as those in the federal government, now have pay determined by a job evaluation system. In comparable worth job evaluation, the employer and employees (and union when there is a collective bargaining agreement) select the criteria on which wages should be based and decide how much weight to assign to each factor. It is important to set the criteria without sex bias. Points are then assigned for every job in a company according to its evaluation system so that a job's total score represents its worth to the employer. Very different jobs might have a similar score. Each job might have salary ranges and the actual salary for any worker would fall into these ranges according to seniority and other qualifications without regard to sex or race. Some examples of jobs that have been ranked the same are seen in Table 1.

Several important court cases have tested the concept of Comparable Worth. In a San Jose, California, case in 1981, municipal workers struck to enforce a job evaluation study that showed that certain jobs dominated by women were underpaid. They received $1.5 million in pay adjustments. In another case, Westinghouse Corporation was sued for having a pay scale that placed women workers in the lowest pay categories. The Corporation was forced to reevaluate their job categories and pay women commensurately. In 1983, women workers in the State of Washington won $800 million in back pay and wage increases on the basis of a Comparable Worth evaluation.

Conservatives argue that Comparable Worth adjustments are expensive and they stress the difficulty of trying to rate jobs with disparate qualifications. Feminists state that there is no other sure way to cope with pay inequities as long as jobs remain largely segregated by sex. They point to the fact that the cost of implementing pay equity in the State of Minnesota was less than 4 percent of the state's payroll budget.

What did not happen after the pay adjustment in Minnesota is significant. No employees had their wages reduced or frozen. There were no strikes or lawsuits. There was no bureaucracy created to manage the program. Contrary to dire warnings that women would stay in all-female fields as pay increased, women still sought jobs in male areas. Collective bargaining was still very important and morale was high. Feminists also state that pay equity will save tax dollars spent now on welfare for women and minorities whose wages are kept low by dis-

TABLE 1

EMPLOYER	OCCUPATION	PREDOMINATE SEX	PAY
Yale University	Administrative Assistant	Female	$13,000
	Truck Driver	Male	$18,000
State of Minnesota	Registered Nurse	Female	$20,676
	Vocational Education Teacher	Male	$27,120
County of Los Angeles	Health Technician	Minority	$13,380
	Evidence Custodian	White	$16,812

SWS/Sociologists for Women in Society, Facts About Pay Equity, April, 1986.

crimination. They emphasize that it will not lower any other workers' wages. Under the Equal Pay Act and Title VII, courts have consistently held that an employer may not lower any employee's pay to eliminate wage discrimination.

A different perspective on comparable worth is proposed by Penelope Ciancanelli and Bettina Berch in their article, "Gender and the GNP." They posit that "Employers are not the only opponents of comparable worth. Large numbers, perhaps even a 'silent majority' of Americans, may be quite uncomfortable with women making as much money as men do as this would encroach on men's social power and disturb existing arrangements."[5]

SEXUAL HARASSMENT

One of the most critical hidden aspects of women's work is sexual harassment. Sexual harassment can be defined in a number of ways. What one person might call a flattering compliment another person might call offensive. Marisa Manley says that, "one person's offhand comment can be another's hostile environment."[6] Ann McGrath emphasizes that the key to the definition of sexual harassment is that it is "unwelcome."[7] A working definition by the Michigan Task Force on Sexual Harassment that encompasses many aspects of sexual harassment states that harassment "includes continual or repeated verbal abuse of a sexual nature, including but not limited to graphic commentaries on the victim's body, sexually suggestive objects or pictures in the workplace, sexually degrading words used to describe the victim, or propositions of a sexual nature. Sexual harassment also includes the threat or insinuation that lack of sexual submission will adversely affect the victim's employment, wages, standing, or other conditions that affect the victim's livelihood."

Sexual harassment has existed for as long as women have worked. In the 19th century young unmarried women who worked in the mills often became pregnant after "succumbing to male supervisors." Instead of action being taken against the perpetrator, the problem was confronted by questioning whether it was immoral for young girls to work alongside men. It was decided that such contact was immoral and women were usually segregated into different jobs, often at lower pay. In domestic work women were also victims of harassment. Louisa May Alcott in 1874 wrote about her experience with sexual harassment in the workplace when she worked as a domestic for a married couple. After propositioning her many times, the husband ordered Alcott to do the hardest manual labor around the house and yard.

One of the most pervasive early forms of sexual harassment was that endured by black women slaves. There is clear documentation that slave women were consistent victims of sexual abuse at the hands of white masters. Minority women are still among the most severely exploited today. As Catherine MacKinnon puts it, in *Sexual Harassment of Working Women*, sexual harassment in this case can be a "sexist way to express racism or a racist way to express sexism."

Types of Harassment

According to legal definition, sexual harassment usually falls into two categories: "quid pro quo" and "hostile environment." The former basically means one thing in return for another (for example, a raise for sex) and the later is anything that is perceived to be an expression of hostility by the person receiving it. Peggy Crull suggests that certain kinds of behaviors usually happen to women according to their field of work. Quid pro quo behavior usually is directed at women in traditional fields of work, places where women are expected to be working. The hostile environment behavior usually happens to women with jobs typically held by men.

Crull believes that the hostile environment is more likely to occur on non-traditional jobs because the perpetrator is likely to be a co-worker who does not necessarily have the power to offer a quid pro quo. To this coworker the woman may symbolize the power on the job which he is losing. In the traditional job Crull says that harassment is more likely to be provoked by what she calls "sex role spillover," in which the roles of the two genders on the job are similar to the roles of a patriarchal family and the boss is acting toward the woman as he would if she were his wife. The woman in the traditional job steps out of her role when she refuses her boss's sexual requests—a threat to patriarchy. Crull points out that sexual harassment is "only the tip of the iceberg and what lies beneath is a whole system of assumptions, practices and structures through which sexuality negatively affects the woman's position in the marketplace."[8]

Rulings against both quid pro quo and hostile environment types of sexual harassment have been upheld by the Supreme Court. In June of 1986, in *Meritor Savings Bank* v. *Michelle Vinson*, an opinion by William Rehnquist stated, "Without question, when a supervisor sexually harasses a subordinate because of a subordinate's sex, that supervisor discriminates on the basis of sex." This ruling paved the way for sexual harassment claims as sex discrimination under Title VII of the 1964 Civil Rights Act.

In spite of this landmark ruling, questions about many areas of sexual harassment have not yet been answered. These center around employer liability, definitions of "unwelcome," and situations in which there was previous consensual sexual activity. Because of the uniqueness of each case, the Court has been deciding each question on a case by case basis.

Questions also exist about whether or not to believe a victim when she complains long after the time of the harassment. In a highly publicized situation, Anita Hill, now a law professor, complained that Judge Clarence

Thomas, then a nominee for the United States Supreme Court, had sexually harassed her when she worked for him years before. She stated that she could not stand to see such a man elevated to the Supreme Court without coming forward with her complaint. Because both Hill and Thomas were black, the cases stimulated a great deal of controversy. African Americans often expressed the opinion that Hill should have kept quiet and not jeopardized the chances of the first black man to be appointed to the court. Most women believed Hill's charges of harassment but many men doubted her, and there were suggestions that the confirmation committee had hushed up her story. In the end, the overwhelmingly male Senate confirmed Thomas as a Supreme Court Justice.

Extent

In the late 1980s several studies were conducted to determine the extent of sexual harassment in the workplace. Between 1985 and 1987, the U.S. Merit Systems Protection Board surveyed over 23,000 federal employees about their experiences. The study found that 42 percent of women federal workers reported being sexually harassed. A survey of 160 companies done by *Working Women* magazine asked about the incidence of specific behaviors and found that 42 percent of the women had experienced teasing sexual comments; 26 percent had experienced touching or leaning over and cornering; 17 percent had experienced pressure for sexual favors; 12 percent had experienced pressure for dates. Such harassment had happened to a diverse group of women from coal miners, factory workers, and police officers to nurses, secretaries, lawyers, and professors. MacKinnon points out that the diversity of occupations supports the hypothesis that harassment occurs because of the group's common characteristic, sex.

By the late 1990s, employers were much more aware of sexual harassment, and training aimed at preventing or combating harassment was commonplace. However, arassment cases continued to surface. One celebrated group of cases concerned military drill sergeants and other officers who used their power to sexually harass female recruits, including forcing them to have sexual intercourse. Women also quit newly integrated military academies after severe hazing by male upperclassmen.

One commonly asked question about harassment is "Doesn't it happen to men, too?" Approximately one-tenth of harassment incidents reported are those where men are victims or harassment is between two people of the same sex: men harassed by women, men by men or women harassed by women. Few women are in positions of authority over men in the workplace, however.

Effects on Women

In many respects women respond to sexual harassment in the same way that they respond to rape. Women may feel a variety of things emotionally, such as embarrassment, intimidation, fear, despair, guilt, shame, and anger. Physiologically, they may experience stomachaches, headaches, loss of appetite, bouts of crying, and insomnia. They may begin to question their own integrity, and ask themselves what they are doing to provoke this behavior. Most women fear repercussions or retaliation in terms of their jobs. Many quit their jobs.

Although black women experience the same emotional and physical reactions as non-minority victims, their actions in response to the harassment may differ. A number of white women will leave their jobs; black women are more likely to take legal action. They have taken such action in disproportionate numbers. MacKinnon hypothesizes that they have no

choice but to act legally due to their "least advantaged position in the economy."

Responding to Sexual Harassment

Clearly both the workplace and women have a stake in ending this unwanted behavior. Businesses cannot afford to have situations causing emotional and physical stress for its employees, and there is always the potential for a lawsuit if an organization does not address the situation. Many experts in the field suggest that confronting the person doing the harassing is important, and may even be enough to end the situation. According to some studies, when a woman just ignores the harassment it intensifies 75 percent of the time. Responding with "I'm not receptive to this" or "Please don't" may be all it takes, says Amy Saltzman.[9] If confrontation does not work, telling someone is the next step. Several experts suggest keeping records of the incidents for reporting purposes as well as for a possible lawsuit. Sexual harassment is still commonplace and widespread. It is an integral part of women's experience in the workforce. Catherine MacKinnon sums up the insidious nature of harassment when she says, "Sexual harassment undercuts woman's potential for social equality in two ways: it uses employment to coerce her sexually and it uses her sexual position to coerce her economically."

OTHER IMPORTANT WORK ISSUES

Family Leaves and Maternity Health Coverage

In 1990, 47 percent of working mothers relied on spouses or relatives to provide child care. There were also an estimated 2.5 million children six to thirteen years of age who were left on their own after school. By 1996, licensed day-care centers accounted for the care of 8.5 million children under six, approximately 10 percent of the children needing care. Another 40 percent were in unlicensed in-home care. For families who earned less than $15,00 and had a young child, day care expenses consumed 23 percent of all household expenditures. Even in states where there was a good supply of day care, access was low in poorer areas. The high cost of day care restricts women's employment opportunities, both in terms of current employment and the amount of time they spend in paid work. The need for child care is greatest among female employees who do not have a family buffer.

Many believe there is a shortage of quality day care. Of an estimated 46,000 mid-to-large-size companies, only 3,300 (5 percent) provided child care in 1988. Many of these programs were informational or referral programs. However, the number of corporations providing on-site day care has increased. Most of the companies that sponsor such care believe it helps reduce absenteeism and improves morale and productivity, although some companies have found that the costs outweigh the benefits. There has recently been a consolidation of employer child-care centers among the major national providers and many believe that employers who offer child care as an employee benefit have focused on innovation and high quality care.

In 1990, the Federal government enacted the Child Care and Development Act, which offered the states grant money to develop quality child care. Those applauding the act still advise caution and careful planning, however. The kind of care developed now will affect care decisions into the next century, with public-private partnerships being suggested. Yet another positive development is the rise of centralized Child Care Resource and Referral networks.

Family Leave

The Federal government also passed the Family and Medical Leave Act (FMLA) in 1993, which allowed covered employers to grant up to 12 weeks of unpaid leave to eligible workers for the birth, adoption, or foster-care of a child, the "serious health condition" of a spouse, son, daughter, or parent, and a "serious health condition" of the employee that renders the employee incapable of performing essential job functions. In addition, one survey showed that large employers often incorporate some maternity benefits in personnel policies, including payments toward health insurance coverage during leave, and at least partial wage replacement. Small employers were more likely to allow women to return to their jobs on a reduced work schedule after childbirth. In spite of these improvements, however, the U.S. lags far behind other industrialized nations in its provision of family leave and child care.

Options to Make Work Time More Flexible

Employers have recently been more willing to allow job-sharing between employees. This allows each employee to spend more time with children and family while having the advantages of a paid job. One of the difficulties that has to be worked out with this employment possibility, however, is how benefits for the job will be allocated. Other increasingly available options are work at home, compressed work weeks, part-time employment, telecommuting, and flextime. However, some warn against the negative effects on one's career that such options may have. Such effects include limited work responsibilities, ineligibility for promotions, no salary increases, lack of pro-rated benefits, and lack of visibility. As many employers are already outsourcing work and using contract employees, these negatives and the possibility of job loss should not be minimized.

Another problem for working women is inadequate pensions. Only about 1/3 of employed women have employer-provided pensions. Moreover, the pensions they do get are about half of what men get, as benefits are largely a function of wages, and women's wages average only

76 percent of men's wages. Women also change jobs more often than men, and can thus miss out on benefits. And part-time work frequently comes without benefits.

Insurance companies have also attempted to reduce monthly pension payments to women, claiming that they live longer than men, and the money they get needs to be spread over a longer period. In addition, companies that provide disability insurance are asking women to pay higher premiums, claiming that women have more disabilities than men.

Other government laws also affect those in the labor force, especially women. Tax and social security laws that penalize two-worker families may make it less rewarding for a woman to work; and veterans' benefits may mean that it is more difficult for a woman to get some jobs, or to get the same benefits as a man would.

IN SUMMARY

Women in the job market suffer lower wages and lower job status than men for a number of reasons. As the result of choice or discrimination, they may not make the investment in their human capital that gives them access to the more prestigious and well-paying jobs. They are likely to enter jobs that are segregated, that pay less, and that may be glutted in the near future. They are also discriminated against for a variety of reasons that include myths and the weight of cultural tradition. As unequal pay "per se" is illegal, the means for this discrimination is usually to place women in jobs with secondary status. Moreover, laws and government policies add to the low status of women workers. Thus, institutional discrimination against women (conscious or unconscious) means that they retain their status as secondary workers with unequal wages and job status.

NOTES

1. William H. Chafe, "Looking Backward in Order to Look Forward," in Juanite Kreps, ed., *Women and the American Economy* (Englewood Cliffs, N.J.: Prentice-Hall, 1976), pp. 15–16.

2. Ibid., p. 25.

3. Felicia Schwartz, *The Harvard Business Review*, quoted in Martha Moore and David Proctor, "USA Firms Facing 'New Facts of Life,'" in *USA Today*, March 11, 1989, p. 1A.

4. Heidi Hartmann, "Capitalism, Patriarchy and Job Segregation by Sex," *Signs* 1, pt. 2 (1976), 137–69.

5. Penelope Ciancanelli and Bettina Berch, pp. 244–266, in Beth Hess and Myra Marx Feree, eds., *Analyzing Gender: A Handbook of Social Science Research* (Beverly Hills, Ca.: Sage, 1987).

6. Marisa Manley, "Dealing with Sexual Harassment," *Inc.* (May 1987), 145–46.

7. Ann McGrath, "The Touchy Issue of Sexual Harassment," *Savvy* (April, 1987), 18–19.

8. Peggy Crull, "Hidden Aspects of Women's Work," in Christine Bose and Roslyn Feldberg, eds., *Hidden Aspects of Women's Work* (New York: Praeger, 1987.)

9. Amy Saltzman, "Hands Off at the Office," *U. S. News and World Report*, August 1, 1988, pp. 56–58.

Inside the Work Worlds of Chicana and Mexican Immigrant Women

Denise A. Segura

Chicanas (Mexican American women) and Mexicanas (immigrant women from Mexico)[1] confront many barriers to employment and job advancement. Securing decent jobs and promotions can be a difficult, if not impossible, task, considering structural features of the labor market (e.g., occupational segregation), social aspects of work, family responsibilities, and individual characteristics. This chapter brings the human dimension of this problem to life through an analysis of in-depth interviews with forty Chicana and Mexicana workers. I argue that labor market structure, particularly occupational segregation by race-ethnicity and gender, shapes Chicanas' and Mexicanas' experiences at work as well as their chances for job mobility. Within these confines, Chicanas and Mexicanas actively seek to develop strategies to maximize their social and economic betterment.

I organize my analysis first to provide a larger picture of Chicana and Mexicana employment and occupational segregation. Usually occupational segregation refers to the disproportionately large concentration of women in low-paying occupations. In this chapter, however, occupational segregation by gender is taken one step further to distinguish between jobs where the work force is primarily White women (White-female-dominated jobs) or pri-

marily racial-ethnic minority women (minority female-dominated jobs). This analytic separation is based on the perceptions of my study informants.[2] Second, I discuss the process whereby the women I interviewed became employed in jobs associated with their gender, or their gender/race-ethnicity, in the San Francisco Bay area of northern California. Third, I use three representative case studies to illustrate key features of the different labor market segments in which the respondents worked, and discuss their implications for occupational mobility. This analysis of the experiences of Chicana and Mexicana workers contributes new research on workplace features and dynamics that reinforce occupational segregation.

CHICANAS AND OCCUPATIONAL SEGREGATION

Chicanas and Mexican immigrant women have historically worked in jobs that have been filled by racial-ethnic minorities, women, and/or women of color. Current employment patterns point to a cumulative effect of race-ethnicity and gender that limits Chicanas' access to better-paying jobs. Table 1 illustrates that in 1990, relatively few Chicano men and Chicana women, vis-à-vis non-Hispanic men and women, worked in the relatively better-paying, prestigious managerial and professional occupations.[3]

Like non-Hispanic women, Chicanas are occupationally segregated in female-dominated technical, sales, or administrative support occupations (see Table 1). In 1990, about 38 percent of Chicana and Mexicana women worked in

TABLE 1   Occupational Distribution of Men and Women of Mexican and Non-Hispanic Origin, Sixteen Years and Over, March 1990[a]

OCCUPATION	MEXICAN ORIGIN[b]		NON-HISPANIC	
	MALE	FEMALE	MALE	FEMALE
Managerial and professional	8.3%	14.2%	27.4%	27.1%
Technical, sales, administrative support	12.6	38.1	21.0	45.3
Services	5.1	23.9	9.2	16.9
Farming, forestry, fishing	11.2	1.8	3.6	1.0
Precision production, craft, repair	21.2	3.2	19.3	2.1
Operators, fabricators, laborers	31.7	18.8	19.5	7.5
Total number (thousands)	3,335	2,006	58,235	49,759

[a]All numbers in this table are estimates.
[b]Includes both Chicano/a and Mexicano/a people.
Source: U.S. Department of Commerce, Bureau of the Census, *The Hispanic Population in the United States, March 1990.* Current Population Reports, Series P-20, no. 449 (Washington, D.C.: U.S. Government Printing Office, 1991).

these jobs. Fewer Chicanas and Mexicanas were employed in these female-dominated jobs, however, than non-Hispanic women. Moreover, research indicates that when Chicanas and Mexicanas work in these female-dominated occupations, they tend to occupy the lower levels (e.g., file clerk rather than supervisor). Also, like other women of color, but unlike White women or Chicano men, Chicanas are overrepresented in low-paying, low-status jobs susceptible to seasonal fluctuations, such as domestic workers, cannery workers, and garment factory seamstresses.

There are other differences in employment between Chicanas/Mexicanas and non-Hispanic men and women. In 1990, the unemployment rate for Chicanas and Mexicanas was 9.8 percent, as opposed to 5.7 percent and 4.9 percent for non-Hispanic men and women, respectively. In 1989, the median earnings of Chicana/ Mexicana workers were $8,874 as opposed to $22,081 for non-Hispanic men and $11,885 for non-Hispanic women. This employment and unemployment profile suggests that Chicanas encounter a unique situation in the labor market, one characterized by jobs that mirror a combination of two sets of statuses—race-ethnicity and gender.

Human capital theory posits a different view, one that emphasizes the importance of individual characteristics for employment and mobility. According to this perspective, wages and mobility reflect an individual's level of educational attainment and job skills. Thus, Chicanos' lower earnings result from their lower levels of human capital relative to White males. In addition, as women, Chicanas and Mexicanas have family roles that may lessen the time they can make available for their jobs and severely hamper their chances to advance on the job. Theoretically, then, women "choose" less prestigious jobs (e.g., clerical) because they are relatively easy to enter and exit, thereby offering a good fit with women's gender roles and expectations. What is problematic in this perspective is the assumption that all workers enjoy equal opportunities to acquire or augment their human capital, have the same access to job information, and act in rational, self-interested ways that are only minimally affected by social relations. Human capital theory also tends to accept uncritically gender ideology and expectations as given rather than socially constructed.

Other research highlights structural barriers to job entry and mobility for Chicanas and

Mexicanas. They are occupationally segregated in operative jobs and lower-level service and clerical jobs. These jobs tend to be located in what many labor economists and sociologists call the "secondary labor market" of semiskilled and unskilled jobs, where high turnover of personnel, instability, low wages, and few avenues for advancement predominate (e.g., garment workers, child care workers). Such occupational segregation can be viewed as a structural feature of the labor market. As such, it is regarded by many as the major barrier to good pay, good working conditions, and job advancement that women of color experience.

Occupational segregation is sustained by a range of social forces. Employer discrimination (by race and gender) is one dynamic that reinforces occupational segregation by limiting Chicanas' and Mexicanas' access to better jobs in the primary labor market, and favoring their entry into jobs traditionally associated with minorities and women. Racial-ethnic-, class-, and/or gender-segregated social networks can also reproduce occupational segregation. Insofar as workers rely on family and friends for job information, they become limited to jobs traditionally filled by these groups—which, in the case of the working class, intensifies the occupational segregation of racial-ethnic minorities.

The organization of the workplace and the work environment also plays a key role in maintaining workers in low-paying jobs. For example, some lower-level (or "secondary") jobs are organized hierarchically in ways that provide a limited degree of mobility to workers. Gradations within lower-level jobs can offer workers a degree of mobility (e.g., moving from sorting fruit to packing fruit, or from piecework wages to hourly wages). While the degree of this mobility may not always be statistically significant, it is qualitatively distinct and important when it helps keep workers in an occupationally segregated work world. When actual job advancement is not likely, positive social relations may reinforce the occupa-

tional segregation of Chicana and Mexicana workers, as this paper will illustrate.

FORTY WOMEN OF MEXICAN DESCENT

For this study, I interviewed twenty Chicanas and twenty resident Mexican immigrant women in 1984–85. All the women were selected from the 1978–79 or 1980–81 CETA (Comprehensive Employment Training Act) cohorts of an adult education and employment training program in the San Francisco Bay area.[4] This program was designed to increase the job skills of participants through educational, language, and specialized vocational training. Participants were usually placed by the program, or found employment via their social networks, in clerical, operative, and service jobs often filled by women and racial-ethnic minorities. Forty-nine Chicanas and Mexicanas had participated in this program during the targeted years. While I tried to contact all forty-nine women, I could locate and interview only forty. Each interview lasted from three to four hours. The interviews were informal and usually took place in the respondent's home. I talked with six women at the training program at their own request. The interviews were open-ended, and were based on an interview guide I developed early in the research. I did not administer a questionnaire but asked general questions that became more specific in the course of the interview. The questions were designed to gather in-depth life and work histories from the Chicana and Mexicana informants to explore (1) why they entered and exited from their jobs, (2) how they perceived and experienced occupational mobility in the labor market, and (3) the barriers to mobility they were experiencing. I defined occupational mobility as an increase in wages and job status, from the first job after leaving the training program to their last/current job.

From their life histories, I discovered that all but one Mexicana and one Chicana grew up in families they described as poor or working class. Forty percent of the Mexicanas had less than a primary school education, and 60 percent had finished elementary school. All but three of the Mexicanas had obtained a high school equivalency diploma by the time they finished the training program. Slightly over half of the Chicanas had not finished high school. By the time they finished the training program, only five did not have either a high school diploma or its equivalent.

Of the forty respondents, thirty-one had been involved in a conjugal relationship (either legal marriage or informal cohabitation with a partner) at some point in their lives before being interviewed. At the time of the interviews, six Chicanas and fourteen Mexicanas were married. Seven Chicanas and four Mexicanas were single parents. All but ten respondents had children.

EMPLOYMENT AND MOBILITY

When the women discussed the dynamics of job choice, I ascertained they were essentially channeled into female-dominated jobs. This finding is an important critique of human capital's emphasis on individual rational choice. Women in this study framed their initial employment not as a matter of choice but as part of a fluid process that was continuously being constructed and reconstructed, depending on institutional practices, family economic need, gender ideology, and other social influences. The women who had attended high school had participated in youth employment programs that had placed them in female-dominated jobs (e.g., clerical aide). None of the women reported being encouraged to consider nontraditional jobs either by secondary school counselors or by family members. In fact, the respondents relied on their social networks and/or the training program for job placements.

The program provided access to male-dominated jobs (paint packer, venetian blind maker, mail carrier) to only three women. Only one woman accepted such a job. Her economic need was acute (her husband was unemployed), whereas the other two women had husbands who were employed and did not want their wives working in male-dominated jobs.[5] The combination of institutional dynamics and family needs and preferences led thirty-nine of the forty respondents (nineteen Mexicanas and twenty Chicanas) to enter jobs where their coworkers were mostly women. This initial job placement reinforced the respondents' occupational segregation in female-dominated jobs and upheld traditional conceptions of gender within this community.

Another critical finding that emerged in the interviews concerned racial-ethnic segregation within the female-dominated jobs held by the respondents (see Table 2). Seventeen respondents (thirteen Chicanas and four Mexicanas) reported working in jobs where a majority of their coworkers were White women. Twenty-two respondents (fifteen Mexicanas and seven Chicanas) worked in jobs where nearly all of their coworkers were women of color.

In the course of the interviews, it became apparent that the jobs where the majority of the work force consisted of White women corresponded to better working conditions, higher salaries, and more advancement opportunities vis-à-vis jobs where a majority of workers were women of color.[6] Salaries were much higher in male-dominated jobs. Of the fourteen women who had become occupationally mobile, ten secured promotions within White-female-dominated clerical occupations. One Mexicana became upwardly mobile within a minority-female-dominated occupation (she went from hotel maid to assistant housekeeping manager). One Chicana and one Mexicana switched from White-female-dominated occupations to a male-dominated occupation. They moved from clerical jobs to mail carriers. The last upwardly mobile woman, a Mexicana, was promoted within a male-dominated occupation (from paint

TABLE 2   Study Informants' Employment

MALE-DOMINATED JOBS	WHITE-FEMALE-DOMINATED JOBS	MINORITY-FEMALE-DOMINATED JOBS
Mail carrier	Clerical	Hotel maid
Line foreman		Bilingual child care worker
Paint packer		Bilingual teacher's assistant
		Seamstress
		Operative (e.g., tool packer)
		Assistant housekeeping manager
		Waitress

Note: Race-ethnic and gender job descriptions are based on informants' reports of the gender and race-ethnicity of coworkers. For male-dominated jobs, less than 10 percent of coworkers were female. For White-female-dominated jobs, less than 10 percent of coworkers were men or women of color. For minority-female-dominated jobs, less than 10 percent of coworkers were White women or men.

packer to line foreman). This mobility profile suggests that the local labor markets accessed by the respondents reinforced larger racial-ethnic and gender hierarchies.

Women's opportunities for occupational advancement often hinged upon the degree to which they felt attached to their jobs. A woman's relationship with her coworkers and the quality of her interaction with supervisors were critical in this regard. The better a woman felt about the social relations at work, the more likely she would be to call on others to devise strategies to manage problematic aspects of the job or to seek out the means for promotion. At the same time, if a woman felt alienated at work, her attachment to her job typically suffered, resulting in her exit from the job as soon as her economic circumstances allowed.

Racial-ethnic and class differences between the respondents and their coworkers/supervisors shaped the contours of the social relations at work. Moreover, the structure of the labor market—the occupational segregation of the respondents into White-female-dominated jobs or minority-female-dominated jobs—restricted their chances to realize occupational mobility in a number of ways. To illustrate in more concrete terms the impact of labor market structure and interactional dynamics at work among Chicana and Mexicana workers, I present three cases: Norma, Laura, and Angela. Each repre-

sents women in a different job situation who confronted and managed structural, individual, and social barriers to occupational mobility.

CASE 1: NORMA

The first case is Norma, a Mexicana who became occupationally mobile in a clerical job. At the time of her interview, Norma was twenty-nine years old and married, with two preschool-aged children. She was promoted from clerical trainee to data entry clerk II in a large research firm. Norma entered her first job through a 1980 affirmative action program that targeted racial-ethnic minorities.

Norma recalled that gaining access to her job had been difficult and stressful. She told me that during her initial job interview, a supervisor told her that her English was inadequate. Norma reported this incident to her job counselor at the training program. The counselor called the supervisor's manager to inform him of Norma's high written and oral English proficiency test scores and to suggest that refusing her employment based on language might be discriminatory. Norma went for a second interview and was hired. While Norma was pleased to obtain the job, she felt that her assertive pursuit of it had made her anathema to some of the supervisory staff. This troubled her, but she maintained that if she had not fought for her employment rights, she would not be working in a "good" clerical job.

Norma contended that her predominantly White female coworkers and supervisors have never accepted her. After five years on the job, she still experiences a sense of social isolation at work:

It has been difficult to get used to working here. The atmosphere is very different [than Mexico]. The customs are different. There is little conversation beyond "hi." Only with their friends do they say more. I realize that these feelings usually happen when one enters a new job. But usually the novelty wears off. For me it has never worn off. The atmosphere still seems very cold. I have thought that perhaps it is the language. But I don't know ... perhaps it's being Latina. The few Latinos they've had there—all of them leave.

Norma told me that she had nearly quit her job after eleven months. She had felt socially isolated from coworkers and had not received much direction, training, or support from her immediate supervisor. Like the other respondents in White-female-dominated clerical jobs, Norma understood that becoming informed about the opportunities for advancement on the job was a critical prerequisite to becoming occupationally mobile. The respondents maintained that jobs posted on bulletin boards were not the best sources of information for promotions. Rather, supervisors, and often coworkers, were key informants in distinguishing jobs that were "really open" from jobs that were already filled. To receive this kind of information, women had to be part of a social network.

After eleven months, Norma despaired of achieving social acceptance at work or getting ahead in her job. Then, she took a six-month maternity leave. Norma returned to her job as scheduled because of her husband's recent job loss. When she returned, she had a new unit supervisor (or manager), a Chicano male. He gave her additional training, advised her to attend specific classes at the local community college, and gave her moral support when she was harassed by coworkers regarding certain small but critical details, such as the pictures she chose to decorate her corner of the office, her makeup, and her accent. He recommended her for the one promotion she obtained. Recently, this manager told her that he would be leaving his job within a year. He advised Norma to start looking for another job while he could still help her.

Norma averred that she was taking this manager's advice to look for a better job. She believed that her painful experiences in her current job will help her do better in subsequent jobs. Norma laughed as she told me that she was no longer "verde" (green) and now understood "more how things work." When I asked her to elaborate on what she had learned, she discussed the importance of "patience," "seeking out people who will help one," and "understanding that there's a lot of racism out there."

Like many of the Mexicana respondents, Norma was initially reluctant to designate problems at work as possible manifestations of racism. Chicanas, on the other hand, were usually quick to identify and condemn racism in the labor market and in society generally. This difference probably reflects Chicanas' experiences and perceptions of themselves as members of a racial-ethnic minority in the United States, whereas Mexicanas were typically unused to characterizing themselves as "minorities." Instead, the Mexicana respondents focused on being immigrants in search of better lives. They rationalized cold or hostile treatment as part of the immigrant experience that would abate as they became culturally and linguistically proficient in English and the American way of life. To Norma and the other Mexicanas, adhering to this rationalization was part of being "green" or a novice in the labor market. The Mexicanas in this study typically lost this idealized view by the end of their first year in their first job in the United States.

CASE 2: LAURA

The second example is Laura, a Chicana who became occupationally mobile by leaving a clerical job and entering a male-dominated job, mail carrier. Laura was twenty-five years old, single, with one year of college education. As part of an intensive affirmative action campaign at a local college, she was hired as a receptionist in its engineering department. There were about seven other clerical workers in her unit, all but one of them White women. Laura's account was similar to Norma's with respect to the sense of social isolation experienced. But while Norma focused on the ways her racial-ethnic or cultural background separated her from her coworkers, Laura emphasized how class differences separate workers socially:

With my coworkers it was difficult. It was a very stuffy environment there at the college. . . . Everyone there, they were from a totally different class. They were more into themselves and others like them—you know, more upper class. So I guess I couldn't relate to them. They used to talk about things I didn't know anything about. I felt really out of place. . . . After I'd been there about three years, I'd reached the top level—for me. Then I got called to the post office. When I told my supervisor that I was leaving, she was shocked. [She laughs with a wicked gleam in her eye.] She said, "Why don't we try for a promotion?" I said, "It's kind of late for that." You see, I'd been trying to transfer and be promoted for about two years.

Laura felt that her working-class background set her apart from her coworkers. When I asked her what she meant by this, she said that the kinds of movies she liked, the jokes she found amusing, and her dress were different from those of her coworkers. In addition, she felt uncomfortable when they used "big" words or discussed events she believed formed part of "White, upper-class culture." Her words suggest that occupational mobility can be problematic if a woman's bearing, including her choice of words, mannerisms, and dress, vary significantly from the workplace norm. Both Norma and Laura discussed the major modifications they had made in

their makeup, hairstyles, and dress. But their less obvious qualities—in particular, their social mannerisms—were much more difficult to modify. Thus, persistently, they felt out of place.

The tensions Laura, Norma, and other respondents felt in White-female-dominated jobs lessened only slowly. Some women, like Norma, adapted to the work environment under the auspices of a supportive supervisor. Others, like Laura, did not receive this kind of support and left the job in search of greener pastures. According to Laura, her supervisor did not regard her as an able worker worthy of additional training and promotion, both of which she had repeatedly asked for. This lack of support, coupled with her social distance from coworkers, contributed to Laura's disengagement from her job. So Laura enrolled in a night course to prepare for the post office exam—a job that was opening up to Hispanics due to a recent consent decree. After three unsatisfactory years as a clerical worker, she entered the high-paying, male-dominated world of the mail carrier.

Laura, Norma, and the other respondents differed with respect to how long a time should elapse before they might reasonably "give up" on establishing rapport with supervisors and coworkers. If a woman felt a great deal of hostility directed at her, she generally left within a year. Other women stayed in White-female-dominated jobs even though they had not been promoted. Their job attachment hinged on two factors: (1) their earnings were critical for their economic survival or that of their families—particularly if they were single parents; and (2) they perceived clerical work as "better" than the low-level factory or service jobs they knew about and had connections to.

CASE 3: ANGELA

The third example is Angela, a Mexicana garment worker who is not occupationally mobile. Angela is thirty-one years old, married, with a ten-year-old child. Her husband works irregularly as a janitor. Angela left the training program in 1980 with a job as a tool packer in a small, local factory. This job paid the minimum wage and offered health benefits to workers but not to their families. After about six months, Angela left this job due to health problems. She quickly found employment as a seamstress in a small shop. That job offered similar wages and benefits, but ended eighteen months later. In 1983, Angela obtained her current job as a seamstress in a medium-sized factory. When I asked her why she chose employment in garment factories, Angela replied, "Here Mexican women are appreciated mainly for their work in the kitchen, taking care of children, and in factories because they are very patient. In other jobs—I'm not so sure."

Although Angela had received clerical training, she was not able to find either a clerical job or a service job that paid her as much as piece-work wages in a sewing factory. When I asked her how long she had looked for a different job, she admitted she had applied to only two or three places.

What was drawing Angela to the sewing factory was a combination of her prior experience as a seamstress, the sense that she would have relatively easy access to a sewing job, and the knowledge that she would work with women she would feel comfortable with. Her current job is sewing small stuffed animals. Because of the extensive detailing on the animals, the job was difficult to learn, but Angela's coworkers assisted her. She described this process warmly: "At the beginning, it [the job] was very difficult for me and I was very slow. My coworkers helped me sometimes so that I could make more money and my quota. We get along well together. Thanks to their support I stayed there, even though my supervisor sometimes says, 'You must hurry yourself up!'"

Angela enjoys a good relationship with her coworkers but feels tense due to pressure from her supervisor to exceed current production levels. She does not feel this is discriminatory harassment, however, since the supervisor urges everyone to increase production. In fact, Angela gave high marks to her supervisor for her even-handed treatment of employees: "She [the supervisor] has more than enough experience and a lot of patience. But when we don't produce the minimum [production level], she tells us we have to hurry—but in a good way."

Angela's supervisor is a Mexican woman, and her coworkers are Latina or Asian immigrant women. Like other women employed in minority-female-dominated jobs in factories, hotels, child care centers, and bilingual classrooms, Angela and her coworkers socialize during lunchtimes, and sometimes after work as well. Angela indicated that she enjoys being able to speak Spanish on the job with her Latina coworkers and Mexican supervisor. She practices her English skills with her Asian coworkers, who are also interested in speaking English. Angela told me that she feels a part of her workplace, and has not been avoided, isolated, or harassed in any way by her coworkers. The warm social relations she described contrasted sharply with the alienation felt by the Chicana and Mexicana respondents in clerical jobs where their coworkers were predominantly White women and men.

Angela and the other respondents understood the unstable nature of factory, hotel, and child care jobs. Nor did they expect to get promoted in these jobs. But economic need and feeling comfortable socially at work enhanced their job attachment. These feelings impeded the respondents' chances to realize occupational mobility because they discouraged them from leaving what they termed "decent-paying jobs" for more lucrative jobs that involved (in their view) a high risk of failure. Moreover, they provided one form of compensation for harsh physical conditions and lack of promotional opportunities.

CONCLUSION

The experiences of the women in this study point to important structural and experiential barriers to employment and mobility. Each case has profound implications for racial-ethnic, class, and gender segregation at work and in society. First, occupational segregation by gender, and by gender/race-ethnicity, was actively created and recreated at the macro and micro levels. Second, occupational segregation limited women's job attachment and mobility. Third, social relations at work played a key role in women's employment options. Fourth, social relations at work were shaped by the social class, race-ethnicity, and gender of coworkers and supervisors.

Occupational segregation was reinforced by a channeling process. Respondents described schooling that did not impart a sense of employment options outside those traditionally ascribed to women. Similarly, the employment training program rarely provided them with access to jobs outside of those occupied by women and/or women of color in the community. Family dynamics (economic need, husband's dislike of wives working with men) also upheld women's participation in female-dominated jobs. This intersection of macro/micro social dynamics posed strong barriers to women's job attachment and mobility.

Employment in jobs occupationally segregated by gender and race-ethnicity restricted the type of occupational mobility the respondents could attain or aspire to. Among the respondents, promotional opportunities were greater in White-female-dominated clerical jobs than in minority-female-dominated service and operative jobs. The quality of social relations at work often intensified existing patterns of occupational segregation. That is, the racial-ethnic and social class background of the respondents often separated them from coworkers and supervisors. It was difficult for both the respondents and their coworkers to establish a rapport if they were from different social worlds.

Social relations within minority-female-dominated jobs typically were much warmer. The relative absence of conflict based on race or class differences in these jobs often attracted

and held the respondents to this structurally unstable arena. In this fashion, positive social relations at work reinforced the occupational clustering of the respondents in low-paying jobs.

Another dilemma many of the respondents faced was disaffection on the part of some coworkers and supervisors, triggered by their recruitment through affirmative action hiring programs. Women usually did not address this predicament directly but tried to outlast the resentment—a task rendered somewhat easier as the respondents adapted to the culture of their work environments or the workplace became more diversified (e.g., Norma's supportive Chicano supervisor). This problem points to the need to prepare workers and managers for a diverse workplace.

It is important to remember that while heterogeneity may promote intergroup relations, moving beyond homogeneity is a difficult and often painful process, as this study has demonstrated. Continuing to explore the human dimensions of this dilemma is essential. As we become more knowledgeable of the ways in which structural forces and micro dynamics uphold class, racial-ethnic, and gender segregation in the labor market, we will be that much closer to developing strategies to promote intergroup relations and erode labor market inequality.

NOTES

1. In this chapter, the term "Chicana" refers to Mexican American women, women of Mexican descent born in the United States (n = 18) or who emigrated to the United States as preschool children (n = 2). "Mexicanas" were women born and raised in Mexico who emigrated as young women or adults (over sixteen years of age). "Hispanic" and "Latino/a" are broader terms that refer to men and women of Spanish origin (both native and foreign born) living in the United States.

2. A job usually is "female-dominated" when women constitute more than their proportion (43 percent) of the labor force. Chicanas and Mexicanas are overrepresented in a job when their participation exceeds

that of their proportion in the labor force (2.5 percent). In this chapter, jobs are considered to be female-dominated if the respondents report that nearly all of their coworkers are women. However, an important finding in this study was that several of the women worked in racial-ethnic/gender-segregated jobs. This means that in several instances nearly all of their coworkers were White women, whereas others reported that all of their coworkers were women of color. This finding led me to subdivide typically female jobs into "White-female-dominated jobs" (jobs filled primarily by White women) and "minority-female-dominated jobs" (jobs filled by women of color), as reported by the study respondents. I present distinguishing features from each segment of the female labor market for their impact on job attachment and occupational mobility.

3. Although this discrepancy is substantial, it actually reflects a modest level of improvement for Chicana/Mexicana women. In 1977, 9.1 percent of Chicanas and Mexicanas were professional, technical, or managerial workers.

4. For additional information on the methods and sample selection, see Segura, "Chicanas and Mexican Immigrant Women in the Labor Market: A Study of Occupational Mobility and Stratification." Ph.D dissertation, University of California, Berkeley, 1986.

5. I explore in-depth husbands' influences on their wives' employment decisions as part of a larger system of patriarchy and Chicano/ Mexicano familism in Segura, "The Interplay of Familism and Patriarchy on the Employment of Chicana and Mexican Immigrant Women." In Renato Rosaldo Lecture Series Monograph 5, pp. 35–53. Tucson: Mexican American Studies Center, University of Arizona, 1989.

6. The overall average monthly wages of the eleven women working in White-female-dominated jobs from January 1984 to January 1985 was $896.54. The fourteen women employed during the same time period who worked in minority-female-dominated jobs earned an average of $772.85 per month, and the three women working in male-dominated jobs earned $1,920.00. If we consider full-time job status, women in White-female-dominated jobs earned an average $1,122.00, while women in minority-female-dominated jobs earned $849.00 and women in male-dominated jobs earned $1,920.00.

Professional Women: How Real Are the Recent Gains?

Debra Renee Kaufman

Today there are just under fifty million women in the civilian labor force. Nearly ten million women, or one out of every five of those employed, hold professional or managerial positions. In law, medicine, postsecondary education, and business, the number of women has increased significantly during the last ten years. But the gains that women have made in the professions have been hard won and may well prove even harder to maintain. As Epstein warned in 1970, "No matter what sphere of work women are hired for or select, like sediment in a wine bottle they seem to settle to the bottom" (1970b, p. 2). What women are allowed to do remains limited, and barriers still restrict their mobility in the professional world. In professions that are as male-dominated today as they were a decade ago, women are still likely to be overrepresented in low-paid and low-prestige subspecialties. However, when men enter female-dominated professions, they usually rise to the top.

Society has various expectations of and beliefs about its professionals. It assumes that they will abide by a code of ethics in dealing with their colleagues and clients and that they will belong to a professional association entrusted with enforcing this code. Since professionals are considered best qualified to judge each other's work, they are expected to submit to the judgment of their colleagues. Professionals are expected to make decisions without pressure from clients, the public, or an employing agency. It is believed that professional work benefits the public.

In many respects, professionals represent the elite cadre of society's work force. Since professions carry a high degree of honor and status in our society, their members can expect greater rewards for their services. Professional prestige is partly attributable to the fact that professionals are highly educated. Their specialized training allows them to draw on a body of knowledge unavailable to lay people. The exclusivity of the professions is also a result of their legal right to exercise a virtual monopoly over the delivery of their service. Professionals are

thought to derive a great deal of fulfillment from their work and to enjoy a high degree of autonomy. It is not clear, however, that professional women enjoy these advantages to the same extent as do their male colleagues. Even when women are willing and able to make the commitment to a professional career, most find themselves located in subsidiary positions within prestige professions or in positions that do not accord them the autonomy, prestige, or pay customarily associated with the professional image (see Table 1).

Table 1 shows that, from the beginning of this century to the present, the professions have been clearly sex-segregated. In the 1990s the prestige professions remain male-dominated: only 8.4 percent of the clergy, 21.4 percent of lawyers and judges, 20.4 percent of physicians, and 40.9 percent of college and university teachers were women. Conversely, the percentages of women who are social workers (68.9 percent), teachers except college and university (74.8 percent), registered nurses (94.3 percent), and librarians (87.6 percent) indicate that those professions remain female-dominated (*Employment and Earnings*, Jan. 1992, Table 22). The male-dominated professions are overwhelmingly white. In the female professions, African-American women are approaching parity with

TABLE 1   Percent Female in Eight Selected Professions, 1900–1990

PROFESSION	1990	1980	1970	1960	1950	1940	1930	1920	1910	1900
Physicians	21.0	13.4	9.3	6.8	6.5	4.7	4.4	5.0	6.0	5.6
Lawyers and judges	24.4	12.8	4.9	3.5	3.5	2.5	2.1	1.4	0.5	.8
Clergy	10.4	5.8	2.9	2.3	4.1	2.7	2.2	1.4	0.5	3.1
Professors	40.5	36.6	28.6	21.9	23.3	26.5	32.5	30.2	18.9	6.3
Social workers	69.0	64.9	62.8	62.7	69.1	64.3	78.7			
Nurses	94.3	95.9	96.1	97.5	97.6	97.8	98.1	96.3	92.9	93.6
Librarians	81.3	82.5	82.0	85.5	88.5	89.5	91.3	88.2	78.5	74.7
Teachers	74.7	70.8	69.5	72.5	78.8	75.3	81.8	84.5	80.1	74.5
Managers[a]	42.2	30.5	18.5							

[a]Managers is from "executive, administrative and managerial occupations," which is a broad category, unlike the professional specialty occupations in this table. In 1980 several management-related occupations were relocated into this category. These were heavily female, which partially accounts for the large increase in percent of female "managers," from 1970.

their proportion of the population. This is not true of Hispanic women (*Employment and Earnings*, Jan. 1993, Table 22). Perhaps even more revealing about women's status in the professions is that the female-dominated occupations, although classified by the Bureau of the Census as professions, are often referred to in the sociological literature as the "semi-professions."

We see that this distinction is more than academic when we realize that the term *profession* seems to be reserved for only those careers structured for the lives that men lead. Such careers are predicated on the notion that the professional is relatively free from child-care and home responsibilities. This permits great investments of time, energy, devotion, and "overtime" work, which are not possible for someone whose primary obligation is to a family. Extensive, difficult, and often expensive schooling is also required for the pursuit of such careers. "Continuity is usually essential," writes Oppenheimer, "and the freedom to move or to stay put, depending on the exigencies of the career, may be an important factor in whether or not success is achieved" (1970, p. 115).

THE FEMALE-DOMINATED PROFESSIONS

While the female-dominated occupations, like other professions, require advanced education and specific credentials, they often lack the authority, autonomy, and monopoly over a knowledge base that characterize the prestige and male-dominated professions. Oppenheimer suggests that the major female-dominated professions stand in direct contrast to the male-dominated ones:

All of [the female-dominated professions] depend on skilled but cheap labor in fairly large quantities . . . most of the training for them is acquired *before* employment, and career continuity is not essential. They exist all over the country, and hence mobility—or the lack of it—is not usually a serious handicap. Diligence and a certain devotion to the job are

required, but long-range commitments and extensive sacrifices of time and energy are not necessary. Employment in most of these occupations relatively infrequently puts the female worker in a supervisory position over male employees, though she may be in a position of relative power over those outside the organization. Nurses, for example, may initiate action for patients, but their authority to do so is derived from the attending physician; furthermore, the authority and the task have a distinctly feminine flavor—that of the nurturing female. Social workers are often in power positions vis-à-vis clients, but these clients are not in the work organization and are in a notoriously poor position to effect changes anyway. (Oppenheimer, 1970, p. 114)

While all women are affected by this pattern, black professional women are especially vulnerable. They are heavily concentrated in the lower-paying specialties in the female-dominated professions, serving black clients and generally poor and working-class people in the public sector.

Men assume the more respected positions of authority and power in female-dominated professions, positions quite consonant with societal views about men's "natural" roles. Male nurses, for instance, tend to be promoted to administrative jobs more frequently than are female nurses. Among teachers, women are more likely to teach at less prestigious levels of education than are men. In 1992, 98.6 percent of prekindergarten and kindergarten and 85.4 percent of elementary-school teachers were women, compared to 55.5 percent of secondary-school teachers.

THE PRESTIGE PROFESSIONS

Despite the increasing number of women earning doctorates, completing professional degrees, and entering the professions, the prestige professions and the prestige specialties within them still remain male-dominated. Medicine, law, academia, science, and management have a similar gender hierarchy.

Medicine

Throughout the first seventy years of this century, the proportion of women among active American physicians remained essentially unchanged, at around 7 percent. Many factors have contributed to this low percentage—from early gender-role socialization to discrimination in admission practices and policies of medical schools. However, in the last two decades, changes in federal law and in custom have helped women more than quadruple their enrollment in medical schools. In 1964–65, 7.7 percent of the first-year medical students in America were women; in 1991–92 women were 39.9 percent. In 1976–77, women accounted for 19.2 percent of all those who obtained medical degrees in America; by 1990–91 they were 35.9 percent. As of 1992, women constituted 20.4 percent of all practicing physicians, and 29.5 percent of all medical residents in America.

However, it is after medical school that the recent gains women have made come into question. Female physicians, for instance, tend to concentrate in such specialties as pediatrics, psychiatry, public health, physical medicine (rehabilitation), and preventive medicine, while men concentrate in high-status and high-pay surgical specialties. Despite steady increases, women are primarily located in the less prestigious areas of the medical profession and consequently earn less in each specialty. In part, this may be because men are more likely to practice in independent or group practices and women are more likely to be found in salaried positions.

Law

Women have made great strides in the legal profession, increasing from 5.3 percent of those receiving law degrees in 1969–70 to 42.6 percent in 1991–92. In 1992, 21.4 percent of all lawyers were women. However, as with medicine, the gains women have made are tempered by the different career patterns women lawyers face compared to those of their male colleagues.

While women have been able to enter areas formerly denied to them—such as small private companies, large corporate firms, law school faculties, and the judiciary—they are still heavily clustered in the less prestigious areas of family law, trusts and estates, and tax. Even their Wall Street advances from associates to partners must be interpreted with caution. Although more women are making gains in the profession, such advancements may have a different meaning now than they would have had earlier.

For women and minority associates, there is a greater chance of becoming partner, but that position may be a junior partnership bringing a proportionately smaller share of profits at the end of the year. It may also have less power and influence attached to it. There is some suspicion on the part of the older women attorneys that this is the kind of partnership young women are likely to get as the firms are feeling pressed to promote their women associates. Although this is definitely a step upward compared to the past, it does not mean that women have "made it" in relation to men who are rising in the hierarchy. (Epstein 1980, p. 308)

Academe

Just over 40 percent of university and college teachers in 1992 were women. Nonetheless, as in other male-dominated professions, many disparities exist between male and female professors. Academic women are concentrated in lower-ranked and nontenured positions; they work mainly in less prestigious institutions and fields; they are often segregated in areas with predominantly female student bodies; and, even within the same academic rank or category of institutional affiliation, they do not earn as much as men do. Even in traditional women's fields, men are more likely to be at the highest levels of the professions. Men direct the libraries, schools of social work, and teacher-training institutions for elementary and secondary education. Outside of education departments, employment of minority women is virtually nonexistent in all types of schools.

Women faculty in the professional schools fare particularly poorly compared to men. In 1991–92, women were only 26.2 percent of full-time and 24.3 percent of part-time faculty in law degree-granting programs but were 42.6 percent of the student body. Women were 28.5 percent of full-time medical school faculty that year, while composing nearly 40 percent of the student body. Irrespective of the professional school and the timing of their first appointment, women are located at the bottom of the academic hierarchy. If women are disproportionately on nontenure track appointments, and if such appointments are in the lower ranks, as the data suggest, it is not certain that women, over time, will achieve either professional security or equality in ranks with men.

Science and Engineering

In 1992, women accounted for 17.5 percent of the science and engineering work force, up from 9 percent in 1976. Women account for a larger share of employment in science than they do in engineering. Again, as with the other male-dominated professions, women are not randomly distributed in science or engineering. Almost half of all women scientists and engineers are concentrated in psychology or in the life and biological sciences. Women represent less than 10 percent of all engineers. Among engineers, only 6.9 percent of aerospace, 6.3 percent of chemical, and 7.9 percent of civil engineers were women.

Sokoloff (1986) suggests that a split is developing in the organization of the professions. Two sets of jobs seem to be emerging: those with high prestige, good pay, autonomy, and opportunity for growth, and those that are more routinized, poorly paid, and less autonomous. She also notes that shifts in sex segregation have been often followed by declines in earnings or career possibilities. Therefore, numeri-

cal growth may not offset segregation patterns within the professions. This has led some authors to conclude that desegregation in the male-dominated professions has not substantially changed the sex-segregation patterns within those professions.

Management

Over the past decade many scholars have argued that managerial careers have become professional careers. Like the professions, managerial careers often require licensing and professional schooling. In 1992, women in the United States represented 41.5 percent of all persons employed in managerial, executive, and administrative occupations, indicating an increase from 26.5 percent in 1978. These gains are also reflected in the dramatic increase in the number of women receiving their bachelor's and master's degrees in business management over the last two decades. In 1970–71, women earned 9.1 percent of the bachelor's and 3.9 percent of the master's degrees awarded. By 1989–90 they earned 46.7 percent of the bachelor's degrees and 34 percent of the master's degrees. Much of this significant gain can be attributed to the women's movement, affirmative action, and the passage in 1972 of Title IX of the Education Amendments, which prohibited sex discrimination in institutions of higher education and thus opened business schools to women who had been excluded or dissuaded from enrolling in them before that time.

However, despite these real gains, closer inspection of women's distribution within this occupational category clearly reflects the same pattern as that in the other prestigious, high-paying, and male-dominated professions: Women are more likely to be managers in areas where the pay and prestige are less and where there are already more women employees at lower levels. Women (and minorities) are more often found in staff (e.g., personnel and labor relations) than in line (marketing and sales) positions. This distinction is important since line positions are considered to be important entry points to upper-management jobs.

Although more women hold management positions than at any other time, few have made the breakthrough to top-level executive positions. Findings from a 1991 study done by the Feminist Majority Foundation indicate that of the 6,502 jobs at the vice-presidential level and higher within the nation's largest corporations, only 175, or 2.6 percent, were held by women. According to a survey of seven hundred companies by Korn Ferry, a leading executive recruiting firm, women and minorities were virtually the same percentage of officials with ranks of vice-president or higher as they were a decade ago.

In conclusion, there are fewer women in the prestige professions than there are men, female professionals generally still occupy the least prestigious specialties within those professions, and females earn less for comparable work. These facts suggest that women still face stern barriers to their entry into and advance through the professional ranks.

SEX-TYPING AND THE PROFESSIONS

Not only have the professions been segregated by sex, but also they have been greatly affected by the even more invidious process of sextyping. When a majority of those in a profession are of one sex, the "normative expectation" develops that this is how it *should* be. The model of the practitioner then takes on the personality and behavioral characteristics associated with that sex. For instance, in our study of accountants, the quality most frequently cited for success and mobility by both young and old, male and female respondents was "executive presence". This term almost perfectly matches what is called in the sociological literature the *male managerial behavioral model*—characterized by aggressiveness, decisiveness, competi-

tiveness, and risk taking. In fact, so identified is *male* with *manager* that one writer has stated: "The good manager is aggressive, authoritative, firm and just. He is not feminine" (McGregor, 1967, p. 23). The high-status professions and the prestige specialties in our society are identified with the instrumental, rigorous, "hardnosed" qualities identified as masculine, not with the "softer," more expressive, nurturing modes of behavior identified as feminine. Since the characteristics associated with the most valued professions are also those associated with men, women fail to meet one of the most important professional criteria: they are not men.

Research on the subject has clearly shown that traits customarily associated with femininity, and consequently with women, are not as highly valued in our society as are traits stereotypically associated with men. The belief in strong gender differences persists, although leading scholars clearly state that the overlap between the sexes on most personality and behavioral measures is extensive. Jacklin and Maccoby, for instance, in a thorough review of the subject, argue that gender differences in fear, timidity, anxiety, competitiveness, and dependence among young children remain open to debate because of insufficient or ambiguous evidence. They also assert that there is little scientific support for gender differences in such areas as achievement motivation, risk taking, task persistence, or other related skills. Yet these traits are typically associated with men in our society and with the pursuit of a successful professional career.

Other studies have revealed a deep conviction in our society that men and women manifest different characteristics, as well as showing that there is a more positive evaluation of those characteristics ascribed to men. Perhaps their most surprising finding was that even mental-health clinicians ascribed specific traits to each sex and agreed that a normal, healthy adult more closely reflects those traits ascribed to a healthy male than it does those ascribed to a healthy female. The clinicians portrayed healthy female adults as more submissive, less independent, less adventurous, less objective, more easily influenced, less aggressive, less competitive, more excitable in minor crises, more emotional generally, more conceited about their appearance, and more apt to have their feelings hurt. This childlike portrait led the authors to remark that "this constellation seems a most unusual way of describing *any* mature healthy individual."

Such stereotypes follow women into the workplace. Even when women do the same work as men, they are not perceived as being as competent as men, and their work is not perceived to be as prestigious. In a fine and thorough review of the social-psychological literature on sex-related stereotypes, O'Leary notes that Feldman-Summers and Kiesler were unable to find a single occupation in which women were expected to outperform males, even in elementary-school teaching and nursing. Touhey emphasizes that anticipating greater participation by women in high-status professions has resulted in a decline in the way both males and females perceive the prestige of those occupations. However, the converse was found when men entered female-dominated professions. In a study by Bass, Krussell, and Alexander, 174 male managers and staff personnel perceived women as unable to supervise men and as less dependable than men. In another study of managers' perceptions of sex differences, particularly perceptions relevant to the promotion of women, Rosen and Jerdee found that male managers and administrators held uniformly more negative perceptions of women compared to men on each of four scales: aptitudes, knowledge, and skills; interest and motivation; temperament; and work habits and attitudes. Generally, women were perceived as having aptitudes, knowledge skills, and interests and motivations compatible with routine clerical roles and not managerial roles. In this study, virtually every perceived difference between male and female employees was unfavorable to women aspiring to higher-level occupations. In contrast, Reskin and Hartmann cite other studies that suggest that negative correlations about women supervisors are weaker among women, well-educated males, and workers with female bosses.

In their study, Rosen and Jerdee found that males and females often were treated differently in their managerial roles. In a simulated situation, "supervisor" subjects promoted men more often, gave men more career development opportunities, trusted men more in handling personnel problems, and granted men leaves of absence for child-care duties less often than they did with hypothetical female counterparts. However, we need not rely on hypothetical supervisors to know that gender biases exist. Women earn less than men do in almost every occupation and within almost all specialties. Perhaps the best indicator that women are less valued in our society simply because they are female comes from a number of studies documenting that women possessing the *identical* qualifications and skills as men fare more poorly in obtaining professional-type jobs.

The Fidell study was particularly eye opening for people just entering graduate school and planning for an academic career. Fidell sent one of two forms to all colleges and universities that were offering graduate degrees in psychology in 1970. Each form contained ten paragraphs describing professional characteristics of ten hypothetical psychologists. The person most closely associated with departmental hiring was asked to participate in the study by judging the "candidates" and their chances of obtaining full-time positions. Form A used masculine first names; form B, feminine first names. Except for the names and pronouns, the wording on both forms was identical. Fidell found that men received higher levels of appointments; the positions were more likely to be on tenure track; and only men were offered full professorships.

Since the prestige professions are sex-typed, the expectations for men and women differ from the moment people make a decision to train for a career. As graduate students, women are not expected to be as dedicated, ambitious, or serious about their studies as men are. It is assumed that marriage and child rearing will eventually interrupt their studies and certainly their careers. The data suggest that such interruptions are indeed more disruptive for women than they are for men. In a reanalysis of a nationwide sample of graduate students, Feldman found that divorced men were unhappier with the graduate-student role than were single or married men, whereas divorced women among all graduate students were the happiest. He concluded that "apparently divorced men are burdened with greater responsibilities than their single or married counterparts, while divorced women have reduced their responsibilities and are thus freer to pursue the student role."

One fact reported in all studies on the division of labor at home among two-earner families is that employed married women spend far more time on housework than employed husbands. Pleck implies that except for the "fun" parts of child care, there has not been a major shift in the division of labor between men and women.

Indeed, professional women, like other working women, see the private sphere as still primarily a woman's responsibility. Cultural norms that reinforce the links between women, personal life, domesticity, and child rearing are deeply entrenched. One study of upper middle-class professionals found that women rated themselves lower on their performance as wives and mothers than men rated themselves as husbands and fathers. One possibility for women's lower ratings is that these professionally employed women used unemployed wives and mothers as the point of comparison for their own behavior. Interestingly, the higher the incomes of successful academic women in this study, the more work they did around the house. However, the more money their husbands made, the more frequently these women absolved their husbands from domestic responsibilities. Businesswomen in this study reported that they were happiest when their husbands' careers took precedence over their own.

The full-time employed wife–mother bears the largest burden for managing the home and children. Her share of domestic activities is three times as great as that of her full-time employed husband. These findings may not simply reflect a generation lag: in Komarovsky's study of Columbia University male students, even the "liberated" males in her sample expressed concern about the combination of motherhood and career for their future wives. The majority of the men believed that home and child-care responsibilities were still primarily the concern of the wife–mother. Professional careers are designed not for women with families, but rather for men who are free of family obligations. For the professional man, frequent absences from home, tardiness for dinner, and "overtime" work are not only expected but also accepted as evidence that he is a good provider and therefore a good parent and spouse. Such is not the case for the professional woman.

Multiple-role conflict is but one area in which differences exist between men and women who pursue professional careers. Another difference has to do with the timing of that endeavor. Hochschild argues that age is measured against one's achievements. Getting there first is an important element of success. "If jobs are scarce and promising reputations important, who wants a 50 year old mother-of-three with a dissertation almost completed?" Referring specifically to the academic arena, Hochschild states that "time is objectified in the academic vita which grows longer with each article and book, and not with each vegetable garden, camping trip, political meeting or child." A successful professional career requires early achievement and uninterrupted competition for continued success—timing based on a male pattern.

In almost every particular, professional life is oriented more toward males than toward females. Because women are expected to behave in a generally "softer" way than are men, they may be perceived as unsuited for the combative style expected from many professionals. Even smiling might be bad for women's business careers because it is interpreted by male coworkers as a sign of submission. This is substantiated by studies suggesting that the way women talk, gesture, smile, touch, sit, walk, and use space communicates their dependent and inferior status in our society. Some feminists have openly challenged the "success ethic" and the values of the professional life, arguing for a more humane (if not feminine) style in the workplace. However, such changes demand a total restructuring of the attitudes and behavior now common in the professions and a redefining and revaluing of what is feminine. The incentives for such change are few, particularly in a tight economy, and, as the following section shows, change generally comes quite slowly.

HISTORICAL REVIEW

The discouraging picture painted in the preceding discussion still represents an improvement over the past. The professions at the top of the American occupational hierarchy—medicine, law, and higher education—began as medieval guilds from which women were virtually excluded. In the thirteenth century, European medicine became firmly established as a secular science, and physicians were trained in the universities. Since females were excluded from the universities, they were denied the key resource to become professionals. However, there was little that we would recognize as science in the late medieval training. Physicians rarely saw any patients, and no experimentation of any kind was taught. Medicine was sharply differentiated from surgery; the dissection of bodies

was considered sacrilegious. In contrast, women healers of the same time, who were often labeled witches, had an experimental and empirical base to their healing. "It was witches who developed an extensive understanding of bones, muscles, herbs, and drugs, while physicians were still deriving their prognoses from astrology"; in fact, "Paracelsus, considered the 'father of modern medicine', burned his text on pharmaceuticals, confessing that he had learned from the Sorceress all he knew" (Ehrenreich and English, 1973, p. 17).

The key point is that neither knowledge, techniques, nor results defined the professional. What defined the professional was access to the universities. Society barred women from practicing medicine as professionals by denying them access to university training. By the fourteenth century, the church had explicitly legitimized the professionalism of male practitioners by denouncing healing without university training as heresy. Medieval writings on the subject asserted that "if a woman dare to cure without having studied, she is a witch and must die" (Ehrenreich and English, 1973, p. 19).

The development of the American medical profession was quite different, but the results were the same—women were effectively barred from the profession. By the early nineteenth century, there were many formally trained doctors—"regular" doctors, as they called themselves. At the same time, the popular health movement and numerous other groups with new medical philosophies were establishing their own schools open to women and to blacks. Frightened by these new movements, the "regulars" established the American Medical Association in 1847, thereby asserting themselves as the only legitimate spokespersons for the medical profession. Noting that by definition a profession has authority to select its own members and to regulate their practice, Ehrenreich and English (1973) emphasize that the "regular" doctors were a formidable obstacle to women. The rare woman who did make it into a "regular" medical school faced a series of "sexist hurdles" that only the most motivated women could manage:

First there was the continuous harassment—often lewd—by the male students. There were professors who wouldn't discuss anatomy with a lady present. There were textbooks like a well-known 1848 obstetrical text which states, "She (Woman) has a head almost too small for intellect but just big enough for love." There were respectable gynecological theories of the injurious effects of intellectual activity on the female reproductive organs.... Having completed her academic work, the would-be woman doctor usually found the next steps blocked. Hospitals were usually closed to women doctors, and even if they weren't, the internships were not open to women. If she did finally make it into practice, she found her brother "regulars" unwilling to refer patients to her and absolutely opposed to her membership in their medical societies. (Ehrenreich and English, 1973, p. 29)

By the early twentieth century, "irregular" schools and their students were routinely closed out of the medical profession. Tough licensing laws, requiring extended college and clinical training, sealed the doctors' monopoly on medical practice (Ehrenreich and English, 1973, p. 33).

Law, like medicine, began as a medieval guild and has been, until very recently, a male bastion. Women in law, until the last decade, have been "sex segregated in an occupational hierarchy: the lawyers and judges are almost invariably men, while the clerks, paralegal workers and secretaries who work for them are usually women" (Patterson and Engleberg, 1978, p. 277).

It was even more difficult for women to enter the legal profession than it was for them to become doctors. The first woman to be admitted to the practice of law in the United States was Belle Mansfield in 1869. Less than one year later, Myra Bradwell was refused admission to the bar in Illinois solely on the basis of her sex. In the nineteenth century, the legal

profession was more highly organized and protected by government than was medicine. Law schools did not admit women until the 1890s, and then did so only reluctantly. And after completing their studies, "even if women did achieve professional acceptance, they usually supported themselves through salaried positions, generally with insurance companies or government agencies, rather than through independent practice" (Brownlee and Brownlee, 1976, p. 289). Patterson and Engleberg note that even now women lawyers are still more likely than are men to turn to government positions. But what is more important, the authors find that when a man enters a government position, he uses it as a stepping-stone into private practice, whereas a woman tends to stay put, making it a career.

Prior to 1920, women's admission to law schools was not critical because preparation to practice law could be done by apprenticeships. In 1920, the American Bar Association officially endorsed law school as the desired preparation for the practice of the profession. But it was not until 1972 that women were finally admitted to *all* law schools.

The recruitment of women into the now female-dominated professions has had a different historical pattern. Shortages of cheap skilled labor—particularly during wars, recessions, and depressions—have accounted for a good deal of the recruitment of women into teaching and nursing. There were several advantages to using females as teachers. Women were available in great numbers, and they were willing to work for low wages. Moreover, this profession did not challenge the cultural ideal of women's "natural" place. Who could be more "naturally" equipped to teach children than women?

Nursing, too, began as an occupation dominated by men. But, when the Civil War created a shortage of male nurses, women entered the field in significant numbers. The Brownlees contend that the transformation of nursing into a woman's profession did not occur until there was a "sustained entry of educated women who reduced wages below what productivity justified" (Brownlee and Brownlee, 1976, p. 264). These were, for the most part, educated women who had been closed out of the prestige professions. Ehrenreich and English, for instance, note that Dorothea Dix and Florence Nightingale did not "begin to carve out their reform careers until they were in their thirties and faced with the prospect of a long useless spinsterhood" (1973, p. 38).

In nursing, female attributes seemed more important than competence or skill; good nurses were essentially ones who looked good and possessed "character." Ehrenreich and English suggest that the "ideal lady" of the nineteenth century was simply transplanted from home to hospital.

To the doctor, she brought the wifely virtue of absolute obedience. To the patient, she brought the selfless devotion of a mother. To the lower level hospital employee she brought the firm but kindly discipline of a household manager accustomed to dealing with servants. (Ehrenreich and English, 1973, pp. 36–37)

Nursing itself was hard labor; therefore, while the educators remained upper class, the practitioners were mostly working-class and middle-class women. When a group of English nurses proposed that nursing model itself after the medical profession, with examinations and licensing, Nightingale claimed that "nurses cannot be examined any more than mothers" (cited in Ehrenreich and English, 1973, p. 37). The occupations of nursing and teaching were extensions of women's "natural" domestic roles.

KEEPING WOMEN DOWN: THE SUBTLE ART OF PRACTICING THE PROFESSIONS

How can we explain women's continuing secondary status within the professions? As we have seen, the prestige professions are defined primarily in terms of men and the lives they lead. The processes that maintain this male model are usually well beyond a woman's control, however committed or dedicated she may be. No matter what her personal characteristics, a woman is often assigned the stereotypical characteristics of her sex, and despite her efforts to transcend these stereotypes, certain structural features of the professions work against her upward mobility.

The invisible barriers found in many professional organizations that appear to block the advancement opportunities of minorities and women in the public and private sectors of the economy are referred to as the "glass ceiling." The glass ceiling is often the result of a failure of professional business organizations to adhere to affirmative action programs, to monitor programs specifically established to promote women and minorities, and/or a failure to make clear the standards of performance and the resources necessary for advancement often obtained through informal mentoring.

In 1989, the Office of Federal Contract Compliance Programs of the Department of Labor interviewed nine Fortune 500 establishments as a pilot study of the glass ceiling phenomenon. Although the researchers had initially intended to study the highest levels of management within those companies, they had to shift their focus downward when they found that there were no minorities or women at the very top levels. The glass ceiling not only existed but also was lower than expected. The study cited the lack of informal mentoring as one of the single most important factors in keeping women in the lowest managerial positions. Other attitudinal and organizational practices that worked against women and minorities included the use of executive search firms that were not aware of affirmative action obligations, the failure to assign minorities and women to career-enhancing assignments, and the lack of a formal system to monitor how personnel were given consideration for development opportunities and for financial compensation by senior-level executives and corporate decision makers. These processes are similar to the mechanisms that operate to keep women out of the top positions in law, medicine, science, and academia.

"Interaction in professions, especially in their top echelons," Epstein points out, "is characterized by a high degree of informality, much of it within an exclusive, club-like context" (1970a, p. 968). Hughes notes that the "very word 'profession' implies a certain social and moral solidarity, a strong dependence of one colleague upon the opinions and judgments of others" (1962, p. 125). Those who bear certain characteristics (black, Jewish, female, etc.) are at an immediate disadvantage in such a collegial context. As Hughes (1945) suggested years ago, such statuses condition what is considered an "appropriate" set of characteristics for acceptance by one's peers as a professional; he describes these as "auxiliary characteristics." Such auxiliary characteristics as race, religion, ethnicity, and sex are "the bases of the colleague group's definition of its common interests, of its informal code, and of selection of those who become the inner fraternity" (p. 355). Hughes's fraternal imagery is apt; like fraternal societies, the collegial group depends on "common background, continual association and affinity of interest" (Epstein, 1970a, p. 972). Almost by definition, women and other low-status groups are excluded from such brotherly associations.

Professional "standards of excellence" allegedly establish the criteria for recruitment and advancement in one's field. Excellence, however, like any other social reality, is not universally manifest, but must be defined and interpreted. As Epstein (1970a) notes, fine distinctions between good and superior performances require subtle judgments, and such judgments are rendered by one's peers. In many ways, one's acceptance into and success within the professions are contingent on one's acceptance into the informal circles.

The professions depend on intense socialization of their members, much of it by immersion in the norms of professional culture even before entry; and later by the professionals' sensitivity to his peers. . . . Not only do contacts with professional colleagues act as a control system, they also provide the wherewithal by which the professional may become equipped to meet the highest standards of professional behavior. (Epstein, 1970a, p. 972)

Those who do not conform because they lack important "auxiliary characteristics" create dilemmas for themselves and for others. For example, the protégé system is one of the mechanisms whereby one's name and work become known in the upper echelons of one's profession. According to Epstein (1970a, 1970b) and White (1970), the men who dominate the top echelons of most professions may be reluctant to adopt female protégés. White claims that "a man . . . may believe that she is less likely to be a good gamble, a risk for him to exert himself for, or that she is financially less dependent upon a job" (p. 414). The man may also fear others' suspicion of a sexual liaison as a byproduct of such close and intense work. Although it is not unusual for a senior executive to be a mentor to a rising male star, this acceptable practice immediately becomes suspect if a young female receives it. A lack of sponsorship means a woman is more likely to be excluded from those crucial arenas where professional identity and recognition are established.

Collegial contacts are important for more than one's professional identity and acceptance into the profession. Social psychologist White (1970) interviewed women scholars at the Radcliffe Institute who had been awarded fellowships to continue their professional interests on a part-time basis while raising their families. The women thought that access to stimulating colleagues was as important as was the opportunity to be intellectually engaged in a project. White concluded that "appraisals of their work by others, coupled with acceptance and recognition by people whose professional opinions were relevant and appropriate, made a significant difference in determining whether a woman felt like a professional, and whether she in turn had a strong sense of commitment to future work" (p. 413). Furthermore, she suggests that "challenging interaction with other professionals is frequently as necessary to creative work as is the opportunity for solitude and thought" (p. 414).

Collegial contacts are also crucial for survival.

There are elaborate social systems in all parts of academic and business life, and purely technical training is rarely enough. The aspiring young scientist must be knowledgeable about many aspects of institutions, journals, professional meetings, methods of obtaining source materials, and funding grant applications. Knowing how to command these technical and institutional facilities requires numerous skills, many unanticipated by the young student. . . . This is the kind of learning we speak of as "caught," and not taught, and it is a valued by-product of acceptance and challenging association with other professionals. (White, 1970, p. 414)

If women are excluded from male networks, they remain not only marginal but also invisible when such important professional decisions as selection for promotion, tenure, research grants, coeditorships, summer teaching, and departmental privileges are under consideration. My research suggests that women academicians are less likely than are men to include people of higher rank in their collegial networks and are more likely to claim their colleague-friends as professionally unimportant to their careers.

It is within the collegial arena that judgments are made and standards are set. It is within the collegial arena that the ongoing dynamics of professional life are carried out. If women are denied access to this arena (even if they have formed their own networks), they are left out of the power centers of their professions. Moreover, their exclusion from male networks prevents the breakdown of myths about professional women. If women and men operate in different networks, gender-role stereotypes remain unchallenged.

CONCLUSION

How real are women's most recent gains in the professions? Despite their increasing numbers in male-dominated professions, women still constitute a disproportionately small percentage of those practicing the professions. Moreover, even in female-dominated professions, women are second to men in that their positions tend to carry less prestige.

Perhaps the most difficult task in assessing women's gains is measuring the "cost" of success. Even when women have been able to achieve high-pay, high-prestige positions within the professions, the costs for such success have been high. Many have had to give up or delay marriage, family, and significant relationships. Those who have not given up family have had to add to their demanding career commitments the major responsibilities of managing home and child-care tasks. In our society, both families and professional careers are "greedy" institutions. Until changes occur, women who want both can expect to face conflicting and overwhelming demands. Moreover, until we change the normative expectations about a woman's place both within the professions and within the home, so that both demands and rewards are equal to those of men, we must continue to question the gains women have made.

REFERENCES

Brownlee, W. E., and Brownlee, M. 1976. *Women in the American Economy: A Documentary History. 1675–1929.* New Haven, Conn.: Yale University Press.

Ehrenreich, Barbara, and English, Dierdre. 1973. *Witches, Midwives, and Nurses: A History of Women Healers.* Old Westbury, N.Y.: Feminist Press.

Employment and Earnings. January 1993. Annual 1992 Averages, Household Data, Table 22, "Employed Civilians by Detailed Occupation, Sex, Race and Hispanic Origin." Washington, D.C.: U.S. Bureau of Labor Statistics.

Epstein, Cynthia. 1970a. "Encountering the Male Establishment: Sex-Status Limits on Women's Careers in the Professions." *American Journal of Sociology* 75(6): 965–82.

Epstein, C. 1970b. *Woman's Place: Options and Limits in Professional Careers.* Berkeley: University of California Press.

Epstein, C. 1980. "The New Women and the Old Establishment." *Sociology of Work and Occupations* 7(3): 291–316.

Hughes, E. 1945. "Dilemmas and Contradiction of Status." *American Journal of Sociology* 50: 353–59.

Hughes, E. 1962. "What Other?" In *Behavior and Social Processes*, ed. A. Rose, 23–28. Boston: Houghton Mifflin Co.

McGregor, D. 1967. *The Professional Manager.* New York: McGraw-Hill Book Co.

Oppenheimer, V. K. 1970. *The Female Labor Force in the U.S.: Demographic and Economic Factors Governing Its Growth and Changing Composition.* University of California at Berkeley Population Monographs, no. 5. Berkeley: University of California.

Patterson, M., and Engleberg, L. 1978. "Women in Male-Dominated Professions." In *Women Working*, ed. A. Stromberg and S. Harkess, 201–25. Palo Alto, Calif.: Mayfield Publishing Co.

Sokoloff, N. 1986. "A Profile of the General Labor Force and the Professions: A Review of the Aggregate Gender and Race Segregation Literature." Paper presented at the American Sociological Association, New York, August 1986.

White, M. 1970. "Psychological and Social Barriers to Women in Science." *Science* 170(3956): 413–16.

The Job of Housewife

Barbara R. Bergmann

To be a housewife is to be a member of a very peculiar occupation, one with characteristics like no other. The nature of the duties to be performed, the method of payment, the form of supervision, the tenure system, the "market" in which the "workers" find "jobs," and the physical hazards are all very different from the way things are in other occupations. The differences are so great that one tends not to think of a housewife as belonging to an occupation in the usual sense. It is sometimes said

that a housewife "doesn't work." The truth is, of course, that a housewife does work, does get a reward for her work, and not infrequently gets fired or quits. One dictionary defines an occupation as "an activity that serves as one's regular source of livelihood." Being a housewife is an activity that gets one food, clothing, and a place to live. It certainly meets the dictionary's definition of having an occupation.

By tradition and by law, the housewife is not counted as working for an "employer." The reward she gets for her work is not legally defined as a "wage." That reward may be access to goods and services rather than cash. This arrangement has implications for her status, her sense of independence, and her participation in planning the family budget. Because she has

From *The Economic Emergence of Women*, by Barbara R. Bergmann, Chapter 9. Copyright © 1986 by Basic Books, Inc. Reprinted by permission.

been considered to be merely an economic and social appendage of her husband, she was never taxed as other workers. Her old-age support was not arranged on the same basis as that of other workers.

In the era when all women were expected to spend their mature years as housewives, when almost all men maintained housewives, and when divorce was uncommon, none of this was thought to merit comment or was considered a problem. Now, however, we are in a transition period in which about half of the married men maintain housewives while the other half have employed spouses. The housewife's pay, taxes, postdivorce support, and provision for old age raise policy questions that paradoxically get more insistent as the housewife occupation dwindles. In some respects, housewives are gravely disadvantaged. In other respects, families with housewives are given extra advantages that families with two earners are denied. The way the tax and Social Security laws treat the housewife need examination and reform. The postdivorce situation of women who have been long-term housewives needs to be improved.

The proportion of adult women who report themselves as engaged exclusively in keeping house has been dwindling throughout this century. But even in its dwindled state, the housewife occupation is very large. In fact, it is still the largest single occupation in the United States economy. In January 1986, a total of 29.9 million women in the United States (or 32 percent of the women aged 16 years or over) described themselves to the census taker as "keeping house."* By comparison, workers of both sexes in professional and managerial occupations—physicians, nurses, lawyers, teachers, engineers, social workers, business executives, government officials—amounted altogether to

only 26.4 million. Workers of both sexes in clerical and allied jobs amounted to 17.5 million.[1]

A housewife is a married woman who holds no paid job and who works within the home performing services for her own family. She may also contribute some unpaid volunteer work. But her principal attention is to child care, food preparation, housecleaning, laundry, grocery shopping, and a host of other chores and errands. Many if not all of these services will be performed whether the family maintains a housewife or not. However, a family that maintains a competent person devoted full time to performing these services generally benefits from having them performed well and carefully and in a timely manner. A one-earner family has a higher standard of living than a two-earner family with the same money income because of the family's greater enjoyment of high-quality services.

While the advantages of having a housewife in the family are considerable, so are the disadvantages. Most obviously, the family loses the money income that the person serving as housewife might contribute to the collective budget. There are other disadvantages, concentrated on the shoulders of the person playing the housewife role. A housewife works alone, or with only the company of small children, and many housewives are, as a result, extremely lonely. The husband of a housewife, with his monopoly of direct access to money, has the opportunity to be tyrannical. Sometimes, he acts violently toward her. He may desert, leaving her unprepared to earn a good living. For all these reasons, the housewife occupation is one of the most problem-ridden in the economy.

Being a housewife is no longer a lifetime vocation for most women. Many of the women who tell the census taker they are not in the labor force because they are "keeping house" are taking a temporary spell in the housewife occupation. The shorter the time a person spends as a housewife, the less severe the problems are likely to be. When looked at objectively, the

---

*In January 1986, 468,000 men reported that they were not in the labor force because they were keeping house.

long-term housewife's occupation turns out to be one of the riskiest, both physically and financially. But even short spells as a housewife can produce severe disadvantages.

The housewife usually is thought of as outside the economy. Housewives' services are not included as part of the gross national product, and housewives lack cash payments designated as wages. But there certainly is an economic side to the housewife role. The nature and value of the productive services delivered by the housewife, the nature and value of the pay, and how these get set raise issues worthy of examination.

While there has been some agitation to include housewives' services in the gross national product and to pay them cash wages, the important issues of public policy with respect to housewives lie elsewhere. The treatment of the "displaced homemaker"—a person who has been a housewife for a long time but whose "job" has ended through separation or divorce—is a national scandal. Another set of important policy questions, debated in the Congress every few years, is the treatment of the housewife and the employed wife in matters of taxation and Social Security. Present laws favor the housewife-maintaining family in important ways and penalize the family with an employed wife. Another issue concerns the wisdom of encouraging women to assume the housewife role after the birth of a baby, by instituting generous maternity-leave policies.

THE DUTIES OF THE HOUSEWIFE

"The hand that rocks the cradle rules the world," goes one attempt to persuade women that they should rest content with being housewives. At the other extreme, John Kenneth Galbraith has called the housewife a "crypto-servant."[2] Both of these are irritating ideas, probably intentionally so.

Many of the housewife's duties are those of the servant, and the servant job is the one clos-

est to the housewife's in the money economy. Unlike the servant, the housewife is a family member and therefore partakes to some degree in whatever deference is due to the bank account, class position, and occupation of the husband. She also partakes, as a servant does not, of whatever luxury the husband's salary affords in living space, food, clothing, and entertainment. She does have more discretion than a servant ordinarily has, and she may have the management of the family's finances in her hands. In some respects the housewife's working conditions are more onerous than the servant's: The housewife works seven days a week and is on call twenty-four hours a day for the service of the whole family.

Personal relations are important in a regular job, but they are a much more important part of the housewife's job. The children she takes care of are her own. The housewife's relation to the husband, including their sexual relation, is a factor in her ability to keep her position as wife. Of course, the feelings of love that the housewife and her husband may share enhance the marriage and may make the performance of her work "a labor of love." Yet sexual relations are notoriously changeable in their tenor. If they go sour, the housewife may lose her position. The connection between the economic and the sexual means that the housewife's economic security is hostage to personal whims.

To continue the servant analogy, female servants in the nineteenth century, and probably throughout the course of history, had sexual duties to the father of the house and possibly to the grown sons as well. This was certainly true if they were slaves or indentured servants. These days, good servants are rare, and if unwelcome attentions are forced on them, they can quit and go elsewhere. Only the prostitute and the housewife now have jobs in which a requirement to engage in sex relations is part of the duties. In any other job, the imposition of such a requirement is considered sexual harassment and is outlawed under the Civil Rights Act.

The sexual part of the housewife's job has become more crucial with the advent of easy and frequent divorce. When marriage was understood to go on until death, falling out of love, or meeting someone you liked better was considered no excuse to end it. In the present era, even an excuse is unnecessary. There are some other jobs besides the housewife's where a person performing competently in the technical aspects of the work will be displaced because the boss develops a sexual desire for another person. But surely, the best ones do not have that characteristic.

A great deal of what we are saying about the housewife also applies, to some degree, to many of the wives who have paid jobs. Most do housework seven days a week, in addition to their paid job. The majority of them have wages that are considerably lower than their husbands'. For a woman in that situation, the continuation of the marriage allows her to have a far higher standard of living than she could achieve independently. In this sense, she, like the housewife, gets part of her livelihood by being her husband's wife and doing whatever is necessary to maintain that status.

THE HOUSEWIFE'S MOBILITY PROBLEMS

The housewife has problems in moving from one job to another that exceed those in other jobs. For most people it is easier to move from one job to another within the same occupation than to change occupations. But the housewife, unlike nurses or carpenters or secretaries or economists, cannot search overtly for other vacancies of a similar type while occupying her present "job." For that matter, even after it has ended, she cannot search overtly for another "meal ticket"—her search must be presented to herself and to others as a search for love. If anything, her experience as a housewife is a hindrance in finding a new spot in the same profession. She now counts as secondhand merchandise, with some expensive appendages—her children by her previous husband—trailing after her. She is no longer as young as she was.

In short, gaining another housewife berth with a new husband is not easy. A survey by the Census Bureau in 1985 found that 35 percent of women who had ever been divorced had not remarried. Of those who did find new partners, the median interval between divorce and remarriage was 4.6 years.[3]

If the housewife wants to move into another occupation—namely, a paying job—the similarity of the duties of the housewife and the duties of the servant create difficulties. Apparently most employers do not consider the experience of the housewife to be valuable in performing paid jobs. Of course, this attitude may grow out of sexism. An equivalent set of duties attached to a man's job might well be thought of as valuable experience, possibly for some managerial jobs.

The nature of the financial arrangements of housewife-maintaining families creates difficulties for the housewife if she wants to "quit her job" by quitting the marriage. It may be difficult or impossible for her to accumulate a cash reserve that would carry her through until she finds some other source of livelihood, usually a job in another occupation. If she can make such an accumulation, it may have to be done by stealth. The "live-in" feature of the housewife's job increases the difficulty of quitting by increasing the size of the cash accumulation needed to change jobs. In most other occupations a person who quits a particular job does not have to move out of his or her living quarters at the time of the quit. Such a person usually can live for a while on the goodwill built up with the landlord and on the stocks of staples in the kitchen.

To the financial difficulties of quitting a marriage must be added the formidable logistical difficulties—finding new residential quarters and arranging to move there. A housewife's lack of credit in her own name may also create problems at such a time. We are speaking here of the difficulties of a transition for the housewife from her present job to some other way of getting a living. The longer-term prospects are not good, either, principally because most of the high-paying jobs are marked off for men.

PHYSICAL HAZARDS

It is estimated that about 14 million women are injured in the home each year.[4] Accidents are not the only source of injury. Large numbers of women are the victims of intentional violence from their husbands. A survey found that 4 percent of women living with a husband or male partner at the time of the survey had in the previous twelve months been kicked, bitten, hit with a fist, hit with an object, been beaten up, threatened with a knife or a gun, or had a knife or gun used against them. Nine percent of the women said that at some time in the past they had been victims of those kinds of abuse from the man they lived with. If we include what the survey characterized as less severe forms of violence—having something thrown at them, or being pushed, grabbed, shoved, or slapped—then 10 percent of the women reported violent abuse in the previous twelve months and 21 percent had at some time experienced it.[5]

Police officers have not considered a husband's violent behavior against his wife to be a crime. If called to a home on a complaint of violence, apparently most police officers consider that the appropriate course of action is to conciliate the matter rather than to arrest the husband and charge him with a criminal offense. Many men, including many police officers, believe that men have the right to beat their wives. A housewife will lose her economic support if her husband has to spend time in jail, and this makes judges reluctant to jail battering husbands. Beaten-up wives themselves worry about this. A housewife often refuses to press charges, or withdraws them if they have been pressed. This kind of behavior reinforces police officers' attitude in refusing to make arrests.

There has been considerable speculation about why wives continue to live with violent spouses. Some have argued that such wives derive a masochistic enjoyment from being hurt, or feel that they have deserved punishment. Whether this is true or not, there is very likely an economic aspect to the wife's behavior. Such a woman will have no immediate way to make money, and is likely to have young children whom she feels she must keep with her and whom she would have to feed and shelter. She may not have relatives in the same city with extra space and money they would be willing to put at her disposal. To such a woman, the difficulties of leaving a violent husband may appear insurmountable. There is literally no place for her to go.

Feminists have opened up an offensive against wife-battering by bringing lawsuits against municipal authorities in cases where the police have failed to protect women from their batterers. Where permanent injury has been sustained, multimillion-dollar judgments have been obtained, and these will certainly motivate authorities to indoctrinate police officers to behave more aggressively against batterers than they have been wont to do in the past.

Feminists also have begun organizing shelters for battered women in many cities throughout the United States. These serve as a place of resort for a woman and her children with nowhere else to go. From the shelter, she can apply for welfare and look for a job and a place to live. The shelter movement has received some financial help from the federal government. Recently there has been an attack on the shelter movement from the religious right wing on the grounds that shelters are "antifamily" and "rest and recreation centers for tired housewives." Those who attack shelters want to shore up the husband's authority in the family and apparently believe that the right to administer physical punishment to his wife is necessary or helpful to the maintenance of that authority.

MEASURING THE ECONOMIC VALUE OF THE HOUSEWIFE

The housewife's activities result in the production of a great many excellent things: meals on the table, clean rooms, clean clothes, and children cared for. We can arrive at measures of the value of the housewife's services by drawing on the obvious parallels between her activities and similar productive activities in the market economy. However, as will become apparent, there is more than one way to arrive at a measurement, and determining which method is the best is no simple matter.

There is no housework task that does not have analogies in the commercial economy. For food preparation and cooking, there are restaurant meals. For housecleaning, there are paid cleaners. For transportation of family members, there are taxis and chauffeurs. There are commercial laundries. The people who perform these tasks for pay are, of course, covered in the U.S. government's tally of production and income, the gross national product accounts. Yet the productive value of the unpaid housework by family members is not covered. Why is that?

The accounts, which were set up for the United States in the 1930s and 1940s, were envisaged primarily as a device for measuring levels of production and income generation in the money economy. Certain items not traded for money did get included, but housework services were not among them. Originally housework may have been excluded from the national income accounts because the changes in the amount performed were thought to be small and to lack relevance to policy. Sexism may also have played a part, considering some

of the nontraded items that room was found for, such as the food grown by farmers that is eaten on farms.

These days, however, when catering to the self-image of housewives is considered good politics both on the right and the left, it probably is the valuation problem that has kept housework from being part of the gross national product. No less than three alternative methodologies suggest themselves for valuing housework. However, any of them if adopted might prove embarrassing to the statistical agency.

One way to estimate the value of the housework performed by a housewife would be to equate it to the salary of a full-time servant. This method of estimation probably would be considered to be in bad taste and certainly would not endear the statistical agency to housewives and their partisans. A major purpose of putting housework in the gross national product is to add dignity to the status of housewives, so such a methodology is worse than useless.

A second method of valuing the housewife's productive contribution goes to the opposite extreme. It involves listing the activities of a housewife and finding the specialized occupation in the money economy that is closest to each one. The list that proponents of this kind of measure get together usually includes cook, dishwasher, chauffeur, cleaner, interior designer, nursemaid, dietician, laundress, and so on. The housewife's time at each activity is then valued at the appropriate specialist's pay scale. Many of the occupations cited are mostly male, and many of them are high-paying, in part because women frequently are excluded from them. Housewives work long hours, so this method can easily produce an estimate higher than the average male salary and two to three times as high as the average pay of a woman working at a full-time job. The Chase Manhattan Bank published an estimate based on this method for 1972 that came to a value of $257.53 for a 100-hour work week. In that year white males employed full time averaged $172 and white females $108.*

A third methodology would equate the value of housework to the wage the housewife herself could earn on a full-time job. This method gives a different value to the housework of the college graduate and that of the high-school graduate, despite the fact that they may be doing identical housework.

Given the problem of measuring the housewife's contribution to the national economy, it certainly is no wonder that the economists and statisticians who compile the national economic accounts have been slow to include those contributions. However, those who are pressing for their inclusion might ask themselves how much real benefit would result.

Up to this point, I have emphasized the similarities between housework and services available for purchase in the money economy. However, a word ought to be said about the differences. Oscar Wilde rightly spoke against those who know the price of everything and the value of nothing. What is it worth to have one's own mother devoted to one's care twenty-four hours a day? On the other hand, what is the true cost of living for and through others, of giving up for a lifetime the possibility of achievements outside the home? Accounting for such benefits and costs by putting price tags on them would not do them justice. However, they need to be in our consciousness as we think about the housewife, contemplate the decline and eventual disappearance of the housewife occupation, and consider what might be done to replace some of the good things that are being lost in the course of that decline.

---

*The Chase Manhattan Bank's calculation is given in A. C. Scott, "The Value of Housework: For Love or Money?" *Ms. Magazine* (June, 1972): 56–58.

PAY FOR HOUSEWIVES

The housewife, despite the productive work she does, receives no sum of money she can call her wage. This lack of a wage has struck many people as an important injustice, which they say ought to be remedied.[6] Perhaps what is most galling is that while the housewife's duties resemble those of a servant, the financial arrangements she has with her husband somewhat resemble those of someone even lower down on the status ladder—namely, the slave. Slaves get no sum of money designated as a wage but do get room, board, and clothing. The legal impunity with which the husband has been able to chastise the wife physically has reinforced the slave analogy. The slave who ran away might be captured and brought back by law. The housewife was constrained to stay by the poverty of the economic and social alternatives open to her. In some cultures, the bridegroom buys the bride for a considerable sum from her father.

The truth of the matter is that both the housewife and the slave do receive a recompense for their work. The slave is at the mercy of the master for the amount of the recompense and for his or her very life. By contrast, custom constrains the husband to allow the wife a standard of living similar to his own. Unless the husband has expensive vices (gambling, drink, and resort to other women are the classic ones), the wife generally cannot complain that the share he accords her is unfair. It is not the lack of recompense but the form it takes that creates practical and psychological problems, especially if the two spouses do not have an amicable relationship.

The housewife's contributions to the family and the return she gets for making them are both obscured by legal and popular ideas that each spouse is unilaterally rendering duties to the other rather than making an exchange of economically valuable services. A husband is seen as having a duty to support the wife, with no conditions specified. The wife is seen as having a duty to keep the house, again unconditionally. The connection between the husband's monetary support and the wife's housework is further obscured by the fact that the standard of living of the wife seems to be inversely related to the amount of housework she does. Those wives who do no housework whatever often enjoy the highest standard of living. Many of those who do the most housework have the lowest standard of living.

The wives of the richest husbands get a pure grant of their living expenses from their husband. Their situation certainly is not typical but seems to have set the pattern for thinking about the economic relations of all husbands and wives. All husbands are thought of as contributing support as a pure grant. Where, as is the usual case, servants cannot be afforded, the wife "has to do the housework." The fraction of wives exempted from housework has always been small; nowadays it is minuscule. The monetary contributions of the husband are in most situations connected to the performance of the housework by the wife. After all, if she stops doing the housework, the marriage will probably end. So there is in reality an exchange of the wife's housework for the husband's continuance in the marriage, and for his continuing to supply her with room, board, and other benefits.

When the husband works, he helps his employer to produce an output and is paid by that employer in money. His income is embodied in his paycheck. Presumably, all of that paycheck becomes the family's income and goes into the family budget. It is consumed when the dollars are used for family members' expenses. The husband's recompense from his employer gets converted into consumer goods for him, consumer goods for other members of the family, and some that are enjoyed jointly, such as the family living quarters.

The housewife's productive activities also contribute to the family's ability to consume, and it is not farfetched to call that contribution an addition on her part to the family income. That contribution is as real as the monetary contribution out of the husband's paycheck. As we have seen, there is more than one way of valuing the housewife's services, but they are real and substantial nonetheless. The income contributed by the wife is consumed almost as it is being produced. By contrast, the income contributed by the husband may linger a bit in the bank before melting away in consumption.

Is the housewife paid? By analogy with the husband, the value of her housework services constitutes an income she has earned. Granted, she immediately and automatically contributes her "income" to the family. But many husbands contribute all of their income to the family, too.

Husband and wife share both the money income and get a benefit from the housework, which we might call the "service income." In the last analysis, the recompense of each for their exertions is their share in both kinds of incomes. The recompense of the housewife includes a share in the goods and services purchased out of the family's cash budget—clothing, a roof over her head, participation in family vacations, travel, medical care, trips to the movies, and so on. She also benefits from her own services, as when she partakes of a family meal she has cooked, or gets satisfaction from the development of a child she has nurtured. She ends up with a certain total level of consumption—and whether we call that her share or her pay should not much matter.

What, then, do the "pay for housework" advocates complain of? It is attitudes they are complaining of more than material deprivation. The husband's money contribution seems more real or important than the wife's service contribution. His contribution is more visible and seems more concrete. Psychologically, a sum of money perhaps is more easily comprehended than a multitude of actions that constitute housework. The nature of the husband's contribution renders him more powerful in the family and creates the impression that he supports her with no return and that she is parasitical. If she had money to contribute to their joint budget, all of those ideas might disappear or at least be softened.

If the housewife had a wage, she might have more say over the way the family's money income gets spent. Of course, there are families in which the husband's pay is all delivered entirely to the wife's control and all spending is controlled by the wife. However, if the husband wants, he can keep control of all the money and dole it out to the wife at his pleasure. She may have no fixed sum that is given to her for her own needs or even for household expenses. She may be in the humiliating position of continually having to ask for small sums. Informal surveys among my students whose mothers are housewives suggest that about 20 percent of them are in that situation. The opportunities for petty tyranny in such an arrangement are endless.

Suppose it became common practice for the husband of a housewife to render up to her some fraction of his cash wage and acknowledge that he was paying her a wage for housework. Each spouse could not go off and spend the money under their control independently. On the contrary, both the husband and the wife would have to put up almost all of that money for food purchases, the rent or the mortgage, car expenses, and so on. Perhaps the wife would feel freer to buy things for herself, but this is far from clear.

Another possible source of a cash wage for housework would be the government. But where would the government get the funds? One possibility would be to put a large special tax on the husbands of housewives. The money collected, with a suitable subtraction for administrative expenses, might be sent by the Internal Revenue Service to the housewives. The housewives' self-esteem might be enhanced by the receipt of the government checks, but the benefits would be entirely in terms of status.

Another scheme, which would have important substantive results, would be to send government paychecks to housewives out of the ordinary revenue of the government. Presumably there would have to be a tax increase to finance it. The additional taxes would be paid by housewife-maintaining families as well as by single people and two-earner couples. However, the latter two groups would receive no benefit from the extra taxes. The net effect would be a transfer of purchasing power from the pockets of single people and two-earner families into the pockets of families that maintained housewives. But single-earner families are already better off in terms of living standards than two-earner couples of identical cash income. Sending the former a check for the wife's housework financed in part by taxes of the latter would be asking the less well off to contribute to the more well off. Such a scheme also would encourage women to become and remain housewives.

To sum up this discussion, those who have sought to put pay for housewives on the feminist agenda appear to have made a mistake.

MATERNITY AND CHILDREARING LEAVE

Most women who enter the housewife occupation do so when they have a baby. Not all new mothers leave their jobs. About a quarter of women currently giving birth to a baby do not leave the labor force at all, and another quarter return before the child's first birthday.

There always has been some sentiment for the allowance of long and generously paid maternity leaves for employed women. Lengths of three months, six months, a year, or even several years have been proposed. Such leaves would allow women with jobs to be housewives for considerable periods, and with pay to boot. Since they would be keeping one foot in the labor market at all times, the appearance of dependency would be avoided. Women in dead-end, boring, arduous jobs would no doubt welcome such leaves, and others might also. The leaves might be considered society's or the employer's contribution to the raising of children. They would make the life of the mother easier, allow her to devote herself to the child entirely, and would keep some very young babies out of day-care centers.

Long paid maternity and child-raising leaves are really another version of pay for housewives. The rhetoric on leaves emphasizes the welfare of the child rather than the worth of the mother's services. But in economic terms the two are very similar. However, the stipend for maternity leave is usually proportional to the wife's wage.

A policy requiring employers to give such paid leaves has important disadvantages for women. If the employer must pay a woman's salary for a long maternity leave, employers will have a further incentive to keep women out of the high-paying fields. Even more than now, women will be confined to jobs in which the duties follow an easily learned routine and in which one person can easily be replaced by another. In such jobs, the pay would be lowered to make up for the cost of the maternity leave. More women would take long maternity leaves, and every woman who has a baby would be under social pressure to take the maternity leave, at possible damage to her career. Another disadvantage of long paid maternity leaves for child-rearing is that they reinforce the idea that child care, and the other family service chores that women do when they stay home, are women's work.

An alternative to long leaves for mothers would be work-reduction arrangements for both spouses that allowed couples to share child care and housework. Both the mother and the father might reduce the intensity of their paid work for a considerable period after the birth of their baby. Perhaps both could go on half-time for two years or so, or perhaps the father and mother might take alternate weeks or months or quarters of a year off. Under such a system, neither mothers nor fathers would sacrifice career opportunities disproportionately.

However, both parents would be at a disadvantage relative to one-earner couples and childless people in highly competitive fields, unless special rules were instituted to take care of that too. Such a system would restore to young children a period of nurturance passed in the quiet and (relatively germ-free) isolation of their own homes, at all times under the attention and care of a parent.*

We might call such a system "two-parent nurturance leave." From many points of view, including probably that of the child, it would be superior both to the housewife-breadwinner setup, and to the two-earners-with-baby setup, with its overextended "supermom." The Swedes have taken modest steps to work toward such a system. In Sweden, the health insurance system provides for paid leave when a baby is born, which mothers and fathers may share. To encourage fathers to participate in child care, the father is entitled to ten days of leave, which does not count against the couple's allotment and which is lost if not taken.[7] However, in Sweden only a small percentage of new fathers currently take advantage of the leave.

The Swedish example shows that instituting such a system would by no means be easy. Men have an interest in continuing to be exempt from household chores, and from career interruption. And as long as wages of women are far inferior to those of men, any scheme that involves men taking unpaid or partly paid leave is relatively expensive for the family.

TAX POLICY AND THE HOUSEWIFE

We turn now to the treatment of housewives and employed wives in matters of taxation.

---

*Currently some parents achieve this by working alternative shifts. However, such arrangements are not available to everyone, and furthermore drastically reduce the time the parents can spend in each other's company.

The United States has consistently followed a system of income taxation based on two principles. One is the principle of progressive taxation—that people with higher incomes should pay higher shares of their incomes to the tax collector. The second is that a married couple should be taxed on the sum of their incomes, and the spouses not be allowed to calculate their taxes as though they were single people. In recent decades, U.S. tax laws have been revised numerous times. However all revisions have kept these principles intact.

A low-income person who marries a high-income person is not allowed by the U.S. tax code to pay the low taxes that would be levied on a low-income person living alone. Rather, such a person is made to pay the higher taxes thought appropriate to a member of an affluent family. While that has a measure of justice to it, it creates a *two-earner marriage penalty*—when two people marry, and both continue to earn income, the taxes they owe as a couple may be greater than the sum of the taxes the two of them owed as single people.

In order to keep the marriage penalty from becoming more than a few thousand dollars per couple, the tax rules have been written so that a married couple with a given income pays less tax than one single person with the same income. That creates a second anomaly—the *housewife bonus*. A man married to a woman with no income pays considerably less than he would as a single person.

There is still a third anomaly in the U.S. tax code—the *single-parent penalty*. A mother who is not currently married, and is the only earner in her family, is not permitted the same generous treatment accorded to the single-earner married couple. She is treated as an intermediate case between singles and marrieds.

These tax anomalies are illustrated in Table 1. The numbers in the table are based on current plans for taxes in 1988. A two-earner couple who as single people would have paid a total of $6,888 in taxes would owe $7,554 after

TABLE 1   How Income Taxes in the United States Vary with Marital Status

The Two-Earner Marriage Penalty

Man with income of $30,000
Woman with income of $20,000

Their taxes as single people ($4,638 + 2,250)	$6,888
Their tax as a married couple	7,554

The Housewife Bonus

Man with income of $30,000

His tax as a single person	$4,638
His tax if married to a housewife, no children	3,150

The Single-Parent Penalty

Tax of single mother earning $40,000, two-person family	$5,712
Tax of married couple earning $40,000, two-person family	4,854

Note: Based on proposals for taxes to take effect in 1988 as detailed in *Tax Reform Act of 1986: Report of the Committee on Finance, United States Senate,* Report 99–313, May 21, 1986. The use of the standard deduction is assumed in all cases.

their marriage, thus suffering a rise in taxes of $666 or almost 10 percent. By contrast, the man who is married to a nonemployed wife would pay $1,488 less than he would as a single person, a tax reduction of almost a third. The single mother supporting a nonearning child in our example is forced to pay $858 more than a man supporting a nonearning wife, an 18 percent tax penalty.

The marriage penalty encourages people who are living together without benefit of formal marriage to stay that way. For those who do get married, the tax system encourages wives to remain housewives or to become housewives. In our example, a couple's taxes increase from $3,150 to $7,554, a sum of $4,404, if the wife takes a job that pays $20,000.

Most couples view the husband's employment as beyond question but view the wife's employment as something on which a decision might be made either way. Thus they would tend to view the $4,404 addition to their tax bill not as an extra burden on both of their salaries but as the tax on the $20,000 that the wife might earn. By that way of thinking, her salary carries a higher tax rate than the rate on her husband's salary, and a rate almost double the rate she paid as a single woman.

The idea behind a progressive tax structure is that better-off people should carry a more-than-proportional share of supporting public expenditure, while the burden on lower-income people should be relatively light. The principle is straightforward when comparing individuals. When comparing individuals with married couples or comparing one- and two-earner families, however, what is fair and what is unfair becomes more problematical.

Should two-earner couples be allowed to pay taxes as though they were single? One argument against the idea is that when people marry, their expenses diminish because they share a dwelling unit, so they can afford higher taxes. These days, however, many couples live together before their marriage. It seems unreasonable to force such couples to pay extra taxes for the act of getting married.

On balance, there is a lot to be said for requiring people to file on the basis of their own incomes without regard to the income of other family members, and for abolishing special tax rates for married people. This is the way taxes are structured in Sweden.[8] If such a system was adopted in the United States, married single earners would have to pay considerably more tax than they currently do.

A more radical proposal, by Rolande Cuvillier,[9] would go farther than getting rid of the tax break currently enjoyed by the one-earner couple. Cuvillier would make the one-earner couple pay extra taxes. They would be required to pay tax on the value of the services performed by the housewife. Cuvillier reasons that having a housewife increases the family's real income. She simply carries the idea of taxation to its logical conclusion and argues that the family should be taxed on that part of its real income consisting of housewife-performed services. After all, says Cuvillier, the housewife is part of the community, and public services are delivered to her at public expense. She, or her husband on her behalf, should pay her share of this public expense.

Presumably only the extra services delivered by the housewife beyond those performed by two-earner couples would be taxed. In computing taxable income, an amount equal to some fraction of a servant's wage would be added to the cash income of couples maintaining a housewife.

SOCIAL SECURITY AND THE HOUSEWIFE

The Social Security system, on which Americans depend to give them income in old age, was established in the 1930s. Each person who has ever held a job covered under Social Security has an individual account in which that person's earnings are recorded. The rhetoric used to convince a basically conservative population that the system was a reasonable one portrayed the benefits as being drawn from a fund that had been built up out of the worker's own contributions as well as contributions by the employer on the worker's behalf. In reality, benefit formulas were constructed to replace a greater portion of the wage income of the lower-earning workers than of high-earning workers, and extra benefits were paid to the retired male workers who were married.*

At the time Social Security was set up and the principles of the benefit formula were established, most women spent their married years out of the labor force. If they were to receive Social Security benefits, they would have to do so in their capacity as wives or widows of male workers. The solution adopted was to

---

*See note to Table 2.

award to each retired couple a "spouse benefit" equal to 50 percent of the husband's benefit. Wives who had earnings in their own right might elect to take benefits based on those earnings, or might elect the spouse benefit, but not both.

The net effect of such arrangements is that the benefits a person gets are not proportional to that person's contributions. People who have had low earnings get more Social Security benefits per dollar of contribution than high wage earners. A married man gets more than a single man who has made the same contributions. Many women who have made contributions to Social Security end up by accepting the spouse benefit, which they could have received with no contributions at all. In a sense, these women receive nothing for their contributions.

Table 2 shows examples of the results of this kind of arrangement, which have been chosen to highlight the features of the system. In the first case shown (Dennis and Deborah), the man's salary had averaged $11,000 in terms of 1985 wage levels, and the wife's salary had been the same. They have a choice of taking the benefits the two of them were entitled to on the basis of their own earnings, or taking the husband's benefit plus the 50 percent spouse benefit. Obviously they would choose the former, giving them a benefit of $10,936. By contrast, the one-earner couple (Edgar and Elsie) can retire on an annual benefit of $13,047, which includes the $8,698 the husband would have been entitled to as a retired single man, plus the 50 percent spouse benefit.

The combined earnings of the first couple are equal to those of the second couple, and the two couples would have paid identical Social Security taxes. Moreover, the first couple would have put out more work effort, and led a less comfortable life than the second couple, who would have had the services of a housewife. Nevertheless, the one-earner couple would be awarded a benefit that was 19 percent higher than that awarded the two-earner couple.

If the two wives in our example become widowed, they would get very different benefits.

TABLE 2 Benefits to Couples Under the Social Security System for People Retiring in 1985

	AVERAGE INDEXED EARNINGS	BENEFITS FOR COUPLES BASED ON	
		OWN EARNINGS	SPOUSE BENEFIT
Dennis	$11,000	$5,468	$5,468
Deborah	11,000	5,468	2,734
Total	$22,000	$10,936	$8,202
Edgar	$22,000	$8,698	$8,698
Elsie	—	—	$4,349
Total	$22,000	$8,698	$13,047

Note: Benefits are based on 1985 formulas for people retiring at 65, which give 90 percent of the first $280 per month of average indexed earnings, 32 percent of earnings between $280 and $1,691, and 15 percent of earnings between $1,691 and $3,291. Average indexed earnings are computed by taking earnings for each of the previous 25 years, adjusting them to account for changes in average salary levels between the year in question and the retirement year, and then taking the average of such adjusted earnings. The lowest 5 years are excluded from the average. Detailed information on benefit structures are contained in U.S. Department of Health and Human Services, *Social Security Handbook,* 8th ed. (1984).

Elsie, who had never contributed to the Social Security system, would get a widow's benefit of $8,698. Deborah would get much less, only $5,468, despite a lifetime of contributions.

These examples suggest that the Social Security system, like the income-tax system, is more generous to families with housewives than to families of employed women. This is certainly the case if we restrict our attention to benefits going to retired married couples and to widows. The system is generous to those housewives who manage to stay married to their husbands. But it is extremely harsh to those housewives who become divorced.

Until 1978, a divorced woman who had been married to a man less than twenty years was entitled to no Social Security benefit whatsoever on the basis of her former marriage. Spouse benefits would have been payable only for the retired ex-husband's new wife, if any. If the divorced wife had been a housewife, or had a poor or spotty earnings record under her own name, her financial situation in old age would be very poor. Currently, divorced women whose marriage lasted for at least ten years qualify for benefits based on the ex-husband's earnings. However, while the ex-husband is alive, a divorced wife receives no benefits until he retires, and then is entitled only to a payment equal to the spouse benefit. Thus if Edgar divorced Elsie, he and a new wife would retire with a benefit of $13,047, but Elsie would be reduced to living on $4,349. However, if Edgar died, Elsie's benefit would rise to $8,698, the same amount the second wife would receive.

The problem of old-age support for divorced housewives has stirred suggestions that the Social Security system should give housewives direct credit for their service at home by putting "earnings" credits into their records. When wives received benefits under such a system, the benefits would be based on the woman's own credits—any earnings the woman had plus her housewife credits.

On what basis would the housewife's credits be computed? Some have suggested that credit for all the earnings of a couple be shared between spouses. Under earnings-sharing, the separate Social Security accounts of the husband and wife each would be credited with one half of their total earnings. Men married to housewives would get credit in their own accounts for only 50 percent of their earnings. This certainly would have the virtue of making explicit the economic partnership implicit in the marriage and of vesting in the wife the right to future benefits based on economic activity during the marriage. But men have been highly vocal against "giving away credits that belong to them." Other schemes that have been suggested to extend explicit coverage to housewives would allow couples to pay for extra credits to the wife's account (as is permitted in some other countries), or alternatively require them to make such payments. Still another would give the husband full credit for his earnings but would award an extra 50 percent to the wife's account. Under the latter scheme, the rest

of the community would continue the current subsidies to housewife-maintaining couples.[10]

All of these schemes involve basing pension checks on each person's "own" account. This might have the effect of giving housewives more dignity; their work would be recognized as worthy of social credit, and they would appear to be less dependent.

A still more fundamental reform of Social Security would reduce the effect of a person's earnings on the size of that person's retirement benefit check. Under a so-called two-tiered or double-decker setup, every old person would get a stipend unrelated to the person's earning history. To that stipend would be added a relatively small amount based on the earnings record. This would make the system more "like welfare" rather than the purely contributory system it appears (falsely) to most people to be. The two-tier system would help the displaced housewife more than any other. It would also reduce the unfair advantage the current system gives to the one-earner over two-earner couples with the same income. For those reasons it is the most desirable of the reforms that have been proposed.

FEMINIST THINKING ABOUT THE FULL-TIME HOMEMAKER

The role of the housewife has a major place in feminist thought. Betty Friedan's book *The Feminine Mystique*, which was influential in initiating the current wave of feminism in the United States, had as its central theme the disadvantages to women from assuming the housewife role. All feminists believe that women should not be forced into assuming that role and that alternative choices should be available.

There is a second strand of feminist thinking concerning housewives that derives from the solidarity feminists feel with all women, housewives included. This solidarity expresses itself in a concern to alleviate injuries (physical, psychological, financial) that housewives have suffered. It also leads feminists to join in efforts to shore up the dignity of the housewife.

There is still a third strand of thought about homemakers. Some people who consider themselves feminists think it would be desirable for even larger numbers of people to assume the stay-at-home housekeeper role than now do so. They see it as indispensable for the proper raising of children. They would prefer it if members of both sexes were candidates for the role, or if mothers and fathers could alternate. However, whether that were possible or not, they favor public policies making it financially easier for families to support a full-time homemaker. They tend to favor multi-year parental leaves with pay for childrearing.

Much of the attention of feminists has gone toward trying to help the housewife. Rolande Cuvillier, quoted earlier in connection with taxation, argues that the net effect of many pro-housewife measures is not to help women at all. Rather, such measures help men to retain someone dedicated to serving them in the home, at the expense of the rest of society. Thus policy measures that encourage women to become or remain housewives, such as tax breaks for housewife-maintaining families, help perpetuate the inequality of the sexes. When the scarce resources of the feminist movement are devoted to pushing measures that have that effect, support and attention are diverted away from reforms that would help the employed woman, the single mother, or the battered housewife.

The disadvantages to playing the role of full-time homemaker are so great that it is unlikely that significant numbers of men would want to serve in it. If the occupation continues to exist, it will continue to be part of the female domain and hence inherently disadvantaged. Since this is the case, equality of the sexes and women's welfare would be better served if younger women were to avoid entering the role even temporarily and if the socially sanctioned "option" to assume the role were to disappear. Policies that reward families for having housewives, or encourage women to assume the housewife role, do harm to women and should be avoided.

After we have passed through a phase where unpaid family care services have been largely replaced by purchased substitutes, and after equality of opportunity has been established in the workplace, it will be time to consider reviving the occupation of full-time homemaker. Then we can see if it can become an honorable, safe, and secure occupation for both mothers and fathers.

NOTES

1. These figures are derived from tables A–4 and A–22, U.S. Bureau of Labor Statistics, *Employment and Earnings* (February 1986).

2. John Kenneth Galbraith, *Economics and the Public Purpose* (Boston, Mass.: Houghton Mifflin, 1973), chap. 4.

3. Unpublished tabulation from the Census' Current Population Surveys.

4. *Statistical Abstract of the United States, 1985* (Washington, D.C.: U.S. Government Printing Office, 1984), table 179, p. 113. The figure is for 1981.

5. U.S. Department of Justice, *A Survey of Spousal Violence Against Women in Kentucky* (Washington, D.C.: Law Enforcement Assistance Administration, 1979).

6. C. Lopate, "Pay for Housework," *Journal of Social Policy*, vol. 5 (January 1974): 27–31.

7. The Swedish Institute, "Child Care Programs in Sweden," *Fact Sheets on Sweden* (Stockholm: September 1984).

8. The Swedish Institute, "Taxes in Sweden," *Fact Sheets on Sweden* (Stockholm: March 1985).

9. Rolande Cuvillier, "The Housewife—An Unjustified Financial Burden on the Community," *Journal of Social Policy*, vol. 8 (January 1979): 1–26.

10. For detailed discussions of all of the major alternatives to the present system of computing Social Security benefits, see Richard V. Burkhauser and Karen C. Holden, eds., *A Challenge to Social Security: The Changing Roles of Women and Men in American Society* (New York: Academic Press, 1982).

The Domestic Scene

Traditionally, marriage has been a lifelong partnership between a man and a woman in which their individual resources, interests, and even identities fully merge. For two-earner as well as one-earner families, marriage has also been an economic partnership in which a woman gives priority to homemaking and child care, while a man gives priority to his career. Over the centuries a distinctive ideology has come to surround not only marriage but also motherhood. This ideology of motherhood finds expression everywhere: in novels and works of art, in the booklets found in obstetricians' waiting rooms, and even in the lectures handed down by mothers and mothers-in-law. According to this ubiquitous ideology, once a woman becomes a mother, she no longer has an identity and interests of her own. Henceforth, she is simply the instrument of her children's needs and wants. No matter what, the "maternal" show must go on, a drama in which each and every mother is supposed to repeat endlessly the small, routine chores of socializing young human beings. Though father may "help out" whenever he feels like it, raising children is mother's responsibility. "Normal" women supposedly love to mother, and there is something "abnormal" about any woman who does not want to sacrifice herself totally in acts of unconditional love for her children.

The ideology of motherhood notwithstanding, some women are not always willing or even able to fulfill its terms. They have other identities besides that of mother and other interests besides those of their children. To the degree that the mothering role conflicts with these other interests and identities, such women may experience their maternal tasks as suffocating. Moreover, they may get physically and psychologically exhausted—tired of the demands made upon them, and resentful of husbands who lift relatively few of their fingers around the house. Nevertheless, these women may also feel guilty precisely because their feelings about mothering are ambivalent. In "Anger and Tenderness," Adrienne Rich articulates these and other maternal feelings. She shares with us her own mothering experiences—her love-hate relationship with her sons. We need, she says, to ask ourselves if there are ways for women to mother that do not demand unconditional surrender to the needs and wants of their children. Under what set of circumstances can mothering be a relatively joyful—or at least healthy—experience for all considered?

If traditional marriage has brought with it problems such as those we have sketched, then perhaps the solution is to replace traditional marriage with a new type of marriage in which the roles of husband and wife are fully equal. Perhaps a married couple should both work outside the home and within the home, thereby overcoming traditional gender roles and responsibilities. In "The Divorce Law Revolution and the Transformation of Legal Marriage," Lenore Weitzman observes that this new ideology of marriage is the one that is implicit in the new no-fault divorce laws. The old divorce laws assumed that a husband's role was to support a wife and children during marriage and to continue to support them after divorce; and that a wife's role was to take care of home and children during marriage and to continue to care for them after divorce.

In contrast, the new divorce laws treat wives and husbands as fully equal partners in marriage *and* divorce. Thus, at divorce both partners are responsible for self-support and child support, and both are eligible for child custody. Alimony is awarded only according to need, and property is divided equally. Moreover, in most states no ground or fault is necessary to obtain a divorce. All that is required, according to the new divorce laws, is the desire of at least one partner in the marriage to end it. This is in sharp contrast to the old divorce laws, according to which a marriage could be dissolved only if at least one of the parties was judged guilty of some serious indiscretion, such as adultery, physical abuse, or mental cruelty. In such cases, the law punished the guilty party and rewarded the innocent one through suitable alimony and property awards.

However beneficial to women the new divorce laws might seem, Weitzman argues that they worsen rather than improve women's condition. Even when both members of a married couple work outside the home, the woman's job is still the second job: the part-time job, the dead-end job, the luxury job. Women still tend to choose family responsibilities over career opportunities when push comes to shove, a tendency that is far less prevalent among men. As a result, at the time of a divorce a woman's earning capacity may have been impaired by the marriage relationship, while a man's earning capacity may have been enhanced. But the new divorce laws do not take this phenomenon into account. No matter what, divorce courts currently treat men and women equally at divorce, and the courts decide property settlements, alimony awards, and child support accordingly. What makes this "new deal" a particularly difficult one for ex-wives, who get child custody 90 percent of the time, is that their ex-husbands rarely pay even half of the expenses associated with rearing a child to adulthood. As a result, women and children tend to experience a sharp decline in their standard of living subsequent to a divorce, while men experience a steady rise in theirs. (Weitzman originally reported an average 73 percent decline in women and children's standard of living in the first year after divorce versus an average 42 percent rise in men's standard of living. However, Saul Hoffman and Greg Duncan suggest that 30 percent may be a more accurate figure for the decline in women and children's standard of living.)

According to Weitzman, another significant consequence of the new divorce laws is that they have "shifted the legal criteria for divorce—and thus for viable marriage—from fidelity to the marriage contract to individual standards of personal satisfaction" (p. 234). As a result, marriage is increasingly understood as a "time-limited, contingent arrangement rather than a lifelong commitment" (p. 234). In addition, the new divorce laws "alter the traditional legal view of marriage as a partnership by rewarding individual achievement rather than investment in the family partnership" (p. 237). Instead of "the traditional vision of a common financial future within marriage," the new laws "convey a new vision of independence for husbands and wives in marriage," and they "confer economic advantages on spouses who invest in themselves at the expense of the marital partnership" (pp. 237–238). Given this new understanding of marriage, Weitzman predicts that fewer people are going to "tie the marriage knot." Therefore, we need to ask ourselves whether the demise of the traditional marriage is an event that we should celebrate with unalloyed glee, or one that we should worry about—if only a bit.

If both the old inegalitarian marriage and the new egalitarian marriage pose problems for women, no marriage at all often poses even greater problems for them. In "Something Old, Something New: Women's Poverty in the 1990s," Diana Pearce points out that 44.5 percent of single-female-headed households with children (56.1 percent if the women are black, and 58.2 percent if the women are Hispanic) are poor, compared with 7.8 percent of married-couple households with children. Moreover, about one million persons in women-maintained families experience homelessness each year, living on the streets, in condemned buildings, abandoned cars, tents, garages, or battered women's shelters. Indeed, most of the homeless families with children are single-female-headed families.

Two major circumstances tend to push women into the ranks of the impoverished. First, women are disadvantaged in the labor market: they rely on part-time, temporary, or dead-end jobs, or full-time jobs in female-dominated occupations (which pay less), or full-time jobs in male-dominated occupations (which still pay less when the job-holders are women). Second, women bear the burden, economic as well as emotional, of raising children. Since these two circumstances are true of women in general, poverty can happen to *any* woman. It happened, for example, to Pearce's own well-educated, middle-class sister. More-over, since housing costs have been rising much faster than wages, more and more woman-maintained families are moving into homelessness. "Most painful of all, single mothers are asked to make difficult and unfair choices. . . . Pay the rent (but leave the kids on their own), pay the child care (and hope to postpone eviction), or eat at soup kitchens (and hope the kids do not get too hungry during the day, especially on nonschool days). . . . Pay to have the ear infections cleared up (but go without new shoes for the children, and school supplies, and. . . .) or buy these necessities and risk hearing loss or even deafness" (p. 248). What needs to be done, concludes Pearce, is to restructure employment in women-friendly ways, and to develop alternative models of housing ownership and design. "Neither the feminization of poverty nor women's poverty is inevitable" (p. 250), she insists, provided we are serious about "reorder[ing] our thinking" and our public policy.

Anger and Tenderness

Adrienne Rich

. . . to understand is always an ascending movement; that is why comprehension ought always to be concrete. (one is never got out of the cave, one comes out of it.)
SIMONE WEIL, *First and Last Notebooks*

Entry from my journal, November 1960

My children cause me the most exquisite suffering of which I have any experience. It is the suffering of ambivalence: the murderous alternation between bitter

resentment and raw-edged nerves, and blissful gratification and tenderness. Sometimes I seem to myself, in my feelings toward these tiny guiltless beings, a monster of selfishness and intolerance. Their voices wear away at my nerves, their constant needs, above all their need for simplicity and patience, fill me with despair at my own failures, despair too at my fate, which is to serve a function for which I was not fitted. And I am weak sometimes from held-in rage.

There are times when I feel only death will free us from one another, when I envy the barren woman who has the luxury of her regrets but lives a life of privacy and freedom.*

And yet at other times I am melted with the sense of their helpless, charming and quite irresistible beauty—their ability to go on loving and trusting—their staunchness and decency and unself-consciousness. *I love them.* But it's in the enormity and inevitability of this love that the sufferings lie.

April 1961

A blissful love for my children engulfs me from time to time and seems almost to suffice—the aesthetic pleasure I have in these little, changing creatures, the sense of being loved, however dependently, the sense too that I'm not an utterly unnatural and shrewish mother—much though I am!

May 1965

To suffer with and for and against a child—maternally, egotistically, neurotically, sometimes with a sense of helplessness, sometimes with the illusion of learning wisdom—but always, everywhere, in body and soul, *with* that child—because that child is a piece of oneself.

To be caught up in waves of love and hate, jealousy even of the child's childhood; hope and fear for its maturity; longing to be free of responsibility, tied by every fibre of one's being.

That curious primitive reaction of protectiveness, the beast defending her cub, when anyone attacks or criticizes him—And yet no one more hard on him than I!

September 1965

Degradation of anger. Anger at a child. How shall I learn to absorb the violence and make explicit only the caring? Exhaustion of anger. Victory of will, too dearly bought—far too dearly!

---

*The term "barren woman" was easy for me to use, unexamined, fifteen years ago. It seems to me now a term both tendentious and meaningless, based on a view of women which sees motherhood as our only positive definition.

March 1966

Perhaps one is a monster—an anti-woman—something driven and without recourse to the normal and appealing consolations of love, motherhood, joy in others. . . .

Unexamined assumptions: First, that a "natural" mother is a person without further identity, one who can find her chief gratification in being all day with small children, living at a pace tuned to theirs; that the isolation of mothers and children together in the home must be taken for granted; that maternal love is, and should be, quite literally selfless; that children and mothers are the "causes" of each others' suffering. I was haunted by the stereotype of the mother whose love is "unconditional"; and by the visual and literary images of motherhood as a single-minded identity. If I knew parts of myself existed that would never cohere to those images, weren't those parts then abnormal, monstrous? And—as my eldest son, now aged twenty-one, remarked on reading the above passages: "You seemed to feel you ought to love us all the time. But there *is* no human relationship where you love the other person at every moment." Yes, I tried to explain to him, but women—above all, mothers—have been supposed to love that way.

From the fifties and early sixties, I remember a cycle. It began when I had picked up a book or began trying to write a letter, or even found myself on the telephone with someone toward whom my voice betrayed eagerness, a rush of sympathetic energy. The child (or children) might be absorbed in busyness, in his own dreamworld; but as soon as he felt me gliding into a world which did not include him, he would come to pull at my hand, ask for help, punch at the typewriter keys. And I would feel his wants at such a moment as fraudulent, as an attempt moreover to defraud me of living even for fifteen minutes as myself. My anger would rise; I would feel the futility of any attempt to salvage myself, and also the inequality between us: my needs always balanced against those of a child, and always losing. I could love so much better, I told myself, after even a quarter-hour of selfishness, of peace, of detachment from my children. A few minutes! But it was as if an invisible thread would pull taut between us and break, to the child's sense of inconsolable abandonment, if I moved—not even physically, but in spirit—into a realm beyond our tightly circumscribed life together. It was as if my placenta had begun to refuse him oxygen. Like so many women, I waited with impatience for the moment when their father would return from work, when for an hour or two at least the circle drawn around mother and children would grow looser, the intensity between us slacken, because there was another adult in the house.

I did not understand that this circle, this magnetic field in which we lived, was not a natural phenomenon.

Intellectually, I must have known it. But the emotion-charged, tradition-heavy form in which I found myself cast as the Mother seemed, then, as ineluctable as the tides. And, because of this form—this microcosm in which my children and I formed a tiny, private emotional cluster, and in which (in bad weather or when someone was ill) we sometimes passed days at a time without seeing another adult except for their father—there *was* authentic need underlying my child's invented claims upon me when I seemed to be wandering away from him. He was reassuring himself that warmth, tenderness, continuity, solidity were still there for him, in my person. My singularity, my uniqueness in the world as *his mother*—perhaps more dimly also as Woman-evoked a need vaster than any single human being could satisfy, except by loving continuously, unconditionally, from dawn to dark, and often in the middle of the night.

2

In a living room in 1975, I spent an evening with a group of women poets, some of whom had children. One had brought hers along, and they slept or played in adjoining rooms. We talked of poetry, and also of infanticide, of the case of a local woman, the mother of eight, who had been in severe depression since the birth of her third child, and who had recently murdered and decapitated her two youngest, on her suburban front lawn. Several women in the group, feeling a direct connection with her desperation, had signed a letter to the local newspaper protesting the way her act was perceived by the press and handled by the community mental health system. Every woman in that room who had children, every poet, could identify with her. We spoke of the wells of anger that her story cleft open in us. We spoke of our own moments of murderous anger at our children, because there was no one and nothing else on which to discharge anger. We spoke in the sometimes tentative, sometimes rising, sometimes bitterly witty, unrhetorical tones and language of women who had met together over our common work, poetry, and who found another common ground in an unacceptable, but undeniable anger. The words are being spoken now, are being written down; the taboos are being broken, the masks of motherhood are cracking through. For centuries no one talked of these feelings. I became a mother in the family-centered, consumer-oriented, Freudian-American world of the 1950s. My husband spoke eagerly of the children we would have; my parents-in-law awaited the birth of their grandchild. I had no idea of what *I* wanted, what *I* could or could not choose. I only knew that to have a child was to assume adult womanhood to the full, to prove myself, to be "like other women."

To be "like other women" had been a problem for me. From the age of thirteen or fourteen, I had felt I was only acting the part of a feminine creature. At the age of sixteen my fingers were almost constantly ink-stained. The lipstick and high heels of the era were difficult-to-manage disguises. In 1945 I was writing poetry seriously, and had a fantasy of going to postwar Europe as a journalist, sleeping among the ruins in bombed cities, recording the rebirth of civilization after the fall of the Nazis. But also, like every other girl I knew, I spent hours trying to apply lipstick more adroitly, straightening the wandering seams of stockings, talking about "boys." There were two different compartments, already, to my life. But writing poetry, and my fantasies of travel and self-sufficiency, seemed more real to me; I felt that as an incipient "real woman" I was a fake. Particularly was I paralyzed when I encountered young children. I think I felt men could be—wished to be—conned into thinking I was truly "feminine"; a child, I suspected, could see through me like a shot. This sense of acting a part created a curious sense of guilt, even though it was a part demanded for survival.

I have a very clear, keen memory of myself the day after I was married: I was sweeping a floor. Probably the floor did not really need to be swept; probably I simply did not know what else to do with myself. But as I swept that floor I thought: "Now I am a woman. This is an age-old action, this is what women have always done." I felt I was bending to some ancient form, too ancient to question. *This is what women have always done.*

As soon as I was visibly and clearly pregnant, I felt, for the first time in my adolescent and adult life, not guilty. The atmosphere of approval in which I was bathed—even by strangers on the street, it seemed—was like an aura I carried with me, in which doubts, fears, misgivings, met with absolute denial. *This is what women have always done.*

Two days before my first son was born, I broke out in a rash which was tentatively diagnosed as measles, and was admitted to a hospital for contagious diseases to await the onset of labor. I felt for the first time a great deal of conscious fear, and guilt toward my unborn child, for having "failed" him with my body in this way. In rooms near mine were patients with polio; no one was allowed to enter my room except in a hospital gown and mask. If during pregnancy I had felt in any vague command of my situation, I felt now totally dependent on my obstetrician, a huge, vigorous, paternal man, abounding with optimism and assurance, and given to pinching my cheek. I had gone through a healthy pregnancy, but as if tranquilized or sleep-walking. I had taken a sewing class in which I produced an unsightly and ill-cut maternity jacket which I never wore; I had made curtains for the baby's room, collected baby clothes, blotted out as much as possible the woman I had been a few months earlier. My second book of poems was in press, but I had stopped writing poetry, and read little except household magazines and books on child-care. I felt myself perceived by the world simply as a pregnant woman, and it seemed easier, less disturbing, to perceive myself so. After my child was born the "measles" were diagnosed as an allergic reaction to pregnancy.

Within two years, I was pregnant again, and writing in a notebook:

November 1956

Whether it's the extreme lassitude of early pregnancy or something more fundamental, I don't know; but of late I've felt, toward poetry, —both reading and writing it—nothing but boredom and indifference. Especially toward my own and that of my immediate contemporaries. When I receive a letter soliciting mss., or someone alludes to my "career," I have a strong sense of wanting to deny all responsibility for and interest in that person who writes—or who wrote.

If there is going to be a real break in my writing life, this is as good a time for it as any. I have been dissatisfied with myself, my work, for a long time.

My husband was a sensitive, affectionate man who wanted children and who—unusual in the professional, academic world of the fifties—was willing to "help." But it was clearly understood that this "help" was an act of generosity; that *his* work, *his* professional life, was the real work in the family; in fact, this was for years not even an issue between us. I understood that my struggles as a writer were a kind of luxury, a peculiarity of mine; my work brought in almost no money: it even cost money, when I hired a household helper to allow me a few hours a week to write. "Whatever I ask he tries to give me," I wrote in March 1958, "but always the initiative has to be mine." I experienced my depressions, bursts of anger, sense of entrapment, as burdens my husband was forced to bear because he loved me; I felt grateful to be loved in spite of bringing him those burdens.

But I was struggling to bring my life into focus. I had never really given up on poetry, nor on gaining some control over my existence. The life of a Cambridge tenement backyard swarming with children, the repetitious cycles of laundry, the night-wakings, the interrupted moments of peace or of engagement with ideas, the ludicrous dinner parties at which young wives, some with advanced degrees, all seriously and intelligently dedicated to their children's welfare and their husbands' careers, attempted to reproduce the amenities of Brahmin Boston, amid French recipes and the pretense of effortlessness—above all, the ultimate lack of seriousness with which women were regarded in that world—all of this defied analysis at that time, but I *knew* I had to remake my own life. I did not then understand that we—the women of that academic community—as in so many middle-class communities of the period—were expected to fill both the part of the Victorian Lady of Leisure, the Angel in the House, and also of the Victorian cook, scullery maid, laundress, governess, and nurse. I only sensed that there were false distractions sucking at me, and I wanted desperately to strip my life down to what was essential.

June 1958

These months I've been all a tangle of irritations deepening to anger: bitterness, disillusion with society and with myself; beating out at the world, re-

jecting out of hand. What, if anything, has been positive? Perhaps the attempt to remake my life, to save it from mere drift and the passage of time. . . .

The work that is before me is serious and difficult and not at all clear even as to plan. Discipline of mind and spirit, uniqueness of expression, ordering of daily existence, the most effective functioning of the human self—these are the chief things I wish to achieve. So far the only beginning I've been able to make is to waste less time. That is what some of the rejection has been all about.

By July of 1958 I was again pregnant. The new life of my third—and, as I determined, my last—child, was a kind of turning for me. I had learned that my body was not under my control; I had not intended to bear a third child. I knew now better than I had ever known what another pregnancy, another new infant, meant for my body and spirit. Yet, I did not think of having an abortion. In a sense, my third son was more actively chosen than either of his brothers; by the time I knew I was pregnant with him, I was not sleepwalking any more.

August 1958 (Vermont)

I write this as the early rays of the sun light up our hillside and eastern windows. Rose with [the baby] at 5:30 A.M. and have fed him and breakfasted. This is one of the few mornings on which I haven't felt terrible mental depression and physical exhaustion.

. . . I have to acknowledge to myself that I would not have chosen to have more children, that I was beginning to look to a time, not too far off, when I should again be free, no longer so physically tired, pursuing a more or less intellectual and creative life. . . . The *only* way I can develop now is through much harder, more continuous, connected work than my present life makes possible. Another child means postponing this for some years longer— and years at my age are significant, not to be tossed lightly away.

And yet, somehow, something, call it Nature or that affirming fatalism of the human creature, makes me aware of the inevitable as already part of me, not to be contended against so much as brought to bear as an additional weapon against drift, stagnation and spiritual death. (For it is really death that I have been fearing—the crumbling to death of that scarcely-born physiognomy which my whole life has been a battle to give birth to—a recognizable, autonomous self, a creation in poetry and in life.)

If more effort has to be made then I will make it. If more despair has to be lived through, I think I can anticipate it correctly and live through it.

Meanwhile, in a curious and unanticipated way, we really do welcome the birth of our child.

There was, of course, an economic as well as a spiritual margin which allowed me to think of a third child's birth not as my own death-warrant but as an "additional weapon against death." My body, despite recurrent flares of arthritis, was a healthy one; I had good prenatal care; we were not living on the edge of malnutrition; I knew that all my children would be fed, clothed, breathe fresh air; in fact it did not occur to me that it could be otherwise. But, in another sense, beyond that physical margin, I knew I was fighting for my life through, against, and with the lives of my children, though very little else was clear to me. I had been trying to give birth to myself; and in some grim, dim way I was determined to use even pregnancy and parturition in that process.

Before my third child was born I decided to have no more children, to be sterilized. (Nothing is removed from a woman's body during this operation; ovulation and menstruation continue. Yet the language suggests a cutting- or burning-away of her essential womanhood, just as the old word "barren" suggests a woman eternally empty and lacking.) My husband, although he supported my decision, asked whether I was sure it would not leave me feeling "less feminine." In order to have the operation at all, I had to present a letter, counter-signed by my husband, assuring the committee of physicians who approved such operations that I had already produced three children, and stating my reasons for having no more. Since I had had rheumatoid arthritis for some years, I could give a reason acceptable to the male panel who sat on my case; my own judgment would not have been acceptable. When I awoke from the operation, twenty-four hours after my child's birth, a young nurse looked at my chart and remarked coldly: "Had yourself spayed, did you?"

The first great birth-control crusader, Margaret Sanger, remarks that of the hundreds of women who wrote to her pleading for contraceptive information in the early part of the twentieth century, all spoke of wanting the health and strength to be better mothers to the children they already had; or of wanting to be physically affectionate to their husbands without dread of conceiving. None was refusing motherhood altogether, or asking for an easy life. These women—mostly poor, many still in their teens, all with several children—simply felt they could no longer do "right" by their families, whom they expected to go on serving and rearing. Yet there always has been, and there remains, intense fear of the suggestion that women shall have the final say as to how our bodies are to be used. It is as if the suffering of the mother, the primary identification of woman *as* the mother—were so necessary to the emotional grounding of human society that the mitigation, or removal, of that suffering, that identification, must be fought at every level, including the level of refusing to question it at all.

3

"Vous travaillez pour l'armée, madame?" (You are working for the army?), a Frenchwoman said to me early in the Vietnam war, on hearing I had three sons.

April 1965

Anger, weariness, demoralization. Sudden bouts of weeping. A sense of insufficiency to the moment and to eternity. . . .

Paralyzed by the sense that there exists a mesh of relations, between e.g. my rejection and anger at [my eldest child], my sensual life, pacifism, sex (I mean in its broadest significance, not merely physical desire)—an interconnectedness which, if I could see it, make it valid, would give me back myself, make it possible to function lucidly and passionately—Yet I grope in and out among these dark webs—

I weep, and weep, and the sense of powerlessness spreads like a cancer through my being.

August 1965, 3:30 A.M.

Necessity for a more unyielding discipline of my life.
> Recognize the uselessness of blind anger.
> Limit society.
> Use children's school hours better, for work & solitude.
> Refuse to be distracted from own style of life.
> Less waste.
> Be harder & harder on poems.

Once in a while someone used to ask me, "Don't you ever write poems about your children?" The male poets of my generation did write poems about their children—especially their daughters. For me, poetry was where I lived as no-one's mother, where I existed as myself.

The bad and the good moments are inseparable for me. I recall the times when, suckling each of my children, I saw his eyes open full to mine, and realized each of us was fastened to the other, not only by mouth and breast, but through our mutual gaze: the depth, calm, passion, of that dark blue, maturely focused look. I recall the physical pleasure of having my full breast suckled at a time when I had no other physical pleasure in the world except the guilt-ridden pleasure of addictive eating. I remember early the sense of conflict, of a battleground none of us had chosen, of being an observer who, like it or not, was also an actor in an endless contest of wills. This was what it meant to me to have three children under the age of seven. But I recall too each child's individual body, his slenderness, wiriness, softness, grace, the beauty of little boys who have not been

taught that the male body must be rigid. I remember moments of peace when for some reason it was possible to go to the bathroom alone. I remember being uprooted from already meager sleep to answer a childish nightmare, pull up a blanket, warm a consoling bottle, lead a half-asleep child to the toilet. I remember going back to bed starkly awake, brittle with anger, knowing that my broken sleep would make next day a hell, that there would be more nightmares, more need for consolation, because out of my weariness I would rage at those children for no reason they could understand. I remember thinking I would never dream again (the unconscious of the young mother—where does it entrust its messages, when dream-sleep is denied her for years?).

For many years I shrank from looking back on the first decade of my children's lives. In snapshots of the period I see a smiling young woman, in maternity clothes or bent over a half-naked baby; gradually she stops smiling, wears a distant, half-melancholy look, as if she were listening for something. In time my sons grew older, I began changing my own life, we began to talk to each other as equals. Together we lived through my leaving the marriage, and through their father's suicide. We became survivors, four distinct people with strong bonds connecting us. Because I always tried to tell them the truth, because their every new independence meant new freedom for me, because we trusted each other even when we wanted different things, they became, at a fairly young age, self-reliant and open to the unfamiliar. Something told me that if they had survived my angers, my self-reproaches, and still trusted my love and each other's, they were strong. Their lives have not been, will not be, easy; but their very existences seem a gift to me, their vitality, humor, intelligence, gentleness, love of life, their separate life-currents which here and there stream into my own. I don't know how we made it from their embattled childhood and my embattled motherhood into a mutual recognition of ourselves and each other. Probably that mutual recognition, overlaid by social and traditional circumstance, was always there, from the first gaze between the mother and the infant at the breast. But I do know that for years I believed I should never have been anyone's mother, that because I felt my own needs acutely and often expressed them violently, I was Kali, Medea, the sow that devours her farrow, the unwomanly woman in flight from womanhood, a Nietzschean monster. Even today, rereading old journals, remembering, I feel grief and anger; but their objects are no longer myself and my children. I feel grief at the waste of myself in those years, anger at the mutilation and manipulation of the relationship between mother and child, which is the great original source and experience of love.

On an early spring day in the 1970s, I meet a young woman friend on the street. She has a tiny infant against her breast, in a bright cotton sling; its face is pressed against her blouse, its tiny hand clutches a piece of the cloth. "How old is she?" I ask. "Just two weeks old," the mother tells me. I am amazed to feel in myself a passionate longing to have, once again, such a small, new being clasped against my body. The baby belongs there, curled, suspended asleep between her mother's breasts, as she belonged curled in the womb. The young mother—who already has a three-year-old—speaks of how quickly one forgets the pure pleasure of having this new creature, immaculate, perfect. And I walk away from her drenched with memory, with envy. Yet I know other things: that her life is far from simple; she is a mathematician who now has two children under the age of four; she is living even now in the rhythms of other lives—not only the regular cry of the infant but her three-year-old's needs, her husband's problems. In the building where I live, women are still raising children alone, living day in and day out within their individual family units, doing the laundry, herding the tricycles to the park, waiting for the husbands to come home.

There is a baby-sitting pool and a children's playroom, young fathers push prams on weekends, but child-care is still the individual responsibility of the individual woman. I envy the sensuality of having an infant of two weeks curled against one's breast; I do not envy the turmoil of the elevator full of small children, babies howling in the laundromat, the apartment in winter where pent-up seven- and eight-year-olds have one adult to look to for their frustrations, reassurances, the grounding of their lives.

4

But, it will be said, this is the human condition, this interpenetration of pain and pleasure, frustration and fulfillment. I might have told myself the same thing, fifteen or eighteen years ago. But the patriarchal institution of motherhood is not the "human condition" any more than rape, prostitution, and slavery are. (Those who speak largely of the human condition are usually those most exempt from its oppressions—whether of sex, race, or servitude.)

Motherhood—unmentioned in the histories of conquest and serfdom, wars and treaties, exploration and imperialism—has a history, it has an ideology, it is more fundamental than tribalism or nationalism. My individual, seemingly private pains as a mother, the individual, seemingly private pains of the mothers around me and before me, whatever our class or color, the regulation of women's reproductive power by men in every totalitarian system and every socialist revolution, the legal and technical control by men of contraception, fertility, abortion, obstetrics, gynecology, and extrauterine reproductive experiments—all are essential to the patriarchal system, as is the negative or suspect status of women who are not mothers.

Throughout patriarchal mythology, dream-symbolism, theology, language, two ideas flow side by side: one, that the female body is impure, corrupt, the site of discharges, bleedings, dangerous to masculinity, a source of moral and physical contamination, "the devil's gateway." On the other hand, as mother the woman is beneficent, sacred, pure, asexual, nourishing; and the physical potential for motherhood—that same body with its bleedings and mysteries—is her single destiny and justification in life. These two ideas have become deeply internalized in women, even in the most independent of us, those who seem to lead the freest lives.

In order to maintain two such notions, each in its contradictory purity, the masculine imagination has had to divide women, to see us, and force us to see ourselves, as polarized into good or evil, fertile or barren, pure or impure. The asexual Victorian angel-wife and the Victorian prostitute were institutions created by this double thinking, which had nothing to do with women's actual sensuality and everything to do with the male's subjective experience of women. The political and economic expediency of this kind of thinking is most unashamedly and dramatically to be found where sexism and racism become one. The social historian A. W. Calhoun describes the encouragement of the rape of black women by the sons of white planters, in a deliberate effort to produce more mulatto slaves, mulattos being considered more valuable. He quotes two mid-nineteenth-century southern writers on the subject of women:

"The heaviest part of the white racial burden in slavery was the African woman of strong sex instincts and devoid of a sexual conscience, at the white man's door, in the white man's dwelling." ... "Under the institution of slavery, the attack against the integrity of white civilization was made by the insidious influence of the lascivious hybrid woman at the point of weakest resistance. In the uncompromising purity of the white mother and wife of the upper classes lay the one assurance of the future purity of the race."[1]

The motherhood created by rape is not only degraded; the raped woman is turned into the criminal, the *attacker*. But who brought the black woman to the white man's door, whose absence of a sexual conscience produced the financially profitable mulatto children? Is it asked whether the "pure" white mother and wife was not also raped by the white planter, since she was assumed to be devoid of "strong sexual instinct?" In the American South, as elsewhere, it was economically necessary that children be produced; the mothers, black and white, were a means to this end.

Neither the "pure" nor the "lascivious" woman, neither the so-called mistress nor the slave woman, neither the woman praised for reducing herself to a brood animal nor the woman scorned and penalized as an "old maid" or a "dyke," has had any real autonomy or selfhood to gain from this subversion of the female body (and hence of the female mind). Yet, because short-term advantages are often the only ones visible to the powerless, we, too, have played our parts in continuing this subversion.

5

Most of the literature of infant care and psychology has assumed that the process toward individuation is essentially the *child's* drama, played out against and with a parent or parents who are, for better or worse, givens. Nothing could have prepared me for the realization that I *was* a mother, one of those givens, when I knew I was still in a state of uncreation myself. That calm, sure, unambivalent woman who moved through the pages of the manuals I read seemed as unlike me as an astronaut. Nothing, to be sure, had prepared me for the intensity of relationship already existing between me and a creature I had carried in my body and now held in my arms and fed from my breasts. Throughout pregnancy and nursing, women are urged to relax, to mime the serenity of madonnas. No one mentions the psychic crisis of bearing a first child, the excitation of long-buried feelings about one's own mother, the sense of confused power and powerlessness, of being taken over on the one hand and of touching new physical and psychic potentialities on the other, a heightened sensibility which can be exhilarating, bewildering and exhausting. No one mentions the strangeness of attraction—which can be as single-minded and overwhelming as the early days of a love affair—to a being so tiny, so dependent, so folded-in to itself—who is, and yet is not, part of oneself.

From the beginning the mother caring for her child is involved in a continually changing dialogue, crystallized in such moments as when, hearing her child's cry, she feels milk rush into her breasts; when, as the child first suckles, the uterus begins contracting and returning to its normal size, and when later, the child's mouth, caressing the nipple, creates waves of sensuality in the womb where it once lay; or when, smelling the breast even in sleep, the child starts to root and grope for the nipple.

The child gains her first sense of her own existence from the mother's responsive gestures and expressions. It's as if, in the mother's eyes, her smile, her stroking touch, the child first reads the message: *You are there!* And the mother, too, is discovering her own existence newly. She is connected with this other being, by the most mundane and the most invisible strands, in a way she can be connected with no one else except in the deep past of her infant connection with her own mother. And she, too, needs to struggle from that one-to-one intensity into new realization, or reaffirmation, of her being-unto-herself.

The act of suckling a child, like a sexual act, may be tense, physically painful, charged with cultural feelings of inadequacy and guilt; or, like a sexual act, it can be a physically delicious, elementally soothing experience, filled with a tender sensuality. But just as lovers have to break apart after sex and become separate individuals again, so the mother has to wean herself from the infant and the infant from herself. In psychologies of child-rearing the emphasis is placed on "letting the child go" for the child's sake. But the mother needs to let it go as much or more for her own.

Motherhood, in the sense of an intense, reciprocal relationship with a particular child, or children, is one part of female process; it is not an identity for all time. The housewife in her mid-forties may jokingly say, "I feel like someone out of a job." But in the eyes of society, once having been mothers, what are we, if not always mothers? The process of "letting-go"—though we are charged with blame if we do not—is an act of revolt against the grain of patriarchal culture. But it is not enough to let our children go; we need selves of our own to return to.

To have borne and reared a child is to have done that thing which patriarchy joins with physiology to render into the definition of femaleness. But also, it can mean the experiencing of one's own body and emotions in a powerful way. We experience not only physical, fleshly changes but the feeling of a change in character. We learn, often through painful self-discipline and self-cauterization, those qualities which are supposed to be "innate" in us: patience, self-sacrifice, the willingness to repeat endlessly the small, routine chores of socializing a human being. We are also, often to our amazement, flooded with feelings both of love and violence intenser and fiercer than any we had ever known. (A well-known pacifist, also a mother, said recently on a platform: "If anyone laid a hand on *my* child, I'd murder him.")

These and similar experiences are not easily put aside. Small wonder that women gritting their teeth at the incessant demands of childcare still find it hard to acknowledge their children's growing independence of them; still feel they must be at home, on the *qui vive*, be that ear always tuned for the sound of emergency, of being needed. Children grow up, not in a smooth ascending curve, but jaggedly, their needs inconstant as weather. Cultural "norms" are marvelously powerless to decide, in a child of eight or ten, what gender s/he will assume on a given day, or how s/he will meet emergency, loneliness, pain, hunger. One is constantly made aware that a human existence is anything but linear, long before the labyrinth of puberty because a human being of six is still a human being.

In a tribal or even a feudal culture a child of six would have serious obligations; ours have none. But also, the woman at home with children is not believed to be doing serious work she is just supposed to be acting out of maternal instinct, doing chores a man would never take on, largely uncritical of the meaning of what she does. So child and mother alike are depreciated, because only grown men and women in the paid labor force are supposed to be "productive."

The power-relations between mother and child are often simply a reflection of power-relations in patriarchal society: "You will do this because I know what is good for you" is difficult to distinguish from "You will do this because I can *make* you." Powerless women have always used mothering as a channel—narrow but deep—for their own human will to power, their need to return upon the world what it has visited on them. The child dragged by the arm across the room to be washed, the child cajoled, bullied, and bribed into taking "one more bite" of a detested food, is more than just a child which must be reared according to cultural traditions of "a good mothering." S/he is a piece of reality, of the world, which can be acted on, even modified, by a woman restricted from acting on anything else except inert materials like dust and food.

6

When I try to return to the body of the young woman of twenty-six, pregnant for the first time, who fled from the physical knowledge of her pregnancy and at the same time from her intellect and vocation, I realize that I was effectively alienated from my real body and my real spirit by the institution—not the fact—of motherhood. This institution—the foundation of human society as we know it—allowed me only certain views, certain expectations, whether embodied in the booklet in my obstetrician's waiting room, the novels I had read,

my mother-in-law's approval, my memories of my own mother, the Sistine Madonna or she of the Michelangelo *Pietà*, the floating notion that a woman pregnant is a woman calm in her fulfillment or, simply, a woman waiting. Women have always been seen as waiting: waiting to be asked, waiting for our menses, in fear lest they do or do not come, waiting for men to come home from wars, or from work, waiting for children to grow up, or for the birth of a new child, or for menopause.

In my own pregnancy I dealt with this waiting, this female fate, by denying every active, powerful aspect of myself. I became dissociated both from my immediate, present, bodily experience and from my reading, thinking, writing life. Like a traveler in an airport where her plane is several hours delayed, who leafs through magazines she would never ordinarily read, surveys shops whose contents do not interest her, I committed myself to an outward serenity and a profound inner boredom. If boredom is simply a mask for anxiety, then I had learned, as a woman, to be supremely bored rather than to examine the anxiety underlying my Sistine tranquility. My body, finally truthful, paid me back in the end: I was allergic to pregnancy.

I have come to believe that female biology—the diffuse, intense sensuality radiating out from clitoris, breasts, uterus, vagina; the lunar cycles of menstruation; the gestation and fruition of life which can take place in the female body—has far more radical implications than we have yet come to appreciate. Patriarchal thought has limited female biology to its own narrow specifications. The feminist vision has recoiled from female biology for these reasons; it will, I believe, come to view our physicality as a resource, rather than a destiny. In order to live a fully human life we require not only *control* of our bodies (though control is a prerequisite); we must touch the unity and resonance of our physicality, our bond with the natural order, the corporeal ground of our intelligence.

The ancient, continuing envy, awe, and dread of the male for the female capacity to create life has repeatedly taken the form of ha-tred for every other female aspect of creativity. Not only have women been told to stick to motherhood, but we have been told that our intellectual or aesthetic creations were inappro-priate, inconsequential, or scandalous, an at-tempt to become "like men," or to escape from the "real" tasks of adult womanhood: marriage and childbearing. To "think like a man" has been both praise and prison for women trying to escape the body-trap. No wonder that many intellectual and creative women have insisted that they were "human beings" first and women only incidentally, have minimized their physi-cality and their bonds with other women. The body has been made so problematic for women that it has often seemed easier to shrug it off and travel as a disembodied spirit.

But this reaction against the body is now coming into synthesis with new inquiries into the actual—as opposed to the culturally warped—power inherent in female biology, however we choose to use it, and by no means limited to the maternal function.

My own story is only one story. What I carried away in the end was a determination to heal—insofar as an individual woman can, and as much as possible with other women—the separation between mind and body; never again to lose myself both psychically and phys-ically in that way. Slowly I came to understand the paradox contained in "my" experience of motherhood; that, although different from many other women's experiences it was not unique; and that only in shedding the illusion of my uniqueness could I hope, as a women, to have any authentic life at all.

NOTE

1. Arthur Calhoun, *A Social History of the American Family from Colonial Times to the Present* (Cleveland, 1917).

The Divorce Law Revolution and the Transformation of Legal Marriage

Lenore J. Weitzman

In 1970, California launched a legal revolution by instituting the first no-fault divorce law in the United States. This pioneering new law promised to free the legal process of divorce from the shackles of outmoded tradition. It embodied "modern" concepts of equity and equality, and was immediately heralded as the family law of the future.

From *Contemporary Marriage: Comparative Perspectives on a Changing Institution*, edited by Kingsley Davis, in association with Amyra Grossbard-Shechtman. Copyright © 1985 by Lenore J. Weitzman. Reprinted by permission.

Note: The issues and data discussed in this chapter are explored in greater depth in my book, The Divorce Revolution: The Unexpected Social and Economic Consequences for Women and Children in America (*New York, Free Press, 1985*).

Before 1970 all states in the United States required fault-based grounds for divorce. One party had to be judged guilty of some marital fault, such as adultery or cruelty, before a divorce could be granted. California rejected this traditional system by permitting parties to divorce when "irreconcilable differences" caused the breakdown of their marriage. This simple change transformed the legal process of divorce. By 1985, just fifteen years later, every state but South Dakota had adopted some form of no-fault divorce law.

These no-fault divorce laws are unique in several respects. First, they eliminate the need for grounds in order to obtain a divorce. (In fact, in many no-fault states it is not even necessary to obtain a spouse's consent in order to obtain a divorce.) Second, they undercut the old system of alimony and property awards for "innocent" spouses. Third, no-fault laws seek to undermine the adversary process and to reduce the acrimony and trauma of the fault system. Finally, new norms for dividing property and awarding alimony eliminate the anachronistic assumptions in the traditional law and treat wives as full and equal partners in the marital partnership.

When I first read about California's new law I was fascinated by the reformers' attempt to alter the social and psychological effects of divorce by changing the legal process. I had just completed two years as a postdoctoral fellow at Yale Law School, with a focus on family law, and I saw California's law as an exciting experiment in legal reform.

I also shared the reformers' optimism and assumed that only good could come from an end to the old fault-based system of divorce. The sham testimony and vilification that were required to prove fault insulted the dignity of the law, the courts, and all the participants. How much better, I thought, to construct a legal procedure that would eliminate vicious scenes and reduce, rather than increase, the antagonism and hostility between divorcing spouses. How much better to lessen the trauma of divorce for both parents and children. And how much better to end a marriage in a non-adversarial process that would enable the parties to fashion fair and equitable financial arrangements. If I, as a researcher, had a personal or political goal beyond my stated aim of analyzing the effects of the new law, it was to help potential reformers in other states learn from the California experience.

In the early 1970s I joined with Herma Hill Kay and Ruth B. Dixon in an interdisciplinary effort to study the social and legal consequences of California's divorce law reforms. We embarked on an analysis of court records, interviews with family law judges and lawyers, and in-depth interviews with recently divorced men and women.

As this research progressed, it became evident that the consequences of the legal reforms extended far beyond the original vision of the reformers. Without fault-based grounds for divorce, and without the need to prove adultery or mental cruelty, the reformers had not only recast the *psychological context* of divorce (and had in fact reduced some of the hostility and acrimony it generated), but they had also transformed the *economic consequences* of divorce and, in the process, had redefined the rights and responsibilities of husbands and wives in legal marriage.

Ends may influence beginnings. In a society where one-half of all first marriages are expected to end in divorce, a radical change in the rules for ending marriage inevitably affects the rules for marriage itself and the intentions and expectations of those who enter it.

THE UNINTENDED CONSEQUENCES

One unanticipated and unintended result of the no-fault reforms has been widespread economic disruption for divorced women and their children. The new rules for alimony, property, and child support shape radically different economic futures for divorced men, on the one hand, and for divorced women and their children on the other. Women, and the minor children in their households—90 percent of the children live with their mothers after divorce[1]—experience a sharp decline in their standard of living after divorce. Men, in contrast, are usually much better off and have a higher standard of living as a result of a no-fault divorce.

How could these simple changes in the rules for divorce have such far-reaching effects? Why would a legal reform designed to create more equitable settlements end up impoverishing divorced women and their children?

In the pages that follow we will see how the new rules, rules designed to treat men and women "equally," have in practice served to deprive divorced women, especially mothers of young children and older homemakers, of the protections that the old law provided. These women have lost both the legitimacy and the financial rewards that the traditional divorce law provided for wives and mothers. Instead of

recognition for their contributions as homemakers and mothers, and instead of compensation for the years of lost opportunities and impaired earning capacities, these women now face a divorce law that treats them "equally" and expects them to be equally capable of supporting themselves after divorce.

Since a woman's ability to support herself is likely to be impaired during marriage, especially if she has been homemaker and mother, she may not be equal to her former husband at the point of divorce. Rules that treat her as if she is equal simply serve to deprive her of the financial support she needs. In fact, marriage itself contributes to the economic inequalities between men and women and to the different structural opportunities that the two spouses face at divorce. While most married women give priority to their family roles, most married men give priority to their careers. She often forgoes further education and occupational

TABLE 1   Summary of Changes in Divorce Law

TRADITIONAL DIVORCE	NO-FAULT DIVORCE
Restrictive law	Permissive law
To protect marriage	To facilitate divorce
Specific grounds	No grounds
Adultery, cruelty, etc.	Marital breakdown
Moral framework	Administrative framework
Guilt vs. innocence	
Fault	No-fault
One party caused divorce	Cause of divorce irrelevant
Consent of innocent spouse needed	No consent
Innocent spouse has "power"	Unilateral divorce
Can prevent/delay divorce	No consent/agreement necessary
Gender-based responsibilities	Gender-neutral responsibilities
Husband responsible for alimony	Both responsible for self-support
Wife responsible for custody	Both eligible for custody
Husband responsible for child support	Both responsible for child support
Financial awards linked to fault	Financial awards based on need and equality
Alimony for "innocent" wife	Alimony based on need
Greater share of property to "innocent" spouse	Property divided equally
Adversarial	Nonadversarial
One party guilty, one innocent	No guilty or innocent party
Financial gain in proving fault	No financial gain in charges
	Amicable resolution encouraged

gains for homemaking and child care, while he often acquires more education and on-the-job experience. As a result, her earning capacity is impaired while his earning capacity is enhanced. In both single-income and two-income families the couple, as a unit, are more likely to have given priority to the husband's career.

If the divorce rules do not allow her to share the fruits of her investment in his career (through alimony and child support awards); and if divorce rules expect her to enter the labor market as his equal—even though she may have fewer job skills, outdated experience, no seniority, and no time for retraining; and if she continues to have the major responsibility for their children after divorce, it is easy to understand why divorced women are likely to be much worse off than their former husbands. Confronted with expectations that they will be "equally" responsible for the financial support of their children and themselves, they have typically been unequally disadvantaged by marriage and have fewer resources to meet those expectations. In addition, rules that require an equal division of marital property often force the sale of the family home and compound the financial dislocations by forcing children to change schools, neighborhoods, and friends just when they most need continuity and stability.

The result is often hardship, impoverishment, and disillusionment for divorced women and their children.

The unintended economic consequences of no-fault divorce provide the first major theme of this paper. The second major theme traces the effects of no-fault divorce on the institution of marriage.

THE TRANSFORMATION OF MARRIAGE

The divorce law revolution transformed more than the prior legal assumptions about divorce. It transformed the legal norms for marriage by articulating, codifying, and legitimating a new understanding of the marital partnership and marital commitment in our society. The new laws reflect, among other things, changing social realities, emerging social norms, and everyday legal practice. Ideally, that is as it should be: if law is to be effective, it must accord with social and practical reality. But the new divorce laws do not adequately or accurately reflect social reality, and they therefore exacerbate some of the grossest inequities in our society.

Traditional family law established a clear moral framework for both marriage and divorce: marriage was a partnership, a lifelong commitment to join together "forsaking all others," for better or for worse. Husbands and wives were assigned specific roles and responsibilities, and these obligations were reinforced by law. The moral obligations of marriage were, in theory, reinforced by alimony and property awards so that spouses who lived up to their marriage contract were rewarded, and those who had not were punished.

Of course, we now know that the reality of divorce settlements often diverged from this theoretical ideal. Alimony was the exception rather than the rule, and fathers often breached their responsibility for child support. But the old structure did give the spouse who wanted to remain married considerable bargaining power, and to that extent it reinforced marriage as against the alternative of divorce. The required grounds and the need to prove fault created barriers to divorce. In addition, because the old structure linked fault to the terms of the economic settlement, divorce was expensive for men of means. If she was "innocent," the wife of a man with money and property could expect to be awarded a lifetime alimony, the family home, and other property to meet her needs. In addition, her husband would remain responsible for her financial support. (So, too, could the guilty wife expect to be punished and be denied alimony and property.)

The new reforms altered each of the major provisions of the traditional law, and in the process, they redefined the norms of legal marriage. No-fault laws abolished the need for grounds and the need to prove fault in order to obtain a divorce. They abandoned the gender-based assumptions of the traditional law in favor of standards for treating men and women "equally" in alimony and property awards. They negated the traditional role that fault played in financial awards and instead decreed that awards should be based on the divorcing parties' current financial needs and resources. And finally, the new rules shifted the legal criteria for divorce—and thus for viable marriage—from fidelity to the marriage contract to individual standards of personal satisfaction. The rules are thereby redefining marriage as a time-limited, contingent arrangement rather than a lifelong commitment.

From State Protection of Marriage to Facilitation of Divorce

The divorce law reforms have moved the state from a position of protecting marriage (by restricting marital dissolution) to one of facilitating divorce.

They adopt a laissez-faire attitude toward both marriage and divorce, leaving both the terms of the marriage contract—and the option to terminate it—squarely in the hands of the individual parties. The pure no-fault states also eliminate any moral dimension from the divorce: guilt and innocence, fidelity and faithlessness, no longer affect the granting of the decree or its financial consequences.

The individual's freedom to end the marriage is further bolstered in some states by no-consent rules that give either party the right to obtain a divorce without the other's agreement. Since pure no-fault–no-consent rules allow one spouse to make a unilateral decision to terminate the marriage, they transfer the economic leverage from the spouse who wants to remain married to the spouse who wants to get divorced. It is an important difference. Under the prior law the party who wanted a divorce might well have to make economic concessions or "buy" a spouse's agreement. But under the no-consent rule it is the one who hopes to preserve the marriage who must do the bargaining. Apart from the economic implications, which are considerable, these laws strengthen the hand of the party who seeks the divorce, increasing the likelihood that divorce will in fact occur.

From a Lifetime Contract to an Optional, Time-Limited Commitment

The new divorce laws no longer view marriage as a lifelong partnership, but as a union that remains only so long as it proves satisfying to both partners. In addition, the traditional obligations of marriage, like the institution itself, are increasingly being redefined by the new divorce laws as optional, time-limited, contingent, open to individual definition, and, most important, terminable upon divorce.

In contrast to the traditional marriage contract whereby a husband undertook lifelong responsibility for his wife's support, the new divorce laws suggest that this and other family responsibilities can—and may—be terminated upon divorce, or soon after divorce, as evident in the new rules for alimony, property, child support, and custody. Short-term alimony awards, discussed above, are evident throughout the United States as courts define women as "dependents" for shorter and shorter periods of time. Current awards in California average two years.

Similar in its effect is the emphasis on a speedy resolution of the spouses' property claims. My research reveals many more forced sales of family homes than in the past, to hasten the day when each spouse can "take his (or her) money and leave." Arrangements that delay the sale of the home so that minor children do not have to move are viewed with disfavor by the courts because they "tie up the father's money." The judges we interviewed asserted that each spouse is entitled to his or her share of the property and should not have to wait for it. There is also a tendency to "cash out" other shared investments such as pensions and retirement benefits to provide a "clean break" between the parties at the time of the divorce.

Even parenting is becoming increasing optional and terminable upon divorce. Indeed, a de facto effect of the current laws is to deprive children of the care, companionship, and support of their fathers. This is evident in the courts' treatment of postdivorce visitation and child support. Furstenberg and colleagues found that 52 percent of the children of divorce in a nationally representative sample had not seen their fathers at all in the past year, and only 17 percent of the children had seen their fathers at least once a week. These data indicate that a majority of divorced fathers are abandoning their parental roles after divorce and are being allowed to do so without legal sanction.

In fact, one of the strongest supports for the assertion that fathers—who are 90 percent of the noncustodial parents—are legally allowed to abandon their children is the lack of a legal course of action to compel a parent to see his or her children. The implicit message is that joint parenting—and even parenting itself—is an "optional" responsibility for divorced fathers.

This message is also reflected by the law's tolerance for fathers who abandon their children financially and in the meager amounts of court-ordered child support. The courts award little child support to begin with, thereby allowing fathers to rid themselves of much of their financial responsibility for their children, and then fail to enforce child support awards once they are made.

The inadequacy of child support awards has been well documented. A 1978 U.S. Census survey found that divorced fathers paid an average of $1,951 per year per child. In 1981 they paid an average of $2,220, which represents a 16 percent decline in real dollars between 1978

and 1981. In California we found that the average child support award was typically less than the cost of day care alone—it did not approach half of the cost of actually raising children.

Past research has also more than amply documented the widespread noncompliance with child support awards. The 1981 Census survey, for example, showed that more than half (53 percent) of the millions of women who are due child support do not receive it.

While child support awards have always been inadequate and poorly enforced, what appears to be unique about the current situation is the willful disregard of court orders among middle-class and upper-middle-class fathers. For example, our California data reveal that fathers with incomes of $30,000 to $50,000 a year are just as likely to avoid child support payments as men with incomes of under $10,000 a year. The explanation for this lies in the legal system's lax enforcement, which has given fathers tacit approval (and financial incentives) for evading court orders.

Although 1984 federal legislation to strengthen the enforcement of child support may alter the present pattern, thus far family law judges and lawyers have been reluctant to bother with enforcement. When we collected our data the California law already contained many of the strict enforcement provisions of the 1984 federal law, but the judges we interviewed preferred not to use them.

Preston contends that the financial and social "disappearing act of fathers" after divorce is part of a larger trend: the conjugal family is gradually divesting itself of care for children in much the same way that it did earlier for the elderly. To date, indications of parental abandonment have focused on fathers. Thus far, most analysts have seen mothers as firmly committed to their children. But as the norms of the new divorce laws permeate popular awareness, this picture also may change.

The import of the new custody laws, especially those that change the maternal presumption to a joint custody preference, undermine women's incentives to invest in their children. As women increasingly recognize that they will be treated "equally" in child custody decisions, that caretaking and nurturance of children find no protection in the law and are punished by the job market, and that joint custody awards may push them into difficult, restrictive, and unrewarding postdivorce custodial arrangements, they may increasingly take to heart the new laws' implied warning that motherhood does not pay.

The optional and time-limited marital commitments embodied in the new divorce laws have a differential effect on men and women. While they free men from the responsibilities they retained under the old system, they "free" women from the security that system provided. Since women's investments in home, family, and children have typically meant lost opportunities in the paid labor force, they are more dependent on the long-term protection and security that the traditional law promised them. It is not surprising that our research finds women "suffering" more under the new laws, for these laws remove the financial safeguards of the old law—with a decline in alimony awards and a decrease in women's share of the community property—at the same time that they increase the financial burdens imposed on women after divorce.

For men, by contrast, the new legal assumption of time-limited commitments means a new freedom from family financial obligations. In fact, the new laws actually give men an incentive to divorce by offering them a release from the financial burdens of marriage. In fact, the wealthier a man is, and the longer he has been married, the more he has to gain financially from divorce.

From Protection for Housewives and Mothers to Gender-Neutral Rules

If the new legal assumptions were accompanied by provisions that enabled both spouses to choose the extent to which they would assume breadwinning and homemaking roles, and if they then gave each spouse "credit" for the roles they in fact assumed during marriage, then the law would accurately reflect the complexity and variety of marital roles in these years of "transition." But the present legal system seems to leave no room for such flexibility.

Rather, it suggests that a woman (or a man) who chooses homemaking and parenting risks a great penalty because she (or he) will pay heavily for that choice in the event of a divorce. Even if two parties agree to form an equal partnership in which they give priority to his career while she assumes the larger share of the housework and child care, and even if they agree that he will share his earnings and career assets with her, their agreement may have no legal standing. The woman will still be expected to be self-sufficient after divorce, and the man's promise of continued support and a share of his earnings—the promise that is implied in most marriages with a traditional division of labor—will be ignored in most courts.

The penalty can be equally severe for the woman who works during marriage, or who works part-time, but who nevertheless gives priority to her family over her work. Her claims to share her husband's income through spousal support fall on deaf ears in courts, which are concerned only with her "ability to engage in gainful employment."

Under the new legal assumptions the average divorced woman in California will be awarded no alimony, only minimal child support (which she probably will not be able to collect), exactly half of the joint tangible assets (an average of less than $10,000 worth of property), and an explicit directive to become immediately self-supporting. Even if she had married under the old law, and lived her life by the letter of the traditional marriage contract, and is 45 or 55 at the time of divorce, chances are that the courts will apply the new standards of self-sufficiency to her as well. Especially disadvantaged by these new assumptions are mothers of young children and older homemakers.

Thus one implication of the present allocation of family resources at divorce is that women had better not forgo any of their own education, training, and career development to devote themselves fully or even partially to domesticity. The law assures that they will not be much rewarded for their devotion, and they will suffer greatly if their marriage dissolves.

The concept of marital roles embodied in the new divorce laws carries an equally sobering message about motherhood. Divorcing mothers of preschool children have experienced a greater decline in alimony awards than any other group of women since the no-fault laws were instituted and the vast majority of these mothers—87 percent—are awarded no alimony at all. They are expected to find jobs immediately, to support themselves completely and, for the most part, to support their children as well.

In addition, since the age of majority children has dropped from age 21 to age 18, the divorced mother of teenage children confronts the fact that her former husband is not legally required to support their children once they reach age 18 even if they are still in their senior year of high school, much less through college. However, both high school and college students in these post–child-support years usually remain financially dependent on their parents. It is their mothers who are much more likely to respond to their needs and to support them, even though they are typically financially less able to do so.

Finally, the woman who has raised her children to maturity and who, as a result of the priority she has given to motherhood, finds herself with no marketable skills when she is divorced at 45 or 55, typically faces the harshest deprivations after divorce. The courts rarely reward her for the job she has done. Rather, the new assumptions imply that her motherhood

years were wasted and worthless, for she, too, is measured against the all-important new criterion of earning capacity.

Thus the new divorce laws are institutionalizing a set of norms that may be as inappropriate in one direction as the old norms were in another. The old law assumed that all married women were first and foremost housewives and mothers. The new law assumes that all married women are employable and equally capable of self-sufficiency after divorce. Both views are overly simplistic, impede women's options, and exert a rigidifying influence on future possibilities.

For most women in our society, marriage and career are no longer either/or choices. Most women do not expect to choose between work and marriage, or between a career and motherhood. The vast majority of American women want all three. But, as Shirley Johnson has observed, when "women who have both worked full time and carried the lioness's share of the household management and child rearing responsibilities, find out that their dual role is not recognized or rewarded in divorce settlements, the effect of the new divorce laws is to encourage women to . . . shift their energies into the labor market" (Johnson 1985). Johnson argues that the economic message in the new divorce laws is that it no longer pays for a woman to "invest in marriage-specific skills" since such investments have a relatively low payoff in a society with a high risk of marital dissolution.

From Partnership to Individualism

The new divorce laws alter the traditional legal view of marriage as a partnership by rewarding individual achievement rather than investment in the family partnership. Instead of the traditional vision of a common financial future within marriage, the no-fault and no-consent standards for divorce, and the new rules for alimony, property, custody, and child support, all convey a new vision of independence for husbands and wives in marriage. In addition, the new laws confer economic advantages on spouses who invest in themselves at the expense of the marital partnership.

This focus on the individual underlies many of the changes discussed above. It reflects not only a shift in the legal relationships between the family and its adult members but also a shift in the courts' attitudes and practices in meting out rewards at divorce.

The traditional law embodied the partnership concept of marriage by rewarding sharing and mutual investments in the marital community. Implicit in the new laws, in contrast, are incentives for investing in oneself, maintaining one's separate identity, and being self-sufficient. The new stress is on individual responsibility for one's future, rather than on joint or reciprocal responsibilities.

Once again, it is easy to see how these new assumptions reflect larger cultural themes: the rise of individualism, the emphasis on personal fulfillment, the belief in personal responsibility, and the importance we attach to individual "rights." These trends have at once been applauded for the freedom they offer and criticized as selfish, narcissistic, and amoral. Whether this change represents a decline or an advance depends on one's personal values: are we concerned with the security and stability that the old order provided or with the misery it caused for those who were forced to remain in unhappy marriages?

Our evaluation will also depend on how we see the past. The belief that the rise of individualism has fostered a decline in the family rests on the assumption that the family was stable and harmonious in the past. But historians have not yet identified an era in which families were stable and harmonious and all family members behaved unselfishly and devoted their efforts to the collective good. That "classical family of western nostalgia," to use William J. Goode's term for the stereotype, has been one

of the major casualties of recent research in family history.

But historical research does suggest a change in the psychological quality of family life and a rise in what Lawrence Stone calls "affective individualism"—a growing focus on individuals as unique personalities and a political emphasis on individual rights. The rise of affective individualism has brought emotional closeness between nuclear family members and a greater appreciation for the individuality of each person in the family. Historically, this trend strengthened the husband–wife unit at the expense of the larger family and the kinship network in which it was embedded. More recently, as rising divorce rates demonstrate, the strength of the husband–wife unit has declined and values of "pure" individualism are emerging. The new divorce laws reflect this evolution in that they encourage notions of personal primacy for both husband and wife. They imply that neither spouse should invest too much in marriage or place marriage above self-interest.

Both the new rules for spousal support and the new rules for property undermine the marital partnership. Despite the partnership principles that underlie the division of property, that is, the idea that property accumulated during marriage is to be shared equally at divorce—the current bases for dividing property belie such principles.

If the major breadwinner is allowed to retain most of the new property or career assets he (or she) has acquired during marriage—assets such as a professional education or good will, or health benefits, or enhanced earning capacity—the law's implicit message is that one's own career is the only safe investment. This encourages both spouses to invest in themselves before investing in each other, or their marriage, or their children.

This is one area in which the new legal assumptions are not congruent with the attitudes and assumptions of the divorced men and women we interviewed. Our interviewees rejected the limited definition of alimony as based on "need" and minimal self-sufficiency, and instead saw alimony as a means of sharing their partnership assets—the income and earning capacity in which they had both invested, and the standard of living they expected to share. These "sharing principles" for alimony were seen as an essential element in their implicit partnership "contract."

One implication of these changes is that marriage is likely to become increasingly less central to the lives of individual men and women. The privileged status of marriage in traditional family law, as well as the protections and restrictions placed on its inception and dissolution, reinforced its importance and encouraged husbands and wives to invest in it and to make it the center of their lives. The new laws, in contrast, discourage shared investments in marriage and thereby encourage both husbands and wives to dissociate from investments in the partnership. As more men and women follow the apparent mandate of the new laws, it seems reasonable to predict that marriage will lose further ground.

Indeed, William J. Goode persuasively argues that the trend is already well in progress. He observes that for both men and women marriage is simply less important today than it was in the past, and he foresees the further "decline of individual investments in family relationships over the coming decade" because investments in one's individual life and career pay off better in modern society (Goode 1984). As more women seek to follow men in the path of acquiring status, self-esteem, and a sense of individual accomplishment from their jobs, the importance of marriage will rest increasingly on its ability to provide individuals with psychic and emotional sustenance. This, Goode observes, is a difficult and fragile bond. In these trends he sees profound implications for the future of intimate relationships and the bearing and rearing of children in Western nations.

The Clouded Status of Children

A final feature of the new divorce laws is their ambiguous message about parental responsibility for children. In the past, the sustained well-being of the children of divorce was assumed to be the state's primary concern in any legal proceedings involving children. Indeed, it was this concern that dictated most of the traditional divorce law protections for women: women were recognized as the primary custodians of children, and in that capacity were to be accorded preferences and support to ensure the fulfillment of their responsibilities. Similarly, women who had devoted the productive years of their lives to child-rearing were to be rewarded for that appropriate and honorable effort.

Under the new laws, the state's concern for the welfare of children is far less in evidence. Rather, it appears that in the law's practical application, at least, the children have been all but forgotten in the courts' preoccupation with parental "equality."

The same rules that facilitate divorce facilitate the disruption of children's lives. The gender-neutral rules that encourage or force mothers to work also deprive children of the care and attention they might otherwise have. (Effectively, the fate of divorcing mothers is still the fate of the children of divorce because, sex-neutral custody standards notwithstanding, mothers still are the primary caretakers of children after divorce.) Also, the actual effects of the current laws deprive children of both the care and the support of their fathers.

In sum, under the present laws divorced fathers *may* participate more in the lives of their children if they choose to do so, but they need not so choose; and mothers *must* work outside the home whether they wish it or not, and thus *must* divide their energies between jobs and children. One might well ask what legal protections remain to insure parenting for children after divorce.

Even as the law over time evolves to reflect social reality, it also serves as a powerful force in creating social reality. Although the divorce law reformers knew that equality between the sexes was not yet a reality when they codified assumptions about equality in the law, they had seen trends in that direction and believed the new law would accelerate those trends. My research shows however, that the law actually slowed any trend toward economic equality that may have been developing. It worsened women's condition, improved men's condition, and widened the income gap between the sexes. The law has moved us toward a new reality, to be sure, but it is not, in the economic sphere at least, the hoped-for reality.

So long as the laws remain in force in their present form and their present application, postdivorce equality between the sexes will remain an illusion.

NOTE

1. Although thirty states have adopted some form of joint custody laws, mother custody awards are still the norm and mothers have the primary responsibility for their children after divorce in the vast majority of the cases. The legal trends and the empirical data on child custody are reviewed in Weitzman 1985, pp. 215–261.

REFERENCES

Goode, William J. "Individual Investments in Family Relationships Over the Coming Decades." *The Tocqueville Review* 6 (1984):51–84.

Johnson, Shirley Lans. "The Economic Position of Divorced Women." *Fair-share*, 1985.

Weitzman, Lenore J. *The Divorce Revolution: The Unexpected Social and Economic Consequences for Women and Children in America.* New York: Free Press, 1985.

Something Old, Something New: Women's Poverty in the 1990s

Diana M. Pearce

Mary came from a fairly typical middle-class family in which her father worked as a mid-level executive and her mother stayed at home for almost all of her growing-up years. She fin-

ished high school and went straight to college, leaving home and living in the dormitories. After graduation, she went to Washington, D.C., and worked for the federal government for several years before getting married to an older man, a Ph.D. agricultural researcher. She left paid employment with the birth of her first child and did not return until after her third child was born, and then only part time (in a job deliberately structured for wives reentering the workforce, but which was dead end). Taking a job was necessitated by her husband's increasingly unstable employment. His intermittent employment coupled with his refusal to share child care or other housework led to escalating tensions and resulted, within a few years, in their separation and divorce. Although she was able to keep the house because it had been bought with her own money (from a settlement from a bad accident in which she had sustained permanent injuries), she sometimes had to borrow money from friends and relatives to buy heating oil or even groceries. Her efforts to obtain child support from her ex-husband were met with threats of violence, as well as threats to sue her for support (since she was working and he was not). Her children began to get into trouble in school and the family social worker urged her to quit work and go on welfare. Instead, she left her part-time job and, using her premarriage experience, moved into a regular career-track government job; she eventually sought and obtained a transfer out of the area, in part to escape the continued threats from her ex-husband.

This story describes how many women come to experience poverty. It also happens to be, with a few minor details changed, my sister's story. It could, of course, be your story—or your sister's, daughter's, mother's, or friend's. It is typical, but not universal: It does not describe the experience of elderly women (although she may yet experience elderly poverty); the stigmatizing experience of going on welfare, even if briefly; or the experience of being a poor woman in a community in which many families experience lifelong poverty.

It is not typical in several ways. First, Mary had three children; two-thirds of poor women maintaining families alone have only one or two children.[1] Three or more is fairly unusual, despite newspaper features suggesting otherwise (a misleading source of information on the poor that I call *Sunday Supplement Sociology*). Second, she owned a house, and it was in her

name. Three out of four women householders rent and pay an average of almost 60 percent of their income for housing.[2] Third, she had a college education. Only about half of women in poverty have finished high school, and less than one-sixth have had any college at all.[3]

However, in five very important ways, she was typical. First, she got married. Most women, in fact about 95 percent of women, get married at some time before they are 65.[4] Second, she had children—again, over 90 percent of women who marry have children.[5] Getting divorced is not as common, but since about 50 percent of marriages end in divorce, she is hardly atypical, either. Fourth, she was in her early thirties when she experienced poverty, which puts her in the largest group of poor mothers maintaining families alone. Over 40 percent of such mothers are 25 to 34 years old, and only 20 percent are less than 25 years old.[6] Finally, although most women who become single parents probably experience poverty-level incomes at some point, as with Mary, most do *not* go on welfare. According to one study, only one-fifth of women who become single parents go on welfare within two years of becoming a single parents;[7] even among unmarried teen mothers, who experience poverty rates of 80 percent and higher, only 30 percent go on welfare within three years of the birth of their child.[8]

What is striking about Mary's story and those of so many others like her is that she did what most women do and, moreover, she did it in the right order. She finished her schooling before entering the work force and she got married before having children—but she still ended up experiencing poverty. Even the ways in which she was atypical balanced each other out; that is, while she had three children, she also had a college education and several years of premarriage and prechildren work experience.

It would, of course, be much easier to understand if the typical Mary story involved dropping out of high school, early and multiple childbearing, lack of marriage, long-term welfare dependency, and little or no labor-force participation. It would further simplify understanding if she were a member of a disadvantaged racial or ethnic group, such as African American, Hispanic, or Native American. Because all of these characteristics are, in fact, highly correlated with poverty, it would be easy to assume that the high and persistent levels of poverty experienced by women are the result of their having made different choices from nonpoor women, perhaps influenced by a culture or underclass milieu in which they reside, and leave it at that. Such a description is not typical of poor women and thus we are left with a much more difficult task in understanding women's poverty. We have to ask why my sister was poor. We cannot ascribe her poverty, or indeed most of women's poverty, to different values, behaviors, and choices; for most poor women, like Mary, have made many of the same choices that nonpoor women make. Instead, we must look beyond individual characteristics and locate the complexities of women's poverty within the context of what is happening in the American economy and specifically within its job structure; within the structural inequalities experienced by women; and, for women of color, within the historical and contemporaneous experience of persistent poverty and racially or ethnically based inequality.

DEMOGRAPHIC CHANGES AND WOMEN'S POVERTY

Determining the cause(s) of women's poverty is halfway to determining the cure(s); equally important, however, is determining which factors can be influenced by public policy and which cannot. This distinction was the key to the effectiveness of reforms that were instigated under the Social Security Act of 1935,[9] our first major antipoverty legislation. Undergirding many of the programs was the then-radical recognition of some new facts of life, brought home by the Depression: Some unemployment

is not due to individual actions or bad character and, in fact, is inevitable. For the elderly, there was an equally important recognition of the right to support after and as a reward for years of working, and a much less clearly articulated recognition of the need for the elderly not to be dependent on their adult children.

Both recognitions were the result of a somewhat belated understanding of the consequences of a shift to an urban industrialized and capitalist society. That is, it was finally accepted that industrial capitalism produced unemployment, especially during economic downturns; it also failed to provide for those too old, disabled, or sick to work. To deny these facts simply meant a lot of hardship and poverty for the unemployed, elderly, and disabled.

Today, the fact of life gradually being recognized and accepted is that single-parent families are a common family form. About one out of five families with children is maintained by a woman alone.[10] The combination of a 50 percent divorce rate and the fact that one out of four children is born out of wedlock means that living in a single-parent family has become extremely common. One demographer estimates that 50 percent of white children and 90 percent of black children will experience living in a single-parent family at some time during their growing-up years.[11]

Assuming that the large numbers of families maintained by a single mother is a new phenomenon, there has been enormous effort expended to find the causes for this change, usually labeled pejoratively as the breakdown in the family, the demise of the intact family, the explosion of broken families, and so on. In spite of numerous efforts, however, researchers have been unable to attribute this widespread phenomenon to such public policies as levels of welfare benefits or ease of getting welfare, or type of divorce law.

On the other hand, women's employment outside the home, women's education, the less stigmatizing label attached to single parenthood, male unemployment, and decreased tolerance of domestic violence and male dominance are all factors that have contributed to the increase in single-parent households. There are undoubtedly other factors as well, but, as in the 1930s, we are faced with a model that involves everything and everybody; that is, all of the forces and characteristics of modern life in an advanced industrialized and urbanized society are the same ones that make it possible for couples to divorce and for mothers and children to survive economically as single-parent families, though often in or near poverty.

There are some who would turn the clock back in terms of law, sex roles, and women's employment—in essence, returning to the nineteenth century when women (except lower-class and immigrant women) had few opportunities for employment outside the home and there was virtually no welfare to support single-parent families. Even then, women became single mothers either because they were widowed or, less commonly, because they left men who were abusive, alcoholic, or not supporting the family; but, because they could not work to support their families and because there was no child care and virtually no public welfare, they often lost their children and thus did not become independent single-parent families. (Even if they did work outside the home, they still often lost their children because they were neglecting them (some even "boarded" their children at orphanages and worked as domestics).

To recognize that single-parent families in modern society are inevitable should not be taken as an implicit endorsement of this family form without reservations. Other things being equal, both economically and emotionally two adults are probably better than one for raising children. However, few would disagree that "other things" are often anything but "equal"; certainly violence, physical and sexual abuse, and constant tension, arguments, and rancor are better lived without if the choice is between

such things and single parenthood—even if the latter means poverty.

To be agnostic on the question of single parenthood is not to be neutral on the question of impoverishment of single-parent families. That is, while we can do very little to decrease the numbers of single-parent families (and most of that is at the individual level, not at the public-policy level), we can do a lot about how poor they are. We know that single parenthood and poverty are not inevitably linked. Two types of comparisons, one with other (poor) groups in the United States historically and the other with single parents in other countries today, make this clear.

Take, for example, two groups that once experienced disproportionately high levels of poverty in the United States: the unemployed and the elderly. Once we decided to do something about unemployment, we created a system, unemployment insurance, that has largely worked (particularly pre-1980) to keep many unemployed workers out of poverty, at least until their benefits are exhausted. Likewise, we created a series of programs—social security, Medicare, and elderly housing—that have dramatically reduced poverty among the elderly (although least effectively for elderly widows).

It is possible, of course, that the poverty of single-parent families is more intractable than that of other groups. Yet, compared to European countries, one of the most striking facts about American society today is how much poorer single-parent families are in the United States and how much we are concentrating poverty among women-maintained families. In European countries, mainly through income-support programs—both means-tested (like our welfare system, but less stigmatized) and universal (such as child allowances that go to *all* children)—the poverty rates of children in single-parent families are reduced to rates that range from 2 percent to 16 percent, compared to 54 percent in the United States.[12] Contrary to the alarms raised by some conservatives, these policies have not increased the prevalence of single parents; indeed, none of these societies has nearly as high a rate of single parenthood as has the United States.

Before we turn to solutions, it is necessary to untangle some of the complexities of women's poverty. Basically, women's poverty revolves around two factors that are distinct for women: their disadvantaged position in the labor force and the burden—economic as well as emotional—of children. Each of these, in turn, is embedded in two larger phenomena: economic trends and women's inequality generally. Let us now consider each of these factors.

THE DISTINCTIVE CHARACTER OF WOMEN'S POVERTY: WOMEN'S LABOR MARKET DISADVANTAGE

While employment is often touted as an all-encompassing key that will unlock women's poverty, the dismal labor-market picture for women suggests that jobs are as much a part of the problem as they are the solution. Three key aspects of this situation deserve attention: occupational sex segregation, women's lower wages, and the disproportionate numbers of women in part-time, temporary, and dead-end jobs.

Occupational Sex Segregation

Although the concentration of women in a few occupations has decreased slowly in recent years, it is still very high and much higher than that of men. About 30 percent (compared to 40 percent a decade ago) of women are in the ten most common occupations for women: bookkeeper/accounting clerk, waitress, nurse, nursing aide/orderly, child-care worker, cashier, elementary school teacher, secretary, retail salesworker, and health technologist (e.g., dental hygienist). All but two of these are nonprofessional and all are poorly paid relative to comparable male-dominated professions requiring similar levels of education, skill, and responsibility.

At the other end of the scale, there is even less positive news regarding women in nontraditional occupations, that is, occupations in which fewer than 25 percent of the workers are women. While women have made substantial inroads in a few professions, such as law and medicine, there has been little change in others, such as engineering and some hard sciences, and losses in some of the craft occupations, such as carpentry, in which the percentage of women has dropped over the 1980s from 1.7 to 1.3. (Even newer occupations, such as airplane mechanic, have gone from 3.8 percent to 2.8 percent female through the 1980s.) Altogether, the proportion of women who are in nontraditional occupations has remained virtually unchanged over the last decade at about 9 percent of women workers.

Lower Wages

Two-thirds of minimum-wage workers are women. Overall, women who are employed full-time, year-round earn 71 cents for each dollar earned by men; the figure for black women workers (compared to all men) is 62 cents, and for Hispanic women workers, is 57 cents.[13] While this is an overall improvement from the 59 cents women earned a decade ago, it is much less of an improvement than it first appears when compared to the wage ratio in 1955, which was 64 cents. The variations reflect not only what is happening to women's wages but what is happening to men's wages as well; in fact, most of the improvement in the wage ratios between men and women workers over the last decade is the result of declining men's wages—due largely to sectoral shifts—rather than to increased wages for women.[14]

Part-Time, Temporary, or Dead-End Jobs

To talk about the wage gap is only half the story for women, literally, for only about half of women work full-time *and* year-round; women workers account for almost two-thirds of part-time workers. Whether by choice or not—and the economic consequences are the same—women who hold jobs that are part time and part year find not only that their earnings are lower, but also that their hourly wages are less and they are likely to have no fringe benefits, including paid holidays, sick leave, and health insurance. Overall, their working conditions are worse and their job security virtually nonexistent. Often by design, their hours and wages are inadequate and their job tenure too short to qualify for unemployment insurance when their job ends, which it frequently does in a relatively short amount of time.

These three characteristics—occupational segregation; lower wages; and part-time, temporary, or dead-end jobs—are the structural inequalities experienced by women in the labor market. It is against these and interacting with them that general economic trends are acting. Since most of these have been discussed elsewhere, they will be only briefly sketched here. Some of the most striking trends through the 1980s include the following:

- There has been a sectoral shift from primary manufacturing and heavy industry to a service-sector economy, including information processing as well as more traditional services.
- There has been an increase in low-wage employment, that is, wages paying less than what would be necessary for someone working full-time to support a family of three above the poverty line. This trend has been termed the *Great U-Turn.*
- Unemployment compensation, created as part of the Depression-era New Deal to prevent unemployed workers from falling into poverty, has been drastically cut: At the height of the current recession (1991–1992), only about 40 percent of unemployed workers are receiving unemployment compensation benefits, compared to about 60 percent at the height of the 1975 recession. During much of the mid- to late-1980s, only about one-third of unemployed workers received benefits.
- There has been an increase in income inequality. For decades, one could summarize American

economic inequality with the *5 and 20 rule*: The bottom 20 percent received about 5 percent of aggregate income, while the top 5 percent received about 20 percent; actually, in 1947, the bottom 20 percent of families had 5.0 percent of the income, but the top 5 percent had only 17.2 percent of the income. In 1970, the bottom fifth had increased their share to 5.5 percent of aggregate income, while the share of the top 5 percent had gone down to 14.4 percent, reflecting a gradual reduction in income inequality during the post-war years. That trend reversed itself dramatically in the 1980s and, by the end of the decade, the bottom 20 percent was receiving just 4.6 percent of the income, a loss of almost one-sixth of its share, while the top 5 percent increased its share by about one-fourth, to 17.9 percent of aggregate income.

- Women workers have steadily increased their participation in the labor force, from 34.5 percent of women in paid employment in 1960 to 61.5 percent in 1990. It is expected that by the year 2000, half of all workers will be female.

Putting together these trends with the structural inequality experienced by women workers, created by occupational segregation and wage discrimination, one gets a clear picture of women's labor-market disadvantage. As new workers, women entering or reentering the work force in recent years have disproportionately taken the new jobs: 60 percent of the jobs taken by the increased number of women entering the labor force during the 1975–1985 decade were low-wage jobs (i.e., paying at or below the poverty wage for a three-person family and assuming full-time, year-round work; that is roughly about $6.00 per hour in today's terms).

Besides being low wage, many of these jobs are seasonal or temporary and do not last long enough (or pay enough) to make the worker eligible for unemployment insurance when the job ends. The average low-wage job, as defined earlier, lasts 1.75 years. Of the women who maintained households alone, worked part of the year, and experienced unemployment part of the year, almost three times as many received welfare as received unemployment compensation during their period of unemployment (30 percent vs. 11 percent). The receipt of unemployment insurance has dropped dramatically for this group of women over the last decade, from 14 percent to 11 percent, almost a one-third drop.

Given the low wages and part-time and part-year nature of employment for women workers, especially women householders, it is not surprising that poverty rates are not much reduced by going into paid employment. The families of one out of three women who are maintaining households alone are poor; if she is employed, the poverty rate drops to about 22 percent; among black women, employment drops the poverty rate from 48 percent to 32 percent, and among Hispanic women householders, the drop is from 48 percent to 28 percent. Only if she manages to hold a job full-time and for the whole year is her poverty rate reduced substantially, to 7 percent (11 percent for black women householders, and 14 percent for Hispanic women householders). By contrast, the poverty rate for married-couple households in which the husband works is only 4.2 percent (and 2.3 percent if he worked full-time, year-round).[15] Even when the householder is not employed, *the poverty rate for married-couple households in which the husband did not work at all is less than the poverty rate for black and Hispanic women-maintained households in which the householder worked full-time year-round.*[16]

THE DISTINCTIVE CHARACTER OF WOMEN'S POVERTY: CHILDREN

Having the economic responsibility for children greatly increases the likelihood of poverty, particularly for women. Of women-maintained families with children (less than 18 years old), 44.5 percent are poor; 56.1 percent of black and 58.2 percent of Hispanic women-maintained families with children are poor. If it is a family without children (e.g., two adult sisters living together), the poverty rate is less than 10 percent.[17] Again, the contrast with married-couple households with children is striking: only 7.8 percent are poor (14.3 percent of black and 20.8 percent of Hispanic married-couple families with children are poor). Moreover, the disparity between women-maintained families with children and all other families has increased; in 1970, the poverty rate for women-maintained families with children was 3.4 times the rate of all other families; today it is more than 5 times as great.

For at least one reason, poverty associated with the economic burden of children should be decreasing. In general, women are having fewer children, and average family size has steadily decreased over the last few decades, from 2.33 children in 1970 to 1.85 children per family in 1990. Likewise, poor women's families have also decreased in size: The average number of children in a woman-maintained family in 1970 was 2.90; in 1992, it is 2.15. Moreover, the proportion of families with four or more children is quite small: Only 15 percent of poor families have four or more children. Indeed, poor married-couple families tend to have more children than poor women-maintained families, averaging 2.47 children per family.

Given that the number of children is clearly not the issue, we must turn to the cost of children. There are two sides to this issue: how much the cost of children is borne by the single mother versus by others (the absent father, the state, etc.) and the actual costs of raising a child—for such things as food, shelter, and health care.

Other sources of funds to cover the cost of children are minimal and have not even kept up with inflation. Child support is only paid to 37 percent of children with absent fathers and, when they do pay, the average annual payment per family, not per child, was only $2,995 in 1989.[18] This was an increase over the average annual payment in 1981 of $2,106, but, when we adjust for inflation, it was actually only a slight increase of 4 percent. Women in poverty, of course, receive even less child support. Only about one-fourth receive child support, averaging $1,889 per family in 1989; although this amounts to over one-third of the income of families receiving child support, it does not lift very many out of poverty. Of 3.2 million single-parent families with an absent father, only 140,000 would be lifted out of poverty if all of child support due was paid.[19]

Women who turn to public assistance find that that too has declined, in real terms, over the 1980s. In the average state, the total of welfare benefits plus the cash value of food stamps only reaches to three-fourths of the poverty level. Over the last decade, the value of those benefits has declined by about 20 percent, and, over the last three decades, the decline has been such that in real terms, welfare benefits are less, in the average state, than they were in 1960.

There are two possible reasons why poverty rates are so high, in spite of the decreasing numbers of children: (1) the children are younger, and (2) housing costs have risen. Younger children have always meant higher poverty rates; thus, the poverty rate for single mothers with children under six years of age was 59.4 percent in 1990, substantially the same as in 1970 (the earliest date for which we have such figures).[20] In addition, because of the high cost of child care, averaging $3,000 per year for the average preschool child, many women cannot earn enough to pay for child care as well as the rent and other essentials. In essence, she must earn an extra $1.50 per hour, more if she is not working full-time, just to pay for the child care. Therefore, many single mothers of very young children are not employed or work only part-time. On the other hand, because no allowance is made for child care, many employed single mothers are not considered poor, even though, once they have paid child care, they have less than a poverty-level income.

Housing costs have increased dramatically in the last decade in absolute terms, much faster than wages or other income sources available to women and their families. This has had three repercussions: First, because single mothers' income has increased very little, the proportion of income that goes to housing has risen from an average of 38 percent to 58 percent.[21] Second, doubling up has increased, particularly among poor women-maintained families, with about one out of four women-maintained families sharing their housing with another family; over half of these families are poor (unpublished 1990 Census Bureau data analyzed by the author).

Finally, some women-maintained families simply cannot pay the rent, or even half of it, and become homeless. One-third to 40 percent of the homeless are homeless families with children, most of which are single-mother families, and it is likely that there are many more not counted (living in abandoned cars, tents, garages, battered women's shelters, etc.). Thus, about one million persons (depending upon your estimate of total numbers of homeless) in women-maintained families experience homelessness each year. Because poverty counts are based on household surveys and do not include those living in shelters, in institutions, or on the streets, many of these women and their children are not counted among the poor.

SUMMARY AND CONCLUSIONS

Of course, the two sets of factors that make women's poverty distinctive—the economic burden of children and women's disadvantaged labor-market status—are only analytically separable. When a woman's wages are inadequate, she cannot pay rent on housing that is large enough for her and her child(ren). When child and other income support is lacking, women are forced into jobs, but the cost and availability of child care often limit her occupational choices and work hours. Moreover, our public policies reinforce the very inequalities that lead to poverty and this is especially true for single parents. There are almost no programs or policies that provide after-school care, for example. This makes it difficult for women to take full-time, better-paying jobs. Welfare programs, in addition to stigmatizing the recipients, offer little access to training or education beyond basic literacy; furthermore, they hurry women into employment, no matter how low the wages or how poor the future prospects, thus continuing the cycle of poverty.

Most painful of all, single mothers are asked to make difficult and unfair choices: work to support the family (be a good worker), but at a job without benefits, thus forgoing health care even when one needs it; or, stay at home to take care of the children, some of whom may be sick, disabled, or traumatized by abuse (be a good parent), and risk societal condemnation for being lazy. Pay the rent (but leave the kids on their own), pay the child care (and hope to postpone eviction), or eat at soup kitchens (and hope the kids do not get too hungry during the day, especially on nonschool days). Often something has to give.

Two areas of public policy will be critical in the 1990s and essentially will determine whether the feminization of poverty is reversed or continues to grow. The first area has to do with paid employment. Many jobs, particularly entry-level jobs in expanding sectors, such as service and information processing, have disappeared during the 1980s. Public policy may simply let that continue and worsen or it can begin to limit employers' ability to structure jobs that not only exploit workers but also make it extremely difficult for them to be both good workers and good parents.

There are four ways that public policy can restructure employment to help alleviate women's poverty. The first, and simplest, is to raise and index the minimum wage. For almost two decades, a full-time, year-round job at the minimum wage would provide enough support for a family of three at the poverty level; now, minimum-wage work will barely support a two-person family at the poverty level.

The second area of public-policy concern should be the limited occupational choices facing women. While there have been many programs developed to facilitate women's entry into nontraditional occupations, few have achieved meaningful numbers and many have simply disappeared. Particularly for noncollege-bound women, there has been little change and, without greater desegregation of occupations, achieving increased earnings and pay equity in more traditional occupations will continue to be difficult.

Third, public policy must reverse the trend toward part-time, part-year, or temporary jobs, which has become the employment ghetto of the 1990s for women workers. This means that benefits received by full-time employees should be extended to part-time employees, such as health insurance, sick leave, and so on. It also means that employers should be restricted from creating jobs with deliberately high turnover, the costs of which are borne almost entirely by workers. Such practices have seriously eroded unemployment insurance, which was originally intended to protect workers against unemployment that was not their fault, but that of business downturns, obsolescence, or capricious employers. Roughly two-thirds of today's workers, when they lose their jobs, do not have this cushion against unemployment.

Finally, it is time for employers to create family-friendly and woman-accepting work environments. Policies that provide child-care support, family and medical leave, unemployment insurance for women who become unemployed as a result of sexual harassment, and simply the flexibility to allow workers to deal with day-to-day crises of being parents (e.g., not being fired for talking to one's child on the telephone) are critical.

The second area of critical concern for women in the 1990s is housing. As women maintaining households alone are forced to spend increasing proportions of income securing housing, their ability to respond to other needs, especially emergency medical care, becomes quite tenuous. For example, what starts as an earache in a young child can easily snowball: If paying for emergency health care precludes making the rent, homelessness can result or, alternatively, if the cost of rent precludes health care, and the ear infection leads to deafness, long-term problems of disability will occur. Thus, when there is little or no margin—that is, too little is left after paying the rent—almost anything can become problematic. As mentioned earlier, increasing numbers of families are reacting to increased housing costs by doubling up, leading to another set of problems and issues: overcrowding, abuse and violence, as well as increased homelessness (due to the unstable nature of doubling-up arrangements).

As with all issues, the structural and interrelated nature of women's poverty affects housing as well; the affordability of housing for women can be increased by either increasing housing subsidies or by raising incomes, mainly through earnings, of women-maintained families. Because of the presence of children, many women with housing problems are reluctant to come forward (for fear they will lose their children to foster care because the housing they have is inadequate, overcrowded, unheated, or nonexistent). Unfortunately, there has been little policy attention directed toward developing alternative models of housing ownership (such as cooperatives or limited equity cooperatives) to control housing costs. Likewise, community-enhanced models of housing, which integrate child care and job training (particularly in nontraditional occupations), would begin to address not only women's poverty but also women's structural inequalities.

Note that some issues are missing from this list, long as it is. For example, nothing has been said about child support, welfare-benefit levels, or such universal programs as child allowances to tax credits (such as the Earned Income Tax Credit [EITC], which reduces taxes for employed low-income families with children). There are three reasons for these omissions. First, they are all now, and are likely to continue to be, insignificant and limited as a means of moving poor women out of poverty. As a society, we are simply not willing to give enough or, in the case of child support, compel absent fathers to give enough, to move more than a very small number of poor women across the poverty line, and then not by much. Even discussions of a refundable child tax credit or expanded tax exemptions would not amount to a substantial hedge against poverty, and some even exclude poor families who receive welfare.

Second, most poverty policy discussions, to the extent that they acknowledge gender at all, end up prescribing income-support programs for women-maintained families (although usually substantially increased, but see the earlier discussion for the political realism of that), and jobs or employment programs for men and their families. Thus, this omission is intended to *gender integrate* the discussion of employment solutions to poverty, so that, in fact, women may benefit from them. Of course, employment solutions (including the training and education programs that lead to jobs) are not only more likely to lead out of poverty but also are more likely to lead to permanent exits from poverty. Income-support programs and tax provisions, on the other hand, are not only historically much less in amount, they are subject to frequent rounds of cutbacks, as we have recently seen. For example, in 1991, 40 states froze or cut back welfare or other income-support programs for the poor (such as general assistance and housing subsidies).

Finally, these programs were omitted from the discussion in this chapter because they are based on a faulty premise; that is, that income supports for these families go to women who are doing nothing. If income-support programs, including tax credits, child support, and welfare, were instead viewed as providing the basics needed and deserved for children and their parents to live decent, healthy lives, then they would be worth supporting. In the latter case, there would be two effects: First, the income supports would be adequate in amount; for example, in the range of what we give foster parents to raise children. Second, they would not be taxed away; that is, mothers could enter employment and not lose by doing so (as of 1992, a dollar of welfare benefits is deducted for each dollar of earnings).

Putting together both the necessary items on the agenda, employment and housing, and the omitted ones, it is clear that addressing women's poverty is about addressing the structural inequalities faced by women, the changing employment and housing picture that developed in the 1980s (and is continuing in the 1990s), and, for women of color, the racism that perpetuates poverty for all people of color.

Many of the issues discussed here are quantitatively worse for black and Hispanic women; where data were available, these differences, or the lack of them, have been noted. This should not be taken to mean that poverty, labor-market disadvantage, or the economic aspects of children (child care, housing, etc.) are simply additive for women of color. Clearly, the historic high rates and the more recent growth of unemployment experienced particularly by black men (and women of color as well) due to racism and racial discrimination give the high rates of poverty and its persistence a different character than that experienced by many white women. At the same time, though difficult and maybe impossible to untangle, gender, as well as race, clearly contributes to the poverty experienced by women of color, and neither issue should be neglected in addressing poverty experienced by these women.

Neither the feminization of poverty nor women's poverty is inevitable. A first step is to reorder our thinking. Just as we switched a half-century ago from talking about *the unemployed* to talking about *unemployment*, and thereby restructured our policies, today we must turn from talking about *the poor* to talking about *poverty*. The second, and crucial step, is to recognize that poverty is gendered, as well as racialized, with different causes and cures when it is experienced by women compared to men and by different racial and ethnic groups. Our task is not about finding out how poor women are different or how *they* need to be changed, but to recognize the universal and embedded nature of women's poverty in the gender, racial, and class inequalities that characterize American society today.

NOTES

1. U.S. Bureau of the Census, "Current Population Reports" (Series P-60, No. 168), *Money Income and Poverty Status in the United States: 1989* (Washington, D.C.: U.S. Government Printing Office, 1990).

2. Low Income Housing Information Service, 1989.

3. U.S. Bureau of the Census, 1990.

4. S. M. Bianchi and D. Spain, *American Women in Transition* (New York: Russell Sage Foundation, 1986), 12.

5. Ibid., 66.

6. U.S. Bureau of the Census, "Current Population Reports" (Series P-60, No. 175), *Poverty in the United States: 1990* (Washington, D.C.: U.S. Government Printing Office, 1991).

7. N. Mudrick, "The Use of AFDC by Previously High-and-Low-Income Households," *Social Service Review* 52 (1978): 111.

8. Committee on Ways and Means, U.S. House of Representatives, *Overview of Entitlement Programs, 1991 Green Book: Background Material and Data on*

Programs within the Jurisdiction of the Committee on Ways and Means (Washington, D.C.: U.S. Government Printing Office, 1990).

9. "The Social Security Act: The First Twenty Years," *Social Security Bulletin* (August 1955): 1–10.

10. U.S. Bureau of the Census, *Poverty*, 1991.

11. L. Bumpass, "Children and Marital Disruption: A Replication and Update," *Demography* 21 (February 1984): 71–82.

12. T. M. Smeeding, "Cross National Perspectives on Income Security Programs," for "The War on Poverty: What Worked?" Testimony for the Congress of the United States, Joint Economic Committee, September 25, 1991:4 and Table 3.

13. U.S. Bureau of the Census, "Current Population Reports" (Series P-60, No. 174), *Money Income of*

Households, Families and Persons in the United States: 1991 (Washington, D.C.: U.S. Government Printing Office, 1991).

14. U.S. Bureau of the Census, *Money Income*, 1991; National Committee on Pay Equity, 1989.

15. U.S. Bureau of the Census, *Money Income*, 1991.

16. Ibid.

17. Ibid.

18. U.S. Department of Commerce, Bureau of the Census, *Child Support and Alimony: 1989* (Series P-60, No. 173) (Washington, D.C.: U.S. Government Printing Office, 1991).

19. Ibid.

20. U.S. Bureau of the Census, *Poverty*, 1991.

21. Low Income Housing Information Service, 1989.

Cultural Invisibility

There are many ways in which one might seek to understand a society. One might interview its members, or analyze the layout and structure of its cities, or study its political organization and kinship systems, or even examine the contents of its garbage (as some anthropologists like to do). Most people, however, would sooner study the society's literature, art, or science; its religions and philosophies; or its history—all of which express the society's "culture": its highest achievements, its spiritual dimensions, its development over time, the best it has to offer.

Unfortunately, in the case of our society, its "best" either fails to include women and the feminine, or includes them in quite negative ways. Consider, for example, our science—particularly physics, the paradigm of the natural sciences. In "Patriarchy, Scientists, and Nuclear Warriors," Brian Easlea points out that physics is dominated by men—a result not of chance, but of strenuous attempts since its beginning to keep women out of it. But Easlea suggests that physics is "masculine" in other ways as well. Indeed, its aim is to "master" nature, a nature conceptualized as female ("mother nature") and, incidentally, as having no moral claim on us. Physics' rational and objective method, moreover, is said to depend on hard experimental facts and mathematical rigor, uncontaminated by "feminine" emotionality, intuitiveness, or subjectivity. In addition, its practitioners, particularly the most successful ones, behave in culturally masculine ways, displaying what one anthropologist of physics (Sharon Traweek) has characterized as "aggressive individualism, haughty self-confidence, and a sharp competi-

tive edge." Finally, physics' research projects frequently are tied to the military, one of the bailiwicks of masculinity.

Our science, typified by physics, is, in short, thoroughly *masculine*; women and the feminine are absent from it. Surprisingly enough, however, our art—the presumed home of feeling, emotion, subjectivity, and everything feminine, the supposed antithesis of our science—is as tied to *masculinity* as our science is. At least this is what Carol Duncan argues in "The MoMA'S Hot Mamas." Duncan suggests that most of the academic world, as well as the public at large, accepts the story of modern art that is told by MoMA's (New York City's Museum of Modern Art's) permanent exhibit. According to this story, the history of modern art consists in the progressive renunciation of representation as the goal of art and the simultaneous search for greater artistic freedom and autonomy. We are told that, through time, a series of ever more abstract artistic styles unfolded—from Cubism, to German Expressionism, to Futurism, and so on, through Dada-Surrealism, and finally to American Abstract Expressionism—each of which eschews the concrete material objects, needs, and goals of everyday life and seeks, instead, "the realm of absolute spirit, manifested as absolute formal and nonrepresentational purity" (p. 269). At the same time that MoMA tells the story of modern art's abandonment of materiality in its quest toward spirituality, however, MoMA tells another story—a very material story—which has everything to do with bodies and very little to do with spirit. Modern art, observes Duncan, is "positively crowded with images of women, most often simply unidentified female bodies or parts of bodies, but also frequently sexualized female bodies—"tarts, prostitutes, artist's models, or low-life entertainers" (p. 271). Many of these images portray "distorted or dangerous-looking creatures, potentially overpowering, devouring, or castrating" or "decadent, corrupt—and therefore *morally* monstrous—women" (pp. 271–272). These images, addressed to men, testify to men's pervasive fear of and ambivalence toward women. They serve, says Duncan, to masculinize the museum as a male social environment where men gather to gaze at women. For that matter, even those works of modern art that do not contain images of women serve to masculinize the museum to the extent that "they mark the larger project of modern art as primarily a male endeavor" (p. 271). Including an adequate number of women artists in the story of modern art would certainly help demasculinize the museum's social environment, but as Duncan implies, it is doubtful that MoMA has any immediate plans to change the contents of its permanent collection.

Thus, modern art, as well as science, as they are presently constituted, are masculine aspects of our culture. Though one might expect organized religion to tell a different story—issues surrounding the divine should, after all, transcend issues of gender—Virginia Sapiro assures us in "Women and Religion" that it does not. Indeed, within organized religion the divine itself is spoken of as male—for example, as Father, King, Lord, and God-He, not as Mother, Queen, Lady, and God-She. And this shapes our conceptions not only of the divine, but also of men and women, fathers and mothers, authority, holiness, and other aspects of religious life. Moreover, in most religious denominations, the religious authorities are male, and it is women's role to accept these male authorities, serving as their good and faithful assistants and helpmates. As it turns out, women have proved to be excellent handmaidens. They

manage their homes in accordance with religious law and custom; they do the unpaid work ministers' wives do; they spend hours doing their churches' volunteer, charity, or philanthropic work; and they cheerfully clean their churches, teach the children's Sunday School classes, and cook for the church picnics. Women's impact in these various activities should not be underestimated since "the social issues and concerns of churches are often manifest largely in the work of women" (p. 294). Yet the fact remains that women are required to remain in the church's background, taking center stage but rarely, and then only with the "permission" of male authorities.

Sue Rosser makes it clear in "Re-visioning Clinical Research: Gender and the Ethics of Experimental Design" that it is not only science, art, and religion which marginalize women. So too does medicine. Since it is predominantly white, middle/upper-class men who determine medicine's agenda in general and its funding priorities in particular, it is not surprising that the focus of contemporary medicine is on men's diseases, disabilities, and dysfunction. Thus it follows that research on specifically female conditions—e.g., dysmenorrhea, incontinency in older women, and nutrition in postmenopausal women—has received low priority, funding, and prestige, and that suggestions for fruitful research questions based on the personal experience of women have also been largely ignored. Moreover, diseases like heart disease that affect both sexes have been defined as "male" diseases, and most of the funding for heart-disease research has been channeled into studies focusing on how the disease progresses and manifests itself in white, middle-aged, middle-class males. Very little funding has been appropriated for studying heart disease in women, despite the fact that it is the Number 1 killer of U. S. women (especially older women and poor black women who have had several children). Finally, the scientific community has often failed to include females in animal studies in basic research as well as in clinical research unless the research has centered on controlling reproduction. When females have been used as experimental subjects, moreover, they have often been treated as less than fully human (as in investigations of the side effects of oral contraceptives on women, in which poor Mexican-American women were not told they were participating in research, or receiving placebos rather than the oral contraceptives they had requested). These types of gender bias raise serious ethical issues. After all, as Sue Rosser puts it: "Health care practitioners must treat the majority of the population, which is female, based on information gathered from clinical research in which drugs may not have been tested on females, in which the etiology of the disease in women has not been studied and in which women's experience has been ignored" (p. 304).

Patriarchy, Scientists, and Nuclear Warriors

Brian Easlea

In a lecture at the University of California in 1980, the Oxford historian Michael Howard accused the world's scientific community, and particularly the Western scientific community, of an inventiveness in the creation and design of weapons that has made, he believes, the pursuit of a "stable nuclear balance" between the superpowers virtually impossible. At the very least, he found it curious that a scientific community that had expressed great anguish over its moral responsibility for the development of the first crude fission weapons "should have ceased to trouble itself over its continuous involvement with weapons-systems whose lethality and effectiveness make the weapons that destroyed Hiroshima and Nagasaki look like clumsy toys."[1] On the other hand, in the compelling pamphlet *It'll Make a Man of You: A Feminist View of the Arms Race*, Penny Strange expresses no surprise at the militarization of science that has occurred since the Second World War. While acknowledging that individual scientists have been people of integrity with a genuine desire for peace, she tersely states that "weapons research is consistent with the attitudes underlying the whole scientific worldview" and that she looks forward to "an escape from the patriarchal science in which the conquest of nature is a projection of sexual dominance."[2] My aim in this article is to explore the psychological attributes of patriarchal science, particularly physics, that contribute so greatly to the apparent readiness of scientists to maintain the inventive momentum of the nuclear arms race.

My own experiences as a physicist were symptomatic of the problems of modern science. So I begin with a brief account of these experiences followed by a look at various aspects of the masculinity of science, particularly physics, paying special attention to the ideology

From *Beyond Patriarchy*, edited by Michael Kaufman. Copyright © 1987 by Oxford University Press. Reprinted by permission of the author.

surrounding the concept of a scientific method and to the kinds of sexual rhetoric used by physicists to describe both their "pure" research and their contributions to weapons design. I conclude with some thoughts on the potential human integrity of a life in science—once patriarchy and its various subsystems have become relics of history.

A PERSONAL EXPERIENCE OF PHYSICS

Growing up in the heart of rural England, I wanted in my early teens to become a professional bird-watcher. However, at the local grammar school I was persuaded that boys who are good at mathematics become scientists: people just don't become bird-watchers. I did in fact have a deep, if romantic, interest in physics, believing that somehow those "great men" like Einstein and Bohr truly understood a world whose secrets I longed to share. So I went to University College London in 1954 to study physics and found it excruciatingly boring. But I studied hard and convinced myself that at the postgraduate level it would be different if only I could "do research"—whatever that mysterious activity really was. It didn't seem remarkable to me at the time that our class consisted of some forty men and only three or four women. At that time, I was both politically conservative and politically naive, a situation not helped by the complete absence of any lectures in the physics curriculum on "science and society" issues.

In my final year it was necessary to think of future employment. Not wanting to make nuclear weapons and preferring to leave such "dirty" work to other people, I considered a career in the "clean and beautiful" simplicity of the electronics industry. I came very close to entering the industry but in the end, to my great happiness, was accepted back at University College to "do research" in mathematical physics. It was while doing this research

that I was to begin my drift away from a career in physics.

One event in my graduate years stands out. As an undergraduate I had only twice ever asked about the nature of reality as presented by modern physics, and both times the presiding lecturer had ridiculed my question. However, one day a notice appeared announcing that a famous physicist, David Bohm, together with a philosopher of science were inviting physics students to spend a weekend in a large country house to discuss fundamental questions of physics. That weekend was an enlightening experience that gave me the confidence to believe that physics was not solely a means for manipulating nature or a path to professional mundane achievement through the publication of numerous, uninteresting papers, but ideally was an essential part of human wisdom.

In the early 1960s, while I was on a two-year NATO Fellowship at the Institute of Theoretical Physics in Copenhagen, the first cracks and dents began to appear in my worldview. I met scientists from around the world, including the Soviet Union, who engaged me in animated political discussions. With a group of physicists I went on a ten-day tour of Leningrad and Moscow and, equipped with a smattering of Russian, I left the group to wander about on my own and kept meeting people who, at this high point of the Cold War, implored me to believe that Russia wanted peace. I couldn't square this image of Russia and the Russian people with what I had become accustomed to in Britain and would soon be exposed to while teaching at the University of Pittsburgh.

It seemed to be a world gone mad: my new university in Pittsburgh awarded honorary degrees to Werner von Braun, the former Nazi missile expert, and to Edward Teller, the father of the H-bomb. The Cuban blockade followed; Kennedy, Khrushchev, and physics were going to bring about the end of the world. I kept asking myself how the seemingly beautiful, breathtaking physics of Rutherford,

Einstein, Heisenberg, and Niels Bohr had come to this.

New experiences followed which deepened my frustration with physics and increased my social and philosophic interests. University appointments in Brazil gave me a first-hand experience with the type of military regime that the United States so liked to support to save the world from communism. In the end I returned to the University of Sussex, where I taught "about science" courses to non-science students and "science and society" courses to science majors.

The more I learned, the more I became convinced that the reason physics was so misused and the reason the nuclear arms race existed was the existence of capitalist societies, principally the United States, that are based on profit making, permanent war economies, and the subjugation of the Third World. My pat conclusion was that if capitalism could be replaced by socialism, human behavior would change dramatically. But I felt uneasy with this belief since oppression and violence had not first appeared in the world in the sixteenth century. As the years went by and the feminist movement developed, I came to explore the profound psychological connections between the discipline of physics and the world of the warriors—connections that are ultimately rooted in the social institutions of patriarchy. That is the focus of this paper.

THE MASCULINITY OF PHYSICS

Indisputably, British and American physics is male-dominated. In Britain in the early 1980s, women made up only 4 percent of the membership of the Institute of Physics, and in the United States women made up only 2 percent of the faculty of the 171 doctorate-awarding physics departments.[3] This male domination of physics has obviously not come about by chance; not until recently have physicists made serious attempts to encourage women to study the discipline and enter the profession. Indeed, in the first decades of the twentieth century strenuous attempts by physicists to keep women out of their male preserve were not unknown. Symbolic of such attempts in the 1930s was that of no less a man than the Nobel laureate Robert Millikan, who in 1936 wrote to the President of Duke University questioning the wisdom of the University's appointment of a woman to a full physics professorship.[4] As the statistics amply demonstrate, the male domination of physics continues despite publicized attempts by physicists to eliminate whatever prejudice still exists against the entry of women into the profession.

A second aspect of the masculinity of physics is that the men who inhabit this scientific world—particularly those who are successful in it—behave in culturally masculine ways. Indeed, as in other hierarchical male-dominated activities, getting to the top invariably entails aggressive, competitive behavior. Scientists themselves recognize that such masculine behavior, though it is considered unseemly to dwell upon it, is a prominent feature of science. The biologist Richard Lewontin even goes so far as to affirm that "science is a form of competitive and aggressive activity, a contest of man against man that provides knowledge as a side-product."[5] Although I wouldn't agree with Lewontin that knowledge is a mere "side-product" of such competition, I would, for example, agree with the anthropologist Sharon Traweek, who writes that those most prestigious of physicists—the members of the high-energy physics "community"—display the highly masculine behavioral traits of "aggressive individualism, haughty self-confidence, and a sharp competitive edge."[6] Moreover, Traweek's verdict is supported by the remarks of the high-energy physicist Heinz Pagels, who justifies such masculine behavior by explaining that a predominant feature in the conduct of scientific research has to be intellectual aggression, since, as he puts it, "no great science was discovered in the spirit of humility."[7] Scientists, then, physicists included, behave socially in a masculine manner.

A third aspect of the masculinity of physics is the pervasiveness of the ideology and practice of the conquest of nature rather than a human goal of respectful interaction and use. Although, of course, many attitudes (including the most gentle) have informed and continue to inform the practice of science, nevertheless a frequently stated masculine objective of science is the conquest of nature. This was expressed prominently by two of the principal promoters and would-be practitioners of the "new science" in the seventeenth century, Francis Bacon and René Descartes, the former even claiming that successful institutionalization of his method would inaugurate the "truly masculine birth of time." Although modern scientists usually attempt to draw a distinction between "pure" and "applied" science, claiming that pure science is the attempt to discover the fundamental (and beautiful) laws of nature without regard to possible application, it is nevertheless widely recognized that it is causal knowledge of nature that is sought, that is, knowledge that in principle gives its possessors power to intervene successfully in natural processes. In any case, most "pure" scientists know very well that their work, if successful, will generally find application in the "conquest of nature." We may recall how the first investigators of nuclear energy wrote enthusiastically in the early years of the twentieth century that their work, if successful, would provide mankind with an almost limitless source of energy. Both the "pure" and the technological challenges posed by the nucleus proved irresistible: the nucleus was there to be conquered and conquest was always incredibly exciting. Even in today's beleaguered domain of nuclear power for "peaceful" purposes, the ideology and practice of the conquest of nature has not disappeared. Thus, rallying the troops in 1979 at the twenty-fifth anniversary of the formation of the UK Atomic Energy Authority, the physicist chairman of the Authority, Sir John Hill, said that we will be judged "upon our achievements and not upon the plaintive cries of the faint-hearted who have lost the courage and ambitions of our forefathers, which made mankind the master of the earth."[8]

The masculine goal of conquest undoubtedly makes its presence felt in our images of nature and beliefs about the nature of reality; this constitutes a fourth aspect of the masculinity of physics and of science in general. That which is to be conquered does not usually emerge in the conqueror's view as possessing intrinsically admirable properties that need to be respected and preserved. Much, of course, could be written on specific images of nature, particularly with respect to "pure" and "applied" research objectives, and the subject does not lend itself to obvious generalizations. Nevertheless, it is clear that from the seventeenth century onwards, natural philosophers, men of science, and scientists tended to see the "matter" of nature as having no initiating, creative powers of its own (a point of view maintained only with some difficulty after the development of evolutionary theory in the nineteenth century). The historian of science, R. S. Westfall, is certainly not wrong when he writes that "whatever the crudities of the seventeenth century's conception of nature, the rigid exclusion of the psychic from physical nature has remained as its permanent legacy."[9] No matter what the cognitive arguments in favor of science's generally reductionist conception of "matter" and nature, it is clear that a nature that is seen as "the mere scurrying of matter to and fro" is a nature not only amenable to conquest but also one that requires no moral self-examination on the part of its would-be conqueror. "Man's place in the physical universe," declared the Nobel laureate physical chemist (and impeccable Cold-War warrior) Willard Libby, "is to be its master . . . to be its king through the power he alone possesses—the Principle of Intelligence."[10]

A fifth aspect of the masculinity of physics lies in the militarization the discipline has undergone in the twentieth century. Optimistically, Francis Bacon had expressed the hope in the seventeenth century that men would cease making war on each other in order to make collective warfare on nature. That hope has not been realized, nor is it likely to be. We may, after all, recall C. S. Lewis's opinion that "what we call Man's power over nature turns out to be a power exercised by some men over other men [and women] with nature as its instrument."[11] In the overall militarization of science that has occurred largely in this century and that was institutionalized during and after the Second World War, physics and its associated disciplines have indeed been in the forefront. For example, in a courageous paper to the *American Journal of Physics*, the physicist E. L. Woollett reported that at the end of the 1970s some 55 percent of physicists and astronomers carrying out research and development in the United States worked on projects of direct military value and he complained bitterly that physics had become a largely silent partner in the nuclear arms race.[12] It is estimated that throughout the world some half million physical scientists work on weapons design and improvement. As the physicist Freeman Dyson has reported, not only is the world of the scientific warriors overwhelmingly male-dominated but he sees the competition between physicists in weapons creation, allied to the (surely masculine) thrill of creating almost limitless destructive power, as being in large part responsible for the continuing qualitative escalation of the nuclear arms race.[13] Moreover, competition between weapons physicists is still a powerful motivating force in the nuclear arms race. Commenting on the rivalry at the Livermore Weapons Laboratory between two physical scientists, Peter Hagelstein and George Chapline, as to who would be the first to achieve a breakthrough in the design of a nuclear-bomb-powered X-ray laser, the head of the Livermore "Star Wars" Group, Lowell Wood, alleged: "It was raw, unabashed competitiveness.

It was amazing—even though I had seen it happen before . . . two relatively young men . . . slugging it out for dominance in this particular technical arena."[14] And he then went on to agree with Richard Lewontin's unflattering description of motivation throughout the world of science:

I would be very surprised if very many major scientific endeavors, maybe even minor ones, happen because a disinterested scientist coolly and dispassionately grinds away in his lab, devoid of thoughts about what this means in terms of competition, peer esteem, his wife and finally, prizes and recognition. I'm afraid I'm sufficiently cynical to think that in excess of 90 percent of all science is done with these considerations in mind. Pushing back the frontiers of knowledge and advancing truth are distinctly secondary considerations.[15]

One might, no doubt naively, like to believe that male scientists do not compete among themselves for the privilege of being the first to create a devastating new weapon. That belief would certainly be quite wrong.

Given such a sobering description of the masculine world of physics in Britain and North America, it isn't altogether surprising if girls, whose gender socialization is quite different from that of boys, are reluctant to study physics at school. What's more, it is in no way irrational, as British science teacher Hazel Grice points out, for girls to reject a subject that appears to offer "as the apex of its achievement a weapon of mass annihilation."[16]

SCIENTIFIC METHOD FOR SCIENTISTS AND WARRIORS

One common description of physics is that it is a "hard," intellectually difficult discipline, as opposed to "soft" ones, such as English or history. The hard-soft spectrum spanning the academic disciplines is, of course, well-known, and within the sciences themselves there is also a notorious hard-soft spectrum, with physics situated at the hard end, chemistry somewhere toward the middle, biology toward the soft end, and psychology beyond. Insofar as mind, reason, and intellect are (in a patriarchy) culturally seen as masculine attributes, the hard-soft spectrum serves to define a spectrum of diminishing masculinity from hard to soft.

But what is held to constitute intellectual difficulty? It seems that the more mathematical a scientific discipline, the more intellectually difficult it is believed to be and hence the "harder" it is. Mathematics not only makes a discipline difficult, it seems: it also makes it rigorous; and the discipline is thus seen to be "hard" in the two connecting senses of difficult and rigorous. The fact that physics, and especially theoretical physics, makes prodigious use of sophisticated mathematics no doubt contributes to their enviable position at the masculine end of the hard-soft spectrum. It is perhaps of more relevance, however, that mathematics and logical rigor are usually seen as essential components of the "scientific method" and it is the extent to which a discipline is able to practice the "scientific method" that determines its ultimate "hardness" in the sense of intellectual difficulty, the rigor of its reasoning, and the reliability and profundity of its findings. Physics, it is widely believed, is not only able to but does make excellent use of the "scientific method," which thus accounts for its spectacular successes both in the understanding of physical processes and in their mastery. While, of course, all the scientific disciplines aspire to practice the "scientific method," it is physics and related disciplines that are held to have succeeded best.

But does such a procedure as the "scientific method" really exist? If it does, it is deemed to enjoy masculine rather than feminine status insofar as it rigorously and inexorably arrives at truth about the natural world and not mere opinion or wishful thinking. Such a method must therefore, it seems, be ideally characterized by logically rigorous thinking aided by mathematics and determined by experimental, that is, "hard" evidence with no contamination by feminine emotion, intuition, and subjective desires. "The scientific attitude of mind," explained Bertrand Russell in 1913, "involves a sweeping away of all other desires in the interests of the desire to know—it involves the suppression of hopes and fears, loves and hates, and the whole subjective emotional life, until we become subdued to the material, able to see it frankly, without preconceptions, without biases, without any wish except to see it as it is."[17] Such a view of the scientific method remains incredibly influential. In 1974 the sociologist Robert Bierstedt could confirm that "the scientist, *as such*, has no ethical, religious, political, literary, philosophical, moral, or marital preferences.... As a scientist he is interested not in what is right or wrong, or good and evil, but only in what is true or false."[18] Numerous examples could be given. Emotion, wishful thinking, intuition, and other such apparent pollutants of cognition are held to betray and subvert the objectivity of the scientific method, which is the hard, ruthless application of logic and experimental evidence to the quest to understand and master the world. Thus while the philosopher of science Hans Reichenbach could tell the world in 1951 that "the scientific philosopher does not want to belittle the value of emotions, nor would he like to live without them" and that the philosopher's own life could be as passionate and sentimental as that of any literary man, nevertheless the truly scientific philosopher "refuses to muddle emotion and cognition, and likes to breathe the pure air of logical insight and penetration."[19] Perhaps that is why the Nobel laureate physicist, Isidor Rabi, then eighty-four years of age, could confide in the early 1980s to Vivian Gornick that women were temperamentally unsuited to science, that the female nervous system was "simply different." "It makes it impossible for them to stay with the thing," he explained. "I'm afraid there's no use quarrelling with it, that's the way it is."[20]

Now the view of successful "scientific method" as masculine logic, rigor, and experimentation necessarily untainted and uncontaminated with feminine emotion, intuition, and wishful thinking is completely and hopelessly wrong. Such a scientific method is as elusive as "pure" masculinity. If nothing else, the invention of theories demands considerable intuition and creative imagination, as every innovative scientist knows and often has proclaimed. Does this therefore mean that the masculine "objectivity" of scientific method is intrinsically compromised? The philosopher of science, Carl Hempel, explains that it doesn't, since "scientific objectivity is safeguarded by the principle that while hypotheses and theories may be freely invented and *proposed* in science [the so-called context of discovery], they can be *accepted* into the body of scientific knowledge only if they pass critical scrutiny [the context of justification], which includes in particular the checking of suitable test implications by careful observation and experiment."[21] Alas for this typical defense of scientific objectivity, for ever since the work of Thomas Kuhn in his 1962 essay *The Structure of Scientific Revolutions*, it is generally accepted that no hard and fast distinction can be readily drawn between such a feminine context of discovery and a masculine context of justification.[22]

For this is what seems to be at issue. Not only does the notion of scientific objectivity appear to entail a clear-cut distinction between the masculine investigator and the world of "feminine" or "female" matter, within the psyche of the masculine investigator there also appears to be a pressing need to establish an inviolable distinction between a masculine mode of "hard," rigorous reasoning determined by logic and experimental evidence and, should it operate at all, a feminine mode characterized by creative imagination, intuition, and emotion-linked preferences. However, such clear-cut distinctions neither exist nor are possible in scientific practice, no matter how much the masculine mode appears paramount in normal research.

What certainly does exist (although not uniformly so) is a very impassioned commitment to deny an evaluative subjective component to scientific practice; we may see such a masculine commitment as stemming from an emotional rejection and repudiation of the feminine within masculine inquiry. In other words, the impassioned claim that there exists an unemotional, value-free scientific method (or context of justification) may be interpreted as an emotional rejection and repudiation of the feminine and, if this is so, it would mean that scientific practice carried out (supposedly) in an "objective," value-free, unemotional way is in fact deeply and emotionally repressive of the feminine. This is a hornets' nest with all kinds of implications, but it may help to explain why much of modern science has, I shall argue, been embraced so uncritically by a society that is misogynistic and, in the case of the war industries, misanthropic as well. It is partly because patriarchal science is fundamentally antifeminine that its practitioners are psychologically vulnerable to the attractions of the "defense" industry.

We learn from Freeman Dyson that the world of the warriors, which comprises military strategists, scientists, and Pentagon officials, is ostentatiously defined by a "deliberately cool," quantitative style that explicitly excludes "overt emotion and rhetoric"—it is a style modelled on "scientific method" and directly opposed to, for example, the "emotional," "anecdotal" style of the anti-nuclear campaigner Helen Caldicott, whose arguments, according to Dyson, the warriors find unacceptable even when they manage to take them seriously.[23] For her part, Helen Caldicott believes that great rage and hatred lie suppressed behind the seemingly imperturbable, "rational" mask of scientific military analysis.[24] The military historian Sue Mansfield has posed the problem at its starkest: the stress placed in the scientific world on "objectivity" and a quantitative approach as a guarantee of truth, together with the relegation of emotions to a peripheral and unconscious existence, has, she maintains, carried "from its beginnings in the seventeenth century the burden of an essential hostility to the body, the feminine, and the natural environment."[25]

SEXUAL RHETORIC BY SCIENTISTS AND WARRIORS

The stereotype of the sober male scientist dispassionately investigating the properties of matter with, obviously, not a single sexual thought in mind is singularly undermined by the extent to which scientists portray nature as female in their informal prose, lectures, and talks. Indeed, according to the historian of science Carolyn Merchant, the most powerful image in Western science is "the identification of nature with the female, especially a female harbouring secrets."[26] Physicists often refer to their "pure" research as a kind of sexual exploration of the secrets of nature—a female nature that not only possesses great subtlety and beauty to be revealed only to her most skillful and determined admirers and lovers, but that is truly fearsome in her awesome powers.

"Nature," wrote the high-energy physicist Frank Close in the *Guardian*, "hides her secrets in subtle ways." By "probing" the deep, mysterious, unexpectedly beautiful submicroscopic world, "we have our eyes opened to her greater glory."[27] The impression is given of a nonviolent, male exploration of the sexual secrets of a mysterious, profoundly wonderful female nature. From the end of the nineteenth century to the middle 1980s, such sentiments have frequently been expressed by famous physicists. Thus, addressing the annual meeting of the British Association in 1898, the physicist Sir William Crookes announced to his audience, "Steadily, unflinchingly, we strive to pierce the inmost heart of nature, from what she is to reconstruct what she has been, and to prophesy what she yet shall be. Veil after veil we have lifted, and her face grows more beautiful,

august, and wonderful, with every barrier that is withdrawn."[28]

But no matter how many veils are lifted, ultimately the fearsome and untameable "femaleness" of the universe will remain.[29] Even if female nature is ultimately untameable, scientific research and application can reveal and make usable many of nature's comparatively lesser secrets. It is striking how successful scientific research is frequently described in the language of sexual intercourse, birth, and claims to paternity in which science or the mind of man is ascribed the phallic role of penetrating or probing into the secrets of nature—with the supposed hardness of successful scientific method now acquiring an obvious phallic connotation. Accounts of the origins of quantum mechanics and nuclear physics in the first decades of the twentieth century illustrate this well. In 1966 the physicist, historian, and philosopher of science, Max Jammer, admiringly announced that those early achievements of physicists in quantum mechanics clearly showed "how far man's intellect can penetrate into the secrets of nature on the basis of comparatively inconspicuous evidence"; indeed, Victor Weisskopf, Nobel laureate, remembers how the physicists at Niels Bohr's institute were held together "by a common urge to penetrate into the secrets of nature."[30] While Frederick Soddy was already proudly convinced by 1908 that "in the discovery of radioactivity ... we had penetrated one of nature's innermost secrets,"[31] it was Soddy's collaborator in those early years, Sir Ernest Rutherford, who has been adjudged by later physicists and historians to have been the truly masculine man behind nuclear physics' spectacular advances in this period. Referring to Rutherford's triumphant hypothesis in 1911 that the atom consisted of an extremely concentrated nucleus of positively charged matter surrounded by a planetary system of orbiting electrons, one of Rutherford's assistants at the time, C. G. Darwin, later wrote that it was one of the "great occurrences" of his life that he was "actually present half-an-hour after the nucleus was born."[32] Successful and deep penetration, birth, and ensuing paternity: these are the hallmarks of great scientific advance.

At first sight it might seem that there is little untoward in such use of sexual, birth, and paternity metaphors, their use merely demonstrating that nuclear research, like scientific research in general, can be unproblematically described by its practitioners as a kind of surrogate sexual activity carried out by male physicists on female nature. However, not only did all the early nuclear pioneers (Rutherford included) realize that enormous quantities of energy lay waiting, as it were, to be exploited by physicists—"it would be rash to predict," wrote Rutherford's collaborator, W. C. D. Whetham, "that our impotence will last for ever"[33]—but, ominously, some of the sexual metaphors were extremely aggressive, reminding one forcibly of the ideology of (masculine) conquest of (female) nature. Indeed, since Rutherford's favorite word appears to have been "attack" it does not seem startling when one of the most distinguished physicists in the United States, George Ellery Hale, who was convinced that "nature has hidden her secrets in an almost impregnable stronghold," wrote admiringly to Rutherford in astonishingly military-sexual language. "The rush of your advance is overpowering," he congratulated him, "and I do not wonder that nature has retreated from trench to trench, and from height to height, until she is now capitulating in her inmost citadel."[34]

The implications of all this were not lost on everyone. Well before the discovery of uranium fission in 1939, the poet and Cambridge historian Thomas Thornely expressed his great apprehension at the consequences of a successful scientific assault on nature's remaining nuclear secrets:

Well may she start and desperate strain,
To thrust the bold besiegers back;
  If they that citadel should gain,

What grisly shapes of death and pain
May rise and follow in their track![35]

Not surprisingly, just as military scientists and strategists have adopted the formal "scientific style" of unemotional, quantitative argument, so they also frequently make informal use of sexual, birth, and paternity metaphors in their research and testing. Now, however, these metaphors become frighteningly aggressive, indeed obscene: military sexual penetration into nature's nuclear secrets will, the metaphors suggest, not only shake nature to her very foundations but at the same time demonstrate indisputable masculine status and military paternity. We learn that the first fission bomb developed at the Los Alamos laboratory was often referred to as a "baby"—a baby boy if a successful explosion, a baby girl if a failure. Secretary of War Henry Stimson received a message at Potsdam after the successful Trinity test of an implosion fission weapon which (after decoding) read:

Doctor has just returned most enthusiastic and confident that the little boy [the uranium bomb] is as husky as his big brother [the tested plutonium bomb]. The light in his eyes discernible from here to Highhold and I could have heard his screams from here to my farm.[36]

Examples are abundant: the two bombs (one uranium and one plutonium) exploded over Japanese cities were given the code names "Little Boy" and "Fat Man"; a third bomb being made ready was given the name "Big Boy." Oppenheimer became known as the Father of the A-Bomb and indeed the National Baby Institution of America made Oppenheimer its Father of the Year. Edward Teller, publicly seen as the principal physicist behind the successful design of the first fusion weapon or H-bomb, seemingly takes pains in his memoirs to draw readers' attention to the fact that it was a "phallic" triumph on his part.[37] After the enormous blast of the first H-bomb obliterated a Pacific island and all its life, Teller sent a triumphant telegram to his Los Alamos colleagues, "It's a boy."[38] Unfortunately for Teller, his paternity status of "Father of the H-Bomb" has been challenged by some physicists who claim that the mathematician Stanislaw Ulam produced the original idea and that all Teller did was to gestate the bomb after Ulam had inseminated him with his idea, thus, they say, making him the mere Mother.

Following the creation of this superbomb, a dispute over two competing plans for a nuclear attack against the Soviet Union occurred between strategists in the RAND think tank and the leading generals of the Strategic Air Command (SAC) of the U.S. Air Force. In a circulated memorandum the famous strategist Bernard Brodie likened his own RAND plan of a limited nuclear strike against military targets while keeping the major part of the nuclear arsenal in reserve to the act of sexual penetration but with withdrawal before ejaculation; he likened the alternative SAC plan to leave the Soviet Union a "smoking radiating ruin at the end of two hours" to sexual intercourse that "goes all the way."[39] His colleague Herman Kahn coined the term "wargasm" to describe the all-out "orgastic spasm of destruction" that the SAC generals supposedly favored.[40] Kahn's book *On Escalation* attempts, like an elaborate scientific sex manual, a precise identification of forty-four (!) stages of increasing tension culminating in the final stage of "spasm war."[41] Such sexual metaphors for nuclear explosions and warfare appear to be still in common use. In 1980 General William Odom, then a military adviser to Zbigniew Brzesinski on the National Security Council, told a Harvard seminar of a strategic plan to release 70 to 80 percent of America's nuclear megatonnage "in one orgasmic whump,"[42] while at a London meeting in 1984, General Daniel Graham, a former head of the Defense Intelligence Agency and a prominent person behind President Reagan's Strategic Defense Initiative, brought some appreciative chuckles from his nearly all-male audience in referring to all-out nuclear "exchange" as the "wargasm."[43]

What is one to make of such metaphors and in particular of an analogy that likens ejaculation of semen during sexual intercourse (an act, one hopes, of mutual pleasure and possibly the first stage in the creation of new life) with a nuclear bombardment intended to render a huge country virtually lifeless, perhaps for millennia to come? And what conception of pleasure was foremost in Kahn's mind when he coined the term "wargasm"—surely the most obscene word in the English language—to describe what he sees as the union between Eros and Thanatos that is nuclear holocaust? I find such comparisons and terminology almost beyond rational comment. Simone de Beauvoir's accurate observation that "the erotic vocabulary of males" has always been drawn from military terminology becomes totally inadequate.[44] Brodie's and Kahn's inventiveness has surely eclipsed Suzanne Lowry's observation in the *Guardian* that "'fuck' is the prime hate word" in the English language.[45] Indeed, given the sexual metaphors used by some of the nuclear warriors, one can understand Susan Griffin's anguished agreement with Norman Mailer's (surprising) description of Western culture as "drawing a rifle sight on an open vagina"—a culture, Griffin continues, "that even within its worship of the female sex goddess hates female sexuality."[46] We may indeed wonder why a picture of Rita Hayworth, "the ubiquitous pinup girl of World War II," was stenciled on the first atomic bomb exploded in the Bikini tests of 1946.[47]

UNCONSCIOUS OBJECTIVES OF PATRIARCHY AND PATRIARCHAL PHYSICS

There has been much analysis of the Catholic Church's dichotomization of women into two stereotypes: the unattainable, asexual, morally pure virgin to which the Christian woman could aspire but never reach and the carnal whore-witch representing uncontrollable sexuality, depravity, wickedness, and the threat of universal chaos and disorder. During the sixteenth and seventeenth centuries such a fear and loathing of women's apparent wickedness came to a head in the European witch craze that was responsible for the inquisition and execution of scores of thousands of victims, over 80 percent of them female. A major historian of the witch craze, H. C. E. Midelfort, has noted that "one cannot begin to understand the European witch craze without recognizing that it displayed a burst of misogyny without parallel in Western history."[48]

Whatever the causes of the European witch craze, what may be particularly significant is that it coincided with the first phase of the scientific revolution, the peak of the witch craze occurring during the decades in which Francis Bacon, René Descartes, Johannes Kepler, and Galileo Galilei made their revolutionary contributions. In *one* of its aspects, I believe that the scientific revolution may be seen as a secularized version of the witch craze in which sophisticated men either, like Francis Bacon, projected powerful and dangerous "femaleness" onto nature or, like René Descartes, declared nature to be feminine and thus totally amenable to manipulation and control by (the mind of) man. We recall how Simone de Beauvoir declared that woman is seemingly "represented, at one time, as pure passivity, available, open, a utensil"—which is surely Descartes's view of "feminine" matter—while "at another time she is regarded as if possessed by alien forces: there is a devil raging in her womb, a serpent lurks in her vagina, eager to devour the male's sperm"—which has more affinity to Francis Bacon's view of "female" matter.[49] Indeed, Bacon likened the experimental investigation of the secrets of "female" nature to the inquisition of witches on the rack and looked forward to the time when masculine science would shake "female" nature to her very foundations. It is, I believe, the purified natural magical tradition advocated by Bacon (with considerable use of very aggressive sexual imagery) that contributed in a major way to the rise of modern science. Believing firmly in the existence of the secrets of nature that could be penetrated by the mind of man, Bacon predicted that eventually the new science would be able to perform near miracles. And indeed the momentous significance of the scientific revolution surely lies in the fact that, unlike the rituals of preliterate societies which in general failed to give their practitioners power over nature (if this is what they sought), the male practitioners of modern science have been rewarded with truly breathtaking powers to intervene successfully in natural phenomena (we have become blasé about the spectacular triumphs of modern science, but what a near miracle is, for example, a television picture). Bacon's prediction that the new science he so passionately advocated would inaugurate the "truly masculine birth of time" and eventually shake nature to her very foundations has been triumphantly borne out by the achievements of modern physics and the sad possibility of devastating nature with environmental destruction, nuclear holocaust, and nuclear winter.

Clearly modern science possesses what might be called a rational component. In this article I am taking for granted the fact that modern science produces knowledge of nature that "works" relative to masculine (and other) expectations and objectives and that the intrinsic interest and fascination of scientific inquiry would render a non-patriarchal science a worthy and central feature of a truly human society. What I am here concerned with is the "truly masculine" nature of scientific inquiry involving the discipline's would-be rigid separation between masculine science and "female" nature and the possibility of an underlying, if for the most part unconscious, hostility to "dangerous femaleness" in the minds of some, or many, of its practitioners—a hostility presumably endemic to patriarchal society. A case can be made—and has been both by Carolyn

Merchant and myself—that a powerful motivating force, but not the only one, behind the rise of modern science was a kind of displaced misogyny.[50] In addition a case can be made that a powerful motivating force behind some (or much) modern science and particularly weapons science is a continuation of the displaced misogyny that helped generate the scientific revolution.

Certainly a counterclaim is possible that modern science might have had some misogynistic origins, but that this has no relevance today. In disagreement with such a counterclaim, however, it can be plausibly argued that the industrialized countries have remained virulently misogynistic, as seen in the prevalence of violence practiced and depicted by men against women. If there is indeed a link between misogyny, insecure masculinity, and our conceptions of science, particularly weapons science, then we are given a way to understand why nuclear violence can be associated in warriors' minds with sexual intercourse and ejaculation. Moreover, not only does Sue Mansfield suggest that at a deep level the scientific mentality has carried from its inception in the seventeenth century "the burden of an essential hostility to the body, the feminine, and the natural environment," but she also points out that, if human life survives at all after a nuclear holocaust, then it will mean the total restoration of the power of weapon-bearing men over women. This leads her to make a significant comment that "though the reenslavement of women and the destruction of nature are not conscious goals of our nuclear stance, the language of our bodies, our postures, and our acts is a critical clue to our unexamined motives and desires."[51]

Of course, at the conscious level the scientific warrior today can, and does, offer a "rational" explanation for his behavior: his creation of fission and fusion weapons, he maintains, has made the deliberate starting of world war unthinkable and certainly has preserved peace

in Europe for the last forty years. Whatever financial gain comes his way is not unappreciated but is secondary to the necessity of maintaining his country's security; likewise whatever scientific interest he experiences in the technological challenge of his work is again secondary to the all-important objective of preserving the balance of terror until world statesmen achieve multilateral disarmament. While well-known arguments can be made against the coherence of such a typical rationalization, what I am suggesting is that at a partly conscious, partly unconscious, level the scientific warrior experiences not only an almost irresistible need to separate his (insecure) masculinity from what he conceives as femininity but also a compulsive desire to create the weapons that unmistakably affirm his masculinity and by means of which what is "female" can, if necessary and as a last resort, be annihilated. (And it must be noted that scientific warriors can be supported by women or even joined by female warriors in their largely unconscious quest to affirm masculine triumph over the feminine and female.)

CONCLUSION

Looking over the history of humanity—the "slaughter-bench of history" as Hegel called it—I feel compelled to identify a factor—beyond economic and territorial rationales—that could help explain this sorry escalation of weaponry oppression, and bloodshed. It seems to me of paramount importance to try to understand why men are generally the direct oppressors, oppressing other men and women, why in general men allow neither themselves nor women the opportunity to realize full humanity.

While the political scientist Jean Bethke Elshtain may well be correct when she writes skeptically that no great movement will ever be fought under the banner of "androgyny," I suggest that it could well be fought under the banner of "a truly human future for everyone."[52] And that would entail the abolition of the *institutionalized* sexual division of labor. Men and women must be allowed the right to become complete human beings and not mutilated into their separate masculine and feminine gender roles. At the same time, I agree with Cynthia Cockburn when she writes in her book *Machinery of Dominance* that "men need more urgently to learn women's skills than women need to learn men's" and that "the revolutionary step will be to bring men down to earth, to domesticate technology and reforge the link between making and nurturing."[53]

In such a world "education" could not remain as it is now in Britain and the United States (and elsewhere). Certainly there would be no "physics" degree as it exists today, although there would be studies that would eventually take "students" to the frontiers of research in "physics." Needless to say, such an educational system would not be male-dominated (or female-dominated), it would not institutionalize and reward socially competitive aggressive behavior, and there would be no objective in "physics" education of the "conquest of nature," although it would certainly recognize the need to find respectful, ecologically sound ways of making use of nature. Moreover, images of nature would, I suspect, undergo some profound changes (with probably major changes to some theories as well), and clearly in a truly human world there would be no militarization of physics. As for the "scientific method," this would be recognized to be a somewhat mysterious activity, perhaps never completely specifiable, certainly an activity making use of the full range of *human* capacities from creative intuition to the most rigorous logical reasoning.

As for sexual imagery, that would surely thrive in the new truly human activity of scientific research, given that sexual relations—deprived of the hatred that now so greatly distorts sexuality—would continue to provide not only much of the motivation but also the metaphors for describing scientific activity (and much

else). Consider, for example, the language of a woman who was awarded just about every honor the discipline of astrophysics could bestow (but only after she spent years challenging blatant sexism and discrimination). The images invoked by Cecilia Payne-Gaposchkin are more directly erotic than the "equivalent" sexual imagery used by male scientists and physicists (not to mention their frequent aggressive imagery); her language was of her friendship, her love, her delight, her ecstasy with the world of "male" stars and galaxies. Writing of nature as female, Payne-Gaposchkin advises her fellow researchers: "Nature has always had a trick of surprising us, and she will continue to surprise us. But she has never let us down yet. We can go forward with confidence,

Knowing that nature never did betray
The heart that loved her.[54]

But it was an embrace of relatedness that Payne-Gaposchkin had sought and which had given her great satisfaction throughout her life, the satisfaction arising, in the words of Peggy Kidwell, from a sustained impassioned, loving endeavor "to unravel the mysteries of the stars."[55] In a truly human world, the principal purpose and result of science, as Erwin Schrödinger once said, will surely be to enhance "the general joy of living."[56]

NOTES

1. Michael Howard, "On Fighting a Nuclear War," in Michael Howard, *The Causes of War and Other Essays* (London: Temple Smith, 1983), 136.

2. Penny Strange, *It'll Make a Man of You* (Nottingham, England: Mushroom Books with Peace News, 1983), 24–5.

3. These statistics are taken from *Girls and Physics: A Report by the Joint Physics Education Committee of the Royal Society and the Institute of Physics* (London, 1982), 8, and Lilli S. Hornig, "Women in Science and Engineering: Why So Few?" *Technology Review* 87 (November/December, 1984) 41.

4. See Margaret W. Rossiter, *Women Scientists in America: Struggles and Strategies to 1940* (Baltimore: Johns Hopkins University Press, 1982), 190–1.

5. Richard Lewontin, "Honest Jim' Watson's Big Thriller, about DNA," Chicago *Sun Times*, 25 Feb. 1968, 1–2, reprinted in James D. Watson, *The Double Helix . . . A New Critical Edition*, edited by Gunther S. Stent (London: Weidenfeld, 1981), 186.

6. Sharon Traweek, "High-Energy Physics: A Male Preserve," *Technology Review* (November/December, 1984), 42–3; see also her *Beamtimes and Lifetimes: The World of High-Energy Physicists* (Boston: Harvard University Press, 1988).

7. Heinz Pagels, *The Cosmic Code: Quantum Physics as the Language of Nature* (London: Michael Joseph, 1982), 338.

8. Sir John Hill, "The Quest for Public Acceptance of Nuclear Power," *Atom*, no. 273 (1979): 166–72.

9. Richard S. Westfall, *The Construction of Modern Science* (1971; Cambridge: Cambridge University Press, 1977), 41. It should be noted, however, that quantum mechanics is essentially an antireductionist theory; see, for example, the (controversial) book by Fritjof Capra, *The Tao of Physics* (London: Fontana, 1976).

10. Willard Libby, "Man's Place in the Physical Universe," in John R. Platt, ed., *New Views of the Nature of Man* (Chicago: University of Chicago Press, 1965), 14–15.

11. C. S. Lewis, *The Abolition of Man* (1943; London: Geoffrey Bles, 1946), 40.

12. E. L. Woollett, "Physics and Modern Warfare: The Awkward Silence," *American Journal of Physics* 48 (1980): 104–11.

13. Freeman Dyson, *Weapons and Hope* (New York: Harper and Row, 1984), 41–2.

14. William J. Broad, *Star Warriors: A Penetrating Look into the Lives of the Young Scientists Behind Our Space Age Weaponry* (New York: Simon and Schuster, 1985), 204.

15. Ibid.

16. Hazel Grice, letter to the *Guardian*, 9 Oct. 1984, 20.

17. Bertrand Russell, "Science in a Liberal Education," the *New Statesman* (1913) reprinted in *Mysticism and Logic and Other Essays* (Harmondsworth: Penguin, 1953), 47–8.

18. Robert Bierstedt, *The Social Order* (1957; New York: McGraw-Hill, 1974), 26.

19. Hans Reichenbach, *The Rise of Scientific Philosophy* (1951; Berkeley and Los Angles: California University Press, 1966), 312.

20. Vivian Gornick, *Women in Science: Portraits from a World in Transition* (New York: Simon and Schuster, 1984), 36.

21. Carl Hempel, *Philosophy of Natural Science* (Englewood Cliffs, N.J.: Prentice-Hall, 1966), 16.

22. See, for example, Imre Lakatos and Alan Musgrave, eds., *Criticism and the Growth of Knowledge* (Cambridge: Cambridge University Press, 1970): Sandra Harding, "Is Gender a Variable in Conceptions of Rationality? A Survey of Issues," *Dialectica: International Journal of Philosphy of Knowledge* 36 (1982): 225–42: and Harry M. Collins, ed., special issue of *Social Studies of Science* 11 (1981): 3–158, "Knowledge and Controversy: Studies of Modern Natural Science."

23. Freeman Dyson, *Weapons and Hope*, 4–6.

24. Helen Caldicott, "Etiology: Missile Envy and Other Psychopathology," in her *Missile Envy: The Arms Race and Nuclear War* (New York: William Morrow, 1984).

25. Sue Mansfield, *The Gestalts of War: An Inquiry into Its Origins and Meaning as a Social Institution* (New York: Dial Press, 1982), 224.

26. Carolyn Merchant, "Isis' Consciousness Raised," *Isis* 73 (1982): 398–409.

27. Frank Close, "And now at last, the quark to top them all," the *Guardian*, 19 July 1984, 13, and "A shining example of what ought to be impossible," the *Guardian*, 8 Aug. 1985, 13.

28. Sir William Crookes, quoted in E. E. Fournier d'Albe, *The Life of Sir William Crookes* (London: Fisher Unwin, 1923), 365.

29. See, for example, the physicist Paul Davies's account of "black holes," "naked singularities," and "cosmic anarchy" in his *The Edge of Infinity: Naked Singularities and the Destruction of Space-time* (London: Dent, 1981), especially 92–3, 114, 145.

30. Victor Weisskopf, "Niels Bohr and International Scientific Collaboration," in S. Rozenthal, ed., *Niels Bohr: His Life and Work as Seen by His Friends and Colleagues* (Amsterdam: North Holland, 1967), 262.

31. Frederick Soddy, *The Interpretation of Radium* (London, 1909), 234.

32. C. G. Darwin quoted in A. S. Eve, *Rutherford* (Cambridge: Cambridge University Press, 1939), 199, 434.

33. W. C. D. Whetham, *The Recent Development of Physical Science* (London: Murray, 1904), 242.

34. G. E. Hale quoted in Helen Wright, *Explorer of the Universe: A Biography of George Ellery Hale* (New York: Dutton, 1966), 283, and in A. S. Eve, *Rutherford*, 231.

35. "The Atom" from *The Collected Verse of Thomas Thornely* (Cambridge: W. Heffer, 1939), 70–1, reprinted in John Heath-Stubbes and Phillips Salmon, eds., *Poems of Science* (Harmondsworth: Penguin, 1984), 245.

36. Richard G. Hewlett and Oscar E. Anderson, *A History of the United States Atomic Energy Commission* (Pennsylvania State University Press, 1962), vol. 1, *The New World*, 1939–1946, 386.

37. Edward Teller with Allen Brown, *The Legacy of Hiroshima* (London: Macmillan, 1962), 51–3.

38. Edward Teller, *Energy from Heaven and Earth* (San Francisco: W. H. Freeman, 1979), 151. See also Norman Moss, *Men Who Play God* (Harmondsworth: Penguin, 1970), 78. For general detail see my *Fathering the Unthinkable: Masculinity, Scientists and the Nuclear Arms Race* (London: Pluto Press, 1983), ch. 3.

39. Bernard Brodie's memorandum is referred to by Fred Kaplan in *The Wizards of Armageddon* (New York: Simon and Schuster, 1983), 222. I have not seen the text of Brodie's memorandum. The chilling phrase "smoking, radiating ruin at the end of two hours" comes from a declassified Navy memorandum on a SAC briefing held in March 1954; see David Alan Rosenberg, "A Smoking Radiating Ruin at the End of Two Hours': Documents on American Plans for Nuclear War with the Soviet Union 1954–55," *International Security* 6 (1981/82), 3–38.

40. Herman Kahn, *On Escalation: Metaphors and Scenarios* (London: Pall Mall, 1965), 194.

41. Note that Gregg Herken in *Counsels of War* (New York: Knopf, 1985), 206, writes that Bernard Brodie objected to Herman Kahn's "levity" in coining the term "wargasm."

42. Quoted in Thomas Powers, "How Nuclear War Could Start," *New York Review of Books*, 17 Jan. 1985, 34.

43. Roger Hutton, (personal communication), who attended the meeting when researching the Star Wars project.

44. Simone de Beauvoir, *The Second Sex* (1949; Harmondsworth: Penguin, 1972), 396.

45. Suzanne Lowry, "O Tempora, O Mores," the *Guardian*, 24 May 1984, 17.

46. Susan Griffin, *Pornography and Silence: Culture's Revenge Against Nature* (London: Women's Press, 1981), 217.

47. Paul Boyer, *By the Bomb's Early Light: American Thought and Culture at the Dawn of the Atomic Age* (New York: Pantheon, 1985), 83.

48. H. C. E. Midelfort, "Heartland of the Witchcraze: Central and Northern Europe," *History Today* 31 (February, 1981): 28.

49. Simone de Beauvoir, *The Second Sex*, 699.

50. See, for example, Carolyn Merchant, *The Death of Nature: Women, Ecology and the Scientific Revolution* (San Francisco: Harper and Row, 1980), and my *Science and Sexual Oppression: Patriarchy's Confrontation with Women and Nature* (London: Weidenfeld, 1981), ch. 3 and *Fathering the Unthinkable*, ch. 1.

51. Sue Mansfield, *The Gestalts of War*, 223.

52. Jean Bethke Elshtain, "Against Androgyny," Telos 47 (1981), 5–22.

53. Cynthia Cockburn, *Machinery of Dominance* (London: Pluto Press, 1985), 256–7.

54. Katherine Haramundanis, ed., *Cecilia Payne-Gaposchkin: An Autobiography and Other Recollections* (Cambridge: Cambridge University Press, 1984), 237.

55. *Ibid.*, 28.

56. "Science, Art and Play," reprinted in E. C. Schrödinger, *Science, Theory and Man* (New York: Dover, 1957), 29; see, for example, Euan Squires, *To Acknowledge the Wonder: The Story of Fundamental Physics* (Bristol: Adam Hilger, 1985).

The MoMA's Hot Mamas

Carol Duncan

When the Museum of Modern Art opened its newly installed and much enlarged permanent collection in 1984, critics were struck with how little things had changed. In the new installation, as in the old, modern art is once again a progression of formally distinct styles. As before, certain moments in this progression are given greater importance than others: Cézanne, the first painter one sees, announces modern art's beginnings. Picasso's dramatically installed *Les Demoiselles d'Avignon* [1] signifies the coming of Cubism—the first giant step twentieth-century art took and the one from which much of the history of modern art proceeds. From Cubism unfolds the other notable avant-garde movements: German Expressionism, Futurism, and so on, through Dada-Surrealism. Finally come the American Abstract Expressionists. After purifying their work of a residue of Surrealist representation, they made the final breakthrough into the realm of absolute spirit, manifested as absolute formal and nonrepresentational purity. It is in reference to their achievement that, according to the MoMA (in its large, new, final gallery), all later significant art in one way or another continues to measure its ambitions and scale.

Probably more than any other institution, the MoMA has promoted this "mainstream modernism," greatly augmenting its authority and prestige through acquisitions, exhibitions, and publications. To be sure, the MoMA's managers

did not independently invent the museum's strictly linear and highly formalist art-historical narrative; but they have embraced it tenaciously, and it is no accident that one can retrace that history in its galleries better and more fully than in any other collection. For some, the museum's retrospective character is a regrettable turnaround from its original role as champion of the new. But the MoMA remains enormously important for the role it plays in maintaining in the present a particular version of the art-historical past. Indeed, for much of the academic world, as for the larger art public, the kind of art history it narrates still constitutes the definitive history of modern art.

Yet, in the MoMA's permanent collection, more meets the eye than this history admits to. According to the established narrative, the history of art is made up of a progression of styles and unfolds along certain irreversible lines: from style to style, it gradually emancipates itself from the imperative to represent convincingly or coherently a natural, presumably objective world. Integral to this narrative is a model of moral action, exemplified by individual artists. As they become liberated from traditional representation, they achieve greater subjectivity and hence greater artistic freedom and autonomy of spirit. As the literature of modern art portrays it, their progressive renunciation of representation, repeatedly and minutely documented in monographs, catalogues, and critical journals, is often achieved through painful or self-sacrificing searching or courageous risk-taking. The disruption of space, the denial of volume, the overthrow of traditional compositional schemes, the discovery of painting as an autonomous surface, the emancipation of color, line, or texture, the occasional transgressions

FIGURE 1   Pablo Picasso, *Les Demoiselles d'Avignon*, 1907. New York, Museum of Modern Art, acquired through the Lillie P. Bliss Bequest.

and reaffirmations of the boundaries of art (as in the adaptation of junk or non-high-art materials), and so on through the liberation of painting from frame and stretcher and thence from the wall itself—all of these advances trans-late into moments of moral as well as artistic choice. As a consequence of his spiritual struggle, the artist finds a new realm of energy and truth beyond the material, visible world that once preoccupied art—as in Cubism's reconstruction of the "fourth dimension," as Apolli-naire called the power of thought itself; Mon-drian's or Kandinsky's visual analogues of abstract, universal forces; Robert Delaun-ay's discovery of cosmic energy; or Miró's re-creations of a limitless and potent psychic field. Ideally and to the extent to which they have as-similated this history, museum visitors reenact these artistic—and hence spiritual—struggles. In this way they ritually perform a drama of enlightenment in which freedom is won by re-peatedly overcoming and moving beyond the visible, material world.

And yet, despite the meaning and value given to such transcendent realms, the history of modern art, as it is written and as it is seen in the MoMA and elsewhere, is positively crowded with images—and most of them are of women. Despite their numbers, their variety is remarkably small. Most often they are sim-ply female bodies or parts of bodies, with no identity beyond their female anatomy—those ever-present "Women" or "Seated Women" or "Reclining Nudes." Or they are tarts, prosti-tutes, artist's models, or low-life entertainers—highly identifiable socially, but at the bottom of the social scale. In the MoMA's authorita-tive collection, Picasso's *Demoiselles d'Avignon*, Léger's *Grand Déjeuner*, Kirchner's scenes of streetwalkers, Duchamp's *Bride*, Severini's Bal Tabarin dancer, de Kooning's *Woman I*, and many other works are often monumental in scale and conspicuously placed. Most critical and art-historical writings give them compara-ble importance.

To be sure, modern artists have often cho-sen to make "big" philosophical or artistic state-ments via the nude. If the MoMA exaggerates this tradition or overstates some aspects of it, it is nevertheless an exaggeration or overstate-ment of something pervasive in modern art practice. Why then has art history not ac-counted for this intense preoccupation with so-cially and sexually available female bodies? What, if anything, do nudes and whores have to

do with modern art's heroic renunciation of representation? And why is this imagery ac-corded such prestige and authority within art history—why is it associated with the highest artistic ambition?

In theory, museums are public spaces ded-icated to the spiritual enhancement of all who visit them. In practice, however, museums are prestigious and powerful engines of ideology. They are modern ritual settings in which visi-tors enact complex and often deep psychic dra-mas about identity—dramas that the museum's stated, consciously intended programs do not and cannot acknowledge overtly. Like those of all great museums, the MoMA's ritual transmits a complex ideological signal. My concern here is with only a portion of that signal—the por-tion that addresses sexual identity. I shall argue that the collection's recurrent images of sexual-ized female bodies actively masculinize the museum as a social environment. Silently and surreptitiously, they specify the museum's ritual of spiritual quest as a male quest, just as they mark the larger project of modern art as pri-marily a male endeavor.

If we understand the modern art museum as a ritual of male transcendence, if we see it as organized around male fears, fantasies, and de-sires, then the quest for spiritual transcendence on the one hand and the obsession with a sex-ualized female body on the other, rather than appearing unrelated or contradictory, can be seen as parts of a larger, psychologically inte-grated whole. How very often images of women in modern art speak of male fears. Many of the works I just mentioned feature distorted or dangerous-looking creatures, potentially over-powering, devouring, or castrating. Indeed, the MoMA's collection of monstrous, threatening females is exceptional: Picasso's *Demoiselles* and *Seated Bather* (the latter a giant praying man-tis); the frozen, metallic odalisques in Léger's *Grand Déjeuner*; several early female figures by Giacometti; sculptures by Gonzáles and

Lipschitz; and Baziotes's *Dwarf,* a mean-looking creature with saw teeth, a single large eye, and a prominent, visible uterus—to name only some. (One could easily expand the category to include works by Kirchner, Severini, Rouault, and others who depicted decadent, corrupt—and therefore *morally* monstrous—women.) In different ways, each of these works testifies to a pervasive fear of and ambivalence about woman. Openly expressed on the plane of culture, this fear and ambivalence, it seems to me, makes the central moral of modern art more intelligible—whether or not it tells us anything about the individual psyches of those who produced these works.

Even work that eschews such imagery and gives itself entirely to the drive for abstract, transcendent truth may also speak of these fears, in the very act of fleeing the realm of matter (*mater*) and biological need that is woman's traditional domain. How often modern masters have sought to make their work speak of *higher* realms—of air, light, the mind, the cosmos—realms that exist above a female, biological earth. Cubism, Kandinsky, Mondrian, the Futurists, Miró, the Abstract Expressionists—all drew artistic life from some nonmaterial energy of the self or the universe. (Léger's ideal of a rational, mechanical order can also be understood as opposed to—and a defense against—the unruly world of nature that it seeks to control.) The peculiar iconoclasm of much modern art, its renunciation of representation and the material world behind it, seems at least in part based in an impulse, common among modern males, to escape not the mother in any literal sense but a psychic image of woman and her earthly domain that seems rooted in infant or childish notions of the mother. Philip Slater noted an "unusual emphasis on mobility and flight as attributes of the hero who struggles against the menacing mother."[1] In the museum's ritual, the recurrent image of a menacing woman adds urgency to such flights to "higher" realms. Hence also the frequent appearance in written art history of monstrous or threatening women or, what is their obverse, powerless or vanquished women. Whether man-killer or murder victim, whether Picasso's deadly *Seated Bather* or Giacometti's *Woman with Her Throat Cut,* their presence both in the museum ritual and in the written (and illustrated) mythology is necessary. In both contexts, they provide the reason for the spiritual and mental flight. Confrontation and escape from them constitute the ordeal's dark center, a darkness that gives meaning and motive to the quest for enlightenment.

Since the heroes of this ordeal are generically men, the presence of women artists in this mythology can be only an anomaly. Women artists, especially if they exceed the standard token number, tend to degender the ritual ordeal. Accordingly, in the MoMA and other museums, their numbers are kept well below the point where they might effectively dilute the masculinity. The female presence is necessary only in the form of imagery. Of course men, too, are occasionally represented. But unlike women, who are seen primarily as sexually accessible bodies, men are portrayed as physically and mentally active beings who creatively shape their world and ponder its meanings. They make music and art, they stride, work, build cities, conquer the air through flight, think, and engage in sports (Cézanne, Rodin, Picasso, Matisse, Léger, La Fresnaye, Boccioni). When male sexuality is broached, it is often presented as the experience of highly self-conscious, psychologically complex beings whose sexual feelings are leavened with poetic pain, poignant frustration, heroic fear, protective irony, or the drive to make art (Picasso, de Chirico, Duchamp, Balthus, Delvaux, Bacon, Lindner).

De Kooning's *Woman I* and Picasso's *Demoiselles d'Avignon* are two of art history's most important female images. They are also key objects in the MoMA's collection and highly effective in maintaining the museum's masculinized environment.

The museum has always hung these works with precise attention to their strategic roles in the story of modern art. Both before and after the 1984 expansion, de Kooning's *Woman I* hung at the threshold to the spaces containing *the* big Abstract Expressionist "breakthroughs"—the New York school's final collective leap into absolutely pure, abstract, nonreferential transcendence: Pollock's artistic and psychic free flights, Rothko's sojourns in the luminous depths of a universal self, Newman's heroic confrontations with the sublime, Still's lonely journeys into the back beyond of culture and consciousness, Reinhardt's solemn and sardonic negations of all that is not Art, and so on. And always seated at the doorway to these moments of ultimate freedom and purity, and literally helping to frame them, has been *Woman I* [2]. So important is her presence just there, that when she has to go on loan, *Woman II* appears to take her place [3]. With good reason. De Kooning's *Women* are exceptionally successful ritual artifacts, and

they masculinize the museum's space with great efficiency.

The woman figure had been emerging gradually in de Kooning's work in the course of the 1940s. By 1951–52, it had fully revealed itself in *Woman I* as a big, bad mama—vulgar, sexual, and dangerous. De Kooning imagines her facing us with iconic frontality—large, bulging eyes; open, toothy mouth; massive breasts [4]. The suggestive pose is just a knee movement away from open-thighed display of the vagina, the self-exposing gesture of mainstream pornography.

These features are not unique in the history of art. They appear in ancient and tribal cultures, as well as in modern pornography and graffiti. Together, they constitute a well-known figure type. The Gorgon of ancient Greek art [5], an instance of that type, bears a striking resemblance to de Kooning's *Woman I* and, like her, simultaneously suggests and avoids the explicit act of sexual self-display that elsewhere characterizes the type. An Etruscan example [6] states more of its essential components as they appeared in a wide range of archaic and tribal cultures—not only the display of genitals, but

FIGURE 2 Willem de Kooning, *Woman I,* 1952, as installed in 1988. New York, Museum of Modern Art (*Carol Duncan*).

FIGURE 3 Willem de Kooning, *Woman II,* 1952, as installed in 1978. New York, Museum of Modern Art (*Carol Duncan*).

FIGURE 4 Willem de Kooning, *Woman I,* 1952. New York, Museum of Modern Art.

also the flanking animals that point to her origins as a fertility or mother goddess. Obviously, the configuration, with or without animals, carries complex symbolic possibilities and can convey many-sided, contradictory, and layered meanings. In her guise as the Gorgon witch, however, the terrible aspect of the mother goddess, her lust for blood and her deadly gaze, is emphasized. Especially today, when the myths and rituals that may have suggested other meanings have been lost—and when modern psychoanalytic ideas are likely to color any interpretation—the figure appears especially intended to conjure up infantile feelings of powerless-ness before the mother and the dread of castration: in the open jaw can be read the *vagina dentata*—the idea of a dangerous, devouring vagina, too horrible to depict, and hence transposed to the toothy mouth.

FIGURE 5 *Gorgon,* clay relief. Syracuse, National Museum.

Feelings of inadequacy and vulnerability before mature women are common (if not always salient) phenomena in male psychic development. Such myths as the story of Perseus and such visual images as the Gorgon can play a role in mediating that development by extending and re-treating on the cultural plane its core psychic experience and accompanying defenses. Thus objectified and communally shared in imagery, myth, and ritual, such individual fears and desires may achieve the status of higher, universal truth. In this sense, the

FIGURE 6 Etruscan *Gorgon,* drawing after a bronze carriage front. Munich, Museum Antiker Kleinkunst.

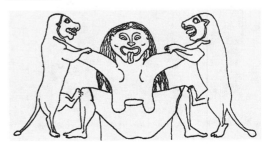

presence of Gorgons on Greek temples, important houses of cult worship (they also appeared on Christian church walls)—is paralleled by *Woman I*'s presence in a high-cultural house of the modern world.

The head of de Kooning's *Woman I* is so like that of the archaic Gorgon that the reference could well be intentional, especially since the artist and his friends placed great store in ancient myths and primitive images and likened themselves to archaic and tribal shamans. Writing about de Kooning's *Women*, Thomas Hess echoed this claim in a passage comparing de Kooning's artistic ordeal to that of Perseus, slayer of the Gorgon. Hess is arguing that de Kooning's *Women* grasp an elusive, dangerous truth "by the throat."

And truth can be touched only by complications, ambiguities and paradox, so, like the hero who looked for Medusa in the mirroring shield, he must study her flat, reflected image every inch of the way.[2]

But then again, the image type is so ubiquitous we needn't try to assign de Kooning's *Woman I* to any particular source in ancient or primitive art. *Woman I* can call up the Medusa as easily as the other way around. Whatever de Kooning knew or sensed about the Gorgon's meanings, and however much or little he took from it, the image type is decidedly present in his work. Suffice it to say that de Kooning was aware, and indeed explicitly claimed, that his *Women* could be assimilated to the long history of goddess imagery.[3] By choosing to place such figures at the center of his most ambitious artistic efforts, he secured for his work an aura of ancient mystery and authority.

The *Woman* is not only monumental and iconic. In high-heeled shoes and brassiere, she is also lewd, her pose indecently teasing. De Kooning acknowledged her oscillating character, claiming for her a likeness not only to serious art—ancient icons and high-art nudes—but also to pinups and girlie pictures of the vulgar

present. He saw her as simultaneously frightening and ludicrous.[4] The ambiguity of the figure, its power to resemble an awesome mother goddess as well as a modern burlesque queen, provides a fine cultural, psychological, and artistic field in which to enact the modern myth of the artist-hero—the hero whose spiritual ordeal becomes the stuff of ritual in the public space of the museum. As a powerful and threatening woman, it is she who must be confronted and transcended—gotten past on the way to enlightenment. At the same time, her vulgarity, her, "girlie" side—de Kooning called it her "silliness"—renders her harmless (or is it contemptible?) and denies the terror and dread of her Medusa features. The ambiguity of the image thus gives the artist (and the viewer) both the experience of danger and a feeling of overcoming it. Meanwhile, the suggestion of pornographic self-display—more explicit in de Kooning's later work but certainly present here—specifically addresses itself to the male viewer. With it, de Kooning knowingly and assertively exercises his patriarchal privilege of objectifying male sexual fantasy as high culture.

An interesting drawing/photomontage by the California artist Robert Heinecken, *Invitation to Metamorphosis* [7], similarly explores the ambiguities of a Gorgon-girlie image. Here the effect of ambiguity is achieved by the use of masks and by combining and superimposing separate negatives. Heinecken's version of the self-displaying woman is a composite consisting of a conventional pornographic nude and a Hollywood movie-type monster. As a well-qualified Gorgon, her attributes include an open, toothy mouth, carnivorous animal jaws, huge bulging eyes, large breasts, exposed genitals, and one very nasty-looking claw. Her body is simultaneously naked and draped, enticing and repulsive, and the second head, to the left of the Gorgon head—the one with the seductive smile—also wears a mask. Like the de Kooning work, Heinecken's *Invitation* sets up a psychologically unstable atmosphere fraught

FIGURE 7   Robert Heinecken, *Invitation to Metamorphosis,* emulsion on canvas and pastel chalk, 1975 (*Robert Heinecken*).

with deception, allure, danger, and wit. The image's various components continually disappear into and reappear out of one another. Behaving something like de Kooning's layered paint surfaces, they invite ever-shifting, multiple readings. In both works, what is covered becomes exposed, what is opaque becomes transparent, and what is revealed conceals something else. Both works fuse the terrible killer-witch with the willing and exhibitionist whore. Both fear and seek danger in desire, and both kid the danger.

Of course before de Kooning or Heinecken created ambiguous self-displaying women, there was Picasso's *Demoiselles d'Avignon* of 1907 [1]. The work was conceived as an extraordinarily ambitious statement—it aspires to revelation— about the meaning of Woman. In it, all women belong to a universal category of being, existing across time and place. Picasso used ancient and tribal art to reveal woman's universal mystery: Egyptian and Iberian sculpture on the left, and African art on the right. The figure on the

lower right looks as if it was directly inspired by some primitive or archaic deity. Picasso would have known such figures from his visits to the ethnographic art collections in the Trocadero. A study for the work in the Musée Picasso in Paris [8] closely follows the type's symmetrical, self-displaying pose. Significantly, Picasso wanted her to be prominent—she is the nearest and largest of all the figures. At this stage, Picasso also planned to include a male student on the left and, in the axial center of the composition, a sailor—a figure of horniness incarnate. The self-displaying woman was to have faced him, her display of genitals turned away from the viewer.

In the finished work, the male presence has been removed from the image and relocated in the viewing space before it. What began as a depicted male-female confrontation thus became a confrontation between viewer and image. The relocation has pulled the lower right-hand figure completely around, so that her stare and her sexually inciting act, although not detailed and less symmetrical than before, are now directed outward. Picasso thus isolated and monumentalized the ultimate men-only situation. As restructured, the work forcefully asserts to both men and women the privileged status of male viewers—they alone are intended to experience the full impact of this most revelatory moment.[5] It also assigns women to a visitors' gallery where they may watch but not enter the central arena of high culture.

Finally, the mystery that Picasso unveils about women is also an art-historical lesson. In the finished work, the women have become stylistically differentiated so that one looks not only at present-tense whores but also back down into the ancient and primitive past, with the art of "darkest Africa" and works representing the beginnings of Western culture (Egyptian and Iberian idols) placed on a single spectrum. Thus does Picasso use art history to argue his thesis: that the awesome goddess, the terrible

FIGURE 8   Pablo Picassso, study for *Les Demoiselles d'Avignon*, 1907. Paris, Musée Picasso. (Oeffentliche Kunstsammlung Basel, Kupferstichkabinett/Oeffentliche Kunstsammlung Basel, Martin Bühler)

witch, and the lewd whore are but facets of a single many-sided creature, in turn threatening and seductive, imposing and self-abasing, dominating and powerless—and always the psychic property of a male imagination. Picasso also implies that truly great, powerful, and revelatory art has always been and must be built upon such exclusively male property.

The museum's installation amplifies the already powerful meanings of the work. Mounted on a freestanding wall in the center of the first Cubist gallery, the painting seizes your attention the moment you turn into the room—the placement of the doorway makes it appear suddenly and dramatically. Physically dominating this intimately scaled gallery, the installation dramatizes the painting's role as progenitor of the surrounding Cubist works and their subsequent art-historical issue. So central is the work to the structure of MoMA's program that recently, when the painting was on loan, the museum felt compelled to post a notice on the freestanding wall explaining the

work's absence—but also invoking its presence. In a gesture unusual for the MoMA, the notice was illustrated by a tiny color reproduction of the missing monument.

The works by de Kooning and Heinecken that I have discussed, along with similar works by many other modern artists, benefit from and reinforce the status won by the *Demoiselles*. They also develop its theme, drawing out different emphases. One of the elements they develop more explicitly than did Picasso is that of pornography. By way of exploring how that pornographic element works in the museum context, I want to look first at how it works outside the museum.

Last year, an advertisement for *Penthouse* magazine appeared on New York City bus-stop shelters [9]. New York City bus shelters are often decorated with near-naked women and sometimes men advertising everything from underwear to real estate. But this was an ad for pornographic images as such—that is, images designed not to sell perfume or bathing suits, but to stimulate erotic desire, primarily in men. Given its provocative intent, the image generates very different and—I think for almost

FIGURE 9   Bus-stop shelter on Fifty-seventh Street, New York City, with advertisement for *Penthouse* magazine, 1988 (*Carol Duncan*).

everyone—more charged meanings than the ads for underwear. At least one passerby had already recorded in red spray paint a terse but coherent response: "For Pigs."

Having a camera with me, I decided to take a shot of it. But as I set about focusing, I began to feel uncomfortable and self-conscious. As I realized only later, I was experiencing some prohibition in my own conditioning, activated not simply by the nature of the ad but by the act of photographing such an ad in public. Even though the anonymous inscription had made it socially safer to photograph—it placed it in a conscious and critical discourse about gender—to photograph it was still to appropriate openly a kind of image that middle-class morality says I'm not supposed to look at or have. But before I could sort that out, a group of boys jumped into the frame. Plainly, they intended to intervene. Did I know what I was doing? one asked me with an air I can only call stern, while another admonished me that I was photographing a *Penthouse* ad—as if I would not knowingly do such a thing.

Apparently, the same culture that had conditioned me to feel uneasy about what I was doing also made *them* uneasy about it. Boys this age know very well what's in *Penthouse*. Knowing what's in *Penthouse* is knowing something meant for men to know; therefore, knowing *Penthouse* is a way of knowing oneself to be a man, or at least a man-to-be, at precisely an age when one needs all the help one can get. I think these boys were trying to protect the capacity of the ad to empower them as men by preventing me from appropriating an image of it. For them, as for many men, the chief (if not the only) value and use of pornography is this power to confirm gender identity and, with that, gender superiority. Pornography affirms their manliness to themselves and to others and proclaims the greater social power of men. Like some ancient and primitive objects forbidden to the female gaze,

the ability of pornography to give its users a feeling of superior male status depends on its being owned or controlled by men and forbidden to, shunned by, or hidden from, women. In other words, in certain situations a female gaze can *pollute* pornography. These boys, already imprinted with the rudimentary gender codes of the culture, knew an infringement when they saw one. (Perhaps they suspected me of defacing the ad.) Their harassment of me constituted an attempt at gender policing, something adult men routinely do to women on city streets.

Not so long ago, such magazines were sold only in sleazy porn stores. Today ads for them can decorate mid-town thoroughfares. Of course, the ad as well as the magazine cover cannot itself be pornography and still be legal (in practice, that tends to mean it can't show genitals), but to work as an ad it must *suggest* it. For different reasons, works of art like de Kooning's *Woman I* or Heinecken's *Invitation* also refer to without actually being pornography—they depend on the viewer "getting" the reference but must stop there. Given those requirements, it shouldn't surprise us that the artists' visual strategies have parallels in the ad [10]. *Woman I* shares a number of features with the ad. Both present frontal, iconic, massive figures seen close up—they fill, even overflow, the picture surface. The photograph's low camera angle and the painting's scale and composition monumentalize and elevate the figures, literally or imaginatively dwarfing the viewer. Painting and photograph alike concentrate attention on head, breasts, and torso. Arms serve to frame the body, while legs are either cropped or, in the de Kooning, undersized and feeble. The figures thus appear powerful and powerless at the same time, with massive bodies made to rest on unstable, weakly rendered, tentatively placed legs. And with both, the viewer is positioned to see it all should the thighs open. And of course, on *Penthouse* pages, thighs do little else but

FIGURE 10 Advertisement for *Penthouse,* using a photograph by Bob Guccione, April 1988 (*Penthouse*).

open. But de Kooning's hot mama has a very different purpose and cultural status from a *Penthouse* "pet."

De Kooning's *Woman I* conveys much more complex and emotionally ambivalent meanings. The work acknowledges more openly the fear of and flight from as well as a quest for the woman. Moreover de Kooning's *Woman I* is always upstaged by the artist's self-display *as an artist*. The manifest purpose of a *Penthouse* photo is, presumably, to arouse desire. If the de Kooning awakens desire in relation to the female body, it does so in order to deflate or conquer its power of attraction and escape its

danger. The viewer is invited to relive a struggle in which the realm of art provides escape from the female's degraded allure. As mediated by art criticism, de Kooning's work speaks ultimately not of male fear but of the triumph of art and a self-creating spirit. In the critical literature, the *Women* figures themselves become catalysts or structural supports for the work's more significant meanings: the artist's heroic self-searching, his existentialist courage, his pursuit of a new pictorial structure or some other artistic or transcendent end.

The work's pornographic moment, now subsumed to its high-cultural import, may (unlike the *Penthouse* ad) do its ideological work with unchallenged prestige and authority. In building their works on a pornographic base and triggering in both men and women deepseated feelings about gender identity and difference, de Kooning, Heinecken, and other artists (most notoriously, David Salle) exercise a privilege that our society has traditionally conferred upon men only. Through their imagery, they lay claim to public space as a realm under masculine control. Transformed into art and displayed in the public space of the museum, the self-displaying poses affirm to male viewers their membership in the more powerful gender group. They also remind women that their status as members of the community, their right to its public space, their share in the common, culturally defined identity, is not quite the same—is somehow less equal—than men's. But these signals must be covert, hidden under the myth of the transcendent artist-hero. Even de Kooning's later *Women* figures, which more openly invite comparison to pornographic photography and graffiti [11], qualify the reference; the closer to pornography, the more overlaid they must be with unambiguously "artistic" gestures and philosophically significant impastos.

Nevertheless, what is true in the street may not be so untrue in the museum, even

FIGURE 11   Willem de Kooning (1904–1997). *The Visit.* 1966–67. © Tate Gallery, London/Art Resource, NY.

though different rules of decorum may make it seem so. Inside or outside, such images wield great authority, structuring and reinforcing the psychic codes that determine and differentiate the real possibilities of women and men.

NOTES

1. Philip Slater, *The Glory of Hera* (Boston, 1968), p. 321.

2. Thomas B. Hess, *Willem de Kooning* (New York, 1959), p. 7. See also Hess, *Willem de Kooning: Drawings* (New York and Greenwich, Conn., 1972), p. 27, on a de Kooning drawing of Elaine de Kooning (ca. 1942) in which the writer finds the features of Medusa—a "menacing" stare and intricate, animated "Medusa hair."

3. As he once said, "The *Women* had to do with the female painted through all the ages. . . . Painting the *Woman* is a thing in art that has been done over and over—the idol, Venus, the nude." Quoted in *Willem de Kooning: The North Atlantic Light, 1960–1983*, exh. cat., Stedelijk Museum, Amsterdam; Louisiana Museum of Modern Art, Humlebaek; and the Moderna Museet, Stockholm, 1983. Sally Yard, "Willem de Kooning's Women," *Arts* 53 (November 1975): 96–101, argues several sources for the *Women* paintings, including Cycladic idols, Sumerian votive figures, Byzantine icons, and Picasso's *Demoiselles*.

4. *Willem de Kooning: The North Atlantic Light* (cited n. 3), p. 77. See also Hess, *Willem de Kooning*, 1959 (cited n. 2), pp. 21 and 29.

5. See, for example, Leo Steinberg, "The Philosophical Brothel," *Art News*, September 1972, pp. 25–26. In Steinberg's ground-breaking reading, the act of looking at these female figures visually re-creates the act of sexually penetrating a woman. The implication is that women are anatomically unequipped to experience the work's full meaning.

Women and Religion

Virginia Sapiro

In 1780 Judith Sargent Murray, an American writer and the daughter of a minister, argued against interpretations of Scripture presenting women as inferior and dangerous. In 1837 the English social observer Harriet Martineau argued that American women's morals were crushed by the repressive teachings of religion. In 1848 the participants at the Seneca Falls convention, a meeting often described as the beginning of the American feminist movement, denounced the treatment of women by organized churches. In the 1880s Elizabeth Cady Stanton, Matilda Joslyn Gage, and many other feminists published attacks on church teachings about women. Emma Goldman declared organized religion one of the most vile oppressors of both men and women. In the 1970s Mary Daly, then a professor of theology at a Roman Catholic college, argued that male religious authorities are guilty of gynocide—murder of women—physically, psychologically, and morally.

American feminists have long criticized organized religion for oppression of women. But American feminist history also includes uncountable figures such as Sarah and Angelina Grimké, Lucretia Mott, and Elizabeth Cady Stanton, who recognized that they derived their political principles, strength and bravery, and their speaking and organizing skills from their religions. Many women have fought from the inside to transform their religions and have demanded the opportunity to become religious leaders and authorities. Others have sought alternative forms of religion more suited to their principles of equality and freedom.

Organized religion is one of the most powerful institutions involved in shaping people's beliefs, attitudes, values, and behavior. Gender is such an important part of the theology, cultural precepts, ceremonies, and rituals of most religions that we could not understand the institutional roots of sex/gender systems without analyzing the role of religion. To do this we look first at teachings about women, gender, and sexuality in the major American religions. We then turn to the role of women in shaping religion and the ways in which women have influenced society through their religious activities. Before examining these issues, however, we must first consider some difficulties involved in any discussion of religion.

"Organized religion" is not a single, homogeneous entity. Even within a single family of religions such as Christianity, we find substantial differences among denominations. Quakers and Roman Catholics are both Christians, both believe in a single deity that sent a son to earth, and both use the Old and New Testaments of the Bible as their chief texts, but beyond this they diverge widely, especially on issues of gender. Nevertheless we cannot consider all American religions in detail here because there are scores of them, ranging from those with millions of members to those with a couple thousand or fewer. Our discussion is limited to considering the denominations that have had the most widespread influence on American society and values because of either their size or their distinctive roles.

Studying religion in American society poses some unique problems and questions. Unlike many other countries the United States does not have an established or national religion.

Even more important, the principles of American law call for a "wall of separation" between religion and government. Despite this wall, foreign observers are often amazed by the central role religion plays not only in the personal life of Americans but also in public life.

Surveys in the mid 1970s showed that 58% of all Americans considered their religious beliefs very important compared with 36% each of Italians and Canadians, 23% of Britons, 22% of French, and 17% of Germans. Moreover, 94% of Americans claimed to believe in God, compared with 89% of Canadians, 88% of Italians, 76% of Britons, and 72% each of French and Germans. And 40% of all Americans claim to go to church regularly. During the 1980s and 1990s religious sentiment rose throughout the country. . . . The majority of Americans find religion a very important part of their lives, and almost half derive day-to-day guidance from religion. . . . Also, at least on some questions, women express greater religiosity than men. They are more likely to find religion important in their lives, pray regularly, and read the Bible. More women than men interpret the Bible as the literal word of God.

Americans do not just find their religions personally important; many believe that religion should play a large role in guiding culture and politics. Indeed, despite the traditional American notion of a wall between religion and government, 34% of Americans say that they favor a constitutional amendment making Christianity the official religion of the United States. This attitude is particularly widespread among Protestants, individuals with less than a high school education, and blacks. The theoretical wall separating church and state is very porous and flexible in practice. Thus it is especially important to understand how religion shapes gender norms and behavior.

Although the long history of each religion is important for understanding its contemporary ideas and practices, we will look primarily at the American religious experience. We will

not ask what Jesus and Paul really said or meant but what American Christians have thought they said and meant, and how these interpretations affect American life. We will not ask about the forms patriarchal principles took among the ancient Israelites but will explore the norms of American Jews.

RELIGIOUS TEACHINGS ABOUT WOMEN AND GENDER

Religion offers guidelines for moral behavior and thought. In many cases, religion prescribes considerably more than simple guidelines, of course; some doctrines are rules that must be followed for fear of punishment. Religious institutions are like social institutions in an important way: They provide both explicit rules and more generalized norms that people internalize and enforce on themselves.

The Bible is an important source of moral norms for both Christians and Jews, but different denominations find very different messages in this same text. Mormons, for example, referred to the biblical patriarchs to support the institution of polygamy until polygamy was made illegal by an act of Congress. Other Christians and Jews, revering the same patriarchs in the same Bible, have regarded polygamy as uncivilized and sinful or contrary to God's law. Orthodox and many Conservative Jews still follow the laws on female pollution found in Leviticus, which defines a woman's natural bodily functions as unclean and prescribes purification rituals. Other denominations, including many that claim to accept literal biblical dictates, do not enforce these biblical laws even if they still think menstruating women are unclean. Muslims base their beliefs on a different book, the Koran, but its words are also interpreted in different ways.

Despite these differences, there are some remarkable similarities among various denominations' traditional views on gender. Among these are the beliefs that (1) women and men have different missions and different standards of behavior and (2) although women and men are equal in the eyes of the deity, women are to some degree subordinated to men. Let us look in more detail at religious definitions of gender and some of the changes now taking place. We begin with a discussion of images of God and then turn to religious prescriptions for everyday life and morality for women. This section ends with a look at some new and alternative views of women.

God Talk: Is It Male?

God the Father. God the King and Lord. The Father, the Son, and the Holy Ghost. If we believe the words used in Judaism, Christianity, or Islam to describe God, the deity is male. Some people argue that the use of *He* to refer to God is a generic term, but it is difficult to say the same of *Father, Lord*, and *King*. To see the importance of "he" words in religion, try taking a religious text or prayer and substituting female-gender words. Think about your reactions as you hear yourself refer to God as *She, the Queen,* or *my Lady*. Adults are not supposed to make the "childish" error of anthropomorphism, that is, seeing God as a human being. Even theological sophistication, however, is not a sufficiently powerful force to eliminate what we might call "andromorphism." God may not be human like us, but "he" is still male.

The gender images of Jesus in Christian theology and tradition are especially interesting. Whereas the character attributed to God has generally been unambiguously masculine, the character of Jesus is considerably more androgynous. God's compassion is often described as *fatherly*, a term that seems less appropriate to describe the compassion of Jesus. Although Jesus was male, his unfailing gentleness, humility, simplicity, and nonviolence; his healing qualities and immediately forgiving nature; and his suffering for others are usually regarded as feminine. Nevertheless, the fact that

Jesus and the disciples were male has often been used to argue that women should not hold the highest positions of religious authority. Many leaders in the Anglican and Episcopal churches used this view to argue against the installation of the first female bishop in the Episcopal church in 1989.

Religious language helps define our conception of God, authority, goodness, and holiness. If God is a Father but not a Mother, that says something not just about our conception of God but also about our conceptions of fathers and mothers and, by extension, men and women. Religious language and thought teaches us not just about our religions but about other aspects of life as well. If we look at American history, we can see the crucial role religion has played in defining the roles of women in American life and culture.

Defining Male and Female

Religion played a crucial role in the formation of American ideology on gender as well as other things during the colonial and early post-Revolution eras. Although the Anglican colonials of the South had a somewhat less stern outlook than the Puritans of the North, a literal reading of the Bible and a patriarchal view of God and society were important bases of thought in either case. When people learned to read, their text was the Bible; even if they could not read, they learned their lessons in church each Sunday or, if they were farther from "civilization," from the traveling preacher.

The Puritans based their views of women on the Old Testament and their interpretation of the patriarchal ancient Hebrew values. Woman's purpose was to be a helpmate for her husband, to be fruitful and to multiply. Both men and women must fear God and Satan (although in different ways), but women should also be submissive to their husbands, the moral authority of the household. Women's work, especially the pain of childbirth, was viewed by

Christians as a punishment for Eve's insubordination: "I will increase your labor and your pain, and in labor you shall bear children. You shall be eager for your husband, and he shall be your master" (Gen. 3:16).[1]

Puritans and others found more warnings for women to submit themselves to their husbands in the New Testament: "For man did not originally spring from woman, but woman was made out of man; and man was not created for woman's sake, but woman for the sake of man" (1 Cor. 11:8–10). Women should be silent in church and learn from their husbands (1 Cor. 14:34–35; 1 Tim. 2:9–15). "Wives, be subject to your husbands as to the Lord; for the man is the head of the woman, just as Christ also is the head of the Church. Christ is, indeed, the Savior of the body; but just as the church is subject to Christ, so must women be to their husbands in everything" (Eph. 5:22–24). Although more egalitarian than other denominations in matters concerning public speaking, even the gentle Friends, or Quakers, accepted the patriarchal view that man is to woman what Christ is to humans.

Religion and the Bible provided examples of female character to serve as lessons for all, particularly in the persons of Eve and Mary. Religious people found proof in Genesis that woman was created as man's auxiliary and also that woman is likely both to sin and to tempt men to sin if left to her own devices. The main lesson of this story has been that if women are not controlled they will reenact the Fall. Rather than providing a maternal image (as the mother of us all), Eve has come to represent woman's treachery. Although Jews interpret the story of the Garden of Eden somewhat differently from Christians (neither the Fall nor Original Sin are part of Jewish theology), women and men are customarily separated in Orthodox synagogues because of the belief that women would otherwise distract men from their piety. In Islam this separation is achieved through veiling and *purdah*.

Within the Christian tradition (especially among Roman Catholics) the primary contrasting female image to Eve is Mary, the mother of Jesus, who, according to some Catholic traditions, was conceived without sin (that is, without recourse to sexual relations) and who most Christians believe conceived Jesus "without sin." She is the ideal woman and, most important for understanding religious norms of womanhood, an unattainable ideal. Although the cult of the Virgin has perhaps never taken hold in the United States to the same degree that it has elsewhere, Mary is a powerful model in Christian life.

Biblical stories are interpreted differently by different people and traditions. Many Jewish and Christian feminists have reinterpreted the story of Eve; they see her as the person responsible for making humans capable of knowledge of good and evil. Jewish feminists have rehabilitated Vashti in the book of Esther in the Apocrypha. Vashti was rejected as a wife by King Ahasuerus in favor of Esther because Vashti refused to dance before her husband and his drunken friends at a party. The feminist intention is not to diminish Esther's accomplishments, but rather to reject the assumption that women who do not unquestioningly submit to their husband are bad. Other commentators point to additional female religious models such as Deborah, the judge, or Ruth and Naomi.

Despite these alternative stories and interpretations, the predominant message of most religions is that women and men have very different roles and characters; that religious authority speaks mostly in a male voice; and that woman's primary role is to accept that authority and to bear and raise children.

It is important to understand how religions presumably dedicated to holiness and justice support such a system of inequality and submission. Many religious authorities of different denominations have argued that the enforcement of these differences does not create or enforce inequality. They argue that although men and women are different they are equal in value in the eyes of God. For denominations with a concept of heaven, religious teachings claim that by fulfilling their different duties women and men earn equal places in heaven. Some religions simply believe that God designed women as inferior beings. Changes in the texts and practices of many denominations over the past century show that the religious principles of female inferiority are being abandoned.

Religious teachings also have direct effects on gender ideology and attitudes toward women. Historically, theologians have elaborated on the theme of separate spheres and characters for women and men and have equated preservation of women's place with preservation of morality and of a civilized (and American) way of life. A sermon delivered in 1837 by a Presbyterian minister demonstrates the degree to which regulation of women's sphere, Christian morality, and attitudes toward civilization were intricately intertwined. The preservation of the moral order, he argued, depended on the preservation of distinct spheres for men and women. Women were responsible for determining whether civilization would rise or fall. Addressing women, he said,

Yours it is to decide, under God, whether we shall be a nation of refined and high-minded Christians, or whether, rejecting the civilities of life, and throwing off the restraints of morality and purity, we should become a fierce race of semi-barbarians, before whom neither order, nor honor, nor chastity can stand (Kraditor 1968, 50).

The morality of separate spheres for the sexes, with women's spheres subordinate to men's, has remained an important religious theme; there are numerous examples of God being called on to reinforce limitations placed on women. In 1887 Senator George Vest of Missouri argued against women's suffrage on the floor of the Senate by saying, "I do not believe that the Great Intelligence ever intended [women] to invade the sphere of work given to

men, tearing down and destroying all the best influences for which God has intended them" (quoted in Kraditor 1968, 195). Making a similar point at the turn of the century, President Grover Cleveland argued, "I believe that trust in Divine Wisdom, and ungrudging submission to divine purposes, will enable dutiful men and women to know the places assigned to them, and will incite them to act well in their parts in the sight of God" (Kraditor 1968, 200). And Senator Sam Ervin called God into battle against the Equal Rights Amendment. During the national discussion of "family values" surrounding the 1992 election, many representatives of the religious political right emphasized that many of the recent changes in women's roles brought with them the destruction of the moral fiber of the country.

The predominant message of most religious denominations has been that both women and men are to be carefully restricted to their distinct spheres and that women's roles on earth are to be good wives and mothers and to preserve traditional moral values, especially the modesty and domesticity of women. The punishments of religious women who transgressed the boundaries of these spheres have been enormous, including death (during colonial times for witchcraft and homosexuality), damnation to hell, separation from the religious community, and charges of responsibility for the downfall of a religion or of civilization as a whole.

Because of these views religious organizations and clergy have often played active roles in resisting feminism. In the 19th century, for example, many church leaders criticized women for publicly speaking on behalf of reform movements. Citing the biblical injunction "suffer women not to speak," some wrote, "We cannot . . . but regret the mistaken conduct of those who encourage females to bear an obtrusive and ostentatious part in measures of reform, and countenance any of that sex who so forget themselves as to itinerate in the character of public lecturers and teachers" (quoted in Rossi 1988, 305–6).

If public speaking was unfeminine, for many church leaders the idea of women's suffrage was even worse. In 1869 an American Transcendentalist leader said, "The conclusive objection to the political enfranchisement is that it would weaken and finally break up and destroy the Christian family" (quoted in Kraditor 1968, 192). "Let the hand which rocks the cradle teach the coming young men and women of America the Lord's Prayer and the Ten Commandments," said a New York politician in 1894, "and you will do more for your emancipation . . . than you can do with both hands full of white ballots" (Kraditor 1968, 198).

Religious organizations have been leading opponents of divorce reform, liberalization of birth control and abortion, educational policies that would reform gender messages in textbooks and make sex education part of the curriculum, legislation supporting civil rights for homosexuals, and the Equal Rights Amendment. In the first decades of the 20th century, some religious organizations opposed the reforms urged by feminist and progressive groups on the grounds that they were socialist and therefore antireligious. Contemporary studies of antifeminist activist groups show that participants in those groups share the characteristics of being particularly attached to religion and particularly antagonistic to communism.

Numerous politically and socially active women have been individually punished or reprimanded by their churches such as Anne Hutchinson and Lucy Stone (1818–1893), who was expelled from the Congregational church for her abolitionist activity. In the 1980s the Mormon church excommunicated Sonia Johnson for her support of the Equal Rights Amendment. In 1983 the Catholic church gave Agnes Mary Mansour the choice of resigning her post as director of social services in Michigan or dismissal from her order of nuns for tolerating the use of federal funds for abortions. She left

the order. In many cases these women were rebuked precisely because they claimed to derive their "deviant" views from their religious values; in these cases they were punished for coming to their own conclusions about spirituality and religiosity.

Research continues to show that religious beliefs help shape people's view of gender and women's roles. Consider the evidence in Table 1, which looks at the relationship between fundamentalist beliefs, religiosity, and attitudes toward gender equality in government, the economy, and the family. It shows that fundamentalists, those who see the Bible as the literal word of God, are more likely than other people to think that men should have more power than women in government, the economy, and the family. It also shows that people who claim they find a great deal of guidance from religion in their day-to-day lives are also more likely to believe in male dominance. If we look at the combined effects of these different aspects of religious belief, we see substantial support for male dominance among religious fundamentalists.

Religious organizations have also helped foster women's activism and even, at times, feminism. Many of the 19th-century suffragists were very involved in their religious communities. In recent decades, women have been actively involved in religion-based feminism. But the power of women to define their own terms, goals, and activities in conventional religious institutions has usually been limited; if their message provided too clear an alternative to traditional religious teachings, they found themselves opposed by the higher, male authorities.

Morality, Sexuality, and Gender

Religious authority regulates sexual morality in ways that have profound effects on women and men and that help further define gender and gender difference. Most denominations regard marriage as the cornerstone of the sexual, moral, and, therefore, social order. . . . Marital law is based very heavily on traditional

TABLE 1   Attitudes Toward Gender Equality, by Religious Fundamentalism and Personal Importance of Religion, 1991

	RELIGION HAS MODERATE/LITTLE IMPORTANCE		RELIGION HAS GREAT IMPORTANCE	
	NOT FUNDAMENTALIST	FUNDAMENTALIST	NOT FUNDAMENTALIST	FUNDAMENTALIST
Men should have more power and influence than women in government and politics.	8	20	21	41
Men should have more power and influence than women in business and industry.	11	22	25	34
Men should have more power and influence that women in the family.	3	16	11	28

Note: People who said that religion provides "a great deal of guidance" in their day-to-day lives are in the Religion Has Great Importance category. Those who agree that "the Bible is God's word and all it says is true" are categorized as fundamentalists. Numbers show proportion of people in each religion category who agreed with the statement to the left. Based on N = 467.
Source: 1991 American National Election Study Pilot Study, analysis by author.

religious views and law. Although their specific views of sexuality and sexual practices vary, most denominations agree that sexual relations may appropriately and rightfully take place only within marriage between a man and a woman. Many—probably most—believe that the primary, if not sole, purpose of sexual relations is reproduction. Two of the Ten Commandments serve as authority here; one forbids adultery, and one forbids a man to covet his neighbor's wife, house, slaves, or other possessions. Notice that the latter not only defines proper sexual relations but also reinforces the idea that women are men's (sexual) property. For some denominations, such as the Roman Catholic church, reproduction is the sole moral reason for sexual activity.

This moral link between sexuality and reproduction has had two important implications. The first is that if only sexual acts that could result in conception are natural and good, sexual acts that could not result in offspring are unnatural and bad. Christians and Jews alike have used religious authority to forbid homosexuality (Lev. 18:22; 1 Cor. 6:9–11), although church authorities were more vigilant in suppressing homosexuality during some historical periods (e.g., the 12th, 13th, and 19th centuries) than in others. American laws against sodomy were based directly on religious teaching and sometimes used the language of the Bible. Although sodomy laws are usually discussed in reference to homosexual activities, they also applied to (and were originally enforced against) heterosexual acts that could not result in conception. These laws were serious in their consequences; early in American history some homosexual acts were punishable by death. The Bible also has been used to declare masturbation (Gen. 38:3–10) and transvestism (Deut. 22:5) sinful and wrong.

Among the mainstream Christian denominations, only the United Church of Christ fully accepts homosexual ministers. Events within the Presbyterian church exemplify the kind of debates and conflicts that have taken place in many denominations in recent years. In 1991 a task force report argued that the Presbyterian church should not condemn sexual acts outside marriage—regardless of whether they involved two people of the same sex or not—if the acts were mutual and caring. Later the same year the Human Sexuality Committee successfully recommended that the Presbyterian General Assembly reject the task force report. In 1992 the highest court of the Presbyterian church nullified the hiring of a lesbian pastor by one church, although it said that if she were celibate she could be hired. At the same time it said an "unrepentent homosexual" could not be ordained. That same year the generally liberal National Council of Churches decided in a divided vote not to give "observer status" to the mostly gay and lesbian Universal Fellowship of Metropolitan Churches, a denomination with about 50,000 members. The most active opposition came from the Eastern Orthodox churches, some of the African American denominations, and the Korean Presbyterian church.

The second implication of basing sexual morality on its reproductive function is that the practice of birth control is considered wrong. Roman Catholic authorities remain adamant that any form of "artificial" birth control is sinful. Most Protestant denominations and Jews, however, officially leave the decision about whether to conceive to individual choice, although many religious authorities informally discourage the use of contraception. Unitarian churches, on the other hand, have often taken very strong stands in favor of birth control.

Abortion is an even more difficult issue than birth control because it involves terminating life that has already begun. Historically, theologians and the common law generally viewed abortion as murder only after quickening of the fetus took place (i.e., when the fetus moves), and abortion was generally tolerated within the first 40 days after conception. In 1869 Pope Pius IX changed the position of the Catholic church, declaring almost all abortions murder and therefore sinful. According to Catholic doctrine it is not acceptable to terminate a life pur-

posely, even to save another life. The Catholic church has remained firm on its stands on both birth control and abortion, although there is widespread controversy within the church, and some Catholics have felt particularly alienated from their religion because of its stands on these matters. Catholics can even be found in the highest ranks of the National Abortion Rights League, an interest group dedicated to reproductive choice for women.

Religions further regulate sexuality and social relations by dictating who may and may not get married. The Bible enumerates forbidden marriages, such as those considered incestuous. Many religious authorities do not allow interfaith marriage within their communities unless the "outsider" agrees to convert or unless they agree to raise the children in their religion. God's law has been used to bar sexual relations and marriage between people of different races (miscegenation), as this quotation from a Virginia court case in the 1960s shows: "Almighty God created the races white, black, yellow, malay, and red, and he placed them on separate continents. And but for the interference with his arrangement there would be no cause for such marriages. The fact that he separated the races shows that he did not intend for the races to mix."[2]

Most denominations have long supported the idea of personal choice with respect to divorce, at least to some degree, although the Eastern Orthodox, Episcopal, Mormon, and Roman Catholic churches have generally held that marriages are indissoluble. Many denominations do not permit divorce except on strict grounds of adultery or desertion; many religious authorities will not remarry a divorced person unless that person was the "innocent" party in the divorce or the ex-spouse is dead. Some denominations (e.g., Congregationalists, Christian Scientists, Jews, and Unitarians) leave the question of divorce to the conscience of the individuals involved; others (e.g., Baptists and Disciples of Christ) leave it to the conscience of the minister.

We should not overestimate the impact of sexually repressive religious teachings on people's behavior. Historians have found ample evidence of "prematurely conceived" (as opposed to prematurely birthed) babies throughout American history. Indeed, even among the sterner of American clergy, attitudes toward sexuality were not necessarily as repressive as they are sometimes painted. Some Puritan ministers carefully pointed out that they differed from Roman Catholics by not extolling the virtues of virginity to the same degree, even while they condemned sex outside marriage. Historian Edmund Morgan found that "the Puritans were not ascetics; they never wished to prevent the enjoyment of earthly delights. They merely demanded that the pleasures of the flesh be subordinated to the greater glory of God: husband and wife must not become 'so transported with affection, that they look at no higher end than marriage itself'" ([1944] 1978, 364). Morgan even found evidence that a church expelled one of its male members for denying "congiugall fellowship unto his wife for the space of 2 years."

Nevertheless, the conflict between being holy and experiencing sexual feelings is an important theme throughout the history of sexuality and religion. Witness, for example, the sentiments expressed in a love letter the feminist Quaker Angelina Grimké wrote to her husband-to-be in 1838:

Ought God to be all in all to us on earth? I tho't so, and am frightened to find that He is not, that is, I feel something else is necessary to my happiness. I laid awake thinking why it was that my heart longed and panted and reached after you as it does. Why my Savior and my God is not enough to satisfy me. Am I sinning, am I ungrateful, am I an IDOLATOR? (Rossi 1988, 289)

The Roman Catholic church further emphasizes a conflict between sexuality and holiness by maintaining that those who dedicate their lives to God by becoming priests or nuns must remain celibate. This rule of celibacy has somewhat different connotations for women and men. Nuns wear wedding rings to symbolize their marriage to Christ. Priests, of course, are not married to Christ; such a relationship, even if spiritual, would imply the sin of homosexuality. It is interesting to note the importance of sexuality and marriage in images of women. While nuns are married to Christ, women who were persecuted for witchcraft were said to be married to or to have sexual relations with the Devil. Thus, even in images of profound goodness or profound evil, women are defined by their relations to male authority.

Contemporary sociological studies show that people's religious orientations do shape their sexual views and behavior. In their study of American couples (which included married and unmarried homosexual and heterosexual couples), Philip Blumstein and Pepper Schwartz found that regular church attenders were more conservative about sexual matters than those who were not as overtly religious. Religious heterosexuals are more opposed to civil rights for homosexuals, for example, than are less religious people. Most research finds that Catholics have a more conservative reproductive ideology than do other people. James Robbins's study of black women who had had abortions found that the more involved these women were with religion, the less happy they were with their own decisions to have abortions. Blumstein and Schwartz found that, although there may be differences in attitudes,

there is very little difference between religious and nonreligious people when it comes to how they act. They have the same amount of sex. They are just as satisfied. They have no more and no less conflict about sex. And they are just as traditional about the woman's right to initiate it. But perhaps the most startling finding is that religious people are as nonmonogamous as anyone else. However attached people may be to religious institutions, they do not seem to be insulated from the temptations of the flesh (1983, 285).

It is not entirely clear whether religious messages about morality have more impact in shaping people's attitudes, behavior, or simply feelings of guilt about doing the same things other people do.

Feminist Alternatives and the Women's Spirituality Movement

A few examples show the types of alternatives many feminists have posed to the more orthodox views of their religious bodies.

Two of the best-known feminist religious thinkers of the 19th century were the Quaker sisters Sarah (1792–1873) and Angelina (1805–1876) Grimké. In Angelina Grimké's most famous work, her 1836 "Appeal to the Christian Women of the South," she urged women to be instrumental in ending slavery, even if their actions brought them suffering, because they had to follow what they knew to be God's will rather than sinful and oppressive laws created by men. Drawing on the New Testament statement that "there is neither male nor female," the Grimké sisters believed that enforcing separate spheres for women and men and withholding religious and political rights for women were un-Christian acts. Their work, like the work of many other feminist religious activists, shows that the same texts and basic ideas can be interpreted in a variety of ways with very different effects.

Certainly many feminist critics of religion offered attacks on what they regarded as misogynist or androcentric theology and practices. Among these are Elizabeth Cady Stanton, Matilda Joslyn Gage, and a committee of other feminists who wrote *The Woman's Bible* ([1895] 1974), an exegesis and criticism of the Bible, which they regarded as a man-made, error-filled document. A more contemporary example is Mary Daly, whose series of critiques and "re-

visions" argue that our understanding of God and religion must be "exorcised" to root out the androcentrism of religion, much as the evil influence of Satan was exorcised by traditional Catholic ritual.

But many writers today also stand in the tradition of the Grimkés in working not just to criticize their religions but also to reconstruct them in a more feminist direction. Among the most well-known of these are Rosemary Ruether, Carol Christ, Judith Plaskow, and Elizabeth Schüssler Fiorenza. These and other thinkers and activists focus on both the substance and the practices of their religions to consider possibilities for change. Their work revolves around two different strategies. One is to remove gender-specific content or rituals, the other is to incorporate more woman-centered language and rituals. Let us look at examples of both.

A common strategy to "de-genderize" religion is to focus on removing gender difference from liturgy and ritual. Formerly gender-segregated rituals are integrated. For example, the important Jewish initiation rite of Bar Mitzvah (Son of the Commandments) historically was a male ritual, but for several decades Reform Jews have celebrated the same ritual for girls, the Bat Mitzvah (Daughter of the Commandments). Traditional Jewish law does not count women among the ten adults whose presence is required to say certain prayers; in more progressive communities women are counted. Traditionally only Jewish men wore prayer shawls and *yarmulkes* (hats); in more progressive communities many women do as well. Women are no longer barred from the rabbinate except among the Orthodox.

One of the most well-known efforts to remove sexist difference within Christianity other than allowing women into the clergy occurred in 1983 when the National Council of Churches began publishing new translations of biblical passages under the title *Inclusive Language Lectionary* amid considerable controversy. The lectionary refers to God as "the

Father and Mother" or "Sovereign" rather than as "Father" or "Lord," and it refers to Jesus as the "Child" rather than as the "Son" of God to reduce the emphasis on male religious imagery. Some churches gave the lectionary a warm reception, and others attacked it as "tampering with the word of God."

While many efforts have focused on removing gender difference from religion as a means toward eliminating subordination of women, others revise religious texts and traditions to incorporate more woman-centered aspects to emphasize a specifically female religious and spiritual experience. Here the intention is largely to empower women, often by rediscovering women-created ideas and rituals and female figures that have been forgotten. Many feminist religious activists also work to create new practices and liturgy focused on women's specific experiences, history, and relationship to religion, morality, and spirituality.

Many such feminists, notably those in the women's spirituality movement, emphasize the symbol of the Goddess, a female conceptualization of the deity. Through Goddess symbolism these feminists try to emphasize a changed conception of God that affirms those parts of the universe more traditionally associated with feminine rather than masculine character. Thus, rather than thinking of God primarily as the "King," "Ruler," and "Judge," providing the constancy of the rule of law, the women's spirituality movement emphasizes the life-giving and sustaining power, and the constant fluidity and change in life found in the life course throughout nature and the change of seasons.[3]

Another branch of feminist spiritualism has turned to witchcraft to find a tradition. This witchcraft has nothing to do with the Wicked Witch of the West or even Glenda the Good Witch, but rather the tradition of witchcraft (which comes from the word *wicce*, meaning "wise ones") that has been the general name for female priestesses, healers, and sages throughout the ages, many of whom have been punished only because they knew how to use medicinal herbs to help people. If women have rejected the long tradition of the *wicce*, they argue, it is not because the tradition is itself bad, but because men have feared and therefore punished it, generally by execution. Sometimes, in our eagerness to reject the violence of these men's actions, we have forgotten that many women have practiced witchcraft, although that practice bears little resemblance to the descriptions in the more orthodox religious texts.

These movements for change involve religious authorities, clergy, and members of traditional religious organizations, as well as people outside these organizations who are attempting to create their own. Although all of these people have different points of view, they are linked by the convictions that (1) religious organizations are among the most forceful institutions that shape and define sex/gender systems; (2) women have had very little control over these powers; and (3) religion should free the human spirit rather than keep it in bondage. Although these movements for change have had wide impact, organized religion has also resisted change very strongly.

WOMEN'S RELIGIOUS ACTIVITIES AND INFLUENCES

Thus far we have looked at some of the ways that religious teachings help define gender, sexuality, and women's roles. We now look more directly at women's religious activity. What roles have women played in American religious life and religious organizations? How have their activities in religious organizations helped them shape their own and other people's lives? To what degree have women's activities influenced religious and spiritual life in the United States?

Everyday Life as Religious Activity

In "The Cult of True Womanhood, 1830–1860" historian Barbara Welter identifies the central historical role white women were expected to play in American religious life:

The nineteenth-century American man was a busy builder of bridges and railroads, at work long hours in a materialist society. The religious values of his forbears were neglected in practice if not in intent, and he occasionally felt some guilt that he had turned this new land, this temple of the chosen people, into one vast countinghouse. But he could salve his conscience by reflecting that he had left behind a hostage, not only to fortune, but to all the values which he held so dear and treated so lightly (1966, 21).

That hostage was woman. Although a good woman was supposed to be submissive to her husband and her Lord, she was also supposed to create a religious home. She was responsible for guarding the spiritual life of her family, which sometimes meant acting outside the home and becoming, in effect, the backbone of church organizations and the occasional upsurges in religious activity.

Historians point out that women were central in the second "Great Awakening" of the 1820s in the East, the remarkable growth in evangelical Protestantism with its famous revival meetings that attracted large numbers of women and drew women into a view of everyday life as a moral mission. In her study of women's roles in the frontier West, Julie Roy Jeffrey found that many of the newly gathered congregations of the mid 19th century were composed primarily of women. "Women not only swelled membership rolls but were quickly recognized as recruiters and forcibly reminded of their responsibilities [by ministers]" (1979, 96). Jeffrey also found evidence that women often gave solace and encouragement to the struggling missionary ministers who were depressed and frustrated by their apparent failures to bring God's word to the frontier. What role might religion play in American life today were it not for the women who populated churches and supported their ministers a century ago?

When we look at women's roles historically it is nearly impossible to separate women's specifically *religious* activities and duties from their other activities. Women's family roles often have been understood as expressions of their religious values and the primary means for enforcing women's piety. Consider, for example, the argument made by Catharine Beecher in her manual for the homemaker, *A Treatise on Domestic Economy* ([1841] 1977). She set her advice on topics as diverse as nutrition, clothing, charity, exercise, and flower cultivation in a deeper philosophical and religious context. She began by arguing that "the democratic institutions of this country are in reality no other than the principles of Christianity carried into operation" (10). She then argued that "the success of democratic institutions (and therefore, by logical extension, Christian institutions) . . . depends upon the intellectual and moral character of the mass of the people" (13). According to Beecher the responsibility for securing this character depends on the woman. "The mother writes the character of the future man; the sister beds the fibers that after are the forest tree; the wife sways the heart, whose energies may turn for good or for evil the destinies of a nation" (13). Because every detail of a household must be arranged according to important basic principles, "These general principles are to be based on Christianity" (145). Thus, the activities of household management are expressions of religious duty and participation.

Similar beliefs are held in other religions. A central tenet of Jewish life is that the wife and mother is responsible for creating a Jewish home; she thereby is responsible for maintaining Jewish life and Judaism itself. Every meal eaten in the home of an Orthodox Jewish family is a reminder of religion and woman's role in it; the woman must carefully follow the laws of *kashrut* in buying, preparing, and serving food, thereby enforcing Jewish law and custom within her family. The conflation of women's religious activity and domestic obligation is especially apparent in Judaism because many important rituals and celebrations take place in the home rather than in the synagogue. The Sabbath meal is itself a religious service and includes traditional foods and the lighting of the Sabbath candles by the woman. Passover, one of the most important Jewish festivals, is celebrated entirely in the home. Much of the woman's work during Passover week is regulated by the fact that it is Passover; her very domestic labor is a ritual act.

For women who are the wives of clergy and missionaries, wifehood is itself a religious occupation. The ministry is one of the many male-dominated jobs in which the wife has special tasks that are unpaid extensions of the husband's job; in fact the husband's job creates nearly a full-time job for his untrained, unsalaried wife. The job of a minister's wife varies from denomination to denomination and from congregation to congregation. Generally, however, she is expected to attend most religious functions (or at least those that allow women), regardless of her own interests. She is expected to serve on committees, especially those that revolve around "women's concerns" such as education and entertainment. When the minister entertains congregants, visiting ministers, and others in his line of duty, she does the work. Above all, the minister's wife is the highly visible representative of her husband and his religious values. Ministers' wives, like the wives of other highly visible authorities, are subject to constant criticism and gossip if their homes, children, clothes, and smiles aren't perfect or appropriate for the values of the congregation. The importance of this job is evidenced by the controversy surrounding ministers' wives who choose to pursue independent careers and therefore do not have the time or the inclination to serve their husbands' congregations full-time.

It is easy to underestimate the religious work and influence of ministers' wives, both historically and today. In the 19th century missionaries sent to the frontier West to "civilize" (meaning to Christianize) the new communities were urged to bring wives for help and support they would need. Julie Jeffrey found that most of the wives thought of themselves as missionaries (as well they might have, given the work they did), even if their husbands and churches regarded them only as helpmates. But, as Jeffrey points out, "Few anticipated the potential conflict between [the roles of wife and missionary]. Nor did their religious enthusiasm and lofty idealism prepare them for the reality of missionary work" (1979, 100).

These women performed the hard duties of frontier women, plus many of the difficult duties of missionary work. They recruited women, taught, organized social events, and were responsible for fund-raising—often through their own labor rather than through collections—so that their husbands could tend to more spiritual needs. They were shuffled from one place to another as their husbands were called to new missions. The toll on these women and their families was often great. It is unfortunate that these hard-working women are often forgotten or remembered only as the wives of the men who tamed the West.

Making a home is regarded as a religious activity of central importance; for many people this is proof enough that women are highly regarded by their religions and are free to pursue a full life within their religious communities and to be influential in them. For many other women—including, of course, those who are not wives and mothers as well as those who simply see wider horizons—this is not enough.

Women's Service Outside the Home

Women have always constituted a substantial portion of the people who have practiced their religious values through public or community service, volunteer work, charity, or philanthropy. For many women bound even by the most traditional domestic values, these service activities and the religious organizations that undertake them have often provided the primary or even sole channel for extrafamilial public action and personal development. Religious organizations have provided ways for women to have an impact on their communities and society that they could not achieve in the male-dominated worlds of politics and the professions.

The 19th century witnessed the development of a religiously based gender ideology that regarded charity and service work a necessary part of a homemaker's life, especially but not exclusively among middle-class women. As Catharine Beecher observed, "It is also one of the plainest requirements of Christianity, that we devote some of our time and efforts to the comfort and improvement of others" ([1841] 1977, 145–46). Such activities were especially appropriate because the focus of women's lives within their families was the comfort and improvement of others. Beecher included service work in her advice to women on how to schedule their time wisely: "The leisure of two afternoons and evenings could be devoted to religious and benevolent objects, such as religious meetings, charitable associations, Sunday school visiting, and attention to the sick and poor" (147).

The impact of women who express the social implications of their religious concerns through organized activities is immeasurable. The number of people who have been fed, clothed, housed, educated, and otherwise comforted by religious organizations of women is uncountable. Through these organizations women have pressed social and political concerns at all ends of the political spectrum and all levels of politics. Indeed, this work became part of the basis on which public welfare policies were constructed. Throughout the 20th century representatives of women's religious organizations have testified frequently before local and state legislatures, as well as before congressional committees. The social issues and concerns of churches are often manifest largely in the work of women.

Women's religiously based service work is important to understand not only because it has had a great impact on American women and U.S. society more broadly, but also because it offers us a good example of the complexities of developing a feminist analysis of the gender basis of social institutions. As Lori Ginzberg writes in her study of 19th-century women's benevolent work, "Ideologies about gender serve broader purposes than either describing or enforcing supposed differences between women and men. It is necessary . . . to understand the uses to which those ideologies are put" (Ginzberg 1990, 216). Women's influence and power in service work stems from a gender ideology of difference. Women were supposed to have moral influence because of their natural moral difference from and superiority over men.

Women or, more accurately, the belief in women's moral superiority perfectly fit the requirement that charitable endeavors appear unmotivated by self- or class interest. As members of a group that seemed to be defined exclusively by gender, women could have no interest other than to fulfill their benevolent destiny; they could be applauded and recognized without calling into question the purity of their motives (Ginzberg 1990, 216).

Charity *did* serve class interests for the middle-class and business-owning-class women who were so active in late 19th-century charity work. As Ginzberg points out, charity played an important role in economic development by mediating "the most blatant harshness and dislocation of nineteenth-century capitalism and urbanization" and helping to foster a moral culture that supported that form of industrial capitalism. Thus the structure of gender relations impacted the structure of class relations.

Another important complexity in understanding the significance of the gender ideology of difference underpinning the ideal of female benevolence is its dual effect on the charitable women themselves. On the one hand it provided an outlet for public and communal activity, and indeed a base for women to exert a considerable degree of influence over their communities and even over government. Ann Douglas claims that women thus were powerful agents in the creation of 19th-century American culture, especially in helping it forsake the harsh Calvinist character of the earlier century in favor of Victorian sentimentalism. Historian Sara Evans argues that women's activities helped forge a new meaning of public and domestic life, in which the moral mission of homemakers reached outward to public works, and public life, they argued, should function to care for people and sustain them morally. Moreover, this notion of the unique spiritual character of women gave them grounds for collective identity, viewing themselves as sisters, and creating the potential for collective action, including the creation of a feminist movement. On the other hand, this gender ideology reinforced the idea of separate spheres, in which women and men had different and, in fact, unequal places. It was an ideology with both a radical and a deeply conservative potential.

Religious organizations continue to provide a means through which women make contributions to others in their communities. Besides the continuing charitable efforts of churches, synagogues, and other religious organizations, many women have participated in efforts to create new forms of spirituality that emphasize a religious basis for accepting public and even political responsibility for justice and social welfare. These women reject what Judith Plaskow calls the "institutionalized separation of spirituality and politics":

The assigned guardian of spirituality has been religion, which is itself relegated to the margins of society and expected to limit its interests to Saturday or Sunday mornings. As spirituality minds its otherworldly business, transformation of social structures is left to the often dirty work of politics, which catches us up in a realm of compromise, power seeking, struggle over what have been defined as limited resources, and confrontation with the distortions and disease in our social system (1990, 212–13).

Plaskow and others want to go beyond the traditional bounds of female benevolence and charity to argue for a spiritualism that is itself committed to transformational politics. She underscores the idea of *tikkun olam*—the responsibility to participate in restoring the world to its wholeness, just as others, such as Pamela Couture emphasize the idea of "shared responsibility" grounded in Christianity. Likewise, in the early 1980s many women became involved in new formulations of the political responsibilities of spirituality in the "sanctuary movement," a religion-based movement to give sanctuary to the victims of government violence in El Salvador. At the time, El Salvador was ruled by a U.S.-backed regime that tortured and killed its opponents, including religious workers.

These notions of responsibility erase the difference between religion and politics. In these cases, religious activists are attempting to link spirituality, feminism, and a progressive political commitment to communal responsibility in the material as well as spiritual world. These more liberal and progressive thinkers are not alone in their arguments for linking spirituality and political action. Those on the right have also done so, for example, in anti-abortion and "rescue" movements, which they also define as based in social justice and social commitments.

Women as Religious Authorities and Leaders

We already have seen that with some exceptions, most Judeo-Christian religions explicitly reserve leadership and positions of authority for men. Nevertheless, women have assumed a variety of leadership roles, and they are pressing for more.

Women have been the founders of a number of American Christian denominations. Among the most important and well known are Ellen White, who founded the Seventh-Day Adventist church and led it for 50 years; Aimee Semple McPherson, a charismatic evangelist who founded the Church of the Foursquare Gospel; and Mary Baker Eddy (1821–1910), who founded the Church of Christ, Scientist, best known for the beliefs that the spirit and mind are the central facts of life and that illness, disease, and death are mere illusions that can be overcome by spirituality.

Another church founder was Ann Lee (1736–1884), an immigrant from England who, as a young woman, belonged to a religious group known as the "Shaking Quakers" because of members' behavior while praying. While imprisoned in England for heresy and accusations of witchcraft, she experienced revelations. Once freed she led a small group of followers who believed her to be a messenger of Christ to New York, where she established the first Shaker community. The Shakers believed that only through celibacy could a person achieve the highest spirituality; the growth of the community thus depended on new converts. The Shaker community was based on sharing and hard work, and it is noted for its well-crafted furniture. By the middle of the 20th century only a handful of old women were left in the community. These women decided to let the Shaker community die a natural death and sought no more converts.

Much attention has been focused on the issue of ordination of women. Antoinette Brown Blackwell (1825–1921) was the first American woman to be ordained as a minister and to have her own congregation. At least three Protestant denominations have ordained women for a century or more, including the United Church of Christ, the American Baptist churches, and the Disciples of Christ. Change has come much more recently in most denominations, however. Sally Priesand was the first woman ordained as

a (Reform) rabbi in 1972. In 1989 Barbara Harris became the first female Episcopal bishop, an event that caused great consternation in some sectors of the worldwide Anglican church. Orthodox Jews still do not ordain women, women still may not become Roman Catholic priests, and some conservative Protestant denominations remain opposed to female ordination. Although women are still a small fraction of all ministers, these numbers are likely to change as more women train for the ministry. In 1989 the National Council of Churches found that of 172 denominations for which information was available, 84 ordained women, 82 did not, and 6 did not have ordained clergy. It also reported that women constituted about 8% of the clergy in denominations that ordained women.

A survey of male and female Protestant clergy showed that their experiences and motivations differed to some degree. Women were more likely to have upper-middle-class backgrounds, highly educated parents, and mothers who were employed. Men were more likely to have attended denominational colleges, partly reflecting the fact that women made their decisions to enter the ministry later than men. Men were more likely to feel that their families and pastors supported their decisions to enter the ministry in the first place. Women entering the ministry tended to have better academic records than men. More women than men said their motivation in seeking clerical training was personal spiritual growth or service to Christ; more men than women said they pursued religious studies to become parish ministers.

The researchers also uncovered other differences. Men were more likely than women to feel that the ordained ministry carried with it particularly high "prestige and dignity." More women than men felt it was very important to "change the sexist nature of the church." Most of the female ministers revealed strongly feminist attitudes toward women in the church, compared with only 24% of the men. Clerical attitudes toward women's roles in the church vary from denomination to denomination. While 39% of the United Church of Christ ministers expressed strongly feminist attitudes, only 15% of the Episcopal clergy did so.

Women in the ministry face some segregation and discrimination just as women do in other jobs. Men find it easier to become ordained after attending the seminary, although this varies by denomination. Ordained women tend to be placed in smaller churches with older members, and their salaries are lower than men's. As we might expect, the congregants in women's churches tend to be less conservative than those in men's, although surveys show that in most denominations, lay leaders tend to be more conservative on gender issues than are the clergy themselves.

As with other jobs, the fact that some women are now working in this male-dominated profession does not mean that their day-to-day experiences are the same as men's. Women and men feel themselves to be especially competent at different aspects of the job. Carroll, Hargrove, and Lummis found that women felt more confident about their abilities to preach, lead worship, and teach children, and men felt more confident about their abilities to manage the church budget. Women and men both felt they got on well with different age and gender groups within their congregations. Most of the female ministers thought their gender played a role in conflicts or difficulties they encountered in their jobs; 27% thought their sex was a very important factor.

Studies suggest that women change the ministry and its imagery merely by pursuing their vocations. Women have somewhat different attitudes than their male colleagues; they could not believe that church authority is necessarily masculine and remain in the career they have chosen. Women in the ministry have become increasingly aware of the problems of women partly through their own experiences. Carroll, Hargrove, and Lummis found that clergywomen are somewhat more likely than clergymen to think that their congregations should get involved in social and political issues, including the rights of women and minorities.

There is growing evidence that women have a different effect on their congregants than men have. Rabbi Laura Geller (1983, 210), for example, reported on the following reaction of two of her congregants:

Rabbi, I can't tell you how different I felt about services because you are a woman. I found myself feeling that if you can be a rabbi, then maybe I could be a rabbi too. For the first time in my life I felt as though I could learn those prayers, I could study Torah, I could lead this service, I could do anything you could do. Knowing that made me feel much more involved in the service-much more involved with Judaism. Also, it made me think about God in a different way. I'm not sure why. (a middle-aged woman)

Rabbi, I realized that if you could be a rabbi, then certainly I could be a rabbi. Knowing that made the service somehow more accessible to me. I didn't need you to "do it" for me. I could "do it," be involved with Jewish tradition, without depending on you. (a young man)

It seems to be an almost universal religious theme that negative aspects of the world can be lessons for the good. Geller's experience might be an object lesson of exactly this sort.

The relatively low status of the female rabbi, at least in these cases, brought people closer to their own spirituality. These two people were reacting in part to women's lower status, to the jarring image of a female leader in a masculine world, to their stereotypes of women. But as Geller noted, "The lessening of social distance and the reduction of the attribution of power and status leads to the breakdown of hierarchy within a religious institution." In this case the breakdown of gender hierarchies did indeed seem to lead to a breakdown of religious institutional hierarchy because the two are interdependent; they mutually reinforce each other. This is, of course, precisely what conservative leaders fear will be the result of the entrance of women into traditionally male leadership roles. But as these quotations also suggest, many people find a new spirituality and a renewed sense of religious affiliation and purpose when the hierarchy of religious institutions is weakened. Geller noted that a female friend of hers who was an Episcopal minister had a similar experience. "When she offers the Eucharist people take it from her differently from the way they would take it from a male priest, even though she follows the identical ritual. People experience her as less foreign, and so the experience is more natural, less mysterious" (1983, 211).

Women take many other leadership roles in religious organizations. Many denominations have long allowed women to be deaconesses, and the Roman Catholic, Eastern Orthodox, and Episcopal churches have orders of nuns. In some cases these women have been instrumental in changing the status of women. Many Roman Catholic sisters have worked for changes within the Church. Most people are aware that many orders of nuns no longer wear habits. But the size and character of the community of Roman Catholic sisters has been changing over the years. First, it is considerably smaller than it once was; while in 1968 there were over 176,000 nuns in the United States, by 1992 the figure was a little over 99,000. Far fewer women enter as novitiates each year. But the women who enter are different also. Today a substantial portion of women who become nuns are much older than in the past; often they are women who have raised families and had careers, sometimes well-paid professional careers. Indeed, many religious orders now discourage younger women from joining in favor of older women with skills and experiences that can benefit the group and their work. At the same time, this trend is likely to exacerbate the discontent of nuns who are already frustrated with the limits placed on them by the male church hierarchy.

Most denominations also allow women to fulfill other organizational leadership roles, such as committee work and leadership in religious education, some of which are designed only for women and some of which are open to both women and men. We should not underestimate the impact women have had in these various roles; however, many of these roles are limited by very specific boundaries, which also limit women's potential impact on religious life. Women who want to reach further within their religious organizations are still forced, for the most part, to ask permission from male authorities, curb their own spiritual needs, or leave.

RELIGION AND SOCIETY

Few subjects stir up as much controversy and passion as the relationship between religion and gender norms. Often those on opposing sides of the debate do agree about one point: Organized religion has been one of the most powerful human institutions for defining and controlling gender, sexuality, and "woman's place." There is strong disagreement, however, about what can and should be done about this power. The solutions offered are wide ranging.

Religious institutions, like the other institutions discussed in this book, are not isolated enclaves; they are integrally linked to the wider society and its values. They both influence and are influenced by it. They are powerful producers and enforcers of gender norms, but they also are affected by changes in these norms in other social institutions. Many aspects of religious teachings and structures depend on specific conceptions of women and their roles; when these begin to change outside of religious institutions, the institutions are also affected.

Religions have promoted inequality between women and men and have supported great violence against women—and men—who step out of their assigned gender and sexual roles. Because women have been assigned the subordinate position, they have been especially subjected to punishments for gender-specific reasons. For example, the crime of the thousands of women accused of witchcraft was not only that they were heretics but also that they had engaged in activities, such as healing, which were part of the province of men. In modern times many religious organizations have formally and officially resisted changes in the status of women, even outside the institutions themselves.

The story of religious institutions is not a simple history of victimization of women. Denominations differ in their treatment of women, and most have changed to some degree in recent years. Millions of women have found strength and inspiration in their religions, which has sometimes allowed them to battle their own religious institutions and to transform themselves and women's roles in subtle ways. A delicate balancing act is required to recognize both the religious power and influence of women especially when it is often so subtle and the very real gender-specific limits that have been placed on women in almost all of their religious activities.

Many women have sought to create a spiritual bond among women through a feminist approach to religion that values women as a group. While this has been an active and important aspect of feminism, the feminist spirituality movement has also made many women more conscious of divisions among women based in their religious beliefs and practices. This is not just because denominations disagree in their beliefs and differ in their practices. The conflict among women in the women's spirituality movement is related to problems of difference. Let us consider two brief examples here: relations between African American and white Christians and between Christians and Jews.

Many Christian feminist writers have begun to identify a number of problems in developing a feminist theology or spirituality that does not deal specifically with race. Just as the sexism inside organized religion both reflects and shapes the sexism in other social institutions, so does its racism. In most communities, African Americans have no more been welcomed by whites into their churches than they have been welcomed into white-dominated neighborhoods and schools. Despite the apparent welcome accorded the Whoopi Goldberg character in the movie *Sister Act*, African American nuns face discrimination.

Ethnic and other aspects of cultural heritage become woven together with religious practices; thus, for example, even within the same denominations the worship styles can differ dramatically in white and black churches. But there are other intellectual and theological differences that can cause race-based conflict in the effort to claim a "women's" Christian spirituality. Among them is the problem of freedom and free will, which looks different depending on which side of slavery and other forms of institutionalized oppression shapes one's history. African American and white views of religious claims of universality and the unity of human beings are also shaped by the realities of relationships of subordination. Another important point of difference is evident in discussing Christology, debates over the nature and place of Jesus in religious thought, including dealing seriously with the significance of Jesus' race and gender. These are each important and emotional issues. These conflicts remind us of the problem of the false sense of universalism that comes from not recognizing difference.

Many thinkers have also dealt with issues that divide Christians and Jews within the feminist spirituality movement. Judith Plaskow has written influential works on the problem of feminist anti-Judaism, especially in the context of apparently ecumenical spirituality discussions. Here she is not just referring to cultural anti-Judaism reflecting norms in the wider society, although she includes that as well. Rather, she points to a fundamental source of anti-Judaism in Christian theology, especially the versions favored by feminists that emphasize the "feminism" and "femaleness" of Jesus. Historically, part of the forcefulness of the Jesus story is its backdrop—the figures with whom Jesus is compared and the significance of that comparison. The Jesus story depends heavily on what to Jewish eyes are the anti-Jewish caricatures found in Christian images of rabbis, Pharisees, and Jewish life and religion generally. This leads Plaskow to write about the "psychological reality that Christians need Jews in a way that Jews do not need Christians" (1990, 101). She notes that in ecumenical dialog Christians are always asking Jews what they think of Jesus and why they reject Jesus as the Messiah. As she writes,

Christians seem to find it almost impossible to hear that Jews *don't* think about Jesus—except when Christian questions and a Christian culture force them to do so—and that they do not reject Jesus, they are simply not interested in him (1990, 101).

Plaskow argues, contrary to the spiritualist urges toward universalism, that Christians should take Judaism seriously as an independent religion on its own terms.

One of the most striking aspects of the study of women and religion is the degree to which given rituals and texts can offer different messages to different people. The same Bible has proven to some people that women and men are equal and that women should take full leadership roles in religions and society and to others that women are inferior, periodically unclean, dangerous, and subordinate to men. Some people take religious prescriptions for women's domestic roles as a sign of the high esteem in which women are held; others find them the primary indications of women's subordination and even enslavement. At the same time, various religions and denominations often take their own unique aspects to be the truth and the potential source for universal-

ism. These variations and similarities are sources both of the stability and resilience of religious institutions and of their potential for change, of their possibilities for oppression and liberation.

NOTES

1. All biblical quotations are from the *New English Bible with the Apocrypha* (New York: Oxford University Press, 1970).

2. This is a quotation from the 1967 Supreme Court case *Loving* v. *Virginia*, which invalidated the Virginia law against miscegenation.

3. For some influential writing about Goddess religion, see Starhawk (1979) and Christ (1987).

REFERENCES

Beecher, Catharine. [1841] 1977. *A Treatise on Domestic Economy*. New York: Schocken.

Blumstein, Philip W., and Pepper Schwartz. 1983. *American Couples: Money, Work, Sex*. New York: William Morrow.

Christ, Carol. 1987. *Laughter of Aphrodite: Reflections on a Journey to the Goddess*. San Francisco: Harper & Row.

Geller, Laura. 1983. "Reactions to a Woman Rabbi." In *On Being a Jewish Feminist*, edited by Susannah Heschel, 210–13. New York: Schocken.

Ginzberg, Lori D. 1990. *Women and the Work of Benevolence: Morality, Politics, and Class in the Nineteenth-Century United States*. New Haven: Yale University Press.

Jeffrey, Julie Roy. 1979. *Frontier Women: The Trans-Mississippi West, 1840–1880*. New York: Hill & Wang.

Kraditor, Aileen, ed. 1968. *Up from the Pedestal: Selected Writings in the History of Feminism*. New York: Quadrangle.

Morgan, Edmund S. [1944] 1978. "The Puritans and Sex." In *The American Family in Historical Perspective*, edited by Michael Gordon, 363–73. New York: St. Martin's.

Plaskow, Judith. 1990. *Standing Again at Sinai.* San Francisco: HarperCollins.

Rossi, Alice, ed. 1988. *The Feminist Papers: From Adams to de Beauvoir.* Boston: Northeastern University Press.

Starhawk. 1979. *The Spiral Dance: A Rebirth of the Ancient Religion of the Great Goddess.* San Francisco: Harper & Row.

Welter, Barbara. 1966. "The Cult of True Womanhood, 1830–1860." *American Quarterly* 18:151–74.

Re-visioning Clinical Research: Gender and the Ethics of Experimental Design

Sue V. Rosser

INTRODUCTION

Since the practice of modern medicine depends heavily on clinical research, flaws and ethical problems in this research are likely to result in poorer health care and inequity in the medical treatment of disadvantaged groups. The first purpose of this paper is to explore some ways in which clinical research has been impaired and compromised by an androcentric focus in its choice and definition of problems studied, approaches and methods used, and theories and conclusions drawn. Second, I shall describe some attempts to correct this biased focus and envision further improvement through feminist perspectives and approaches.

In scientific research, it is rarely admitted that data have been gathered and interpreted from a particular perspective. Since scientific

From *Hypatia* vol. 4, no. 2 (Summer 1989), pp. 125–139. Copyright © 1989 by Sue V. Rosser. Reprinted by permission.

research centers on the physical and natural world, it is presumed "objective"; therefore, the term perspective does not apply to it. However, the decisions, either conscious or unconscious, regarding what questions are asked, who is allowed to do the asking, what information is collected, and who interprets that information create a particular vantage point from which the knowledge or truth is perceived.

Historians of science, particularly Thomas Kuhn and his followers, have pointed out that scientific theories are not objective and value-free but are paradigms that reflect the historical and social context in which they are conceived. In our culture, the institutionalized power, authority, and domination of men frequently result in acceptance of the male world view or androcentrism as the norm. Recognizing the influence of this androcentric perspective is particularly difficult for scientists because of their traditional belief in the objectivity of science which makes it difficult for them to admit that they actually hold any perspectives which may influence their data, approaches, and theories.

Feminist philosophers of science have described the specific ways in which the very objectivity said to be characteristic of scientific knowledge and the dichotomy between subject and object are, in fact, male ways of relating to the world, which specifically exclude women. Research has also become a masculine province in its choice and definition of problems studied, methods and experimental subjects used, and interpretation and application of experimental results.

Revealing the distortions in clinical research that emanate from the androcentric biases uncovers points at which a feminist ethics might influence this research. Feminist scientists and philosphers have called for more people-oriented and patient-centered research which would be likely to provide better health care for all.

CHOICE AND DEFINITION
OF PROBLEMS STUDIED

With the expense of sophisticated equipment, maintenance of laboratory animals and facilities, and salaries for qualified technicians and researchers, virtually no medical research is undertaken today without Federal or foundation support. Gone are the days when individuals had laboratories in their homes or made significant discoveries working in isolation using homemade equipment. In fiscal 1987, the National Institutes of Health (NIH) funded approximately $6.1 billion of research (*Science and Government Report* 1988). Private foundations and state governments funded a smaller portion of the research (*NSF Science and Engineering Indicators* 1987).

The choice of problems for study in medical research is substantially determined by a national agenda that defines what is worthy of study, i.e. funding. As Marxist, African-American and feminist critics of scientific re-

search have pointed out, the scientific research that is undertaken reflects the societal bias towards the powerful who are overwhelmingly white, middle/upper class, and male in the United States. Obviously, the members of Congress who appropriate the funds for NIH and other Federal agencies are overwhelmingly white, middle/upper class, and male; they are more likely to vote funds for research which they view as beneficial to health needs, as defined from their perspective.

It may be argued that actual priorities for medical research and allocations of funds are not set by members of Congress but by leaders in medical research who are employees of NIH or other Federal agencies or who are brought in as consultants. Unfortunately the same descriptors—white, middle/upper class, and male—must be used to characterize the individuals in the theoretical and decision-making positions within the medical hierarchy and scientific establishment.

Women are lacking even at the level of the peer review committee, which is how NIH determines which of the competitive proposals submitted by researchers in a given area are funded. In the ten year interval 1975–1984, women went from 16.9 percent of NIH peer review committee members to only 17.9 percent; during this time, the total number of members nearly doubled from 733 to 1,264 (Filner 1986). Because the percentage of women post-doctoral fellows increased by 32 percent during the same time period, it seems likely that qualified women were available, but not used.

I believe that the results of having a huge preponderance of male leaders setting the priorities for medical research have definite effects on the choice and definition of problems for research:

1) Hypotheses are not formulated to focus on gender as a crucial part of the question being asked. Since it is clear that many diseases have different frequencies (heart disease, lupus), symptoms (gonorrhea), or complications (most

sexually transmitted diseases) in the two sexes, scientists should routinely consider and test for differences or lack of differences based on gender in any hypothesis being tested. For example, when exploring the metabolism of a particular drug, one should routinely run tests in both males and females. Two dramatic, widely publicized recent examples demonstrate that sex differences are *not* routinely considered as part of the question asked. In a longitudinal study of the effects of cholesterol lowering drugs, gender differences were not tested since the drug was tested on 3,806 men and no women (Hamilton 1985). In a similar test of the effects of aspirin on cardiovascular disease, which is now used widely by the pharmaceutical industry to support "taking one aspirin each day to prevent heart attacks," no females were included. (Science and Government Report 1988).

2) Some diseases which affect both sexes are defined as male diseases. Heart disease is the best example of a disease that has been so designated because of the fact that heart disease occurs more frequently in men at younger ages than women. Therefore, most of the funding for heart disease has been appropriated for research on predisposing factors for the disease (such as cholesterol level, lack of exercise, stress, smoking, and weight) using white, middle-aged, middle-class males.

This "male disease" designation has resulted in very little research being directed towards high risk groups of women. Heart disease is a leading cause of death in older women who live an average of 8 years longer than men. It is also frequent in poor black women who have had several children. Virtually no research has explored predisposing factors for these groups who fall outside the disease definition established from an androcentric perspective. Recent data indicate that the designation of AIDS as a disease of male homosexuals and drug users has led researchers and health care practitioners to fail to understand the etiology and diagnosis of AIDS in women (Norwood 1988).

3) Research on conditions specific to females receives low priority, funding, and prestige. Some examples include dysmenorrhea, incontinency in older women, and nutrition in post-menopausal women. Effects of exercise level and duration upon alleviation of menstrual discomfort and length and amount of exposure to VDTs that have resulted in the "cluster pregnancies" of women giving birth to deformed babies in certain industries have also received low priority. In contrast, significant amounts of time and money are expended upon clinical research on women's bodies in connection with other aspects of reproduction. In this century up until the 1970s considerable attention was devoted to the development of devices for females rather than for males. Furthermore, substantial clinical research has resulted in increasing medicalization and control of pregnancy, labor, and childbirth. Feminists have critiqued the conversion of a normal, natural process controlled by women into a clinical, and often surgical, procedure controlled by men. More recently, the new reproductive technologies such as amniocentesis, *in vitro* fertilization, and artificial insemination have become a major focus as means are sought to overcome infertility. Feminists have warned of the extent to which these technologies place pressure upon women to produce the "perfect" child while placing control in the hands of the male medical establishment.

These examples suggest that considerable resources and attention are devoted to women's health issues when those issues are directly related to men's interest in controlling production of children. Contraceptive research may permit men to have sexual pleasure without the production of children; research on infertility, pregnancy, and childbirth has allowed men to assert more control over the production of more "perfect" children and over an aspect of women's lives over which they previously held less power.

4) Suggestions of fruitful questions for research based on the personal experience of

women have also been ignored. In the health care area, women have often reported (and accepted among themselves) experiences that could not be documented by scientific experiments or were not accepted as valid by the researchers of the day. For decades, dysmenorrhea was attributed by most health care researchers and practitioners to psychological or social factors despite the reports from an overwhelming number of women that these were monthly experiences in their lives. Only after prostaglandins were "discovered" was there widespread acceptance among the male medical establishment that this experience reported by women had a biological component (Kirschstein 1985).

These four types of bias raise ethical issues: Health care practitioners must treat the majority of the population, which is female, based on information gathered from clinical research in which drugs may not have been tested on females, in which the etiology of the disease in women has not been studied and in which women's experience has been ignored.

APPROACHES AND METHODS

1) The scientific community has often failed to include females in animal studies in basic research as well as in clinical research unless the research centered on controlling the production of children. The reasons for the exclusion (cleaner data from males due to lack of interference from estrus or menstrual cycles, fear of inducing fetal deformities in pregnant subjects, and higher incidence of some diseases in males) are practical when viewed from a financial standpoint. However, the exclusion results in drugs that have not been adequately tested in women subjects before being marketed and lack of information about the etiology of some diseases in women.

2) Using the male as the experimental subject not only ignores the fact that females may respond differently to the variable tested, it may also lead to less accurate models even in

the male. Models which *more accurately* simulate functioning complex biological systems may be derived from using female rats as subjects in experiments. Women scientists such as Joan Hoffman have questioned the tradition of using male rats or primates as subjects. With the exception of insulin and the hormones of the female reproductive cycle, traditional endocrinological theory assumed that most of the 20-odd human hormones are kept constant in level in both males and females. Thus, the male of the species, whether rodent or primate, was chosen as the experimental subject because of his noncyclicity. However, new techniques of measuring blood hormone levels have demonstrated episodic, rather than steady, patterns of secretion of virtually all hormones in both males and females. As Hoffman points out, the rhythmic cycle of hormone secretion as also portrayed in the cycling female rat appears to be a more accurate model for the secretion of most hormones (Hoffman 1982).

3) When females have been used as experimental subjects, often they are treated as not fully human. In his attempts to investigate the side effects (Goldzieher *et al*, 1971a) nervousness and depression (Goldzieher *et al*, 1971b) attributable to oral contraceptives, Goldzieher gave dummy pills to 76 women who sought treatment at a San Antonio clinic to prevent further pregnancies. None of the women was told that she was participating in research or receiving placebos. The women in Goldzieher's study were primarily poor, multiparous Mexican Americans. Research that raises similar issues about the ethics of informed consent was carried out on poor Puerto Rican women during the initial phases of testing the effectiveness of the pill as a contraceptive (Zimmerman 1980).

Frequently it is difficult to determine whether these women are treated as less than human because of their gender or whether race and class are more significant variables. From the Tuskegee Syphilis Experiment in which the effects of untreated syphilis were studied in 399 men over a period of forty years (Jones 1981), it is clear that men who are black and poor may not receive appropriate treatment or information about the experiment in which they are participating. Feminist scholars have begun to explore the extent to which gender, race and class become complex, interlocking political variables that may affect access to and quality of healthcare.

4) Current clinical research sets up a distance between the observer and the human object being studied. Several feminist philosophers have characterized this distancing as an androcentric approach. Distance between the observer and experimental subject may be more comfortable for men who are reared to feel more comfortable with autonomy and distance than for women who tend to value relationship and interdependency.

5) Using only the methods traditional to a particular discipline may result in limited approaches that fail to reveal sufficient information about the problem being explored. This may be a particular difficulty for research surrounding medical problems of pregnancy, childbirth, menstruation, and menopause for which the methods of one discipline are clearly inadequate.

Methods which cross disciplinary boundaries or include combinations of methods traditionally used in separate fields may provide more appropriate approaches. For example, if the topic of research is occupational exposures that present a risk to the pregnant woman working in a plant where toxic chemicals are manufactured, a combination of methods traditionally used in social science research with methods frequently used in biology and chemistry may be the best approach. Checking the chromosomes of any miscarried fetuses, chemical analysis of placentae after birth, Apgar Scores of the babies at birth, and blood samples of the newborns to determine trace amounts of the toxic chemicals would be appropriate bio-

logical and chemical methods used to gather data about the problem. In depth interviews with women to discuss how they are feeling and any irregularities they detect during each month of the pregnancy, or evaluation using weekly written questionnaires regarding the pregnancy progress are methods more traditionally used in the social sciences for problems of this sort.

Jean Hamilton has called for interactive models that draw on both the social and natural sciences to explain complex problems:

Particularly for understanding human, gender-related health, we need more interactive and contextual models that address the actual complexity of the phenomenon that is the subject of explanation. One example is the need for more phenomenological definitions of symptoms, along with increased recognition that psychology, behavioral studies, and sociology are among the 'basic sciences' for health research. Research on heart disease is one example of a field where it is recognized that both psychological stress and behaviors such as eating and cigarette smoking influence the onset and natural course of a disease process. (1985, IV-62).

Perhaps more women holding decision-making positions in designing and funding clinical research would result in more interdisciplinary research to study issues of women's health care such as menstruation, pregnancy, childbirth, lactation, and menopause. Those complex phenomena fall outside the range of methods of study provided by a sole discipline. The interdisciplinary approaches developed to solve these problems might then be applied to other complex problems to benefit all health care consumers, both male and female.

THEORIES AND CONCLUSIONS DRAWN FROM THE RESEARCH

The rationale which is traditionally presented in support of the "objective" methods is that they prevent bias. Emphasis upon traditional disciplinary approaches that are quantitative and maintain the distance between observer and experimental subject supposedly removes the bias of the researcher. Ironically, to the extent that these "objective" approaches are in fact synonymous with a masculine approach to the world, they may introduce bias. Specifically, androcentric bias may permeate the theories and conclusions drawn from the research in several ways:

1) First, theories may be presented in androcentric language. Much feminist scholarship has focussed on problems of sexism in language and the extent to which patriarchal language has excluded and limited women. Sexist language is a symptom of underlying sexism, but language also shapes our concepts and provides the framework through which we express our ideas. The awareness of sexism and the limitations of a patriarchal language that feminist researchers have might allow them to describe their observations in less gender-biased terms.

An awareness of language should aid experimenters in avoiding the use of terms such as "tomboyism" (Money and Erhardt 1972), "aggression" and "hysteria" that reflect assumptions about sex-appropriate behavior (Hamilton 1985) that permeate behavioral descriptions in clinical research. Once the bias in the terminology is exposed, the next step is to ask whether that terminology leads to a constraint or bias in the theory itself.

2) An androcentric perspective may lead to formulating theories and conclusions drawn from medical research to support the status quo of inequality for women and other oppressed groups. Building upon their awareness of these biases, women scientists have critiqued the studies of brain-hormone interaction (Bleier 1984) for their biological determinism used to justify women's socially inferior position. Bleier has repeatedly warned against extrapolating from one species to another in biochemical as well as behavioral traits. Perhaps male researchers are less likely to see flaws in

and question biologically deterministic theories that provide scientific justification for men's superior status in society because they as men gain social power and status from such theories. Researchers from outside the mainstream (women for example) are much more likely to be critical of such theories since they lose power from those theories. In order to eliminate bias, the community of scientists undertaking clinical research needs to include individuals from backgrounds of as much variety and diversity as possible with regard to race, class, gender, and sexual preference. Only then is it less likely that the perspective of one group will bias research design, approaches, subjects, and interpretations.

HINTS OF RE-VISIONING

Some changes in clinical research have come about because of the recognition of flaws and ethical problems for women discussed in this paper. Some of the changes are the result of critiques made by feminists and women scientists; some of the changes have been initiated by men.

1) The rise of the women's health movement in the 1970s encouraged women to question established medical authority, take responsibility for their own bodies and express new demands for clinical research and for access to health care. Feminist demands have led to increased availability of health related information to women consumers. Litigation and federal affirmative action programs have resulted in an increase from about 6% to about 40% of women medical students from 1960 to the present (Altekruse and Rosser 1992). Consumer complaints and suggestions have fostered minor reforms in obstetrical care. The decor, ambiance, and regimens of birthing facilities have improved to provide personal and psychological support for the mother and to promote infant-parent bonding. However, concurrent with modest obstetrical modifications

in hospitals, nurse midwives in most states have felt the backlash of professional efforts to control their practice and licensure status (Altekruse and Rosser 1992). Efforts to increase the understanding of the biology of birth and translate that knowledge into clinical care expressed as acceptable infant mortality rates remain inadequate.

2) Guidelines have been developed that require any research project that is Federally funded to insure humane treatment of human subjects and fully informed consent. The impetus for the formation of the National Commission for the Protection of Human Subjects of Biomedical and Behavioral Research was the revelation of the abuses of human subjects during the Nuremberg War Crimes Trials and the Tuskegee Syphilis Experiments (Belmont Report 1978). However, the attention drawn by men such as Veatch (1971) to unethical issues surrounding the testing of oral contraceptives in women helped to insure that women, especially pregnant women, were given particular consideration in the papers forming the basis of the Belmont Report.

3) In recent years U.S. government agencies have shown increased sensitivity to clinical research surrounding women's health issues and the difficult ethical issues of including women in pharmacological research. The Public Health Service (PHS) Task Force on Women's Health Issues was commissioned to aid the PHS "as the agency works within its areas of jurisdiction and expertise to improve the health and well-being of women in the United States" (U.S. Department of Health and Human Services 1985). In her insightful commissioned paper "Avoiding Methodological and Policy-Making Biases in Gender-Related Health Research" for the Report to the Task Force, Jean Hamilton makes strong recommendations:

PHS consensus-development conference on "Gender-related Methods for Health Research" (for the development of guidelines) should be held.... The feasibility of including women in certain types of research needs to be reexamined.... A number of working groups should be formed: A working-group to reconsider the difficult ethical issues of including women in pharmacological research (e.g., extra-protection for women as research subjects, versus other means for informed consent) ... A working-group to identify and to consider mechanisms to enhance the kind of multi-center, *collaborative* or *clinical research center* studies that would be most efficient in advancing our understanding of women and their health ... A working group or committee to consider ways to foster subject-selection in a way that allows for an examination of possible age, sex, and hormonal status effects (Hamilton 1985, IV-63-64).

4) Some attempts at patient involvement in research design and implementation have provided a mechanism to shorten the distance between the observer and subjects observed. Elizabeth Fee describes an account of occupational health research in an Italian factory:

Prior to 1969, occupational health research was done by specialists who would be asked by management to investigate a potential problem in the factory.... The procedure was rigorously objective, the results were submitted to management. The workers were the individualized and passive objects of this kind of research. In 1969, however, when workers' committees were established in the factories, they refused to allow this type of investigation.... Occupational health specialists had to discuss the ideas and procedures of research with workers' assemblies and see their "objective" expertise measured against the "subjective" experience of the workers. The mutual validation of data took place by testing in terms of the workers' experience of reality and not simply by statistical methods; the subjectivity of the workers' experience was involved at each level in the definition of the problem, the method of research, and the evaluation of solutions. Their collective experience was understood to be much more than the statistical combination of individual data; the workers had become the active subjects of research, involved in the production, evaluation, and uses of the knowledge relating to their own experience (1983, 24).[1]

CONCLUSION

Replacing the androcentrism in the practice of medical research and the androcentric bias in the questions asked, methods used, theories and conclusions drawn from data gathered with a feminist approach represents a major change with profound ethical implications. Lynda Birke, a feminist scientist, suggests that feminism will change science and medicine from research that is oppressive to women and potentially destructive to all towards liberation and improvement for everyone.

Perhaps this discussion of creating a feminist science seems hopelessly utopian. Perhaps. But feminism is, above all else, about wanting and working for change, change towards a better society in which women of all kinds are not devalued, or oppressed in any way. Working for change has to include changing science, which not only perpetuates our oppression at present, but threatens also to destroy humanity and all the other species with whom we share this earth (1986, 171).

I have described some hints of the re-visioning of clinical research, prompted by liberation movements of the 1970s and 1980s, that have made health care somewhat less elitist, more humane, and more accessible to all. If a stronger feminist presence were to be felt in design and interpretation of research, who knows what additional improvements might occur? Bound by my own training in traditional science, I wear the blinders provided by the society to individuals of my class, race, and gender in the late-1980s. How can those of us, living with the current reality, visualize the new reality that can come about by the changes we are beginning?

Suzette Haden Elgin in her futuristic novel *Native Tongue* describes the impossibility of envisioning the new reality:

"Perceive this . . . there was only one reason for the Encoding Project, really, other than just the joy of it.

The hypothesis was that if we put the project into effect it would change reality."

"Go on."

"Well . . . you weren't taking that hypothesis seriously. I was."

"We were."

"No. No, you weren't. Because all your plans were based on the old reality. The one before the change."

"But Nazareth, how can you plan for a new reality when you don't have the remotest idea what it would be like?"

Aquina demanded indignantly. "That's not possible!"

"Precisely," said Nazareth. "We have no science for that. We have pseudo-sciences, in which we extrapolate for reality that would be nothing more than a minor variation on the one we have . . . but the science of actual reality change has not yet been even proposed, much less formalized" (1984, 294).

NOTE

1. This example challenges more than the quality of information garnered by objective research methods in which distance is maintained between the observer and the subject. It also raises questions addressed partially by the Belmont Report (1975) regarding the ethics of "double blind" experiments: Why shouldn't individuals whose health may be affected have a right to know what is being done for them and why? Is it ethical to give one group of individuals a placebo if the drug being tested is likely to cure a health problem they have or if withholding the drug will exacerbate the health problem? It also raises the more radical idea of subject involvement in experimental design and interpretation: Shouldn't the subjects be involved in defining what the problem is and the best approaches to solving the problem?

REFERENCES

Altekruse, Joan and Rosser, Sue V. (1992). Women in the biomedical and health care industry. In *The Knowledge Explosion: Generations of Feminist Scholarship*, Dale Spender and Cheris Kramarae (eds.). New York: Teachers College Press.

Belmont Report. 1978. Washington, DC: Department of Health Education and Welfare. (Publication No. OS 78-0012).

Birke, Lynda. 1986. *Women, Feminism, and Biology.* New York: Methuen.

Bleier, Ruth. 1984. *Science and Gender: A Critique of Biology and Its Theories on Women.* New York: Pergamon Press.

Elgin, Suzette H. 1984. *Native Tongue.* New York: Daw Book, Inc.

Fee, Elizabeth. 1983. Women's nature and scientific objectivity. In *Woman's Nature, Rationalizations of Inequality*, Marian Lowe and Ruth Hubbard (eds.). New York: Pergamon Press.

Filner, B. 1986. President's remarks. *AWIS*: XV (4), July/Aug.

Goldzieher, Joseph W., Louis Moses, Eugene Averkin, Cora Scheel, and Ben Taber. 1971a. A placebo-controlled double-blind crossover investigation of the side effects attributed to oral contraceptives. *Fertility and Sterility* 22 (9): 609–623.

Goldzieher, Joseph W., Louis Moses, Eugene Averkin, Cora Scheel, and Ben Taber. 1971b. Nervousness and depression attributed to oral contraceptives: A double-blind, placebo-controlled study. *American Journal of Obstetrics and Gynecology* 22, 1013–1020.

Hamilton, Jean. 1985. Avoiding methodological biases in gender-related research. In *Women's Health Report of the Public Health Service Task Force on Women's Health Issues.* Washington, DC: U.S. Dept. of Health and Human Services Public Service.

Hoffman, J.C. 1982. Biorhythms in human reproduction: The not-so-steady states. *Signs: Journal of Women in Culture and Society* 7 (4): 829–844.

Jones, James H. 1981. *Bad Blood: The Tuskegee Syphilis Experiment.* New York: The Free Press.

Kirschstein, Ruth L. 1985. *Women's Health: Report of the Public Health Service Task Force on Women's Health Issues.* Vol. 2. Washington, DC: U.S. Department of Health and Human Services Public Health Service.

Money, John and Anke Erhardt. 1972. *Man and Woman, Boy and Girl.* Baltimore: Johns Hopkins University Press.

National Science Foundation Science and Engineering Indicators. 1987. Washington, DC (NSB-1, Appendix Table 4–10).

Norwood, Chris. 1988. Alarming Rise in Deaths. *Ms.* July, 65–67.

Science and Government Report. 1988. Washington, D.C. March 1, 18(4):1. Steering Committee of the Physician's Health Study Research Group. 1988. Special report: Preliminary report of findings from the aspirin component of the ongoing physician's health study. *New England Journal of Medicine* 318, 4, 262–264.

U.S. Department of Health and Human Services. 1985. *Women's Health: Report of the Public Health Service Task Force on Women's Issues.* vol. 2. Washington, D.C.: Public Health Service.

Veatch, Robert M. 1971. Experimental Pregnancy. *Hastings Center Report.* 1: 2–3.

Zimmerman, B. et al. 1980. People's science. In *Science and Liberation*, Rita Arditti, Pat Brennan, and Steven Cavrak, (eds.). Boston: South End Press, (299–319).

Part Two

FEMINIST THEORIES AND APPLICATIONS: EXPLAINING THE PRESENT AND CHANGING THE FUTURE

Liberal Feminism

Liberal feminism is probably the most widely recognized mode of feminist thought. The overall claim of liberal feminists is that female subordination is rooted in a set of customary and legal restraints that block women's entrance and/or success in the public world. Excluded, as many women are, from the academy, the forum, the marketplace, and the operating room, their true potential goes unfulfilled. Only when society grants women the same educational and occupational opportunities it grants men will women become men's equals. Because liberal feminists are revisionists, not revolutionaries, they propose reformist measures that expand opportunities for women within the so-called "System." For example, they advocate affirmative-action and comparable-worth laws as well as laws that crack down on sexual harassers, rapists, and women-batterers.

Among the most cogent contemporary spokespersons for liberal feminism is political theorist Susan Okin. In "Justice, Gender, and the Family" Okin expresses the regret that although our society preaches the gospel of "liberty and justice for all," radical gender inequalities persist. Women are not men's equals in economic terms or on the political front. Nor are women men's equals at home, where women assume the primary responsibility for all domestic tasks, especially child care. As Okin sees it, of all the causes that contribute to this gender-inequitable state of affairs none is greater than the institution of gender-structured marriage. Grounding this institution are two common, *inconsistent* presumptions: "that women are primarily responsible for the rearing of children; and that serious and committed members of the work force (regardless of class) do not have primary responsibility, or

310

even shared responsibility, for the rearing of children" (p. 314). Family women with jobs outside the home are simultaneously supposed to *be* and *not be* their children's primary rearers, while family men with jobs outside the home are not supposed to *be* their children primary rearers. Thus, men work a single workday, while women work a double workday. As a result, women work at a disadvantage and find themselves forever lagging behind men in the "race" for power, status, prestige, and material goods and services.

Concerned about the way in which our society has used the institution of gender-structured marriage to keep women subordinate to men, Okin faults today's political theorists for not challenging this institution as fundamentally unjust. Okin claims that the best way for a political theorist to address our society's gender inequalities is not by his using the pronoun "she" as frequently as the pronoun "he," but by his recognizing that it is injustices in the so-called private realm that create and/or compound gender injustices in the so-called public realm.

Okin argues that any sound and complete theory of justice must accomplish three tasks. First, it must recognize the dissimilarities as well as the similarities between men and women so that we learn when and when not to treat women and men exactly alike. It made absolutely no human sense, for example, when the Supreme Court ruled that the exclusion of pregnancy-related disabilities from employees' disability insurance plans was "not a gender-based discrimination at all" because such plans drew a distinction between pregnant women and "non-pregnant *persons*." Second, an adequate theory of justice must emphasize that in our society women's *opportunities* are not equal to men's precisely because the structure and practices of family life, especially the practice of female primary parenting, work against women's doing as well as men do economically, politically, and socially. So long as women

suffer the exhaustion produced by working a double day or by hustling (and I choose this word deliberately) to feed their children on a meager welfare check, true equality of opportunity will remain a figment of liberal philosophers' imagination. Third, and most important, an adequate theory of justice must insist that justice as well as charity begins at *home*. It is within the family that our children learn about the values of equality and fairness; and until our society decides to eliminate the unjust institution of gender-structured marriage, our children, says Okin, will continue to learn some very false lessons about these two values. Comments Okin: "What is a child of either sex to learn about fairness in the average household with two full-time working parents, where the mother does, at the very least, twice as much family work as the father? What is a child to learn about the value of nurturing and domestic work in a home with a traditional division of labor in which the father either subtly or not so subtly uses the fact that he is the wage earner to 'pull rank' on or to abuse his wife?" (pp. 319–320). My guess is that that child will learn that, no matter what enlightened liberal rhetoric teaches, women are not men's equals after all.

Like Okin, James P. Sterba focuses on the topic of justice, and what it means and requires to treat women as men's equals. He claims that most contemporary [liberal] feminists believe that we must support "the political ideal of a gender-free or androgynous society" in order to end male domination and achieve women's liberation. Sterba makes the excellent point that there are two ways to interpret this feminist political ideal. A merely *negative* way is simply to note that a gender-free or genderless society is "one where basic rights and duties are not assigned on the basis of a person's biological sex." (p. 331) but on "(natural) ability, rational expectation, and choice" (p. 333). A more informative, *positive* way is to claim that a gender-free society is an inherently androgynous one which provides that its desirable traits are "equally open to (equally qualified) women and men," and that its virtues are "equally expected of (equally capable) women and men" (p. 332). (Stress mine)

Getting from our actual, non-feminist, unjust world to an ideal, feminist, just world will require a number of important, gender-related changes, according to Sterba. First, our society must support programs of affirmative action and comparable worth. Second, our society must devise policies that will "put an end to the overt violence against women that takes the form of rape, battery, and sexual abuse." Third, our society must implement policies aimed at eliminating sexual harassment in the workplace. Interestingly, each of the reforms Sterba proposes requires men to change their attitudes toward and/or relationships with women. Men must adjust to women who earn as much as or even more than they do, whose "nos" really mean "no"; and who prefer to relate to their male colleagues as coworkers rather than sexual partners. Concomitantly, women must adjust to men who prefer to stay at home with the children, who sit by the phone, hoping that the woman of their dreams will phone them for a date, and who are truly more interested in women's minds than women's bodies. Clearly, the challenges of a gender-free or androgynous society will be many, but the reward of meeting them will be the achievement of a truly just social order.

In "Outrageous Acts and Everyday Rebellions," Gloria Steinem reinforces Okin's and Sterba's point that our society has much work to do before we or our children experience gender justice. When the suffragists finally won the right to vote in 1918, little did they suspect that their great-great-granddaughters would reach adulthood without witnessing the passage of an Equal Rights Amendment. No wonder that Steinem exhorts contemporary feminists to learn the lessons that will help them survive the next stages of women's liberation. The lessons are somber ones: (1) feminists must realize that to the extent that they are resisted, to that same extent they are being successful; (2) feminists must resist the type of thinking that focuses on a woman's "political correctness" rather than on her sincere desire to improve women's everyday lot; (3) feminists must be historians who derive plans of action as well as inspiration from their foremothers; and (4) feminists must realize that not moving ahead is the same as falling behind.

That women have come a long way is certain, but women's long march to freedom is far from over. This is not the time for women to rest on their laurels, in feminists' estimation. On the contrary, it is time for women to push for those reforms in the workplace, in the schools, and in marriage and divorce laws that will finally enable men and women to spend approximately the same time in both the private and the public realm.

Justice, Gender, and the Family

Susan Moller Okin

JUSTICE AND GENDER

We as a society pride ourselves on our democratic values. We don't believe people should be constrained by innate differences from being able to achieve desired positions of influence or to improve their well-being; equality of opportunity is our professed aim. The Preamble to our Constitution stresses the importance of justice, as well as the general welfare and the blessings of liberty. The Pledge of Allegiance asserts that our republic preserves "liberty and justice for all."

Yet substantial inequalities between the sexes still exist in our society. In economic terms, full-time working women (after some very recent improvement) earn on average 71 percent of the earnings of full-time working men. One-half of poor and three-fifths of chronically poor households with dependent children are maintained by a single female parent. The poverty rate for elderly women is nearly twice that for elderly men. On the political front, two out of a hundred U.S. senators are women, one out of nine justices seems to be considered sufficient female representation on the Supreme Court, and the number of men chosen in each congressional election far exceeds the number of women elected in the entire history of the country. Underlying and intertwined with all these inequalities is the unequal distribution of the unpaid labor of the family.

An equal sharing between the sexes of family responsibilities, especially child care, is "the great revolution that has not happened." Women, including mothers of young children, are, of course, working outside the household far more than their mothers did. And the small proportion of women who reach high-level positions in politics, business, and the professions command a vastly disproportionate amount of space in the media, compared with the millions of women who work at low-paying, dead-end jobs, the millions who do part-time work with its lack of benefits, and the millions of others who stay home performing for no pay what is frequently not even acknowledged as work. Certainly, the fact that women are doing more paid work does not imply that they are more equal. It is often said that we are living in a postfeminist era. This claim, due in part to the distorted emphasis on women who have "made it," is false, no matter which of its meanings is intended. It is certainly not true that feminism has been vanquished, and equally untrue that it is no longer needed because its aims have been fulfilled. Until there is justice within the family, women will not be able to gain equality in politics, at work, or in any other sphere.

The typical current practices of family life, structured to a large extent by gender, are not just. Both the expectation and the experience of the division of labor by sex make women vulnerable. As I shall show, a cycle of power relations and decisions pervades both family and workplace, each reinforcing the inequalities between the sexes that already exist within the other. Not only women, but children of both sexes, too, are often made vulnerable by gender-structured marriage. One-quarter of children in the United States now live in families with only one parent—in almost 90 percent of cases, the mother. Contrary to common perceptions—in which the situation of never-married mothers looms largest—65 percent of single-parent families are a result of marital separation or divorce. Recent research in a number of states has shown that, in the average case, the standard of living of divorced women and the children who live with them plummets after divorce, whereas the economic situation of divorced men tends to be better than when they were married.

A central source of injustice for women these days is that the law, most noticeably in the event of divorce, treats more or less as equals those whom custom, workplace discrimination, and the still conventional division of labor within the family have made very unequal. Central to this socially created inequality are two commonly made but inconsistent presumptions: that women are primarily responsible for the rearing of children; and that serious and committed members of the work force (regardless of class) do not have primary responsibility, or even shared responsibility, for the rearing of children. The old assumption of the workplace, still implicit, is that workers have wives at home. It is built not only into the structure and expectations of the workplace but into other crucial social institutions, such as schools, which make no attempt to take account, in their scheduled hours or vacations, of the fact that parents are likely to hold jobs.

Now, of course, many wage workers do not have wives at home. Often, they *are* wives and mothers, or single, separated, or divorced mothers of small children. But neither the family nor the workplace has taken much account of this fact. Employed wives still do by far the greatest proportion of unpaid family work, such as child care and housework. Women are far more likely to take time out of the workplace or to work part-time because of family responsibilities than are their husbands or male partners.

And they are much more likely to move because of their husbands' employment needs or opportunities than their own. All these tendencies, which are due to a number of factors, including the sex segregation and discrimination of the workplace itself, tend to be cyclical in their effects: wives advance more slowly than their husbands at work and thus gain less seniority, and the discrepancy between their wages increases over time. Then, because both the power structure of the family and what is regarded as consensual "rational" family decision making reflect the fact that the husband usually earns more, it will become even less likely as time goes on that the unpaid work of the family will be shared between the spouses. Thus the cycle of inequality is perpetuated. Often hidden from view within a marriage, it is in the increasingly likely event of marital breakdown that the socially constructed inequality of married women is at its most visible.

This is what I mean when I say that gender-structured marriage *makes* women vulnerable. These are not matters of natural necessity, as some people would believe. Surely nothing in our natures dictates that men should not be equal participants in the rearing of their children. Nothing in the nature of work makes it impossible to adjust it to the fact that people are parents as well as workers. That these things have not happened is part of the historically, socially constructed differentiation between the sexes that feminists have come to call *gender*. We live in a society that has over the years regarded the innate characteristic of sex as one of the clearest legitimizers of different rights and restrictions, both formal and informal. While the legal sanctions that uphold male dominance have begun to be eroded in the past century, and more rapidly in the last twenty years, the heavy weight of tradition, combined with the effects of socialization, still works powerfully to reinforce sex roles that are commonly regarded as of unequal prestige and worth. The sexual division of labor has not only been a fundamental part of the marriage contract, but so deeply influences us in our formative years that feminists of both sexes who try to reject it can find themselves struggling against it with varying degrees of ambivalence. Based on this linchpin, "gender"—by which I mean *the deeply entrenched institutionalization of sexual difference*—still permeates our society.

GENDER AS AN ISSUE OF JUSTICE

Counting Women In

When we turn to the great tradition of Western political thought with questions about the justice of the treatment of the sexes in mind, it is to little avail. Bold feminists like Mary Astell, Mary Wollstonecraft, William Thompson, Harriet Taylor, and George Bernard Shaw have occasionally challenged the tradition, often using its own premises and arguments to overturn its explicit or implicit justification of the inequality of women. But John Stuart Mill is a rare exception to the rule that those who hold central positions in the tradition almost never question the justice of the subordination of women. This phenomenon is undoubtedly due in part to the fact that Aristotle, whose theory of justice has been so influential, relegated women to a sphere of "household justice"—populated by persons who are not fundamentally equal to the free men who participate in political justice, but inferiors whose natural function is to serve those who are more fully human. The liberal tradition, despite its supposed foundation of individual rights and human equality, is more Aristotelian in this respect than is generally acknowledged. In one way or another, almost all liberal theorists have assumed that the "individual" who is the basic subject of the theories is the male head of a patriarchal household. Thus they have not usually considered applying the principles of justice to women or to relations between the sexes.

When we turn to contemporary theories of justice, however, we expect to find more illumi-

nating and positive contributions to the subject of gender and justice. However, mainstream contemporary theories of justice do not address the subject any better than those of the past. Theories of justice that apply to only half of us simply won't do; the inclusiveness falsely implied by the current use of gender-neutral terms must become real. Theories of justice must apply to all of us, and to all of human life, instead of *assuming* silently that half of us take care of whole areas of life that are considered outside the scope of social justice. In a just society, the structure and practices of families must afford women the same opportunities as men to develop their capacities, to participate in political power, to influence social choices, and to be economically as well as physically secure.

Gender and Equality of Opportunity

The family is a crucial determinant of our opportunities in life, of what we "become." It has frequently been acknowledged by those concerned with real equality of opportunity that the family presents a problem. But though they have discerned a serious problem, these theorists have underestimated it because they have seen only half of it. They have seen that the disparity among families in terms of the physical and emotional environment, motivation, and material advantages they can give their children has a tremendous effect upon children's opportunities in life. We are not born as isolated, equal individuals in our society, but into family situations: some in the social middle, some poor and homeless, and some superaffluent; some to a single or soon-to-be-separated parent, some to parents whose marriage is fraught with conflict, some to pare~ who will stay together in love and h~ Any claims that equal opport~ therefore completely unf neglect of the poor, espe~ and Hispanic households, ~ policies of the Reagan years, farther from the principles of equal opportunity. To come close to them would require, for example, a high and uniform standard of public education and the provision of equal social services—including health care, employment training, job opportunities, drug rehabilitation, and decent housing—for all who need them. In addition to redistributive taxation, only massive reallocations of resources from the military to social services could make these things possible.

But even if all these disparities were somehow eliminated, we would still not attain equal opportunity for all. This is because what has not been recognized as an equal opportunity problem, except in feminist literature and circles, is the disparity *within* the family, the fact that its gender structure is itself a major obstacle to equality of opportunity. This is very important in itself, since one of the factors with most influence on our opportunities in life is the social significance attributed to our sex. The opportunities of girls and women are centrally affected by the structure and practices of family life, particularly by the fact that women are almost invariably primary parents. What nonfeminists who see in the family an obstacle to equal opportunity have *not* seen is that the extent to which a family is gender-structured can make the sex we belong to a relatively insignificant aspect of our identity and our life prospects or an all-pervading one. This is because so much of the social construction of gender takes place in the family, and particularly in the institution of female parenting.

Moreover, especially in recent years, with the increased rates of single motherhood, separation, and divorce, the inequalities between the sexes have *compounded* the first part of the problem. The disparity among families has grown largely because of the impoverishment of many women and children after separation or divorce. The division of labor in the typical family leaves most women far less capable than of supporting themselves, and this dispar-

ity is accentuated by the fact that children of separated or divorced parents usually live with their mothers. The inadequacy—and frequent nonpayment—of child support has become recognized as a major social problem. Thus the inequalities of gender are now directly harming many children of both sexes as well as women themselves. Enhancing equal opportunity for women, important as it is in itself, is also a crucial way of improving the opportunities of many of the most disadvantaged children.

As there is a connection among the parts of this problem, so is there a connection among some of the solutions: much of what needs to be done to end the inequalities of gender, and to work in the direction of ending gender itself, will also help to equalize opportunity from one family to another. Subsidized, high-quality day care is obviously one such thing; another is the adaptation of the workplace to the needs of parents. These and other relevant policy issues will be addressed.

The Family as a School of Justice

One of the things that theorists who have argued that families need not or cannot be just, or who have simply neglected them, have failed to explain is how, within a formative social environment that is *not* founded upon principles of justice, children can learn to develop that sense of justice they will require as citizens of a just society. Rather than being one among many co-equal institutions of a just society, a just family is its essential foundation.

It may seem uncontroversial, even obvious, that families must be just because of the vast influence they have on the moral development of children. But this is clearly not the case. I shall argue that unless the first and most formative example of adult interaction usually experienced by children is one of justice and reciprocity, rather than one of domination and manipulation or of unequal altruism and one-sided self-sacrifice, and unless they themselves are treated with concern and respect, they are likely to be considerably hindered in becoming people who are guided by principles of justice. Moreover, I claim, the sharing of roles by men and women, rather than the division of roles between them, would have a further positive impact because the experience of *being* a physical and psychological nurturer—whether of a child or of another adult—would increase that capacity to identify with and fully comprehend the viewpoints of others that is important to a sense of justice. In a society that minimized gender this would be more likely to be the experience of all of us.

Almost every person in our society starts life in a family of some sort or other. Fewer of these families now fit the usual, though by no means universal, standard of previous generations, that is, wage-working father, homemaking mother, and children. More families these days are headed by a single parent; lesbian and gay parenting is no longer so rare; many children have two wage-working parents, and receive at least some of their early care outside the home. While its forms are varied, the family in which a child is raised, especially in the earliest years, is clearly a crucial place for early moral development and for the formation of our basic attitudes to others. It is, potentially, a place where we can *learn to be just*. It is especially important for the development of a sense of justice that grows from sharing the experiences of others and becoming aware of the points of view of others who are different in some respects from ourselves, but with whom we clearly have some interests in common.

The importance of the family for the moral development of individuals was far more often recognized by political theorists of the past than it is by those of the present. Hegel, Rousseau, Tocqueville, Mill, and Dewey are obvious examples that come to mind. Rousseau, for example, shocked by Plato's proposal to abolish the family, says that it is

as though there were no need for a natural base on which to form conventional ties; as though the love of one's nearest were not the principle of the love one owes the state; as though it were not by means of the small fatherland which is the family that the heart attaches itself to the large one.

Defenders of both autocratic and democratic regimes have recognized the political importance of different family forms for the formation of citizens. On the one hand, the nineteenth-century monarchist Louis de Bonald argued against the divorce reforms of the French Revolution, which he claimed had weakened the patriarchal family, on the grounds that "in order to keep the state out of the hands of the people, it is necessary to keep the family out of the hands of women and children." Taking this same line of thought in the opposite direction, the U.S. Supreme Court decided in 1879 in *Reynolds v. Nebraska* that familial patriarchy fostered despotism and was therefore intolerable. Denying Mormon men the freedom to practice polygamy, the Court asserted that it was an offense "subversive of good order" that "leads to the patriarchal principle, . . . [and] when applied to large communities, fetters the people in stationary despotism, while that principle cannot long exist in connection with monogamy."

However, while de Bonald was consistent in his adherence to an hierarchical family structure as necessary for an undemocratic political system, the Supreme Court was by no means consistent in promoting an egalitarian family as an essential underpinning for political democracy. For in other decisions of the same period—such as *Bradwell v. Illinois*, the famous 1872 case that upheld the exclusion of women from the practice of law—the Court rejected women's claims to legal equality, in the name of a thoroughly patriarchal, though monogamous, family that was held to require the dependence of women and their exclusion from civil and political life. While bigamy was considered patriarchal, and as such a threat to republican, democratic government, the refusal to allow a married woman to employ her talents and to make use of her qualifications to earn an independent living was not considered patriarchal. It was so far from being a threat to the civil order, in fact, that it was deemed necessary for it, and as such was ordained by both God and nature. Clearly, in both *Reynolds* and *Bradwell*, "state authorities enforced family forms preferred by those in power and justified as necessary to stability and order." The Court noticed the despotic potential of polygamy, but was blind to the despotic potential of patriarchal monogamy. This was perfectly acceptable to them as a training ground for citizens.

Most theorists of the past who stressed the importance of the family and its practices for the wider world of moral and political life by no means insisted on congruence between the structures or practices of the family and those of the outside world. Though concerned with moral development, they bifurcated public from private life to such an extent that they had no trouble reconciling inegalitarian, sometimes admittedly unjust, relations founded upon sentiment within the family with a more just, even egalitarian, social structure outside the family. Rousseau, Hegel, Tocqueville—all thought the family was centrally important for the development of morality in citizens, but all defended the hierarchy of the marital structure while spurning such a degree of hierarchy in institutions and practices outside the household. Preferring instead to rely on love, altruism, and generosity as the basis for family relations, none of these theorists argued for *just* family structures as necessary for socializing children into citizenship in a just society.

The position that justice within the family is irrelevant to the development of just citizens was not plausible even when only men were citizens. John Stuart Mill, in *The Subjection of Women*, takes an impassioned stand against it.

He argues that the inequality of women within the family is deeply subversive of justice in general in the wider social world, because it subverts the moral potential of men. Mill's first answer to the question, "For whose good are all these changes in women's rights to be undertaken?" is: "the advantage of having the most universal and pervading of all human relations regulated by justice instead of injustice." Making marriage a relationship of equals, he argues, would transform this central part of daily life from "a school of despotism" into "a school of moral cultivation." He goes on to discuss, in the strongest of terms, the noxious effect of growing up in a family not regulated by justice. Consider, he says, "the self-worship, the unjust self-preference," nourished in a boy growing up in a household in which "by the mere fact of being born a male he is by right the superior of all and every one of an entire half of the human race." Mill concludes that the example set by perpetuating a marital structure "contradictory to the first principles of social justice" must have such "a perverting influence" that it is hard even to imagine the good effects of changing it. All other attempts to educate people to respect and practice justice, Mill claims, will be superficial "as long as the citadel of the enemy is not attacked." Mill felt as much hope for what the family might be as he felt despair at what it was not. "The family, justly constituted, would be the real school of the virtues of freedom," primary among which was "justice, . . . grounded as before on equal, but now also on sympathetic association." Mill both saw clearly and had the courage to address what so many other political philosophers either could not see, or saw and turned away from.

Despite the strength and fervor of his advocacy of women's rights, however, Mill's idea of a just family structure falls far short of that of many feminists even of his own time, including his wife, Harriet Taylor. In spite of the fact that Mill recognized both the empowering effect of earnings on one's position in the family and the limiting effect of domestic responsibility on women's opportunities, he balked at questioning the traditional division of labor between the sexes. For him, a woman's choice of marriage was parallel to a man's choice of a profession: unless and until she had fulfilled her obligations to her husband and children, she should not undertake anything else. But clearly, however equal the legal rights of husbands and wives, this position largely undermines Mill's own insistence upon the importance of marital equality for a just society. His acceptance of the traditional division of labor, without making any provision for wives who were thereby made economically dependent upon their husbands, largely undermines his insistence upon family justice as the necessary foundation for social justice.

Thus even those political theorists of the past who have perceived the family as an important school of moral development have rarely acknowledged the need for congruence between the family and the wider social order, which suggests that families themselves need to be just. Even when they have, as with Mill, they have been unwilling to push hard on the traditional division of labor within the family in the name of justice or equality.

Contemporary theorists of justice, with few exceptions, have paid little or no attention to the question of moral development—of how we are to *become* just. Most of them seem to think, to adapt slightly Hobbes's notable phrase, that just men spring like mushrooms from the earth. Not surprisingly, then, it is far less often acknowledged in recent than in past theories that the family is important for moral development, and especially for instilling a sense of justice. As I have already noted, many theorists pay no attention at all to either the family or gender. In the rare case that the issue of justice within the family is given any sustained attention, the family is not viewed as a potential school of social justice. In the rare case that a theorist pays any sustained attention

to the development of a sense of justice or morality, little if any attention is likely to be paid to the family. Even in the rare event that theorists pay considerable attention to the family *as* the first major locus of moral socialization, they do not refer to the fact that families are almost all still thoroughly gender-structured institutions.

In a just society, the structure and practices of families must give women the same opportunities as men to develop their capacities, to participate in political power and influence social choices, and to be economically secure. But in addition to this, families must be just because of the vast influence that they have on the moral development of children. The family is the primary institution of formative moral development. And the structure and practices of the family must parallel those of the larger society if the sense of justice is to be fostered and maintained. While many theorists of justice, both past and present, appear to have denied the importance of at least one of these factors, my own view is that both are absolutely crucial. A society that is committed to equal respect for all of its members, and to justice in social distributions of benefits and responsibilities, can neither neglect the family nor accept family structures and practices that violate these norms, as do current gender-based structures and practices. It is essential that children who are to develop into adults with a strong sense of justice and commitment to just institutions spend their earliest and most formative years in an environment in which they are loved and nurtured, *and* in which principles of justice are abided by and respected. What is a child of either sex to learn about fairness in the average household with two full-time working parents, where the mother does, at the very least, twice as much family work as the father? What is a child to learn about the value of nurturing and domestic work in a home with a traditional division of labor in which the father either subtly or not so subtly uses the fact that he is the wage earner to "pull rank" on or to abuse his wife? What is a child to learn about responsibility for others in a family in which, after many years of arranging her life around the needs of her husband and children, a woman is faced with having to provide for herself and her children but is totally ill-equipped for the task by the life she agreed to lead, has led, and expected to go on leading?

TOWARD A HUMANIST JUSTICE

The family is the linchpin of gender, reproducing it from one generation to the next. As we have seen, family life as typically practiced in our society is not just, either to women or to children. Moreover, it is not conducive to the rearing of citizens with a strong sense of justice. In spite of all the rhetoric about equality between the sexes, the traditional or quasi-traditional division of family labor still prevails. Women are made vulnerable by constructing their lives around the expectation that they will be primary parents; they become more vulnerable within marriages in which they fulfill this expectation, whether or not they also work for wages; and they are most vulnerable in the event of separation or divorce, when they usually take over responsibility for children without adequate support from their ex-husbands. Since approximately half of all marriages end in divorce, about half of our children are likely to experience its dislocations, often made far more traumatic by the socioeconomic consequences of both gender-structured marriage and divorce settlements that fail to take account of it. I have suggested that, for very important reasons, the family *needs* to be a just institution, and have shown that contemporary theories of justice neglect women and ignore gender. How can we address this injustice?

This is a complex question. It is particularly so because we place great value on our freedom to live different kinds of lives, there is no current consensus on many aspects of gender, and

we have good reason to suspect that many of our beliefs about sexual difference and appropriate sex roles are heavily influenced by the very fact that we grew up in a gender-structured society. All of us have been affected, in our very psychological structures, by the fact of gender in our personal pasts, just as our society has been deeply affected by its strong influence in our collective past. Because of the lack of shared meanings about gender, it constitutes a particularly hard case for those who care deeply about both personal freedom and social justice. The way we divide the labor and responsibilities in our personal lives seems to be one of those things that people should be free to work out for themselves, but because of its vast repercussions it belongs clearly within the scope of things that must be governed by principles of justice. Which is to say, in the language of political and moral theory, that it belongs both to the sphere of "the good" and to that of "the right."

I shall argue here that any just and fair solution to the urgent problem of women's and children's vulnerability must encourage and facilitate the equal sharing by men and women of paid and unpaid work, of productive and reproductive labor. We must work toward a future in which all will be likely to choose this mode of life. A just future would be one without gender. In its social structures and practices, one's sex would have no more relevance than one's eye color or the length of one's toes. No assumptions would be made about "male" and "female" roles; childbearing would be so conceptually separated from child rearing and other family responsibilities that it would be a cause for surprise, and no little concern, if men and women were not equally responsible for domestic life or if children were to spend much more time with one parent than the other. It would be a future in which men and women participated in more or less equal numbers in every sphere of life, from infant care to different kinds of paid work to high-level politics.

Thus it would no longer be the case that having no experience of raising children would be the practical prerequisite for attaining positions of the greatest social influence. Decisions about abortion and rape, about divorce settlements and sexual harassment, or about any other crucial social issues would not be made, as they often are now, by legislatures and benches of judges overwhelmingly populated by men whose power is in large part due to their advantaged position in the gender structure. If we are to be at all true to our democratic ideals, moving away from gender is essential. Obviously, the attainment of such a social world requires major changes in a multitude of institutions and social settings outside the home, as well as within it.

Such changes will not happen overnight. Moreover, any present solution to the vulnerability of women and children that is just and respects individual freedom must take into account that most people currently live in ways that are greatly affected by gender, and most still favor many aspects of current, gendered practices. Sociological studies confirm what most of us already infer from our own personal and professional acquaintances: there are no currently shared meanings in this country about the extent to which differences between the sexes are innate or environmental, about the appropriate roles of men and women, and about which family forms and divisions of labor are most beneficial for partners, parents, and children. There are those, at one extreme, for whom the different roles of the two sexes, especially as parents, are deeply held tenets of religious belief. At the other end of the spectrum are those of us for whom the sooner all social differentiation between the sexes vanishes, the better it will be for all of us. And there are a thousand varieties of view in between. Public policies must respect people's views and choices. But they must do so only insofar as it can be ensured that these choices do not result, as they now do, in the vulnera-

bility of women and children. Special protections must be built into our laws and public policies to ensure that, for those who choose it, the division of labor between the sexes does not result in injustice. In the face of these difficulties—balancing freedom and the effects of past choices against the needs of justice—I do not pretend to have arrived at any complete or fully satisfactory answers. But I shall attempt in this chapter to suggest some social reforms, including changes in public policies and reforms of family law, that may help us work toward a solution to the injustices of gender.

Marriage has become an increasingly peculiar contract, a complex and ambiguous combination of anachronism and present-day reality. There is no longer the kind of agreement that once prevailed about what is expected of the parties to a marriage. Clearly, at least in the United States, it is no longer reasonable to assume that marriage will last a lifetime, since only half of current marriages are expected to. And yet, in spite of the increasing legal equality of men and women and the highly publicized figures about married women's increased participation in the labor force, many couples continue to adhere to more or less traditional patterns of role differentiation. As a recent article put it, women are "out of the house but not out of the kitchen." Consequently, often working part-time or taking time out from wage work to care for family members, especially children, most wives are in a very different position from their husbands in their ability to be economically self-supporting. This is reflected, as we have seen, in power differentials between the sexes within the family. It means also, in the increasingly common event of divorce, usually by mutual agreement, that it is the mother who in 90 percent of cases will have physical custody of the children. But whereas the greater need for money goes one way, the bulk of the earning power almost always goes the other. This is one of the most important causes of the feminization of poverty, which is affecting the life chances of ever larger numbers of children as well as their mothers. The division of labor within families has always adversely affected women, by making them economically dependent on men. Because of the increasing instability of marriage, its effects on children have now reached crisis proportions.

Some who are critical of the present structure and practices of marriage have suggested that men and women simply be made free to make their own agreements about family life, contracting with each other, much as business contracts are made. But this takes insufficient account of the history of gender in our culture and our own psychologies, of the present substantive inequalities between the sexes, and, most important, of the well-being of the children who result from the relationship. As has long been recognized in the realm of labor relations, justice is by no means always enhanced by the maximization of freedom of contract, if the individuals involved are in unequal positions to start with. Some have even suggested that it is consistent with justice to leave spouses to work out their own divorce settlement. By this time, however, the two people ending a marriage are likely to be far *more* unequal. Such a practice would be even more catastrophic for most women and children than is the present system. Wives in any but the rare cases in which they as individuals have remained their husbands' socioeconomic equals could hardly be expected to reach a just solution if left "free" to "bargain" the terms of financial support or child custody. What would they have to bargain *with*?

There are many directions that public policy can and should take in order to make relations between men and women more just. In discussing these, I shall look to some of the contemporary ways of thinking about justice that I find most convincing. I draw particularly on John Rawls's idea of the original position and Michael Walzer's conception of the complex equality found in separate spheres of justice, between which I find no inconsistency. I also keep in mind critical legal theorists' critique of contract, and the related idea that rights to privacy that are to be valuable to all of us can be enjoyed only insofar as the sphere of life in which we enjoy them ensures the equality of its adult members and protects children. Let us begin by asking what kind of arrangements persons in a Rawlsian original position would agree to regarding marriage, parental and other domestic responsibilities, and divorce. What kinds of policies would they agree to for other aspects of social life, such as the workplace and schools, that affect men, women, and children and relations among them? And let us consider whether these arrangements would satisfy Walzer's separate spheres test—that inequalities in one sphere of life not be allowed to overflow into another. Will they foster equality within the sphere of family life? For the protection of the privacy of a domestic sphere in which inequality exists is the protection of the right of the strong to exploit and abuse the weak.

Let us first try to imagine ourselves, as far as possible, in the original position, knowing neither what our sex nor any other of our personal characteristics will be once the veil of ignorance is lifted.* Neither do we know our place in society or our particular conception of the good life. Particularly relevant in this context, of course, is our lack of knowledge of our beliefs about the characteristics of men and women and our related convictions about the appropriate division of labor between the sexes.

---

*I say "so far as possible" because given the deep effects of gender on our psychologies, it is probably more difficult for us, having grown up in a gender-structured society, to imagine not knowing our sex than anything else about ourselves. Nevertheless, this should not prevent us from trying.

Thus the positions we represent must include a wide variety of beliefs on these matters. We may, once the veil of ignorance is lifted, find ourselves feminist men or feminist women whose conception of the good life includes the minimization of social differentiation between the sexes. Or we may find ourselves traditionalist men or women, whose conception of the good life, for religious or other reasons, is bound up in an adherence to the conventional division of labor between the sexes. The challenge is to arrive at and apply principles of justice having to do with the family and the division of labor between the sexes that can satisfy these vastly disparate points of view and the many that fall between.

There are some traditionalist positions so extreme that they ought not be admitted for consideration, since they violate such fundamentals as equal basic liberty and self-respect. We need not, and should not, that is to say, admit for consideration views based on the notion that women are inherently inferior beings whose function is to fulfill the needs of men. Such a view is no more admissible in the construction of just institutions for a modern pluralist society than is the view, however deeply held, that some are naturally slaves and others naturally and justifiably their masters. We need not, therefore, consider approaches to marriage that view it as an inherently and desirably hierarchical structure of dominance and subordination. Even if it were conceivable that a person who did not know whether he or she would turn out to be a man or a woman in the society being planned would subscribe to such views, they are not admissible. Even if there were no other reasons to refuse to admit such views, they must be excluded for the sake of children, for everyone in the original position has a high personal stake in the quality of childhood. Marriages of dominance and submission are bad for children as well as for their mothers, and the socioeconomic outcome of divorce after such a marriage is very likely to damage their lives and seriously restrict their opportunities.

With this proviso, what social structures and public policies regarding relations between the sexes, and the family in particular, could we agree on in the original position? I think we would arrive at a basic model that would absolutely minimize gender. I shall first give an account of some of what this would consist in. We would also, however, build in carefully protective institutions for those who wished to follow gender-structured modes of life. These too I shall try to spell out in some detail.

MOVING AWAY FROM GENDER

First, public policies and laws should generally assume no social differentiation of the sexes. Shared parental responsibility for child care would be both assumed and facilitated. Few people outside of feminist circles seem willing to acknowledge that society does not have to choose between a system of female parenting that renders women and children seriously vulnerable and a system of total reliance on day care provided outside the home. While high-quality day care, subsidized so as to be equally available to all children, certainly constitutes an important part of the response that society should make in order to provide justice for women and children, it is only one part. If we start out with the reasonable assumption that women and men are equally parents of their children, and have equal responsibility for both the unpaid effort that goes into caring for them and their economic support, then we must rethink the demands of work life throughout the period in which a worker of either sex is a parent of a small child. We can no longer cling to the by now largely mythical assumption that every worker has "someone else" at home to raise "his" children.

The facilitation and encouragement of equally shared parenting would require substantial changes. It would mean major changes in the workplace, all of which could be provided on an entirely (and not falsely) gender-neutral basis. Employers must be required by law not only completely to eradicate sex discrimination, including sexual harassment, they should also be required to make positive provision for the fact that most workers, for differing lengths of time in their working lives, are also parents, and are sometimes required to nurture other family members, such as their own aging parents. Because children are borne by women but can (and, I contend, should) be raised by both parents equally, policies relating to pregnancy and birth should be quite distinct from those relating to parenting. Pregnancy and childbirth, to whatever varying extent they require leave from work, should be regarded as temporarily disabling conditions like any others, and employers should be mandated to provide leave for all such conditions. Of course, pregnancy and childbirth are far *more* than simply "disabling conditions," but they should be treated as such for leave purposes, in part because their disabling effects vary from one woman to another. It seems unfair to mandate, say, eight or more weeks of leave for a condition that disables many women for less time and some for much longer, while *not* mandating leave for illnesses or other disabling conditions. Surely a society as rich as ours can afford to do both.

Parental leave during the postbirth months must be available to mothers and fathers on the same terms, to facilitate shared parenting; they might take sequential leaves or each might take half-time leave. All workers should have the right, without prejudice to their jobs, seniority, benefits, and so on, to work less than full-time during the first year of a child's life, and to work flexible or somewhat reduced hours at least until the child reaches the age of seven. Correspondingly greater flexibility of hours must be provided for the parents of a child with any health problem or disabling condition. The professions whose greatest demands (such as tenure in academia or the partnership hurdle in

law) coincide with the peak period of child rearing must restructure their demands or provide considerable flexibility for those of their workers who are also participating parents. Large-scale employers should also be required to provide high-quality on-site day care for children from infancy up to school age. And to ensure equal quality of day care for all young children, *direct government subsidies* (not tax credits, which benefit the better-off) should make up the difference between the cost of high-quality day care and what less well paid parents could reasonably be expected to pay.

There are a number of things that schools, too, must do to promote the minimization of gender. As Amy Gutmann has recently noted, in their present authority structures (84 percent of elementary school teachers are female, while 99 percent of school superintendents are male), "schools do not simply reflect, they perpetuate the social reality of gender preferences when they educate children in a system in which men rule women and women rule children." She argues that, since such sex stereotyping is "a formidable obstacle" to children's rational deliberation about the lives they wish to lead, sex should be regarded as a relevant qualification in the hiring of both teachers and administrators, until these proportions have become much more equal.

An equally important role of our schools must be to ensure in the course of children's education that they become fully aware of the politics of gender. This does not only mean ensuring that women's experience and women's writing are included in the curriculum, although this in itself is undoubtedly important. Its political significance has become obvious from the amount of protest that it has provoked. Children need also to be taught about the present inequalities, ambiguities, and uncertainties of marriage, the facts of workplace discrimination and segregation, and the likely consequences of making life choices based on assumptions about gender. They should be discouraged from thinking about their futures as *determined* by the sex to which they happen to belong. For many children, of course, personal experience has already "brought home" the devastating effects of the traditional division of labor between the sexes. But they do not necessarily come away from this experience with positive ideas about how to structure their own future family lives differently. As Anita Shreve has recently suggested, "the old home-economics courses that used to teach girls how to cook and sew might give way to the new home economics: teaching girls *and boys* how to combine working and parenting." Finally, schools should be required to provide high-quality after-school programs, where children can play safely, do their homework, or participate in creative activities.

The implementation of all these policies would significantly help parents to share the earning and the domestic responsibilities of their families, and children to grow up prepared for a future in which the significance of sex difference is greatly diminished. Men could participate equally in the nurturance of their children, from infancy and throughout childhood, with predictably great effects on themselves, their wives or partners, and their children. And women need not become vulnerable through economic dependence. In addition, such arrangements would alleviate the qualms many people have about the long hours that some children spend in day care. If one parent of a preschooler worked, for example, from eight to four o'clock and the other from ten to six o'clock, a preschool child would be at day care for only six hours (including nap time), and with each one or both of her or his parents the rest of the day. If each parent were able to work a six-hour day, or a four-day week, still less day care would be needed. Moreover, on-site provision of day care would enable mothers to continue to nurse, if they chose, beyond the time of their parental leave.

The situation of single parents and their children is more complicated, but it seems that it too, for a number of reasons, would be much improved in a society in which sex difference was accorded an absolute minimum of social significance. Let us begin by looking at the situation of never-married mothers and their children. First, the occurrence of pregnancy among single teenagers, which is almost entirely unintended, would presumably be reduced if girls grew up more assertive and self-protective, and with less tendency to perceive their futures primarily in terms of motherhood. It could also be significantly reduced by the wide availability of sex education and contraception. Second, the added weight of responsibility given to fatherhood in a gender-free society would surely give young men more incentive than they now have not to incur the results of careless sexual behavior until they were ready to take on the responsibilities of being parents. David Ellwood has outlined a policy for establishing the paternity of all children of single mothers at the time of birth, and for enforcing the requirement that their fathers contribute to their support throughout childhood, with provision for governmental backup support in cases where the father is unable to pay. These proposals seem eminently fair and sensible, although the minimum levels of support suggested ($1,500 to $2,000 per year) are inadequate, especially since the mother is presumed to be either taking care of the child herself or paying for day care (which often costs far more than this) while she works.

Third, never-married mothers would benefit greatly from a work structure that took parenthood seriously into account, as well as from the subsidization of high-quality day care. Women who grew up with the expectation that their work lives would be as important a part of their futures as the work lives of men would be less likely to enter dead-ended, low-skilled occupations, and would be better able to cope economically with parenthood without marriage.

Most single parenthood results, however, not from single mothers giving birth, but from marital separation and divorce. And this too would be significantly altered in a society not structured along the lines of gender. Even if rates of divorce were to remain unchanged (which is impossible to predict), it seems inconceivable that separated and divorced fathers who had shared equally in the nurturance of their children from the outset would be as likely to neglect them, by not seeing them or not contributing to their support, as many do today. It seems reasonable to expect that children after divorce would still have two actively involved parents, and two working adults economically responsible for them. Because these parents had shared equally the paid work and the family work, their incomes would be much more equal than those of most divorcing parents today. Even if they were quite equal, however, the parent without physical custody should be required to contribute to the child's support, *to the point where the standards of living of the two households were the same.* This would be very different from the situation of many children of divorced parents today, dependent for both their nurturance and their economic support solely on mothers whose wage work has been interrupted by primary parenting.

It is impossible to predict all the effects of moving toward a society without gender. Major current injustices to women and children would end. Men would experience both the joys and the responsibilities of far closer and more sustained contact with their children than many have today. Many immensely influential spheres of life—notably politics and the professional occupations—would for the first time be populated more or less equally by men and women, most of whom were also actively participating parents. This would be in great contrast to today, when most of those who rise to influential positions are either men who, if fathers, have minimal contact with their children, or women who have either forgone motherhood

altogether or hired others as full-time caretakers for their children because of the demands of their careers. These are the people who make policy at the highest levels—policies not only *about* families and their welfare and about the education of children, but about the foreign policies, the wars and the weapons that will determine the future or the lack of future for all these families and children. Yet they are almost all people who gain the influence they do in part by never having had the day-to-day experience of nurturing a child. This is probably the most significant aspect of our gendered division of labor, though the least possible to grasp. The effects of changing it could be momentous.

PROTECTING THE VULNERABLE

The pluralism of beliefs and modes of life is fundamental to our society, and the genderless society I have just outlined would certainly not be agreed upon by all as desirable. Thus when we think about constructing relations between the sexes that could be agreed upon in the original position, and are therefore just from all points of view, we must also design institutions and practices acceptable to those with more traditional beliefs about the characteristics of men and women, and the appropriate division of labor between them. It is essential, if men and women are to be allowed to so divide their labor, as they must be if we are to respect the current pluralism of beliefs, that society protect the vulnerable. Without such protection, the marriage contract seriously exacerbates the initial inequalities of those who entered into it, and too many women and children live perilously close to economic disaster and serious social dislocation; too many also live with violence or the continual threat of it. It should be noted here that the rights and obligations that the law would need to promote and mandate in order to protect the vulnerable need not—and should not—be designated in accordance with sex, but in terms of different functions or roles performed. There are only a minute percentage of "househusbands" in this country, and a very small number of men whose work lives take second priority after their wives'. But they can quite readily be protected by the same institutional structures that can protect traditional and quasi-traditional wives, so long as these are designed without reference to sex.

Gender-structured marriage, then, needs to be regarded as a currently necessary institution (because still chosen by some) but one that is socially problematic. It should be subjected to a number of legal requirements, at least when there are children.* Most important, there is no need for the division of labor between the sexes to involve the economic dependence, either complete or partial, of one partner on the other. Such dependence can be avoided if both partners have *equal legal entitlement* to all earnings coming into the household. The clearest and simplest way of doing this would be to have employers make out wage checks equally divided between the earner and the partner who provides all or most of his or her unpaid domestic services. In many cases, of course, this would not change the way couples actually manage their finances; it would simply codify what they already agree on—that the household income is rightly shared, because in a real sense jointly earned. Such couples recognize the fact that the wage-earning spouse is no more supporting the homemaking and child-rearing spouse than the latter is supporting the former; the form of support each offers the family is simply different. Such couples might well take both checks, deposit them in a joint account, and really share the income, just as they now do with the earnings that come into the household.

In the case of some couples, however, altering the entitlement of spouses to the earned income of the household as I have suggested *would* make a significant difference. It would make a difference in cases where the earning or higher-earning partner now directly exploits this power, by refusing to make significant spending decisions jointly, by failing to share the income, or by psychologically or physically abusing the nonearning or low-earning partner, reinforced by the notion that she (almost always the wife) has little option but to put up with such abuse or to take herself and her children into a state of destitution. It would make a difference, too, in cases where the higher-earning partner indirectly exploits this earning power in order to perpetuate the existing division of labor in the family. In such instances considerable changes in the balance of power would be likely to result from the legal and societal recognition that the partner who does most of the domestic work of the family contributes to its well-being just as much, and therefore rightly *earns* just as much, as the partner who does most of the workplace work.

What I am suggesting is *not* that the wage-working partner pay the homemaking partner for services rendered. I do not mean to introduce the cash nexus into a personal relationship where it is inappropriate. I have simply suggested that since both partners in a traditional or quasi-traditional marriage work, there is no reason why only one of them should get paid, or why one should be paid far more than the other. The equal splitting of wages would constitute public recognition of the fact that the currently unpaid labor of families is just as important as the paid labor. If we do *not* believe this, then we should insist on the complete and equal sharing of both paid and unpaid labor, as occurs in the genderless model of marriage and parenting described earlier. It is only if we *do* believe it that society can justly allow couples to distribute the two types of labor so unevenly. But in such cases, given the

---

*I see no reason why what I propose here should be restricted to couples who are legally married. It should apply equally to "common law" relationships that produce children, and in which a division of labor is practiced.

enormous significance our society attaches to money and earnings, we should insist that the earnings be recognized as equally earned by the two persons. To call on Walzer's language, we should do this in order to help prevent the inequality of family members in the sphere of wage work to invade their domestic sphere.

It is also important to point out that this proposal does not constitute unwarranted invasion of privacy or any more state intervention into the life of families than currently exists. It would involve only the same kind of invasion of privacy as is now required by such things as registration of marriages and births, and the filing of tax returns declaring numbers and names of dependents. And it *seems* like intervention in families only because it would alter the existing relations of power within them. If a person's capacity to fulfill the terms of his or her work is dependent on having a spouse at home who raises the children and in other ways sustains that worker's day-to-day life, then it is no more interventionist to pay both equally for their contributions than only to pay one.

The same fundamental principle should apply to separation and divorce, to the extent that the division of labor has been practiced within a marriage. Under current divorce laws, as we have seen, the terms of exit from marriage are disadvantageous for almost all women in traditional or quasi-traditional marriages. Regardless of the consensus that existed about the division of the family labor, these women lose most of the income that has supported them *and* the social status that attached to them because of their husband's income and employment, often at the same time as suddenly becoming single parents, and prospective wage workers for the first time in many years. This combination of prospects would seem to be enough to put most traditional wives off the idea of divorcing even if they had good cause to do so. In addition, since divorce in the great majority of states no longer requires the consent of both spouses, it seems likely that wives

for whom divorce would spell economic and social catastrophe would be inhibited in voicing their dissatisfactions or needs within marriage. The terms of exit are very likely to affect the use and the power of voice in the ongoing relationship. At worst, these women may be rendered virtually defenseless in the face of physical or psychological abuse. This is not a system of marriage and divorce that could possibly be agreed to by persons in an original position in which they did not know whether they were to be male or female, traditionalist or not. It is a fraudulent contract, presented as beneficial to all but in fact to the benefit only of the more powerful.

For all these reasons, it seems essential that the terms of divorce be redrawn so as to reflect the gendered or nongendered character of the marriage that is ending, to a far greater extent than they do now. The legal system of a society that allows couples to divide the labor of families in a traditional or quasi-traditional manner *must* take responsibility for the vulnerable position in which marital breakdown places the partner who has completely or partially lost the capacity to be economically self-supporting. When such a marriage ends, it seems wholly reasonable to expect a person whose career has been largely unencumbered by domestic responsibilities to support financially the partner who undertook these responsibilities. This support, in the form of combined alimony and child support, should be far more substantial than the token levels often ordered by the courts now. *Both postdivorce households should enjoy the same standard of living.* Alimony should not end after a few years, as the (patronizingly named) "rehabilitative alimony" of today does; it should continue for at least as long as the traditional division of labor in the marriage did and, in the case of short-term marriages that produced children, until the youngest child enters first grade and the custodial parent has a real chance of making his or her own living. After that point, child support should continue at a level that enables the children to enjoy a standard of living equal to that of the noncustodial parent. There can be no reason consistent with principles of justice that some should suffer economically vastly more than others from the breakup of a relationship whose asymmetric division of labor was mutually agreed on.

I have suggested two basic models of family rights and responsibilities, both of which are currently needed because this is a time of great transition for men and women and great disagreement about gender. Families in which roles and responsibilities are equally shared regardless of sex are far more in accord with principles of justice than are typical families today. So are families in which those who undertake more traditional domestic roles are protected from the risks they presently incur. In either case, justice as a whole will benefit from the changes. Of the two, however, I claim that the genderless family is more just, in the three important respects that I spelled out at the beginning: it is more just to women; it is more conducive to equal opportunity both for women and for children of both sexes; and it creates a more favorable environment for the rearing of citizens of a just society. Thus, while protecting those whom gender now makes vulnerable, we must also put our best efforts into promoting the elimination of gender.

The increased justice to women that would result from moving away from gender is readily apparent. Standards for just social institutions could no longer take for granted and exclude from considerations of justice much of what women now do, since men would share in it equally. Such central components of justice as what counts as productive labor, and what count as needs and deserts, would be greatly affected by this change. Standards of justice would become *humanist*, as they have never been before. One of the most important effects of this would be to change radically the situation of women as citizens. With egalitarian families, and with institutions such as workplaces and schools designed to accommodate the needs of parents and children, rather than being based as they now are on the traditional assumption that "someone else" is at home, mothers would not be virtually excluded from positions of influence in politics and the workplace. They would be represented at every level in approximately equal numbers with men.

In a genderless society, children too would benefit. They would not suffer in the ways that they do now because of the injustices done to women. It is undeniable that the family in which each of us grows up has a deeply formative influence on us—on the kind of persons we want to be as well as the kind of persons we are. This is one of the reasons why one *cannot* reasonably leave the family out of "the basic structure of society," to which the principles of justice are to apply. Equality of opportunity to become what we want to be would be enhanced in two important ways by the development of families without gender and by the public policies necessary to support their development. First, the growing gap between the economic well-being of children in single-parent and those in two-parent families would be reduced. Children in single-parent families would benefit significantly if fathers were held equally responsible for supporting their children, whether married to their mothers or not; if more mothers had sustained labor force attachment; if high-quality day care were subsidized; and if the workplace were designed to accommodate parenting. These children would be far less likely to spend their formative years in conditions of poverty, with one parent struggling to fulfill the functions of two. Their life chances would be significantly enhanced.

Second, children of both sexes in gender-free families would have (as some already have) much more opportunity for self-development free from sex-role expectations and sex-typed personalities than most do now. Girls and boys who grow up in highly traditional families, in which sex difference is regarded as a determinant of everything from roles, responsibilities, and privileges to acceptable dress, speech, and modes of behavior, clearly have far less freedom to develop into whatever kind of person they want to be than do those who are raised without such constraints. It is too early for us to know a lot about the developmental outcomes and life choices of children who are equally parented by mothers and fathers, since the practice is still so recent and so rare. Persuasive theories such as Chodorow's, however, would lead us to expect much less differentiation between the sexes to result from truly shared parenting. Even now, in most cases without men's equal fathering, both the daughters and the sons of wage-working mothers have been found to have a more positive view of women and less rigid views of sex roles; the daughters (like their mothers) tend to have greater self-esteem and a more positive view of themselves as workers, and the sons, to expect equality and shared roles in their own future marriages. We might well expect that with mothers in the labor force *and* with fathers as equal parents, children's attitudes and psychologies will become even less correlated with their sex. In a very crucial sense, their opportunities to become the persons they want to be will be enlarged.

Finally, it seems undeniable that the enhancement of justice that accompanies the disappearance of gender will make the family a much better place for children to develop a sense of justice. We can no longer deny the importance of the fact that families are where we first learn, by example and by how we are treated, not only how people do relate to each other but also how they *should*. How would families not built on gender be better schools of moral development? First, the example of co-equal parents with shared roles, combining love with justice, would provide a far better example of human relations for children than the domination and dependence that often occur in traditional marriage. The fairness of the distribution of labor, the equal respect, and the *inter*dependence of his or her parents would surely be a powerful first example to a child in a family with equally shared roles. Second, as I have argued, having a sense of justice requires that we be able to empathize, to abstract from our own situation and to think about moral and political issues from the points of view of others. We cannot come to either just principles or just specific decisions by thinking, as it were, as if we were nobody, or thinking from nowhere; we must, therefore, learn to think from the point of view of others, including others who are different from ourselves.

To the extent that gender is de-emphasized in our nurturing practices, this capacity would seem to be enhanced, for two reasons. First, if female primary parenting leads, as it seems to, to less distinct ego boundaries and greater capacity for empathy in female children, and to a greater tendency to self-definition and abstraction in males, then might we not expect to find the two capacities better combined in children of both sexes who are reared by parents of both sexes? Second, the experience of *being* nurturers, throughout a significant portion of our lives, also seems likely to result in an increase in empathy, and in the combination of personal moral capacities, fusing feelings with reason, that just citizens need.

For those whose response to what I have argued here is the practical objection that it is unrealistic and will cost too much, I have some answers and some questions. Some of what I have suggested would not cost anything, in terms of public spending, though it would redistribute the costs and other responsibilities of rearing children more evenly between men and women. Some policies I have endorsed, such as adequate public support for children whose fathers cannot contribute, may cost more than present policies, but may not, depending on how well they work. Some, such as subsidized

high-quality day care, would b   that women who have
themselves, but also might soo   of their lives nurturing
other savings, since they woul   d like used goods? How
who would otherwise be full-ti   one-quarter of our chil-
to be at least part-time workers.   dren, in one of the richest countries in the

All in all, it seems highly u   w much do we care
long-term costs of such progran   ldren, *because* of this
count only monetary costs, not   pportunities to develop
terms—would outweigh the long   ial, and very little influ-
In many cases, the cycle of po   lues and direction? How
broken—and children enabled t   t the family, our most inti-
or to avoid falling into, it—throu   ng, is often a school of day-
ter early start in life. But even if   low much do we *want* the just
would cost, and cost a lot, we ha   l produce the kind of citizens
much do we care about the injust   re ever to achieve a just society?

Feminist Justice
and Sexual Harassment

James P. Sterba

THE IDEAL OF FEMINIST JUSTICE

Contemporary feminists almost by definition seek to put an end to male domination and to secure women's liberation. To achieve these goals, many feminists support the political ideal of a gender-free or androgynous society.[1] According to these feminists, all assignments of rights and duties are ultimately to accord with the ideal of a gender-free or androgynous society. Since a conception of justice is usually thought to provide the ultimate grounds for the assignment of rights and duties, I shall refer

From *The Journal of Social Philosophy*, Vol. 27 No. 1, Spring, 1996, pp. 103–122. Copyright © 1996 by the *Journal of Social Philosophy*. Reprinted by permission.

to this ideal of a gender-free or androgynous society as "feminist justice."

But how is this ideal to be interpreted? A gender-free or genderless society is one where basic rights and duties are not assigned on the basis of a person's biological sex. Being male or female is not the grounds for determining what basic rights and duties a person has in a gender-free or genderless society. But this is to characterize the feminist ideal only negatively. It tells us what we need to get rid of, not what we need to put in its place. A more positive characterization is provided by the ideal of androgyny. Putting the ideal of feminist justice more positively in terms of the ideal of androgyny also helps to bring out why men should be attracted to feminist justice.

In a well-known article, Joyce Trebilcot distinguishes two forms of androgyny.[2] The first form postulates the same ideal for everyone. According to this form of androgyny, the ideal person "combines characteristics usually attributed to men with characteristics usually attributed to women." Thus, we should expect both nurturance and mastery, openness and objectivity, compassion and competitiveness from each and every person who has the capacities for these traits.

By contrast, the second form of androgyny does not advocate the same ideal for everyone but rather a variety of options from "pure" femininity to "pure" masculinity. As Trebilcot points out, this form of androgyny shares with the first the view that biological sex should not be the basis for determining the appropriateness of gender characterization. It differs in that it holds that "all alternatives with respect to gender should be equally available to and equally approved for everyone, regardless of sex."

It would be a mistake, however, to sharply distinguish between these two forms of androgyny. Properly understood, they are simply two different facets of a single ideal. For, as Mary Ann Warren has argued, the second form of androgyny is appropriate *only* "with respect to feminine and masculine traits which are largely matters of personal style and preference and which have little direct moral significance."[3] However, when we consider so-called feminine and masculine *virtues*, it is the first form of androgyny that is required because, then, other things being equal, the same virtues are appropriate for everyone.

We can even formulate the ideal of androgyny more abstractly so that it is no longer specified in terms of so-called feminine and masculine traits. We can specify the ideal as requiring no more than that the traits that are truly desirable in society be equally available to both women and men, or in the case of virtues, equally expected of both women and men.

There is a problem, of course, in determining which traits of character are virtues and which traits are largely matters of personal style

and preference. To make this determination, Trebilcot has suggested that we seek to bring about the second form of androgyny, where people have the option of acquiring the full range of so-called feminine and masculine traits.[4] But surely when we already have good grounds for thinking that certain traits are virtues, such as courage and compassion, fairness and openness, there is no reason to adopt such a laissez-faire approach to moral education. Although, as Trebilcot rightly points out, proscribing certain options will involve a loss of freedom, nevertheless, we should be able to determine at least with respect to some character traits when a gain in virtue is worth the loss of freedom. It may even be the case that the loss of freedom suffered by an individual now will be compensated for by a gain of freedom to that same individual in the future once the relevant virtue or virtues have been acquired.

So understood, the class of virtues will turn out to be those desirable traits that can be reasonably expected of both women and men. Admittedly, this is a restrictive use of the term "virtue." In normal usage, the term "virtue" is almost synonymous with the term "desirable trait."[5] But there is good reason to focus on those desirable traits that can be reasonably expected of both women and men, and, for present purposes, I will refer to this class of desirable traits as virtues.

Unfortunately, many of the challenges to the ideal of androgyny fail to appreciate how the ideal can be interpreted to combine an expected set of virtues with equal choice from among other desirable traits. For example, some challenges interpret the ideal as attempting to achieve "a proper balance of moderation" among opposing feminine and masculine traits and then question whether stereotypical traits like feminine gullibility or masculine brutality could ever be combined with opposing traits to achieve such a balance.[6] Other challenges interpret the ideal as permitting unrestricted choice of personal traits and then regard the possibility of Total Women and Hells Angels androgynes as a *reductio ad absurdum* of the ideal.[7] But once it is recognized that the ideal of androgyny cannot only be interpreted to expect of everyone a set of virtues (which need not be a mean between opposing extreme traits), but can also be interpreted to limit everyone's choice to desirable traits, then such challenges to the ideal clearly lose their force.

Actually, the main challenge raised by feminists to the ideal of androgyny is that the ideal is self-defeating in that it seeks to eliminate sexual stereotyping of human beings at the same time that it is formulated in terms of the very same stereotypical concepts it seeks to eliminate.[8] Or as Warren has put it, "Is it not at least mildly paradoxical to urge people to cultivate both 'feminine' and 'masculine' virtues, while at the same time holding that virtues ought not to be sexually stereotyped?"

But in response to this challenge, it can be argued that to build a better society we must begin where we are now, and where we are now people still speak of feminine and masculine character traits. Consequently, if we want to easily refer to such traits and to formulate an ideal with respect to how they should be distributed in society, it is plausible to refer to them in the way that people presently refer to them, that is, as feminine or masculine traits.

Alternatively, to avoid misunderstanding altogether, the ideal could be formulated in the more abstract way I suggested earlier so that it no longer specifically refers to so-called feminine or masculine traits. So formulated, the ideal requires that the traits that are truly desirable in society be equally available to both women and men, or in the case of virtues, equally expected of both women and men.

So characterized, the ideal of androgyny represents neither a revolt against so-called feminine virtues and traits nor their exaltation over so-called masculine virtues and traits.[9] Accordingly, the ideal of androgyny does not view women's liberation as *simply* the freeing of

women from the confines of traditional roles, thus making it possible for them to develop in ways heretofore reserved for men. Nor does the ideal view women's liberation as *simply* the revaluation and glorification of so-called feminine activities like housekeeping or mothering or so-called feminine modes of thinking as reflected in an ethic of caring. The first perspective ignores or devalues genuine virtues and desirable traits traditionally associated with women while the second ignores or devalues genuine virtues and desirable traits traditionally associated with men. By contrast, the ideal of androgyny seeks a broader-based ideal for both women and men that combines virtues and desirable traits traditionally associated with women with virtues and desirable traits traditionally associated with men. Nevertheless, the ideal of androgyny will clearly reject any so-called virtues or desirable traits traditionally associated with women or men that have been supportive of discrimination or oppression against women or men. In general, the ideal of androgyny substitutes a socialization based on natural ability, reasonable expectation, and choice for a socialization based on sexual difference.[10]

Of course, in proposing to characterize feminist justice in terms of the ideal of a gender-free or androgynous society, I recognize that not all feminists start off endorsing this ideal. Christina Sommers, for example, has attracted attention recently by distinguishing liberal feminism which she endorses from androgynous feminism which she opposes.[11] But as one gets clearer and clearer about the liberal feminism that Sommers endorses, it begins to look more and more like the androgynous feminism that she says she opposes. There is nothing surprising about this, however. We cannot have the genuine equal opportunity for men and women that Sommers wants without reforming the present distribution of gender traits. Women cannot be passive, submissive, dependent, indecisive, and weak and still enjoy the same opportunities enjoyed by men who are aggressive, dominant, independent, decisive, and strong. So I contend that liberal feminism and androgynous feminism go together because genuine equal opportunity requires the feminist ideal of a gender-free or androgynous society.

Recently, Alison Jaggar has objected to my characterization of feminist justice in terms of the ideal of androgyny on the grounds that feminist justice is an ideal for reforming social structures whereas androgyny is an ideal for reforming individuals.[12] She writes:

[A] commitment to abolishing gender [is a matter primarily of changing social structures] since gender is essentially a system of social norms prescribing different behavior for individuals of different sexes. By contrast, androgyny is an ideal of individual development and a commitment to achieving androgyny is a commitment to changing people.[13]

Yet, as I indicated to Jaggar in earlier correspondence, the ideal of androgyny, as I define it, closely resembles the ideal of equal opportunity, and since the ideal of equal opportunity is thought to be an ideal for reforming social structures the same should be true of the ideal of androgyny as I define it.[14]

Moreover, while she claims to reject the ideal of androgyny, Jaggar herself endorses an ideal that looks very much like the ideal of androgyny as I define it. She writes:

Just as the incorporation of feminine values does not render FPD (Feminist Practical Dialogue) feminist, neither does FPD become feminist by adding masculine values to the feminine in a mix. . . . Instead I regard FPD as feminist primarily because it revises both feminine and masculine values in the light of a distinctively feminist commitment to ending women's subordination.[15]

Now compare this passage with my characterization of the ideal of androgyny that appears in the fourth paragraph preceding this one. This same characterization of androgyny appeared in all three versions of my account of feminist justice on which Jaggar has commented. Given the similarities between the two passages, therefore, Jaggar and I appear to be defending the very same ideal, only naming it differently. I call the ideal "androgyny," while Jaggar does not, but the only difference between us is verbal.

It also seems that those who claim that we cannot escape a gendered society are simply confused about what a gender-free society would be like.[16] For they seem to agree with those who favor a gender-free or androgynous society that the assignments of roles in society should be based on (natural) ability, rational expectation, and choice. But what they also hold is that some of these assignments will be based on sex as well because some of the natural abilities that people have will be determined by their sex. But even assuming this were the case, it wouldn't show that society would be gendered in the sense that its roles were based on sex *rather than* being based on (natural) ability, rational expectation, and choice. And this is the only sense of gendered society to which defenders of feminist justice would be objecting.[17] So once the notion of a gender-free society is clarified, there should be widespread agreement that the assignments of roles in society should be based on (natural) ability, rational expectation, and choice. The ideal of androgyny simply specifies this notion of a gender-free society a bit further by requiring that the traits that are truly desirable in society be equally open to (equally qualified) women and men, or in the case of virtues, equally expected of (equally capable) women and men.

Of course, insofar as natural abilities are a function of sexual difference, there will be differences in the desirable traits and virtues that women and men acquire even in a gender-free or androgynous society. And some contend that these differences will be substantial.[18] But given that we have been slow to implement the degree of equal opportunity required by the ideal of a gender-free or androgynous society, it is difficult to know what differences will emerge that are both sex-based and natural ability-based. What we can be sure of is that given the variety and types of discrimination employed against women in existing societies, a gender-free or androgynous society will look quite different from the societies that we presently know.[19]

APPLYING THE IDEAL

One locus for the radical restructuring required by the ideal of a gender-free or androgynous society is the distribution of economic power in the society. In the United States, the percentage of women in the labor force has risen steadily for three decades, from 35 percent (of those aged sixteen or over) in 1960 to 59 percent in 1995. Roughly 70 percent of women with children were employed in 1995, including more than 58 percent of mothers with children under the age of six and 53 percent of mothers with children under the age of one.[20]

Yet in 1991 women employed full-time still earned $.70 for every dollar men earned, up from the $.60 for every dollar that held from the 1960s through the 1980s. Earnings do increase with education for all workers, but all women as well as men of color earn less than white men at every level of education. For example, women with four years of college education earn less on average than men who have not completed high school.[21]

Sometimes women and men working in the same job category have different incomes. For example, while female secretaries earned a median wage of $278 per week in 1985, the median wage for male secretaries was $365.[22] More frequently, however, women and men tend to be employed in different job categories which are paid differently. According to one study done a few years ago in the state of Washington, women employed as clerk typists earned less than men employed as truck drivers

or warehouse workers. In another study done in Denver, women employed as nurses earned less than men employed as tree cutters. While in each of these cases, the women earned about 20 percent less than the men, the women's jobs when evaluated in terms of skill, responsibility, effort, and working conditions were given equal or higher scores than the men's jobs with which they were compared. Clearly, denying women the opportunity to earn the same as men do for equal or comparable work is a basic injustice in our society, and it will be a very costly one to correct.[23]

It is sometimes assumed that the problem of unequal pay for comparable work will be solved once women move into male-dominated occupations.[24] Unfortunately, as the feminization of certain occupations occurs, we are seeing a subsequent drop in pay for men. For example, as the percentage of women bartenders increased 23 points, men's pay dropped 16 percent and as the percentage of women pharmacists increased 12 points, men's pay fell 11 percent.[25] So the discrimination against women in the economic arena is a far more entrenched problem than is sometimes thought.

The problem assumes even greater proportions when we consider the world at large. According to a United Nations report, although women are responsible for 66 percent of all work produced in the world (paid and unpaid), they receive only 10 percent of the salaries.[26] The same report shows that men own 99 percent of all the property in the world, and women only 1 percent. Clearly, we have a long way to go to achieve the equality required by feminist justice.

It is also important to recognize that the equality required by feminist justice cannot be achieved on men's terms. It is not an equality in which men's values prevail and women's values are lost. As an example of what needs to be avoided, consider the integration of Girl Scouts and Boy Scouts into the same troops in Norway.[27] Before integration, many women had been troop leaders of the Girl Scouts, but after the integration, almost all troops were led by men and the former women leaders became assistant leaders. In addition, an analysis of the activities in the former Girl Scouts compared to the activities of the former Boy Scouts revealed that the activities of the girls were of a more cooperative nature than those of the boys. The boys had activities in which they competed more against each other or against other groups of boys. After integration, the competitive activities of the boys became the activities of both girls and boys. The cooperative activities of the girls were abandoned. The integration was made on the boys' terms.[28] But feminist justice is not a one-way street. If it is to be achieved, each person who is capable must be expected to have the virtues that are now typically associated with women (e.g., nurtuance, caring, sensitivity, compassion) as well as virtues that are now typically associated with men (e.g., self-reliance, courage, decisiveness).

To remedy these inequalities suffered by women in the economic arena will require programs of affirmative action and comparable worth. Affirmative action is needed to place qualified women into positions they deserve to occupy because of past discrimination. Without affirmative action, the structural violence of past discrimination will not be rectified. Only with affirmative action can the competition for desirable jobs and positions be made fair again given our history of past discrimination. There are even cases where affirmative action candidates are clearly the most qualified; nevertheless, those in charge of hiring, because of their prejudice, could only see the candidates as simply qualified, but not the most qualified candidates.[29]

Comparable worth is also needed because, without it, women will not receive the salaries they deserve. They will do work that is judged equal or comparable to the work that men are doing in male-dominated occupations, but, without comparable worth, they will be paid

less than the men are being paid. Paying for comparable worth programs will not be easy. A settlement in the state of Washington granted nearly $500 million to women workers to achieve pay equity.[30] Even larger settlements are anticipated as Canada begins to implement extensive comparable worth programs.[31]

A second locus of change required by the ideal of a gender-free or androgynous society is the overt violence perpetrated against women in our society. According to former surgeon general Antonia Novello, "The home is actually a more dangerous place for the American woman than the city streets." "One-third of the women slain in the U.S.," she continues, "die at the hands of husbands and boyfriends."[32] In addition, women in the United States live in fear of rape. Forty-four percent of women are subjected to rape or attempted rape at some point in their lives, according to a recent study, and almost 50 percent of male college students say they would commit rape if they were certain that they could get away with it.[33] Not infrequently, women are beaten by their own husbands and lovers (between one quarter and one third of women are battered in their homes by husbands and lovers).[34] One third of all women who require emergency-room hospital treatment are there as a result of domestic violence.[35] Thirty-eight percent of little girls are sexually molested inside or outside the family.[36] Since most of these crimes are minimally prosecuted in our society, women in our society can be raped, battered, or sexually abused as a child and little, if anything, will be done about it. What this shows is that the condition of women in our society is actually that of being subordinate to men by force.

This problem is not confined to the U.S. S. Opdebeeck reports that 40 percent of Belgian women between thirty and forty years old experienced some form of physical and/or sexual family violence, and Bert Young notes that wife assault is the leading cause of homicide in Canada.[37] Obviously, this subordination of women must end if we are to achieve the ideal of a gender-free or androgynous society.

Feminist justice requires that we put an end to the overt violence against women that takes the distinctive form of rape, battery, and sexual abuse. This overt violence is in every way as destructive as the other forms of violence we oppose. So we cannot in consistency fail to oppose this form of violence done to women in our society. According to one cross-cultural study of ninety-five societies, 47 percent of them were free of rape.[38] What this shows is that it is possible to eliminate or, at least, drastically to reduce overt violence against women.

One way to help bring about this result is to ban hard-core pornography, which celebrates and legitimizes rape, battery, and the sexual abuse of children, as the Supreme Court of Canada has done.[39] Catharine MacKinnon has argued that pornography of this sort causes harm to women by increasing discriminatory attitudes and behavior in men toward women that takes both violent and nonviolent forms.[40]

Another way to decrease violence against women is to deemphasize violent sports like boxing and football. To see why this would help, all one needs to do is consider the evidence. For example, an exhaustive study of heavyweight prizefights held between 1973 and 1978 and subsequent homicide statistics showed that homicides in the U.S. increased by over 12 percent directly after heavyweight championship prizefights. In fact, the increase was greatest after heavily publicized prizefights.[41] In addition, a study of 24 cases of campus gang rapes indicated that 9 of them were by athletes, and in an investigation of sexual assaults on college campuses which included interviewing over 150 campus police, it turned out that football and basketball players were involved in 38 percent of the reported cases.[42] There is also a 40 percent increase of batteries by husbands and boyfriends associated with the yearly Superbowl football game. In the Chicago area, a local radio station went so far as to recommend that women "take a walk" during the game in order to avoid being assaulted in their homes.[43]

A third way to help reduce violence against women is to teach conflict resolution, childcare, and the history of peace-making in our schools. Several schools have experimented with teaching conflict resolution and child care to elementary and high school children with impressive results, especially for boys.[44] The history of peace-making could also provide our children with a new and better set of models than the history of war-making has done.[45]

Another locus of change required by the ideal of a gender-free or androgynous society overlaps the previous two. It is rooted in the distribution of economic power in society and it frequently takes the form of overt violence against women. It is the problem of sexual harassment, and, given its importance, I want to devote some time to discussing it.

Actually, sexual harassment was not recognized as an offense by U.S. trial courts until the late 1970s, and it was only affirmed by the U.S. Supreme Court as an offense in the 1980s. The term "sexual harassment" itself was not even coined until the 1970s. So the moral problem of sexual harassment is one that many people have only recently come to recognize. The Senate Judiciary Committee hearings on Anita Hill's charge that Clarence Thomas had sexually harassed her obviously heightened people's awareness of this problem.

According to various studies done over the last few years, sexual harassment is a widespread problem. In research by psychologists, 50 percent of women questioned in the workplace said they had been sexually harassed. According to the U.S. Merit Systems Protection Board, within the federal government, 56 percent of 8,500 female workers surveyed claimed to have experienced sexual harassment. According to the *National Law Journal*, 64 percent of women in "pink-collar" jobs reported being sexually harassed and 60 percent of 3,000 women lawyers at 250 top law firms said that they had been harassed at some point in their careers. In a recent survey by *Working Women* magazine, 60 percent of high-ranking corporate women said they have been harassed; 33 percent more knew of others who had been.[46]

According to Ellen Bravo and Ellen Cassedy, "humiliation" is the term most commonly used by those who see themselves as sexually harassed to describe their experience.[47] They see themselves as demeaned and devalued, and treated as sexual playthings. Many find themselves in a doublebind. If they fight, they could lose their jobs or alienate their boss or coworkers. If they don't fight, they could lose their self-respect. Many experience stress-related ailments: depression, sleep or eating disorders, headaches and fatigue, and take more days off from work as a result.[48] The economic consequences for employers are also significant. A 1988 survey of 160 large manufacturing and service companies found this startling result: A typical Fortune 500 company with 23,750 employees loses $6.7 million a year because of sexual harassment. And this loss doesn't even include lawsuits. What it does include are financial losses due to absenteeism, lower productivity, and employee turnover. Another 1988 study showed that sexual harassment cost the federal government $267 million between 1985 and 1987. It cost $37 million to replace federal workers who left their jobs, $26 million in medical leave due to stress from sexual harassment, and $204 million in lost productivity.[49]

Given the seriousness of the problem, it is important to clarify what constitutes, or should constitute, sexual harassment. In 1980, the Equal Employment Opportunity Commission (EEOC) issued guidelines finding harassment on the basis of sex to be a violation of Title VII of the Civil Rights Act of 1964 and defining sexual harassment as "unwelcome sexual advances, requests for sexual favors, and other verbal or physical conduct of a sexual nature"

when such behavior occurred in any of three circumstances:

1. where submission to such conduct is made either explicitly or implicitly a term or condition of an individual's employment,
2. where submission to or rejection of such conduct by an individual is used as the basis for employment decisions affecting the individual, or
3. where such conduct has the purpose or effect of unreasonably interfering with an individual's work performance or creating an intimidating, hostile, or offensive working environment.[50]

In 1986, the U.S. Supreme Court in *Meritor Savings Bank v. Vinson* agreed with the EEOC, ruling that there could be two types of sexual harassment: harassment that conditions concrete employment benefits on granting sexual favors (often called the quid pro quo type) and harassment that creates a hostile or offensive work environment without affecting economic benefits (the hostile environment type).[51]

Nevertheless, the Supreme Court made it difficult for a plaintiff to establish that either of these types of sexual harassment had occurred. For example, a polite verbal "no" does not suffice to show that sexual advances are unwelcome; a woman's entire conduct both inside and outside the workplace is subject to appraisal to determine whether or not she welcomed the advances. For example, in the *Vinson* case there was "voluminous testimony regarding Vinson's dress and personal fantasies," and in the Senate Judiciary Committee hearings, Anita Hill was not able to prevent intensive examination of her private life, although Clarence Thomas was able to declare key areas of his private life as off-limits, such as his practice of viewing and discussing pornographic films.

The Supreme Court also made it difficult to classify work environments as hostile to women unless the harassment is sufficiently severe or pervasive. Applying the Supreme Court's standard, a lower court in *Christoforou v. Ryder Truck Rental* judged a supervisor's actions of fondling a plaintiff's rear end and breasts, propositioning her, and trying to force a kiss at a Christmas party to be "too sporadic and innocuous" to support a finding of a hostile work environment.[52] Similarly, in *Rabidue v. Osceola Refining Co.* a workplace where pictures of nude and scantily clad women abounded (including one that hung on a wall for eight years of a woman with a golf ball on her breasts and a man with his golf club, standing over her and yelling "fore") and where a coworker, never disciplined despite repeated complaints, routinely referred to women as "whores," "cunts," "pussies," and "tits" was judged by a lower court not to be sufficiently hostile an environment to constitute sexual harassment.[53] Notice, *by contrast*, that the Senate Arms Services Committee, in its recent hearings, regarded an environment in which known homosexuals are simply doing their duty in the military to be *too hostile* an environment to ask particularly male heterosexuals to serve in.

Yet why should we accept the Supreme Court's characterization of sexual harassment, especially given its unwelcomeness and pervasiveness requirements?[54] As the Supreme Court interprets sexual harassment, a person's behavior must be unwelcome in a fairly strong sense before it constitutes sexual harassment. But why should a woman have to prove that the offer "If you don't sleep with me, you will be fired" is unwelcome before it constitutes sexual harassment?[55] Isn't such an offer objectively unwelcome? Isn't it just the kind of offer that those in positions of power should not be making to their subordinates—offers that purport to make their continuing employment conditional upon providing sexual favors? Surely, unless we are dealing with some form of legalized prostitution, and maybe not even then, such offers are objectively unwelcome.[56]

Given, then, that such offers are objectively unwelcome, why is there any need to show that they are also subjectively unwelcome before

regarding them as violations of Title VII of the Civil Rights Act? The requirement of subjective unwelcomeness is simply a gratuitous obstacle, which makes the plaintiff's case far more difficult to prove than it should be.[57]

In addition, if the plaintiff is fired after refusing such an offer, the Supreme Court requires the plaintiff to prove that the firing occurred because the offer was refused, which is very difficult to do unless one is a perfect employee. Wouldn't it be fairer, then, to require the employer to prove that the plaintiff would have been fired even if she had said "yes" to the offer?[58] Of course, employers could avoid this burden of proof simply by not making any such offers in the first place.[59] But when they do make objectively unwelcome offers, why shouldn't the burden of proof be on them to show that any subsequent firing was clearly unrelated to the plaintiff's refusal of such an offer? Fairness is particularly relevant in this context because we are committed to equal opportunity in the workplace, which requires employing women and men on equal terms. Accordingly, we must guard against imposing special burdens on women in the workplace, when there are no comparable burdens imposed on men. Feminist justice with its ideal of a gender-free or androgynous society will be satisfied with nothing less.[60]

The demand for equal opportunity in the workplace also appears to conflict with the Supreme Court's pervasiveness requirement for establishing a hostile environment. Citing a lower court, the Supreme Court contends that to be actionable, sexual harassment "must be sufficiently severe or pervasive 'to alter the conditions of the [victim's] employment and create an abusive working environment'"[61] But as this standard has been interpreted by lower courts, the pervasiveness of certain forms of harassment in the workplace has become grounds for tolerating them. In Rabidue, the majority argued

[I]t cannot seriously be disputed that in some work environments, humor and language are rough hewn and vulgar. Sexual jokes, sexual conversations and girlie magazines abound. Title VII was not meant to—or can—change this. Title VII is the federal court mainstay in the struggle for equal employment opportunity for the female workers of America. But it is quite different to claim that Title VII was designed to bring about a magical transformation in the social mores of American workers.[62]

The Supreme Court itself seems to sound a similar theme by emphasizing the application of Title VII to only extreme cases of sexual harassment as found in *Vinson*.

However, as the EEOC interprets Title VII, the law has a broader scope. Title VII affords employees the right to work in an environment free from discriminatory intimidation, ridicule, and insult. According to the EEOC, sexual harassment violates Title VII where conduct creates an intimidating, hostile, or offensive environment or where it unreasonably interferes with work performance.[63]

But how are we to determine what unreasonably interferes with work performance? In *Rabidue*, the majority looked to prevailing standards in the workplace to determine what is reasonable or unreasonable. Yet Justice Keith, in dissent, questioned this endorsement of the status quo, arguing that just as a Jewish employee can rightfully demand a change in her working environment if her employer maintains an anti-Semitic work force and tolerates a workplace in which "kike" jokes, displays of Nazi literature, and anti-Jewish conversation "may abound," surely women can rightfully demand a change in the sexist practices that prevail in their working environments.[64] In *Henson v. Dundee*, the majority also drew an analogy between sexual harassment and racial harassment:

Sexual harassment which creates a hostile or offensive environment for members of one sex is every bit the arbitrary barrier to sexual equality at the workplace that racial harassment is to racial equality. Surely, a requirement that a man or woman run a gauntlet of sexual abuse in return for the privilege of being allowed to work and make a living can be as demeaning and disconcerting as the harshest of racial epithets.[65]

And this passage is also quoted approvingly by the Supreme Court in *Vinson*.

Moved by such arguments, the majority in *Ellison v. Brady* proposed that rather than look to prevailing standards to determine what is reasonable, we should look to the standard of a reasonable victim, or given that most victims of sexual harassment are women, the standard of a reasonable woman.[66] They contend that this standard may be different from the standard of a "reasonable man." For example, what male superiors may think is "harmless social interaction" may be experienced by female subordinates as offensive and threatening.[67]

Nevertheless, if we are concerned to establish the equal opportunity in the workplace that feminist justice with its ideal of a gender-free or androgynous society demands, there should be no question about what standard of reasonableness to use here. It is not that of a reasonable woman nor that of a reasonable man for that matter, but the standard of what is reasonable for everyone to accept. For equal opportunity is a moral requirement, and moral requirements are those that are reasonable for everyone to accept. This assumes that apparent conflicts over what is reasonable to accept, e.g., conflicts between the standard of a reasonable woman and the standard of a reasonable man, are conflicts that can and should be resolved by showing that one of these perspectives is more reasonable than the other, or by showing that some still other perspective is even more reasonable. However, at least in the context of sexual harassment, this standard of what is reasonable for everyone to accept will accord closely with the standard of a reasonable woman, given that once women's perspectives are adequately taken into account, the contrasting perspective of a reasonable man will be seen as not so reasonable after all.

In its decision in *Teresa Harris v. Forklift* (1993), the Supreme Court took an important step toward a more reasonable stance on sexual harassment. In this case, Teresa Harris worked as a rental manager at Forklift Systems. Charles Hardy, Forklift's president, told Harris on several occasions, in the presence of other employees, "You're a woman, what do you know?" and "We need a man as the rental manager." Again in front of others, he suggested that the two of them "go to the Holiday Inn to negotiate [Harris's] raise." Hardy occasionally asked Harris and other female employees to get coins from his front pants pockets. On other occasions, he threw objects on the ground in front of Harris and other women, and asked them to pick the objects up. He made sexual innuendos about Harris's and other women's clothing. On one occasion, while Harris was arranging a deal with one of Forklift's customers, Hardy asked Harris in front of other employees, "What did you do, promise some (sex) Saturday night?" Soon after, Harris quit her job at Forklift.

In this case, the Supreme Court struck down the district court's requirement that in order for sexual harassment to be established, Harris needed to show that Hardy's conduct had "seriously affected her psychological well-being." This was an important decision, but obviously it does not go far enough in establishing a reasonable standard for sexual harassment.

It is also important to recognize here that achieving equal opportunity in the workplace as required by the ideal of a gender-free or androgynous society will conflict, to some degree, with freedom of speech. Consider the recent case of *Robinson v. Jacksonville Shipyards*, in which a United States District Court upheld claims of sexual harassment on hostile work environment grounds, and issued extensive remedial orders.[68] Plaintiff Lois Robinson was one of a very small number of female skilled craftworkers employed at the Shipyards—one of 6 of 832 craftworkers. Her allegations of sexual harassment centered around "the presence in the workplace of pictures of women in various stages of undress and in sexually suggestive or submissive poses, as well as remarks by male employees and supervisors which demean women." Although there was some evidence of several incidents in which the sexually suggestive pictures and comments were directed explicitly at Robinson, most were not.

In analyzing this case, Nadine Strossen, past president of the American Civil Liberties Union, argues that even sexually offensive speech should be protected unless it is explicitly directed at a particular individual or a particular group of individuals.[69] Accordingly, Strossen endorses the ACLU's amicus brief in the *Robinson v. Jacksonville Shipyards* case, which regarded the court's ban on the public display of sexually suggestive material without regard to whether the expressive activity was explicitly directed at any employee as too broad. However, in light of the fact that Jacksonville Shipyards had itself banned all public displays of expressive activity except sexual materials, the amicus brief went on to favor the imposition of a workplace rule that would right the balance and permit the posting of other materials as well—materials critical of such sexual expression, as well as other political and religious or social messages that are currently banned. Such a rule would implement a "more speech" approach to counter offensive speech.

But would such a rule work? Would it work to protect the basic interests of women, especially their right to equal opportunity in the workplace? It is not clear that it would work in male-dominated workplaces like Jacksonville Shipyards, where women are a tiny minority of the workforce, and so they are likely to have their voices drowned out in the free market of expression that this rule would permit.

Nor does Strossen's distinction between offensive speech explicitly directed at a particular person or group and offensive speech that is not so directed seem all that useful, given that most sexual harassment is directed at women not because they are Jane Doe or Lois Robinson, but because they are women. So why should we distinguish between sexual harassment that is explicitly directed at some particular woman because she is a woman and sexual harassment that is only directed at some particular woman because it is explicitly directed at all women? Of course, sexually harassing speech can be more or less offensive, and maybe its offensiveness does correlate, to some degree, with the manner in which that harassment is directed at women. Nevertheless, what is crucial here is that the offensiveness of sexually harassing speech becomes unacceptable from the standpoint of feminist justice when it undermines the equal opportunity of women in the workplace—that is, when it imposes special burdens on women in the workplace where there are no comparable burdens on men. It is at that point that feminist justice requires that we impose whatever limitations on sexually harassing speech are needed to secure equal opportunity in the workplace.

I have argued in this paper that the achievement of feminist justice requires a number of important changes in our society. It requires changes in the distribution of economic power in our society through programs of affirmative action and comparable worth that remove the structural violence against women. It requires changes that are necessary to put an end to the overt violence against women that takes the form of rape, battery, and sexual abuse. Last, it requires changes that implement new programs against sexual harassment in the workplace in order to achieve the equal opportunity that feminist justice promises to everyone. All of these changes, and more, are required by feminist justice's ideal of a gender-free and androgynous society.

NOTES

1. For feminists who have endorsed the ideal of a gender-free or androgynous society see, for example, Ann Ferguson, "Androgyny as an Ideal for Human Development," in *Feminism and Philosophy*, ed. Mary Vetterling-Braggin et al. (Totowa, 1977), pp. 45–69; Mary Ann Warren, "Is Androgyny the Answer to Sexual Stereotyping?" in *"Femininity," "Masculinity," and "Androgyny,"* ed. Mary Vetterling-Braggin (Totowa, 1982), pp. 170–86; A. G. Kaplan and J. Bean, eds. *Beyond Sex-Role Stereotypes: Reading Toward a Psychology of Androgyny* (Totowa, 1976); Andrea Dworkin, *Women Hating* (New York, 1974), Part 4; Carol Gould, "Privacy Rights and Public Virtues: Women, the Family and Democracy," in Carol Gould, *Beyond Domination* (Totowa, 1983), pp. 3–18; Carol Gould, "Women and Freedom," *The Journal of Social Philosophy.* (1984), pp. 20–34; Linda Lindsey, *Gender Roles* (Englewood Cliffs, 1990); Marilyn Friedman, "Does Sommers like Women?" *Journal of Social Philosophy* (1991), pp. 75–90. For feminists who oppose the ideal of androgyny, see Mary Daly, *Gyn-Ecology: The Meta-Ethics of Radical Feminism* (Boston, 1978); Kathryn Paula Morgan, "Androgyny: A Conceptual Critique," *Social Theory and Practice* (1982); Jean Bethke Elstain, "Against Androgyny," *Telos* 47 (1981).

2. Joyce Trebilcot, "Two Forms of Androgynism," reprinted in *Feminism and Philosophy*, Mary Vetterling-Braggin, Frederick Ellison, and Jane English (Totowa, 1977), pp. 70–78.

3. Warren, pp. 178–79.

4. Trebilcot, pp. 74–77.

5. On this point, see Edmund Pincoffs, *Quandaries and Virtue* (Lawrence, 1986), Chap. 5.

6. See, for example, Kathryn Paula Morgan, "Androgyny: A Conceptual Critique," *Social Theory and Practice* (1982), pp. 256–57.

7. See, for example, Daly, *Gyn-Ecology*, p. xi.

8. Margrit Erchler, *The Double Standard* (New York, 1980), pp. 69–71; Elizabeth Lane Beardsley, "On Curing Conceptual Confusion," in *"Feminity," "Masculinity" and "Androgyny,"* pp. 197–202; Mary Daly, "The Qualitative Leap Beyond Patriarchal Religion," *Quest* Vol. 1 (1975), pp. 20–40; Janice Raymond, "The Illusion of Androgyny," *Quest* Vol. 2 (1975), pp. 57–66.

9. For a valuable discussion and critique of these two viewpoints, see Iris Young, "Humanism, Gynocentrism and Feminist Politics, *Women's Studies International Forum* (1985) Vol. 8, no. 3, pp. 173–83.

10. For further defenses of the ideal of androgyny which relate it to the equal opportunity endorsed by welfare liberals and the equal self-development endorsed by socialists, see my *How To Make People Just* (Totowa, 1988), Chap. 5.

11. See Christina Sommers, "Philosophers Against the Family," in George Graham and Hugh LaFollette, *Person to Person* (Philadelphia, 1989), pp. 82–105; "Do These Feminists like Women?" *Journal of Social Philosophy* (1990), pp. 66–74; "Argumentum Ad Feminam," *Journal of Social Philosophy* (1991), pp. 5–19.

12. James P. Sterba, Alision Jaggar, et al., *Morality and Social Justice*, Rowman and Littlefield (1995). In responding to Jaggar when she raised this same objection to a symposium paper I presented to the APA Central Division Meeting in 1992, I claimed that there was no tendency in my work to focus on changing people rather than changing social institutions, and noted further Jaggar's approval of my discussion of how the ideal of androgyny would require significant changes in family structures.

13. Ibid.

14. Private correspondence, Nov. 10, 1993.

15. Ibid. The omitted words are "that might be called androgynous." Does the omission of these words make a difference? It would seem that what Jaggar is really objecting to is my use of the word "androgyny" and not the ideal I use the word to stand for.

16. Elizabeth Wolgast, *Equality and the Rights of Women* (Ithaca, 1980).

17. Moreover, given that the basic rights that we have in society, e.g., a right to equal opportunity, are equal for all citizens and are not based on our differing natural abilities, these rights are not even in this derivative sense based on one's sex.

18. Anne Moir and David Jessel, *Brain Sex* (New York, 1991).

19. Nothing I have said is opposed to the view that the native abilities we recognize are a function of the kind of society in which we live. My point is simply that we will not be able to know who, in fact, has these abilities in our society unless we give both women and men the same opportunities to develop them.

20. See *The New York Times*, Oct. 6, 18, and 19, 1992; See also Phyllis Moen, *Women's Roles* (New York, 1992).

21. Elaine Sorensen, "The Comparable Worth Debate," in *Morality in Practice*.

22. See Susan Okin, *Justice, Gender and the Family* (New York, 1989), Chap. 7.

23. See Jerry Jacobs and Ronnie Steinberg, "Compensating Differentials and the Male-Female Wage Gap," *Social Forces*, Vol. 69, No. 2 (Dec., 1990).

24. Clifford Hackett, "Comparable Worth: Better From a Distance," *Commonweal* May 31, 1985.

25. *Rapid City Journal*, Oct. 20, 1992.

26. Report on the World Conference of the United Nations Decade for Women, Copenhagen, 14–30 July, 1981.

27. Birgit Brock-Utne, pp. 100–101.

28. Similarly, Deborah Tannen contends that when men and women get together in groups, they are likely to talk in ways more familiar and comfortable to men. See Deborah Tannen, *You Just Don't Understand* (New York, 1990).

29. Gertrude Ezorsky, *Racism and Justice* (Ithaca, 1991).

30. Ellen Paul, *Equity and Gender* (New Brunswick, 1989), p. 83. By 1987, ten states had implemented some form of pay equity policies and 27 states and 166 localities had begun comparable-worth studies. Among states that have taken action, Minnesota has most completely adopted and implemented a comparable-worth scheme for public employees. See Mary Ann Mason, "Beyond Equal Opportunity: A New Vision for Women Workers," *Notre Dame Journal of Law, Ethics and Public Policy* (1992), p. 403.

31. *Financial Post*, March 3, 1990.

32. *The New York Times*, Oct. 17, 1991.

33. See Catherine MacKinnon, *Feminism Unmodified* (Cambridge, 1987), and Bert Young, "Masculinity and Violence," presented at the Second World Congress on Violence and Human Coexistence, Montreal, July 12–17, 1992.

34. MacKinnon, op. cit.

35. Deirdre English, "Through the Glass Ceiling," *Mother Jones*, Nov., 1992.

36. MacKinnon, op. cit.

37. See S. Opdebeeck, "Determinants of Leaving an Abusing Partner," presented at the Second World Congress on Violence and Human Coexistence, Montreal, July 12–17, 1992. See Bert Young, op. cit.

38. Myriam Miedzian, *Boys Will Be Boys* (New York, 1991), p. 74.

39. *Donald Victor Butler v. Her Majesty The Queen.*

40. Catharine MacKinnon, op.cit.

41. David Phillips, "The Impact of Mass Media Violence on U.S. Homicides," *American Sociological Review* (1983), pp. 560–68.

42. Miedzian, op.cit. pp. 203–204.

43. WBBM, Jan. 31, 1993. Playing football also impacts negatively on the life expectancies of football players themselves. The average life expectancy of National Football League players in the United States is 54, nearly two decades below the overall male mean. See Don Sabo, "Sport, Patriarchy and Male Identity," *The Arena Review* (1985), pp. 1–30.

44. Ibid., Chaps. 6 and 7.

45. Duane Cady, *From Warism to Pacifism* (Philadelphia, 1989), Chap. 1; Brock-Utne, *Feminist Perspectives on Peace and Peace Education* (New York, 1989), pp. 162–63.

46. Gomez-Preston, Charles, *When No Means No* (New York: Carol Publishing, 1993), pp. 35–36. Ellen Bravo and Ellen Cassedy, *The 9–5 Guide to Combating Sexual Harassment* (New York, 1992), pp. 4–5. The problem is international as well as national. A three-year study of women in Estonia, Finland, Sweden, and the Soviet Union showed that nearly 50 percent of all working women experience sexual harassment. A survey released in 1991 by the Santama Group to Consider Sexual Harassment at Work showed that about 70 percent of Japanese women say they have experienced some type of sexual harassment on the job. See Susan Webb, *Step Forward* (1991), pp. xiv, xvii.

47. Bravo and Cassedy, pp. 43ff.

48. Ibid.

49. Op. cit., pp. 49–50.

50. "EEOC 1980 Guidelines on Sexual Harassment," in *Fair Employment Practices, Labor Relations Reporter.* The Bureau of National Affairs, Inc.

51. *Meritor Savings Bank.* 477 U.S. 57, 106 S. Ct. 2399, 91 L.Ed. 49 (1983).

52. *Christoforou v. Ryder Truck Rental.* 668 F. Supp.294 (S.D.N.Y. 1987).

53. *Rabidue v. Osceola Refining Co.* 805 F.2d 611, 620 (6th Cir. 1986).

54. In a recent study, Barbara A. Getek determined that a number of factors influence whether people tend to classify certain behavior as sexual harassment. They are:

1) How intrusive and persistent the behavior (the more physically intrusive and persistent the behavior is, the more likely that it will be defined as sexual harassment).

2) The nature of the relationship between the actors (the better the actors know each other, the less likely the behavior will be labeled sexual harassment).

3) The characteristics of the observer (men and people in authority are less likely to label behavior as sexual harassment).

4) The inequality in the relationship (the greater the inequality, the more likely the behavior will be labeled sexual harassment). Barbara Getek, "Understanding Sexual Harassment at Work," *Notre Dame Journal of Law, Ethics and Public Policy* (1992).

55. Obviously most offers of this sort will be more subtle, but if they are going to serve their purpose their message must still be relatively easy to discern.

56. Even where there is legalized prostitution, such offers may still be objectively unwelcome.

57. There is an an analogous requirement of subjective consent in the law concerning rape that is similarly indefensible. See Susan Estrich, "Sex at Work," *Stanford Law Review* (1991).

58. A reviewer of this paper was concerned that this suggestion might undercut an appropriate presumption of innocence. But the presumption of innocence is weaker for civil cases than for criminal cases. Thus, in a civil law sexual harassment case, it would seem that making an objectively unwanted sexual offer and then firing the person who refused that offer would be sufficient grounds for removing that presumption.

59. Or they could simply not fire those to whom they make the offers.

60. Barbara Getek contends that sexual harassment is caused by the fact that women are stereotypically identified as sexual objects in ways that men are not. She notes that women are stereotypically characterized as sexy, affectionate, and attractive, whereas men are stereotypically characterized as competent and active. These stereotypes, Getek claims, spill over into the workplace, making it difficult for

women to be perceived as fellow workers rather than sex objects, and it is these perceptions that foster sexual harassment. Op. cit. It would seem, therefore, that eliminating the problem of sexual harassment from our society will require breaking down these stereotypes. But this, of course, is just what the ideal of a gender-free or androgynous society hopes to do.

61. *Meritor Savings Bank v. Vinson*, p. 67.

62. Op. cit.

63. Op. cit.

64. Op. cit.

65. *Henson v. Dundee*, 682 F.2d 897, 904 (11th Cir. 1982).

66. *Ellison v. Brady*, 924 f.2d 872 (9th Cir. 1991).

67. As one of Getek's studies shows, reasonable men and reasonable women can disagree over what constitutes sexual harassment in the workplace. In this study, 67.2% of men as compared to 16.8% of women would be flattered if asked to have sex, while 15% of the men and 62.8% of the women said they would be insulted by such an offer. Op. cit.

68. *Robinson v. Jacksonville Shipyards*, 760 F. Supp. 1486 (M.D. Fla. 1991).

69. Nadine Strossen, "Regulating Workplace Sexual Harassment and Upholding the First Amendment—Avoiding a Collision, *Villanova Law Review*, Vol 37 (forthcoming).

Outrageous Acts and Everyday Rebellions

Gloria Steinem

The great strength of feminism—like that of the black movement here, the Gandhian movement in India, and all the organic struggles for self-rule and simple justice—has always been encouragement for each of us to act, without waiting and theorizing about some future takeover at the top. It's no accident that, when some small group does accomplish a momentous top-down revolution, the change seems to benefit only those who made it. Even with the best intentions of giving "power to the people," the revolution is betrayed.

Power can be taken, but not given. The process of the taking is empowerment in itself.

So we ask ourselves: What might a spectrum of diverse, mutually supportive tactics really look like for us as individuals, for family and community groups, for men who care about equality, for children, and for political movements as a whole? Some actions will always be unique to particular situations and thus unforeseeable. Others will be suited to times of great energy in our lives, and still others will make sense for those who are burnt out and need to know that a time of contemplation and assessment is okay. But here are some that may inspire action, if only to say, "No, that's not right. But this is what I choose to do instead."

AS INDIVIDUALS

In the early 1970s when I was traveling and lecturing with feminist lawyer and black activist Florynce Kennedy, one of her many epigrams went like this: "Unity in a movement situation is overrated. If you were the Establishment, which would you rather see coming in the door, five hundred mice or one lion?"

Mindful of her teaching, I now often end lectures with an organizer's deal. If each person in the room promises that in the twenty-four hours beginning the very next day she or he will do at least *one outrageous thing* in the cause of simple justice, then I promise I will, too. It doesn't matter whether the act is as small as saying, "Pick it up yourself" (a major step for those of us who have been our family's servants) or as large as calling a strike. The point is that, if each of us does as promised, we can be pretty sure of two results. First, the world one day later won't be quite the same. Second, we will have such a good time that we will never again get up in the morning saying, "*Will* I do anything outrageous?" but only "*What* outrageous act will I do today?"

Here are some samples I've recorded from the outrageous acts of real life.

- Announced a permanent refusal to contribute more money to a church or synagogue until women too can become priests, ministers, and rabbis.
- Asked for a long-deserved raise, or, in the case of men and/or white folks, refused an undeserved one that is being given over the heads of others because of their race or sex.
- Written a well-reasoned critique of a sexist or racist textbook and passed it out on campus.
- Challenged some bit of woman-hating humor or imagery with the seriousness more often reserved for slurs based on religion or race.
- Shared with colleagues the knowledge of each other's salaries so that unfairnesses can be calculated. (It's interesting that employers try to keep us from telling the one fact we know.)
- Cared for a child or children so that an overworked mother could have a day that is her own. (This is especially revolutionary when done by a man.)
- Returned to a birth name or, in the case of a man, gave his children both parents' names.

- Left home for a week so that the father of your young child could learn to be a parent. (As one woman later reported calmly, "When I came home, my husband and the baby had bonded, just the way women and babies do.")
- Petitioned for a Women's Studies section in a local library or bookstore.
- Checked a corporate employer's giving programs, see if they are really inclusive by benefiting women with at least half of their dollars, and made suggestions if not.
- Personally talked to a politician who needed persuasion to support, or reward for helping, issues of equality.
- Redivided a conventional house so that each person has a space for which he or she is solely responsible, with turns taken caring for kitchen, bathroom, and other shared rooms.
- Got married to an equal, or divorced from an unequal.
- Left a violent lover or husband.
- Led a walkout from a movie that presents rape scenes or other violence as titillating and just fine.
- Made a formal complaint about working (or living) in a white ghetto. White people are also being culturally deprived.
- Told the truth to a child, or a parent.
- Said proudly, "I am a feminist." (Because this word means a believer in equality, it's especially helpful when said by a man.)
- Organized a block, apartment house, or dormitory to register and vote.
- Personally picketed and/or sued a bigoted employer/teacher/athletic coach/foreman/union boss.

In addition to one-time outrageous acts, these are also the regular ones that should be the bottom line for each of us: writing five letters a week to lobby, criticize, or praise anything from TV shows to a senator; giving 10 percent of our incomes to social justice; going to one demonstration a month or one consciousness-raising group a week just to keep support and energy up; and figuring out how to lead our daily lives in a way that reflects what we believe. People who actually incorporate such day-by-day changes into their lives report that it isn't difficult: five lobbying letters can be written while watching "The Late Show"; giving 10 percent of their incomes often turns out to be the best investment they ever made; meetings create a free space, friends, and an antidote to isolation; and trying to transform a job or a family or a life-style in order to reflect beliefs, instead of the other way around, gives a satisfying sense of affecting the world.

If each of us only reached out and changed *five other people in our lifetimes*, the spiral of revolution would widen enormously—and we can do much more than that.

IN GROUPS

Some of the most effective group actions are the simplest:

- Dividing membership lists according to political district, from precinct level up, so we can inform and get out the pro-equality vote.
- Asking each organization we belong to, whether community or professional, union or religious, to support issues of equality in their formal agendas.
- Making sure that the nonfeminist groups we're supporting don't have mostly women doing the work and mostly men on their boards.
- Making feminist groups *feminist*; that is, relevant to women of the widest diversity of age, race, economics, life-styles, and political labels practical for the work at hand. (An inclusiveness that's best begun among the founders. It's much tougher to start any group and only later reach out to "others.")
- Offering support where it's needed without being asked—for instance, to the school librarian who's fighting right-wing censorship of feminist and other books; or to the new family feeling racially isolated in the neighborhood. (Would you want to have to ask people to help you?)
- Identifying groups for coalitions and allies for issues.
- Streamlining communications. If there were an emergency next week—a victim of discrimination who needed defending, a piece of sinister legislation gliding through city council—could your membership be alerted?
- Putting the group's money where its heart is, and not where it isn't. That may mean contributing to

the local battered women's shelter and protesting a community fund that gives far more to Boy Scouts than to Girl Scouts; or publishing a directory of women-owned businesses; or withholding student-activity fees from a campus program that invites mostly white male speakers. (Be sure and let the other side know how much money they're missing. To be more forceful, put your contributions in an escrow account, with payment contingent on a specific improvement.)

- Organizing speak-outs and press conferences. There's nothing like personal testimonies from the people who have experienced the problem first-hand.
- Giving public awards and dinners to women (and men) who've made a positive difference.
- Bringing in speakers or Women's Studies courses to inform your members; running speakers' bureaus so your group's message gets out to the community.
- Making sure new members feel invited and welcome once they arrive, with old members assigned to brief them and transfer group knowledge.
- Connecting with other groups like yours regionally or nationally for shared experience, actions, and some insurance against reinventing the wheel.

Obviously, we must be able to choose the appropriate action from a full vocabulary of tactics, from voting to civil disobedience, from supporting women in the trades to economic boycotts and tax revolts, from congressional hearings to zap actions with humor and an eye to the evening news.

Given the feminization of poverty, however, groups are also assuming another importance. Since women are an underdeveloped, undercapitalized labor force with an unequal knowledge of technology—in other words, a Third World country wherever we are—we're beginning to realize that the Horatio Alger model of individualistic economic progress doesn't work very well for us. Probably we have more to learn about economic development from our sisters in countries recognized as the Third World. Cooperative ownership forms and communal capital formation may be as important to our future as concepts of equal pay.

So far, these experiments have started small: three single mothers who combine children and resources to buy a house not one of them could afford alone; two women who buy a truck for long-distance hauling jobs; a dozen women who pool their savings to start a bakery or a housecleaning service, or single mothers and feminist architects who transform old buildings into new homes.

But we're beginning to look at Third World examples of bigger efforts. If the poorest women in rural Kenya can pool their savings for years, buy a bus, make money from passengers, and build a cooperative store, why can't we with our greater resources help each other to do the same? If illiterate women in India can found and run their own credit cooperative, thus giving them low-interest loans for the goods they sell in the streets, how dare American women be immobilized by a poor economy? It's also a healthy reversal of the usual flow of expertise from developed to underdeveloped country that may help feminists build bridges across national chasms of condescension and mistrust. Groups and organizations have been the base of our issue-oriented, electoral, consciousness-raising, and direct-action progress. In the future, they may be our economic base as well.

AS STRATEGISTS

We've spent the first decade or so of the second wave of feminism on the riverbank, rescuing each other from drowning. In the survival areas of rape, battery, and other terrorist violence against women, for instance, we've begun to organize help through shelters, hot lines, pressure on police to provide protection, reforms in social services and legislation, and an insistence that society stop blaming the victim.

Now, some of us must go to the head of the river and keep the victims from falling in.

For instance, we can pursue new strategies that have proved effective in treating wife batterers and other violent men. Such strategies have been successful precisely because they came from experiences and feminist insight: violence is an addiction that a male-dominant society creates by teaching us that "real men" must dominate and control the world in general and women in particular. When some men inevitably become addicted to violence to prove their masculinity, conventional Freudian-style treatment has only said: "Yes, men are natural aggressors, but you must learn to control the degree." That's like telling a drug addict that he can have just a little heroin.

Treatment based on experience, on the other hand, says: "No, men are not natural aggressors; you must unhook your sense of identity and masculinity from violence, and kick the habit completely."

The few such programs that exist have been helpful to batterers, rapists and other violent men, criminals, and dangerous citizens who have been judged untreatable precisely because they saw themselves as normal men. This fundamental challenge to cultural ideas of masculinity might also hold hope for less violent ways of solving conflicts on this fragile Spaceship Earth.

That's one of hundreds of futurist examples. There are many other strategies centered around four great goals: *reproductive freedom; work redefined; democratic families; and depoliticized culture.*

Clearly, these goals can only be reached a long distance in the future. We are very far from the opposite shore.

But the image of crossing a river may be too linear to describe the reality we experience. In fact, we repeat similar struggles that seem cyclical and discouraging in the short run, yet each one is on slightly changed territory. One full revolution is not complete until it has passed through the superficiality of novelty and even law to become an accepted part of the culture. Only when we look back over a long passage of time do we see that each of these cycles has been moving in a direction. We see the spiral of history.

In my first days of activism, I thought I would do this ("this" being feminism) for a few years and then return to my real life (what my "real life" might be, I did not know). Partly, that was a naïve belief that injustice only had to be pointed out in order to be cured. Partly, it was a simple lack of courage.

But like so many others now and in movements past, I've learned that this is not just something we care about for a year or two or three. We are in it for life—and for our lives. Not even the spiral of history is needed to show the distance traveled. We have only to look back at the less complete people we ourselves used to be.

And that is the last Survival Lesson: *we look at how far we've come, and then we know— there can be no turning back.*

Radical Feminism

Radical feminists believe that their liberal sisters have not gone far enough. They argue that it is patriarchy that oppresses women: a system characterized by power, dominance, hierarchy, and competition—a system that cannot be reformed but only extirpated root and branch. It is not just patriarchy's legal, political, and economic structures that must be overturned; it is also its social and cultural institutions (especially the family, the Church, and the academy).

Although radical feminist writings are as distinct as they are myriad, many of them trace the effects of female biology on women's self-perception, status, and function in the private and public domains. When an antifeminist says that biology is destiny, that individual means that (1) people are born with the hormones, anatomy, and chromosomes of either a male or a female; (2) females are destined to have a much more burdensome reproductive role than males are; (3) males will, other things being equal, exhibit "masculine" psychological traits, whereas females will, other things being equal, exhibit "feminine" psychological traits; and (4) society should preserve this natural order, making sure that its men remain dominant and its women subordinate. Radical feminists, however, have no interest in preserving a status quo that relegates women to second-sex status. Rather, their aim is to overcome whatever negative effects biology has had on women and perhaps also on men.

ugh most radical feminists now view
iology and psychology as potential
women's liberation, they initially
the actual causes of women's en-
The Dialectic of Sex, Shulamith

Firestone argues that no matter how much educational, legal, political, and economic equality women achieve, nothing fundamental will change for women as long as biological reproduction remains the rule rather than the exception. As Firestone sees it, biological reproduction is neither in women's nor in children's best interests. She claims that the joy of giving birth—invoked so frequently in this society—is a patriarchal myth. In fact, pregnancy is "barbaric," and natural childbirth is "at best necessary and tolerable," at worst, "like shitting a pumpkin." Moreover, biological motherhood is the root of further evils, especially the vice of possessiveness that generates feelings of hostility and jealously among human beings. Favoring one child over another on account of its being the product of one's ovum or sperm is inequalitarian. In order to secure not only women's liberation from men but also all people's liberation from divisive hierarchies, we must stop focusing on what is "mine" and what is "yours."

Whether women's monopoly over the power to give birth is the paradigm for power relations is controversial both inside and outside the radical feminist community. So too is the notion that bearing and rearing children are necessarily oppressive. Most radical feminists no longer agree with Firestone that the "technological fix" of artificial reproduction will secure women's liberation. What is oppressive is not female biology per se, but rather that men have controlled women as bearers and rearers of children. Thus, if women are to be liberated, each woman must determine for herself when to use or not to use reproduction-controlling technologies (for example, contraception, sterilization, abortion) and reproduction-aiding technologies (artificial insemination by donor and *in vitro* fertilization). Each woman also must determine for herself whether she is going to rear her children alone or in collaboration with a spouse, some relative(s), some friend(s), and/or some privately paid or publicly subsidized employees (babysitters, nannies, day-care professionals, nursery teachers).

Not all radical feminists focus on the biological origins of women's oppression, however. Indeed, most of them stress the ways in which gender (rigid ideas about femininity) and sexuality (rigid ideas about heterosexuality) have been used to subordinate women to men. Although radical feminists seldom separate their discussions of gender and sexuality, preferring instead to discuss the sex/gender system in toto, moments of emphasis do punctuate their writings. Like many liberal feminists, many radical feminists have espoused a nurture theory of gender differences according to which "masculine" and "feminine" traits are the products of socialization. However, unlike liberal feminists, who claim "that men are simply fellow victims of sex-role conditioning," radical feminists insist that men have guided the social construction of gender and sexuality for their own purposes. Through education, law, and economics; through pornography, prostitution, sexual harassment, rape, and woman battering; and through foot binding, suttee, purdah, clitoridectomy, witch-burning, and gynecology, men have controlled women's feminine traits and sexuality for male pleasure.

Given the ways in which society has permitted men to abuse and misuse women, it is no wonder that some radical feminists have insisted that women must (1) reinterpret femininity as a female way of being that is independent of masculinity; and (2) escape the confines of heterosexuality, creating an exclusively female sexuality through celibacy, autoeroticism, or lesbianism. Alone, or with other women, a woman can discover the true pleasures of sex.

Women must learn how to stand separate from men so as to experience the fullness of their female persons.

To be certain, "separatism" is an idea that threatens not only men but many women. In her brilliant essay, "Some Reflections on Separatism and Power," Marilyn Frye approaches separatism as something practiced by a variety of individuals—especially those concerned with social change. We all participate in a multitude of relations, most often unreflectively. When we begin to question the "goodness" of some of these relations, we also begin to question the value of our participating in them. To reject some relations—to resist paying income tax for nuclear weapons, to divest from South African stock, or to engage in conscientious objection, for example—is to engage in noncooperation, in nonparticipation, in separatism. What distinguishes feminist from non-feminist separatism, says Frye, is that the former is a separation "from men and from institutions, relationships, roles and activities which are male-defined, male-dominated and operating for the benefit of males and the maintenance of male privilege—this separation being initiated or maintained at will, *by women*" (p. 360). By refusing to approve the status quo for women, and by creating women's consciousness-raising groups, rape crisis centers, all-women social events, battered-women's shelters, and women's art galleries, feminists engage in acts of separatism.

Of course, feminist separation takes forms other than these. Some feminists refuse to change their career plans simply because the men in their lives ask them to; they refuse to have sexual intercourse with their boyfriends or husbands on demand; they refuse to say yes simply because the men in their lives wish they would. Indeed, as Frye sees it, "access is the crucial battle to be fought in the struggle for women's liberation from patriarchy, for the "Patriarchal Imperative" teaches that "males must have access to women" (p. 363). Women must remove (redirect, reallocate) goods and services from men in order to weaken, and even destroy, patriarchal power. Because the most vital goods and services that women have provided for men have tended to be sexual in nature, a call for feminist separatism sometimes leads to a call for lesbian separatism (nonparticipation in the institution of heterosexuality). Although radical feminists agree that female sexuality should not be defined in terms of men's needs and wants, very few radical feminists insist that lesbianism be mandatory for all women. On the contrary, as most radical feminists see it, no specific kind of sexual experience should be prescribed as the best kind for a liberated woman. Every woman should be encouraged to experiment sexually with herself, with other women, and even with men. As dangerous as heterosexuality is for a woman within a patriarchal society—that is, as difficult as it can be for a woman to know whether she wants to say yes or no to a man's sexual advances—she must feel free to follow the lead of her own desires.

One of the most debated issues in the radical feminist community is related to what sorts of sexual desires men and women should feel free to follow. Should men and, for that matter, women have access to pornographic material—a continuum that ranges from pulpy romance novels, which tell stories of thinly disguised male domination and female submission, to soft-core magazines such as *Playboy,* which feature depictions of quivering young bunnies disrobing in front of elderly Great White Hunters, to hard-core magazines such as *Bondage,* which highlight scenes of men torturing women (for example, photos of businessmen systematically applying hot irons, scissors, torches, and knives to the breasts and vaginas of their secretaries)? As some feminists, including some radical feminists, see it, both men and women should have access to this material provided that it benefits them in some way; for example, by helping them to overcome so-called sexual hang-ups. As other feminists, including the majority of radical feminists, see it, however, pornography never benefits women. Rather, it always harms them. How could it be otherwise, asks Catharine MacKinnon, since pornography is:

the graphic sexually explicit subordination of women through pictures or words that also includes women dehumanized as sexual objects, things or commodities; enjoying pain or humiliation or rape; being tied up, cut up, mutilated, bruised, or physically hurt; in postures of sexual submission or servility or display; reduced to body parts, penetrated by objects or animals, or presented in scenarios of degradation, injury, torture; shown as filthy or inferior, bleeding, bruised, or hurt in a context that makes these conditions sexual. (p. 372)

Pornography is not about free speech and the First Amendment, says MacKinnon. Rather, it is about civil rights and the Fourteenth Amendment. Premised as it is on inequality, pornography leads men (and to some degree women) not only to think less of women, but to treat women as second-class citizens, or less than fully human persons. For this reason, MacKinnon argues that pornography can and ought to be controlled as a civil rights violation. Any woman—or man, child, or transsexual used in the place of a woman—should be granted a legal cause of action if that individual is coerced into a pornographic performance, has pornography forced on her, or has been assaulted or attacked because of a particular piece of pornography. Further, any woman should be able to bring suit against traffickers in pornography on behalf of all women.

Clearly, MacKinnon's ideas and those of Andrea Dworkin, her collaborator, are controversial. To their credit, MacKinnon and Dworkin have noticed what we all should have noticed years ago: that the pornographic imagination distorts, degrades, and demeans the bodies of women far more than those of men. With rare exception, pornography is something men do to women. Nevertheless, many feminists, especially liberal feminists, resist the argument that pornography is central to women's subordination. To suggest that pornography contributes to women's oppression more than

does lack of access to good jobs, affordable child care, and quality education is, they insist, to suggest something about which the typical woman on welfare can only shake her head in disbelief.

The Dialectic of Sex

Shulamith Firestone

Sex class is so deep as to be invisible. Or it may appear as a superficial inequality, one that can be solved by merely a few reforms, or perhaps by the full integration of women into the labor force. But the reaction of the common man, woman, and child—"*That?* Why you can't change *that!* You must be out of your mind!"—is the closest to the truth. We are talking about something every bit as deep as that. This gut reaction—the assumption that, even when they don't know it, feminists are talking about changing a fundamental biological condition—is an honest one. That so profound a change cannot be easily fit into traditional categories of thought, e.g., "political," is not because these categories do not apply but because they are not big enough: radical feminism bursts through them. If there were another word more all-embracing than *revolution* we would use it.

Until a certain level of evolution had been reached and technology had achieved its present sophistication, to question fundamental biological conditions was insanity. Why should a woman give up her precious seat in the cattle

car for a bloody struggle she could not hope to win? But, for the first time in some countries, the preconditions for feminist revolution exist—indeed, the situation is beginning to *demand* such a revolution.

The first women are fleeing the massacre, and, shaking and tottering, are beginning to find each other. Their first move is a careful joint observation, to resensitize a fractured consciousness. This is painful: No matter how many levels of consciousness one reaches, the problem always goes deeper. It is everywhere. The division yin and yang pervades all culture, history, economics, nature itself; modern Western versions of sex discrimination are only the most recent layer. To so heighten one's sensitivity to sexism presents problems far worse than the black militant's new awareness of racism. Feminists have to question, not just all of *Western* culture, but the organization of culture itself, and further, even the very organization of nature. Many women give up in despair: If *that's* how deep it goes they don't want to know. Others continue strengthening and enlarging the movement, their painful sensitivity to female oppression existing for a purpose: eventually to eliminate it.

Before we can act to change a situation, however, we must know how it has arisen and evolved, and through what institutions it now operates. Engels: "We must examine the historic succession of events from which the antagonism has sprung in order to discover in the conditions thus created the means of ending the conflict." For feminist revolution we shall need an analysis of the dynamics of sex war as comprehensive as the Marx-Engels analysis of class antagonism was for the economic revolution. More comprehensive. For we are dealing with a larger problem, with an oppression that goes back beyond recorded history to the animal kingdom itself.

In creating such an analysis we can learn a lot from Marx and Engels: Not their literal opinions about women—about the condition of women as an oppressed class they know next to nothing, recognizing it only where it overlaps with economics—but rather their analytic *method*.

Marx and Engels outdid their socialist forerunners in that they developed a method of analysis which was both *dialectical* and *materialist*. The first in centuries to view history dialectically, they saw the world as process, a natural flux of action and reaction, of opposites yet inseparable and interpenetrating. Because they were able to perceive history as movie other than as snapshot, they attempted to avoid falling into the stagnant "metaphysical" view that had trapped so many other great minds . . . They combined this view of the dynamic interplay of historical forces with a materialist one, that is, they attempted for the first time to put historical and cultural change on a real basis, to trace the development of economic classes to organic causes. By understanding thoroughly the mechanics of history, they hoped to show men how to master it.

Socialist thinkers prior to Marx and Engels, such as Fourier, Owen, and Bebel, had been able to do no more than moralize about existing social inequalities, positing an ideal world where class privilege and exploitation should not exist—in the same way that early feminist thinkers posited a world where male privilege and exploitation ought not exist—by mere virtue of good will. In both cases, because the early thinkers did not really understand how the social injustice had evolved, maintained itself, or could be eliminated, their ideas existed in a cultural vacuum, utopian. Marx and Engels, on the other hand, attempted a scientific approach to history. They traced the class conflict to its real economic origins, projecting an economic solution based on objective economic preconditions already present: the seizure by the proletariat of the means of production would lead to a communism in which government had withered away, no longer needed to repress the lower class for the sake of the higher. In the classless society the interests of every individual would be synonymous with those of the larger society.

But the doctrine of historical materialism, much as it was a brilliant advance over previous historical analysis, was not the complete answer, as later events bore out. For though Marx and Engels grounded their theory in reality, it was only a *partial* reality. Here is Engels' strictly economic definition of historical materialism from *Socialism: Utopian or Scientific*:

Historical materialism is that view of the course of history which seeks the *ultimate* cause and the great moving power of all historical events in the economic development of society, in the changes of the modes of production and exchange, in the consequent division of society into distinct classes, and in the struggles of these classes against one another. (Italics mine)

Further, he claims:

. . . that all past history with the exception of the primitive stages was the history of class struggles; that these warring classes of society are always the products of the modes of production and exchange—in a word, of the economic conditions of their time; that the *economic* structure of society always furnishes the real basis, starting from which we can alone work out the *ultimate* explanation of the whole superstructure of juridical and political institutions as well as of the religious, philosophical, and other ideas of a given historical period. (Italics mine)

It would be a mistake to attempt to explain the oppression of women according to this strictly economic interpretation. The class analysis is a beautiful piece of work, but limited: although correct in a linear sense, it does not go deep enough. There is a whole sexual substratum of the historical dialectic that Engels at times dimly perceives, but because he can see sexuality only through an economic filter, reducing everything to that, he is unable to evaluate in its own right.

Engels did observe that the original division of labor was between man and woman for the purposes of childbreeding; that within the family the husband was the owner, the wife the means of production, the children the labor; and that reproduction of the human species was an important economic system distinct from the means of production. . . .

But Engels has been given too much credit for these scattered recognitions of the oppression of women as a class. In fact he acknowledged the sexual class system only where it overlapped and illuminated his economic construct. Engels didn't do so well even in this respect. But Marx was worse: There is a growing recognition of Marx's bias against women (a cultural bias shared by Freud as well as all men of culture), dangerous if one attempts to squeeze feminism into an orthodox Marxist framework—freezing what were only incidental insights of Marx and Engels about sex class into dogma. Instead, we must enlarge historical materialism to *include* the strictly Marxian, in the same way that the physics of relativity did not invalidate Newtonian physics so much as it drew a circle around it, limiting its application—but only through comparison—to a smaller sphere. For an economic diagnosis traced to ownership of the means of production, even of the means of reproduction, does not explain everything. There is a level of reality that does not stem directly from economics.

The assumption that, beneath economics, reality is psychosexual is often rejected as ahistorical by those who accept a dialectical materialist view of history because it seems to land us back where Marx began: groping through a fog of utopian hypotheses, philosophical systems that might be right, that might be wrong (there is no way to tell), systems that explain concrete historical developments by *a priori* categories of thought: historical materialism, however, attempted to explain "knowing" by "being" and not vice versa.

But there is still an untried third alternative: We can attempt to develop a materialist view of history based on sex itself. . . .

Let us try to develop an analysis in which biology itself—procreation—is at the origin of the dualism. The immediate assumption of the layman that the unequal division of the sexes is "natural" may be well-founded. We need not immediately look beyond this. Unlike economic class, sex class sprang directly from a biological reality: men and women were created different, and not equally privileged. Although, as De Beauvoir points out, this difference of itself did not necessitate the development of a class system—the domination of one group by another—the reproductive *functions* of these differences did. The biological family is an inherently unequal power distribution. The need for power leading to the development of classes arises from the psychosexual formation of each individual according to this basic imbalance, rather than, as Freud, Norman O. Brown, and others have, once again overshooting their mark, postulated, some irreducible conflict of Life against Death, Eros vs. Thanatos.

The *biological family*—the basic reproductive unit of male/female/infant, in whatever form of social organization—is characterized by these fundamental—if not immutable—facts:

1. That women throughout history before the advent of birth control were at the continual mercy of their biology—menstruation, menopause, and "female ills," constant painful childbirth, wet-nursing and care of infants, all of which made them dependent on males (whether brother, father, husband, lover, or clan, government, community-at-large) for physical survival.

2. That human infants take an even longer time to grow up than animals, and thus are helpless and, for some short period at least, dependent on adults for physical survival.

3. That a basic mother child interdependency has existed in some form in every society, past or present, and thus has shaped the psychology of every mature female and every infant.

4. That the natural reproductive difference between the sexes led directly to the first division of labor at the origins of class, as well as furnishing the paradigm of caste (discrimination based on biological characteristics).

These biological contingencies of the human family cannot be covered over with anthropological sophistries. Anyone observing animals mating, reproducing, and caring for their young will have a hard time accepting the "cultural relativity" line. For no matter how many tribes in Oceania you can find where the connection of the father to fertility is not known, no matter how many matrilineages, no matter how many cases of sex-role reversal, male housewifery, or even empathic labor pains, these facts prove only one thing: the amazing *flexibility* of human nature. But human nature is adaptable *to* something, it is, yes, determined by its environmental conditions. And the biological family that we have described has existed everywhere throughout time. Even in matriarchies where woman's fertility is worshipped, and the father's role is unknown or unimportant, if perhaps not on the genetic father, there is still some dependence of the female and the infant on the male. And though it is true that the nuclear family is only a recent development, one which, as I shall attempt to show, only intensifies the psycholog-

ical penalties of the biological family, though it is true that throughout history there have been many variations on this biological family, the contingencies I have described existed in all of them, causing specific psychosexual distortions in the human personality.

But to grant that the sexual imbalance of power is biologically based is not to lose our case. We are no longer just animals. And the Kingdom of Nature does not reign absolute. . . .

The "natural" is not necessarily a "human" value. Humanity has begun to outgrow nature: we can no longer justify the maintenance of a discriminatory sex class system on grounds of its origins in Nature. Indeed, for pragmatic reasons alone it is beginning to look as if we *must* get rid of it.

The problem becomes political, demanding more than a comprehensive historical analysis, when one realizes that, though man is increasingly capable of freeing himself from the biological conditions that created his tyranny over women and children, he has little reason to want to give this tyranny up. As Engels said, in the context of economic revolution:

It is the law of division of labor that lies at the basis of the division into classes [Note that this division itself grew out of a fundamental biological division]. But this does not prevent the ruling class, once having the upper hand, from consolidating its power at the expense of the working class, from turning its social leadership into an intensified exploitation of the masses.

Though the sex class system may have originated in fundamental biological conditions, this does not guarantee once the biological basis of their oppression has been swept away that women and children will be freed. On the contrary, the new technology, especially fertility control, may be used against them to reinforce the entrenched system of exploitation.

So that just as to assure elimination of economic classes requires the revolt of the underclass (the proletariat) and, in a temporary dictatorship, their seizure of the means of *pro-duction*, so to assure the elimination of sexual classes requires the revolt of the underclass (women) and the seizure of control of *repro-duction*: not only the full restoration to women of ownership of their own bodies, but also their (temporary) seizure of control of human fertil-ity—the new population biology as well as all the social institutions of childbearing and child-rearing. And just as the end goal of socialist revolution was not only the elimination of the economic class *privilege* but of the economic class *distinction* itself, so the end goal of femi-nist revolution must be, unlike that of the first feminist movement, not just the elimination of male *privilege* but of the sex *distinction* itself: genital differences between human beings would no longer matter culturally. (A reversion to an unobstructed *pansexuality*—Freud's "polymor-phous perversity"—would probably supersede hetero/homo/bisexuality.) The reproduction of the species by one sex for the benefit of both would be replaced by (at least the option of) artificial reproduction: children would be born to both sexes equally, or independently of ei-ther, however one chooses to look at it; the de-pendence of the child on the mother (and vice versa) would give way to a greatly shortened dependence on a small group of others in gen-eral, and any remaining inferiority to adults in physical strength would be compensated for culturally. The division of labor would be ended by the elimination of labor altogether (cybernation). The tyranny of the biological family would be broken. . . .

STRUCTURAL IMPERATIVES

Before we talk about revolutionary alternatives, let's summarize—to determine the specifics that must be carefully excluded from any new struc-tures. Then we can go on to "utopian specula-tion" directed by at least negative guidelines.

We have seen how women, biologically distinguished from men, are culturally distin-guished from "human." Nature produced the fundamental inequality—half the human race must bear and rear the children of all of them—which was later consolidated, institu-tionalized, in the interests of men. Reproduc-tion of the species cost women dearly, not only emotionally, psychologically, culturally but even in strictly material (physical) terms: before re-cent methods of contraception, continuous childbirth led to constant "female trouble," early aging, and death. Women were the slave class that maintained the species in order to free the other half for the business of the world—admittedly often its drudge aspects, but certainly all its creative aspects as well.

This natural division of labor was contin-ued only at great cultural sacrifice: men and women developed only half of themselves, at the expense of the other half. The division of the psyche into male and female to better reinforce the reproductive division was tragic: the hyper-trophy in men of rationalism, aggressive drive, the atrophy of their emotional sensitivity was a physical (war) as well as a cultural disaster. The emotionalism and passivity of women increased their suffering (we cannot speak of them in a symmetrical way, since they were vic-timized as a class by the division). Sexually men and women were channeled into a highly or-dered—time, place, procedure, even dialogue— heterosexuality restricted to the genitals, rather than diffused over the entire physical being.

I submit, then, that the first demand for any alternative system must be:

1. *The freeing of women from the tyranny of their reproductive biology by even means avail-able, and the diffusion of the childbearing and childrearing role to the society as a whole, men as well as women.* There are many degrees of this. Already we have a (hard-won) acceptance of "family planning," if not contraception for its own sake. Proposals are imminent for day-care centers, perhaps even twenty-four-hour child-care centers staffed by men as well as women. But this, in my opinion, is timid if not entirely

worthless as a transition. We're talking about *radical* change. And though indeed it cannot come all at once, radical goals must be kept in sight at all times. Day-care centers buy women off. They ease the immediate pressure without asking why that pressure is on *women.*

At the other extreme there are the more distant solutions based on the potentials of modern embryology, that is, artificial reproduction, possibilities still so frightening that they are seldom discussed seriously. We have seen that the fear is to some extent justified: in the hands of our current society and under the direction of current scientists (few of whom are female or even feminist), any attempted use of technology to "free" anybody is suspect. But we are speculating about post-revolutionary systems, and for the purposes of our discussion we shall assume flexibility and good intentions in those working out the change.

To thus free women from their biology would be to threaten the *social* unit that is organized around biological reproduction and the subjection of women to their biological destiny, the family. Our second demand will come also as a basic contradiction to the family, this time the family as an *economic* unit:

2. *The full self-determination, including economic independence, of both women and children.* To achieve this goal would require fundamental changes in our social and economic structure. This is why we must talk about a feminist socialism: in the immediate future, under capitalism, there could be at best a token integration of women into the labor force. For women have been found exceedingly useful and cheap as a transient, often highly skilled labor supply,[1] not to mention the economic value of their traditional function, the reproduction and rearing of the next generation of children, a job for which they are now patronized (literally and thus figuratively) rather than paid. But whether or not officially recognized, these are essential economic functions. Women, in this present capacity, are the very foundation of the economic superstructure, vital to its existence.[2] The paeans to self-sacrificing motherhood have a basis in reality: Mom *is* vital to the American way of life, considerably more than apple pie. She is an institution without which the system really *would* fall apart. In official capitalist terms, the bill for her economic services[3] might run as high as one-fifth of the gross national product. But payment is not the answer. To pay her, as is often discussed seriously in Sweden, is a reform that does not challenge the basic division of labor and thus could never eradicate the disastrous psychological and cultural consequences of that division of labor.

As for the economic independence of children, that is really a pipe dream, realized as yet nowhere in the world. And, in the case of children too, we are talking about more than a fair integration into the labor force; we are talking about the abolition of the labor force itself under a cybernetic socialism, the radical restructuring of the economy to make "work," i.e., wage labor, no longer necessary. In our post-revolutionary society adults as well as children would be provided for—irrespective of their social contributions—in the first equal distribution of wealth in history.

We have now attacked the family on a double front, challenging that around which it is organized: reproduction of the species by females and its outgrowth, the physical dependence of women and children. To eliminate these would be enough to destroy the family, which breeds the power psychology.

NOTES

1. Most bosses would fail badly had they to take over their secretaries' job, or do without them. I know several secretaries who sign without a thought their bosses names to their own (often brilliant) solutions. The skills of college women especially would cost a fortune reckoned in material terms of male labor.

2. Margaret Benston ("The Political Economy of Women's Liberation," *Monthly Review*, September

1969), in attempting to show that women's oppression is indeed economic—though previous economic analysis has been incorrect—distinguishes between the male superstructure economy based on *commodity* production (capitalist ownership of the means of production, and wage labor), and the pre-industrial reduplicative economy of the family, production for immediate *use*. Because the latter is not part of the *official* contemporary economy, its function at the basis of that economy is often overlooked. Talk of drafting women into the superstructure commod-

ity economy fails to deal with the tremendous amount of necessary production of the traditional kind now performed by women without pay: Who will do it?

3. The Chase Manhattan Bank estimates a woman's over-all domestic work week at 99.6 hours. Margaret Benston gives her minimal estimate for a *childless* married woman at 16 hours, close to half of a regular work week; a *mother* must spend at least six or seven days a week working close to 12 hours.

Some Reflections on Separatism and Power

Marilyn Frye

I have been trying to write something about separatism almost since my first dawning of feminist consciousness, but it has always been for me somehow a mercurial topic which, when I tried to grasp it, would softly shatter into many other topics like sexuality, man-hating, so-called reverse discrimination, apocalyptic utopianism, and so on. What I have to share with you today is my latest attempt to get to the heart of the matter.

In my life, and within feminism as I understand it, separatism is not a theory or a doctrine, nor a demand for certain specific behaviors on the part of feminists, though it is undeniably connected with lesbianism. Feminism seems to me to be kaleidoscopic—something whose shapes, structures and patterns alter with every turn of feminist creativity; and one element

which is present through all the changes is an element of separation. This element has different roles and relations in different turns of the glass—it assumes different meanings, is variously conspicuous, variously determined or determining, depending on how the pieces fall and who is the beholder. The theme of separation, in its multitude variations, is there in everything from divorce to exclusive lesbian separatist communities, from shelters for battered women to witch covens, from women's studies programs to women's bars, from expansion of daycare to abortion on demand. The presence of this theme is vigorously obscured, trivialized, mystified and outright denied by many feminist apologists, who seem to find it embarrassing, while it is embraced, explored, expanded and ramified by most of the more inspiring theorists and activists. The theme of separation is noticeably absent or heavily qualified in most of the things I take to be personal solutions and band-aid projects, like legalization of prostitution, liberal marriage contracts, improvement of the treatment of rape victims and affirmative action. It is clear to me, in my own case at least, that the contrariety of assimilation and separation is one of the main things that guides or determines assessments of various theories, actions and practices as reformist or radical, as going to the root of the thing or being relatively superficial. So my topical question comes to this: What is it about separation, in any or all of its many forms and degrees, that makes it so basic and so sinister, so exciting and so repellent?

Feminist separation is, of course, separation of various sorts or modes from men and from institutions, relationships, roles and activities which are male-defined, male-dominated and operating for the benefit of males and the maintenance of male privilege—this separation being initiated or maintained, at will, *by women*. (Masculist separatism is the partial segregation of women from men and male domains *at the will of men*. This difference is crucial.) The feminist separation can take many forms. Breaking up or avoiding close relationships or working relationships; forbidding someone to enter your house; excluding someone from your company, or from your meeting; withdrawal from participation in some activity or institution, or avoidance of participation; avoidance of communications and influence from certain quarters (not listening to music with sexist lyrics, not watching TV); withholding commitment or support; rejection of or rudeness toward obnoxious individuals.* Some separations are subtle realignments of identification, priorities and commitments, or working with agendas which only incidently coincide with the agendas of the institution one works in. Ceasing to be loyal to something or someone is a separation; and ceasing to love. The feminist's separations are rarely if ever sought or maintained directly as ultimate personal or political ends. The closest we come to that, I think, is the separation which is the instinctive and self-preserving recoil from the systematic misogyny that surrounds us.** Generally, the separations are brought about and maintained for the sake of something else like independence, liberty, growth, invention, sisterhood, safety, health, or the practice of novel or heretical customs.[1] Often the separations in question evolve, unpremeditated, as one goes one's way and finds various persons, institutions or relationships useless, obstructive or noisome and leaves them aside or behind. Sometimes the separations are consciously planned and cultivated as necessary prerequisites or conditions for getting on with one's business. Sometimes the separations are accomplished or maintained easily, or with a sense of relief, or even joy; sometimes they are accomplished or maintained with difficulty, by dint of constant vigilance, or with anxiety, pain or grief.

Most feminists, probably all, practice some separation from males and male-dominated institutions. A separatist practices separation consciously, systematically, and probably more generally than the others, and advocates thorough and "broad-spectrum" separation as part of the conscious strategy of liberation. And,

---

*Adrienne Rich: ". . . *makes me question the whole idea of 'courtesy' or 'rudeness'—surely their constructs, since women become 'rude' when we ignore or reject male obnoxiousness, while male 'rudeness' is usually punctuated with the 'Haven't you a sense of humor' tactic.*" Yes; me too. I embrace rudeness; our compulsive/compulsory politeness so often is what coerces us into their "fellowship."

**Ti-Grace Atkinson: *Should give more attention here to our vulnerability to assault and degradation, and to separation as protection.* Okay, but then we have to re-emphasize that it has to be separation at *our* behest—we've had enough of their imposed separation for our "protection." (There's no denying that in my real-life life, protection and maintenance of places for healing are major motives for separation.)

contrary to the image of the separatist as a cowardly escapist, hers is the life and program which inspires the greatest hostility, disparagement, insult and confrontation and generally she is the one against whom economic sanctions operate most conclusively. The penalty for refusing to work with or for men is usually starvation (or, at the very least, doing without medical insurance); and if one's policy of non-cooperation is more subtle, one's livelihood is still constantly on the line, since one is not a loyal partisan, a proper member of the team, or what have you. The penalties for being a lesbian are ostracism, harassment and job insecurity or joblessness. The penalty for rejecting men's sexual advances is often rape and, perhaps even more often, forfeit of such things as professional or job opportunities. And the separatist lives with the added burden of being assumed by many to be a morally depraved man-hating bigot. But there is a clue here: if you are doing something that is so strictly forbidden by the patriarchs, you must be doing something right.

There is an idea floating around in both feminist and anti-feminist literature to the effect that females and males generally live in a relation of parasitism,[2] a parasitism of the male on the female . . . that it is, generally speaking, the strength, energy, inspiration and nurturance of women that keeps men going, and not the strength, aggression, spirituality and hunting of men that keeps women going.

It is sometimes said that the parasitism goes the other way around, that the female is the parasite. But one can conjure the appearance of the female as parasite only if one takes a very narrow view of human living—historically parochial, narrow with respect to class and race, and limited in conception of what are the necessary goods. Generally, the female's contribution to her material support is and always has been substantial; in many times and places it has been independently sufficient. One can and should distinguish between a partial and contingent material dependence created by a certain sort of money economy and class structure, and the nearly ubiquitous spiritual, emotional and material dependence of males on females. Males presently provide, off and on, a portion of the material support of women, within circumstances apparently designed to make it difficult for women to provide them for themselves. But females provide and generally have provided for males the energy and spirit for living; the males are nurtured by the females. And this the males apparently cannot do for themselves, even partially.

The parasitism of males on females is, as I see it, demonstrated by the panic, rage and hysteria generated in so many of them by the thought of being abandoned by women. But it is demonstrated in a way that is perhaps more generally persuasive by both literary and sociological evidence. Evidence cited in Jesse Bernard's work in *The Future of Marriage* and in George Gilder's *Sexual Suicide* and *Men Alone* convincingly shows that males tend in shockingly significant numbers and in alarming degree to fall into mental illness, petty crime, alcoholism, physical infirmity, chronic unemployment, drug addiction and neurosis when deprived of the care and companionship of a female mate, or keeper. (While on the other hand, women without male mates are significantly healthier and happier than women with male mates.) And masculist literature is abundant with indications of male cannibalism, of males deriving essential sustenance from females. Cannibalistic imagery, visual and verbal, is common in pornography: images likening women to food, and sex to eating. And, as documented in Millett's *Sexual Politics* and many other feminist analyses of masculist literature, the theme of men getting high off beating, raping or killing women (or merely bullying them) is common. These interactions with women, or rather, these actions upon women, make men feel good, walk tall, feel refreshed, in*vigor*ated. Men are drained and depleted by their living by themselves and with and among other men, and are revived and refreshed, re-created, by going home and being served dinner, changing to clean clothes, having sex with the wife; or by dropping by the apartment of a woman friend to be served coffee or a drink and stroked in one way or another; or by picking up a prostitute for a quicky or for a dip in favorite sexual escape fantasies; or by raping refugees from their wars (foreign and domestic). The ministrations of women, be they willing or unwilling, free or paid for, are what restore in men the strength, will and confidence to go on with what they call living.

If it is true that a fundamental aspect of the relations between the sexes is male parasitism, it might help to explain why certain issues are particularly exciting to patriarchal loyalists. For instance, in view of the obvious advantages of easy abortion to population control, to control of welfare rolls, and to ensuring sexual availability of women to men, it is a little surprising that the loyalists are so adamant and riled up in their objection to it. But look. . .

The fetus lives parasitically. It is a distinct animal surviving off the life (the blood) of another animal creature. It is incapable of surviving on its own resources, of independent nutrition; incapable even of symbiosis. If it is true that males live parasitically upon females, it seems reasonable to suppose that many of them and those loyal to them are in some way sensitive to the parallelism between their situation and that of the fetus. They could easily identify with the fetus. The woman who is free to see the fetus as a parasite* might be free to see the man as a parasite. The woman's willing-

---

Caroline Whitbeck: Cross-cultural evidence suggests it's not the fetus that gets rejected in cultures where abortion is common, it is the role of motherhood, the burden, in particular, of "illegitimacy"; where the institution of illegitimacy does not exist, abortion rates are pretty low. This suggests to me that the woman's rejection of the fetus is even more directly a rejection of the male and his world than I had thought.

ness to cut off the life line to one parasite suggests a willingness to cut off the life line to another parasite. The woman who is capable (legally, psychologically, physically) of decisively, self-interestedly, independently rejecting the one parasite, is capable of rejecting, with the same decisiveness and independence, the like burden of the other parasite. In the eyes of the other parasite, the image of the wholly self-determined abortion, involving not even a ritual submission to male veto power, is the mirror image of death.

Another clue here is that one line of argument against free and easy abortion is the slippery slope argument that if fetuses are to be freely dispensed with, old people will be next. Old people? Why are old people next? And why the great concern for them? Most old people are women, indeed, and patriarchal loyalists are not generally so solicitous of the welfare of any women. Why old people? Because, I think, in the modern patriarchal divisions of labor, old people too are parasites on women. The anti-abortion folks seem not to worry about wife beating and wife murder—there is no broad or emotional popular support for stopping these violences. They do not worry about murder and involuntary sterilization in prisons, nor murder in war, nor murder by pollution and industrial accidents. Either these are not real to them or they cannot identify with the victims; but anyway, killing in general is not what they oppose. They worry about the rejection *by women, at women's discretion,* of something which lives parasitically on women. I suspect that they fret not because old people are next, but because men are next.

There are other reasons, of course, why patriarchal loyalists should be disturbed about abortion on demand; a major one being that it would be a significant form of female control of reproduction, and at least from certain angles it looks like the progress of patriarchy *is* the progress toward male control of reproduction, starting with possession of wives and continuing through the invention of obstetrics and the technology of extrauterine gestation. Giving up that control would be giving up patriarchy. But such an objection to abortion is too abstract, and requires too historical a vision, to generate the hysteria there is now in the reaction against abortion. The hysteria is, I think, to be accounted for more in terms of a much more immediate and personal presentiment of ejection by the woman-womb.

I discuss abortion here because it seems to me to be the most publicly emotional and most physically dramatic ground on which the theme of separation and male parasitism is presently being played out. But there are other locales for this play. For instance, women with newly raised consciousnesses tend to leave marriages and families, either completely through divorce, or partially, through unavailability of their cooking, housekeeping and sexual services. And women academics tend to become alienated from their colleagues and male mentors and no longer serve as sounding board, ego booster, editor, mistress or proofreader. Many awakening women become celibate or lesbian, and the others become a very great deal more choosy about when, where and in what relationships they will have sex with men. And the men affected by these separations generally react with defensive hostility, anxiety and guilt-tripping, not to mention descents into illogical argument which match and exceed their own most fanciful images of female irrationality. My claim is that they are very afraid because they depend very heavily upon the goods they receive from women, and these separations cut them off from those goods.

Male parasitism means that males *must have access* to women; it is the Patriarchal Imperative. But feminist no-saying is more than a substantial removal (redirection, reallocation) of goods and services because Access is one of the faces of Power. Female denial of male access to females substantially cuts off a flow of ben-

efits, but it has also the form and full portent of assumption of power.

Differences of power are always manifested in asymmetrical access. The President of the United States has access to almost everybody for almost anything he might want of them, and almost nobody has access to him. The super-rich have access to almost everybody; almost nobody has access to them. The resources of the employee are available to the boss as the resources of the boss are not to the employee. The parent has unconditional access to the child's room; the child does not have similar access to the parent's room. Students adjust to professors' office hours; professors do not adjust to students' conference hours. The child is required not to lie; the parent is free to close out the child with lies at her discretion. The slave is unconditionally accessible to the master. Total power is unconditional access; total powerlessness is being unconditionally accessible. The creation and manipulation of power is constituted of the manipulation and control of access.

All-woman groups, meetings, projects seem to be great things for causing controversy and confrontation. Many women are offended by them; many are afraid to be the one to announce the exclusion of men; it is seen as a device whose use needs much elaborate justification. I think this is because conscious and deliberate exclusion of men by women, from anything, is blatant insubordination, and generates in women fear of punishment and reprisal (fear which is often well-justified). Our own timidity and desire to avoid confrontations generally keep us from doing very much in the way of all-woman groups and meetings. But when we do, we invariably run into the male champion who challenges our right to do it. Only a small minority of men go crazy when an event is advertised to be for women only— just one man tried to crash our women-only Rape Speak-Out, and only a few hid under the auditorium seats to try to spy on a women-only meeting at a NOW convention in Philadelphia.

But these few are onto something their less rabid compatriots are missing. The woman-only meeting is a fundamental challenge to the structure of power. It is always the privilege of the master to enter the slave's hut. The slave who decides to exclude the master from her hut is declaring herself not a slave. The exclusion of men from the meeting not only deprives them of certain benefits (which they might survive without); it is a controlling of access, hence an assumption of power. It is not only mean, it is arrogant.

It becomes clearer now why there is always an off-putting aura of negativity about separatism—one which offends the feminine pollyanna in us and smacks of the purely defensive to the political theorist in us. It is this: First: When those who control access have made you totally accessible, your first act of taking control must be denying access, or must have denial of access as one of its aspects. This is not because you are charged up with (unfeminine or politically incorrect) negativity; it is because of the logic of the situation. When we start from a position of total accessibility there *must* be an aspect of no-saying (which is the beginning of control) in *every effective* act and strategy, the effective ones being precisely those which *shift power*, i.e., ones which involve manipulation and control of access. Second: Whether or not one says "no," or withholds or closes out or rejects, on this occasion or that, the capacity and ability to say "no" (with effect) is logically necessary to control. When we are in control of access to ourselves there will be some no-saying, and when we are more accustomed to it, when it is more common, an ordinary part of living, it will not seem so prominent, obvious, or strained . . . we will not strike ourselves or others as being particularly negative. In this aspect of ourselves and our lives, we will strike ourselves pleasingly as active beings with momentum of our own, with sufficient shape and structure—with sufficient integrity— to generate friction. Our experience of our

no-saying will be an aspect of our experience of our definition.

When our feminist acts or practices have an aspect of separation, we are assuming power by controlling access and simultaneously by undertaking definition. The slave who excludes the master from her hut thereby declares herself *not a slave*. And *definition* is another face of power.

The powerful normally determine what is said and sayable. When the powerful label something or dub it or baptize it, the thing becomes what they call it. When the Secretary of Defense calls something a peace negotiation, for instance, then whatever it is that he called a peace negotiation is an instance of negotiating peace. If the activity in question is the working out of terms of a trade-off of nuclear reactors and territorial redistributions, complete with arrangements for the resulting refugees, that is peacemaking. People laud it, and the negotiators get Noble Peace Prizes for it. On the other hand, when I call a certain speech act a rape, my "calling" it does not make it so. At best, I have to explain and justify and make clear exactly what it is about this speech act which is assaultive in just what way, and then the others acquiesce in saying the act was *like* rape or could figuratively be called a rape. My counterassault will not be counted a simple case of self-defense. And what I called rejection of parasitism, they call the loss of the womanly virtues of compassion and "caring." And generally, when renegade women call something one thing and patriarchal loyalists call it another, the loyalists get their way.*

---

*This paragraph and the succeeding one are the passage which has provoked the most substantial questions from women who read the paper. One thing that causes trouble here is that I am talking from a stance or position that is ambiguous—it is located in two different and noncommunicating systems of thought-action.
(footnote continues)

Women generally are not the people who do the defining, and we cannot from our isolation and powerlessness simply commence saying different things than others say and make it stick. There is a humpty-dumpty problem in that. But we are able to arrogate definition to ourselves when we re-pattern access. Assuming

---

Re the patriarchy and the English language, there is general usage over which I/we do not have the control that elite males have (with the cooperation of all the ordinary patriarchal loyalists). *Re* the new being and meaning which are being created now by lesbian-feminists, we *do* have semantic authority, and, collectively, can and do define with effect. I think it is only by maintaining our boundaries through controlling concrete access to us that we can enforce on those who are not-us our definitions of ourselves, hence force on them *the fact of our existence* and thence open up the *possibility* of our having semantic authority with them. (I wrote some stuff that's relevant to this in the last section of my paper "Male Chauvinism—A Conceptual Analysis.")[3] Our unintelligibility to patriarchal loyalists is a source of pride and delight, in some contexts; but if we don't have an effect on their usage while we continue, willy nilly, to be subject to theirs, being totally unintelligible to them could be fatal. (A friend of mine had a dream where the women were meeting in a cabin at the edge of town, and they had a sort of inspiration through the vision of one of them that they should put a sign on the door which would connect with the patriarchs' meaning-system, for otherwise the men would be too curious/frightened about them and would break the door down to get in. They put a picture of a fish on the door.) Of course, you might say that *being* intelligible to them might be fatal. Well, perhaps it's best to be in a position to make tactical decisions about when and how to be intelligible and unintelligible.

control of access, we draw new boundaries and create new roles and relationships. This, though it causes some strain, puzzlement and hostility, is to a fair extent within the scope of individuals and small gangs, as outright verbal redefinition is not, at least in the first instance.

One may see access as coming in two sorts, "natural" and humanly arranged. A grizzly bear has what you might call natural access to the picnic basket of the unarmed human. The access of the boss to the personal services of the secretary is humanly arranged access; the boss exercises institutional power. It looks to me, looking from a certain angle, like institutions *are* humanly designed patterns of access—access to persons and their services. But institutions are artifacts of definition. In the case of intentionally and formally designed institutions, this is very clear, for the relevant definitions are explicitly set forth in by-laws and constitutions, regulations and rules. When one defines the term "president," one defines presidents in terms of what they can do and what is owed them by other offices, and "what they can do" is a matter of their access to the services of others. Similarly, definitions of *dean, student, judge,* and *cop* set forth patterns of access, and definitions of *writer, child, owner,* and of course, *husband, wife,* and *man* and *girl.* When one changes the pattern of access, one forces new uses of words on those affected. The term "man" has to shift in meaning when rape is no longer possible. When we take control of sexual access to us, of access to our nurturance and to our reproductive function, access to mothering and sistering, we redefine the word "woman." The shift of usage is pressed on others by a change in social reality; it does not await their recognition of our definitional authority.

When women separate (withdraw, break out, regroup, transcend, shove aside, step outside, migrate, say *no*), we are simultaneously controlling access and defining. We are doubly insubordinate, since neither of these is permitted. And access and definition are fundamental ingredients in the alchemy of power, so we are doubly, and radically, insubordinate.

If these, then, are some of the ways in which separation is at the heart of our struggle, it helps to explain why separation is such a hot topic. If there is one thing women are queasy about it is *actually taking power*. As long as one stops just short of that, the patriarchs will for the most part take an indulgent attitude. We are afraid of what will happen to us when we really frighten them. This is not an irrational fear. It is our experience in the movement generally that the defensiveness, nastiness, violence, hostility and irrationality of the reaction to feminism tends to correlate with the blatancy of the element of separation in the strategy or project which triggers the reaction. The separations involved in women leaving homes, marriages and boyfriends, separations from fetuses, and the separation of lesbianism are all pretty dramatic. That is, they are dramatic and blatant when perceived from within the framework provided by the patriarchal world view and male parasitism. Matters pertaining to marriage and divorce, lesbianism and abortion touch individual men (and their sympathizers) because they can feel the relevance of these to themselves—they can feel the threat that they might be the next. Hence, heterosexuality, marriage and motherhood, which are the institutions which most obviously and individually maintain female accessibility to males, form the core

triad of antifeminist ideology; and all-woman spaces, all-woman organizations, all-woman meetings, all-woman classes, are outlawed, suppressed, harassed, ridiculed and punished—in the name of that other fine and enduring patriarchal institution, Sex Equality.

To some of us these issues can seem almost foreign . . . strange ones to be occupying center stage. We are busily engaged in what seem to *us* our blatant insubordinations: living our own lives, taking care of ourselves and one another, doing our work, and in particular, telling it as we see it. Still, the original sin is the separation which these presuppose, and it is that, not our art or philosophy, not our speechmaking, nor our "sexual acts" (or abstinences), for which we will be persecuted, when worse comes to worst.

NOTES

1. See Chris Pierce and Sara Ann Ketchum, "Separatism and Sexual Relationships," in *A Philosophical Approach to Women's Liberation*, eds. S. Hill and M. Weinzweig (Belmont, California: Wadsworth, 1978).

2. I first noticed this when reading *Beyond God the Father*, by Mary Daly (Boston: Beacon Press, 1973). See also *Women's Evolution*, by Evelyn Reed (New York: Pathfinder Press, 1975) for rich hints about male cannibalism and male dependence.

3. In (improbably enough) *Philosophy and Sex*, edited by Robert Baker and Frederick Elliston (Buffalo, New York: Prometheus Books, 1976).

Pornography, Civil Rights, and Speech

Catharine MacKinnon

There is a belief that this is a society in which women and men are basically equals. Room for marginal corrections is conceded, flaws are known to exist, attempts are made to correct what are conceived as occasional lapses from the basic condition of sex equality. Sex discrimination law has concentrated most of its focus on these occasional lapses. It is difficult to overestimate the extent to which this belief in equality is an article of faith for most people, including most women, who wish to live in self-respect in an internal universe, even (perhaps especially) if not in the world. It is also partly an expression of natural law thinking: if we are inalienably equal, we can't "really" be degraded.

This is a world in which it is worth trying. In this world of presumptive equality, people make money based on their training or abilities or diligence or qualifications. They are employed and advanced on the basis of merit. In this world of just deserts, if someone is abused, it is thought to violate the basic rules of the community. If it doesn't, victims are seen to have done something they could have chosen to do differently, by exercise of will or better judgment. Maybe such people have placed themselves in a situation of vulnerability to physical abuse. Maybe they have done something provocative. Or maybe they were just unusually unlucky. In such a world, if such a

person has an experience, there are words for it. When they speak and say it, they are listened to. If they write about it, they will be published. If certain experiences are never spoken about, if certain people or issues are seldom heard from, it is supposed that silence has been chosen. The law, including much of the law of sex discrimination and the First Amendment, operates largely within the realm of these beliefs.

Feminism is the discovery that women do not live in this world, that the person occupying this realm is a man, so much more a man if he is white and wealthy. This world of potential credibility, authority, security, and just rewards, recognition of one's identity and capacity, is a world that some people do inhabit as a condition of birth, with variations among them. It is not a basic condition accorded humanity in this society, but a prerogative of status, a privilege, among other things, of gender.

I call this a discovery because it has not been an assumption. Feminism is the first theory, the first practice, the first movement, to take seriously the situation of all women from the point of view of all women, both on our situation and on social life as a whole. The discovery has therefore been made that the implicit social content of humanism, as well as the standpoint from which legal method has been designed and injuries have been defined, has not been women's standpoint. Defining feminism in a way that connects epistemology with power as the politics of women's point of view, this discovery can be summed up by saying that women live in another world:

specifically, a world of *not* equality, a world of inequality.

Looking at the world from this point of view, a whole shadow world of previously invisible silent abuse has been discerned. Rape, battery, sexual harassment, forced prostitution, and the sexual abuse of children emerge as common and systematic. We find that rape happens to women in all contexts, from the family, including rape of girls and babies, to students and women in the workplace, on the streets, at home, in their own bedrooms by men they do not know and by men they do know, by men they are married to, men they have had a social conversation with, and, least often, men they have never seen before. Overwhelmingly, rape is something that men do or attempt to do to women (44 percent of American women according to a recent study) at some point in our lives. Sexual harassment of women by men is common in workplaces and educational institutions. Based on reports in one study of the federal workforce, up to 85 percent of women will experience it, many in physical forms. Between a quarter and a third of women are battered in their homes by men. Thirty-eight percent of little girls are sexually molested inside or outside the family. Until women listened to women, this world of sexual abuse was *not spoken* of. It was the unspeakable. What I am saying is, if you *are* the tree falling in the epistemological forest, your demise doesn't make a sound if no one is listening. Women did not "report" these events, and overwhelmingly do not today, because no one is listening, because no one believes us. This silence does not mean nothing happened, and it does not mean consent. It is the silence of women of which Adrienne Rich has written, "Do not confuse it with any kind of absence."

Believing women who say we are sexually violated has been a radical departure, both methodologically and legally. The extent and nature of rape, marital rape, and sexual harassment itself, were discovered in this way. Domestic battery as a syndrome, almost a habit, was discovered through refusing to believe that when a woman is assaulted by a man to whom she is connected, that it is not an assault. The sexual abuse of children was uncovered, Freud notwithstanding, by believing that children were not making up all this sexual abuse. Now what is striking is that when each discovery is made, and somehow made real in the world, the response has been: it happens to men too. If women are hurt, men are hurt. If women are raped, men are raped. If women are sexually harassed, men are sexually harassed. If women are battered, men are battered. Symmetry must be reasserted. Neutrality must be reclaimed. Equality must be reestablished.

The only areas where the available evidence supports this, where anything like what happens to women also happens to men, involve children—little boys are sexually abused—and prison. The liberty of prisoners is restricted, their freedom restrained, their humanity systematically diminished, their bodies and emotions confined, defined, and regulated. If paid at all, they are paid starvation wages. They can be tortured at will, and it is passed off as discipline or as means to a just end. They become compliant. They can be raped at will, at any moment, and nothing will be done about it. When they scream, nobody hears. To be a prisoner means to be defined as a member of a group for whom the rules of what can be done to you, of what is seen as abuse of you, are reduced as part of the definition of your status. To be a woman is that kind of definition and has that kind of meaning.

Men *are* damaged by sexism. (By men I mean the status of masculinity that is accorded to males on the basis of their biology but is not itself biological.) But whatever the damage of sexism to men, the condition of being a man is not defined as subordinate to women by force. Looking at the facts of the abuses of women all at once, you see that a woman is socially defined as a person who, whether or not she is or has been, can be treated in these ways by men at any time, and little, if anything, will be done about it. This is what it means when feminists say that maleness is a form of power and femaleness is a form of powerlessness.

In this context, all of this "men too" stuff means that people don't really believe that the things I have just said are true, though there really is little question about their empirical accuracy. The data are extremely simple, like women's pay figure of fifty-nine cents on the dollar. People don't really seem to believe that either. Yet there is no question of its empirical validity. This is the workplace story: what women do is seen as not worth much, or what is not worth much is seen as something for women to do. *Women* are seen as not worth much, is the thing. Now why are these basic realities of the subordination of women to men, for example, that only 7.8 percent of women have never been sexually assaulted, not effectively believed, not perceived as real in the face of all this evidence? Why don't *women* believe our own experiences? In the face of all this evidence, especially of systematic sexual abuse—subjection to violence with impunity is one extreme expression, although not the only expression, of a degraded status—the view that basically the sexes are equal in this society remains unchallenged and unchanged. The day I got this was the day I understood its real message, its real coherence: *This is equality for us.*

I could describe this, but I couldn't explain it until I started studying a lot of pornography. In pornography, there it is, in one place, all of the abuses that women had to struggle so long even to begin to articulate, all the *unspeakable* abuse: the rape, the battery, the sexual harassment, the prostitution, and the sexual abuse of children. Only in the pornography it is called something else: sex, sex, sex, sex, and sex, respectively. Pornography sexualizes rape, battery, sexual harassment, prostitution, and child sexual abuse; it thereby celebrates, promotes, authorizes, and legitimizes them. More generally,

it eroticizes the dominance and submission that is the dynamic common to them all. It makes hierarchy sexy and calls that "the truth about sex" or just a mirror of reality. Through this process pornography constructs what a woman is as what men want from sex. This is what the pornography means.

Pornography constructs what a woman is in terms of its view of what men want sexually, such that acts of rape, battery, sexual harassment, prostitution, and sexual abuse of children become acts of sexual equality. Pornography's world of equality is a harmonious and balanced place. Men and women are perfectly complementary and perfectly bipolar. Women's desire to be fucked by men is equal to men's desire to fuck women. All the ways men love to take and violate women, women love to be taken and violated. The women who most love this are most men's equals, the most liberated; the most participatory child is the most grown-up, the most equal to an adult. Their consent merely expresses or ratifies these preexisting facts.

The content of pornography is one thing. There, women substantively desire dispossession and cruelty. We desperately want to be bound, battered, tortured, humiliated, and killed. Or, to be fair to the soft core, merely taken and used. This is erotic to the male point of view. Subjection itself, with self-determination ecstatically relinquished, is the content of women's sexual desire and desirability. Women are there to be violated and possessed, men to violate and possess us, either on screen or by camera or pen on behalf of the consumer. On a simple descriptive level, the inequality of hierarchy, of which gender is the primary one, seems necessary for sexual arousal to work. Other added inequalities identify various pornographic genres or subthemes, although they are always added through gender: age, disability, homosexuality, animals, objects, race (including anti-Semitism), and so on. Gender is never irrelevant.

What pornography *does* goes beyond its content: it eroticizes hierarchy, it sexualizes inequality. It makes dominance and submission into sex. Inequality is its central dynamic; the illusion of freedom coming together with the reality of force is central to its working. Perhaps because this is a bourgeois culture, the victim must look free, appear to be freely acting. Choice is how she got there. Willing is what she is when she is being equal. It seems equally important that then and there she actually be forced and that forcing be communicated on some level, even if only through still photos of her in postures of receptivity and access, available for penetration. Pornography in this view is a form of forced sex, a practice of sexual politics, an institution of gender inequality.

From this perspective, pornography is neither harmless fantasy nor a corrupt and confused misrepresentation of an otherwise natural and healthy sexual situation. It institutionalizes the sexuality of male supremacy, fusing the erotization of dominance and submission with the social construction of male and female. To the extent that gender is sexual, pornography is part of constituting the meaning of that sexuality. Men treat women as who they see women as being. Pornography constructs who that is. Men's power over women means that the way men see women defines who women can be. Pornography is that way. Pornography is not imagery in some relation to a reality elsewhere constructed. It is not a distortion, reflection, projection, expression, fantasy, representation, or symbol either. It is a sexual reality.

In Andrea Dworkin's definitive work, *Pornography: Men Possessing Women*, sexuality itself is a social construct gendered to the ground. Male dominance here is not an artificial overlay upon an underlying inalterable substratum of uncorrupted essential sexual being. Dworkin presents a sexual theory of gender inequality of which pornography is a constitutive practice. The way pornography produces its meaning constructs and defines men and women as such. Gender has no basis in anything other than the social reality its

hegemony constructs. Gender is what gender means. The process that gives sexuality its male supremacist meaning is the same process through which gender inequality becomes socially real.

In this approach, the experience of the (overwhelmingly) male audiences who consume pornography is therefore not fantasy or simulation or catharsis but sexual reality, the level of reality on which sex itself largely operates. Understanding this dimension of the problem does not require noticing that pornography models are real women to whom, in most cases, something real is being done; nor does it even require inquiring into the systematic infliction of pornography and its sexuality upon women, although it helps. What matters is the way in which the pornography itself provides what those who consume it want. Pornography *participates* in its audience's eroticism through creating an accessible sexual object, the possession and consumption of which *is* male sexuality, as socially constructed; to be consumed and possessed as which, *is* female sexuality, as socially constructed; pornography is a process that constructs it that way.

The object world is constructed according to how it looks with respect to its possible uses. Pornography defines women by how we look according to how we can be sexually used. Pornography codes how to look at women, so you know what you can do with one when you see one. Gender is an assignment made visually, both originally and in everyday life. A sex object is defined on the basis of its looks, in terms of its usability for sexual pleasure, such that both the looking—the quality of the gaze, including its point of view—and the definition according to use become eroticized as part of the sex itself. This is what the feminist concept "sex object" means. In this sense, sex in life is no less mediated than it is in art. Men have sex with their image of a woman. It is not that life and art imitate each other; in this sexuality, they *are* each other.

To give a set of rough epistemological translations, to defend pornography as consistent with the equality of the sexes is to defend the subordination of women to men as sexual equality. What in the pornographic view is love and romance looks a great deal like hatred and torture to the feminist. Pleasure and eroticism become violation. Desire appears as lust for dominance and submission. The vulnerability of women's projected sexual availability, that acting we are allowed (that is, asking to be acted upon), is victimization. Play conforms to scripted roles. Fantasy expresses ideology, is not exempt from it. Admiration of natural physical beauty becomes objectification. Harmlessness becomes harm. Pornography is a harm of male supremacy made difficult to see because of its pervasiveness, potency, and principally, because of its success in making the world a pornographic place. Specifically, its harm cannot be discerned, and will not be addressed, if viewed and approached neutrally, because it is so much of "what is." In other words, to the extent pornography succeeds in constructing social reality, it becomes invisible as harm. If we live in a world that pornography creates through the power of men in a male-dominated situation, the issue is not what the harm of pornography is, but how that harm is to become visible.

Obscenity law provides a very different analysis and conception of the problem of pornography. In 1973 the legal definition of obscenity became that which the average person, applying contemporary community standards, would find that, taken as a whole, appeals to the prurient interest; that which depicts or describes in a patently offensive way—you feel like you're a cop reading someone's *Miranda* rights—sexual conduct specifically defined by the applicable state law; and that which, taken as a whole, lacks serious literary, artistic, political or scientific value. Feminism doubts whether the average person gender-neutral exists; has more questions about the content and process of defining what community standards are than it does about deviations from them; wonders why prurience counts but powerlessness does not and why sensibilities are better protected from offense than women are from exploitation; defines sexuality, and thus its violation and expropriation, more broadly than does state law: and questions why a body of law that has not in practice been able to tell rape from intercourse should, without further guidance, be entrusted with telling pornography from anything less. Taking the work "as a whole" ignores that which the victims of pornography have long known: legitimate settings diminish the perception of injury done to those whose trivialization and objectification they contextualize. Besides, and this is a heavy one, if a woman is subjected, why should it matter that the work has other value? Maybe what redeems the work's value is what enhances its injury to women, not to mention that existing standards of literature, art, science, and politics, examined in a feminist light, are remarkably consonant with pornography's mode, meaning, and message. And finally—first and foremost, actually—although the subject of these materials is overwhelmingly women, their contents almost entirely made up of women's bodies, our invisibility has been such, our equation as a sex *with* sex has been such, that the law of obscenity has never even considered pornography a women's issue.

Obscenity, in this light, is a moral idea, an idea about judgments of good and bad. Pornography, by contrast, is a political practice, a practice of power and powerlessness. Obscenity is ideational and abstract; pornography is concrete and substantive. The two concepts represent two entirely different things. Nudity, excess of candor, arousal or excitement, prurient appeal, illegality of the acts depicted, and unnaturalness or perversion are all qualities that bother obscenity law when sex is depicted or portrayed. Sex forced on real women so that it can be sold at a profit and

forced on other real women; women's bodies
trussed and maimed and raped and made into
things to be hurt and obtained and accessed,
and this presented as the nature of women in
a way that is acted on and acted out, over and
over; the coercion that is visible and the coercion that has become invisible—this and more
bothers feminists about pornography. Obscenity as such probably does little harm. Pornography is integral to attitudes and behaviors of
violence and discrimination that define the
treatment and status of half the population.

At the request of the city of Minneapolis,
Andrea Dworkin and I conceived and designed
a local human rights ordinance in accordance
with our approach to the pornography issue.
We define pornography as a practice of sex discrimination, a violation of women's civil rights,
the opposite of sexual equality. Its point is to
hold those who profit from and benefit from
that injury accountable to those who are injured. It means that women's injury—our damage, our pain, our enforced inferiority—should
outweigh their pleasure and their profits, or sex
equality is meaningless.

We define pornography as the graphic
sexually explicit subordination of women
through pictures or words that also includes
women dehumanized as sexual objects,
things, or commodities; enjoying pain or
humiliation or rape; being tied up, cut up,
mutilated, bruised, or physically hurt; in postures of sexual submission or servility or display; reduced to body parts, penetrated by
objects or animals, or presented in scenarios
of degradation, injury, torture; shown as filthy
or inferior; bleeding, bruised, or hurt in a
context that makes these conditions sexual.
Erotica, defined by distinction as not this,
might be sexually explicit materials premised
on equality. We also provide that the use of
men, children, or transsexuals in the place
of women is pornography. The definition is
substantive in that it is sex-specific, but it

covers everyone in a sex-specific way, so is
gender neutral in overall design. . . .

This law aspires to guarantee women's
rights consistent with the First Amendment by
making visible a conflict of rights between the
equality guaranteed to all women and what, in
some legal sense, is now the freedom of the
pornographers to make and sell, and their consumers to have access to, the materials this ordinance defines. Judicial resolution of this
conflict, if the judges do for women what they
have done for others, is likely to entail a balancing of the rights of women arguing that
our lives and opportunities, including our freedom of speech and action, are constrained
by—and in many cases flatly precluded by, in
and through—pornography, against those who
argue that the pornography is harmless, or
harmful only in part but not in the whole of
the definition; or that it is more important to
preserve the pornography than it is to prevent
or remedy whatever harm it does.

In predicting how a court would balance
these interests, it is important to understand
that this ordinance cannot now be said to be
either conclusively legal or illegal under existing law or precedent, although I think the
weight of authority is on our side. This ordinance enunciates a new form of the previously
recognized governmental interest in sex equality. Many laws make sex equality a governmental interest. Our law is designed to further
the equality of the sexes, to help make sex
equality real. Pornography is a practice of discrimination on the basis of sex, on one level
because of its role in creating and maintaining
sex as a basis for discrimination. It harms
many women one at a time and helps keep all
women in an inferior status by defining our
subordination as our sexuality and equating
that with our gender. It is also sex discrimination because its victims, including men, are
selected for victimization on the basis of
their gender. But for their sex, they would not
be so treated.

The harm of pornography, broadly speak-ing, is the harm of the civil inequality of the sexes made invisible as harm because it has become accepted as the sex difference. Consider this analogy with race: if you see Black people as different, there is no harm to segregation; it is merely a recognition of that difference. To neutral principles, separate but equal was equal. The injury of racial separation to Blacks arises "solely because [they] choose to put that construction upon it." Epistemologically translated: how you see it is not the way it is. Similarly, if you see women as just different, even or especially if you don't know that you do, subordination will not look like subordination at all, much less like harm. It will merely look like an appropriate recognition of the sex difference.

Pornography does treat the sexes differently, so the case for sex differentiation can be made here. But men as a group do not tend to be (although some individuals may be) treated the way women are treated in pornography. As a social group, men are not hurt by pornography the way women as a social group are. Their social status is not defined as *less* by it. So the major argument does not turn on mistaken differentiation, particularly since the treatment of women according to pornography's dictates makes it all too often accurate. The salient quality of a distinction between the top and the bottom in a hierarchy is not difference, although top is certainly different from bottom; it is power. So the major argument is: subordinate but equal is not equal.

Particularly since this is a new legal theory, a new law, and "new" facts, perhaps the situation of women it newly exposes deserves to be considered on its own terms. Why do the problems of 53 percent of the population have to look like somebody else's problems before they can be recognized as existing? Then, too, they can't be addressed if they do look like other people's problems, about which something might have to be done if something is done about these. This construction of the

situation truly deserves inquiry. Limiting the justification for this law to the situation of the sexes would serve to limit the precedential value of a favorable ruling.

Its particularity to one side, the *approach* to the injury is supported by a whole array of prior decisions that have justified exceptions to First Amendment guarantees when something that matters is seen to be directly at stake. What unites many cases in which speech interests are raised and implicated but not, on balance, protected, is harm, harm that counts. In some existing exceptions, the definitions are much more open-ended than ours. In some the sanctions are more severe, or potentially more so. For instance, ours is a civil law; most others, although not all, are criminal. Almost no other exceptions show as many people directly affected. Evidence of harm in other cases tends to be vastly less concrete and more conjectural, which is not to say that there is necessarily less of it. None of the previous cases addresses a problem of this scope or magnitude—for instance, an eight-billion-dollar-a-year industry. Nor do other cases address an abuse that has such widespread legitimacy. Courts have seen harm in other cases. The question is, will they see it here, especially given that the pornographers got there first. I will confine myself here to arguing from cases on harm to people, on the supposition that, the pornographers notwithstanding, women are not flags. . . .

To reach the magnitude of this problem on the scale it exists, our law makes trafficking in pornography—production, sale, exhibition, or distribution—actionable. Under the obscenity rubric, much legal and psychological scholarship has centered on a search for the elusive link between harm and pornography defined as obscenity. Although they were not very clear on what obscenity was, it was its harm they truly could not find. They looked high and low—in the mind of the male consumer, in society or in its "moral fabric," in correlations between variations in levels of antisocial acts and liberalization of obscenity laws. The only harm they have found has been harm to "the social interest in order and morality." Until recently, no one looked very persistently for harm to women, particularly harm to women through men. The rather obvious fact that the sexes *relate* has been overlooked in the inquiry into the male consumer and his mind. The pornography doesn't just drop out of the sky, go into his head, and stop there. Specifically, men rape, batter, prostitute, molest, and sexually harass women. Under conditions of inequality, they also hire, fire, promote, and grade women, decide how much or whether we are worth paying and for what, define and approve and disapprove of women in ways that count, that determine our lives.

If women are not just born to be sexually used, the fact that we are seen and treated as though that is what we are born for becomes something in need of explanation. If we see that men relate to women in a pattern of who they see women as being, and that forms a pattern of inequality, it becomes important to ask where that view came from or, minimally, how it is perpetuated or escalated. Asking this requires asking different questions about pornography than the ones obscenity law made salient.

Now I'm going to talk about causality in its narrowest sense. Recent experimental research on pornography shows that the materials covered by our definition cause measurable harm to women through increasing men's attitudes and behaviors of discrimination in both violent and nonviolent forms. Exposure to some of the pornography in our definition increases the immediately subsequent willingness of normal men to aggress against women under laboratory conditions. It makes normal men more closely resemble convicted rapists attitudinally, although as a group they don't look all that different from them to start with. Exposure to pornography also significantly increases attitudinal measures known to correlate with rape and self-reports of aggressive acts, measures such as hostility toward women, propensity to rape, condoning rape, and predicting that one would rape or force sex on a woman if one knew one would not get caught. On this latter measure, by the way, about a third of all men predict that they would rape, and half would force sex on a woman.

As to that pornography covered by our definition in which normal research subjects seldom perceive violence, long-term exposure still makes them see women as more worthless, trivial, nonhuman, and objectlike, that is, the way those who are discriminated against are seen by those who discriminate against them. Crucially, all pornography by our definition acts dynamically over time to diminish the consumer's ability to distinguish sex from violence. The materials work behaviorally to diminish the capacity of men (but not women) to perceive that an account of a rape is an account of a rape. The so-called sex-only materials, those in which subjects perceive no force, also increase perceptions that a rape victim is worthless and decrease the perception that she was harmed. The overall direction of current research suggests that the more expressly violent materials accomplish with less exposure what the less overtly violent—that is, the so-called sex-only materials—accomplish over the longer term. Women are rendered fit for use and targeted for abuse. The only thing that the research cannot document is which individual women will be next on the list. (This cannot be documented experimentally because of ethics constraints on the researchers—constraints that do not operate in life.) Although the targeting is systematic on the basis of sex, for individuals it is random. They are selected on a roulette basis. Pornography can no longer be said to be just a mirror. It does not just reflect the world or some people's perceptions. It *moves* them. It increases attitudes that are lived out, circumscribing the status of half the population.

What the experimental data predict will happen actually does happen in women's real lives. You know, it's fairly frustrating that women have known for some time that these things do happen. As Ed Donnerstein, an experimental researcher in this area, often puts it, "We just quantify the obvious." It is women, primarily, to whom the research results have been the obvious, because we live them. But not until a laboratory study predicts that these things *will* happen do people begin to believe you when you say they *did* happen to you. There is no—*not any*—inconsistency between the patterns the laboratory studies predict and the data on what actually happens to real women. Show me an abuse of women in society, I'll show it to you made sex in the pornography. If you want to know who is being hurt in this society, go see what is being done and to whom in pornography and then go look for them other places in the world. You will find them being hurt in just that way. We did in our hearings.

In our hearings women spoke, to my knowledge for the first time in history in public, about the damage pornography does to them. We learned that pornography is used to break women, to train women to sexual submission, to season women, to terrorize women, and to silence their dissent. It is this that has previously been termed "having no effect." The way men inflict on women the sex they experience through the pornography gives women no choice about seeing the pornography or doing the sex. Asked if anyone ever tried to inflict unwanted sex acts on them that they knew came from pornography, 10 percent of women in a recent random study said yes. Among married women, 24 percent said yes. That is a lot of women. A lot more don't know. Some of those who do testified in Minneapolis. One wife said of her ex-husband, "He would read from the pornography like a textbook, like a journal. In fact when he asked me to be bound, when he finally convinced me to do it, he read in the magazine how to tie the knots." Another

woman said of her boyfriend, "[H]e went to this party, saw pornography, got an erection, got me . . . to inflict his erection on. . . . There is a direct causal relationship there." One woman, who said her husband had rape and bondage magazines all over the house, discovered two suitcases full of Barbie dolls with rope tied on their arms and legs and with tape across their mouths. Now think about the silence of women. She said, "He used to tie me up and he tried those things on me." A therapist in private practice reported:

Presently or recently I have worked with clients who have been sodomized by broom handles, forced to have sex with over 20 dogs in the back seat of their car, tied up and then electrocuted on their genitals. These are children, [all] in the ages of 14 to 18, all of whom [have been directly affected by pornography,] [e]ither where the perpetrator has read the manuals and manuscripts at night and used these as recipe books by day or had the pornography present at the time of the sexual violence.[1]

One woman, testifying that all the women in a group of exprostitutes were brought into prostitution as children through pornography, characterized their collective experience: "[I]n my experience there was not one situation where a client was not using pornography while he was using me or that he had not just watched pornography or that it was verbally referred to and directed me to pornography." "Men," she continued, "witness the abuse of women in pornography constantly and if they can't engage in that behavior with their wives, girlfriends or children, they force a whore to do it."

Men also testified about how pornography hurts them. One young gay man who had seen *Playboy* and *Penthouse* as a child said of such heterosexual pornography: "It was one of the places I learned about sex and it showed me that sex was violence. What I saw there was a specific relationship between men and women. . . . [T]he woman was to be used, objectified, humiliated and hurt; the man was in a superior position, a position to be violent. In pornography I learned that what it meant to be sexual with a man or to be loved by a man was to accept his violence." For this reason, when he was battered by his first lover, which he described as "one of the most profoundly destructive experiences of my life," he accepted it.

Pornography also hurts men's capacity to relate to women. One young man spoke about this in a way that connects pornography—not the prohibition on pornography—with fascism. He spoke of his struggle to repudiate the thrill of dominance, of his difficulty finding connection with a woman to whom he is close. He said: "My point is that if women in a society filled by pornography must be wary for their physical selves, a man, even a man of good intentions, must be wary for his mind. . . . I do not want to be a mechanical, goose-stepping follower of the *Playboy* bunny, because that is what I think it is. . . . [T]hese are the experiments a master race perpetuates on those slated for extinction." The woman he lives with is Jewish. There was a very brutal rape near their house. She was afraid; she tried to joke. It didn't work. "She was still afraid. And just as a well-meaning German was afraid in 1933, I am also very much afraid."

Pornography stimulates and reinforces, it does not cathect or minor, the connection between one-sided freely available sexual access to women and masculine sexual excitement and sexual satisfaction. The catharsis hypothesis is fantasy. The fantasy theory is fantasy. Reality is: pornography conditions male orgasm to female subordination. It tells men what sex means, what a real woman is, and codes them together in a way that is behaviorally reinforcing. This is a real five-dollar sentence, but I'm going to say it anyway: pornography is a set of hermeneutical equivalences that work on the epistemological level. Substantively, pornography defines the meaning of what a woman is

seen to be by connecting access to her sexuality with masculinity through orgasm. What pornography means *is* what it does.

So far, opposition to our ordinance centers on the trafficking provision. This means not only that it is difficult to comprehend a group injury in a liberal culture—that what it *means* to be a woman is defined by this and that it is an injury for all women, even if not for all women equally. It is not only that the pornography has got to be accessible, which is the bottom line of virtually every objection to this law. It is also that power, as I said, is when you say something, it is taken for reality. If you talk about rape, it will be agreed that rape is awful. But rape is a conclusion. If a victim describes the facts of a rape, maybe she was asking for it or enjoyed it or at least consented to it, or the man might have thought she did, or maybe she had had sex before. It is now agreed that there is something wrong with sexual harassment. But describe what happened to you, and it may be trivial or personal or paranoid, or maybe you should have worn a bra that day. People are against discrimination. But describe the situation of a real woman, and they are not so sure she wasn't just unqualified. In law, all these disjunctions between women's perspective on our injuries and the standards we have to meet go under dignified legal rubrics like burden of proof, credibility, defenses, elements of the crime, and so on. These standards all contain a definition of what a woman is in terms of what sex is and the low value placed on us through it. They reduce injuries done to us to authentic expressions of who we are. Our silence is written all over them. So is the pornography.

We have as yet encountered comparatively little objection to the coercion, force, or assault provisions of our ordinance. I think that's partly because the people who make and approve laws may not yet see what they do as that. They *know* they use the pornography as we have described it in this law, and our law defines that, the reality of pornography, as a harm to women. If they suspect that they might on occasion engage in or benefit from coercion or force or assault, they may think that the victims won't be able to prove it—and they're right. Women who charge men with sexual abuse are not believed. The pornographic view of them is: they want it; they all want it. When women bring charges of sexual assault, motives such as venality or sexual repression must be invented, because we cannot really have been hurt. Under the trafficking provision, women's lack of credibility cannot be relied upon to negate the harm. There's no woman's story, to destroy, no credibility-based decision on what happened. The hearings establish the harm. The definition sets the standard. The grounds of reality definition are authoritatively shifted. Pornography is bigotry, *period*. We are now—the world pornography has decisively defined—having to meet the burden of proving, once and for all, for all of the rape and torture and battery, all of the sexual harassment, all of the child sexual abuse, all of the forced prostitution, *all* of it that the pornography is part of and that is part of the pornography, that the harm *does happen* and that when it happens it looks like this. Which may be why all this evidence never seems to be enough.

It is worth considering what evidence has been enough when other harms involving other purported speech interests have been allowed to be legislated against. By comparison to our trafficking provision, analytically similar restrictions have been allowed under the First Amendment, with a legislative basis far less massive, detailed, concrete, and conclusive. Our statutory language is more ordinary, objective, and precise and covers a harm far narrower than the legislative record substantiates. Under *Miller*, obscenity was allowed to be made criminal in the name of the "danger of offending the sensibilities of unwilling recipients or expo-

sure to juveniles." Under our law, we have direct evidence of harm, not just a conjectural danger, that unwilling women in considerable numbers are not simply offended in their sensibilities, but are violated in their persons and restricted in their options. Obscenity law also suggests that the applicable standard for legal adequacy in measuring such connections may not be statistical certainty. The Supreme Court has said that it is not their job to resolve empirical uncertainties that underlie state obscenity legislation. Rather, it is for them to determine whether a legislature could reasonably have determined that a connection might exist between the prohibited material and harm of a kind in which the state has legitimate interest. Equality should be such an area. The Supreme Court recently recognized that prevention of sexual exploitation and abuse of children is, in their words, "a governmental objective of surpassing importance." This might also be the case for sexual exploitation and abuse of women, although I think a civil remedy is initially more appropriate to the goal of empowering adult women than a criminal prohibition would be.

Other rubrics provide further support for the argument that this law is narrowly tailored to further a legitimate governmental interest consistent with the goals underlying the First Amendment. Exceptions to the First Amendment—you may have gathered from this—exist. The reason they exist is that the harm done by some speech outweighs its expressive value, if any. In our law a legislature recognizes that pornography, as defined and made actionable, undermines sex equality. One can say—and I have—that pornography is a causal factor in violations of women; one can also say that women will be violated so long as pornography exists; but one can also say simply that pornography violates women. Perhaps this is what the woman had in mind who testified at our hearings that for her the question is not just whether pornography causes violent acts to be perpetrated against some women. "Porn is already a violent act against women. It is our mothers, our daughters, our sisters, and our wives that are for sale for pocket change at the newsstands in this country." *Chaplinsky v. New Hampshire* recognized the ability to restrict as "fighting words" speech which, "by [its] very utterance inflicts injury." Perhaps the only reason that pornography has not been "fighting words"—in the sense of words that by their utterance tend to incite immediate breach of the peace—is that women have seldom fought back, yet.

Some concerns that are close to those of this ordinance underlie group libel laws, although the differences are equally important. In group libel law, as Justice Frankfurter's opinion in *Beauharnais* illustrates, it has been understood that an individual's treatment and alternatives in life may depend as much on the reputation of the group to which that person belongs as on their own merit. Not even a partial analogy can be made to group libel doctrine without examining the point made by Justice Brandeis and recently underlined by Larry Tribe: would more speech, rather than less, remedy the harm? In the end, the answer may be yes, but not under the abstract system of free speech, which only enhances the power of the pornographers while doing nothing substantively to guarantee the free speech of women, for which we need civil equality. The situation in which women presently find ourselves with respect to the pornography is one in which more *pornography* is inconsistent with rectifying or even counterbalancing its damage through speech, because so long as the pornography exists in the way it does there *will not be more speech by women.* Pornography strips and devastates women of credibility, from our accounts of sexual assault to our everyday reality of sexual subordination. We are stripped of authority and reduced and devalidated and silenced. Silenced here means that the purposes

of the First Amendment, premised upon conditions presumed and promoted by protecting free speech, do not pertain to women because they are not our conditions. Consider them: individual self-fulfillment—how does pornography promote our individual self-fulfillment? How does sexual inequality even permit it? Even if she can form words, who listens to a woman with a penis in her mouth? Facilitating consensus—to the extent pornography does so, it does so one-sided by silencing protest over the injustice of sexual subordination. Participation in civic life—central to Professor Meiklejohn's theory—how does pornography enhance women's participation in civic life? Anyone who cannot walk down the street or even lie down in her own bed without keeping her eyes cast down and her body clenched against assault is unlikely to have much to say about the issues of the day, still less will she become Tolstoy. Facilitating change—*this law* facilitates the change that existing First Amendment theory had been used to throttle. Any system of freedom of expression that does not address a problem where the free speech of men silences the free speech of women, a real conflict between speech interests as well as between people, is not serious about securing freedom of expression in this country.

For those of you who still think pornography is only an idea, consider the possibility that obscenity law got one thing right. Pornography is more actlike than thoughtlike. The fact that pornography, in a feminist view, furthers the idea of the sexual inferiority of women, which is a political idea, doesn't make the pornography itself into a political idea. One can express the idea a practice embodies. That does not make the practice into an idea. Segregation expresses the idea of the inferiority of one group to another on the basis of race. That does not make segregation an idea. A sign that says "Whites Only" is only words. Is it therefore protected by the First Amendment? Is it not an act, a practice, of segregation because what it means is inseparable from what it does? *Law is only words.*

The issue here is whether the fact that words and pictures are the central link in the cycle of abuse will immunize that entire cycle, about which we cannot do anything without doing something about the pornography. As Justice Stewart said in *Ginsburg*, "When expression occurs in a setting where the capacity to make a choice is absent, government regulation of that expression may coexist with and *even implement* First Amendment guarantees." I would even go so far as to say that the pattern of evidence we have closely approaches Justice Douglas' requirement that "freedom of expression can be suppressed if, and to the extent that, it is so closely brigaded with illegal action as to be an inseparable part of it." Those of you who have been trying to separate the acts from the speech—that's an act, that's an act, there's a law against that act, regulate that act, don't touch the speech—notice here that the illegality of the acts involved doesn't mean that the speech that is "brigaded with" it *cannot* be regulated. This is when it *can* be.

I take one of two penultimate points from Andrea Dworkin, who has often said that pornography is not speech for women, it is the silence of women. Remember the mouth taped, the woman gagged, "Smile, I can get a lot of money for that." The smile is not her expression, it is her silence. It is not her expression not because it didn't happen, but because it *did* happen. The screams of the women in pornography are silence, like the screams of Kitty Genovese, whose plight was misinterpreted by some onlookers as a lovers' quarrel. The flat expressionless voice of the woman in the New Bedford gang rape, testifying, is silence. She was raped as men cheered and watched, as they do in and with the pornography. When women resist and men say, "Like this, you stupid bitch, here is how to do it" and shove their faces into

the pornography, this "truth of sex" is the silence of women. When they say, "If you love me, you'll try," the enjoyment we fake, the enjoyment we learn is silence. Women who submit because there is more dignity in it than in losing the fight over and over live in silence. Having to sleep with your publisher or director to get access to what men call speech is silence. Being humiliated on the basis of your appearance, whether by approval or disapproval, because you have to look a certain way for a certain job, whether you get the job or not, is silence. The absence of a woman's voice, everywhere that it cannot be heard, is silence. And anyone who thinks that what women say in pornography is women's speech—the "Fuck me, do it to me, harder," all of that—has never heard the sound of a woman's voice.

The most basic assumption underlying First Amendment adjudication is that, socially, speech is free. The First Amendment says Congress shall not abridge the freedom of speech. Free speech, get it, *exists.* Those who wrote the First Amendment *had* speech—they wrote the Constitution. *Their* problem was to keep it free from the only power that realistically threatened it: the federal government. They designed the First Amendment to prevent government from constraining that which, if unconstrained by government, was free, meaning *accessible to them.* At the same time, we can't tell much about the intent of the framers with regard to the question of women's speech, because I don't think we crossed their minds. It is consistent with this analysis that their posture toward freedom of speech tends to presuppose that whole segments of the population are not systematically silenced socially, prior to government action. If everyone's power were equal to theirs, if this were a nonhierarchical society, that might make sense. But the place of pornography in the ·inequality of the sexes makes the assumption of equal power untrue.

This is a hard question. It involves risks. Classically, opposition to censorship has involved keeping government off the backs of people. Our law is about getting some people off the backs of other people. The risks that it will be misused have to be measured against the risks of the status quo. Women will never have that dignity, security, compensation that is[^] the promise of equality so long as the pornography exists as it does now. The situation of women suggests that the urgent issue of our freedom of speech is not primarily the avoidance of state intervention as such, but getting affirmative access to speech for those to whom it has been denied.

NOTE

1. *Public Hearings on Ordinances to Add Pornography as Discrimination Against Women,* Committee on Governmental Operations. City Council, Minneapolis MN, December 12–13, 1983.

Cultural Feminism

The term "cultural feminist" has been used to denote at least two schools of feminist thought. As Linda Alcoff and Alice Echols use the term, it applies to a distinction within radical feminist thought. As we use the term "cultural feminist" here, it denotes that school of feminist thought which believes that, either by nature (biology), or by nurture (socialization), or by some combination of nature and nurture, men and women have developed different sets of value. According to this view, on the average, women put a premium on creating and maintaining intense, intimate, and caring relationships with others, whereas men are more interested in asserting their individuality and controlling their own and others' destinies. Thus, cultural feminists reject what they perceive as a masculine chase for political power, corporate status, and medical expertise. Indeed, they argue, as long as our society's institutions are dominated by the male drive to control others, many women will be unable to survive, let alone thrive, in them. Cultural feminists wish to transform competitive institutional relations based on furthering each individual's interests into cooperative institutional relations based on achieving a common goal. They are convinced that women's ability to weave thick relational networks is the source of whatever power women *do* have in both the private and public realms. They admit, however, that within a patriarchal society, women's caring posture can mutate into a masochistic posture. Women who are convinced that their interests are not as important as men's or even children's interests may end up trading self-respect for servility. Thus, most cultural feminists take very

seriously Sheila Mullett's advice that until gender equity is achieved, women must continually ask themselves whether the kind of caring in which they are engaged:

1. fulfills the one caring
2. calls upon the unique and particular individuality of the one caring
3. is not produced by a person in a role because of gender, with one gender engaging in nurturing behavior and the other engaging in instrumental behavior
4. is reciprocated with caring, and not merely with the satisfaction of seeing the ones cared-for flourishing and pursuing other projects
5. takes place within the framework of consciousness-raising practice and conversation

In her groundbreaking work *In a Different Voice* Carol Gilligan claimed that on the average, and for a variety of cultural reasons, women in this society tend to espouse an ethics of care that stresses relationships and responsibilities, whereas men tend to espouse an ethics of justice that stresses rules and rights. For women ethics is about attachment and connection, about not hurting other people, about intimacy and love. For men ethics is about separation and autonomy, about taking a stand, about identity and work. Refusing to privilege masculine over feminine ethics, Gilligan observes in "Visions of Maturity" that our society tends to think women are less moral than men because it largely subscribes to a *male* model of moral development, according to which a truly moral person is a separate individual who does his duty for duty's sake and who is willing to sacrifice everything everyone that is precious to him to uphold the law or to serve a cause he deems "noble." Thus, notes Gilligan, "Luther in his devotion to Faith, like Gandhi in his devotion to Truth, ignore the people most closely around them while working instead toward the glory of God" (p. 386). Measured against this male model of moral development, most women fare poorly, largely because, for women, such abstractions as "Faith" and "Truth" are not nearly as important as the flesh-and-blood people in their lives. But, asks Gilligan, does this necessarily mean that women are less morally developed than men, or does it instead suggest that we need to rethink our concept of a fully developed moral person? Although she does not propose to substitute Mother Teresa for Gandhi and Luther, Gilligan insists that society should listen to women's moral voice with the same attentiveness that it listens to men's moral voice. As important as it is for us to recognize the premise of equality—that everyone should be treated the same—it is equally as important for us to recognize the premise of nonviolence—that no one should be hurt. The morally mature person knows how to mediate between sameness and difference. He or she comes to understand "that just as inequality adversely affects both parties in an unequal relationship, so too violence is destructive for everyone involved" (p. 397). As Gilligan sees it, a dialogue between fairness and care will help us understand that humans need both separation from and attachment to others.

Nel Noddings also draws a distinction between an ethics of justice and an ethics of care, identifying the former with men and the latter with women. She diverges from Gilligan, however, in her insistence that care is *more* fundamental than justice, thus implying that, in our society at least, men have to catch up with women morally.

Noddings contrasts the legend of Ceres with the Biblical story of Abraham and Isaac to underscore the limits of "male" morality. She interprets the legend of Ceres as "a fable of caring and being cared-for" (p. 399). Recalling that Ceres was the goddess responsible for the Earth's well-being, Noddings stresses that despite her duty to her beloved Earth, Ceres abandons her post to search for her daughter Proserpine after she is abducted by Pluto, god of the underworld. Ceres refuses to put her job, so to speak, above her daughter. In contrast to Ceres, Abraham puts abstract duty above concrete love. For him, doing one's duty—specified in his case as obeying God's will—is the ultimate moral imperative. When God commands Abraham to sacrifice his son Isaac to Him, Abraham prepares to do so even though he cannot understand why God would command such an atrocious act. Noddings is distinctly unimpressed by Abraham's blind faith. She claims that the "one-caring can only describe his act—'You would kill your own son!'—and refuse him forgiveness" (p. 400). Any person who has any moral sensitivity at all knows that refusing to sacrifice a particular person—especially a vulnerable person who is in one's care—to a general cause, however worthy, is not a sign of moral weakness but of moral strength.

In addition to Noddings, so-called maternal thinkers have used the mother-child relationship as a springboard for discussing the necessary and sufficient conditions for any and all moral human relationships. Maternal thinker Sara Ruddick argues that from the work mothers do for their children emerges a distinct mode of moral reasoning best termed "maternal thinking." In order to meet the three fundamental goals of maternal practice—namely, the preservation, growth, and social acceptability of children—mothers must cultivate a multitude of very specific virtues, the most important of which is the metavirtue of attentive love. This metavirtue, which is at once cognitive and affective, enables mothers to really know their children. Realizing what is bad as well as good about their children, *good* mothers try to help their children eliminate their vices and weaknesses, slowly replacing them with virtues and strengths.

Ruddick stresses that maternal thinking is part of a so-called feminist standpoint. A standpoint, says Ruddick, is "an engaged vision of the world opposed and superior to dominant ways of thinking. As a proletarian standpoint is a superior vision produced by the experience and oppressive conditions of labor, a feminist standpoint is a superior vision produced by the political conditions and distinctive work of women" (p. 406). In other words, because they have a vested interest in maintaining the status quo, the bourgeois/men see what they want to see. For them, the world, as it is, is the best possible world. In contrast, because the proletariat/women have anything but a strong desire to maintain things as they are, their status as the victimized enables them to see what is wrong about some people using other people as mere means to serve their own selfish ends. As part of a feminist standpoint, therefore, maternal thinking is a clearer way of moral thinking than the kind of patriarchal thinking exhibited by Abraham, for example.

Concerned that men of *goodwill* might feel that, by virtue of their XY chromosome, they cannot think "maternally," Ruddick notes that *all* human beings are capable of thinking in terms of preserving each other, helping each other grow, and making each other socially acceptable. To survive as a human species and to thrive as individual human beings, we all need to think "maternally." Ruddick asks her readers to consider that because women have been excluded from the public realm until relatively recently, maternal thinking has not been prevalent in government, medicine, law, business, the church, and the academy. Instead a very nonmaternal kind of thinking has dominated the public realm—the kind of thinking that leads to ecological disorder, to social injustice, and especially to war. People who do not think like mothers, suggests Ruddick, do not see like mothers. They do not make a connection, for example, between war in the abstract and war in the concrete. For them, war is about winning, defending one's way of live, and establishing one's position of power. For a maternal thinker, war is about destroying that boy or girl whom one has spent years preserving, nurturing, and training: a unique human person who cannot be replaced. In sum, for a maternal thinker, war is about death—about canceling out the "product(s)" of maternal practice, and such a realization catapults maternal thinkers in the direction of peace activities.

Visions of Maturity

Carol Gilligan

Attachment and separation anchor the cycle of human life, describing the biology of human reproduction and the psychology of human development. The concepts of attachment and separation that depict the nature and sequence of infant development appear in adolescence as identity and intimacy and then in adulthood as love and work. This reiterative counterpoint in human experience, however, when molded into a developmental ordering, tends to disappear in the course of its linear reduction into the equation of development with separation. This disappearance can be traced in part to the focus on child and adolescent development, where progress can readily be charted by measuring the distance between mother and child. The limitation of this rendition is most apparent in the absence of women from accounts of adult development.

Choosing like Virgil to "sing of arms and the man," psychologists describing adulthood have focused on the development of self and work. While the apogee of separation in adolescence is presumed to be followed in adulthood by the return of attachment and care, recent depictions of adult development, in their seamless emergence from studies of men, provide scanty illumination of a life spent in intimate and generative relationships. Daniel Levinson (1978), despite his evident distress about the exclusion of women from his necessarily small sample, sets out on the basis of an all-male study "to create an overarching conception of development that could encompass the diverse biological, psychological and social changes occurring in adult life" (p. 8).

Levinson's conception is informed by the idea of "the Dream," which orders the seasons of a man's life in the same way that Jupiter's prophecy of a glorious destiny steers the course of Aeneas' journey. The Dream about which Levinson writes is also a vision of glorious achievement whose realization or modification will shape the character and life of the man. In the salient relationships in Levinson's analysis, the "mentor" facilitates the realization of the Dream, while the "special woman" is the helpmate who encourages the hero to shape and live out his vision: "As the novice adult tries to separate from his family and pre-adult world, and to enter an adult world, he must form significant relationships with other adults who will facilitate his work on the Dream. Two of the most important figures in this drama are the 'mentor' and the 'special woman'" (p. 93).

The significant relationships of early adulthood are thus construed as the means to an end of individual achievement, and these "transitional figures" must be cast off or reconstructed following the realization of success. If in the process, however, they become, like Dido, an impediment to the fulfillment of the Dream, then the relationship must be renounced, "to allow the developmental process" to continue. This process is defined by Levinson explicitly as one of individuation: "throughout the life cycle, but especially in the key transition periods ... the developmental process of *individuation* is going on." The process refers "to the changes in a person's relationships to himself and to the external world," the relationships that constitute his "Life Structure" (p. 195).

If in the course of "Becoming One's Own Man," this structure is discovered to be flawed and threatens the great expectations of the Dream, then in order to avert "serious Failure or Decline," the man must "break out" to salvage his Dream. This act of breaking out is consummated by a "marker event" of separation, such as "leaving his wife, quitting his job, or moving to another region" (p. 206). Thus the road to mid-life salvation runs through either achievement or separation.

From the array of human experience, Levinson's choice is the same as Virgil's, charting the progress of adult development as an arduous struggle toward a glorious destiny. Like pious Aeneas on his way to found Rome, the men in Levinson's study steady their lives by their devotion to realizing their dream, measuring their progress in terms of their distance from the shores of its promised success. Thus in the stories that Levinson recounts, relationships, whatever their particular intensity, play a relatively subordinate role in the individual drama of adult development.

The focus on work is also apparent in George Vaillant's (1977) account of adaptation to life. The variables that correlate with adult adjustment, like the interview that generates the data, bear predominantly on occupation and call for an expansion of Erikson's stages. Filling in what he sees as "an uncharted period of development" which Erikson left "between the decades of the twenties and forties," Vaillant describes the years of the thirties as the era of "Career Consolidation," the time when the men in his sample sought, "like Shakespeare's soldier, 'the bauble Reputation'" (p. 202). With this analogy to Shakespeare's Rome, the continuity of intimacy and generativity is interrupted to make room for a stage of further individuation and achievement, realized by work and consummated by a success that brings societal recognition.

Erikson's (1950) notion of generativity, however, is changed in the process of this recasting. Conceiving generativity as "the concern in establishing and guiding the next generation,"

Erikson takes the "*productivity* and *creativity*" of parenthood in its literal or symbolic realization to be a metaphor for an adulthood centered on relationships and devoted to the activity of taking care (p. 267). In Erikson's account, generativity is the central stage of adult development, encompassing "man's relationship to his production as well as to his progeny" (p. 268). In Vaillant's data, this relationship is relegated instead to mid-life.

Asserting that generativity is "not just a stage for making little things grow," Vaillant argues against Erikson's metaphor of parenthood by cautioning that "the world is filled with irresponsible mothers who are marvellous at bearing and loving children up to the age of two and then despair of taking the process further." Generativity, in order to exclude such women, is uprooted from its earthy redolence and redefined as "responsibility for the growth, leadership, and well-being of one's fellow creatures, not just raising crops or children" (p. 202). Thus, the expanse of Erikson's conception is narrowed to development in mid-adulthood and in the process is made more restrictive in its definition of care.

As a result, Vaillant emphasizes the relation of self to society and minimizes attachment to others. In an interview about work, health, stress, death, and a variety of family relationships, Vaillant says to the men in his study that "the hardest question" he will ask is, "Can you describe your wife?" This prefatory caution presumably arose from his experience with this particular sample of men but points to the limits of their adaptation, or perhaps to its psychological expense.

Thus the "models for a healthy life cycle" are men who seem distant in their relationships, finding it difficult to describe their wives, whose importance in their lives they nevertheless acknowledge. The same sense of distance between self and others is evident in Levinson's conclusion that, "In our interviews, friendship was largely noticeable by its absence. As a tentative generalization we would say that close friend-ship with a man or a woman is rarely exper-ienced by American men." Caught by this impression, Levinson pauses in his discussion of the three "tasks" of adulthood (Building and Modifying the Life Structure, Working on Single Components of the Life Structure, and Becoming More Individuated), to offer an elab-oration: "A man may have a wide social network in which he has amicable, 'friendly' relation-ships with many men and perhaps a few women. In general, however, most men do not have an intimate male friend of the kind that they recall fondly from boyhood or youth. Many men have had casual dating relationships with women, and perhaps a few complex love-sex relationships, but most men have not had an intimate non-sexual friendship with a woman. We need to understand why friendship is so rare, and what consequences this depriva-tion has for adult life" (p. 335).

Thus, there are studies, on the one hand, that convey a view of adulthood where rela-tionships are subordinated to the ongoing pro-cess of individuation and achievement, whose progress, however, is predicated on prior at-tachments and thought to enhance the capacity for intimacy. On the other hand, there is the observation that among those men whose lives have served as the model for adult develop-ment, the capacity for relationships is in some sense diminished and the men are constricted in their emotional expression. Relationships often are cast in the language of achievement, characterized by their success or failure, and impoverished in their affective range:

At forty-five, Lucky, enjoyed one of the best mar-riages in the Study, but probably not as perfect as he implied when he wrote, "You may not believe me when I say we've never had a disagreement, large or small."

The biography of Dr. Carson illustrates his halting passage from identity to intimacy, through career consolidation, and, finally, into the capacity to *care* in

its fullest sense . . . he had gone through divorce, re-marriage, and a shift from research to private practice. His personal metamorphosis had continued. The mousy researcher had become a charming clini-cian . . . suave, untroubled, kindly and in control . . . The vibrant energy that had characterized his ado-lescence had returned . . . now his depression was clearly an *affect*, and he was anything but fatigued. In the next breath he confessed, "I'm very highly sexed and that's a problem, too." He then provided me with an exciting narrative as he told me not only of recent romantic entanglements but also of his warm fatherly concern for patients (Vaillant, 1977, pp. 129, 203–206).

The notion that separation leads to attach-ment and that individuation eventuates in mu-tuality, while reiterated by both Vaillant and Levinson, is belied by the lives they put forth as support. Similarly, in Erikson's studies of Luther and Gandhi, while the relationship be-tween self and society is achieved in magnifi-cent articulation, both men are compromised in their capacity for intimacy and live at great personal distance from others. Thus Luther in his devotion to Faith, like Gandhi in his devo-tion to Truth, ignore the people most closely around them while working instead toward the glory of God. These men resemble in remark-able detail pious Aeneas in Virgil's epic, who also overcame the bonds of attachment that impeded the progress of his journey to Rome.

In all these accounts the women are silent, except for the sorrowful voice of Dido who, im-ploring and threatening Aeneas in vain, in the end silences herself upon his sword. Thus there seems to be a line of development missing from current depictions of adult development, a fail-ure to describe the progression of relationships toward a maturity of interdependence. Though the truth of separation is recognized in most developmental texts, the reality of continuing connection is lost or relegated to the back-ground where the figures of women appear. In this way, the emerging conception of adult de-velopment casts a familiar shadow on women's lives, pointing again toward the incompleteness of their separation, depicting them as mired in relationships. For women, the developmental markers of separation and attachment, allocated sequentially to adolescence and adulthood, seem in some sense to be fused. However, while this fusion leaves women at risk in a society that rewards separation, it also points to a more general truth currently obscured in psychological texts.

In young adulthood, when identity and intimacy converge in dilemmas of conflicting commitment, the relationship between self and other is exposed. That this relationship differs in the experience of men and women is a steady theme in the literature on human development and a finding of my research. From the different dynamics of separation and attachment in their gender identity formation through the divergence of identity and intimacy that marks their experience in the adolescent years, male and female voices typically speak of the importance of different truths, the former of the role of separation as it defines and empowers the self, the latter of the ongoing process of attachment that creates and sustains the human community.

Since this dialogue contains the dialectic that creates the tension of human development, the silence of women in the narrative of adult development distorts the conception of its stages and sequence. Thus, I want to restore in part the missing text of women's development, as they describe their conceptions of self and morality in the early adult years. In focusing primarily on the differences between the accounts of women and men, my aim is to enlarge developmental understanding by including the perspectives of both of the sexes. While the judgments considered come from a small and highly educated sample, they elucidate a contrast and make it possible to recognize not only what is missing in women's development but also what is there.

This problem of recognition was illustrated in a literature class at a women's college where the students were discussing the moral dilemma described in the novels of Mary McCarthy and James Joyce:

I felt caught in a dilemma that was new to me then but which since has become horribly familiar: the trap of adult life, in which you are held, wriggling, powerless to act because you can see both sides. On that occasion, as generally in the future, I compromised.

(*Memories of a Catholic Girlhood*)

I will not serve that in which I no longer believe, whether it calls itself my home, my fatherland or my church: and I will try to express myself in some mode of life or art as freely as I can and as wholly as I can, using for my defense the only arms I allow myself to use—silence, exile and cunning.

(*A Portrait of the Artist as a Young Man*)

Comparing the clarity of Stephen's *non serviam* with Mary McCarthy's "zigzag course," the women were unanimous in their decision that Stephen's was the better choice. Stephen was powerful in his certainty of belief and armed with strategies to avoid confrontation; the shape of his identity was clear and tied to a compelling justification. He had, in any case, taken a stand.

Wishing that they could be more like Stephen, in his clarity of decision and certainty of desire, the women saw themselves instead like Mary McCarthy, helpless, powerless, and constantly compromised. The contrasting images of helplessness and power in their explicit tie to attachment and separation caught the dilemma of the women's development, the conflict between integrity and care. In Stephen's simpler construction, separation seemed the empowering condition of free and full self-expression, while attachment appeared a paralyzing entrapment and caring an inevitable prelude to compromise. To the students, Mary McCarthy's portrayal confirmed their own endorsement of this account.

In the novels, however, contrasting descriptions of the road to adult life appear.

For Stephen, leaving childhood means renouncing relationships in order to protect his freedom of self-expression. For Mary, "farewell to childhood" means relinquishing the freedom of self-expression in order to protect others and preserve relationships: "A sense of power and Caeserlike magnanimity filled me. I was going to equivocate, not for selfish reasons but in the interests of the community, like a grown-up responsible person" (p. 162). These divergent constructions of identity, in self-expression or in self-sacrifice, create different problems for further development—the former a problem of human connection, and the latter a problem of truth. These seemingly disparate problems, however, are intimately related, since the shrinking from truth creates distance in relationship, and separation removes part of the truth. In the college student study which spanned the years of early adulthood, the men's return from exile and silence parallels the women's return from equivocation, until intimacy and truth converge in the discovery of the connection between integrity and care. Then only a difference in tone reveals what men and women know from the beginning and what they only later discover through experience.

The instant choice of self-deprecation in the preference for Stephen by the women in the English class is matched by a childlike readiness for apology in the women in the college student study. The participants in this study were an unequal number of men and women, representing the distribution of males and females in the class on moral and political choice. At age twenty-seven, the five women in the study all were actively pursuing careers—two in medicine, one in law, one in graduate study, and one as an organizer of labor unions. In the five years following their graduation from college, three had married and one had a child.

When they were asked at age twenty-seven, "How would you describe yourself to yourself?" one of the women refused to reply, but the other four gave as their responses to the interviewer's question:

This sounds sort of strange, but I think maternal, with all its connotations. I see myself in a nurturing role, maybe not right now, but whenever that might be, as a physician, as a mother . . . It's hard for me to think of myself without thinking about other people around me that I'm giving to.

(Claire)

I am fairly hard-working and fairly thorough and fairly responsible, and in terms of weaknesses, I am sometimes hesitant about making decisions and unsure of myself and afraid of doing things and taking responsibility, and I think maybe that is one of the biggest conflicts I have had . . . The other very important aspect of my life is my husband and trying to make his life easier and trying to help him out.

(Leslie)

I am a hysteric. I am intense. I am warm. I am very smart about people . . . I have a lot more soft feelings than hard feelings. I am a lot easier to get to be kind than to get mad. If I had to say one word, and to me it incorporates a lot, *adopted*.

(Erica)

I have sort of changed a lot. At the point of the last interview [age twenty-two] I felt like I was the kind of person who was interested in growth and trying hard, and it seems to me that the last couple of years, the not trying is someone who is not growing, and I think that is the thing that bothers me the most, the thing that I keep thinking about, that I am not growing. It's not true, I am, but what seems to be a failure partially is the way that Tom and I broke up. The thing with Tom feels to me like I am not growing . . . The thing I am running into lately is that the way I describe myself, my behavior doesn't sometimes come out that way. Like I hurt Tom a lot, and that bothers me. So I am thinking of myself as somebody who tried not to hurt people, but I ended up hurting him a lot, and so that is something that weighs on me, that I am somebody who unintentionally hurts people. Or a feeling, lately, that it is simple to sit down and say what your principles are, what your values are, and what I think about myself, but the way it sort of works out in actuality is sometimes very different. You can say you try not to hurt people, but you might because of things about yourself, or you can say this is my principle, but when the situation comes up, you don't really behave the way you would like . . . So I consider myself contradictory and confused.

(Nan)

The fusion of identity and intimacy, noted repeatedly in women's development, is perhaps nowhere more clearly articulated than in these self-descriptions. In response to the request to describe themselves, all of the women describe a relationship, depicting their identity *in* the connection of future mother, present wife, adopted child, or past lover. Similarly, the standard of moral judgment that informs their assessment of self is a standard of relationship, an ethic of nurturance, responsibility, and care. Measuring their strength in the activity of attachment ("giving to," "helping out," "being kind," "not hurting"), these highly successful and achieving women do not mention their academic and professional distinction in the context of describing themselves. If anything, they regard their professional activities as jeopardizing their own sense of themselves, and the conflict they encounter between achievement and care leaves them either divided in judgment or feeling betrayed. Nan explains:

When I first applied to medical school, my feeling was that I was a person who was concerned with other people and being able to care for them in some way or another, and I was running into problems the last few years as far as my being able to give of myself, my time, and what I am doing to other people. And medicine, even though it seems that profession is set up to do exactly that, seems to more or less interfere with your doing it. To me it felt like I wasn't really growing, that I was just treading water, trying to cope with what I was doing that made me very angry in some ways because it wasn't the way that I wanted things to go.

Thus in all of the women's descriptions, identity is defined in a context of relationship and judged by a standard of responsibility and care. Similarly, morality is seen by these women as arising from the experience of connection and conceived as a problem of inclusion rather than one of balancing claims. The underlying assumption that morality stems from attachment is explicitly stated by Claire in her response to Heinz's dilemma of whether or not to steal an overpriced drug in order to save his wife. Explaining why Heinz should steal, she elaborates the view of social reality on which her judgment is based:

By yourself, there is little sense to things. It is like the sound of one hand clapping, the sound of one man or one woman, there is something lacking. It is the collective that is important to me, and that collective is based on certain guiding principles, one of which is that everybody belongs to it and that you all come from it. You have to love someone else, because while you may not like them, you are inseparable from them. In a way, it is like loving your right hand. *They are part of you*; that other person is part of that giant collection of people that you are connected to.

To this aspiring maternal physician, the sound of one hand clapping does not seem a miraculous transcendence but rather a human absurdity, the illusion of a person standing alone in a reality of interconnection.

For the men, the tone of identity is different, clearer, more direct, more distinct and sharp-edged. Even when disparaging the concept itself, they radiate the confidence of certain truth. Although the world of the self that men describe at times includes "people" and "deep attachments," no particular person or relationship is mentioned, nor is the activity of relationship portrayed in the context of self-description. Replacing the women's verbs of attachment are adjectives of separation— "intelligent," "logical," "imaginative," "honest," sometimes even "arrogant" and "cocky." Thus the male "I" is defined in separation, although the men speak of having "real contacts" and "deep emotions" or otherwise wishing for them.

In a randomly selected half of the sample, men who were situated similarly to the women in occupational and marital position give as their initial responses to the request for self-description:

Logical, compromising, outwardly calm. If it seems like my statements are short and abrupt, it is because of my background and training. Architectural statements have to be very concise and short. Accepting. Those are all on an emotional level. I consider myself educated, reasonably intelligent.

I would describe myself as an enthusiastic, passionate person who is slightly arrogant. Concerned, committed, very tired right now because I didn't get much sleep last night.

I would describe myself as a person who is well developed intellectually and emotionally. Relatively narrow circle of friends, acquaintances, persons with whom I have real contacts as opposed to professional contacts or community contacts. And relatively proud of the intellectual skills and development, content with the emotional development as such, as a not very actively pursued goal. Desiring to broaden that one, the emotional aspect.

Intelligent, perceptive—I am being brutally honest now—still somewhat reserved, unrealistic about a number of social situations which involve other people, particularly authorities. Improving, looser, less tense and hung up than I used to be. Somewhat lazy, although it is hard to say how much of that is tied up with other conflicts. Imaginative, sometimes too much so. A little dilletantish, interested in a lot of things without necessarily going into them in depth, although I am moving toward correcting that.

I would tend to describe myself first by recounting a personal history, where I was born, grew up, and that kind of thing, but I am dissatisfied with that, having done it thousands of times. It doesn't seem to capture the essence of what I am, I would probably decide after another futile attempt, because there is no such thing as the essence of what I am, and be very bored by the whole thing . . . I don't think that there is any such thing as myself. There is myself sitting here, there is myself tomorrow, and so on.

Evolving and honest.

I guess on the surface I seem a little easy-going and laid back, but I think I am probably a bit more wound up than that. I tend to get wound up very easily. Kind of smart aleck, a little bit, or cocky maybe. Not as thorough as I should be. A little bit hard-ass, I guess, and a guy that is not swayed by emotions and feelings. I have deep emotions, but I am not a person who has a lot of different people. I have attachments to a few people, very deep attachments. Or attachments to a lot of things, at least in the demonstrable sense.

I guess I think I am kind of creative and also a little bit schizophrenic . . . A lot of it is a result of how I grew up. There is a kind of longing for the pastoral life and, at the same time, a desire for the flash, prestige, and recognition that you get by going out and hustling.

Two of the men begin more tentatively by talking about people in general, but they return in the end to great ideas or a need for distinctive achievement:

I think I am basically a decent person. I think I like people a lot and I like liking people. I like doing things with pleasure from just people, from their existence, almost. Even people I don't know well. When I said I was a decent person, I think that is almost the thing that makes me a decent person, that is a decent quality, a good quality. I think I am very bright. I think I am a little lost, not acting quite like I am inspired—whether it is just a question of lack of inspiration, I don't know—but not accomplishing things, not achieving things, and not knowing where I want to go or what I'm doing. I think most people especially doctors, have some idea of what they are going to be doing in four years. I [an intern] really have a blank . . . I have great ideas . . . but I can't imagine me in them.

I guess the things that I like to think are important to me are I am aware of what is going on around me, other people's needs around me, and the fact that I enjoy doing things for other people and I feel good about it. I suppose it's nice in my situation, but I am not sure that is true for everybody. I think some people do things for other people and it doesn't make them feel good. Once in awhile that is true of me too, for instance working around the house, and I am always doing the same old things that everyone else is doing and eventually I build up some resentment toward that.

In these men's descriptions of self, involvement with others is tied to a qualification of identity rather than to its realization. Instead of attachment, individual achievement rivets the male imagination, and great ideas or distinctive activity defines the standard of self-assessment and success.

Thus the sequential ordering of identity and intimacy in the transition from adolescence to adulthood better fits the development of men than it does the development of women. Power and separation secure the man in an identity achieved through work, but they leave him at a distance from others, who seem in some sense out of his sight. Cranly, urging Stephen Daedalus to perform his Easter duty for his mother's sake, reminds him:

Your mother must have gone through a good deal of suffering . . . Would you not try to save her from suffering more even if—or would you?

If I could, Stephen said, that would cost me very little.

Given this distance, intimacy becomes the critical experience that brings the self back into connection with others, making it possible to see both sides—to discover the effects of actions on others as well as their cost to the self. The experience of relationship brings an end to isolation, which otherwise hardens into indifference, an absence of active concern for others, though perhaps a willingness to respect their rights. For this reason, intimacy is the transformative experience for men through which adolescent identity turns into the generativity of adult love and work. In the process, as Erikson (1964) observes, the knowledge gained through intimacy changes the ideological morality of adolescence into the adult ethic of taking care.

Since women, however, define their identity through relationships of intimacy and care, the moral problems that they encounter pertain to issues of a different sort. When relationships are secured by masking desire and conflict is avoided by equivocation, then confusion arises about the locus of responsibility and truth. McCarthy, describing her "representations" to her grandparents, explains:

Whatever I told them was usually so blurred and glossed, in the effort to meet their approval (for, aside from anything else, I was fond of them and tried to accommodate myself to their perspective), that except when answering a direct question, I hardly knew whether what I was saying was true or false. I really tried, or so I thought, to avoid lying, but it seemed to me that they forced it on me by the difference in their vision of things, so that I was always transposing reality for them into terms they could understand. To keep matters straight with my conscience, I shrank, whenever possible, from the lie absolute, just as, from a sense of precaution, I shrank from the plain truth.

The critical experience then becomes not intimacy but choice, creating an encounter with self that clarifies the understanding of responsibility and truth.

Thus in the transition from adolescence to adulthood, the dilemma itself is the same for both sexes, a conflict between integrity and care. But approached from different perspectives, this dilemma generates the recognition of opposite truths. These different perspectives are reflected in two different moral ideologies, since separation is justified by an ethic of rights while attachment is supported by an ethic of care.

The morality of rights is predicated on equality and centered on the understanding of fairness, while the ethic of responsibility relies on the concept of equity, the recognition of differences in need. While the ethic of rights is a manifestation of equal respect, balancing the claims of other and self, the ethic of responsibility rests on an understanding that gives rise to compassion and care. Thus the counterpoint of identity and intimacy that marks the time between childhood and adulthood is articulated through two different moralities whose complementarity is the discovery of maturity.

The discovery of this complementarity is traced in the study by questions about personal experiences of moral conflict and choice. Two lawyers chosen from the sample illustrate how the divergence in judgment between the sexes is resolved through the discovery by each of the other's perspective and of the relationship between integrity and care.

The dilemma of responsibility and truth that McCarthy describes is reiterated by Hilary, a lawyer and the woman who said she found it too hard to describe herself at the end of what "really has been a rough week." She too, like McCarthy, considers self-sacrificing acts "courageous" and "praiseworthy," explaining that "if everyone on earth behaved in a way that showed care for others and courage, the world would be a much better place, you wouldn't have crime and you might not have poverty." However, this moral ideal of self-sacrifice and care ran into trouble not only in a relationship where the conflicting truths of each person's feelings made it impossible to avoid hurt, but also in court where, despite her concern for the client on the other side, she decided not to help her opponent win his case.

In both instances, she found the absolute injunction against hurting others to be an inadequate guide to resolving the actual dilemmas she faced. Her discovery of the disparity between intention and consequence and of the actual constraints of choice led her to realize that there is, in some situations, no way not to hurt. In confronting such dilemmas in both her personal and professional life, she does not abdicate responsibility for choice but rather claims the right to include herself among the people whom she considers it moral not to hurt. Her more inclusive morality now contains the injunction to be true to herself, leaving her with two principles of judgment whose integration she cannot yet clearly envision. What she does recognize is that both integrity and care must be included in a morality that can encompass the dilemmas of love and work that arise in adult life.

The move toward tolerance that accompanies the abandonment of absolutes is considered by William Perry (1968) to chart the course of intellectual and ethical development during the early adult years. Perry describes the changes in thinking that mark the transition from a belief that knowledge is absolute and answers clearly right or wrong to an understanding of the contextual relativity of both truth and choice. This transition and its impact on moral judgment can be discerned in the changes in moral understanding that occur in both men and women during the five years following college (Gilligan and Murphy, 1979; Murphy and Gilligan, 1980). Though both sexes move away from absolutes in this time, the absolutes themselves differ for each. In women's development, the absolute of care, defined initially as not hurting others, becomes complicated through a recognition of the need for personal integrity. This recognition gives rise to the claim for equality embodied in the concept of rights, which changes the understanding of relationships and transforms the definition of care. For men, the absolutes of truth and fairness, defined by the concepts of equality and reciprocity, are called into question by experiences that demonstrate the existence of differences between other and self. Then the awareness of multiple truths leads to a relativizing of equality in the direction of equity and gives rise to an ethic of generosity and care. For both sexes the existence of two contexts for moral decision makes judgment by definition contextually relative and leads to a new understanding of responsibility and choice.

The discovery of the reality of differences and thus of the contextual nature of morality and truth is described by Alex, a lawyer in the college student study, who began in law school "to realize that you really don't know everything" and "you don't ever know that there is any absolute. I don't think that you ever know that there is an absolute right. What you do know is you have to come down one way or the other. You have got to make a decision."

The awareness that he did not know everything arose more painfully in a relationship whose ending took him completely by surprise. In his belated discovery that the woman's experience had differed from his own, he realized how distant he had been in a relationship he considered close. Then the logical hierarchy of moral values, whose absolute truth he formerly proclaimed, came to seem a barrier to intimacy rather than a fortress of personal integrity. As his conception of morality began to change, his thinking focused on issues of relationship, and his concern with injustice was complicated by a new understanding of human attachment. Describing "the principle of attachment" that began to inform his way of looking at moral problems, Alex sees the need for morality to extend beyond considerations of fairness to concern with relationships:

People have real emotional needs to be attached to something, and equality doesn't give you attachment. Equality fractures society and places on every person the burden of standing on his own two feet.

Although "equality is a crisp thing that you could hang onto," it alone cannot adequately resolve the dilemmas of choice that arise in life. Given his new awareness of responsibility and of the actual consequences of choice, Alex says:

"You don't want to look at just equality. You want to look at how people are going to be able to handle their lives." Recognizing the need for two contexts for judgment, he nevertheless finds that their integration "is hard to work through," since sometimes "no matter which way you go, somebody is going to be hurt and somebody is going to be hurt forever." Then, he says, "you have reached the point where there is an irresolvable conflict," and choice becomes a matter of "choosing the victim" rather than enacting the good. With the recognition of the responsibility that such choices entail, his judgment becomes more attuned to the psychological and social consequences of action, to the reality of people's lives in an historical world.

Thus, starting from very different points, from the different ideologies of justice and care, the men and women in the study come, in the course of becoming adult, to a greater understanding of both points of view and thus to a greater convergence in judgment. Recognizing the dual contexts of justice and care, they realize that judgment depends on the way in which the problem is framed.

But in this light, the conception of development itself also depends on the context in which it is framed, and the vision of maturity can be seen to shift when adulthood is portrayed by women rather than men. When women construct the adult domain, the world of relationships emerges and becomes the focus of attention and concern. McClelland (1975), noting this shift in women's fantasies of power, observes that "women are more concerned than men with both sides of an interdependent relationship" and are "quicker to recognize their own interdependence" (pp. 85–86). This focus on interdependence is manifest in fantasies that equate power with giving and care. McClelland reports that while men represent powerful activity as assertion and aggression, women in contrast portray acts of nurturance as acts of strength. Considering his research on power to deal "in particular with the characteristics of maturity," he suggests that mature women and men may relate to the world in a different style.

That women differ in their orientation to power is also the theme of Jean Baker Miller's analysis. Focusing on relationships of dominance and subordination, she finds women's situation in these relationships to provide "a crucial key to understanding the psychological order." This order arises from the relationships of difference, between man and woman and parent and child, that create "the milieu—the family—in which the human mind as we know it has been formed" (1976, p. 1). Because these relationships of difference contain, in most instances, a factor of inequality, they assume a moral dimension pertaining to the way in which power is used. On this basis, Miller distinguishes between relationships of temporary and permanent inequality, the former representing the context of human development, the latter, the condition of oppression. In relationships of temporary inequality, such as parent and child or teacher and student, power ideally is used to foster the development that removes the initial disparity. In relationships of permanent inequality, power cements dominance and subordination, and oppression is rationalized by theories that "explain" the need for its continuation.

Miller, focusing in this way on the dimension of inequality in human life, identifies the distinctive psychology of women as arising from the combination of their positions in relationships of temporary and permanent inequality. Dominant in temporary relationships of nurturance that dissolve with the dissolution of inequality, women are subservient in relationships of permanently unequal social status and power. In addition, though subordinate in social position to men, women are at the same time centrally entwined with them in the intimate and intense relationships of adult sexuality and family life. Thus women's psychology reflects both sides of relationships of interde-

pendence and the range of moral possibilities to which such relationships give rise. Women, therefore, are ideally situated to observe the potential in human connection both for care and for oppression.

This distinct observational perspective informs the work of Carol Stack (1974) and Lillian Rubin (1976) who, entering worlds previously known through men's eyes, return to give a different report. In the urban black ghetto, where others have seen social disorder and family disarray, Stack finds networks of domestic exchange that describe the organization of the black family in poverty. Rubin, observing the families of the white working class, dispels the myth of "the affluent and happy worker" by charting the "worlds of pain" that it costs to raise a family in conditions of social and economic disadvantage. Both women describe an adulthood of relationships that sustain the family functions of protection and care, but also a social system of relationships that sustain economic dependence and social subordination. Thus they indicate how class, race, and ethnicity are used to justify and rationalize the continuing inequality of an economic system that benefits some at others' expense.

In their separate spheres of analysis, these women find order where others saw chaos—in the psychology of women, the urban black family, and the reproduction of social class. These discoveries required new modes of analysis and a more ethnographic approach in order to derive constructs that could give order and meaning to the adult life they saw. Until Stack redefined "family" as "the smallest organized, durable network of kin and non-kin who interact daily, providing the domestic needs of children and assuring their survival," she could not find "families" in the world of "The Flats." Only the "culturally specific definitions of certain concepts such as family, kin, parent, and friend that emerged during this study made much of the subsequent analysis possible . . . An arbitrary imposition of widely accepted definitions of the family . . . blocks the way to understanding how people in The Flats describe and order the world in which they live" (p. 31).

Similarly, Miller calls for "a new psychology of women" that recognizes the different starting point for women's development, the fact that "women stay with, build on, and develop in a context of attachment and affiliation with others," that "women's sense of self becomes very much organized around being able to make, and then to maintain, affiliations and relationships," and that "eventually, for many women, the threat of disruption of an affiliation is perceived not just as a loss of a relationship but as something closer to a total loss of self." Although this psychic structuring is by now familiar from descriptions of women's psychopathology, it has not been recognized that "this psychic starting point contains the possibilities for an entirely different (and more advanced) approach to living and functioning ... [in which] affiliation is valued as highly as, or more highly than, self-enhancement" (p. 83). Thus, Miller points to a psychology of adulthood which recognizes that development does not displace the value of ongoing attachment and the continuing importance of care in relationships.

The limitations of previous standards of measurement and the need for a more contextual mode of interpretation are evident as well in Rubin's approach. Rubin dispels the illusion that family life is everywhere the same or that subcultural differences can be assessed independently of the socioeconomic realities of class. Thus, working-class families "reproduce themselves not because they are somehow deficient or their culture aberrant, but because there are no alternatives for most of their children," despite "the mobility myth we cherish so dearly" (pp. 210–211). The temporary inequality of the working-class child thus turns into the permanent inequality of the working-class adult, caught in an ebb-tide of social mobility that erodes the quality of family life.

Like the stories that delineate women's fantasies of power, women's descriptions of adulthood convey a different sense of its social reality.

In their portrayal of relationships, women replace the bias of men toward separation with a representation of the interdependence of self and other, both in love and in work. By changing the lens of developmental observation from individual achievement to relationships of care, women depict ongoing attachment as the path that leads to maturity. Thus the parameters of development shift toward marking the progress of affiliative relationship.

The implications of this shift are evident in considering the situation of women at mid-life. Given the tendency to chart the unfamiliar waters of adult development with the familiar markers of adolescent separation and growth, the middle years of women's lives readily appear as a time of return to the unfinished business of adolescence. This interpretation has been particularly compelling since life-cycle descriptions, derived primarily from studies of men, have generated a perspective from which women, insofar as they differ, appear deficient in their development. The deviance of female development has been especially marked in the adolescent years when girls appear to confuse identity with intimacy by defining themselves through relationships with others. The legacy left from this mode of identity definition is considered to be a self that is vulnerable to the issues of separation that arise at mid-life.

But this construction reveals the limitation in an account which measures women's development against a male standard and ignores the possibility of a different truth. In this light, the observation that women's embeddedness in lives of relationship, their orientation to interdependence, their subordination of achievement to care, and their conflicts over competitive success leave them personally at risk in mid-life seems more a commentary on the society than a problem in women's development.

The construction of mid-life in adolescent terms, as a similar crisis of identity and separation, ignores the reality of what has happened in the years between and tears up the history of love and of work. For generativity to begin at mid-life, as Vaillant's data on men suggest, seems from a woman's perspective too late for both sexes, given that the bearing and raising of children take place primarily in the preceding years. Similarly, the image of women arriving at mid-life childlike and dependent on others is belied by the activity of their care in nurturing and sustaining family relationships. Thus the problem appears to be one of construction, an issue of judgment rather than truth.

In view of the evidence that women perceive and construe social reality differently from men and that these differences center around experiences of attachment and separation, life transitions that invariably engage these experiences can be expected to involve women in a distinctive way. And because women's sense of integrity appears to be entwined with an ethic of care, so that to see themselves as women is to see themselves in a relationship of connection, the major transitions in women's lives would seem to involve changes in the understanding and activities of care. Certainly the shift from childhood to adulthood witnesses a major redefinition of care. When the distinction between helping and pleasing frees the activity of taking care from the wish for approval by others, the ethic of responsibility can become a self-chosen anchor of personal integrity and strength.

In the same vein, however, the events of mid-life—the menopause and changes in family and work—can alter a woman's activities of care in ways that affect her sense of herself. If mid-life brings an end to relationships, to the sense of connection on which she relies, as well as to the activities of care through which she judges her worth, then the mourning that accompanies all life transitions can give way to the melancholia of self-deprecation and despair. The meaning of mid-life events for a woman thus reflects the interaction between the structures of her thought and the realities of her life.

When a distinction between neurotic and real conflict is made and the reluctance to choose is differentiated from the reality of hav-

ing no choice, then it becomes possible to see more clearly how women's experience provides a key to understanding central truths of adult life. Rather than viewing her anatomy as destined to leave her with a scar of inferiority (Freud, 1931), one can see instead how it gives rise to experiences which illuminate a reality common to both of the sexes: the fact that in life you never see it all, that things unseen undergo change through time, that there is more than one path to gratification, and that the boundaries between self and other are less clear than they sometimes seem.

Thus women not only reach mid-life with a psychological history different from men's and face at that time a different social reality having different possibilities for love and for work, but they also make a different sense of experience, based on their knowledge of human relationships. Since the reality of connection is experienced by women as given rather than as freely contracted, they arrive at an understanding of life that reflects the limits of autonomy and control. As a result, women's development delineates the path not only to a less violent life but also to a maturity realized through interdependence and taking care.

In his studies of children's moral judgment, Piaget (1932/1965) describes a three-stage progression through which constraint turns into cooperation and cooperation into generosity. In doing so, he points out how long it takes before children in the same class at school, playing with each other every day, come to agree in their understanding of the rules of their games. This agreement, however, signals the completion of a major reorientation of action and thought through which the morality of constraint turns into the morality of cooperation. But he also notes how children's recognition of differences between others and themselves leads to a relativizing of equality in the direction of equity, signifying a fusion of justice and love.

There seems at present to be only partial agreement between men and women about the adulthood they commonly share. In the absence of mutual understanding, relationships between the sexes continue in varying degrees of constraint, manifesting the "paradox of egocentrism" which Piaget describes, a mystical respect for rules combined with everyone playing more or less as he pleases and paying no attention to his neighbor (p. 61). For a life-cycle understanding to address the development in adulthood of relationships characterized by cooperation, generosity, and care, that understanding must include the lives of women as well as of men.

Among the most pressing items on the agenda for research on adult development is the need to delineate *in women's own terms* the experience of their adult life. My own work in that direction indicates that the inclusion of women's experience brings to developmental understanding a new perspective on relationships that changes the basic constructs of interpretation. The concept of identity expands to include the experience of interconnection. The moral domain is similarly enlarged by the inclusion of responsibility and care in relationships. And the underlying epistemology correspondingly shifts from the Greek ideal of knowledge as a correspondence between mind and form to the Biblical conception of knowing as a process of human relationship.

Given the evidence of different perspectives in the representation of adulthood by women and men, there is a need for research that elucidates the effects of these differences in marriage, family, and work relationships. My research suggests that men and women may speak different languages that they assume are the same, using similar words to encode disparate experiences of self and social relationships. Because these languages share an overlapping moral vocabulary, they contain a propensity for systematic mistranslation, creating misunderstandings which impede communication and limit the potential for cooperation and care in relationships. At the same time, however, these languages articulate with one another in critical ways. Just as the language of responsibilities provides a weblike imagery of relationships to replace a hierarchical ordering that dissolves with the coming of equality, so the language of rights underlines the importance of including in the network of care not only the other but also the self.

As we have listened for centuries to the voices of men and the theories of development that their experience informs, so we have come more recently to notice not only the silence of women but the difficulty in hearing what they say when they speak. Yet in the different voice of women lies the truth of an ethic of care, the tie between relationship and responsibility, and the origins of aggression in the failure of connection. The failure to see the different reality of women's lives and to hear the differences in their voices stems in part from the assumption that there is a single mode of social experience and interpretation. By positing instead two different modes, we arrive at a more complex rendition of human experience which sees the truth of separation and attachment in the lives of women and men and recognizes how these truths are carried by different modes of language and thought.

To understand how the tension between responsibilities and rights sustains the dialectic of human development is to see the integrity of two disparate modes of experience that are in the end connected. While an ethic of justice proceeds from the premise of equality—that everyone should be treated the same—an ethic of care rests on the premise of nonviolence—that no one should be hurt. In the representation of maturity, both perspectives converge in the realization that just as inequality adversely affects both parties in an unequal relationship, so too violence is destructive for everyone involved. This dialogue between fairness and care not only provides a better understanding of relations between the sexes but also gives rise to a more comprehensive portrayal of adult work and family relationships.

As Freud and Piaget call our attention to the differences in children's feelings and thought, enabling us to respond to children with greater care and respect, so a recognition of the differences in women's experience and understanding expands our vision of maturity and points to the contextual nature of developmental truths. Through this expansion in perspective, we can begin to envision how a marriage between adult development as it is currently portrayed and women's development as it begins to be seen could lead to a changed understanding of human development and a more generative view of human life.

REFERENCES

Erikson, Erik H. *Childhood and Society.* New York: W. W. Norton, 1950.

————. *Young Man Luther.* New York: W. W. Norton, 1958.

————. *Insight and Responsibility.* New York: W. W. Norton, 1964.

————. *Gandhi's Truth.* New York: W. W. Norton, 1969.

Freud, Sigmund. "Female Sexuality" (1931) in *The Standard Edition of the Complete Psychological Works of Sigmund Freud,* trans. and ed. James Strachy. London: The Hogarth Press 1961. Vol. XXI.

Gilligan, Carol, and Murphy, John Michael. "Development from Adolescence to Adulthood: The Philosopher and the 'Dilemma of the Fact.'" In D. Kuhn, ed., *Intellectual Development Beyond Childhood.* New Directions for Child Development, no. 5. San Francisco: Jossey-Bass, 1979.

Joyce, James. *A Portrait of the Artist as a Young Man* (1916). New York: The Viking Press, 1956.

Levinson, Daniel J. *The Seasons of a Man's Life.* New York: Alfred A. Knopf, 1978.

McCarthy, Mary. *Memories of a Catholic Girlhood.* New York: Harcourt Brace Jovanovich, 1946.

McClelland, David C. *Power: The Inner Experience.* New York: Irvington, 1975.

Miller, Jean Baker. *Toward a New Psychology of Women.* Boston: Beacon Press, 1976.

Murphy, J. M., and Gilligan, C. "Moral Development in Late Adolescence and Adulthood: A Critique and Reconstruction of Kohlberg's Theory." *Human Development* 23 (1980): 77–104.

Perry, William. *Forms of Intellectual and Ethical Development in the College Years.* New York: Holt, Rinehart and Winston, 1968.

Piaget, Jean. *The Moral Judgment of the Child* (1932). New York: The Free Press, 1965.

Rubin, Lillian. *Worlds of Pain.* New York: Basic Books, 1976.

Stack, Carol B. *All Our Kin.* New York: Harper and Row, 1974.

Vaillant, George E. *Adaptation to Life.* Boston: Little, Brown, 1977.

Women and Caring

Nel Noddings

Women often define themselves as both persons and moral agents in terms of their capacity to care. When we move from natural caring to an ethic of caring, we shall consider the deep psychological structures that may be responsible for this mode of definition. Here I wish to concentrate on the caring itself—on particular examples of feminine courage in relating and remaining related and on the typical differences between men and women in their search for the ethical in human relationships.

From *Caring: A Feminine Approach to Ethics and Moral Education,* by Nel Noddings, pp. 40–48. Copyright © 1984 by the Regents of the University of California. Reprinted by permission.

We may find the sorts of examples and contrasts we seek in legend, Biblical accounts, biography, and fiction. I shall do no more than sample the possibilities here. The legend of Ceres, for example, can be interpreted beautifully to illustrate the attitude and conflicts of one-caring.[1] Recall that Ceres was the goddess who cared for the earth. It was she who made the fields fertile and watched over the maturation and harvest of crops. She had a daughter, Proserpine, whom she dearly loved. One day, Pluto, god of the underworld, crazed by love from Cupid's arrow, snatched Proserpine from her play and abducted her to his underground kingdom. Ceres searched the world for her daughter without success and was grief-stricken. Next something happens in the legend that is especially instructive for the one-caring: Ceres, in all her misery, is approached by an old man, Celeus, and his little girl. They respond to her grief and invite her to visit their cottage; indeed, they respond by weeping with her. Ceres is moved by this show of compassion and accompanies them. Here is a concrete illustration of the power of the cared-for in contributing to the caring relation. Ceres knows that she is the one-caring, that she has the power to confer good or ill on these passersby. But, in her misery, she needs the active response of the cared-for to maintain herself as one-caring. Typical of one-caring who would be one-caring, she answers Celeus by saying: "Lead on, . . . I cannot resist that appeal."[2]

Arriving at the cottage, Ceres finds a little boy very ill, probably dying. She is received, however, by the child's mother, Metanira, and moved to pity, Ceres cures the child with a kiss. Later, when Ceres tries to make the child immortal by tempering his body in flaming ashes, Metanira snatches the child fearfully from her. Ceres chides the mother for depriving her son of immortality but, still, she assures Metanira that he will nevertheless be "great and useful." The boy, Triptolemus, will someday teach humankind the secrets of agriculture as revealed to him by Ceres. Here, then, is a second facet of the ideal for one-caring. The cared-for shall be blessed not with riches, luck, and power but with the great gift of *usefulness*. The conversation between Ceres intending immortality for Triptolemus and Metanira afraid to risk her son in the flames is illustrative, again, of the feminine striving for an attainable ideal. It stands in bold contrast to the story we shall consider next—that of Abraham's willingness to sacrifice his son to divine command.

Eventually, Ceres finds the place where Proserpine was swallowed up by the earth, but she mistakenly supposes that the earth itself did this terrible thing. She is stricken by a double grief. Not only has she lost her beloved Proserpine but another cared-for, her fruitful earth, has turned against her. Now Ceres does not fly into a destructive rage and visit the earth with lightning, fire and flood. She merely ceases to care; she withdraws as one-caring, and the earth dries up in mud and weeds and brambles. Ceres, the one-caring, has nothing to sustain her in caring. Here, we see foreshadowed the power of the cared-for in maintaining the caring relationship.

Finally, Ceres learns the truth and entreats Jove to intercede on her behalf with Pluto. As you may recall, Pluto, in fear of losing his kingdom entirely, agrees to return Proserpine but induces her to eat some pomegranate seeds so that she will be unable to spend more than half of each year with her mother. When Proserpine returns each spring, Ceres bestows great fruitfulness on the earth and, when she leaves each fall, Ceres is overcome by grief and allows winter to settle on the earth.

This story is widely understood as an allegory of the seasons, of sleeping grain and awakening fruitfulness, but it may be interpreted also as a fable of caring and being cared-for.[3] It illustrates the vulnerability of the one-caring, her reception of the proximate stranger, her generosity upon being herself received, and the munificent displacement of motivation that occurs when she is sustained as one-caring.

Now, someone is sure to point out that, in contrast to the legend of one-caring as the pinnacle of feminine sensibility, feminine skullduggery lies at the root of the problem described in the legend.[4] It was, after all, Venus who prompted her son, Cupid, to shoot Pluto with the arrow of love. I am not denying the reality of this dark side of feminine character,[5] but I am rejecting it in my quest for the ethical. I am not, after all, suggesting a will to power but rather a commitment to care as the guide to an ethical ideal.

This commitment to care and to define oneself in terms of the capacity to care represent a feminine alternative to Kohlberg's "stage six" morality.[6] At stage six, the moral thinker transcends particular moral principles by appealing to a highest principle—one that allows a rearrangement of the hierarchy in order to give proper place-value to human love, loyalty, and the relief of suffering. But women, as ones-caring, are not so much concerned with the rearrangement of priorities among principles; they are concerned, rather, with maintaining and enhancing caring. They do not abstract away from the concrete situation those elements that allow a formulation of deductive argument; rather, they remain in the situation as sensitive, receptive, and responsible agents. As a result of this caring orientation, they are perceived by Kohlberg as "being stuck" at stage three—that stage in which the moral agent wants to be a "good boy or girl." The desire to be good, however, to be one-caring in response to these cared-fors here and now, provides a sound and lovely alternative foundation for ethical behavior. Like Ceres, the one-caring will not turn from the real human beings who address her. Her caring is the foundation of—and not a mere manifestation of—her morality.

In contrast to the story of Ceres, who could not abandon her child even for the sake of her beloved Earth, we may consider Abraham. In obedience to God, Abraham traveled with his son, Isaac, to Moriah, there to offer him as a sacrifice: "And they came to the place which God had told him of; and Abraham built an altar there, and laid the wood in order, and bound Isaac his son, and laid him on the altar upon the wood. And Abraham stretched forth his hand, and took the knife to slay his son."[7]

Kierkegaard interprets Abraham's action as supra-ethical, that is, as the action of an individual who is justified by his connection to God, the absolute. For him, as for us, the individual is higher than the universal, but for him that "higher" status is derived from "absolute duty toward God." Hence a paradox is produced. Out of duty to God, we may be required to do to our neighbor what is ethically forbidden. The ethical is, for Kierkegaard, the universal, and the individual directly obedient to God is superior to the universal. He says: "In the story of Abraham we find such a paradox. His relation to Isaac, ethically expressed, is this, that the father should love the son. This ethical relation is reduced to a relative position in contrast with the absolute relation to God."[8]

But for the mother, for us, this is horrendous. Our relation to our children is not governed first by the ethical but by natural caring. We love not because we are required to love but because our natural relatedness gives natural birth to love. It is this love, this natural caring, that makes the ethical possible. For us, then, Abraham's decision is not only ethically unjustified but it is in basest violation of the supra-ethical—of caring. The one-caring can only describe his act—"You would kill your own son!"—and refuse him forgiveness. Abraham's obedience fled for protection under the skirts of an unseeable God. Under the gaze of an abstract and untouchable God, he would destroy *this* touchable child whose real eyes were turned upon him in trust, and love, and fear. I suspect no woman could have written either *Genesis* or *Fear and Trembling*, but perhaps I should speak only for myself on that. The one-caring, male or female, does not seek security in abstractions cast either as principles or entities. She remains responsible here and now for this cared-for and this situation and for the forseeable futures projected by herself and the cared-for.

Now, of course, the scholar may argue that I have interpreted the story too literally, and even that Kierkegaard did so in an agony of faith against ethical reason. He will point out that, on another interpretation, God used Abraham and Isaac to teach His people that human sacrifice was unacceptable to Him and, henceforth, forbidden. This interpretation will not satisfy the mother. The mother in Abraham's position would respond to the fear and trust of her child—not to the voice of abstraction. The Mother-as-God would not use a parent and child so fearfully and painfully to teach a welcome lesson to her other children. The Mother-God must respond caringly to Abraham as cared-for and to Isaac as cared-for, and she must preserve Abraham as one-caring in relation to Isaac.

Everything that is built on this sacrificial impulse is anathema to woman. Here, says woman, is my child. I will not sacrifice him for God, or for the greatest good, or for these ten others. Let us find some other way.

The devotion to "something beyond" that is revealed in traditional, masculine ethics is often devotion to deity, but sometimes it is devotion to principle. Recall the story of Manlius, a Roman commander who laid down harsh laws for the conduct of his legions. One of the first to disobey a rule about leaving camp to engage in individual combat was his own son. In compliance with the rules, Manlius ordered the execution of his son. A principle had been violated; for this violation, X must be executed. That "X" was replaced by "my son" gave Manlius no release from obedience to the principle. Why, then, did he not think concretely before establishing the rule? Why do men so often lay out their own clear paths to tragedy? The one-caring would want to think carefully about the establishment of rules and even more carefully about the prescription of penalties. Indeed, she would prefer to establish a climate of cooperative "we-ness" so that rules and penalties might be kept to a minimum. For her, the hypothetical is filled with real persons, and, thus, her rules are tempered a priori with thoughts of those in her inner circle. A stranger might, then, be spared death because she would not visit death upon her own child. She does not, in whatever personal agony, inflict death upon her child in devotion to either principle or abstract entity.

History, legend, and biography might profitably be reinterpreted in light of feminine experience. Both men and women may participate in the "feminine" as I am developing it, but women have suffered acutely from its lack of explication. They have felt and suffered and held fast, but they have—as a result—been accused of deficiency in abstract reasoning, of capricious behavior, of emotional reaction. Even in parenting, perhaps especially in parenting, the typical differences between concrete and abstract, between here-and-now and here-and-after, between flesh-and-blood and spirit, stand out in life and literature. In Robert Frost's "Home Burial," the conflict between man and woman in the loss of their child is dramatic. He tries to relieve his grief by speaking of ordinary things; she is convinced because of this that he feels no grief. He makes matters worse by saying:

What was it brought you up to think it the thing
To take your mother-loss of a first child
So inconsolably—in the face of love.
You'd think his memory might be satisfied—[9]

What is the man doing here? He is not callous, and he has not escaped suffering, but he has not met his wife on the level of feeling. He accuses her of thinking "it the thing" to grieve deeply; he speaks of "mother-loss" and "first child," but he avoids the child's name and any concrete reference to him. He speaks of "his memory" but not of the small, warm body his wife nurtured. It is this difference in language and direction of reference that forms the difference between an ethic of caring and an ethic of principle.

Examples appear in real life as well as in poetry and fiction. Pearl Buck describes the difference in her own parents.

> The fascinating thing about Andrew and Carie was that from the two of them we always got entirely different stories about the same incident. They never saw the same things or felt the same way about anything, and it was as though they had not gone to the same place or seen the same people.[10]

Andrew was spirit—all heaven and abstraction; Carie was completely human. He was a preacher, a missionary in China, and cared for the souls of his parishioners. Carie cared for them as persons, ministering to their bodies and earthly minds. She had no preconceived notion of what her children should be; she did not cast them in the image of a catechism-produced God. Rather, she loved their warm bodies, cherished their laughter and childish pranks, nurtured their earthly courage and compassion for each other. The greatest joy in her life came through her children, and her greatest suffering was incurred by their loss. When Andrew was seventy years old, some time after Carie had died, he wrote the story of his life. The record fit into twenty-five pages. His daughter remarks:

> It was the story of his soul, his unchanging soul. Once he mentioned the fact of his marriage to Carie, his wife. Once he listed the children he had had with her, but in the listing he forgot entirely a little son who lived to be five years old and was Carie's favorite child, and he made no comment on any of them.[11]

Yet all of her life Carie was made to feel spiritually inferior to her husband and, as she lay near death, he expressed concern about her soul!

Today we are asked to believe that women's "lack of experience in the world" keeps them at an inferior stage in moral development. I am suggesting, to the contrary, that a powerful and coherent ethic and, indeed, a different sort of world may be built on the natural caring so familiar to women.

CIRCLES AND CHAINS

We find ourselves at the center of concentric circles of caring. In the inner, intimate circle, we care because we love. In particularly trying situations we may act out of ethical sense even here. After all, sometimes we are tired, the other has behaved abominably, and our love is frayed. Then we remind ourselves of the other's location in our system of circles: He is (was) my friend; she is my child; he is my father. The engrossment remains, although its color changes, and we may vacillate between the once natural caring for other to growing concern for ourselves.

As we move outward in the circles, we encounter those for whom we have personal regard. Here, as in the more intimate circles, we are guided in what we do by at least three considerations: how we feel, what the other expects of us, and what the situational relationship requires of us. Persons in these circles do not, in the usual course of events, require from us what our families naturally demand, and the situations in which we find ourselves have, usually, their own rules of conduct. We are comfortable in these circles if we are in compliance with the rules of the game. Again, these rules do not compel us, but they have an instrumental force that is easily recognized. I listen with a certain ready appreciation to colleagues, and I respond in a polite, acceptable fashion. But I must not forget that the rules are only aids to smooth passage through unproblematic events. They protect and insulate me. They are a reflection of someone's sense of relatedness institutionalized in our culture. But they do not put me in touch; they do not guarantee the relation itself. Thus rules will not be decisive for us in critical situations, but they will be acknowledged as economies of a sort. As such they will be even less important than the "illuminative maxims" described by Joseph Fletcher.[12] For us, the destructive role of rules and principles must be clarified and acknowledged.

Beyond the circles of proximate others are those I have not yet encountered. Some of these are linked to the inner circle by personal or formal relations. Out there is a young man who will be my daughter's husband; I am prepared to acknowledge the transitivity of my love. He enters my life with potential love. Out there, also, are future students; they are linked formally to those I already care for and they, too, enter my life potentially cared-for. Chains of caring are established, some linking unknown individuals to those already anchored in the inner circles and some forming whole new circles of potential caring. I am "prepared to care" through recognition of these chains.

But what of the stranger, one who comes to me without the bonds established in my chains of caring? Is there any sense in which I can be prepared to care for him? I can remain receptive. As in the beginning, I may recognize the internal "I must," that natural imperative that arises as I receive the other, but this becomes more and more difficult as my world grows more complex. I may be bombarded with stimuli that arouse the "I must," and I learn to reduce the load. As we have seen, a standard fashion of controlling what comes in is to rely on situational rules. These protect me. What, under normal circumstances, I must do for a colleague is different from what I must do for my child. I may come to rely almost completely on external rules and, if I do, I become detached from the very heart of morality: the sensibility that calls forth caring. In an important sense, the stranger has an enormous claim on me, because I do not know where he fits, what requests he has a formal right to

make, or what personal needs he will pass on to me. I can meet him only in a state of wary anticipation and rusty grace, for my original innocent grace is gone and, aware of my finiteness, I fear a request I cannot meet without hardship. Indeed, the caring person, one who in this way is prepared to care, dreads the proximate stranger, for she cannot easily reject the claim he has on her. She would prefer that the stray cat not appear at the back door—or the stray teenager at the front. But if either presents himself, he must be received not by formula but as individual.

The strain on one who would care can be great. Literature is filled with descriptions of encounters of this sort: the legitimate dread of the one-caring and the ultimate acceptance or rejection of the internal "I must." One thinks of John Steinbeck's Carl Tiflin and Mr. Gitano in *The Red Pony*.[13] In defiance of a loud and insistent "I must," Tiflin diminishes his ethical ideal and turns the old man away. In contrast, Robert Frost has the farm wife, Mary, express the one-caring as she accepts the "hired man" into her home:

Yes, what else but home? It all depends on
   what you mean by home.
Of course he's nothing to us, any more
Than was the hound that came a stranger to us
Out of the woods, worn out upon the trail.
Home is the place where, when you have to go there,
They have to take you in.[14]

Both imperatives expressed here, the "have to's" of the one-caring and the cared-for, are internal imperatives. An observer can see alternatives clearly, but the "I must" suggests itself as binding upon the one in whom it occurs. We are both free and bound in our circles and chains.

NOTES

1. Carol Gilligan cites D. McClelland as interpreting the myth as a description of the feminine attitude toward power. See Gilligan, "Woman's Place in

Man's Life Cycle," *Harvard Educational Review* 49 (1979), 445.

2. Thomas Bulfinch, *Mythology: The Age of Fable* (New York: The New American Library, Inc., 1962), p. 86.

3. The legend of Ceres has been variously interpreted. The ancient myth clearly referred to the conferral of special gifts on young males by creative and powerful female figures. In this sense, we find a long-standing tradition for the interpretation of Ceres as one-caring, bestowing the gifts of competence and usefulness on her protégés. See Erich Neumann, *The Great Mother* (Princeton: Princeton University Press, 1955). On p. 321, Neumann states: "This investiture is not an 'agricultural' rite, although in the earliest primordial age it was probably bound up with such a rite. In the mysteries at least, it has a far more profound significance. It is the investiture of the male with his chthonic and spiritual fecundating function, which is transmitted to him by woman."

4. See the account in Bulfinch, *Mythology: The Age of Fable.*

5. For a fascinating account of the dark and light in feminine thinking and legend, see M. Esther Harding, *Woman's Mysteries* (New York: Harper and Row, Publishers, 1971).

6. See Lawrence Kohlberg and R. Kramer, "Continuities and Discontinuities in Childhood and Adult Moral Development," *Human Development* 12 (1969), 93–120.

7. Genesis 22: 9, 10.

8. Søren Kierkegaard, *Fear and Trembling,* trans. Walter Lowrie (Princeton: Princeton University Press, 1941), p. 81.

9. Robert Frost, "Home Burial," in *The Complete Poems of Robert Frost* (New York: Henry Holt and Company, 1949), p. 71.

10. Pearl S. Buck, *Fighting Angel* (New York: Pocket Books, Inc., 1964), p. 38.

11. Ibid., p. 2.

12. Joseph Fletcher, *Situation Ethics* (Philadelphia: The Westminster Press, 1966).

13. John Steinbeck, *The Red Pony* (New York: The Viking Press, Inc., 1945).

14. Robert Frost, "The Death of the Hired Man," in *The Complete Poems of Robert Frost,* p. 53.

Maternal Thinking as a Feminist Standpoint

Sara Ruddick

I have written of maternal thinking as if it were only one discipline among others—no ax to grind, no particular story to impose upon the many stories people tell, no meta-message in the quilt that different artists make together. To be sure, women's and mothers' voices have been

silenced, their thinking distorted and sentimentalized. Hence it will take sustained political and intellectual effort before maternal thinking is truly heard. Well-intentioned generosity and space and time to speak are not enough. Nonetheless, I have envisioned a future in which maternal thinkers are respected and self-respecting without making for them/us any claims of moral and political advantage.

Temperamentally I am a pluralist. From grade school, I welcomed the idea that there were many perspectives and hence many truths. In my childhood, it was Nazis, white supremacists, and later McCarthyites who claimed to speak from a privileged standpoint. Not surprisingly, when I studied philosophy I was drawn to traditions that rejected the ambition, pervasive among philosophers, of ordering ways of knowing from the least to the most adequate. I learned that to imagine a language—or a discipline—was to imagine what Wittgenstein called a "form of life."[1] If there was no God, then there was also no philosopher who stood outside or at the beginning, giving grounds, justifying evidence, making a place for epistemological and moral certainty. Reasons begin in and ultimately end in action. To quote Wittgenstein again:

Giving grounds, however, justifying the evidence, comes to an end; but the end is not certain propositions striking us immediately as true, i.e., it is not a kind of seeing on our part; it is our *acting*, which lies at the bottom of the language game.[2]

If the statement "A child's life must be protected" strikes us as immediately true, this is because we daily act protectively and our true statement expresses as it reveals our commitment. What the sentence expresses and the commitment reveals is not only the truth that children are deserving of protection but also the form of life in which that truth is indubitable. Preservative love is a "form of life": "What has to be accepted, the given, is—so one could say—*Forms of Life*."[3]

In feminism too I have applauded those who reject the large picture for multiple perspectives. Catherine MacKinnon, for example, expresses my epistemological stance:

Feminism not only challenges masculine partiality but questions the universality imperative itself. A perspectivity is revealed as a strategy of male hegemony. . . . Nor is feminism objective, abstract, or universal. . . . Feminism does not begin with the premise that it is unpremised. It does not desire to persuade an unpremised audience because there is no such audience.[4]

I continue to share the epistemological prejudices of the *Women's Ways of Knowing* collective, whose members celebrate women for recognizing "that all knowledge is constructed . . . that answers to all questions vary depending on the context in which they are asked and on the frame of reference of the person doing the asking."[5]

Nonetheless, only a few years after I began writing about maternal thinking, my pluralism began to give way to angry and insistent claims of superiority. My son was reaching draft age in a country whose government was prone to invade the islands, gulfs, and governments of peoples and resources it wished to control. If conscripted, my son would serve a "defense" establishment that deliberately "targets" millions of strangers with weapons no one could survive and devises war plans that no one could live long enough to execute. I became preoccupied with the immorality—and the madness—of organized, deliberate violence. I read the works of pacifists, just-war theorists, and military historians, began teaching seminars on the choice between violence and nonviolence, joined a women's peace group, and took part in a working conference of philosophers, defense department analysts, and defense sociologists who were charged with studying conscription but often spent their time planning and remembering war. Soon I had frightened myself thoroughly. For a time I felt as if I were pathologically obsessed and hopelessly sentimental.

I didn't raise my son to be a soldier
I brought him up to be my pride and joy
Who dares to put a musket on his shoulder
To kill some other mother's darling boy?[6]

It was in this mood that I received a copy of an article by Nancy Hartsock that both developed and transformed the Marxian notion of a privileged political and epistemological "standpoint." A standpoint is an engaged vision of the world opposed and superior to dominant ways of thinking. As a proletarian standpoint is a superior vision produced by the experience and oppressive conditions of labor, a feminist standpoint is a superior vision produced by the political conditions and distinctive work of women. Although the epistemological and moral values of any standpoint are obscured by dominant ideals of reason and despised by dominant peoples, subordination can be overturned through political and intellectual struggle. Even now, the vision offered by a feminist standpoint reveals that dominant ways of knowing are, in Hartsock's words, "partial and perverse."

By "women's work"—the basis for a feminist standpoint—Hartsock has in mind "caring labor": birthing labor and lactation; production and preparation of food; mothering; kin work; housework; nursing; many kinds of teaching; and care of the frail elderly, work that is characteristically performed in exploitative and oppressive circumstances. I believe that it is at least premature to assimilate these different kinds of work as maternal work. Nonetheless, it is certainly the case that maternal practices make up a central part of caring labor, and hence maternal thinking in its many variations could be considered a constituent element of the standpoint that Hartsock envisions. Or, to put the point romantically—adapting Foucault—maternal thinking is a "subjugated knowledge," "lost in an all-encompassing theoretical framework or erased in a triumphal history of ideas"—"regarded with disdain by intellectuals as being either primitive or woefully incomplete" yet likely to become "insurrectionary."[7]

This invigorating language is more than rhetoric. Hartsock not only proclaimed the worth of caring labor; she substantiated her claim by detailing characteristics of caring labor that were responsible for the standpoint's superiority. Caretakers are immersed in the materials of the physical world. The physical phenomena of human and other bodies must be interpreted in relation to the demands of caretaking. It is not useful to abstract to "air, earth, fire, and water," let alone to electrons. Whether care workers are cleaning toilet bowls, attending to the incontinence of dying patients, or toilet training children; whether they nurse a baby, invent a sauce, or mash potatoes thin enough to allow a toothless, elderly person to feed herself, care workers depend on a practical knowledge of the qualities of the material world, including the human bodily world, in which they deal.

This means that the material world, seen under the aspect of caring labor, is organized in terms of people's needs and pleasures and, by extension, of the needs and pleasures of any animal or plant that is instrumental in human caring or is tended for its own sake. The value of objects and accomplishments turns on their usefulness in satisfying needs and giving pleasures rather than on the money to be made by selling them or the prestige by owning them or the attention by displaying them. Finally, caretakers work with subjects; they give birth to and tend self-generating, autonomously willing lives. A defining task of their work is to maintain mutually helpful connections with another person—or animal—whose separateness they create and respect. Hence they are continuously involved with issues of connection, separation, development, change, and the limits of control.

If this characterization of caring labor sounds like the maternal practices and thinking I have described, this is not coincidental. Reading Hartsock from a perspective influenced by my own concerns, I felt as if "maternal thinking" were given both an epistemological and political base; moreover, from the time I first read "The Feminist Standpoint," my understanding of maternal practice has been deepened by Hartsock's account of the characteristics of caring labor. Even more heartening, by looking and acting from a feminist standpoint, dominant ways of thinking—and I had in mind primarily militarist thinking —were revealed to be as abstract and destructive as I suspected. This gave maternal thinking, as part of the feminist standpoint, a critical power I had not imagined.

To diagnose and account for the destructiveness of dominant modes of thought that the standpoint reveals, Hartsock constructed an account of the "abstract masculinity" that characterizes dominant views, adapting a well-known story to her purposes. According to this now familiar story, in societies where young children are tended almost entirely by women, where authority and power are ascribed to men, and where independence is valued over the capacity to sustain relations of mutual interdependence, young children associate with women the dependence and care they both fear and desire and the achievement of independence with masculinity. In these societies, boys and girls value masculinity, both because of its association with independence and because of its distance from fearsome, desirable female bodies and care. But boys, who are meant to become "masculine," are more apt than girls to define themselves as not-maternal-female. To a degree that girls do not, boys fortify themselves against the needs and pleasures of care that they depended on as infants and will rely on more or less intensely throughout their lives. Their incipiently misogynist fear of women and repudiation of "feminine" care is exacerbated if, as men, they are able to exploit the caring labor of others rather than undertaking it themselves.

According to this story, especially "masculine" men (and sometimes women), fearful of the physicality and needs of care, develop a fantasy of transcendence based on a "tradition of freeing the thinking brain from the depths of the most pressing situations and sending it off to some (fictive) summit for a panoramic overview."[8] From this perch they promulgate views that are inimical to the values of caring labor. They imagine a truth abstracted from

bodies and a self detached from feelings. When faced with concrete sensuousness, they measure and quantify. Only partially protected by veils of ignorance that never quite hide frightening differences and dependencies, they forge agreements of reason and regiment dissent by rules and fair fights. Fearful of the dependencies in which connection begins, they become attached to detachment, developing ideals of objectivity that turn on separation and distance. Beset by needs they are ill equipped to name or satisfy and faced with an anarchically lively, caring world on which they fearfully depend, they misdescribe in abstractly sentimental or demeaning ways what they insist on labeling "women's work." At worst, from their fictive summit they deliver abstract understandings that systematically invert "the proper valuation of human experience."[9] They might, for example, accord superiority not "to the sex that brings forth but to that which kills," considering the "sacrifice" of a child in an abstract cause to be the vindication of caring labor.[10] Or, as in violent pornography and rape, they might transform "the force of life in sexuality" into fearful relations of dominance and submission.[11]

Feminist standpoint philosophers—among them philosophically minded and feminist maternal thinkers—directly oppose this "masculine" fantasy of transcendence. Their task is to redefine reason and restructure its priorities so that thoughtful people will be able to "generalize the potentiality made available by the activity of women"—i.e., caring labor—to society as a whole.[12] Since they actively participate in caring labor and therefore know firsthand the temptations, failures, and subtle intellectual challenges of their work, they will not idealize caretakers. What they have been taught by Hartsock, they will recognize daily: "[masculine] men's power to structure social relations in their own image means that women [and other caring laborers] too must participate in social relations which manifest and express abstract masculinity."[13] However alienated they are by the discrepancy between their experiences and the sentimental and abstract conceptual schemes that distort them, maternal thinkers know that they have learned to speak in the dominant languages, as do all members of a culture. To articulate maternal thinking they have had to cling to realities that they were in danger of forgetting and at the same time forge a way of thinking that is new. They will bring this heritage to the philosophical task of articulating standpoint theory, setting themselves to resist the lure of abstraction and the social rewards that "transcendence" brings. Together with other standpoint theorists, they work to articulate an engaged vision that must be "struggled for and represents an achievement."[14]

These standpoint theorists are feminists. The work that they believe should be the basis of an alternative moral and epistemological vision has been performed by women and has created "women" as they are. As feminists, standpoint theorists fight against the exploitation and abuse of women caretakers while valuing the particular knowledge that women acquire from their suffering of and resistance to oppression. But their focus is not in the first place on gender but on the work itself and the political conditions in which it is undertaken. Their attention to exploitative and unequal power does not stop artificially with men's abuse of women; many women, and not only those advantaged by attachments to privileged men, exploit the caring labor of others, usually, but not always, of other women. Men as well as women caretakers are besieged by violences and abstractions that overwhelm their vision and mock their efforts to provide and protect.

Standpoint theorists are also feminists in virtue of their political ambition to generalize the values of caring labor that are, for reasons of history, inextricably bound up with the lives and values of women. But their aim is not to create a future that is female. In the "fully human community"[15] they envision, institutionalized gender differences of power and property disappear, replaced by inclusive playful, inventive variations on sexual identities.

Although standpoint theorists ground themselves in the values of caring labor, they reject a division of all human activities into caring labor and everything else, a division that has been so debilitating to caretakers and women. Most of what goes on in our minds and lives eludes the conceptual division between care and abstract masculinity. Standpoint theorists, like anyone else, enjoy singing, computing, storytelling, and argument and heartily commit themselves to philosophy, farming, business administration, ballet, and all other disciplines, contesting only the dominance in any discipline of abstractly masculine values. They do not, for example, give up science but limit its domain so that detachment and abstraction take their rightful place; better still, they imbue science itself with the values of care. Certainly the maternal thinkers among them have no patience with the idea that a person's identity is wholly formed by her principal work or, still more confining, by the gender identity a particular society expects. If nothing else, on the basis of their knowledge of adolescent children they assert that a rigid insistence on being either a caretaker *or* scientist, either philosopher *or* poet, either man *or* woman, is a sign of personal anxiety and social coercion. Their task, as they have learned from the work of training children, is to articulate conditions of respect for unpredictable and as yet unimagined difference and variety among and within people.

Despite their rejection of dualisms and their respect for difference, these standpoint philosophers seem very different from the Wittgensteinian pluralist who imagined maternal thinking as one discipline among others. Standpoint thinkers are ready, as the Wittgensteinian pluralist would never be, to declare that dominant values are destructive and perverse and that the feminist standpoint represents the "real" appropriately human order of life. One might say that standpoint theorists, including the maternal thinkers among them, have seen the Truth—and, indeed, many of the standpoint theorists whose invigorating work I have found indispensable seem to say just that.

Although I count myself among standpoint theorists, I do not take the final step that some appear to take of claiming for one standpoint a Truth that is exhaustive and absolute. Epistemologically, I continue to believe that all reasons are tested by the practices from which they arise; hence justifications end in the commitments with which they begin. Although I envision a world organized by the values of caring labor, I cannot identify the grounds, reason, or god that would legitimate that vision. There is, for example, nothing above or below preservative love, only the ongoing intellectual-practical acts of seeing children as vulnerable and responding to that vulnerability with a determination to protect rather than to abandon or assault.

I am also suspicious of any dualistic ordering of appearance and reality, perversion and utopia. The values of care do not stand to dominant values of abstract masculinity as the one reality stands to appearance; standpoint theorists know this, of course, but any dualistic formulations tend to reduce the richness and unpredictability both of the world and of the ways in which we think about it. I also fear that despite their stated convictions, standpoint theorists or their followers will lose sight of the failures and temptations of the caretakers they celebrate. It would then be easy to slip into a formulation of a feminine/feminist standpoint as an achievement rather than a place from which to create a sturdy, sane vision of the natural and social world. Perhaps most worrisome, being on the side of good can foster a repressive self-righteousness that legitimates killing or, alternatively, condemns violence without attending to the despair and abuse from which it arises. Directly to the point of my project, dualistic righteousness encourages a mythical division between women's peacefulness and men's wars that is belied by history and obscures the flawed, complex peacefulness that is latent in maternal practice and thinking.

In the last few years I have consciously assessed moral and political decisions in the light of the values of care and then in turn reassessed those values. I am confident that persistent efforts to see and act from the standpoint of care will reveal the greater safety, pleasure, and justice of a world where the values of care are dominant. But I realize that for those who are not already committed to the values of caring labor, a case must be made for the moral and epistemological superiority of the kind of thinking to which it gives rise. This requires specific oppositional comparisons between particular concepts and values of caring labor and their counterparts in dominant, abstractly masculine ways of knowing—for example, comparisons of maternal and military concepts of the body and of control. These specific comparisons will reveal incrementally the superiority of the rationality of care to the abstract masculine ways of knowing that dominate our lives.

I bring maternal thinking to bear on military thinking. As part of a feminist standpoint, I take maternal thinking to be an engaged critical and visionary perspective that illuminates both the destructiveness of war and the requirements of peace. Yet one of my principal points is that maternal thinking itself is often militarist. Like the standpoint of which it is a part, an antimilitarist maternal perspective is an engaged vision that must be achieved through struggle and change.

Accordingly, I reassess the mythical division between men's wars and women's peace. Although distinctly maternal desires and capacities for peacemaking exist, it is through maternal *efforts* to be peaceful rather than an achieved peacefulness that I find resources for creating a less violent world. I discuss ideals of nonviolence that govern some maternal practices and propose a maternal conception of birth and bodily life that symbolizes nonviolent connection. I repeatedly contrast maternal concepts with their military analogues. At the same time, I identify characteristics of distinctly maternal militarism and underline the limitations of maternal nonviolence. I look for ways to re-create maternal practice as a sturdier, more reliable instrument of peace. I celebrate two transformative social movements, women's politics of resistance and feminism. Each movement transforms the practice of mothers who engage in it. Together, they work on the maternal imagination, inspiring new powers to know, care, and act.

I do not think maternal thinking, any more than the standpoint of which it is a part, represents a True or Total discourse. Nor are mothers, any more than other women, the quintessential revolutionary subjects. It is enough to say that there is a peacefulness latent in maternal practice and that a transformed maternal thinking could make a distinctive contribution to peace politics. Given the violence we live in and the disasters that threaten us, enough seems a feast.

A NOTE ABOUT PEACE

Peace, like mothering, is sentimentally honored and often secretly despised. Like mothers, peacemakers are scorned as powerless appeasers who are innocent of the real world. Just because mothering and peace have been so long and so sentimentally married, a critical understanding of mothering and maternal nonviolence will itself contribute to the reconception of "peace." Peace activists themselves often speak of the need to create more active, robust images of peace. One of my aims is to contribute to this task. It is not, however, only from mothering that I gain a sense of what peace might look like. On the contrary, as I attempt to articulate maternal struggles to become peaceful, I implicitly assume an understanding of peacefulness derived from reading, listening to, and

observing nonviolent activists. It is the peacefulness of nonviolent activism to which I hope mothers, along with other women and men, can contribute and that I believe is latent in maternal practice. The idea of peacefulness implicit in nonviolent action is different from what is usually called pacifism. To forestall misunderstandings, I want to clarify this difference.

Peace is not sharply distinguished from war. Wars are prepared for in a time of "peace" that includes many violences and is often secured by violence. One of the central tasks of peacemaking is to identify violences wherever they occur—in boardrooms, bedrooms, factories, classrooms, and battlefields. Peacemakers do not turn away from violence but ferret it out, asking in detail who is hurt and how. Indeed, the light of imagined peace reveals to peacemakers violations of body and spirit that are mystified, disguised, and invisible to the realist eye. A defining characteristic of peacemakers is their commitment to resist the violences that a lively appreciation of peacefulness reveals.

Peace requires a sturdy suspicion of violence even in the best of causes. The effectiveness of violence is repeatedly exaggerated, while its moral, social, political, economic, psychological, and physical costs are minimized or ignored. Peacemakers set themselves to reveal and count the costs while questioning, at every turn, the benefits. But—and here is the primary difference with pacifists—a sturdy suspicion of violence does not betoken absolute renunciation. Although pacifists perform an essential service among peace activists by requiring every act of violence to be critically appraised, it is unnecessary and divisive to require of all peacemakers an absolute commitment not to kill. Nor does a sturdy suspicion of violence require self-righteous condemnation of others' violent acts or a prizing of violence from historical situations such as in Nazi Germany or South Africa. Peacemakers can remain sturdily suspicious of violence and able to count its costs in the best of causes yet refuse to judge from a distance the violent response of others to violent assault on them. Although she will never celebrate violence, a peacemaker may herself act violently in careful, conscientious knowledge of the hurt she inflicts and of its cost to her as well as her victim. Alice Walker and Jane Lazarre speak about this kind of conscientious knowledge. Alice Walker's heroine Meridean speaks from the civil rights movement:

And certainly to boast about this new capacity to kill —which she did not, after all, admire—would be to destroy the understanding she had acquired with it. Namely, this: that even the contemplation of murder required incredible delicacy as it required incredible spiritual work and the historical background and present setting must be right. Only in a church surrounded by the righteous guardians of the people's memories could she even approach the concept of retaliatory murder. Only among the pious could this idea both comfort and uplift.[16]

Jane Lazarre describes the "full knowledge" that should be part of every violent act:

The denial of ambivalence—whatever *action* one takes—is the beginning of tyranny. The soldier who said that it had been easy for him to kill was saying something not only about himself, but about the nature of war. My father fought in the Spanish Civil War—a just war if there is any just war. He said exactly the same thing to me about killing in Spain. If I were ever in a situation in which I had to kill that man who found it easy to kill Vietnamese, or the man who said he would drop a nuclear bomb tomorrow if so ordered, I would rather kill him in full knowledge of his humanity, thinking about the son he loves, the father he lost as a little boy, than to kill under the illusion that I was doing nothing more than extinguishing a butcher or a pig. It's an illusion which would accelerate my trigger finger, but stop my heart.[17]

The sturdiest suspicion of violence is of no avail to threatened peoples who do not have al-

ternative nonviolent ways of protecting what they love and getting what they need. Thus peacemakers must invent myriad nonviolent actions and then name, describe, and support them. Whenever a collective decides to invest in the weapons and the training that organized violence requires, it is also choosing against the nonviolent alternatives. Only a people sturdily suspicious of violence will be able to hold the choice between violence and nonviolence in mind. Of these people, only those who have multiplied and strengthened strategies of nonviolent resistance and change will be able to invent the myriad actions and connections of "peace."

Although peace can be hinted at in a general vocabulary, peacemaking is always specific. Social and military violence are rooted in particular technological, economic, and military conditions, and so is resistance to them. In the United States, the plans and rhetoric of war are permeated with a distinctive blend of abstract fanaticism, professionalized bureaucracy, and complicated high technology that leaves many citizens helpless. I grope for images of peace and strategies of peacemaking responsive to this incarnation of militarism—for ways to make manifest in the United States now a maternal resource for peace.

NOTES

1. Ludwig Wittgenstein, *Philosophical Investigations*, no. 19.

2. Wittgenstein, *On Certainty*, no. 204.

3. Wittgenstein, *Philosophical Investigations*, Part II, p. 226.

4. Catherine A. MacKinnon, "Feminism, Marxism, Method, and the State: An Agenda for Theory," *Signs*, vol. 7, no. 3, p. 534.

5. Mary Belenky, Blythe Clichy, Nancy Goldberger, and Jill Tarule, *Women's Ways of Knowing* (New York: Basic Books, 1986), pp. 137–38.

6. Adela Pankhurst, "I Didn't Raise My Son to Be a Soldier," in *My Country Is the Whole World*, ed. Cam-

bridge Women's Peace Collective (London: Pandora Press, 1984), p. 100.

7. Michael Foucault, *Power/Knowledge* (New York: Pantheon, 1985). pp. 81–82.

8. Klaus Thewelweit, *Male Fantasies* (Minneapolis: University of Minnesota Press, 1987), p. 364.

9. Hartsock, "Feminist Standpoint," p. 299.

10. Simone de Beauvoir, *The Second Sex* (New York: Vintage, 1974); also cited by Hartsock, "Feminist Standpoint."

11. Hartsock, "Feminist Standpoint," p. 301.

12. Hartsock, "Feminist Standpoint," p. 304.

13. Hartsock, "Feminist Standpoint," p. 302.

14. Hartsock, "Feminist Standpoint," pp. 288, 302.

15. Hartsock, "Feminist Standpoint," p. 305.

16. Alice Walker, *Meridian* (New York: Washington Square Press, 1976), p. 200.

17. Jane Lazarre, Letter to the New School for Social Research (New York City) faculty, Spring 1985.

Marxist/Socialist Feminism

Rather than choosing between the liberal and radical feminist explanations for women's oppression, some feminists seek to weave these strands of feminist theory together. This task seems to have been taken up most effectively by socialist feminists. Although the socialist feminist approach to women's oppression differs from the Marxist feminist approach, it shares enough ideas with its historic antecedent to warrant a discussion of Evelyn Reed's "Women: Caste, Class or Oppressed Sex?" Like all Marxist feminists, Reed claims that women's oppression originated in the introduction of private property, an institution that ended whatever equality the human community had previously enjoyed. Private ownership of the means of production by relatively few persons, originally all male, inaugurated a class system whose contemporary manifestations are corporate capitalism and imperialism. Reflection on this state of affairs suggests that not patriarchy but capitalism is the root cause of women's oppression. If all women—not just the relatively privileged or exceptional ones—are ever to be liberated, the capitalist system must be replaced by a socialist system in which the means of production belong to one and all and the whole community takes care of each other's fundamental needs "from the cradle to the grave" (p. 417). Because each person would have enough not only to survive but also to thrive under socialism, toiling men and women would no longer be the duped *puppets* of capitalist exploiters. On the contrary, they would be persons free to shape their own destinies in concert with each other.

Stressing that the same *capitalist* social forces and relations that "have brought about the oppression of one class by another, one race by another, and one nation by another" (p. 420) have also brought about the oppression of women, Reed resists the view that women are oppressed simply because they are *female*. Although Reed agrees that relative to men women occupy a subordinate position in a patriarchal or male-dominated society, she does not think that the way for women to improve their position relative to men is for women to wage a "caste war" against men (p. 421). Rather she urges oppressed women to join oppressed men in a "class war" against their common oppressors, some of whom are female. Reed thinks it is ridiculous to insist that *all* women, simply be virtue of possessing two x chromosomes, belong to the same class. On the contrary, she maintains that "*women, like men, are a multiclass sex*" (p. 422) who have less in common with each other than with members of the class to which they belong. For example, rich women are their husbands' economic, social and political partners as well as their husbands' *sexual* bedmates. They are united with their husbands "in defense of private property, profiteering, militarism, racism—and the exploitation of other women" (p. 422). When the proletariat revolts against the bourgeois, women will be found on both sides of the struggle, according to Reed.

Oppressed women must unite with oppressed men to fight against their common enemy—the powers of capitalism. Marxists are not *pessimists* about male-female relations. They do not think that feminism requires the two sexes to be perpetually at war or totally separated, and they certainly do not believe that women's liberation depends on the liquidation or elimination of men. On the contrary, insists Reed, Marxists are *optimists* about male-female relations. They maintain that "[f]ar from being eternal, woman's subjection and the bitter hostility between the sexes are no more than a few thousand years old. They were produced by the drastic social charges which brought the family, private property, and the state into existence" (p. 424). With the end of capitalism will come the end of patriarchy, a social system that militates against the basic desire of human beings to cooperate with each other in communities of care.

Not entirely convinced by Reed's brand of Marxist feminism, socialist feminist Heidi Hartmann observes that however well the categories of Marxist analysis—for example, "class," "reserve army of labor," "wage laborer"—help explain the creation of a particular occupational structure, they leave largely unexplained why *women* rather than men play the subordinate and submissive roles in both the workplace and in the home. To understand women's relation to men as well as workers' relation to capital, says Hartmann, a feminist analysis of patriarchy must accompany a Marxist analysis of capitalism. In her estimation, the partnership between patriarchy and capitalism is complex because patriarchy's interests in women are not always the same as capitalism's interests. In the nineteenth century, for example, male *workers* wanted women to stay at home where they could "personally service" them (p. 428), whereas male *capitalists* wanted women (excluding their own, of course) to work for "pin money" in the wage-labor market. Only if male workers and male capitalists could find some mutually agreeable way to handle this particular "woman question" could the interests of patriarchy and capitalism be harmonized.

Initially, the way was for male capitalists to pay male workers a "family wage" large enough to permit them to keep their wives and children at home. Male capitalists struck this bargain with male workers because they believed that

(1) stay-at-home housewives would produce and maintain healthier, happier, and therefore more *productive* male workers than would working wives; and (2) women and children could always be persuaded at a later date to reenter the work force for low wages should men demand high wages. As it so happens, many women and children are currently entering the work force for low wages not so much because men are demanding too much in the way of remuneration, but simply because many families can no longer make it on one family income—even a good one.

However, the move of women into the workplace has not fundamentally diminished men's power over women. Through the sexual division of labor, patriarchy maintains the subordinate status of women in the workplace as well as in the home. In a workplace that is divided into high-paying, male-dominated jobs and low-paying, female-dominated jobs, men earn $1.00 for every $.70 women earn. In the home, working women, but not working men, experience the stresses and strains of the "double day." Numerous studies show that the husbands of working women do not do much more work around the house than do the husbands of stay-at-home housewives. Most working women have two full-time jobs: one in the home and one outside the home.

Reflecting on the present sexual division of labor, which results in women getting the "short end of the stick" in the home and/or the workplace, Hartmann concludes that men's desire to control women is at least as strong as capitalism's desire to control workers. Capitalism and patriarchy must be fought simultaneously. However, since a war on two fronts is enormously taxing, women must pick their battles carefully. And given that it is easier for working women to form coalitions with each other than it is for housewives to do so, women might as well begin their "war" in the workplace by demanding that they be paid as well as men are paid. Women must demand not only "equal wages for equal work," but also "comparable wages for comparable work," for only then will the workplace be truly socialized rather than merely liberalized.

As many socialist feminists see it, the ultimate aim of the so-called "comparable worth movement" is not simply to make women the economic equals of men but to break down what is an increasingly scandalous hierarchy of wages, providing some people with seven-figure salaries and others with a pittance. The justification generally given for this skewed state of affairs is that the market pays the highest price to those who do the most valuable work. But as socialist feminists see it, it is doubtful that the market always rewards the "right" people; and it is even more doubtful that anyone's work is worth *astronomically* more than anyone else's.

To be sure, it will be difficult for mainstream Americans to accept not only that women deserve as much pay as men do for comparable work, but also that no one really deserves that much more money than anyone else. But even if Americans accept only the first of these arguments, capitalism and patriarchy will be weakened. For example, because nearly half of all poor families are female-headed, and because women are the primary recipients of food stamps, legal services, and publicly subsidized healthcare, if wage-earning women were paid what their jobs are worth, these women would be able to support themselves and their children adequately without being forced, in one way or another, to attach themselves to possibly abusive men simply because they offer an additional source of income.

Women: Caste, Class or Oppressed Sex?

Evelyn Reed

The new stage in the struggle for women's liberation already stands on a higher ideological level than did the feminist movement of the last century. Many of the participants today respect the Marxist analysis of capitalism and subscribe to Engels's classic explanation of the origins of women's oppression. It came about through the development of class society, founded upon the family, private property, and the state.

But there still remain considerable misunderstandings and misinterpretations of Marxist positions, which have led some women who consider themselves radicals or socialists to go off course and become theoretically disoriented. Influenced by the myth that women have always been handicapped by their childbearing functions, they tend to attribute the roots of women's oppression, at least in part, to biological sexual differences. In actuality its causes are exclusively historical and social in character.

Some of these theorists maintain that women constitute a special class or caste. Such definitions are not only alien to the views of Marxism but lead to the false conclusion that it is not the capitalist system but men who are the prime enemy of women. I propose to challenge this contention.

The findings of the Marxist method, which have laid the groundwork for explaining the genesis of woman's degradation, can be summed up in the following propositions:

> *First, women were not always the oppressed or "second" sex. Anthropology, or the study of prehistory, tells us the contrary. Throughout primitive society, which was the epoch of tribal collectivism, women were the equals of men and recognized by man as such.*
>
> *Second, the downfall of women coincided with the breakup of the matriarchal clan commune and its replacement by class-divided society with its institutions of the patriarchal family, private property and state power.*

The key factors which brought about this reversal in woman's social status came out of the transition from a hunting and food-gathering economy to a far higher mode of production based upon agriculture, stock raising and urban crafts. The primitive division of labor between the sexes was replaced by a more complex social division of labor. The greater efficiency of labor gave rise to a sizable surplus product, which led first to differentiations and then to deepgoing divisions among the various segments of society.

By virtue of the directing roles played by men in large-scale agriculture, irrigation and construction projects, as well as in stock raising, this surplus wealth was gradually appropriated by a hierarchy of men as their private property. This, in turn, required the institution of marriage and the family to fix the legal ownership and inheritance of a man's property. Through monogamous marriage the wife was brought under the complete control of her husband who was thereby assured of legitimate sons to inherit his wealth.

As men took over most of the activities of social production, and with the rise of the family institution, women became relegated to the home to serve their husbands and families. The state apparatus came into existence to fortify and legalize the institutions of private property, male dominion and the father-family, which later were sanctified by religion.

This, briefly, is the Marxist approach to the origins of woman's oppression. Her subordination did not come about through any biological deficiency as a sex. It was the result of the revolutionary social changes which destroyed the equalitarian society of the matriarchal gens or clan and replaced it with a patriarchal class society which, from its birth, was stamped with discriminations and inequalities of many kinds, including the inequality of the sexes. The growth of this inherently oppressive type of socioeconomic organization was responsible for the historic downfall of women.

But the downfall of women cannot be fully understood, nor can a correct social and political solution be worked out for their liberation, without seeing what happened at the same time to men. It is too often overlooked that the patriarchal class system which crushed the matriarchy and its communal social relations also shattered its male counterpart, the fratriarchy— or tribal brotherhood of men. Woman's overthrow went hand in hand with the subjugation of the mass of toiling men to the master class of men.

The import of these developments can be more clearly seen if we examine the basic character of the tribal structure which Morgan, Engels and others described as a system of "primitive communism." The clan commune was both a sisterhood of women and a brotherhood of men. The sisterhood of women, which was the essence of the matriarchy, denoted its collectivist character. The women worked together as a community of sisters; their social labors largely sustained the whole community. They also raised their children in common. An individual mother did not draw distinctions between her own and her clan sisters' progeny, and the children in turn regarded all the older sisters as their mutual mothers. In other words, communal production and communal possessions were accompanied by communal child-raising.

The male counterpart of this sisterhood was the brotherhood, which was molded in the same communal pattern as the sisterhood. Each clan or phratry of clans comprising the tribe was regarded as a "brotherhood" from the male standpoint just as it was viewed as a "sisterhood" or "motherhood" from the female standpoint. In this matriarchal-brotherhood the adults of both sexes not only produced the necessities of life together but also provided for and protected the children of the community. These features made the sisterhood and brotherhood a system of "primitive communism."

Thus, before the family that had the individual father standing at its head came into existence, the functions of fatherhood were a *social*, and not a *family* function of men. More than this, the earliest men who performed the services of fatherhood were not the mates or "husbands" of the clan sisters but rather their clan brothers. This was not simply because the processes of physiological paternity were unknown in ancient society. More decisively, this fact was irrelevant in a society founded upon collectivist relations of production and communal child-raising.

However odd it may seem to people today, who are so accustomed to the family form of child-raising, it was perfectly natural in the primitive commune for the clan brothers, or "mothers' brothers," to perform the paternal functions for their sisters' children that were later taken over by the individual father for his wife's children.

The first change in this sister-brother clan system came with the growing tendency for pairing couples, or "pairing families" as Morgan and Engels called them, to live together in the same community and household. However, this simple cohabitation did not substantially alter the former collectivist relations or the productive role of the women in the community. The sexual division of labor which had formerly been allotted between clan sisters and brothers became gradually transformed into a sexual division of labor between husbands and wives.

But so long as collectivist relations prevailed and women continued to participate in social production, the original equality between the sexes more or less persisted. The whole community continued to sustain the pairing units, just as each individual member of these units made his and her contribution to the labor activities.

Consequently, the pairing family, which appeared at the dawn of the family system, differed radically from the nuclear family of our times. In our ruthless competitive capitalist system every tiny family must sink or swim through its own efforts—it cannot count on assistance from outside sources. The wife is dependent upon the husband while the children must look to the parents for their subsistence, even if the wage earners who support them are stricken by unemployment, sickness or death. In the period of the pairing family, however, there was no such system of dependency upon "family economics," since the whole community took care of each individual's basic needs from the cradle to the grave.

This was the material basis for the absence, in the primitive commune, of those social oppressions and family antagonisms with which we are so familiar.

It is sometimes said or implied that male domination has always existed and that women have always been brutally treated by men. Contrariwise, it is also widely believed that the relations between the sexes in matriarchal society were merely the reverse of our own—with women dominating men. Neither of these propositions is borne out by the anthropological evidence.

It is not my intention to glorify the epoch of savagery nor advocate a romantic return to some past "golden age." An economy founded upon hunting and food-gathering is the lowliest stage in human development, and its living conditions were rude, crude and harsh. Nevertheless, we must recognize that male and female relations in that kind of society were fundamentally different from ours.

Under the clan system of the sisterhood of women and the brotherhood of men there was no more possibility for one sex to dominate the other than there was for one class to exploit another. Women occupied the most eminent position because they were the chief producers of the necessities of life as well as the procreators of new life. But this did not make them the oppressors of men. Their communal society excluded class, racial or sexual tyranny.

As Engels pointed out, with the rise of private property, monogamous marriage and the patriarchal family, new social forces came into play in both society at large and the family setup which destroyed the rights exercised by earliest womankind. From simple cohabitation of pairing couples there arose the rigidly fixed, legal system of monogamous marriage. This brought the wife and children under the complete control of the husband and father who gave the family his name and determined their conditions of life and destiny.

Women, who had once lived and worked together as a community of sisters and raised their children in common, now became dispersed as wives of individual men serving their lords and masters in individual households. The former equalitarian sexual division of labor between the men and women of the commune gave way to a family division of labor in which the woman was more and more removed from social production to serve as a household drudge for husband, home and family. Thus women, once "governesses" of society, were degraded under the class formations to become the governess of a man's children and his chief housemaid.

This abasement of women has been a permanent feature of all three stages of class society,

from slavery through feudalism to capitalism. So long as women led or participated in the productive work of the whole community, they commanded respect and esteem. But once they were dismembered into separate family units and occupied a servile position in home and family, they lost their prestige along with their influence and power.

Is it any wonder that such social changes should bring about intense and long-enduring antagonism between the sexes? As Engels says:

Monogamy then does by no means enter history as a reconciliation of man and wife, and still less as the highest form of marriage. On the contrary, it enters as the subjugation of one sex by the other, as the proclamation of an antagonism between the sexes unknown in all preceding history. . . . The first class antagonism appearing in history coincides with the development of the antagonism of man and wife in monogamy, and the first class oppression with that of the female by the male sex (*Origin of the Family, Private Property, and the State*).

Here it is necessary to note a distinction between two degrees of women's oppression in monogamous family life under the system of private property. In the productive farm family of the preindustrial age, women held a higher status and were accorded more respect than they receive in the consumer family of our own city life, the nuclear family.

So long as agriculture and craft industry remained dominant in the economy, the farm family, which was a large or "extended" family, remained a viable productive unit. All its members had vital functions to perform according to sex and age. The women in the family helped cultivate the ground and engaged in home industries as well as bearing children, while the children and older folks produced their share according to ability.

This changed with the rise of industrial and monopoly capitalism and the nuclear family. Once masses of men were dispossessed from the land and small businesses to become wage earners in factories, they had nothing but their labor power to sell to the capitalist bosses for their means of subsistence. The wives of these wage earners, ousted from their former productive farm and homecraft labors, became utterly dependent upon their husbands for the support of themselves and their children. As men became dependent upon their bosses, the wives became more dependent upon their husbands.

By degrees, therefore, as women were stripped of their economic self-dependence, they fell ever lower in social esteem. At the beginning of class society they had been removed from *social* production and social leadership to become farm-family producers, working through their husbands for home and family. But with the displacement of the productive farm family by the nuclear family of industrial city life, they were driven from their last foothold on solid ground.

Women were then given two dismal alternatives. They could either seek a husband as provider and be penned up thereafter as housewives in city tenements or apartments to raise the next generation of wage slaves. Or the poorest and most unfortunate could go as marginal workers into the mills and factories (along with the children) and be sweated as the most downtrodden and underpaid section of the labor force.

Over the past generations women wage workers have conducted their own labor struggles or fought along with men for improvements in their wages and working conditions. But women as dependent housewives have had no such means of social struggle. They could only resort to complaints or wrangles with husband and children over the miseries of their lives. The friction between the sexes became deeper and sharper with the abject dependency of women and their subservience to men.

Despite the hypocritical homage paid to womankind as the "sacred mother" and devoted homemaker, the *worth* of women sank to its lowest point under capitalism. Since housewives do not produce commodities for the market nor create any surplus value for the profiteers, they are not central to the operations of capitalism. Only three justifications for their existence remain under this system: as breeders, as household janitors, and as buyers of consumer goods for the family.

While wealthy women can hire servants to do the dull chores for them, poor women are riveted to an endless grind for their whole lives. Their condition of servitude is compounded when they are obliged to take an outside job to help sustain the family. Shouldering two responsibilities instead of one, they are the "doubly oppressed."

Even middle-class housewives in the Western world, despite their economic advantages, are victimized by capitalism. The isolated, monotonous, trivial circumstances of their lives lead them to "living through" their children—a relationship which fosters many of the neuroses that afflict family life today. Seeking to allay their boredom, they can be played upon and preyed upon by the profiteers in the consumer goods fields. This exploitation of women as consumers is part and parcel of a system that grew up in the first place for the exploitation of men as producers.

The capitalists have ample reason for glorifying the nuclear family. Its petty household is a goldmine for all sorts of hucksters from real estate agents to the manufacturers of detergents and cosmetics. Just as automobiles are produced for individual use instead of developing adequate mass transportation, so the big corporations can make more money by selling small homes on private lots to be equipped with individual washing machines, refrigerators, and other such items. They find this more profitable than building large-scale housing at low rentals or developing community services and child-care centers.

In the second place, the isolation of women, each enclosed in a private home and tied to the same kitchen and nursery chores, hinders them from banding together and becoming a strong social force or a serious political threat to the Establishment.

What is the most instructive lesson to be drawn from this highly condensed survey of the long imprisonment of womankind in the home and family of class society—which stands in such marked contrast to their stronger, more independent position in preclass society? It shows that the inferior status of the female sex is not the result of their biological makeup or the fact that they are the childbearers. Childbearing was no handicap in the primitive commune; it *became* a handicap, above all, in the nuclear family of our times. Poor women are torn apart by the conflicting obligations of taking care of their children at home while at the same time working outside to help sustain the family. Women, then, have been condemned to their oppressed status by the same social forces and relations which have brought about the oppression of one class by another, one race by another, and one nation by another. It is the capitalist system—the ultimate stage in the development of class society—which is the fundamental source of the degradation and oppression of women.

Some women in the liberation movement dispute these fundamental theses of Marxism. They say that the female sex represents a separate caste or class. Ti-Grace Atkinson, for example, takes the position that women are a separate *class*; Roxanne Dunbar says that they comprise a separate *caste*. Let us examine these two theoretical positions and the conclusions that flow from them.

First, are women a caste? The caste hierarchy came first in history and was the prototype and predecessor of the class system. It arose after the breakup of the tribal commune with the emergence of the first marked differentiations of segments of society according to the new divisions of labor and social functions. Membership in a superior or inferior

station was established by being born into that caste.

It is important to note, however, that the caste system was also inherently and at birth a class system. Furthermore, while the caste system reached its fullest development only in certain regions of the world, such as India, the class system evolved far beyond it to become a world system, which engulfed the caste system.

This can be clearly seen in India itself, where each of the four chief castes—the Brahmans or priests, the soldiers, the farmers and merchants, and the laborers, along with the "out-castes" or pariahs—had their appropriate places in an exploitative society. In India today, where the ancient caste system survives in decadent forms, capitalist relations and power prevail over all the inherited precapitalist institutions, including the caste relics.

However, those regions of the world which advanced fastest and farthest on the road to civilization bypassed or overleaped the caste system altogether. Western civilization, which started with ancient Greece and Rome, developed from slavery through feudalism to the maturest stage of class society, capitalism.

Neither in the caste system nor the class system—nor in their combinations—have women comprised a separate caste or class. Women themselves have been separated into the various castes and classes which made up these social formations.

The fact that women occupy an inferior status as a *sex* does not *ipso facto* make women either an inferior caste or class. Even in ancient India women belonged to different castes, just as they belong to different classes in contemporary capitalist society. In the one case their social status was determined by birth into a caste; in the other it is determined by their own or their husband's wealth. But the two can be fused—for women as for men. Both sexes can belong to a superior caste and possess superior wealth, power and status.

What, then, does Roxanne Dunbar want to convey when she refers to all women (regardless of class) as comprising a separate caste? And what consequences for action does she draw from this characterization? The exact content of both her premise and her conclusions are not clear to me, and perhaps to many others. They therefore deserve closer examination.

Speaking in a loose and popular way, it is possible to refer to women as an inferior "caste"—as is sometimes done when they are also called "slaves" or "serfs"—when the intent is merely to indicate that they occupy the subordinate position in male-dominated society. The use of the term "caste" would then only expose the impoverishment of our language, which has no special word to indicate womankind as the oppressed sex. But more than this seems to be involved, if we judge from the paper by Roxanne Dunbar dated February 1970 which supersedes her previous positions on this question.

In that document she says that her characterization of women as an exploited caste is nothing new; that Marx and Engels likewise "analyzed the position of the female sex in just such a way." This is simply not the case. Neither Marx in *Capital*, nor Engels in *The Origin of the Family, Private Property, and the State*, nor in any writings by noted Marxists from Lenin to Luxemburg on this matter, has woman been defined by virtue of her sex as a "caste." Therefore this is not a mere verbal squabble over the misuse of a term. It is a distinct departure from Marxism, although presented in the name of Marxism.

I would like clarification from Roxanne Dunbar on the conclusions she draws from her theory. For, if all women belong to an inferior caste, and all men belong to the superior caste, it would consistently follow that the central axis of a struggle for liberation would be a "caste war" of all women against all men to bring about the liberation of women. This conclusion would seem to be confirmed by her statement

that "we live under an international caste system. . . ."

This assertion is equally non-Marxist. What Marxists say is that we live under an international *class* system. And they further state that it will require not a caste war, but a *class struggle*—of all the oppressed, male and female alike—to consummate women's liberation along with the liberation of all the oppressed masses. Does Roxanne Dunbar agree or disagree with this viewpoint on the paramount role of the class struggle?

Her confusion points up the necessity for using precise language in a scientific exposition. However downtrodden women are under capitalism, they are not chattel slaves any more than they are feudal serfs or members of an inferior caste. The social categories of slave, serf and caste refer to stages and features of past history and do not correctly define the position of women in our society.

If we are to be precise and scientific, women should be defined as an "oppressed *sex*."

Turning to the other position, it is even more incorrect to characterize women as a special "class." In Marxist sociology a class is defined in two interrelated ways: by the role it plays in the processes of production and by the stake it has in the ownership of property. Thus the capitalists are the major power in our society because they own the means of production and thereby control the state and direct the economy. The wage workers who create the wealth own nothing but their labor power, which they have to sell to the bosses to stay alive.

Where do women stand in relation to these polar class forces? They belong to all strata of the social pyramid. The few at the top are part of the plutocratic class; more among us belong to the middle class; most of us belong to the proletarian layers of the population. There is an enormous spread from the few wealthy women of the Rockefeller, Morgan and Ford families to the millions of poor women who subsist on welfare dole. *In short, women, like men, are a multiclass sex.*

This is not an attempt to divide women from one another but simply to recognize the actual divisions that exist. The notion that all women as a sex have more in common than do members of the same class with one another is false. Upper-class women are not simply bed-mates of their wealthy husbands. As a rule they have more compelling ties which bind them to-gether. They are economic, social and political bedmates, united in defense of private property, profiteering, militarism, racism—and the ex-ploitation of other women.

To be sure, there can be individual excep-tions to this rule, especially among young women today. We remember that Mrs. Frank Leslie, for example, left a $2 million bequest to further the cause of women's suffrage, and other upper-class women have devoted their means to secure civil rights for our sex. But it is quite another matter to expect any large number of wealthy women to endorse or sup-port a revolutionary struggle which threatens their capitalist interests and privileges. Most of them scorn the liberation movement, saying openly or implicitly, "What do we need to be liberated from?"

Is it really necessary to stress this point? Tens of thousands of women went to the Wash-ington antiwar demonstrations in November 1969 and again in May 1970. Did they have more in common with the militant men marching beside them on that life-and-death issue—or with Mrs. Nixon, her daughters, and the wife of the attorney general, Mrs. Mitchell, who peered uneasily out of her window and saw the specter of another Russian Revolution in those protesting masses? Will the wives of bankers, generals, corporation lawyers, and big industrialists be firmer allies of women fighting for liberation than working-class men, black and white, who are fighting for theirs? Won't there be both men and women on both sides of the class struggle? If not, is the struggle to be

directed against men as a sex rather than against the capitalist system?

It is true that all forms of class society have been male-dominated and that men are trained from the cradle on to be chauvinistic. But it is not true that men as such represent the main enemy of women. This crosses out the multi-tudes of downtrodden, exploited men who are themselves oppressed by the main enemy of women, which is the capitalist system. These men likewise have a stake in the liberation struggle of the women; they can and will be-come our allies.

Although the struggle against male chau-vinism is an essential part of the tasks that women must carry out through their liberation movement, it is incorrect to make that the central issue. This tends to conceal or overlook the role of the ruling powers who not only breed and benefit from all forms of discrim-ination and oppression but are also responsible for breeding and sustaining male chauvinism. Let us remember that male supremacy did not exist in the primitive commune, founded upon sisterhood and brotherhood. Sexism, like racism, has its roots in the private property system.

A false theoretical position easily leads to a false strategy in the struggle for women's liber-ation. Such is the case with a segment of the Redstockings who state in their *Manifesto* that "women are an oppressed *class.*" If all women compose a class then all men must form a counterclass—the oppressor class. What con-clusion flows from this premise? That there are no men in the oppressed class? Where does this leave the millions of oppressed white working men who, like the oppressed blacks, Chicanos and other minorities, are exploited by the mo-nopolists? Don't they have a central place in the struggle for social revolution? At what point and under what banner do these oppressed peoples of all races and both sexes join together for common action against their common enemy? To oppose women as a class against men as a class can only result in a diversion of the real class struggle.

Isn't there a suggestion of this same line in Roxanne Dunbar's assertion that female liberation is the basis for social revolution? This is far from Marxist strategy since it turns the real situation on its head. Marxists say that social revolution is the basis for full female liberation—just as it is the basis for the liberation of the whole working class. In the last analysis the real allies of women's liberation are all those forces which are impelled for their own reasons to struggle against and throw off the shackles of the imperialist masters.

The underlying source of women's oppression, which is capitalism, cannot be abolished by women alone, nor by a coalition of women drawn from all classes. It will require a worldwide struggle for socialism by the working masses, female and male alike, together with every other section of the oppressed, to overthrow the power of capitalism, which is centered today in the United States.

In conclusion, we must ask, what are the connections between the struggle for women's liberation and the struggle for socialism?

First, even though the full goal of women's liberation cannot be achieved short of the socialist revolution, this does not mean that the struggle to secure reforms must be postponed until then. It is imperative for Marxist women to fight shoulder to shoulder with all our embattled sisters in organized actions for specific objectives from now on. This has been our policy ever since the new phase of the women's liberation movement surfaced a year or so ago, and even before.

The women's movement begins, like other movements for liberation, by putting forward elementary demands. These are: equal opportunities with men in education and jobs; equal pay for equal work; free abortions on demand; and child-care centers financed by the government but controlled by the community. Mobilizing women behind these issues not only gives us the possibility of securing some improvements but also exposes, curbs and modifies the worst aspects of our subordination in this society.

Second, why do women have to lead their own struggles for liberation, even though in the end the combined anticapitalist offensive of the whole working class will be required for the victory of the socialist revolution? The reason is that no segment of society which has been subjected to oppression, whether it consists of Third World people or of women, can delegate the leadership and promotion of their fight for freedom to other forces—even though other forces can act as their allies. We reject the attitude of some political tendencies that say they are Marxists but refuse to acknowledge that women have to lead and organize their own independent struggle for emancipation, just as they cannot understand why blacks must do the same.

The maxim of the Irish revolutionists—"who would be free themselves must strike the blow"—fully applies to the cause of women's liberation. Women must themselves strike the blows to gain their freedom. And this holds true after the anticapitalist revolution triumphs as well as before.

In the course of our struggle, and as part of it, we will reeducate men who have been brainwashed into believing that women are naturally the inferior sex due to some flaws in their biological makeup. Men will have to learn that, in the hierarchy of oppressions created by capitalism, their chauvinism and dominance is another weapon in the hands of the master class for maintaining its rule. The exploited worker, confronted by the even worse plight of his dependent housewife, cannot be complacent about it—he must be made to see the source of the oppressive power that has degraded them both.

Finally, to say that women form a separate caste or class must logically lead to extremely pessimistic conclusions with regard to the antagonism between the sexes in contrast with the revolutionary optimism of the Marxists. For unless the two sexes are to be totally separated, or the men liquidated, it would seem that they will have to remain forever at war with each other.

As Marxists we have a more realistic and hopeful message. We deny that women's inferiority was predestined by her biological makeup or has always existed. Far from being eternal, woman's subjugation and the bitter hostility between the sexes are no more than a few thousand years old. They were produced by the drastic social changes which brought the family, private property and the state into existence.

This view of history points up the necessity for a no less thoroughgoing revolution in socioeconomic relations to uproot the causes of inequality and achieve full emancipation for our sex. This is the purpose and promise of the socialist program, and this is what we are fighting for.

The Unhappy Marriage of Marxism and Feminism: Towards a More Progressive Union

Heidi Hartmann

The "marriage" of marxism and feminism has been like the marriage of husband and wife depicted in English common law: marxism and feminism are one, and that one is marxism. Recent attempts to integrate marxism and feminism are unsatisfactory to us as feminists because they subsume the feminist struggle into the "larger" struggle against capital. To continue our simile further, either we need a healthier marriage or we need a divorce.

The inequalities in this marriage, like most social phenomena, are no accident. Many marxists typically argue that feminism is at best less important than class conflict and at worst divisive of the working class. This political stance produces an analysis that absorbs feminism into the class struggle. Moreover, the analytic power of marxism with respect to capital has obscured its limitations with respect to sexism. We will argue here that while marxist analysis provides essential insight into the laws of historical development, and those of capital in particular, the categories of marxism are sex-blind. Only a specifically feminist analysis reveals the systemic character of relations between men and women. Yet feminist analysis by itself is inadequate because it has been blind to history and insufficiently materialist. Both marxist analysis, particularly its historical and materialist

From *Women and Revolution*, edited by Lydia Sargent. Copyright © 1981 by Lydia Sargent. Reprinted by permission.

method, and feminist analysis, especially the identification of patriarchy as a social and historical structure, must be drawn upon if we are to understand the development of western capitalist societies and the predicament of women within them. In this essay we suggest a new direction for marxist feminist analysis.

I. MARXISM AND THE WOMAN QUESTION

The woman question has never been the "feminist question." The feminist question is directed at the causes of sexual inequality between women and men, of male dominance over women. Most marxist analyses of women's position take as their question the relationship of women to the economic system, rather than that of women to men, apparently assuming the latter will be explained in their discussion of the former. Marxist analysis of the woman question has taken several forms. All see women's oppression in our connection (or lack of it) to production. Defining women as part of the working class, these analyses consistently subsume women's relation to men under workers' relation to capital.

All attempt to include women in the category working class and to understand women's oppression as another aspect of class oppression. In doing so all give short shrift to the object of feminist analysis, the relations between women and men. While our "problems" have been elegantly analyzed, they have been misunderstood. The focus of marxist analysis has been class relations; the object of marxist analysis has been understanding the laws of motion of capitalist society. While we believe marxist methodology *can* be used to formulate feminist strategy, these marxist feminist approaches clearly do not do so; their marxism clearly dominates their feminism.

This is due in part to the analytical power of marxism itself. Marxism is a theory of the development of class society, of the accumulation process in capitalist societies, of the reproduction of class dominance, and of the development of contradictions and class struggle. Capitalist societies are driven by the demands of the accumulation process, most succinctly summarized by the fact that production is oriented to exchange, not use. In a capitalist system production is important only insofar as it contributes to the making of profits, and the use value of products is only an incidental consideration. Profits derive from the capitalists' ability to exploit labor power, to pay laborers less than the value of what they produce. The accumulation of profits systematically transforms social structure as it transforms the relations of production. The reserve army of labor, the poverty of great numbers of people and the near-poverty of still more, these human reproaches to capital are by-products of the accumulation process itself. From the capitalist's point of view, the reproduction of the working class may "safely be left to itself." At the same time, capital creates an ideology, which grows up along side it, of individualism, competitiveness, domination, and in our time, consumption of a particular kind. Whatever one's theory of the genesis of ideology one must recognize these as the dominant values of capitalist societies.

Marxism enables us to understand many aspects of capitalist societies: the structure of production, the generation of a particular occupational structure, and the nature of the dominant ideology. Marx's theory of the development of capitalism is a theory of the development of "empty places." Marx predicted, for example, the growth of the proletariat and the demise of the petit bourgeoisie. More precisely and in more detail, Braverman among others has explained the creation of the "places" clerical worker and service worker in advanced capitalist societies. Just as capital creates these places indifferent to the individuals who fill them, the categories of marxist analysis, class, reserve army of labor, wage-laborer, do not explain why particular people fill particular places. They give no clues about why *women* are subordinate to *men* inside and outside the family and why it is not the other way around. *Marxist categories, like capital itself, are sex-blind.* The categories of marxism cannot tell us who will fill the empty places. Marxist analysis of the woman question has suffered from this basic problem.

II. RADICAL FEMINISM AND PATRIARCHY

The great thrust of radical feminist writing has been directed to the documentation of the slogan "the personal is political." Women's discontent, radical feminists argued, is not the neurotic lament of the maladjusted, but a response to a social structure in which women are systematically dominated, exploited, and oppressed. Women's inferior position in the labor market, the male-centered emotional structure of middle class marriage, the use of women in advertising, the so-called understanding of women's psyche as neurotic—popularized by academic and clinical psychology—aspect after aspect of women's lives in advanced capitalist society was researched and analyzed. The radical feminist literature is enormous and defies easy summary. At the same time, its focus on psychology is consistent. The New York Radical Feminists' organizing document was "The Politics of the Ego." "The personal is political" means for radical feminists, that the original and basic class division is between the sexes, and that the motive force of history is the striving of men for power and domination over women, the dialectic of sex.

Accordingly, Firestone rewrote Freud to understand the development of boys and girls into men and women in terms of power. Her characterizations of what are "male" and "female" character traits are typical of radical feminist writing. The male seeks power and domination; he is egocentric and individualis-

tic, competitive and pragmatic; the "technological mode," according to Firestone, is male. The female is nurturant, artistic, and philosophical; the "aesthetic mode" is female.

No doubt, the idea that the aesthetic mode is female would have come as quite a shock to the ancient Greeks. Here lies the error of radical feminist analysis: the dialectic of sex as radical feminists present it projects male and female characteristics as they appear in the present back into all of history. Radical feminist analysis has greatest strength in its insights into the present. Its greatest weakness is a focus on the psychological which blinds it to history.

The reason for this lies not only in radical feminist method, but also in the nature of patriarchy itself, for patriarchy is a strikingly resilient form of social organization. Radical feminists use patriarchy to refer to a social system characterized by male domination over women. Kate Millett's definition is classic:

our society . . . is a patriarchy. The fact is evident at once if one recalls that the military, industry, technology, universities, science, political offices, finances—in short, every avenue of power within the society, including the coercive force of the police, is entirely in male hands.[1]

This radical feminist definition of patriarchy applies to most societies we know of and cannot distinguish among them. The use of history by radical feminists is typically limited to providing examples of the existence of patriarchy in all times and places. For both marxist and mainstream social scientists before the women's movement, patriarchy referred to a system of relations between men, which formed the political and economic outlines of feudal and some pre-feudal societies, in which hierarchy followed ascribed characteristics. Capitalist societies are understood as meritocratic, bureaucratic, and impersonal by bourgeois social scientists; marxists see capitalist societies as systems of class domination. For both kinds of social scientists neither the historical patriarchal societies nor today's western capitalist societies are understood as systems of relations between men that enable them to dominate women.

Towards a Definition of Patriarchy

We can usefully define patriarchy as a set of social relations between men, which have a material base, and which, though hierarchical, establish or create interdependence and solidarity among men that enable them to dominate women. Though patriarchy is hierarchical and men of different classes, races, or ethnic groups have different places in the patriarchy, they also are united in their shared relationship of dominance over their women; they are dependent on each other to maintain that domination. Hierarchies "work" at least in part because they create vested interests in the status quo. Those at the higher levels can "buy off" those at the lower levels by offering them power over those still lower. In the hierarchy of patriarchy, all men, whatever their rank in the patriarchy, are bought off by being able to control at least some women. There is some evidence to suggest that when patriarchy was first institutionalized in state societies, the ascending rulers literally made men the heads of their families (enforcing their control over their wives and children) in exchange for the men's ceding some of their tribal resources to the new rulers. Men are dependent on one another (despite their hierarchical ordering) to maintain their control over women.

The material base upon which patriarchy rests lies most fundamentally in men's control over women's labor power. Men maintain this control by excluding women from access to some essential productive resources (in capitalist societies, for example, jobs that pay living wages) and by restricting women's sexuality. Monogamous heterosexual marriage is one relatively recent and efficient form that seems to allow men to control both these areas. Controlling women's access to resources and their sexuality, in turn, allows men to control women's labor power, both for the purpose of serving men in many personal and sexual ways and for the purpose of rearing children. The services women render men, and which exonerate men from having to perform many unpleasant tasks (like cleaning toilets) occur outside as well as inside the family setting. Examples outside the family include the harassment of women workers and students by male bosses and professors as well as the common use of secretaries to run personal errands, make coffee, and provide "sexy" surroundings. Rearing children, whether or not the children's labor power is of immediate benefit to their fathers, is nevertheless a crucial task in perpetuating patriarchy as a system. Just as class society must be reproduced by schools, work places, consumption norms, etc., so must patriarchal social relations. In our society children are generally reared by women at home, women socially defined and recognized as inferior to men, while men appear in the domestic picture only rarely. Children raised in this way generally learn their places in the gender hierarchy well. Central to this process, however, are the areas outside the home where patriarchal behaviors are taught and the inferior position of women enforced and reinforced: churches, schools, sports, clubs, unions, armies, factories, offices, health centers, the media, etc.

The material base of patriarchy, then, does not rest solely on childrearing in the family, but on all the social structures that enable men to control women's labor. While we believe that most known societies have been patriarchal, we do not view patriarchy as a universal, unchanging phenomenon. Rather patriarchy, the set of interrelations among men that allow men to dominate women, has changed in form and intensity over time. It is crucial that the hierarchy among men, and their differential access to patriarchal benefits, be examined. Surely, class, race, nationality, and even marital status and sexual orientation, as well as the obvious age, come into play here. And women of different class, race, national, marital status, or sexual orientation groups are subjected to different degrees of patriarchal power. Women may themselves exercise class, race, or national power, or even patriarchal power (through their family connections) over men lower in the patriarchal hierarchy than their own male kin.

To recapitulate, we define patriarchy as a set of social relations which has a material base and in which there are hierarchical relations between men and solidarity among them which enable them in turn to dominate women. The material base of patriarchy is men's control over women's labor power. That control is maintained by excluding women from access to necessary economically productive resources and by restricting women's sexuality. Men exercise their control in receiving personal service work from women, in not having to do housework or rear children, in having access to women's bodies for sex, and in feeling powerful and being powerful. The crucial elements of patriarchy as we *currently* experience them are: heterosexual marriage (and consequent homophobia), female childrearing and housework, women's economic dependence on men (enforced by arrangements in the labor market), the state, and numerous institutions based on social relations among men—clubs, sports, unions, professions, universities, churches, corporations, and armies. All of these elements need to be examined if we are to understand patriarchal capitalism.

Both hierarchy and interdependence among men and the subordination of women are *integral* to the functioning of our society; that is, these relationships are *systemic*. We leave aside the question of the creation of these relations and ask, can we recognize patriarchal relations in capitalist societies? Can we understand how these relations among men are perpetuated in capitalist societies? Can we identify

ways in which patriarchy has shaped the course of capitalist development?

III. THE PARTNERSHIP OF PATRIARCHY AND CAPITAL

How are we to recognize patriarchal social relations in capitalist societies? It appears as if each woman is oppressed by her own man alone; her oppression seems a private affair. Relationships among men and among families seem equally fragmented. It is hard to recognize relationships among men, and between men and women, as *systematically* patriarchal. We argue, however, that patriarchy as a system of relations between men and women exists in capitalism, and that in capitalist societies a healthy and strong partnership exists between patriarchy and capital. Yet if one begins with the concept of patriarchy and an understanding of the capitalist mode of production, one recognizes immediately that the partnership of patriarchy and capital was not inevitable; men and capitalists often have conflicting interests, particularly over the use of women's labor power. Here is one way in which this conflict might manifest itself: the vast majority of men might want their women at home to personally service them. A smaller number of men, who are capitalists, might want most women (not their own) to work in the wage labor market. In examining the tensions of this conflict over women's labor power historically, we will be able to identify the material base of patriarchal relations in capitalist societies, as well as the basis for the partnership between capital and patriarchy.

Industrialization and the Development of Family Wages

Marxists made quite logical inferences from a selection of the social phenomena they witnessed in the nineteenth century. But marxists ultimately underestimated the strength of the preexisting patriarchal social forces with which fledgling capital had to contend and the need for capital to adjust to these forces. The industrial revolution was drawing all people into the labor force, including women and children: in fact the first factories used child and female labor almost exclusively. That women and children could earn wages separately from men both undermined authority relations and kept wages low for everyone. Kautsky, writing in 1892, describes the process this way:

Then with the wife and young children of the working-man ... able to take care of themselves, the wages of the male worker can safely be reduced to the level of his own personal needs without the risk of stopping the fresh supply of labor power.

The labor of women and children, moreover, affords the additional advantage that these are less capable of resistance than men [sic]; and their introduction into the ranks of the workers increases tremendously the quantity of labor that is offered for sale in the market.

Accordingly, the labor of women and children ... also diminishes [the] capacity of the male worker for resistance in that it overstocks the market: owing to both these circumstances it lowers the wages of the working-man.[2]

The terrible effects on working class family life of low wages and of forced participation of all family members in the labor force were recognized by marxists. Kautsky wrote:

The capitalist system of production does not in most cases destroy the single household of the working-man, but robs it of all but its unpleasant features. The activity of woman today in industrial pursuits ... means an increase of her former burden by a new one. *But one cannot serve two masters.* The household of the working-man suffers whenever his wife must help to earn the daily bread.[3]

Working men as well as Kautsky recognized the disadvantages of female wage labor. Not only were women "cheap competition" but working women were their very wives, who could not "serve two masters" well.

Male workers resisted the wholesale entrance of women and children into the labor force, and sought to exclude them from union membership and the labor force as well. In 1846 the *Ten Hours' Advocate* stated:

It is needless for us to say, that all attempts to improve the morals and physical condition of female factory workers will be abortive, unless their hours are materially reduced. Indeed we may go so far as to say, that married females would be much better occupied in performing the domestic duties of the household, than following the never-tiring motion of machinery. We therefore hope the day is not distant, when the husband will be able to provide for his wife and family, without sending the former to endure the drudgery of a cotton mill.[4]

In the United States in 1854 the National Typographical Union resolved not to "encourage by its act the employment of female compositors." Male unionists did not want to afford union protection to women workers; they tried to exclude them instead. In 1879 Adolph Strasser, president of the Cigarmakers International Union, said: "We cannot drive the females out of the trade, but we can restrict their daily quota of labor through factory laws."

While the problem of cheap competition could have been solved by organizing the wage earning women and youths, the problem of disrupted family life could not be. Men reserved union protection for men and argued for protective labor laws for women and children. Protective labor laws, while they may have ameliorated some of the worst abuses of female and child labor, also limited the participation of adult women in many "male" jobs. Men sought to keep high wage jobs for themselves and to raise male wages generally. They argued for wages sufficient for their wage labor alone to support their families. This "family wage" system gradually came to be the norm for stable working class families at the end of the nineteenth century and the beginning of the twentieth. Several observers have declared the nonwage-working wife to be part of the standard of living of male workers. Instead of fighting for equal wages for men and women, male workers sought the family wage, wanting to retain their wives' services at home. In the absence of patriarchy a unified working class might have confronted capitalism, but patriarchal social relations divided the working class, allowing one part (men) to be bought off at the expense of the other (women). Both the hierarchy between men and the solidarity among them were crucial in this process of resolution. Family wages may be understood as a resolution of the conflict over women's labor power which was occurring between patriarchal and capitalist interests at that time.

Family wages for most adult men imply men's acceptance, and collusion in, lower wages for others, young people, women and socially defined inferior men as well (Irish, blacks, etc., the lowest groups in the patriarchal hierarchy who are denied many of the patriarchal benefits). Lower wages for women and children and inferior men are enforced by job segregation in the labor market, in turn maintained by unions and management as well as by auxiliary institutions like schools, training programs, and even families. Job segregation by sex, by insuring that women have the lower paid jobs, both assures women's economic dependence on men and reinforces notions of appropriate spheres for women and men. For most men, then, the development of family wages, secured the material base of male domination in two ways. First, men have the better jobs in the labor market and earn higher wages than women. The lower pay women receive in the labor market both perpetuates men's material advantage over women and encourages women to choose wifery as a career. Second, then, women do housework, childcare, and perform other services at home which benefit men directly. Women's home responsibilities in turn reinforce their inferior labor market position.

The resolution that developed in the early twentieth century can be seen to benefit capitalist interests as well as patriarchal interests. Capitalists, it is often argued, recognized that in the extreme conditions which prevailed in the early nineteenth century industrialization, working class families could not adequately reproduce themselves. They realized that housewives produced and maintained healthier workers than wage-working wives and that educated children became better workers than noneducated ones. The bargain, paying family wages to men and keeping women home, suited the capitalists at the time as well as the male workers. Although the terms of the bargain have altered over time, it is still true that the family and women's work in the family serve capital by providing a labor force and serve men as the space in which they exercise their privilege. Women, working to serve men and their families, also serve capital as consumers. The family is also the place where dominance and submission are learned, as Firestone, the Frankfurt School, and many others have explained. Obedient children become obedient workers; girls and boys each learn their proper roles.

While the family wage shows that capitalism adjusts to patriarchy, the changing status of children shows that patriarchy adjusts to capital. Children, like women, came to be excluded from wage labor. As children's ability to earn money declined, their legal relationship to their parents changed. At the beginning of the industrial era in the United States, fulfilling children's need for their fathers was thought to be crucial, even primary, to their happy development; fathers had legal priority in cases of contested custody. As children's ability to contribute to the economic well-being of the family declined, mothers came increasingly to be viewed as crucial to the happy development of their children, and gained legal priority in cases of contested custody. Here patriarchy adapted to the changing economic role of children when children were productive, men claimed them; as children became unproductive, they were given to women.

The Family and the Family Wage Today

We argued above, that, with respect to capitalism and patriarchy, the adaptation, or mutual accommodation, took the form of the development of the family wage in the early twentieth century. The family wage cemented the partnership between patriarchy and capital. Despite women's increased labor force participation, particularly rapid since World War II, the family wage is still, we argue, the cornerstone of the present sexual division of labor—in which women are primarily responsible for housework and men primarily for wage work. Women's lower wages in the labor market (combined with the need for children to be reared by someone) assure the continued existence of the family as a necessary income pooling unit. The family, supported by the family wage, thus allows the control of women's labor by men both within and without the family.

Though women's increased wage work may cause stress for the family (similar to the stress Kautsky and Engels noted in the nineteenth century), it would be wrong to think that as a consequence, the concepts and the realities of the family and of the sexual division of labor will soon disappear. The sexual division of labor reappears in the labor market, where women work at women's jobs, often the very jobs they used to do only at home—food preparation and service, cleaning of all kinds, caring for people, and so on. As these jobs are low-status and low-paying patriarchal relations remain intact, though their material base shifts somewhat from the family to the wage differential, from family-based to industrially-based patriarchy.

Industrially based patriarchal relations are enforced in a variety of ways. Union contracts which specify lower wages, lesser benefits, and fewer advancement opportunities for women are not just atavistic hangovers—a case of sexist attitudes or male supremacist ideology—they maintain the material base of the patriarchal system. While some would go so far as to argue that patriarchy is already absent from the family (see, for example, Stewart Ewen, *Captains of Consciousness*), we would not. Although the terms of the compromise between capital and patriarchy are changing as additional tasks formerly located in the family are capitalized, and the location of the deployment of women's labor power shifts, it is nevertheless true, as we have argued above, that the wage differential caused by extreme job segregation in the labor market reinforces the family, and, with it, the domestic division of labor, by encouraging women to marry. The "ideal" of the family wage—that a man can earn enough to support an entire family—may be giving way to a new ideal that both men and women contribute through wage earning to the cash income of the family. The wage differential, then, will become increasingly necessary in perpetuating patriarchy, the male control of women's labor power. The wage differential will aid in *defining* women's work as secondary to men's at the same time as it necessitates women's actual continued economic dependence on men. The sexual division of labor in the labor market and elsewhere should be understood as a manifestation of patriarchy which serves to perpetuate it.

Ideology in the Twentieth Century

If we examine the characteristics of men as radical feminists describe them—competitive, rationalistic, dominating—they are much like our description of the dominant values of capitalist society.

This "coincidence" may be explained in two ways. In the first instance, men, as wage laborers, are absorbed in capitalist social relations at work, driven into the competition these relations prescribe, and absorb the corresponding values. The radical feminist description of men was not altogether out of line for capitalist societies. Secondly, even when men and women do not actually behave in the way sexual norms prescribe, men *claim for themselves* those characteristics which are valued in the dominant ideology. So, for example, the authors of *Crestwood Heights* found that while the men, who were professionals, spent their days manipulating subordinates (often using techniques that appeal to fundamentally irrational motives to elicit the preferred behavior), men and women characterized men as "rational and pragmatic." And while the women devoted great energies to studying scientific methods of child-rearing and child development, men and women in Crestwood Heights characterized women as "irrational and emotional."

This helps to account not only for "male" and "female" characteristics in capitalist societies, but for the particular form sexist ideology takes in capitalist societies. Just as women's work serves the dual purpose of perpetuating male domination and capitalist production, so sexist ideology serves the dual purpose of glorifying male characteristics/capitalist values, and denigrating female characteristics/social need. If women were degraded or powerless in other societies, the reasons (rationalizations) men had for this were different. Only in a capitalist society does it make sense to look down on women as emotional or irrational. As epithets, they would not have made sense in the renaissance. Only in a capitalist society does it make sense to look down on women as "dependent." "Dependent" as an epithet would not make sense in feudal societies. Since the division of labor ensures that women as wives and mothers in the family are largely concerned with the production of use values, the denigration of these activities obscures capital's inability to meet socially determined need at the same time that it degrades women in the eyes

of men, providing a rationale for male dominance. An example of this may be seen in the peculiar ambivalence of television commercials. On one hand, they address themselves to the real obstacles to providing for socially determined needs: detergents that destroy clothes and irritate skin, shoddily made goods of all sorts. On the other hand, concern with these problems must be denigrated: this is accomplished by mocking women, the workers who must deal with these problems.

A parallel argument demonstrating the partnership of patriarchy and capitalism may be made about the sexual division of labor in the work force. The sexual division of labor places women in low-paying jobs, and in tasks thought to be appropriate to women's role. Women are teachers, welfare workers, and the great majority of workers in the health fields. The nurturant roles that women play in these jobs are of low status because capitalism emphasizes personal independence and the ability of private enterprise to meet social needs, emphases contradicted by the need for collectively provided social services. As long as the social importance of nurturant tasks can be denigrated because women perform them, the confrontation of capital's priority on exchange value by a demand for use values can be avoided. In this way, it is not feminism, but sexism that divides and debilitates the working class.

IV. TOWARDS A MORE PROGRESSIVE UNION

Many problems remain for us to explore. Patriarchy as we have used it here remains more a descriptive term than an analytic one. If we think marxism alone inadequate, and radical feminism itself insufficient, then we need to develop new categories. What makes our task a difficult one is that the same features, such as the division of labor, often reinforce both patriarchy and capitalism, and in a thoroughly patriarchal capitalist society, it is hard to isolate the mechanisms of patriarchy. Nevertheless, this is what we must do. We have pointed to some starting places: looking at who benefits from women's labor power, uncovering the material base of patriarchy, investigating the mechanisms of hierarchy and solidarity among men. The questions we must ask are endless.

Feminism and the Class Struggle

The struggle against capital and patriarchy cannot be successful if the study and practice of the issues of feminism is abandoned. A struggle aimed only at capitalist relations of oppression will fail, since their underlying supports in patriarchal relations of oppression will be overlooked. And the analysis of patriarchy is essential to a definition of the kind of socialism useful to women. While men and women share a need to overthrow capitalism they retain interests particular to their gender group. It is not clear—from our sketch, from history, or from male socialists—that the socialism being struggled for is the same for both men and women. For a humane socialism would require not only consensus on what the new society should look like and what a healthy person should look like, but more concretely, it would require that men relinquish their privilege.

As women we must not allow ourselves to be talked out of the urgency and importance of our tasks, as we have so many times in the past. We must fight the attempted coercion, both subtle and not so subtle, to abandon feminist objectives.

This suggests two strategic considerations. First, a struggle to establish socialism must be a struggle in which groups with different interests form an alliance. Women should not trust men to liberate them after the revolution, in part, because there is no reason to think

they would know how; in part, because there is no necessity for them to do so. In fact their immediate self-interest lies in our continued oppression. Instead we must have our own organizations and our own power base. Second, we think the sexual division of labor within capitalism has given women a practice in which we have learned to understand what human interdependence and needs are. While men have long struggled *against* capital, women know what to struggle *for*. As a general rule, men's position in patriarchy and capitalism prevents them from recognizing both human needs for nurturance, sharing, and growth, and the potential for meeting those needs in a nonhierarchical, nonpatriarchal society. But even if we raise their consciousness, men might assess the potential gains against the potential losses and choose the status quo. Men have more to lose than their chains.

As feminist socialists, we must organize a practice which addresses both the struggle against patriarchy and the struggle against capitalism. We must insist that the society we want to create is a society in which recognition of interdependence is liberation rather than shame, nurturance is a universal, not an oppressive practice, and in which women do not continue to support the false as well as the concrete freedoms of men.

NOTES

1. Kate Millett, *Sexual Politics* (New York: Avon Books, 1971), p. 25.

2. Karl Kautsky, *The Class Struggle* (New York: Norton, 1971), pp. 25–26.

3. We might add, "outside the household," Kautsky, *Class Struggle*, p. 26, our emphasis.

4. Cited in Neil Smelser, *Social Change and the Industrial Revolution* (Chicago: University of Chicago Press. 1959), p. 301.

Postmodern Feminism

Interestingly, the standard feminist effort to find integration and agreement, to establish one specifically feminist standpoint that could represent how women see the world, has not gone unchallenged. Postmodern feminists regard this effort as yet another example of "phallologocentric" thought. It is typical "male thinking" to seek the "one, true, feminist story of reality." For postmodernists, such a synthesis is neither feasible nor desirable. It is not feasible because women's experiences differ across class, racial, and cultural lines. It is not desirable because the "One" and the "True" are philosophical myths that culture has used to club into submission the differences that, in point of empirical fact, constitute the human condition. That feminism is many and not one is to be expected because women are many and not one. The more feminist thoughts, the better.

By refusing to center, congeal, and cement separate thoughts into a unified and inflexible truth, postmodern feminists claim to resist patriarchal dogma. Seeing difference everywhere, including some of the general differences between men and women, they make fascinating connections between the ways in which women's "sexuality" and women's "textuality" merge, for example. In her article "Woman's Word," Annie Leclerc claims that the fact that men's sexuality is linear and unitary, doggedly focused on the penis's penetration of the vagina, is not unrelated to the fact that men's writing is overly regimented (ideas are marshaled, organized, and bound together). Likewise, the fact that women's sexuality is cyclical and multifaceted is not unrelated to that fact that women's writing is without definite boundaries.

Leclerc's ideas are more fully developed by Hélène Cixous who objects to masculine writing and thinking because they are cast in binary oppositions. Man has unnecessarily segmented reality by coupling concepts and terms in pairs of polar opposites, one of which is always privileged over the other. In her essay "Sorties," Cixous lists some of these dichotomous pairs:

> Activity/passivity
> Sun/Moon
> Culture/Nature
> Day/Night
>
> Thought has always worked by opposition
> Speech/Writing
> Parole/Ecriture
> High/Low
>
> By dual, hierarchized *oppositions* (p. 440).

In Cixous's view, all of these dichotomies find their inspiration in the fundamental dichotomous couple—man/woman—in which man is associated with all that is active, cultural, light, high, or generally positive, and woman with all that is passive, natural, dark, low, or generally negative. Moreover, the first term of the man/woman dichotomy is the term from which the second departs or deviates. Man is the self; woman is his Other. Thus, woman exists in man's world on his terms. She is either the Other for man, or she is "unthinkable," "unthought" (p. 441).

Cixous challenges women to write themselves out of the world that men have constructed for them by putting into words the unthinkable/unthought. The type of writing that

Cixous identifies as woman's own—marking, scratching, scribbling, jotting down—connotes movements that bring to mind Heraclitus's ever-changing river. In contrast, the type of writing that Cixous associates with man connotes Parmenides's static world: what is has always been and will always be. Once it is stamped with the official seal of patriarchal approval, a thought is no longer permitted to move or change. Thus, for Cixous, feminine writing is not merely a new style of writing; it is "the very possibility of change, the space that can serve as a springboard for subversive thought, the precursory movement of a transformation of social and cultural standards."

In the process of further distinguishing between men's and women's writing, Cixous draws many connections between male sexuality and masculine writing on the one hand and female sexuality and feminine writing on the other. Male sexuality, which centers on what Cixous call the "big dick," is ultimately boring in its pointedness and singularity. Like male sexuality, masculine writing, usually termed "phallocentric" writing by Cixous, is also ultimately boring. Men write the same old things with their "little pocket signifier"—the trio of penis/phallus/pen. Fearing the multiplicity and chaos that exist outside their Symbolic Order, men always write in black ink, carefully containing their thoughts in a sharply defined and rigidly imposed structure. In contrast, female sexuality is, for Cixous, anything but boring; and just as exciting as female sexuality is feminine writing that is open and multiple, varied and rhythmic, full of pleasures and, perhaps more importantly, of possibilities. When a woman writes, said Cixous, she writes in "white ink," letting her words flow freely where she wishes them to go.

Luce Irigaray ("Questions") agrees with Cixous that female sexuality is the inspiration for feminine writing, but she resists what she regards as the temptation to define the "feminine feminine." As Irigaray sees it, any state-

ment that definitively asserts what the real, or true "feminine" is will re-create the "phallic," or "masculine" feminine: "To claim that the feminine can be expressed in the form of a concept is to allow oneself to be caught up again in a system of 'masculine' representations, in which women are trapped in a system or meaning which serves the auto-affection of the (masculine) subject (p. 445)." What obstructs the progression of women's thoughts out of this trap is the concept of Sameness, the ideational result of masculine narcissism and singularity.

Although Irigaray finds traces of Sameness everywhere in Western philosophy and psychoanalysis, she finds it omnipresent in the work of Sigmund Freud, especially in Freud's writings on female sexuality. According to Irigaray, Freud sees the little girl not as feminine in any positive sense but only in her negativity, as a "little man" without a penis. Freud suppresses the notion of difference instead, characterizing the feminine as a lack of something. Woman is a reflection of man, the Same as a man, except in her sexuality. Female sexuality, because it does not mirror the male's, is an absence, or lack of the male's sexuality. Where woman does not reflect man, she does not exist and, suggests Irigaray, will never exist until the Oedipus complex is exploded and the "feminine feminine" released from its repression.

In realizing that Western culture is loathe to abandon accounts of how the self—that is, the male self—is constituted, Irigaray suggests several strategies aimed at enabling woman to experience herself as something other than "waste" or "excess" in the structured margins of a dominant ideology. One of these strategies is to mime the mimes men have imposed on women. If women exist only in men's eyes, as images, women should take those images and reflect them back to men in magnified proportions. As Toril Moi notes, through miming, women can "undo the effects of phallocentric discourse simply by overdoing them." For example, if men view women as sex objects, fetishizing women's breasts in particular, then women should pump up their breasts as big as possible and walk into church on Sunday with them fully exposed, in all their naked glory, as if to say, "Here boys, we know what's on your minds. So look. See if we care." To be sure, concedes Irigaray, miming is not without its perils.

The distinction between miming the patriarchal definition of woman in order to subvert it and merely fulfilling this definition is not clear. In their attempts to *overdo* this definition, women may be drawn back into it. Nevertheless, despite this risk, no female should lose the opportunity to break out of the male straitjackets that have misshaped her female form.

Woman's Word

Annie Leclerc

Nothing exists that has not been made by man—not thought, not language, not words. Even now, there is nothing that has not been made by man, not even me: especially not me.

We have to invent everything anew. Things made by man are not just stupid, deceitful and oppressive. More than anything else, they are sad, sad enough to kill us with boredom and despair.

We have to invent a woman's word. But not "of" woman, "about" woman, in the way that man's language speaks "of" woman. Any woman who wants to use a language that is specifically her own, cannot avoid this extraordinary, urgent task: we must invent woman.

It is crazy, I know. But it is the only thing that keeps me sane.

Whose voice is speaking these words? Whose voice has always spoken? Deafening tumult of important voices; and not one a woman's voice. I haven't forgotten the names of the great talkers. Plato, Aristotle and Montaigne, Marx and Freud and Nietzsche. I know them because I've lived among them and among them alone. These strong voices are also those who have reduced me the most effectively to silence. It is these superb speakers who, more than any others, have forced me into silence.

Whose voice do we hear in those great, wise books we find in libraries? Who speaks in the Capitol? Who speaks in the temple? Who speaks in the lawcourts and whose voice is it that we hear in laws? Men's.

The world is man's word. Man is the word of the world.

No, no, I'm not making any demands. I am not tempted by the dignity of Man's status; it amuses me. When I consider Man, I am only playing.

And I say to myself: Man? What is Man? Man is what man brings into the world. We made children, they made Man.

They turned the specific into the universal. And the universal looks just like the specific.

Universality became their favourite ploy. One voice for all. With one voice, only one can speak. Man.

From *French Connections: Voices from the Women's Movement in France*, ed., trans. by Claire Duchen. Copyright © 1987 by Claire Duchen. Reprinted by permission.

All I want is my voice.

You let me speak, yes, but I don't want your voice. I want my own voice, I don't trust yours any more.

It is no longer enough to speak *about* myself for me to find a voice that is my own. Woman's literature: feminine literature, very feminine, with its exquisite feminine sensitivity. Man's literature is not masculine, with its exquisite masculine sensitivity. A man speaks in the name of Man. A woman in the name of women. But as it is man who has set out the 'truth' about us all, the truth about women, it is still man who speaks through woman's mouth.

The whole of feminine literature has been whispered to women in man's language. The whole range, all the melodies, of femininity, have already been played out.

Is it possible to invent anything new?

We have to invent: otherwise we'll perish.

This stupid, military, evil-smelling world marches on alone towards its destruction. Man's voice is a fabric full of holes, torn, frayed; a burned out voice.

However wide we open our eyes, however far we stretch our ears, from now on, the summits from where laws are made, male summits with all their sacred values, are lost in the thick fog of indifference and boredom. Which is when women open their mouths and begin to speak. From now on, no man's voice will come to cover up the multiple, vigorous voices of women.

But we still aren't there. In fact we won't get there unless woman manages to weave a fabric, whole and new, made of a voice springing from within herself. Because the voice can be new, but the words worn out. Watch out woman, pay attention to your words.

Let me say first of all where all this comes from. It comes from me, woman, from my woman's belly. It began in my belly, with small, slight, signs, hardly audible, when I was pregnant. I began to listen to this timid voice which had no words.

Who could tell me, could I ever express (and what words would I use), to speak of the extraordinary joy of pregnancy, the immense, terrible joy of childbirth.

That is how I first learned that my woman's body was the site of Dionysian celebrations of life.

So then I looked at men. For man, there is only one celebration of sexuality: intercourse. He doesn't want to hear about the others, the multiple celebrations of my body.

And this one celebration of his, he wants it all for himself. He demands that my necessary presence remain discreet and totally devoted to his pleasure.

Well it's too bad for him, but I must talk about the pleasures of my body, no, not those of my soul, my virtue or my feminine sensitivity, but the pleasures of my woman's belly, my woman's vagina, my woman's breasts, luxuriant pleasures that you can't even imagine.

I must talk about it, because only by talking about it will a new language be born, a woman's word.

I have to reveal everything that you have so determinedly hidden, because it was with that repression that all the others began. Everything that was ours, you converted to dirt, pain, duty, bitchiness, small-mindedness, servitude.

Once you had silenced us, you could do whatever you wanted with us, turn us into maid, goddess, plaything, mother hen, *femme fatale*. The only thing you demand really insistently is our silence: in fact, you could hardly demand anything more; beyond silence, you would have to demand our death.

It is our silence and the triumphant sound of your voice that authorized the theft of our labour, the rape of our bodies and all our silent slavery, our silent martyrdom. How can it be that we are now coming out of our coma, and that our tongues, though still sticky with respect for your values, are loosening up, slowly?

You had proclaimed the universality of your language. Very good for asserting your power, but not so good for keeping it.

We listen, convinced, to those who say 'All men are born free and remain equal in their rights.'

And slowly we discover that the person who has nothing, has the right to nothing. Not to equality, nor to freedom. And we end up by demanding the letter of the law. Equality. Freedom.

My body flows with the vast rhythmic pulsation of life. My body experiences a cycle of changes. Its perception of time is cyclical, but never closed or repetitive.

Men, as far as I can judge, have a linear perception of time. From their birth to their death, the segment of time they occupy is straight. Nothing in their flesh is aware of time's curves. Their eyes, their pulse, neglect the seasons. They can only see History, they fight only for History. Their sexuality is linear: their penis becomes erect, stretches, ejaculates and becomes limp. That which makes them live kills them. They escape death only by a new life that, in turn, kills them again.

My body speaks to me of another sense of time, another adventure. Thirteen times a year, I experience the cyclical changes of my body. Sometimes my body is completely forgotten. Not thinking about its pains or its pleasures, I come, I go, I work, I speak and my body is an abstraction. Sometimes, my body is there, present.

Ten, twelve days before my period, my breasts swell, become hardened. This seems, in my case, to follow ovulation, fertility. I can't say that this is always so, because other women say they experience this during their period or just before.

The nipple is tender, bright red, very sensitive. The slightest contact makes it harder. You say, friends say to each other, "My breasts are sore." Especially if you are worried that your period is late, and you are looking for any hopeful signs, you weigh your breasts in your hands, feel them, press them with anxious care, trying to force them to admit that they hurt, you say, you repeat, oh yes, they are sore. But it's not that. They don't hurt, it's just that we can feel them. They are alive, aroused, open to pain but not sore. They are also open to caresses, much more so than usual; continually caressable, strangely open to pleasure. When my period is due, my breasts are loving, avid, sensitive.

I haven't finished talking about my body yet. For it experiences still more wonders. Just because you aren't involved with them, does it mean that I must hide them under a hideous mask of pain and suffering? Do I have to feel bad because I take pleasure in experiences you can't know, to the point of denying myself this pleasure too?

You have poisoned my life. For centuries. Deprived of my body, I only knew how to live through you. Badly, hardly living. Slaving away, enduring, being silent and being pretty. My body there for work and for pleasing you; never for my own pleasure. My body, never my own, for me. Mouth sewn up, face made up. Vagina open when you want it, closed up with Tampax. Scoured, scraped, made hygienic, deodorized and re-odorized with rose-smelling perfume, it's too much, it's stifling me, I need my own body. That is what I mean by living.

You could say, well what are women complaining about since you say there are so many possibilities for them to be happy? It is because these possibilities that we have here and now are merely an anticipation of what could be possible in a radically different society, in which woman's status would also be changed. As would the way in which she is perceived by others.

I'm not saying to women, be happy; but only, do you know that you are capable of happiness?

But we have to understand everything that denies women's happiness—and which is not only her economic, sexual and familial oppression.

We know full well, because it is glaringly obvious, that women are denied happiness because they are overburdened with domestic tasks and with anxieties that postpone their pleasure in life indefinitely, almost until her death. When does a woman really have the chance to take pleasure in herself, in man, in the sun, the rain, the wind, in children, in the seasons, even in the home, when she is constantly harassed by the need to take care of— the housework, the dishes, the washing, the shopping, the ironing, the cooking?

When can she even glimpse the possibility of happiness when, already rushed off her feet, she adds the hardship and humiliation of a badly paid job? We can't pretend that we don't know about all this, because it can't be hidden, we can *see it*.

But do we know enough about what else denies a woman happiness, maybe even more radically? Do we know the extent of a tyranny we can't see—we can't see it because we can see neither the person exercising it nor how it operates, nor exactly on what it operates?

Do we understand that, excluded from her body, kept in ignorance about the pleasures it contains, it is the ability to experience happiness that is missing?

If women are so politically apathetic, so persistently conservative, is it not also because they are incapable of imagining what their pleasure in living could be?

The only bodily pleasure they are aware of missing is the one which they see men indulge in, more often and better than they do: a properly sexual pleasure. But is their imagination so limited that they can't think of other pleasures? Are they so shortsighted that they can't see the source of their problems? Are they too humble, too lazy? If only they learned to find in themselves those joys from which the world is cut off, would their struggle not acquire a new vigor and a new, indispensable rigor? If only they knew that, if man made this world which is an oppressive world, it is up to women to prepare the coming of a different world, which would at last be a world of life.

Women will not be liberated as long as they do not also want to be liberating, by denouncing and by fighting *all* oppression, those that come from man, from power, from work, but also those that come from themselves and operate on themselves, on others and particularly on their children: disincarnated women, de-sexualized women, disinfected, disaffected, glossy magazine women, puppet women, but also women who are men's accomplices, accomplices of the strong man, the husband, boss, cop, and also jealous women, capricious and vengeful, bourgeois women, mean women, finally and above all, women the dragon of the family, women martyrs of devotion, voracious mother-hens, possessive and murderous mothers, odious step-mothers.

As long as we are somehow in complicity with man's oppressions, as long as we perpetuate them on to our children, turning them into vigorous oppressors or into docile victims, we will never, never be free.

Sorties

Hélène Cixous

Where is she?

Activity/passivity,
Sun/Moon,
Culture/Nature,
Day/Night,

Father/Mother,
Head/heart,
Intelligible/sensitive,
Logos/Pathos.

Form, convex, step, advance, seed, progress.
Matter, concave, ground—which supports the step,
receptacle.

Man
—————————
Woman

Always the same metaphor: we follow it, it transports us, in all of its forms, wherever a discourse is organized. The same thread, or double tress leads us, whether we are reading or speaking, through literature, philosophy, criticism, centuries of representation, of reflection.

Thought has always worked by opposition,
Speech/Writing
High/Low

By dual, *hierarchized* oppositions. Superior/Inferior. Myths, legends, books. Philosophical systems. Wherever an ordering intervenes, a law organizes the thinkable by (dual, irreconcilable; or mitigable, dialectical) oppositions. And all

the couples of oppositions are *couples*. Does this mean something? Is the fact that logocentrism subjects thought—all of the concepts, the codes, the values—to a two-term system, related to "the" couple man/woman?

Nature/History,
Nature/Art,
Nature/Mind,
Passion/Action.

Theory of culture, theory of society, the ensemble of symbolic systems—art, religion, family, language, —everything elaborates the same systems. And the movement by which each opposition is set up to produce meaning is the movement by which the couple is destroyed. A universal battlefield. Each time a war breaks out. Death is always at work.

Father/son	Relationships of authority, of privilege, of force.
Logos/writing	Relationships: opposition, conflict, relief, reversion.
Master/slave	Violence. Repression.

And we perceive that the "victory" always amounts to the same thing: it is hierarchized. The hierarchization subjects the entire conceptual organization to man. A male privilege, which can be seen in the opposition by which it sustains itself, between *activity* and *passivity*. Traditionally, the question of sexual difference is coupled with the same opposition: activity/passivity.

That goes a long way. If we examine the history of philosophy—in so far as philosophical discourse orders and reproduces all thought—we perceive that: it is marked by an absolute constant, the orchestrator of values, which is precisely the opposition activity/ passivity.

In philosophy, woman is always on the side of passivity. Every time the question comes up; when we examine kinship structures; whenever a family model is brought into play; in fact as soon as the ontological question is raised; as soon as you ask yourself what is meant by the question "What is it?"; as soon as there is a will to say something. A will: desire, authority, you examine that, and you are led right back—to the father. You can even fail to notice that there's no place at all for women in the operation! In the extreme the world of "being" can function to the exclusion of the mother. No need for mother—provided that there is something of the maternal: and it is the father then who acts as—is—the mother. Either the woman is passive; or she doesn't exist. What is left is unthinkable, unthought of. She does not enter into the oppositions, she is not coupled with the father (who is coupled with the son).

There is Mallarmé's[1] tragic dream, a father lamenting the mystery of paternity, which mourning tears out of the poet, the mourning of mournings, the death of the beloved son: this dream of a union between the father and the son—and no mother then. Man's dream is the face of death. Which always threatens him differently than it threatens woman.

"an alliance
a union, superb
—and the life

remaining in me
I shall use it to—

so no mother then?"

And dream of masculine filiation, dream of God the father
emerging from himself
in his son, —and no mother then

She does not exist, she may be nonexistent; but there must be something of her. Of woman, upon whom he no longer depends, he retains only this space, always virginal, matter subjected to the desire that he wishes to imprint.

And if you examine literary history, it's the same story. It all refers back to man to *his* torment, his desire to be (at) the origin. Back to the father. There is an intrinsic bond between the philosophical and the literary (to the extent that it signifies, literature is commanded by the philosophical) and phallocentrism. The philosophical constructs itself starting with the abasement of woman. Subordination of the feminine to the masculine order which appears to be the condition for the functioning of the machine.

The challenging of this solidarity of logocentrism and phallocentrism has today become insistent enough—the bringing to light of the fate which has been imposed upon woman, of her burial—to threaten the stability of the masculine edifice which passed itself off as eternal-natural; by bringing forth from the world of femininity reflections, hypotheses which are necessarily ruinous for the bastion which still holds the authority. What would become of logocentrism, of the great philosophical systems, of world order in general if the rock upon which they founded their church were to crumble?

If it were to come out in a new day that the logocentric project had always been, undeniably, to *found* (fund)[2] phallocentrism, to insure for masculine order a rationale equal to history itself?

Then all the stories would have to be told differently, the future would be incalculable, the historical forces would, will, change hands, bodies; another thinking as yet not thinkable will transform the functioning of all society. Well, we are living through this very period when the conceptual foundation of a millenial culture is in process of being undermined by millions of a species of mole as yet not recognized.

When they awaken from among the dead, from among the words, from among the laws. . . .

What does one give?

The specific difference that has determined the movement of history as a movement of property is articulated between two economies that define themselves in relation to the problematics of giving.

The (political) economy of the masculine and of the feminine is organized by different requirements and constraints, which, when socialized and metaphorized, produce signs, relationships of power, relationships of production and of reproduction, an entire immense system of cultural inscription readable as masculine or feminine.

I am careful here to use the *qualifiers* of sexual difference, in order to avoid the confusion man/masculine, woman/feminine: for there are men who do not repress their femininity, women who more or less forcefully inscribe their masculinity. The difference is not, of course, distributed according to socially determined "sexes." Furthermore, when I speak of political economy and of libidinal economy, in putting the two together, I am not bringing into play the false question of origin, that tall tale sustained by male privilege. We must guard against falling complacently or blindly into the essentialist ideological interpretation, as, for example, Freud and Jones, in different ways, ventured to do; in their quarrel over the subject of feminine sexuality, both of them, starting from opposite points of view, came to support the awesome thesis of a "natural," anatomical determination of sexual difference-opposition. And from there on, both implicitly support phallocentrism's position of power.

Let us review the main points of the opposing positions: [Ernest] Jones (in *Early Feminine Sexuality*), using an ambiguous approach, attacks the Freudian theses that make of woman an imperfect man.

For Freud:

1. the "fatality" of the feminine situation is a result of an anatomical "defectiveness."
2. there is only one libido, and its essence is male; the inscription of sexual difference begins only with a phallic phase which both boys and girls go through. Until then, the girl has been a sort of little boy: the genital organization of the infantile libido is articulated by the equivalence activity/masculinity; the vagina has not as yet been "discovered."
3. the first love object being, for both sexes, the mother, it is only for the boy that love of the opposite sex is "natural."

For Jones: Femininity is an autonomous "essence."

From the outset (starting from the age of six months) the girl has a *feminine* desire for her father; an analysis of the little girl's earliest fantasms would in fact show that, in place of the breast which is perceived as disappointing, it is the penis that is desired, or an object of the same form (by an analogical displacement). It follows, since we are already into the chain of substitutions, that in the series of partial objects, in place of the penis, would come the child—for in order to counter Freud, Jones docilely returns to the Freudian terrain. And then some. From the equation breast-penis-child, he concludes that the little girl experiences with regard to the father a primary desire. (And this would include the desire to have a child by the father as well.) And, of course, the girl also has a primary love for the opposite sex. She too, then, has a right to her Oedipal complex as a primary formation, and to the threat of mutilation by the mother. At last she is a woman, anatomically, without defect: her clitoris is not a minipenis. Clitoral masturbation is not, as Freud claims, a masculine practice. And it would seem in light of precocious fantasms that the vagina is discovered very early.

In fact, in affirming that there is a specific femininity (while in other respects preserving the theses of an orthodoxy) it is still phallocentrism that Jones reinforces, on the pretext of taking the part of femininity (and of God, who he recalls created them male and female—!). And bisexuality vanishes into the unbridged abyss that separates the opponents here.

As for Freud, if we subscribe to what he sets forth when he identifies with Napoleon in his article of 1933 on *The Disappearance of the Oedipus Complex*: "anatomy is destiny," then we participate in the sentencing to death of woman. And in the completion of all History.

That the difference between the sexes may have psychic consequences is undeniable. But they are surely not reducible to those designated by a Freudian analysis. Starting with the relationship of the two sexes to the Oedipal complex, the boy and the girl are oriented toward a division of social roles so that women "inescapably" have a lesser productivity, because they "sublimate" less than men and because symbolic activity, hence the production of culture, is men's doing.[3]

Freud moreover starts from what he calls the *anatomical* difference between the sexes. And we know how that is pictured in his eyes: as the difference between having/not having the phallus. With reference to these precious parts. Starting from what will be specified, by Lacan, as the transcendental signifier.

But *sexual difference* is not determined merely by the fantasized relationship to anatomy, which is based, to a great extent, upon the point of *view*, therefore upon a strange importance accorded [by Freud and Lacan] to exteriority and to the specular in the elaboration of sexuality. A voyeur's theory, of course.

No, it is at the level of sexual pleasure [*jouissance*] in my opinion that the difference makes itself most clearly apparent in as far as woman's libidinal economy is neither identifiable by a man nor referable to the masculine economy.

For me, the question "What does she want?" that they ask of woman, a question that in fact woman asks herself because they ask it of her, because precisely there is so little place in society for her desire that she ends up by dint of not knowing what to do with it, no longer knowing where to put it, or if she has any, conceals the most immediate and the most urgent question: "How do I experience sexual pleasure?" What is feminine *sexual pleasure*,

where does it take place, how is it inscribed at the level of her body, of her unconscious? And then how is it put into writing?

We can go on at length about a hypothetical prehistory and about a matriarchal era. Or we can, as did Bachofen,[4] attempt to reconstitute a gynecocratic society, and to deduce from it poetic and mythical effects that have a powerfully subversive import with regard to the family and to male power.

All the other ways of depicting the history of power, property, masculine domination, the constitution of the State, the ideological apparatus have their effectiveness. But the change taking place has nothing to do with question of "origin." Phallocentrism *is*. History has never produced, recorded anything but that. Which does not mean that this form is inevitable or natural. Phallocentrism is the enemy. Of *everyone*. Men stand to lose by it, differently but as seriously as women. And it is time to transform. To invent the other history.

There is no such thing as "destiny," "nature," or essence, but living structures, caught up, sometimes frozen within historicocultural limits which intermingle with the historical scene to such a degree that it has long been impossible and is still difficult to think or even to imagine something else. At present, we are living through a transitional period—where the classical structure appears as if it might crack.

To predict what will happen to sexual difference—in another time (in two or three hundred years?) is impossible. But there should be no misunderstanding: men and women are caught up in a network of millenial cultural determinations of a complexity that is practically unanalyzable: we can no more talk about "woman" than about "man" without getting caught up in an ideological theater where the multiplication of representations, images, reflections, myths, identifications constantly transforms, deforms, alters each person's imaginary order and in advance, renders all conceptualization null and void.

There is no reason to exclude the possibility of radical transformations of behavior, mentalities, roles, and political economy. The effects of these transformations on the libidinal economy are unthinkable today. Let us imagine simultaneously a *general* change in all of the structures of formation, education, framework, hence of reproduction, of ideological effects, and let us imagine a real liberation of sexuality, that is, a transformation of our relationship to our body (—and to another body), an approximation of the immense material organic sensual universe that we are, this not being possible, of course, without equally radical political transformations (imagine!). Then "femininity," "masculinity," would inscribe their effects of difference, their economy, their relationships to expenditure, to deficit, to giving, quite differently. That which appears as "feminine" or "masculine" today would no longer amount to the same thing. The general logic of difference would no longer fit into the opposition that still dominates. The difference would be a crowning display of new differences.

But we are still floundering about—with certain exceptions—in the Old order.

The masculine future:

There are exceptions. There always have been those uncertain, poetic beings, who have not let themselves be reduced to the state of coded mannequins by the relentless repression of the homosexual component. Men or women, complex, mobile, open beings. Admitting the component of the other sex makes them at once much richer, plural, strong, and to the extent of this mobility, very fragile. We invent only on this condition: thinkers, artists, creators of new values, "philosophers" of the mad Nietzschen sort, inventors and destroyers of concepts, of forms, the changers of life cannot but be agitated by singularities—complementary or contradictory. This does not mean that in order to create you must be homosexual. But there is no *invention*

possible, whether it be philosophical or poetic, without the presence in the inventing subject of an abundance of the other, of the diverse: persons-detached, persons-thought, peoples born of the unconscious, and in each desert, suddenly animated, a springing forth of self that we did not know about—our women, our monsters, our jackals, our Arabs, our fellow-creatures, our fears.[5] But there is no invention of other I's, no poetry, no fiction without a certain homosexuality (interplay therefore of bisexuality) making in me a crystallized work of my ultrasubjectivities. I is this matter, personal, exuberant, lively masculine, feminine, or other in which I delights me and distresses me. And in the concert of personalizations called I, at the same time that you repress a certain homosexuality, symbolically, substitutively, it comes out through various signs—traits, comportments, manners, gestures—and it is seen still more clearly in writing.

Thus, under the name of Jean Genet, what is inscribed in the movement of a text which divides itself, breaks itself into bits, regroups itself, is an abundant, maternal, pederastic femininity. A phantasmatical mingling of men, of males, of messieurs, of monarchs, princes, orphans, flowers, mothers, breasts, gravitates around a marvelous "sun of energy" love, which bombards and disintegrates these ephemeral amorous singularities so that they may recompose themselves in other bodies for new passions. . . .

NOTES

1. *Pour un tombeau d' Anatole* (Editions du Seuil, 1961, p. 138) tomb in which Mallarmé preserves his son, guards him, he himself the mother, from death.

2. *Fonder* in French means both "to found" and "to fund."—Translator.

3. Freud's thesis is the following: when the Oedipal complex disappears the superego becomes its heir. At the moment when the boy begins to feel the threat of castration, he begins to overcome the Oedipus

complex, with the help of a very severe superego. The Oedipus complex for the boy is a primary process: his first love object, as for the girl, is the mother. But the girl's development is inevitably controlled by the pressure of a less severe superego: the discovery of her castration results in a less vigorous superego. She never completely overcomes the Oedipus complex. The feminine Oedipus complex is not a primary process: the pre-Oedipal attachment to the mother entails for the girl a difficulty from which, says Freud, she never recovers: the necessity of changing objects (to love the father), in midstream is a painful conversion, which is accompanied by an additional renunciation: the passage from pre-Oedipal sexuality to "normal" sexuality implies the abandonment of the clitoris in order to move on to the vagina. When this "destiny" is fulfilled, women have a reduced symbolic activity: they have nothing to lose, to gain, to defend.

4. J.-J. Bachofen (1815–1887) Swiss historian of "gynecocracy," "historian" of a nonhistory. His project is to demonstrate that the nations (Greek, Roman, Hebrew) went through an age of "gynecocracy," the reign of the Mother, before arriving at a patriarchy. This epoch can only be deduced, as it has no history. Bachofen advances that this state of affairs, humiliating for men, must have been repressed, covered over by historical forgetfulness. And he attempts to create (in *Das Mutterrecht* in particular, 1861) an archaeology of the matriarchal system, of great beauty, starting with a reading of the first historical texts, at the level of the symptom, of their unsaid. Gynecocracy, he says, is well-ordered materialism.

5. The French here, *nos semblables, nos frayeurs*, plays on and with the last line of Baudelaire's famous poem "Au lecteur" [To the reader]: "*Hypocrite lecteur,—mon semblable,—mon frère.*"—Translator.

Questions

Luce Irigaray

What is a woman?

I believe I've already answered that there is no way I would "answer" that question. The question "what is . . .?" is the question—the metaphysical question—to which the feminine does not allow itself to submit. . . .

Over and beyond the deconstruction of the Freudian theory of femininity, can one (can you) elaborate another concept of femininity: with a different symbolics, a different unconscious, that would be "of woman" (that is, entirely other and not the inverse, the nega-

tive, the complement of that of man)? Can you sketch its content?

Can anyone, can I, elaborate another, a different, concept of femininity? There is no question of another *concept* of femininity.

To claim that the feminine can be expressed in the form of a concept is to allow oneself to be caught up again in a system of "masculine" representations, in which women are trapped in a system of meaning which serves the auto-affection of the (masculine) subject. If it is really a matter of calling "femininity" into question, there is still no need to elaborate another "concept"—unless a woman is renouncing her sex and wants to speak like men. For the elaboration of a theory of woman, men, I think, suffice. In a woman('s) language, the concept as such would have no place. . . .

Strictly speaking, political practice, at least currently, is masculine through and through. In order for women to be able to make themselves heard, a "radical" evolution in our way of conceptualizing and managing the political realm is required. This, of course, cannot be achieved in a single "stroke."

What mode of action is possible today, then, for women? Must their interventions remain marginal with respect to social structure as a whole?

What do you mean by "marginal"?

I am thinking especially about *women's liberation movements*. Something is being elaborated there that has to do with the "feminine," with what women-among-themselves might be, what a "women's society" might mean. If I speak of marginality, it is because, first of all, these movements to some extent keep themselves deliberately apart from institutions and from the play of forces in power, and so forth. "Outside" the already-existing power relations. Sometimes they even reject intervention—including intervention "from without"—against any institution whatsoever.

This "position" is explained by the difficulties women encounter when they try to make their voices heard in places already fixed within and by a society that has simultaneously used and excluded them, and that continues in particular to ignore the specificity of their "demands" even as it recuperates some of their themes, their very slogans. This position can be understood, too, through women's need to constitute a place to be among themselves, in order to learn to formulate their desires, in the absence of overly immediate pressures and oppressions.

Of course, certain things have been achieved for women, in large part owing to the libera-

tion movements: liberalized contraception, abortion, and so on. These gains make it possible to raise again, differently, the question of what the social status of women might be—in particular through its differentiation from a simple reproductive-maternal function. But these contributions may always just as easily be turned against women. In other words, we cannot yet speak, in this connection, of a feminine politics, but only of certain conditions under which it may be possible. The first being an end to silence concerning the exploitation experienced by women: the systematic refusal to "keep quiet" practiced by the liberation movements. . . .

In the interview with Liberation, *you object to the notion of equality. We agree. What do you think of the notion of "woman power"? If woman were to come to pass (in history and in the unconscious . . .) what would result: would a feminine power be purely and simply substituted for masculine power? Or would there be peaceful coexistence? Or what?*

It clearly cannot be a matter of substituting feminine power for masculine power. Because this reversal would still be caught up in the economy of the same, in the same economy—in which, of course, what I am trying to designate as "feminine" would not emerge. There would be a phallic "seizure of power." Which, moreover, seems impossible: women may "dream" of it, it may sometimes be accomplished marginally, in limited groups, but for society as a whole, such a substitution of power, such a reversal of power, is impossible.

Peaceful Coexistence? I don't know just what that means. I don't think peaceful coexistence exists. It is the decoy of an economy of power and war. The question we might raise instead is this one: even though everything is in place and operating as if there could be nothing but the desire for "sameness," *why would there be no desire for "otherness"?* No desire for a difference that would not be repeatedly and eternally co-opted and trapped within an economy of "sameness." You may very well say that that is my dream, that it is just another dream. But why? Once again, the reversal or transfer of power would not signify the "advent" of the other, of a "feminine" other. But why would it be impossible for there to be any desire for difference, any desire for the other? Moreover, does not all reabsorption of otherness in the discourse of sameness signify a desire for difference, but a desire that would always—to speak a shamefully psychological language— "be frightening"? And which by that token would always keep "veiled"—in its phobia—the question of the difference between the sexes and of the sexual relation.

Why speak (dialogue) here with a man, and a man whose craft is after all philosophy?

Why try to speak with a man? Because what I want, in fact, is not to create a theory of woman, but to secure a place for the feminine within sexual difference. That difference—masculine/feminine—has always operated "within" systems that are representative, self-representative, of the (masculine) subject. Moreover, these systems have produced many other differences that appear articulated to compensate for an operative sexual indifference. For one sex and its lack, its atrophy, its negative, still does not add up to two. In other words, the feminine has never been defined except as the inverse, indeed the underside, of the masculine. So for woman it is not a matter of installing herself within this lack, this negative, even by denouncing it, nor of reversing the economy of sameness by turning the feminine into *the standard for "sexual difference"*; it is rather a matter of trying to practice that difference. Hence these questions: what other mode of reading or writing, of interpretation and affirmation, may be mine inasmuch as I am a woman, with respect to you, a man? Is it possible that the difference might not be reduced once again to a process of *hier-*

archization? Of subordinating the other to the same?

As for philosophy, so far as the question of woman is concerned—and it comes down to the question of sexual difference—this is indeed what has to be brought into question. Unless we are to agree naively—or perhaps strategically—to limit ourselves to some narrow sphere, some marginal area that would leave intact the discourse that lays down the law to all the others: philosophical discourse. The philosophical order is indeed the one that has to be questioned, and *disturbed*, inasmuch as it covers over sexual difference. . . .

What is the signification of this gesture with respect to everything that may be called today, on whatever basis, a "women's liberation movement"? Why is this separatist breaking away of "women-among-themselves"?

The signification of this gesture with respect to women's liberation movements? Let's say that at first glance it may look like a breaking away, as you put it. This would mean that the empirical fact of remaining always and only among women would be necessary and even sufficient to put one on the side of "women's liberation," politically. . . . But wouldn't it still be maintaining an idealist logic to pose the alternative in those terms: women either function alongside men, where they will be no more than objects, images, ideas, aspects of a feeling-matter appropriated by and for men, or else— but isn't this "or else" in danger of amounting finally to the same thing?—women remain among themselves. Which is not to say that they have no compelling need to do this. As a political tactic in particular. Women—as the stakes of private property, of appropriation by and for discourse—have always been put in a position of mutual rivalry. So to make their own efforts more effective, they have had to constitute a place where they could be "among themselves." A place for individual and collective "consciousness-raising" concerning the specific oppression of women, a place where the desire of women by and for each other could be recognized, a place for them to regroup. But, for me, that place is in danger of becoming a utopia of historical reversal, a dream of reappropriation of power—particularly phallic power—by women if it closes itself in on the circle of its demands and even desires. And besides, it would just be copying the society of men among themselves, with women remaining once again in the role assigned to them. Except that women could do without men while they are elaborating their own society?

So the "breaking away" of which you speak—and which, for me, is not one—seems strategically necessary, too, for two reasons at least (1) Women cannot work on the question of their own oppression without an analysis and even an experience of institutions—institutions governed by men. (2) What poses a problem—a fundamental one?—for the feminine, hence the necessity and usefulness of this angle of approach, is the operation of discursive logic. For example, in its oppositions, its schisms, between empirical and transcendental, perceptible and intelligible, matter and idea, and so on. That hierarchical structure has always put the feminine in a position of inferiority, of exploitation, of exclusion with respect to language. But, in the same stroke, as it were, it has confirmed the impracticable character of the sexual relation. For this relation boils down to man's self-affection mediated by the feminine, which he has appropriated into his language. The reciprocal not being "true." Thus it is necessary to turn again to this "proper" character of language, analyzing it not only in its dual movement of appropriation and disappropriation with respect to the masculine subject alone, but also in what remains mute, and deprived of any possibility of "self-affection," of "self-representation," for the feminine. If the only response to men-among-themselves is women-among-themselves, whatever subtends the functioning of the logic of presence, of

being, of property—and thus maintains the effacement of the difference between the sexes—is very likely to perpetuate and even reinforce itself. Rather than maintaining the masculine-feminine opposition, it would be appropriate to seek a possibility of *nonhierarchical* articulation of that difference in language. This explains what you call the breaking away of "women-among-themselves"; such a break is equally necessary where "men-among-themselves" are concerned, even though it is more difficult to bring about, since that state of affairs underlies the contemporary forms of their power.

One cannot fail to have at least a sense that your first concern is to avoid a naive positioning of "the question of women." One that would be, for example, a pure and simple reversal of the masculine positioning of the question (a pure and simple reversal of "phallogocentrism," and so forth).

To this question I think I have in fact already replied, both in answering the preceding questions and in writing *Speculum*. Which is obviously not a book *about* woman; and it is still less—whatever one may think about it, or even project from it as a hope for the reversal of values—a "studied gynecocentrism," a "place of the monopolization of the symbolic" to the benefit of a woman, or of some women. Such naive judgments overlook the fact that from a feminine locus nothing can be articulated without a questioning of the symbolic itself. But we do not escape so easily from reversal. We do not escape, in particular, by thinking we can dispense with a rigorous interpretation of phallogocentrism. There is no simple manageable way to leap to the outside of phallogocentrism, *nor any possible way to situate oneself there, that would result from the simple fact of being a woman.* And in *Speculum*, if I was attempting to move back through the "masculine" imaginary, that is, our cultural imaginary, it is because that move imposed itself, both in order to demarcate the possible "outside" of this imaginary and to allow me to situate myself with respect to it as a woman, implicated in it and at the same time exceeding its limits. But I see this excess, of course, as what makes the sexual relation possible, and not as a reversal of phallic power. And my "first" reaction to this excess is to laugh. Isn't laughter the first form of liberation from a secular oppression? *Isn't the phallic tantamount to the seriousness of meaning?* Perhaps woman, and the sexual relation, transcend it "first" in laughter?

Besides, women among themselves begin by laughing. To escape from a pure and simple reversal of the masculine position means in any case not to forget to laugh. Not to forget that the dimension of desire, of pleasure, is untranslatable, unrepresentable, irrecuperable, in the "seriousness"—the adequacy, the univocity, the truth . . .—of a discourse that claims to state its meaning. Whether it is produced by men or women. Which is not to assert that one has to give in to saying just anything at all, but that *speaking the truth constitutes the prohibition on woman's pleasure, and thus on the sexual relation.* The covering-up of its forcefulness, of force itself, under the lawmaking power of discourse. Moreover, it is right here that the most virulent issue at stake in the oppression of women is located today: men want to hold onto the initiative of discourse about sexual pleasure, and thus also about *her* pleasure.

Can you say something about your work in relation to the women's liberation movement?

Before attempting to answer your question, I should like to clarify two things:

—First, that I can't tell you what is happening in the liberation movement. Even granting that I might wish to answer your question, what is happening in the women's liberation movement cannot simply be surveyed, described, related "from the outside."

—Second, that I prefer to speak, in the plural, of women's liberation movements. In fact, there are multiple groups and tendencies in women's struggles today, and to reduce them to a single movement involves a risk of introducing phenomena of hierarchization, claims of orthodoxy, and so on.

To come back to my work: I am trying, as I have already indicated, to go back through the masculine imaginary, to interpret the way it has reduced us to silence, to muteness or mimicry, and I am attempting, from that starting-point and at the same time, to (re)discover a possible space for the feminine imaginary.

But it is obviously not simply an "individual" task. A long history has put all women in the same sexual, social, and cultural condition. Whatever inequalities may exist among women, they all undergo, even without clearly realizing it, the same oppression, the same exploitation of their body, the same denial of their desire.

That is why it is very important for women to be able to join together, and to join together "among themselves." In order to begin to escape from the spaces, roles, and gestures that they have been assigned and taught by the society of men. In order to love each other, even though men have organized a *de facto* rivalry among women. In order to discover a form of "social existence" other than the one that has always been imposed upon them. The first issue facing liberation movements is that of making each woman "conscious" of the fact that what she has felt in her personal experience is a condition shared by all women, thus *allowing that experience to be politicized.*

But what does "political" mean, here? No "women's politics" exists, not yet, at least not in the broad sense. And, if such a politics comes into existence one of these days, it will be very different from the politics instituted by men. For the questions raised by the exploitation of women's bodies exceed the stakes, the schemas, and of course the "parties" of the politics known and practiced up to now. Obviously, that does not prevent political parties from wanting to "co-opt" the woman question by granting women a place in their ranks, with the aim of aligning them—one more time . . .—with their "programs," which, most of the time, have nothing to do with them, in the sense that these programs fail to take into consideration the *specific exploitation* of women. For the exploitation of women does not constitute a *limited* question, within politics, one which would concern only a "sector" of the population, or a "part" of the "body politic." When women want to escape from exploitation, they do not merely destroy a few "prejudices," they disrupt the entire order of dominant values, economic, social, moral, and sexual. They call into question all existing theory, all thought, all language, inasmuch as these are monopolized by men and men alone. They challenge *the very foundation of our social and cultural order*, whose organization has been prescribed by the patriarchal system.

The patriarchal foundation of our social existence is in fact overlooked in contemporary politics, even leftist politics. Up to now *even Marxism has paid very little attention to the problems of the specific exploitation of women, and women's struggles most often seem to disturb the Marxists.* Even though these struggles could be interpreted with the help of the schemas for the analysis of social exploitation to which Marxist political programs lay specific claim. Provided, of course, that these schemas be used differently. But no politics has, up to now, questioned its own relation to phallocratic power . . .

In concrete terms, that means that women must of course continue to struggle for equal wages and social rights, against discrimination in employment and education, and so forth. But that is not enough: women merely "equal" to men would be "like them," therefore not women. Once more, the difference between the sexes would be in that way canceled out, ignored, papered over. So it is essential for women among themselves to invent new modes of organization, new forms of struggle, new challenges. The various liberation movements have already begun to do this, and a "women's international" is beginning to take shape. But here too, innovation is necessary: institutions, hierarchy, and authority—that is, the existing forms of politics—are men's affairs. Not ours.

That explains certain difficulties encountered by the liberation movements. If women allow themselves to be caught in the trap of power, in the game of authority, if they allow themselves to be contaminated by the "paranoid" operations of masculine politics, they have nothing more to say or do *as women*. That is why one of the tasks in France today is to try to regroup the movement's various tendencies around a certain number of specific themes and actions: rape, abortion, the challenge to the prerogative of the father's name in the case of juridical decisions that determine "to whom children belong," the full-fledged participation of women in legislative decisions and actions, and so on. And yet all that must never disguise the fact that it is in order to bring their difference to light that women are demanding their rights.

For my part, I refuse to let myself be locked into a single "group" within the women's liberation movement. Especially if such a group becomes ensnared in the exercise of power, if it purports to determine the "truth" of the feminine, to legislate as to what it means to "be a woman," and to condemn women who might have immediate objectives that differ from theirs. I think the most important thing to do is to expose the exploitation common to all women and to find the struggles that are appropriate for each woman, right where she is, depending upon her nationality, her job, her social class, her sexual experience, that is, upon the form of oppression that is for her the most immediately unbearable.

Ecological Feminism

More than any other school of feminist thought, ecofeminism strives to show the connections between the myriad forms of oppression, rooting them all in human beings' efforts to control nature. Ecological feminists or ecofeminists claim that the dualism between nature and culture, the separation of the biological ("animal") world from the social ("human") world, the splits between men and women, and the cross-cultural association of women with nature, reproduction, matter, and otherness, and of men with culture, production, form, and selfhood, are all part of the same western patriarchal ideology that has been used to justify the degrading and raping of both nature and women.

Although ecofeminists are amazingly diverse, most of them fall into one of two broad categories. So-called social-constructionist ecofeminists see the association of women with nature and men with culture as the origin of both men's subordination of women and human beings' exploitation of nature. They claim that the dualistic ideology that supports patriarchy is so powerful that *women* as well as men believe that women belong in the private realm, there to rear the children they have birthed, whereas men belong in the public realm, there to work productively and creatively to shape society, first with their hands and minds and later with their machines and computers. The challenge for social-constructionist feminists, among whom Karen Warren stands, is, then, to disengage women from *limiting* associations with nature and reproduction without demeaning nature as inferior to culture or reproduction as less valuable than production.

In "The Power and the Promise of Ecological Feminism," Warren argues that:

(1) Feminism is a movement to end sexism.
(2) But sexism is conceptually linked with naturism (through an oppressive conceptual framework characterized by a logic of domination).
(3) Thus, feminism is (also) a movement to end naturism (p. 457).

Claiming that the nature/culture dichotomy as well as the woman/man hierarchy must be destroyed does not in Warren's estimation entail our denying the differences between nature and culture on the one hand or women and men on the other. Just because all human beings are rational/emotional, mind/body wholes does not mean that there are no differences between men and women or between human beings, animals, and plants. To recognize difference is not to insist that any one way of being is better than or superior to any other way of being. It is, however, to suggest that, depending on their capacities for deliberation, some members of the ecological community should assume primary responsibility for coordinating its complex interrelationships. Their role will be to enable less deliberate members of the ecological community to perform their "tasks"—i.e., to be respectfully used for the good of the entire ecosystem.

In contrast to social-constructionist feminists, so-called nature ecofeminists believe that women have special qualities stemming from their biological connection to the natural processes of reproduction. Instead of denying their connections to nature, women should celebrate them, adamantly insisting that nature not culture, reproduction not production, is the sine qua non for life. This view is espoused by ecofeminists like Marti Kheel, who believe that because of their natural, female experiences women tend to put a premium on relationships and particular individuals. They stress caring, nurturing, and emotions, and they strive to replace conflict and assertion of individual rights with cooperation and community.

Kheel contrasts what she terms "heroic ethics" with "holistic ethics," suggesting that the former is male, masculine, or masculinist and that the latter is female, feminine, or feminist. Practitioners of heroic ethics are well-intentioned. After all, they want to rescue women/nature: to stop the raping of women, the slaughter of animals, and the pollution of the environment. Armed with the instrument of reason, heroic ethicists propose to protect women and nature with the shield of a rational ethics.

They promise to determine which members of the ecosystem have (don't have) interests and rights, and to take care of the ones that do.

As Kheel sees it, however, heroic ethics is part of the problem, not part of the solution. It is as male, masculine, or masculinist as the patriarchal culture that produced it. It needs, she says, to be replaced by the kind of female, feminine, or feminist ethics that looks at the ecosystem holistically—one that uses the emotions to help the diverse members of the ecosystem harmonize. Holistic ethics uses sense and sensibility to fill in the blanks that rational argumentation leaves empty; it tells the whole moral story. For example, if a person is debating whether or not it is wrong to kill animals for *unnecessary* meat consumption, she should spend the day touring a slaughterhouse rather than reading a treatise on animal rights.

The Power and the Promise of Ecological Feminism

Karen J. Warren

INTRODUCTION

Ecological feminism (ecofeminism) has begun to receive a fair amount of attention lately as an alternative feminism and environmental ethic. Since Francoise d'Eaubonne introduced the term *ecofeminisme* in 1974 to bring attention to women's potential for bringing about an ecological revolution, the term has been used in a variety of ways. As I use the term in this paper, ecological feminism is the position that there

From *Environmental Ethics* 12 (1990): 125–46. Reprinted by permission of Karen Warren.

are important connections—historical, experiential, symbolic, theoretical—between the domination of women and the domination of nature, an understanding of which is crucial to both feminism and environmental ethics. I argue that the promise and power of ecological feminism is that *it provides a distinctive framework both for reconceiving feminism and for developing an environmental ethic which takes seriously connections between the domination of women and the domination of nature.* I do so by discussing the nature of a feminist ethic and the ways in which ecofeminism provides a feminist and environmental ethic. I conclude that any feminist theory *and* any environmental ethic which fails to take seriously the twin and interconnected dominations of women and nature is at best incomplete and at worst simply inadequate.

FEMINISM, ECOLOGICAL FEMINISM, AND CONCEPTUAL FRAMEWORKS

Whatever else it is, feminism is at least the movement to end sexist oppression. It involves the elimination of any and all factors that contribute to the continued and systematic domination or subordination of women. While feminists disagree about the nature of and solutions to the subordination of women, all feminists agree that sexist oppression exists, is wrong, and must be abolished.

A "feminist issue" is any issue that contributes in some way to understanding the oppression of women. Equal rights, comparable pay for comparable work, and food production are feminist issues wherever and whenever an understanding of them contributes to an understanding of the continued exploitation or subjugation of women. Carrying water and searching for firewood are feminist issues wherever and whenever women's primary responsibility for these tasks contributes to their lack of full participation in decision making, income producing, or high status positions engaged in by men. What counts as a feminist issue, then, depends largely on context, particularly the historical and material conditions of women's lives.

Environmental degradation and exploitation are feminist issues because an understanding of them contributes to an understanding of the oppression of women. In India, for example, both deforestation and reforestation through the introduction of a monoculture species tree (e.g., eucalyptus) intended for commercial production are feminist issues because the loss of indigenous forests and multiple species of trees has drastically affected rural

Indian women's ability to maintain a subsistence household. Indigenous forests provide a variety of trees for food, fuel, fodder, household utensils, dyes, medicines, and income-generating uses, while monoculture-species forests do not. Although I do not argue for this claim here, a look at the global impact of environmental degradation on women's lives suggests important respects in which environmental degradation is a feminist issue.

Feminist philosophers claim that some of the most important feminist issues are *conceptual* ones: these issues concern how one conceptualizes such mainstay philosophical notions as reason and rationality, ethics, and what it is to be human. Ecofeminists extend this feminist philosophical concern to nature. They argue that, ultimately, some of the most important connections between the domination of women and the domination of nature are conceptual. To see this, consider the nature of conceptual frameworks.

A *conceptual framework* is a set of *basic* beliefs, values, attitudes, and assumptions which shape and reflect how one views oneself and one's world. It is a socially constructed lens through which we perceive ourselves and others. It is affected by such factors as gender, race, class, age, affectional orientation, nationality, and religious background.

Some conceptual frameworks are oppressive. An *oppressive conceptual framework* is one that explains, justifies, and maintains relationships of domination and subordination. When an oppressive conceptual framework is *patriarchal*, it explains, justifies, and maintains the subordination of women by men.

I have argued elsewhere that there are three significant features of oppressive conceptual frameworks: (1) value-hierarchical thinking, i.e., "up-down" thinking which places higher value, status, or prestige on what is "up" rather than on what is "down"; (2) value dualisms, i.e., disjunctive pairs in which the disjuncts are seen as oppositional (rather than as complementary) and exclusive (rather than as inclusive), and which place higher value (status, prestige) on one disjunct rather than the other (e.g., dualisms which give higher value or status to that which has historically been identified as "mind," "reason," and "male" than to that which has historically been identified as "body," "emotion," and "female"); and (3) logic of domination, i.e., a structure of argumentation which leads to a justification of subordination.

The third feature of oppressive conceptual frameworks is the most significant. A logic of domination is not *just* a logical structure. It also involves a substantive value system, since an ethical premise is needed to permit or sanction the "just" subordination of that which is subordinate. This justification typically is given on grounds of some alleged characteristic (e.g., rationality) which the dominant (e.g., men) have and the subordinate (e.g., women) lack.

Contrary to what many feminists and ecofeminists have said or suggested, there may be nothing *inherently* problematic about "hierarchical thinking" or even "value-hierarchical thinking" in contexts other than contexts of oppression. Hierarchical thinking is important in daily living for classifying data, comparing information, and organizing material. Taxonomies (e.g., plant taxonomies) and biological nomenclature seem to require *some* form of "hierarchical thinking." Even "value-hierarchical thinking" may be quite acceptable in certain contexts. (The same may be said of "value dualisms" in non-oppressive contexts.) For example, suppose it is true that what is unique about humans is our conscious capacity to radically reshape our social environments (or "societies"), as Murray Bookchin suggests. Then one could truthfully say that humans are better equipped to radically reshape their environments than are rocks or plants—a "value-hierarchical" way of speaking.

The problem is not simply *that* value-hierarchical thinking and value dualisms are used, but *the way* in which each has been used

in oppressive conceptual frameworks to establish inferiority and to justify subordination.[1] It is the logic of domination, *coupled* with value-hierarchical thinking and value dualisms, which "justifies" subordination. What is explanatorily basic, then, about the nature of oppressive conceptual frameworks is the logic of domination.

For ecofeminism, that a logic of domination is explanatorily basic is important for at least three reasons. First, without a logic of domination, a description of similarities and differences would be just that—a description of similarities and differences. Consider the claim, "Humans are different from plants and rocks in that humans can (and plants and rocks cannot) consciously and radically reshape the communities in which they live; humans are similar to plants and rocks in that they are both members of an ecological community." Even if humans are "better" than plants and rocks with respect to the conscious ability of humans to radically transform communities, one does not *thereby* get any *morally* relevant distinction between humans and nonhumans, or an argument for the domination of plants and rocks by humans. To get *those* conclusions one needs to add at least two powerful assumptions, viz., (A2) and (A4) in argument A below:

(A1)   Humans do, and plants and rocks do not, have the capacity to consciously and radically change the community in which they live.

(A2)   Whatever has the capacity to consciously and radically change the community in which it lives is morally superior to whatever lacks this capacity.

(A3)   Thus, humans are morally superior to plants and rocks.

(A4)   For any X and Y, if X is morally superior to Y, then X is morally justified in subordinating Y.

(A5)   Thus, humans are morally justified in subordinating plants and rocks.

Without the two assumptions that *humans are morally superior* to (at least some) nonhumans, (A2), and that *superiority justifies subordina-*

tion, (A4), all one has is some difference between humans and some nonhumans. This is true *even if* that difference is given in terms of superiority. Thus, it is the logic of domination, (A4), which is the bottom line in ecofeminist discussions of oppression.

Second, ecofeminists argue that, at least in Western societies, the oppressive conceptual framework which sanctions the twin dominations of women and nature is a patriarchal one characterized by all three features of an oppressive conceptual framework. Many ecofeminists claim that, historically, within at least the dominant Western culture, a patriarchal conceptual framework has sanctioned the following argument B:

(B1)   Women are identified with nature and the realm of the physical; men are identified with the "human" and the realm of the mental.

(B2)   Whatever is identified with nature and the realm of the physical is inferior to ("below") whatever is identified with the "human" and the realm of the mental; or, conversely, the latter is superior to ("above") the former.

(B3)   Thus, women are inferior to ("below") men; or, conversely, men are superior to ("above") women.

(B4)   For any X and Y, if X is superior to Y, then X is justified in subordinating Y.

(B5)   Thus, men are justified in subordinating women.

If sound, argument B establishes *patriarchy*, i.e., the conclusion given at (B5) that the systematic domination of women by men is justified. But according to ecofeminists, (B5) is justified by just those three features of an oppressive conceptual framework identified earlier: value-hierarchical thinking, the assumption at (B2); value dualisms, the assumed dualism of the mental and the physical at (B1) and the assumed inferiority of the physical vis-à-vis the mental at (B2); and a logic of domination, the assumption at (B4), the same as the previous premise (A4). Hence, according to

ecofeminists, insofar as an oppressive patriarchal conceptual framework has functioned historically (within at least dominant Western culture) to sanction the twin dominations of women and nature (argument B), both argument B and the patriarchal conceptual framework, from whence it comes, ought to be rejected.

Of course, the preceding does not identify which premises of B are false. What is the status of premises (B1) and (B2)? Most, if not all, feminists claim that (B1), and many ecofeminists claim that (B2), have been assumed or asserted within the dominant Western philosophical and intellectual tradition.[2] As such, these feminists assert, as a matter of historical fact, that the dominant Western philosophical tradition has assumed the truth of (B1) and (B2). Ecofeminists, however, either deny (B2) or do not affirm (B2). Furthermore, because some ecofeminists are anxious to deny any historical identification of women with nature, some ecofeminists deny (B1) when (B1) is used to support anything other than a strictly historical claim about what has been asserted or assumed to be true within patriarchal culture— e.g., when (B1) is used to assert that women properly are identified with the realm of nature and the physical.[3] Thus, from an ecofeminist perspective, (B1) and (B2) are properly viewed as problematic though historically sanctioned claims: they are problematic precisely because of the way they have functioned historically in a patriarchal conceptual framework and culture to sanction the dominations of women and nature.

What *all* ecofeminists agree about, then, is the way in which *the logic of domination* has functioned historically within patriarchy to sustain and justify the twin dominations of women and nature.[4] Since *all* feminists (and not just ecofeminists) oppose patriarchy, the conclusion given at (B5), all feminists (including ecofeminists) must oppose at least the logic of domination, premise (B4), on which argument B rests—whatever the truth-value status of (B1) and (B2) *outside* of a patriarchal context.

That *all* feminists must oppose the logic of domination shows the breadth and depth of the ecofeminist critique of B: it is a critique not only of the three assumptions on which this argument for the domination of women and nature rests, viz., the assumptions at (B1), (B2), and (B4); it is also a critique of patriarchal conceptual frameworks generally, i.e., of those oppressive conceptual frameworks which put men "up" and women "down," allege some way in which women are morally inferior to men, and use that alleged difference to justify the subordination of women by men. Therefore, ecofeminism is necessary to *any* feminist critique of patriarchy, and, hence, necessary to feminism (a point I discuss again later).

Third, ecofeminism clarifies why the logic of domination, and any conceptual framework which gives rise to it, must be abolished in order both to make possible a meaningful notion of difference which does not breed domination and to prevent feminism from becoming a "support" movement based primarily on shared experiences. In contemporary society, there is no one "woman's voice," no *woman* (or *human*) *simpliciter*: every woman (or human) is a woman (or human) of some race, class, age, affectional orientation, marital status, regional or national background, and so forth. Because there are no "monolithic experiences" that all women share, feminism must be a "solidarity movement" based on shared beliefs and interests rather than a "unity in sameness" movement based on shared experiences and shared victimization. In the words of Maria Lugones, "Unity—not to be confused with solidarity—is understood as conceptually tied to domination."

Ecofeminists insist that the sort of logic of domination used to justify the domination of humans by gender, racial or ethnic, or class status is also used to justify the domination of nature. Because eliminating a logic of domination is part of a feminist critique—whether a critique of patriarchy, white supremacist culture, or imperialism—ecofeminists insist that *naturism* is properly viewed as an integral part of any feminist solidarity movement to end sexist oppression and the logic of domination which conceptually grounds it.

ECOFEMINISM RECONCEIVES FEMINISM

The discussion so far has focused on some of the oppressive conceptual features of patriarchy. As I use the phrase, the "logic of traditional feminism" refers to the location of the conceptual roots of sexist oppression, at least in Western societies, in an oppressive patriarchal conceptual framework characterized by a logic of domination. Insofar as other systems of oppression (e.g., racism, classism, ageism, heterosexism) are also conceptually maintained by a logic of domination, appeal to the logic of traditional feminism ultimately locates the basic conceptual interconnections among *all* systems of oppression in the logic of domination. It thereby explains at a *conceptual* level why the eradication of sexist oppression requires the eradication of the other forms of oppression. It is by clarifying this conceptual connection between systems of oppression that a movement to end sexist oppression—traditionally the special turf of feminist theory and practice—leads to a reconceiving of feminism as *a movement to end all forms of oppression.*

Suppose one agrees that the logic of traditional feminism requires the expansion of feminism to include other social systems of domination (e.g., racism and classism). What warrants the inclusion of nature in these "social systems of domination"? Why must the logic of traditional feminism include the abolition of "naturism" (i.e., the domination or oppression of nonhuman nature) among the "isms" feminism must confront? The conceptual justification for expanding feminism to include ecofeminism is twofold. One basis has already been suggested: by showing that the conceptual connections between the dual dominations of women and nature are located in an oppressive and, at least in Western societies, patriarchal conceptual framework characterized by a logic of domination, ecofeminism explains how and why feminism, conceived as a movement to end sexist oppression, must be expanded and reconceived as also a movement to end naturism. This is made explicit by the following argument C:

(C1)   Feminism is a movement to end sexism.
(C2)   But Sexism is conceptually linked with naturism (through an oppressive conceptual framework characterized by a logic of domination).
(C3)   Thus, Feminism is (also) a movement to end naturism.

Because, ultimately, these connections between sexism and naturism are conceptual—embedded in an oppressive conceptual framework—the logic of traditional feminism leads to the embracement of ecological feminism.

The other justification for reconceiving feminism to include ecofeminism has to do with the concepts of gender and nature. Just as conceptions of gender are socially constructed, so are conceptions of nature. Of course, the claim that women and nature are social constructions does not require anyone to deny that there are actual humans and actual trees, rivers, and plants. It simply implies that *how* women and nature are conceived is a matter of historical and social reality. These conceptions vary cross-culturally and by historical time period. As a result, any discussion of the "oppression or domination of nature" involves reference to historically specific forms of social domination of nonhuman nature by humans, just as discussion of the "domination of women" refers to historically specific forms of social domination of women by men. Although I do not argue for it here, an ecofeminist defense of the historical connections between the dominations of women and of nature, claims (B1) and (B2) in argument B,

involves showing that within patriarchy the feminization of nature and the naturalization of women have been crucial to the historically successful subordinations of both.

If ecofeminism promises to reconceive traditional feminism in ways which include naturism as a legitimate feminist issue, does ecofeminism also promise to reconceive environmental ethics in ways which are feminist? I think so. This is the subject of the remainder of the paper.

CLIMBING FROM ECOFEMINISM TO ENVIRONMENTAL ETHICS

Many feminists and some environmental ethicists have begun to explore the use of first-person narrative as a way of raising philosophically germane issues in ethics often lost or underplayed in mainstream philosophical ethics. Why is this so? What is it about narrative which makes it a significant resource for theory and practice in feminism and environmental ethics? Even if appeal to first-person narrative is a helpful literary device for describing ineffable experience or a legitimate social science methodology for documenting personal and social history, how is first-person narrative a valuable vehicle of argumentation for ethical decision making and theory building? One fruitful way to begin answering these questions is to ask them of a particular first-person narrative.

Consider the following first-person narrative about rock climbing:

For my very first rock climbing experience, I chose a somewhat private spot, away from other climbers and on-lookers. After studying "the chimney," I focused all my energy on making it to the top. I climbed with intense determination, using whatever strength and skills I had to accomplish this challenging feat. By midway I was exhausted and anxious. I couldn't see what to do next—where to put my hands or feet. Growing increasingly more weary as I clung somewhat desperately to the rock, I made a move. It didn't work. I fell. There I was, dangling midair above the rocky ground below, frightened but terribly relieved that the belay rope had held me. I knew I was safe. I took a look up at the climb that remained. I was determined to make it to the top. With renewed confidence and concentration, I finished the climb to the top.

On my second day of climbing, I rappelled down about 200 feet from the top of the Palisades at Lake Superior to just a few feet above the water level. I could see no one—not my belayer, not the other climbers, no one. I unhooked slowly from the rappel rope and took a deep cleansing breath. I looked all around me—really looked—and listened. I heard a cacophony of voices—birds, trickles of water on the rock before me, waves lapping against the rocks below. I closed my eyes and began to feel the rock with my hands—the cracks and crannies, the raised lichen and mosses, the almost imperceptible nubs that might provide a resting place for my fingers and toes when I began to climb. At that moment I was bathed in serenity. I began to talk to the rock in an almost inaudible, child-like way, as if the rock were my friend. I felt an overwhelming sense of gratitude for what it offered me—a chance to know myself and the rock differently, to appreciate unforeseen miracles like the tiny flowers growing in the even tinier cracks in the rock's surface, and to come to know a sense of *being in relationship* with the natural environment. It felt as if the rock and I were silent conversational partners in a longstanding friendship. I realized then that I had come to care about this cliff which was so different from me, so unmovable and invincible, independent and seemingly indifferent to my presence. I wanted to be with the rock as I climbed. Gone was the determination to conquer the rock, to forcefully impose my will on it; I wanted simply to work respectfully with the rock as I climbed. And as I climbed, that is what I felt. I felt myself *caring* for this rock and feeling thankful that climbing provided the opportunity for me to know it and myself in this new way.

There are at least four reasons why use of such a first-person narrative is important to feminism and environmental ethics. First, such a narrative gives voice to a felt sensitivity often lacking in traditional analytical ethical discourse, viz., a sensitivity to conceiving of oneself as fundamentally "in relationship with" others,

including the nonhuman environment. It is a modality which *takes relationships themselves seriously*. It thereby stands in contrast to a strictly reductionist modality that takes relationships seriously only or primarily because of the nature of the *relators* or parties to those relationships (e.g., relators conceived as moral agents, right holders, interest carriers, or sentient beings). In the rock-climbing narrative above, it is the climber's relationship with the rock she climbs which takes on special significance—which is itself a locus of value—in addition to whatever moral status or moral considerability she or the rock or any other parties to the relationship may also have.[5]

Second, such a first-person narrative gives expression to a variety of ethical attitudes and behaviors often overlooked or underplayed in mainstream Western ethics, e.g., the difference in attitudes and behaviors toward a rock when one is "making it to the top" and when one thinks of oneself as "friends with" or "caring about" the rock one climbs.[6] These different attitudes and behaviors suggest an ethically germane contrast between two different types of relationship humans or climbers may have toward a rock: an imposed conqueror-type relationship, and an emergent caring-type relationship. This contrast grows out of, and is faithful to, felt, lived experience.

The difference between conquering and caring attitudes and behaviors in relation to the natural environment provides a third reason why the use of first-person narrative is important to feminism and environmental ethics: it provides a way of conceiving of ethics and ethical meaning as *emerging out of* particular situations moral agents find themselves in, rather than as being *imposed on* those situations (e.g., as a derivation or instantiation of some predetermined abstract principle or rule). This emergent feature of narrative centralizes the importance of *voice*. When a multiplicity of cross-cultural *voices* are centralized, narrative is able to give expression to a range of attitudes, values, beliefs, and behaviors which may be overlooked or silenced by imposed ethical meaning and theory. As a reflection of and on felt, lived experiences, the use of narrative in ethics provides a stance from which ethical discourse can be held accountable to the historical, material, and social realities in which moral subjects find themselves.

Lastly, and for our purposes perhaps most importantly, the use of narrative has argumentative significance. Jim Cheney calls attention to this feature of narrative when he claims, "To contextualize ethical deliberation is, in some sense, to provide a narrative or story, from which the solution to the ethical dilemma emerges as the fitting conclusion." Narrative has argumentative force by suggesting *what counts* as an appropriate conclusion to an ethical situation. One ethical conclusion suggested by the climbing narrative is that what counts as a proper ethical attitude toward mountains and rocks is an attitude of respect and care (whatever that turns out to be or involve), not one of domination and conquest.

In an essay entitled "In and Out of Harm's Way: Arrogance and Love," feminist philosopher Marilyn Frye distinguishes between "arrogant" and "loving" perception as one way of getting at this difference in the ethical attitudes of care and conquest. Frye writes:

The loving eye is a contrary of the arrogant eye.

The loving eye knows the independence of the other. It is the eye of a seer who knows that nature is indifferent. It is the eye of one who knows that to know the seen, one must consult something other than one's own will and interests and fears and imagination. One must look at the thing. One must look and listen and check and question.

The loving eye is one that pays a certain sort of attention. This attention can require a discipline but *not* a self-denial. The discipline is one of self-knowledge, knowledge of the scope and boundary of the self. . . . In particular, it is a matter of being able to tell one's own interests from those of others and of knowing where one's self leaves off and another begins. . . .

The loving eye does not make the object of perception into something edible, does not try to assimilate it, does not reduce it to the size of the seer's desire, fear and imagination, and hence does not have to simplify. It knows the complexity of the other as something which will forever present new things to be known. The science of the loving eye would favor The Complexity Theory of Truth [in contrast to The Simplicity Theory of Truth] and presuppose The Endless Interestingness of the Universe.

According to Frye, the loving eye is not an invasive, coercive eye which annexes others to itself, but one which "knows the complexity of the other as something which will forever present new things to be known."

When one climbs a rock as a conqueror, one climbs with an arrogant eye. When one climbs with a loving eye, one constantly "must look and listen and check and question." One recognizes the rock as something very different, something perhaps totally indifferent to one's own presence, and finds in that difference joyous occasion for celebration. One knows "the boundary of the self," where the self—the "I," the climber—leaves off and the rock begins. There is no fusion of two into one, but a complement of two entities *acknowledged* as separate, different, independent, yet *in relationship*; they are in relationship *if only* because the loving eye is perceiving it, responding to it, noticing it, attending to it.

An ecofeminist perspective about both women and nature involves this shift in attitude from "arrogant perception" to "loving perception" of the nonhuman world. Arrogant perception of nonhumans by humans presupposes and maintains *sameness* in such a way that it expands the moral community to those beings who are thought to resemble (be like, similar to, or the same as) humans in some morally significant way. Any environmental movement or ethic based on arrogant perception builds a moral hierarchy of beings and assumes some common denominator of moral considerability in virtue of which like beings deserve similar treatment or moral consideration and unlike beings do not. Such environmental ethics are or generate a "unity in sameness." In contrast, "loving perception" presupposes and maintains *difference*—a distinction between the self and other, between human and at least some non-humans—in such a way that perception of the other as other *is* an expression of love for one who/which is recognized at the outset as independent, dissimilar, different. As Maria Lugones says, in loving perception, "Love is seen not as fusion and erasure of difference but as incompatible with them." "Unity in sameness" alone is an *erasure of difference*.

"Loving perception" of the nonhuman natural world is an attempt to understand what it means *for humans* to care about the nonhuman world, a world *acknowledged* as being independent, different, perhaps even indifferent to humans. Humans *are* different from rocks in important ways, even if they are also both members of some ecological community. A moral community based on loving perception of oneself *in relationship with* a rock, or with the natural environment as a whole, is one which acknowledges and respects difference, whatever "sameness" also exists. The limits of loving perception are determined only by the limits of one's (e.g., a person's, a community's) ability to respond lovingly (or with appropriate care, trust, or friendship)—whether it is to other humans or to the nonhuman world and elements of it.

If what I have said so far is correct, then there are very different ways to climb a mountain and *how* one climbs it and *how* one narrates the experience of climbing it matter ethically. If one climbs with "arrogant perception," with an attitude of "conquer and control," one keeps intact the very sorts of thinking that characterize a logic of domination and an oppressive conceptual framework. Since the oppressive conceptual framework which sanctions the domination of nature is a patriarchal one, one also thereby keeps intact, even if unwittingly, a patriarchal conceptual framework. Because the dismantling of patriarchal conceptual frameworks is a feminist issue, *how* one climbs

a mountain and *how* one narrates—or tells the story—about the experience of climbing also are *feminist issues*. In this way, ecofeminism makes visible why, at a conceptual level, environmental ethics is a feminist issue.

CONCLUSION

I have argued in this paper that ecofeminism provides a framework for a distinctively feminist and environmental ethic. Ecofeminism grows out of the felt and theorized about connections between the domination of women and the domination of nature. As a contextualist ethic, ecofeminism refocuses environmental ethics on what nature might mean, morally speaking, *for* humans, and on how the relational attitudes of humans to others—humans as well as nonhumans—sculpt both what it is to be human and the nature and ground of human responsibilities to the nonhuman environment. Part of what this refocusing does is to take seriously the voices of women and other oppressed persons in the construction of that ethic.

A Sioux elder once told me a story about his son. He sent his seven-year-old son to live with the child's grandparents on a Sioux reservation so that he could "learn the Indian ways." Part of what the grandparents taught the son was how to hunt the four-leggeds of the forest. As I heard the story, the boy was taught, "to shoot your four-legged brother in his hind area, slowing it down but not killing it. Then, take the four legged's head in your hands, and look into his eyes. The eyes are where all the suffering is. Look into your brother's eyes and feel his pain. Then, take your knife and cut the four-legged under his chin, here, on his neck, so that he dies quickly. And as you do, ask your brother, the four-legged, for forgiveness for what you do. Offer also a prayer of thanks to your four-legged kin for offering his body to you just now, when you need food to eat and clothing to wear. And promise the four-legged that you will put yourself back into the earth when you die, to become nourishment for the earth, and for the sister flowers, and for the brother deer. It is appropriate that you should offer this blessing for the four-legged and, in due time, reciprocate in turn with your body in this way, as the four-legged gives life to you for your survival." As I reflect upon that story, I am struck by the power of the environmental ethic that grows out of and takes seriously narrative, context, and such values and relational attitudes as care, loving perception, and appropriate reciprocity, and doing what is appropriate in a given situation—however that notion of appropriateness eventually gets filled out. I am also struck by what one is able to see, once one begins to explore some of the historical and conceptual connections between the dominations of women and of nature. A *reconceiving* and *re-visioning* of both feminism and environmental ethics, is, I think, the power and promise of ecofeminism.

NOTES

1. It may be that in contemporary Western society, which is so thoroughly structured by categories of gender, race, class, age, and affectional orientation, there simply is no meaningful notion of "value-hierarchical thinking" which does not function in an oppressive context. For purposes of this paper, I leave that question open.

2. Many feminists who argue for the historical point that claims (B1) and (B2) have been asserted or assumed to be true within the dominant Western philosophical tradition do so by discussion of that tradition's conceptions of reason, rationality, and science. For a sampling of the sorts of claims made within that context, see "Reason, Rationality, and Gender," ed. Nancy Tuana and Karen J. Warren, a special issue of the American Philosophical Association's *Newsletter on Feminism and Philosophy* 88, no. 2 (March 1989): 17–71. Ecofeminists who claim that (B2) has been assumed to be true within the dominant Western philosophical tradition include: Gray, *Green Paradise Lost*; Griffin, *Woman and Nature: The Roaring Inside Her*; Merchant, *The Death of Nature*; Ruether, *New Woman/New Earth*. For a discussion of

some of these ecofeminist historical accounts, see Plumwood, "Ecofeminism." While I agree that the historical connections between the domination of women and the domination of nature is a crucial one, I do not argue for that claim here.

3. Ecofeminists who deny (B1) when (B1) is offered as anything other than a true, descriptive, historical claim about patriarchal culture often do so on grounds that an objectionable sort of biological determinism, or at least harmful female sex-gender stereotypes, underlie (B1). For a discussion of this "split" among those ecofeminists ("nature feminists") who assert and those ecofeminists ("social feminists") who deny (B1) as anything other than a true historical claim about how women are described in patriarchal culture, see Griscom, "On Healing the Nature/History Split."

4. I make no attempt here to defend the historically sanctioned truth of these premises.

5. Suppose, as I think is the case, that a necessary condition for the existence of a moral relationship is that at least one party to the relationship is a moral being (leaving open for our purposes what counts as a "moral being"). If this is so, then the Mona Lisa cannot properly be said to have or stand in a moral relationship with the wall on which she hangs, and a wolf cannot have or properly be said to have or stand in a moral relationship with a moose. Such a necessary-condition account leaves open the question whether *both* parties to the relationship must be moral beings. My point here is simply that however one resolves *that* question, recognition of the relationships themselves as a locus of value is a recognition of a source of value that is different from and not reducible to the values of the "moral beings" in those relationships.

6. It is interesting to note that the image of being friends with the Earth is one which cytogeneticist Barbara McClintock uses when she describes the importance of having "a feeling for the organism," "listening to the material [in this case the corn plant]," in one's work as a scientist. See Evelyn Fox Keller, "Women, Science, and Popular Mythology," in *Machina Ex Dea: Feminist Perspectives on Technology*, ed. Joan Rothschild (New York: Pergamon Press, 1983), and Evelyn Fox Keller, *A Feeling For the Organism: The Life and Work of Barbara McClintock* (San Francisco: W. H. Freeman, 1983).

From Heroic to Holistic Ethics: The Ecofeminist Challenge

Marti Kheel

As the destruction of the natural world proceeds at breakneck speed, nature ethicists have found themselves in search of a theory that can serve to bring this destruction to a halt. Just as the prototypical hero in patriarchal stories must rescue the proverbial "damsel in distress," so, too, the sought-after theory must demonstrate heroic qualities. It must, singlehandedly, rescue the ailing body of "Mother Nature" from the villains who have bound and subdued her. The theoretical underpinnings of environmental and animal liberation philosophies are seen by many ethical theorists as having the necessary "intellectual muscle" to perform this heroic feat. But is a heroic ethic a helpful response to the domination of nature, or is it another conqueror in a new disguise?

It is significant that ecofeminists have, by and large, declined to join the "hunt" for an environmental ethic or "savior theory." The writings within ecofeminism have largely ignored the heated debates engaged in by (predominantly) male philosophers over what should constitute the basis of an appropriate ethic for the natural world. A glance at the vast majority of ecofeminist writings reveals, instead, a tendency to concentrate on exposing the underlying mentality of exploitation that is directed against women and nature within the patriarchal world. Whereas nature ethicists have tended to concentrate on "rescuing" the "damsel in distress," ecofeminists have been more likely to ask how and why the "damsel" arrived at her present plight.

Clearly ecofeminists have taken a different approach to the current crisis in nature. No single theory is sought or expected to emerge, through reasoned competition with the others, as the most powerful or compelling one. In fact, no single ethical theory seems to be sought at all. What have been emerging, rather, are a number of theories or stories that, when woven together into a fabric or tapestry, help to provide a picture or "portrait" of the world in which we currently live. Whereas mainstream nature ethicists have based much of their analysis on abstract principles and universal rules, ecofeminists have tended to highlight the role of metaphors and images of nature. The emphasis has been not on developing razor-sharp theories that can be used to dictate future conduct, but rather on painting a "landscape" (or "mindscape") of the world.

This is not to say that ecofeminists have merely described our current problems, showing no interest in changing the world. On the contrary, ecofeminists have been deeply committed to social transformation. The method of transformation that ecofeminists have subscribed to, however, is premised on the insight that one cannot change what one does not understand. Understanding the inner workings of patriarchal society is emphasized precisely so that society might be transformed. The transformation that ecofeminists wish to bring about is, thus, often implicit in their critiques. If the images of women and nature under patriarchal society have facilitated the exploitation and abuse of both, then, clearly, new ways of perceiving the world must be sought. The natural world will be "saved" not by the sword of ethical theory, but rather through a transformed consciousness toward all of life.

The emphasis on developing new ways of perceiving the world is in keeping with much of the recent work in feminist moral theory. Feminist moral theorists have begun to show that ethics is not so much the imposition of obligations and rights, but rather a natural outgrowth of how one views the self, including one's relation to the rest of the world. Before one can change the current destructive relation to nature, we must, therefore, understand the world view upon which this relation rests. Just as a health-care practitioner would not attempt to treat an illness without understanding the nature and history of the disease, many feminists would argue that it is not possible to transform the current world view of patriarchy without understanding the disease that has infected the patriarchal mind. What, then, is the world view that patriarchy has bequeathed us?

THE CONQUEST OF NATURE: THE DAMSEL IS DISTRESSED

The predominant image of nature throughout the Western, patriarchal world has been that of an alien force. Nature, which has been imaged as female, has been depicted as the "other," the raw material out of which culture and masculine self-identity are formed. Two major images have been used to achieve separation from nature. One of the most common images has been that of the Beast. The Beast is conceived as a symbol for all that is not human, for that which is evil, irrational, and wild. Civilization is thus achieved by driving out or killing the Beast. On an inward level, this involves driving

out all vestiges of our own animality—the attempt to obliterate the knowledge that we are animals ourselves. Outwardly, the triumph over the Beast has been enacted through the conquest of wilderness, with its concomitant claim to the lives of millions of animals driven from their lands.

The triumph over the demonic Beast has been a recurring theme throughout the mythologies of the patriarchal world. Typically, the slain Beast is a former divinity from the earlier matriarchal world. The serpents, dragons, and horned gods, who were at one time worshiped as divine, are transformed in patriarchal mythology into devils and monsters that must be slain. Thus, Apollo slays Gaia's python; Perseus kills the three-headed Medusa (the triple goddess), who is described as having snakes writhing from her head; Hercules defeats the terrible multiheaded Hydra; and the pharaohs of later Egypt slay the dragon Apophys. In the Middle Ages, there were countless renditions of St. George's prowess in killing the dragon—again, to rescue the "damsel in distress."

Frequently the death of the Beast is said to herald the birth of light and order, either at the beginning or the end of time. Thus, in the Sumero-Babylonian *Epic of Gilgamesh*, Marduk kills his mother, the goddess Tiamat, the great whale-dragon or cosmic serpent, and from her body the universe is made. Both Judaism and Christianity continue the dragon-slaying tradition. According to St. John the Divine, at the world's end an angel with a key will subdue the dragon that is Satan. And in the Hebrew legend, the death of the serpentlike Leviathan is prophesied for the Day of Judgment. In Christianity, the task of killing the dragonlike monster was transferred from gods and heroes to saints and archangels. The archangel Michael was a notable dragon-slayer. Faith, prayer, and divine intervention came to be seen as the new dragon-slayers whose task it is to restore the world of order.

These myths of violence and conquest contrast sharply with the mythologies of prepatriarchal cultures. The cosmological stories of these societies typically depicted the beginning of life as emerging from a female-imaged goddess who embodied the earth. Thus, Gaia, in the earliest Greek myths, was thought to give birth to the universe by herself. And the snake, so much feared in our current culture, was worshiped in such societies as divine. By the time of the biblical story of the Garden of Eden, a totally new world view had emerged. Both a woman and an animal were by this time depicted as the source of all evil in the world. And "Man," above all other forms of life, was claimed to have a special relation to the divine.

Today, the heroic battle against unruly nature is reenacted as ritual drama in such masculine ventures as sport-hunting, bullfights, and rodeos. A similar mentality can be seen in the ritual degradation of women in pornography and rape. As Susan Griffin points out, pornography is ritual drama. It is the heroic struggle of the masculine ego to deny the knowledge of bodily feelings and one's dependence upon women and all of the natural world.

The second image of nature appears less heroic but is equally violent in its own way. It is the image of nature as mindless matter, which exists to serve the needs of superior, rational "Man." In this image, animals are depicted as having different, unequal natures rather than as wild or evil creatures that must be conquered and subdued. They are not so much irrational as nonrational beings. Along with women, they are viewed as mere "matter" (a word that, significantly, derives from the same root word as "mother").

Both Aristotelian and Platonic philosophy contributed to the conception of nature as inert or mindless matter. It was the Aristotelian notion of purpose and function, however, that especially helped to shape the Western world's instrumental treatment of women and nature. According to Aristotle, there was a natural hierarchical ordering to the world, within which each being moved toward fulfillment of its own particular end. Since the highest end of "Man" was the state of happiness achieved through rational contemplation, the rest of nature was conveniently ordered to free "Man" to attain this contemplative goal. Thus, plants existed to give subsistence to animals, and animals to give it to "Man"; and the specific function of women, animals, and slaves was to serve as instruments for the attainment of the highest happiness of free, adult men. There is no need to conquer nature in this conception, since nature has already been safely relegated to an inferior realm.

The Jewish-Christian tradition has also contributed to an instrumental and hierarchical conception of nature. The Genesis account of Creation must bear a large share of the guilt for this state of affairs. In the priestly account of the Genesis story of Creation, we are told that God gave "Man" "dominion over every living thing that moveth upon the earth" (Genesis 1:26). And in the Yahwist version, chronologically an earlier account, we are told that non-human animals were created by God to be helpers or companions for Adam, and when they were seen as unfit, Eve was created to fulfill this role (Genesis 2:22). Both stories, in their distinct ways, reinforce the notion that women and nature exist only for the purpose of serving "Man."

The conception of nature as an object for "Man's" use was carried to an ultimate extreme by Cartesian philosophy. According to Descartes, since animals were lacking in "consciousness" or "reason," they were mere machines that could feel no pain. Smashing the legs of a monkey, Descartes "reasoned," would hurt no more than removing the hands of a clock. With Cartesian philosophy, the wild, demonic aspect of nature was, thus, finally laid to rest, and the image of nature as a machine was born.

The image of nature (and women) as mindless objects is typically employed for more practical goals—profit, convenience, and knowledge. Division and control, not conquest, are the guiding motives; the rationality of the detached observer replaces the pleasure of conquest as the psychological mode. The use of animals in laboratories, factory farms, and fur ranches exemplifies this frame of mind, as does the image and use of women as "housewives" and "breeding machines." In the earlier (Beastly) image, nature is seen as a harlot; in this conception, nature is more like a slave or wife.

Although the two images of nature may seem unrelated, they merely represent different points along a single scale. In one image, nature is seen as a demonic being who must be conquered and subdued. In the other image, nature has been subdued to the point of death. Behind both images, however, lies a single theme—namely, the notion of nature as the "other," a mental construct in opposition to which a masculine, autonomous self is attained. In one, the violence appears to be perpetrated by an aggressive masculine will; in the other, through the use of reason. But the underlying theme remains the same—namely, the notion of the aggressive establishment of the masculine self through its opposition to all of the natural world.

Feminist psychoanalytic theory has helped to shed light on the psychological motives that lie behind the need men feel to separate violently from the female world. According to object-relations theory, both the boy and the girl child's earliest experience is that of an undifferentiated oneness with the mother figure. Although both must come to see themselves as separate from the mother figure, the boy child, unlike the girl, must come to see himself as opposed to all that is female as well. Thus, the mother figure, and by extension all women, become not just *an* other, but *the* other—the object against which the boy child's identity is formed and defined.

Object-relations theorists, such as Dorothy Dinnerstein, have also argued that it is not just

women who become an object against which men establish their sense of self, but that nature becomes objectified as well. Women and nature both come to represent the world of contingency and vulnerability that men must transcend. The twin need to separate from women and from nature can be discerned in typical male rituals of initiation into adulthood. A boy's entrance into manhood is typically marked by separation from women and often by violence toward the nonhuman world. In many tribal cultures a boy is initiated into manhood by being sent off to hunt and kill an animal. In other cultures, "baptisms of blood" occur when a young man goes to war or sexually penetrates a woman for the first time.

THE PROTECTION OF NATURE: THE DAMSEL IS REDRESSED

If the cult of masculinity has been modeled on the image of predation, the field of nature ethics has been modeled on that of protection. Both animal liberation and environmental ethics spring from a common defensive reaction to the willful aggression perpetrated upon the natural world. Animal liberationists concentrate much of their energies on protecting those animals reduced to the status of inert matter or machines—that is, animals in laboratories and factory farms. Environmental ethicists, by contrast, devote themselves primarily to protecting those parts of nature that are still "wild." But the underlying motive remains the same—namely, the urge to defend and protect.

Various modalities have been proposed for how the defense of nature might best be waged. Typically, nature ethicists have felt compelled to arm themselves with the force of philosophical theory in coming to nature's defense. Whereas patriarchal society has sought to destroy the natural world, nature ethicists have sought to place it under the protective wing of ethical theory. However, as Sarah Hoagland points out, predation and protection are twin aspects of the same world view: "Protection objectifies just as much as predation."

In their attempt to forge iron-clad theories to defend the natural world, nature ethicists have come to rely on the power and strength of a reasoned defense. Reason is enlisted as the new hero to fight on nature's behalf. In the past, humans (primarily men) have conceived of themselves as proprietors of the object-laden natural world. Today, many nature ethicists conceive of themselves not as the owners of nature, but as the owners of value, which it is their prerogative to mete out with a theoretical sweep of their pens. Ethical deliberation on the value of nature is conceived more or less like a competitive sport. Thus, nature ethicists commonly view themselves as "judges" in a game that features competing values out of which a hierarchy must be formed. The outcome is that some must win and others must lose. If a part of nature is accorded high value (typically by being assigned a quality that human beings are said to possess, such as sentience, consciousness, rationality, autonomy), then it is allowed entrance into the world of "moral considerability." If, on the other hand, it scores low (typically by being judged devoid of human qualities), it is relegated to the realm of "objects" or "things," and seen as unworthy of "interests" or "rights." The conferral of value in ethical deliberation is conceived as the conferral of power. "Inherent value" or "inherent worth" (the highest values) accrue to nature to the extent that nature can be rescued from the object world. Much of the heated debate among nature ethicists occurs over what class of entities may rightfully be granted admittance to the subject realm. The presumption behind this conceptual scheme is that if an entity is not graced with the status of "subject," it will become the "object" of abuse.

Both animal liberationists and environmental ethicists seek to curb the willful destruction of the natural world through another act of human will. Reason is, once again, elevated

above the natural instincts and asked to control our aggressive wills. The same reason that was used to take value out of nature (through objectification and the imposition of hierarchy) is now asked to give it value once again. A sound ethic, according to this view, must transcend the realm of contingency and particularity, grounding itself not in our untrustworthy instincts, but rather in rationally derived principles and abstract rules. It must stand on its own as an autonomous construct, distinct from our personal inclinations and desires, which it is designed to control. Ethics is intended to operate much like a machine. Feelings are considered, at best, as irrelevant, and at worst, as hazardous intrusions that clog the "ethical machinery." Basing an argument on love or compassion is tantamount to having no argument at all. As Peter Singer boasts in his well-known *Animal Liberation*, nowhere in his book will readers find an appeal to emotion where it cannot be substantiated by rational argument.

In their attempt to forge iron-clad theories to defend the natural world, nature ethicists have, in many ways, come to replicate the aggressive or predatory conception of nature that they seek to oppose. They leave intact a Hobbesian world view in which nature is conceived as "red in tooth and claw," with self-interest as the only rule of human conduct. The presumption is that only reason compels people to submit to sovereign rule—in this case, not that of a king, but that of ethical theory. Ethics, according to this world view, comes to replicate the same instrumental mentality that has characterized our interaction with the natural world. It is reduced to the status of a tool, designed to restrain what is perceived as an inherently aggressive will.

The notion that ethical conduct involves restraining the errant or immoral passions can be found not only in Western philosophy but in Western religion as well. The Christian church changed the focus of morality from prudence to obedience. The sentiments of the Church fathers are aptly captured by Sarah Hoagland—namely, that "evil results when passion runs out of (their) [i.e., the Church fathers'] control." The Church was (and is) fond of buttressing this notion with appeals to biblical authority. We are told that in the biblical story of Genesis, Adam's sin is precisely a failure of will. Adam's failure to obey God's command is attributed to Eve, and Eve's lapse of obedience is in turn ascribed to the snake. Eve has gone down in history as the embodiment of evil for having trusted the word of an animal over God's command.

Obedience to a transcendent God or abstract concept has been one of the most common conceptions of ethics in the Western world. Behind this notion lies the even more fundamental notion of ethics as restraint. Indeed, the model of ethics as a form of restraint can be seen in the Jewish-Christian God Himself. Thus, feeling remorse for having destroyed most of the world, God forges a covenant with Noah after the flood to restrain Himself from further outbursts of this kind.

Frequently, aggressive conduct is not prohibited under patriarchy, merely restrained and controlled. Often aggression is explicitly condoned if it is properly channeled into ritualized form. In many cultures, killing a totem animal is customarily condemned, but honored on rare occasions when performed as a sacrifice to a god. Similarly, the laws of Kashrut sanction the killing of animals as long as it is done in a restrained and ritualized fashion, according to "God's command."

The institutionalization of violence in modern society serves a legitimating function similar to that of ritual violence. For example, it is illegal for someone to beat a dog wantonly on the street, but if an experimenter beats the same dog in the protective confines of a laboratory, while counting the number of times the dog "vocalizes," it is considered an honorable activity and called "science." The rules of the experiment operate, like the rules of ritual, to lend legitimacy to the violent act. Animal experimentation is accorded additional legitimation by borrowing the language of ritual. Animals are said to be "sacrificed" in laboratories, not killed. Behind this obfuscation of language lies the tragic belief that somehow, if animals are killed at the altars of science, human beings will be allowed to live.

Aggression is often condoned under patriarchy in the name of an abstract ideal, typically "the greater good." We are told that killing (whether in laboratories, in warfare, or in razing land) is necessary for the greater good of "Mankind." Again, the Christian God Himself provides a perfect example of this conduct. Through the killing of his son, "God" is said to have sought the redemption of "Man," and hence the greater good.

Since the Enlightenment, ethical theory has tended to be based less on the Word of God and more on the god of Reason. The theme of controlling the unwieldy passions, however, has remained intact, receiving its most refined expression in the thought of Kant. While science and technology were mining nature for her riches, Kant, in analogous fashion, was attempting to strip human ethical conduct of its immersion in the natural world. As he writes, "To behold virtue in her proper shape is nothing other than to show morality stripped of all admixture with the sensuous and of all the spurious adornments of reward or self love." Moral individuals, according to Kant, rise above their personal inclinations or nature, and act out of duty. Duty is determined first by pure reason or logic, stripped of all feeling, and then by the exercise of the will.

The conception of morality as the rational control of irrational and aggressive desires contrasts sharply with the way in which many women have described their ethical behavior and thought. Research by Carol Gilligan suggests that women's ethical conduct and thought tend to derive more from a sense of connection with others and from the feelings of care and responsibility that such connection entails. Men's sense of morality, on the other hand, tends to derive more from an abstract sense of obligations and rights. According to one of Gilligan's respondents, Amy, "Responsibility signifies response, an extension rather than a limitation of action. Thus, it connotes an act of care, rather than restraint of aggression." For Jake, by contrast, responsibility "pertains to a limitation of action, a restraint of aggression."

For many women, what needs to be explained is not how and why people should be compelled to behave in moral ways, but how and why compassion and moral behavior fail to be sustained. As Alison Jaggar states, "Because we expect humans to be aggressive, we find the idea of cooperation puzzling. If, instead of focusing on antagonistic interactions, we focused on cooperative interaction, we would find the idea of competition puzzling."

TRUNCATED NARRATIVES

The founding of ethics on the twin pillars of human reason and human will is an act of violence in its own right. By denigrating instinctive and intuitive knowledge, it severs our ties to the natural world. But the violence of abstraction operates in other ways as well. Wrenching an ethical problem out of its embedded context severs the problem from its roots. Most nature ethicists debate the value of nature on an abstract or theoretical plane. Typically, they weigh the value of nature against the value of a human goal or plan. For example, we are asked to weigh the value of an animal used for research in a laboratory against the value of a human being who is ill. The problem is conventionally posed in a static, linear fashion, detached from the context in which it was formed. In a sense, we are given truncated stories and then asked what we think the ending should be. However, if we do not understand the world view that produced the dilemma that we are asked to consider, we have

no way of evaluating the situation except on its own terms.

What, for example, is a mother to say when she is told that the only way that her child can be saved is through the "sacrifice" of animal life? The urgency of the situation leads the mother to believe what she is told and to feel that it is "right" that the animal should die to save her child's life. It is understandable that the mother would choose her daughter's life over that of an anonymous animal. It would also be understandable, however, if the mother chose the life of her daughter over that of an anonymous *child*. This, however, is not the ethical dilemma that she is asked to consider. No one has asked her to juxtapose the life of one human against that of another. Although it would clearly be more helpful to experiment on a human child to help save the life of another child, no one is proposing this. Animals, however, have been relegated to the status of objects or property. As such, their bodies can easily be conscripted into this tragic human story.

The mother of the ailing daughter consumes this story; she does not create it or even enact it. *She* is not the one who will be injecting poisons into animals and watching their bodies writhe in pain. *She* is not the one who will slice into their brains to see what bits of knowledge might lie therein. She is the consumer of a narrative or story from which these details have been conveniently excised.

Currently, ethics is conceived as a tool for making dramatic decisions at the point at which a crisis has occurred. Little if any thought is given to why the crisis or conflict arose to begin with. Just as Western allopathic medicine is designed to treat illness, rather than maintain health, Western ethical theory is designed to remedy crisis, not maintain peace. But the word "ethics" implies something far less dramatic and heroic—namely, an "ethos" or way of life.

According to Iris Murdoch, moral behavior is not a matter of weighing competing values and making the proper, rational choice. Rather, as she argues, what is crucial in the moral life is the act of attention *before* a moral choice is made. In her words, the moral life is "not something that is switched off in between the occurrence of explicit moral choices. What happens between such choices is indeed what is crucial." Murdoch contends: "If we consider what the work of attention is like, how continuously it goes on and how imperceptibly it builds up structures of values round about us, we shall not be surprised that at crucial moments of choice most of the business of choosing is already over." Morality, for Murdoch, is far from the notion of the rational control of an inherently aggressive will. When one directs a "patient, loving regard" upon "a person, a thing, a situation," according to Murdoch, the will is presented not as "unimpeded movement," but rather as "something very much more like obedience."

It is precisely this loving regard that patriarchal culture has failed to attain. Rather, in the patriarchal "look," nature has been reduced to a set of objects or symbols that are used to attain a sense of self that is detached from the rest of the natural world. Nature is imaged as wild and demonic, passive and inert, but never as a community of living beings with instincts, desires, and interests of their own.

The patriarchal mind has managed to look, but not see, act but not feel, think but not know. Claude Bernard, considered by many to be the founder of modern medicine and the widespread use of animals in research, embodies this failure of perception. According to Bernard: "The physiologist is not an ordinary man: he is a scientist, possessed and absorbed by the scientific idea that he pursues. He does not hear the cries of animals, he does not see their flowing blood, he sees nothing but his idea, and is aware of nothing but an organism that conceals from him the problem he is seeking to resolve."

It is this fixation on abstraction (God, Reason, ideas, or the "Word") that has hampered the patriarchal mind from perceiving other forms of life in caring ways. In order to disengage from this fixation on abstraction, it is necessary to engage in practice. If ecofeminists are serious about transforming the patriarchal world view, we must begin to take our own experiences and practices seriously. We might, for example, decide, on an abstract plane, that we are justified in eating meat. But if we are dedicated to an ecofeminist praxis, we must put our abstract beliefs to the practical test. We must ask ourselves how we would feel if we were to visit a slaughterhouse or factory farm. And how would we feel if we were to kill the animal ourselves? Ethics, according to this approach, begins with our own instinctive responses. It occurs in a holistic context in which we know the whole story within which our actions take place. It means rethinking the stories that we have come to believe under patriarchy, such as the belief that we must experiment on animals to save human life, or the belief that we must eat meat to lead healthy lives. As Carol Adams points out, we are brought up to accept that being eaten is the logical ending to the story of a farm animal's life. But stories such as these can only be conceived by a patriarchal mind that is unable to conceive of nature as important apart from human use.

Patriarchal society is adept at truncating stories and then adapting them to its own needs. It is true, for example, that *some* animals are predators; however, the vast majority are not. Most of the animals that humans eat are, in fact, vegetarian (cows, pigs, chickens). We are asked, under patriarchy, to model our behavior not after the vegetarian animals but after the predators. The narrative of predation thus becomes a convenient "pretext" to justify a wide range of violent acts. No other species of animal confines, enslaves, and breeds other animals to satisfy its taste for flesh. Yet, under patriarchy, *this* story remains untold. Nor are we told that predatory animals generally kill other animals only for survival reasons; that, unlike humans, these animals would not survive without eating meat. The story of predation is wrenched out of the larger context and served to us to consume.

Since we live in a fragmented world, we will need to stretch our imaginations to put it back together again. It is often difficult for us to conceive of the impact that our personal conduct has beyond our individual lives. Reason is easily divided from emotion when our emotions are divided from experience. Much of the violence that is perpetrated against the natural world occurs behind closed doors or out of our view. Most of us will never see a slaughterhouse, fur ranch, or animal research laboratory. If we are to engage in an ecofeminist praxis, the least we can do is inform ourselves of what transpires in these places. If we are to make holistic choices, the whole story must be known.

The story of meat eating must include not only the brutal treatment of animals on factory farms and in slaughterhouses, not only the devastating impact of meat eating on the ecology of the earth, on world hunger, and on human health—it must include *all* these and other details, which it must then weave together into a whole. Only when we have all the details of this and other stories will we be able to act holistically with our bodies, minds, and souls. It is the details that we need to live moral lives, not obedience to abstract principles and rules.

Holistic medicine provides a fitting paradigm for holistic ethics. Just as holistic medicine seeks to discover the whole story behind disease, so, too, holistic ethics seeks to discover the whole story behind ethical dilemmas. Western allopathic ethics, on the other hand, is designed to treat the symptoms of patriarchy (its dilemmas and conflicts), rather than the disease embodied in its total world view. Allopathic ethics, like allopathic medicine, operates on the notion of heroism. Just as Western heroic medicine spends most of its time, money, and resources on battling advanced stages of disease

and emergency situations, so, too, Western heroic ethics is designed to treat problems at an advanced stage of their history—namely, at the point at which conflict has occurred. It is not difficult to discern why allopathic medicine spends little to no research money on prevention. Prevention is simply not a very heroic undertaking. How can you fight a battle if the enemy does not yet exist? It is far more dramatic to allow disease and conflict to develop and then to call in the troops and declare war. The drama of illness is seen to lead ineluctably to the climax of a heroic, technological fix.

Heroic medicine, like heroic ethics, runs counter to one of the most basic principles in ecology—namely, that everything is interconnected. Ecology teaches us that no part of nature can be understood in isolation, apart from its context or ecological niche. So, too, I would argue, our moral conduct cannot be understood apart from the context (or moral soil) in which it grows. By uprooting ethical dilemmas from the environment that produced them, heroic ethics sees only random, isolated problems, rather than an entire diseased world view. But until the entire diseased world view is uprooted, we will always face moral crises of the same kind. There is an ecology to ethics, just as to every aspect of the natural world. If we do not care for our moral landscape, we cannot expect it to bear fruit.

WEAVING NEW STORIES

The "environmental crisis" is, above all, a crisis of perception. It is a crisis not only by virtue of what our culture sees, but by virtue of what it does not see. Adrienne Rich has shown how "lies, secrecy, and silence" have been used to perpetuate the exploitation of women. The same may be said to apply to the exploitation of all of the natural world as well. If we are to transform the destructive consciousness that pervades our current culture, we must break through the lies, secrecy, and silence. This is not an individual endeavor. Holistic ethics is a collective undertaking, not a solitary task. It is a process of helping one another to piece together the wider stories of which our lives form a part. It means filling in the missing links. It may mean approaching a woman on the street who is wearing a fur coat and asking her if she is aware of how many animals died to make her coat, and if she is aware of how much suffering the animals had to endure. At the same time, it means understanding the cultural context that leads this woman to see glamour where others see death. She is the product of a society that robs women of their own self-image and then sells it back to them in distorted form. She thinks that she is "dressed to kill"; we must let her know that others have been killed for her to dress.

In order to engage in holistic ethics, we must also disengage from patriarchal discourse. Patriarchal discourse creates dilemmas that it then invites us to resolve. Thus, animal experimenters typically invite us to answer the question, "Who would we save if we had to choose between our drowning daughter and a drowning dog?" The crisis scenario is designed to lead us to believe that only one life can be saved, and only at the other's expense. Disengaging from patriarchal discourse means that we must refuse to dignify these dualistic questions with a response. Even to consider such questions is to give support and validity to the patriarchal world view. The best response to such questions is, perhaps, to pose a question of our own. We might ask why the child is ill to begin with. Was it due to the hormones found in the meat she was fed, or was it perhaps due to the consumption of drugs that had proved "safe" after testing on animals? And why was the proverbial dog touted by research scientists "drowning" to begin with? Had someone thrown the dog in the water (or, rather, the laboratory) in the pathetic belief that somehow, through the dog's death, a young child's life would be saved? And how and why did we

develop a culture in which death is seen as a medical failure, rather than as a natural part of life?

As we disengage from patriarchal discourse, we begin to hear larger and fuller stories. Hearing these bigger stories means learning to listen to nature. The voice of women and the voice of nature have been muted under patriarchy. Women and nature are considered objects under patriarchy, and objects do not speak, objects do not feel, and objects have no needs. Objects exist only to serve the needs of others. But despite our society's refusal to listen, nature has been increasingly communicating her needs to us. Nature is telling us in myriad ways that we cannot continue to poison her rivers, forests, and streams, that she is not invulnerable, and that the violence and abuse must be stopped. Nature *is* speaking to us. The question is whether we are willing or able to hear.

The notion of obligations, responsibilities, and rights is one of the tools used by heroic ethics. But genuine responsibility for nature begins with the root meaning of the word—"our capacity for response." Learning to respond to nature in caring ways is not an abstract exercise in reasoning. It is, above all, a form of psychic and emotional health. Heroic ethics cannot manufacture health out of the void of abstraction. Psychic and emotional health cannot be manufactured at all. It can only be nurtured through the development of a favorable environment or context within which it can grow. The moral "climate" must be right.

Ecofeminists and other nature writers have often proclaimed the importance of a "holistic world view." By "holism" they refer to the notion of the "interdependence of all of life." But interdependence is hardly an ideal in and of itself. A master and slave may be said to be interconnected, but clearly that is not the kind of relation that ecofeminists wish to promote. The *quality* of relation is more important than the fact that a relation of some kind exists. If our society is to regain a sense of psychic health, we must learn to attend to the *quality* of relations and interactions, not just the *existence* of relations in themselves. Thus, when hunters claim to promote the well-being of the "whole" by killing individual animals, or to "love" the animals that they kill, we must challenge their story. Our own notion of holistic ethics must contain a respect for the "whole" *as well as* individual beings.

Re-specting nature literally involves "looking again." We cannot attend to the quality of relations that we engage in unless we know the details that surround our actions and relations. If ecofeminists are sincere in their desire to live in a world of peace and nonviolence for all living beings, we must help each other through the pains-taking process of piecing together the fragmented world view that we have inherited. But the pieces cannot simply be patched together. What is needed is a reweaving of all the old stories and narratives into a multifaceted tapestry.

As this tapestry begins to take shape, I stretch my imagination into the future and spin the following narrative. Many, many years from now, I am sitting by the fireside with my sister's grandchild. She turns to me and asks me to tell her a story of how things used to be, in the distant past. I turn to her and speak the following words:

"Once upon a time," I tell her, "there existed a period we now call the Age of Treason. During this time, men came to fear nature and revolted against the earlier matriarchal societies which had lived in harmony with the natural world as we do now. Many terrible things occurred during this time that will be difficult for you to understand. Women were raped and the earth was poisoned and warfare became routine.

"Animals were tortured throughout the land. They were trapped and clubbed so people could dress in their furs. They were enslaved in cages—in zoos, in laboratories, and on factory farms. People ate the flesh of animals and were frequently ill. Researchers told people that if they 'sacrificed' animals in laboratories they would be cured of disease. People no longer trusted in their own power to heal themselves and so they believed what they were told.

"The men had forgotten that they had formerly worshipped the animals they now reviled. Instead they worshipped a God that told them they had a special place in Creation, above all the other animals on earth. They found great comfort in this thought. And so they continued their cruel-hearted ways."

As I conclude my fantasy, I imagine my grandniece turning to me with a look of disbelief.

"Did they *really* used to eat animals?" she queries.

"Yes," I answer gently, "and much, much worse. But now that is all a matter of history. Like a very bad dream. Now, at long last, we can live in peace and harmony with all the creatures of the earth. The Age of Treason has passed."

Toward Multicultural Feminism

As attractive as the postmodern approach to feminism may be, some feminist theorists worry that an overemphasis on difference and a rejection of unity may lead to intellectual and political disintegration. If feminism is to be without any standpoint whatsoever, it becomes difficult to ground feminist claims about what is good for women. Contemporary feminism's major challenge is, therefore, to reconcile the pressures for diversity and difference with those for integration and commonality. Feminists need a home in which each woman has a room of her own, but one in which the walls are thin enough to permit a conversation, a community of friends in virtue and partners in action. Only in such a community are feminist ethics and politics possible.

Contemporary feminists do not shirk from this challenge. Indeed, in "Have We Got a Theory for You! Feminist Theory, Cultural Imperialism and the Demand for 'The Woman's Voice,'" multicultural feminists Maria Lugones and Elizabeth Spelman challenge feminists to do what has never been done before—to conceive a theory that celebrates women's different ways of thinking, doing, and being without separating women from each other on account of these differences. In particular they invite feminists, the majority of whom are still white and privileged, to consider the forms oppression takes for women of color—racial and ethnic minorities—and for poor women in the United States. Writing from the perspective of an Argentinean woman who has lived in the United States for many years, Lugones stresses that in the United States a Hispanic woman is likely to experience herself as "a self" within her own family and friendship circle, but as "the other" outside of her home boundaries. Lugones observes that although Hispanics have to participate in the Anglo world, Anglos do not have to participate in the Hispanic world. An Anglo woman can go to a Hispanic neighborhood for a church festival, for example, and if she finds the rituals and music overwhelming, she can simply get in her car, drive home, and forget the evening. There is no way, however, that a Hispanic woman can escape Anglo culture so easily, for the dominant culture sets the basic parameters for her survival as one of its minority members.

What most concerns Lugones and also Spelman about the relations between Hispanic and Anglo women is that Anglo women, especially Anglo feminist theorists, tend to miss the fact that cultural differences create a *different* experience for the Hispanic woman. Thus they urge feminist theorists to ferret out the racism, classism, ethnocentrism, imperialism, and heterosexism in feminist writings—"isms" that prevent a diverse group of women from becoming friends and learning how to use the pronoun "we" appropriately. "Sisterhood" may be powerful, but it is also difficult to achieve in a multicultural society.

In "Sisterhood: Political Solidarity between Women," bell hooks reminds feminists that confronting one's own ugly "isms" is not only a difficult process but also a painful one. Hurtful words will be shouted and angry glances will be exchanged. Yet as hooks sees it, "sustained woman bonding" between blacks and white women, or between Anglo-American and Hispanic women, or between any two women who really differ from each other, will never occur unless all women learn to do what Lugones and Spelman have obviously learned to do—namely, to confront each other's limits lovingly.

The type of multicultural feminist theory that Spelman, Lugones, and hooks envision is in the process of being written. It is slow work as it demands feminists to overcome their own narrownesses of mind and constrictions of heart, and that, says Lugones and Spelman, takes "openness . . . , sensitivity, concentration, self-questioning" (p. 486). To say "*we* women think" is both a privilege and an achievement. Only friends can say "we"—proudly, defiantly, joyfully, angrily, hopefully. It is not always easy to make friends, but friendship is precisely what feminists are committed to creating.

Have We Got a Theory for You! Feminist Theory, Cultural Imperialism and the Demand for "The Woman's Voice"

Maria Lugones
Elizabeth Spelman

Prologue

(*In an Hispana voice*)

A veces quisiera mezclar en una voz el sonido canyenge, tristón y urbano del porteñismo que llevo adentro con la candecia apacible, serrana y llena de corage de la hispana nuevo mejicana. Contrastar y unir

el piolin y la cuerda
el traé y el pepéname

el camión y la troca
la lluvia y el llanto

Pero este querer se me va cuando veo que he confundido la solidaridad con la falta de diferencia. La solidaridad requiere el reconocer, comprender, respetar y amar lo que nos lleva a llorar en distintas cadencias. El imperialismo cultural desea lo contrario, por eso necesitamos muchas voces. Porque una sola voz nos mata a las dos.

No quiero hablar por ti sino contigo. Pero si no aprendo tus modos y tu los mios la conversación es sólo aparente. Y la apariencia se levanta como una barrera sin sentido entre las

From *Women's Studies International Forum*, Vol. 6, No. 6 (1983), pp. 573–581. Reprinted by permission of Pergamon Press.

dos. Sin sentido y sin sentimiento. Por eso no me debes dejar que te dicte tu ser y no me dictes el mio. Porque entonces ya no dialogamos. El diálogo entre nosotras requiere dos voces y no una.

Tal vez un día jugaremos juntas y nos hablaremos no en una lengua universal sino que vos me habalarás mi voz y yo la tuya.

Preface

This paper is the result of our dialogue, of our thinking together about differences among women and how these differences are silenced. (Think, for example, of all the silences there are connected with the fact that this paper is in English—for that is a borrowed tongue for one of us.) In the process of our talking and writing together, we saw that the differences between us did not permit our speaking in one voice. For example, when we agreed we expressed the thought differently; there were some things that both of us thought were true but could not express as true of each of us; sometimes we could not say "we"; and sometimes one of us could not express the thought in the first person singular, and to express it in the third person would be to present an outsider's and not an insider's perspective. Thus the use of two voices is central both to the process of constructing this paper and to the substance of it. We are both the authors of this paper and not just sections of it but we write together without presupposing unity of expression or of experience. So when we speak in unison it means just that—there are two voices and not just one.

I. INTRODUCTION

(In the voice of a white/Anglo woman who has been teaching and writing about feminist theory)

Feminism is, among other things, a response to the fact that women either have been left out of, or included in demeaning and disfiguring ways in what has been an almost exclusively male account of the world. And so while part of what feminists want and demand for women is the right to move and to act in accordance with our own wills and not against them, another part is the desire and insistence that we give our *own* accounts of these movements and actions. For it matters to us what is said about us, who says it, and to whom it is said: having the opportunity to talk about one's life, to give an account of it, to interpret it, is integral to leading that life rather than being led through it; hence our distrust of the male monopoly over accounts of women's lives. To put the same point slightly differently, part of human life, human living, is talking about it, and we can be sure that being silenced in one's own account of one's life is a kind of amputation that signals oppression. Another reason for not divorcing life from the telling of it or talking about it is that as humans our experiences are deeply influenced by what is said about them, by ourselves or powerful (as opposed to significant) others. Indeed, the phenomenon of internalized oppression is only possible because this is so: one experiences her life in terms of the impoverished and degrading concepts others have found it convenient to use to describe her. We can't separate lives from the accounts given of them; the articulation of our experience is part of our experience.

Sometimes feminists have made even stronger claims about the importance of speaking about our own lives and the destructiveness of others presuming to speak about us or for us. First of all, the claim has been made that on the whole men's accounts of women's lives have been at best false, a function of ignorance; and at worst malicious lies, a function of a knowledgeable desire to exploit and oppress. Since it matters to us that falsehood and lies not be told about us, we demand, of those who have been responsible for those falsehoods and lies, or those who continue to transmit them, not just that we speak but that they learn to be able to hear us. It has also been claimed that talking about one's life, telling one's story, in the company of those doing the same (as in consciousness-raising sessions), is constitutive of feminist method.

And so the demand that the woman's voice be heard and attended to has been made for a variety of reasons: not just so as to greatly increase the chances that true accounts of women's lives will be given, but also because the articulation of experience (in myriad ways) is among the hallmarks of a self-determining individual or community. There are not just epistemological, but moral and political reasons for demanding that the woman's voice be heard, after centuries of androcentric din.

But what more exactly is the feminist demand that the woman's voice be heard? There are several crucial notes to make about it. First of all, the demand grows out of a complaint, and in order to understand the scope and focus of the demand we have to look at the scope and focus of the complaint. The complaint does not specify *which* women have been silenced, and in one way this is appropriate to the conditions it is a complaint about: virtually no women have had a voice, whatever their race, class, ethnicity, religion, sexual alliance, whatever place and period in history they lived. And if it is as women that women have been silenced, then of course the demand must be that women as women have a voice. But in another way the complaint is very misleading, insofar as it suggests that it is women as women who have been silenced, and that whether a woman is rich or poor, Black, brown or white, etc. is irrelevant to what it means for her to be a woman. For the demand thus simply made ignores at least two related points: (1) it is only possible for a woman who does not feel highly vulnerable with respect to other parts of her identity, e.g. race, class, ethnicity, religion, sexual alliance, etc., to conceive of her voice simply or essentially as a "woman's voice"; (2) just because not all women are equally vulnerable with respect

to race, class, etc., some women's voices are more likely to be heard than others by those who have heretofore been giving—or silencing—the accounts of women's lives. For all these reasons, the women's voices most likely to come forth and the women's voices most likely to be heard are, in the US anyway, those of white, middle-class, heterosexual Christian (or anyway not self-identified non-Christian) women. Indeed, many Hispanas, Black women, Jewish women—to name a few groups—have felt it an invitation to silence rather than speech to be requested—if they are requested at all—to speak about being "women" (with the plain wrapper—as if there were one) in distinction from speaking about being Hispana, Black, Jewish, working-class, etc., women.

The demand that the "woman's voice" be heard, and the search for the "woman's voice" as central to feminist methodology, reflects nascent feminist theory. It reflects nascent empirical theory insofar as it presupposes that the silencing of women is systematic, shows up in regular, patterned ways, and that there are discoverable causes of this widespread observable phenomenon; the demand reflects nascent political theory insofar as it presupposes that the silencing of women reveals a systematic pattern of power and authority; and it reflects nascent moral theory insofar as it presupposes that the silencing is unjust and that there are particular ways of remedying this injustice. Indeed, whatever else we know feminism to include—e.g., concrete direct political action—theorizing is integral to it: theories about the nature of oppression, the causes of it, the relation of the oppression of women to other forms of oppression. And certainly the concept of the woman's voice is itself a theoretical concept, in the sense that it presupposes a theory according to which our identities as human beings are actually compound identities, a kind of fusion or confusion of our otherwise separate identities as women or men, as Black or brown or white, etc. That is no less a theoretical stance than

Plato's division of the person into soul and body or Aristotle's parcelling of the soul into various functions.

The demand that the "woman's voice" be heard also invites some further directions in the exploration of women's lives and discourages or excludes others. For reasons mentioned above, systematic, sustained reflection on being a woman—the kind of contemplation that "doing theory" requires—is most likely to be done by women who vis-à-vis other women enjoy a certain amount of political, social and economic privilege because of their skin color, class membership, ethnic identity. There is a relationship between the content of our contemplation and the fact that we have the time to engage in it at some length—otherwise we shall have to say that it is a mere accident of history that white middle-class women in the United States have in the main developed "feminist theory" (as opposed to "Black feminist theory," "Chicana feminist theory," etc.) and that so much of the theory has failed to be relevant to the lives of women who are not white or middle class. Feminist theory—of all kinds—is to be based on, or anyway touch base with, the variety of real life stories women provide about themselves. But in fact, because, among other things, of the structural political and social and economic inequalities among women, the tail has been wagging the dog: feminist theory has not for the most part arisen out of a medley of women's voices; instead, the theory has arisen out of the voices, the experiences, of a fairly small handful of women, and if other women's voices do not sing in harmony with the theory, they aren't counted as women's voices—rather, they are the voices of the woman as Hispana, Black, Jew, etc. There is another sense in which the tail is wagging the dog, too: it is presumed to be the case that those who do the theory know more about those who are theorized than vice versa: hence it ought to be the case that if it is white/Anglo women who write for and about all other

women, then white/Anglo women must know more about all other women than other women know about them. But in fact just in order to survive, brown and Black women have to know a lot more about white/Anglo women—not through the sustained contemplation theory requires, but through the sharp observation stark exigency demands.

(*In an Hispana voice*)

I think it necessary to explain why in so many cases when women of color appear in front of white/Anglo women to talk about feminism and women of color, we mainly raise a complaint: the complaint of exclusion, of silencing, of being included in a universe we have not chosen. We usually raise the complaint with a certain amount of disguised or undisguised anger. I can only attempt to explain this phenomenon from a Hispanic viewpoint and a fairly narrow one at that: the viewpoint of an Argentinian woman who has lived in the US for sixteen years, who has attempted to come to terms with the devaluation of things Hispanic and Hispanic people in "America" and who is most familiar with Hispano life in the Southwest of the US. I am quite unfamiliar with daily Hispano life in the urban centers, though not with some of the themes and some of the salient experiences of urban Hispano life.

When I say "we," I am referring to Hispanas. I am accustomed to use the "we" in this way. I am also pained by the tenuousness of this "we" given that I am not a native of the US. Through the years I have come to be recognized and I have come to recognize myself more and more firmly as part of this "we." I also have a profound yearning for this firmness since I am a displaced person and I am conscious of not being of and I am unwilling to make myself of—even if this were possible—the white/Anglo community.

When I say "you" I mean not the non-Hispanic but the white/Anglo women that I address. "We" and "you" do not capture my relation to other non-white women. The complexity of that relation is not addressed here, but it is vivid to me as I write down my thoughts on the subject at hand.

I see two related reasons for our complaintfull discourse with white/Anglo women. Both of these reasons plague our world, they contaminate it through and through. It takes some hardening of oneself, some self-acceptance of our own anger to face them, for to face them is to decide that maybe we can change our situation in self-constructive ways and we know fully well that the possibilities are minimal. We know that we cannot rest from facing these reasons, that the tenderness towards others in us undermines our possibilities, that we have to fight our own niceness because it clouds our minds and hearts. Yet we know that a thoroughgoing hardening would dehumanize us. So, we have to walk through our days in a peculiarly fragile psychic state, one that we have to struggle to maintain, one that we do not often succeed in maintaining.

We and you do not talk the same language. When we talk to you we use your language: the language of your experience and of your theories. We try to use it to communicate our world of experience. But since your language and your theories are inadequate in expressing our experiences, we only succeed in communicating our experience of exclusion. We cannot talk to you in our language because you do not understand it. So the brute facts that we understand your language and that the place where most theorizing about women is taking place is your place, both combine to require that we either use your language and distort our experience not just in the speaking about it, but in the living of it, or that we remain silent. Complaining about exclusion is a way of remaining silent.

You are ill at ease in our world. You are ill at ease in our world in a very different way than we are ill at ease in yours. You are not of our world and again, you are not of our world in a very different way than we are not of yours. In the intimacy of a personal relationship we appear to you many times to be wholly there, to have broken through or to have dissipated the barriers that separate us because you are Anglo and we are *raza*. When we let go of the psychic state that I referred to above in the direction of sympathy, we appear to ourselves equally whole in your presence but our intimacy is thoroughly incomplete. When we are in your world many times you remake us in your own image, although sometimes you clearly and explicitly acknowledge that we are not wholly there in our being with you. When we are in your world we ourselves feel the discomfort of having our own being Hispanas disfigured or not understood. And yet, we have had to be in your world and learn its ways. We have to participate in it, make a living in it, live in it, be mistreated in it, be ignored in it, and rarely, be appreciated in it. In learning to do these things or in learning to suffer them or in learning to enjoy what is to be enjoyed or in learning to understand your conception of us, we have had to learn your culture and thus your language and self-conceptions. But there is nothing that necessitates that you understand our world: understand, that is, not as an observer understands things, but as a participant, as someone who has a stake in them understands them. So your being ill at ease in our world lacks the features of our being ill at ease in yours precisely because you can leave and you can always tell yourselves that you will be soon out of there and because the wholeness of your selves is never touched by us, we have no tendency to remake you in our image.

But you theorize about women and we are women, so you understand yourselves to be theorizing about us and we understand you to be theorizing about us. Yet none of the feminist theories developed so far seem to me to help Hispanas in the articulation of our experience. We have a sense that in using them we are distorting our experiences. Most Hispanas cannot even understand the language used in these theories—and only in some cases the reason is that the Hispana cannot understand English. We do not recognize ourselves in these theories. They create in us a schizophrenic split between our concern for ourselves as women and ourselves as Hispanas, one that we do not feel otherwise. Thus they seem to us to force us to assimilate to some version of Anglo culture, however revised that version may be. They seem to ask that we leave our communities or that we become alienated so completely in them that we feel hollow. When we see that you feel alienated in your own communities, this confuses us because we think that maybe every feminist has to suffer this alienation. But we see that recognition of your alienation leads many of you to be empowered into the remaking of your culture, while we are paralyzed into a state of displacement with no place to go.

So I think that we need to think carefully about the relation between the articulation of our own experience, the interpretation of our own experience, and theory making by us and other non-Hispanic women about themselves and other "women."

The only motive that makes sense to me for your joining us in this investigation is the motive of friendship, out of friendship. A non-imperialist feminism requires that you make a real space for our articulating, interpreting, theorizing and reflecting about the connections among them—a real space must be a noncoerced space—and/or that you follow us into our world out of friendship. I see the "out of friendship" as the only sensible motivation for this following because the task at hand for you is one of extraordinary difficulty. It requires that you be willing to devote a great part of your life to it and that you be willing to suffer alienation and self-disruption. Self-interest has been proposed as a possible motive for entering this task. But self-interest does not seem to me to be a realistic motive, since whatever the benefits you may accrue from such a journey, they

cannot be concrete enough for you at this time and they may not be worth your while. I do not think that you have any obligation to understand us. You do have an obligation to abandon your imperialism, your universal claims, your reduction of us to your selves simply because they seriously harm us.

I think that the fact that we are so ill at ease with your theorizing in the ways indicated above does indicate that there is something wrong with these theories. But what is it that is wrong? Is it simply that the theories are flawed if meant to be universal but accurate so long as they are confined to your particular group(s)? Is it that the theories are not really flawed but need to be translated? Can they be translated? Is it something about the process of theorizing that is flawed? How do the two reasons for our complaint-full discourse affect the validity of your theories? Where do *we* begin? To what extent are our experience and its articulation affected by our being a colonized people, and thus by your culture, theories and conceptions? Should we theorize in community and thus as part of community life and outside the academy and other intellectual circles? What is the point of making theory? Is theory making a good thing for us to do at this time? When are we making theory and when are we just articulating and/or interpreting our experiences?

II. SOME QUESTIONABLE ASSUMPTIONS ABOUT FEMINIST THEORIZING

(*Unproblematically in Maria's and Vicky's voice*)

Feminist theories aren't just about what happens to the female population in any given society or across all societies; they are about the meaning of those experiences in the lives of women. They are about beings who give their own accounts of what is happening to them or of what they are doing, who have culturally constructed ways of reflecting on their lives.

But how can the theorizer get at the meaning of those experiences? What should the relation be between a woman's own account of her experiences and the theorizer's account of it?

Let us describe two different ways of arriving at an account of another woman's experience. It is one thing for both me and you to observe you and come up with our different accounts of what you are doing; it is quite another for me to observe myself and others much like me culturally and in other ways and to develop an account of myself and then use that account to give an account of you. In the first case you are the "insider" and I am the "outsider." When the outsider makes clear that she is an outsider and that this is an outsider's account of your behavior, there is a touch of honesty about what she is doing. Most of the time the "interpretation by an outsider" is left understood and most of the time the distance of outsidedness is understood to mark objectivity in the interpretation. But why is the outsider as an outsider interpreting your behavior? Is she doing it so that you can understand how she sees you? Is she doing it so that other outsiders will understand how you *are*? Is she doing it so that *you* will understand how you are? It would seem that if the outsider wants you to understand how she sees you and you have given your account of how you see yourself to her, there is a possibility of genuine dialogue between the two. It also seems that the lack of reciprocity could bar genuine dialogue. For why should you engage in such a one-sided dialogue? As soon as we ask this question, a host of other conditions for the possibility of a genuine dialogue between us arise: conditions having to do with your position relative to me in the various social, political and economic structures in which we might come across each other or in which you may run face to face with my account of you and my use of your account of yourself. Is this kind of dialogue necessary for me to get at the meaning of your experiences? That is, is this kind of dialogue neces-

sary for feminist theorizing that is not seriously flawed?

Obviously the most dangerous of the understanding of what I—an outsider—am doing in giving an account of your experience is the one that describes what I'm doing as giving an account of who and how you are whether it be given to you or to other outsiders. Why should you or anyone else believe me; that is why should you or anyone else believe that you are as I say you are? Could I be right? What conditions would have to obtain for my being right? That many women are put in the position of not knowing whether or not to believe outsiders' accounts of their experiences is clear. The pressures to believe these accounts are enormous even when the woman in question does not see herself in the account. She is thus led to doubt her own judgment and to doubt all interpretation of her experience. This leads her to experience her life differently. Since the consequences of outsiders' accounts can be so significant, it is crucial that we reflect on whether or not this type of account can ever be right and if so, under what conditions.

The last point leads us to the second way of arriving at an account of another woman's experience, viz. the case in which I observe myself and others like me culturally and in other ways and use that account to give an account of you. In doing this, I remake you in my own image. Feminist theorizing approaches this remaking insofar as it depends on the concept of women as women. For it has not arrived at this concept as a consequence of dialogue with many women who are culturally different, or by any other kind of investigation of cultural differences which may include different conceptions of what it is to be a woman; it has simply presupposed this concept.

Our suggestion in this paper, and at this time it is no more than a suggestion, is that only when genuine and reciprocal dialogue takes place between "outsiders" and "insiders" can we trust the outsider's account. At first sight it may appear that the insider/outsider distinction disappears in the dialogue, but it is important to notice that all that happens is that we are now both outsider and insider with respect to each other. The dialogue puts us both in position to give a better account of each other's and our own experience. Here we should again note that white/Anglo women are much less prepared for this dialogue with women of color than women of color are for dialogue with them in that women of color have had to learn white/Anglo ways, self-conceptions, and conceptions of them.

But both the possibility and the desirability of this dialogue are very much in question. We need to think about the possible motivations for engaging in this dialogue, whether doing theory jointly would be a good thing, in what ways and for whom, and whether doing theory is in itself a good thing at this time for women of color or white/Anglo women. In motivating the last question let us remember the hierarchical distinctions between theorizers and those theorized about and between theorizers and doers. These distinctions are endorsed by the same views and institutions which endorse and support hierarchical distinctions between men/women, master race/inferior race, intellectuals/manual workers. Of what use is the activity of theorizing to those of us who are women of color engaged day in and day out in the task of empowering women and men of color face to face with them? Should we be articulating and interpreting their experience for them with the aid of theories? Whose theories?

III. WAYS OF TALKING OR BEING TALKED ABOUT THAT ARE HELPFUL, ILLUMINATING, EMPOWERING, RESPECTFUL

(*Unproblematically in Maria's and Vicky's voice*)

Feminists have been quite diligent about pointing out the ways in which empirical, philosophical and moral theories have been androcentric. They have thought it crucial to ask, with respect to such theories: who makes them? for whom do they make them? about what or whom are the theories? why? how are theories tested? what are the criteria for such tests and where did the criteria come from? Without posing such questions and trying to answer them, we'd never have been able to begin to mount evidence for our claims that particular theories are androcentric, sexist, biased, paternalistic, etc. Certain philosophers have become fond of—indeed, have made their careers on—pointing out that characterizing a statement as true or false is only one of many ways possible of characterizing it; it might also be, oh, rude, funny, disarming, etc.; it may be intended to soothe or to hurt; or it may have the effect, intended or not, of soothing or hurting. Similarly, theories appear to be the kinds of things that are true or false; but they also are the kinds of things that can be, e.g., useless, arrogant, disrespectful, ignorant, ethnocentric, imperialistic. The immediate point is that feminist theory is no less immune to such characterizations than, say, Plato's political theory, or Freud's theory of female psychosexual development. Of course this is not to say that if feminist theory manages to be respectful or helpful it will follow that it must be true. But if, say, an empirical theory is purported to be about "women" and in fact is only about certain women, it is certainly false, probably ethnocentric, and of dubious usefulness except to those whose position in the world it strengthens (and theories, as we know, don't have to be true in order to be used to strengthen people's positions in the world).

Many reasons can be and have been given for the production of accounts of people's lives that plainly have nothing to do with illuminating those lives for the benefit of those living them. It is likely that both the method of investigation and the content of many accounts would be different if illuminating the lives of the people the accounts are about were the aim of the studies. Though we cannot say ahead of time how feminist theory-making would be different if all (or many more) of those people it is meant to be about were more intimately part of the theory-making process, we do suggest some specific ways being talked about can be helpful:

1. The theory or account can be helpful if it enables one to see how parts of one's life fit together, for example, to see connection among parts of one's life one hasn't seen before. No account can do this if it doesn't get the parts right to begin with, and this cannot happen if the concepts used to describe a life are utterly foreign.

2. A useful theory will help one locate oneself concretely in the world, rather than add to the mystification of the world and one's location in it. New concepts may be of significance here, but they will not be useful if there is no way they can be translated into already existing concepts. Suppose a theory locates you in the home, because you are a woman, but you know full well that is not where you spend most of your time? Or suppose you can't locate yourself easily in any particular class as defined by some version of marxist theory?

3. A theory or account not only ought to accurately locate one in the world but also enable one to think about the extent to which one is responsible or not for being in that location. Otherwise, for those whose location is as oppressed peoples, it usually occurs that the oppressed have no way to see themselves as in any way self-determining, as having any sense of being worthwhile or having grounds for pride, and paradoxically at the same time feeling at fault for the position they are in. A useful theory will help people sort out just what is and is not due to themselves and their own activities as opposed to those who have power over them.

It may seem odd to make these criteria of a useful theory, if the usefulness is not to be at odds with the issue of the truth of the theory: for the focus on feeling worthwhile or having

pride seems to rule out the possibility that the truth might just be that such-and-such a group of people has been under the control of others for centuries and that the only explanation of that is that they are worthless and weak people, and will never be able to change that. Feminist theorizing seems implicitly if not explicitly committed to the moral view that women *are* worthwhile beings, and the metaphysical theory that we are beings capable of bringing about a change in our situations. Does this mean feminist theory is "biased"? Not any more than any other theory, e.g., psychoanalytic theory. What is odd here is not the feminist presupposition that women are worthwhile but rather that feminist theory (and other theory) often has the effect of empowering one group and demoralizing another.

Aspects of feminist theory are as unabashedly value-laden as other political and moral theories. It is not just an examination of women's positions, for it includes, indeed begins with, moral and political judgements about the injustice (or, where relevant, justice) of them. This means that there are implicit or explicit judgements also about what kind of changes constitute a better or worse situation for women.

4. In this connection a theory that is useful will provide criteria for change and make suggestions for modes of resistance that don't merely reflect the situation and values of the theorizer. A theory that is respectful of those about whom it is a theory will not assume that changes that are perceived as making life better for some women are changes that will make, and will be perceived as making, life better for other women. This is NOT to say that if some women do not find a situation oppressive, other women ought never to suggest to the contrary that there might be very good reasons to think that the situation nevertheless *is* oppressive. But it is to say that, e.g., the prescription that life for women will be better when we're in the workforce rather than at home, when we are completely free of religious beliefs

with patriarchal origins, when we live in complete separation from men, etc., are seen as slaps in the face to women whose life would be better if they could spend more time at home, whose identity is inseparable from their religious beliefs and cultural practices (which is not to say those beliefs and practices are to remain completely uncriticized and unchanged), who have ties to men—whether erotic or not—such that to have them severed in the name of some vision of what is "better" is, at that time and for those women, absurd. Our visions of what is better are always informed by our perception of what is bad about our present situation. Surely we've learned enough from the history of clumsy missionaries, and the white suffragists of the nineteenth century (who couldn't imagine why Black women "couldn't see" how crucial getting the vote for "women" was) to know that we can clobber people to destruction with our visions, our versions, of what is better. BUT: this does not mean women are not to offer supportive and tentative criticism of one another. But there is a very important difference between (a) developing ideas together, in a "pre-theoretical" stage, engaged as equals in joint enquiry, and (b) one group developing, on the basis of their own experience, a set of criteria for good change for women— and then reluctantly making revisions in the criteria at the insistence of women to whom such criteria seem ethnocentric and arrogant. The deck is stacked when one group takes it upon itself to develop the theory and then have others criticize it. Categories are quick to congeal, and the experiences of women whose lives do not fit the categories will appear as anomalous when in fact the theory should have grown out of them as much as others from the beginning. This, of course, is why any organization or conference having to do with "women"—with no qualification—that seriously does not want to be "solipsistic" will from the beginning be multicultural or state the appropriate qualifications. How we think and what we think about does depend in large part

on who is there—not to mention who is expected or encouraged to speak. (Recall the boys in the *Symposium* sending the flute girls out.) Conversations and criticism take place in particular circumstances. Turf matters. So does the fact of who if anyone already has set up the terms of the conversations.

5. Theory cannot be useful to anyone interested in resistance and change unless there is reason to believe that knowing what a theory means and believing it to be true have some connection to resistance and change. As we make theory and offer it up to others, what do we assume is the connection between theory and consciousness? Do we expect others to read theory, understand it, believe it, and have their consciousness and lives thereby transformed? If we really want theory to make a difference to people's lives, how ought we to present it? Do we think people come to consciousness by reading? only by reading? Speaking to people through theory (orally or in writing) is a *very* specific context-dependent activity. That is, theory-makers and their methods and concepts constitute a community of people and of shared meanings. Their language can be just as opaque and foreign to those not in the community as a foreign tongue or dialect. Why do we engage in *this* activity and what effect do we think it ought to have? As Helen Longino has asked: "Is 'doing theory' just a bonding ritual for academic or educationally privileged feminists/women?" Again, whom does our theory-making serve?

IV. SOME SUGGESTIONS ABOUT HOW TO DO THEORY THAT IS NOT IMPERIALISTIC, ETHNOCENTRIC, DISRESPECTFUL

(*Problematically in the voice of a woman of color*)

What are the things we need to know about others, and about ourselves, in order to speak intelligently, intelligibly, sensitively, and helpfully about their lives? We can show respect, or lack of it, in writing theoretically about others no less than in talking directly with them. This is not to say that here we have a well-worked out concept of respect, but only to suggest that together all of us consider what it would mean to theorize in a respectful way.

When we speak, write, and publish our theories, to whom do we think we are accountable? Are the concerns we have in being accountable to "the profession" at odds with the concerns we have in being accountable to those about whom we theorize? Do commitments to "the profession," method, getting something published, getting tenure, lead us to talk and act in ways at odds with what we ourselves (let alone others) would regard as ordinary, decent behavior? To what extent do we presuppose that really understanding another person or culture requires our behaving in ways that are disrespectful, even violent? That is, to what extent do we presuppose that getting and/or publishing the requisite information requires or may require disregarding the wishes of others, lying to them, wresting information from them against their wills? Why and how do we think theorizing about others provides *understanding* of them? Is there any sense in which theorizing about others is a short-cut to understanding them?

Finally, if we think doing theory is an important activity, and we think that some conditions lead to better theorizing than others, what are we going to do about creating those conditions? If we think it not just desirable but necessary for women of different racial and ethnic identities to create feminist theory jointly, how shall that be arranged for? It may be the case that at this particular point we ought not even try to do that—that feminist theory by and for Hispanas needs to be done separately from feminist theory by and for Black women, white women, etc. But it must be recognized that white/Anglo women have more power and privilege than Hispanas, Black women, etc., and at the very least they can use such advantage

to provide space and time for other women to speak (with the above caveats about implicit restrictions on what counts as "the woman's voice"). And once again it is important to remember that the power of white/Anglo women vis-à-vis Hispanas and Black women is in inverse proportion to their working knowledge of each other.

This asymmetry is a crucial fact about the background of possible relationships between white women and women of color, whether as political co-workers, professional colleagues, or friends.

If white/Anglo women and women of color are to do theory jointly, in helpful, respectful, illuminating and empowering ways, the task ahead of white/Anglo women because of this asymmetry is a very hard task. The task is a very complex one. In part, to make an analogy, the task can be compared to learning a text without the aid of teachers. We all know the lack of contact felt when we want to discuss a particular issue that requires knowledge of a text with someone who does not know the text at all. Or the discomfort and impatience that arise in us when we are discussing an issue that presupposes a text and someone walks into the conversation who does not know the text. That person is either left out or will impose herself on us and either try to engage in the discussion or try to change the subject. Women of color are put in these situations by white/Anglo women and men constantly. Now imagine yourself simply left out but wanting to do theory with us. The first thing to recognize and accept is that you disturb our own dialogues by putting yourself in the left-out position and not leaving us in some meaningful sense to ourselves.

You must also recognize and accept that you must learn the text. But the text is an extraordinarily complex one: viz. our many different cultures. You are asking us to make ourselves more vulnerable to you than we already are before we have any reason to trust that you will not take advantage of this vulnerability. So you need to learn to become unintrusive, unimportant, patient to the point of tears, while at the same time open to learning any possible lessons. You will also have to come to terms with the sense of alienation, of not belonging, of having your world thoroughly disrupted, having it criticized and scrutinized from the point of view of those who have been harmed by it, having important concepts central to it dismissed, being viewed with mistrust, being seen as of no consequence except as an object of mistrust.

Why would any white/Anglo woman engage in this task? Out of self-interest? What in engaging in this task would be, not just in her interest, but perceived as such by her before the task is completed or well underway? Why should we want you to come into our world out of self-interest? Two points need to be made here. The task as described could be entered into with the intention of finding out as much as possible about us so as to better dominate us. The person engaged in this task would act as a spy. The motivation is not unfamiliar to us. We have heard it said that now that Third World countries are more powerful as a bloc, westerners need to learn more about them, that it is in their self-interest to do so. Obviously there is no reason why people of color should welcome white/Anglo women into their world for the carrying out of this intention. It is also obvious that white/Anglo feminists should not engage in this task under this description since the task under this description would not lead to joint theorizing of the desired sort: respectful, illuminating, helpful and empowering. It would be helpful and empowering only in a one-sided way.

Self-interest is also mentioned as a possible motive in another way. White/Anglo women sometimes say that the task of understanding women of color would entail self-growth or self-expansion. If the task is conceived as described here, then one should doubt that

growth or expansion will be the result. The severe self-disruption that the task entails should place a doubt in anyone who takes the task seriously about her possibilities of coming out of the task whole, with a self that is not as fragile as the selves of those who have been the victims of racism. But also, why should women of color embrace white/Anglo women's self-betterment without reciprocity? At this time women of color cannot afford this generous affirmation of white/Anglo women.

Another possible motive for engaging in this task is the motive of duty, "out of obligation," because white/Anglos have done people of color wrong. Here again two considerations: coming into Hispano, Black, Native American worlds out of obligation puts white/Anglos in a morally self-righteous position that is inappropriate. You are active, we are passive. We become the vehicles of your own redemption. Secondly, we couldn't want you to come into our worlds "out of obligation." That is like wanting someone to make love to you out of obligation. So, whether or not you have an obligation to do this (and we would deny that you do), or whether this task could even be done out of obligation, this is an inappropriate motive.

Out of obligation you should stay out of our way, respect us and our distance, and forego the use of whatever power you have over us—for example, the power to use your language in our meetings, the power to overwhelm us with your education, the power to intrude in our communities in order to research us and to record the supposed dying of our cultures, the power to engrain in us a sense that we are members of dying cultures and are doomed to assimilate, the power to keep us in a defensive posture with respect to our own cultures.

So the motive of friendship remains as both the only appropriate and understandable motive for white/Anglo feminists engaging in the task as described above. If you enter the task out of friendship with us, then you will be moved to attain the appropriate reciprocity of

care for your and our well-being as whole beings, you will have a stake in us and in our
world, you will be moved to satisfy the need for
reciprocity of understanding that will enable
you to follow us in our experiences as we are
able to follow you in yours.

We are not suggesting that if the learning
of the text is to be done out of friendship, you
must enter into a friendship with a whole community and for the purpose of making theory.
In order to understand what it is that we are
suggesting, it is important to remember that
during the description of her experience of exclusion, the Hispana voice said that Hispanas
experience the intimacy of friendship with
white/Anglo women friends as thoroughly incomplete. It is not until this fact is acknowledged by our white/Anglo women friends and
felt as a profound lack in our experience of
each other that white/Anglo women can begin
to see us. Seeing us in our communities will
make clear and concrete to you how incomplete we really are in our relationships with
you. It is this beginning that forms the proper
background for the yearning to understand
the text of our cultures that can lead to joint
theory-making.

Thus, the suggestion made here is that if
white/Anglo women are to understand our
voices, they must understand our communities

and us in them. Again, this is not to suggest
that you set out to make friends with our communities, though you may become friends with
some of the members, nor is it to suggest that
you should try to befriend us for the purpose
of making theory, with us. The latter would be
a perversion of friendship. Rather, from within
friendship you may be moved by friendship to
undergo the very difficult task of understanding the text of our cultures by understanding
our lives in our communities. This learning
calls for circumspection, for questioning of
yourselves and your roles in your own culture.
it necessitates a striving to understand while in
the comfortable position of not having an official calling card (as "scientific" observers of our
communities have); it demands recognition
that you do not have the authority of knowledge; it requires coming to the task without
ready-made theories to frame our lives. This
learning is then extremely hard because it requires openness (including openness to severe
criticism of the white/Anglo world), sensitivity,
concentration, self-questioning, circumspection. It should be clear that it does not consist
in a passive immersion in our cultures, but in a
striving to understand what it is that our voices
are saying. Only then can we engage in a mutual
dialogue that does not reduce each one of us to
instances of the abstraction called "women."

Sisterhood: Political Solidarity between Women

bell hooks

Women are the group most victimized by sexist oppression. As with other forms of group oppression, sexism is perpetuated by institutional and social structures; by the individuals who dominate, exploit, or oppress; and by the victims themselves, who are socialized to behave in ways that make them act in complicity with the status quo. Male supremacist ideology encourages women to believe we are valueless and obtain value only by relating to or bonding with men. We are taught that our relationships with one another diminish rather than enrich our experience. We are taught that women are "natural" enemies, that solidarity will never exist between us because we cannot, should not, and do not bond with one another. We have learned these lessons well. We must unlearn them if we are to build a sustained feminist movement. We must learn to live and work in solidarity. We must learn the true meaning and value of Sisterhood.

Although contemporary feminist movement should have provided a training ground for women to learn about political solidarity, Sisterhood was not viewed as a revolutionary accomplishment women would work and struggle to obtain. The vision of Sisterhood evoked by women's liberationists was based on the idea of common oppression. Needless to say, it was primarily bourgeois white women, both liberal and radical in perspective, who professed belief in the notion of common op-

pression. The idea of "common oppression" was a false and corrupt platform disguising and mystifying the true nature of women's varied and complex social reality. Women are divided by sexist attitudes, racism, class privilege, and a host of other prejudices. Sustained woman bonding can occur only when these divisions are confronted and the necessary steps are taken to eliminate them. Divisions will not be eliminated by wishful thinking or romantic reverie about common oppression despite the value of highlighting experiences all women share.

In recent years Sisterhood as slogan, motto, rallying cry no longer evokes the spirit of power in unity. Some feminists now seem to feel that unity between women is impossible given our differences. Abandoning the idea of Sisterhood as an expression of political solidarity weakens and diminishes feminist movement. Solidarity strengthens resistance struggle. There can be no mass-based feminist movement to end sexist oppression without a united front—women must take the initiative and demonstrate the power of solidarity. Unless we can show that barriers separating women can be eliminated, that solidarity can exist, we cannot hope to change and transform society as a whole. The shift away from an emphasis on Sisterhood has occurred because many women, angered by the insistence on "common oppression," shared identity, sameness, criticized or dismissed feminist movement altogether. The emphasis on Sisterhood was often seen as the emotional appeal masking the opportunism of manipulative bourgeois white women. It was seen as a cover-up hiding the fact that many women exploit and oppress other women. Black woman activist lawyer Florynce Kennedy wrote an essay, published in the anthology *Sisterhood is Powerful*, voicing her suspicions about the existence of solidarity between women as early as 1970:

It is for this reason that I have considerable difficulty with the sisterhood mystique: "We are sisters," "Don't criticize a 'sister' publicly," etc. When a female judge asks my client where the bruises are when she complains about being assaulted by her husband (as did Family Court Judge Sylvia Jaffin Liese), and makes smart remarks about her being overweight, and when another female judge is so hostile that she disqualifies herself but refuses to order a combative husband out of the house (even though he owns property elsewhere with suitable living quarters)—these judges are not my sisters.

Women were wise to reject a false Sisterhood based on shallow notions of bonding. We are mistaken if we allow these distortions or the women who created them (many of whom now tell us bonding between women is unimportant) to lead us to devalue Sisterhood.

Women are enriched when we bond with one another but we cannot develop sustaining ties or political solidarity using the model of Sisterhood created by bourgeois women's liberationists. According to their analysis, the basis for bonding was shared victimization, hence the emphasis on common oppression. This concept of bonding directly reflects male supremacist thinking. Sexist ideology teaches women that to be female is to be a victim. Rather than repudiate this equation (which mystifies female experience—in their daily lives most women are not continually passive, helpless, or powerless "victims"), women's liberationists embraced it, making shared victimization the basis for woman bonding. This meant that women had to conceive of themselves as "victims" in order to feel that feminist movement was relevant to their lives. Bonding as victims created a situation in which assertive, self-affirming women were often seen as having no place in feminist movement. It was this logic

that led white women activists (along with black men) to suggest that black women were so "strong" they did not need to be active in feminist movement. It was this logic that led many white women activities to abandon feminist movement when they no longer embraced the victim identity. Ironically, the women who were most eager to be seen as "victims," who overwhelmingly stressed the role of victim, were more privileged and powerful than the vast majority of women in our society. An example of this tendency is some writing about violence against women. Women who are exploited and oppressed daily cannot afford to relinquish the belief that they exercise some measure of control, however relative, over their lives. They cannot afford to see themselves solely as "victims" because their survival depends on continued exercise of whatever personal powers they possess. It would be psychologically demoralizing for these women to bond with other women on the basis of shared victimization. They bond with other women on the basis of shared strengths and resources. This is the woman bonding feminist movement should encourage. It is this type of bonding that is the essence of Sisterhood.

Bonding as "victims," white women liberationists were not required to assume responsibility for confronting the complexity of their own experience. They were not challenging one another to examine their sexist attitudes towards women unlike themselves or exploring the impact of race and class privilege on their relationships to women outside their race/class groups. Identifying as "victims," they could abdicate responsibility for their role in the maintenance and perpetuation of sexism, racism, and classism, which they did by insisting that only men were the enemy. They did not acknowledge and confront the enemy within. They were not prepared to forego privilege and do the "dirty work" (the struggle and confrontation necessary to build political awareness as well as the many tedious tasks to be accomplished in day to day organizing) that is necessary in the development of radical political consciousness.* Sisterhood became yet another shield against reality, another support system. Their version of Sisterhood was informed by racist and classist assumption about white womanhood, that the white "lady" (that is to say bourgeois woman) should be protected from all that might upset or discomfort her and shielded from negative realities that might lead to confrontation. Their version of Sisterhood dictated that sisters were to "unconditionally" love one another; that they were to avoid conflict and minimize disagreement; that they were not to criticize one other, especially in public. For a time these mandates created an illusion of unity suppressing the competition, hostility, perpetual disagreement, and abusive criticism (trashing) that was often the norm in feminist groups. Today many splinter groups who share common identities (e.g., Wasp working class; white academic faculty women; anarchist feminists, etc.) use this same model of Sisterhood, but participants in these groups endeavor to support, affirm, and protect one another while demonstrating hostility (usually through excessive trashing) towards women outside the chosen sphere. Bonding between a chosen circle of women who strengthen their ties by excluding and devaluing women outside their group closely resembles the type of personal bonding between women that has always occurred under patriarchy: the one difference being the interest in feminism.

To develop political solidarity between women, feminist activists cannot bond on the terms set by the dominant ideology of the culture. We must define our own terms. Rather than bond on the basis of shared victimization or in response to a false sense of a common

enemy, we can bond on the basis of our political commitment to a feminist movement that aims to end sexist oppression. Given such a commitment, our energies would not be concentrated on the issue of equality with men or solely on the struggle to resist male domination. We would no longer accept a simplistic good girls/bad boys account of the structure of sexist oppression. Before we can resist male domination we must break our attachment to sexism; we must work to transform female consciousness. Working together to expose, examine, and eliminate sexist socialization within ourselves, women would strengthen and affirm one another and build a solid foundation for developing political solidarity.

Between women and men, sexism is most often expressed in the form of male domination which leads to discrimination, exploitation, or oppression. Between women, male supremacist values are expressed through suspicious, defensive, competitive behavior. It is sexism that leads women to feel threatened by one another without cause. While sexism teaches women to be sex objects for men, it is also manifest when women who have repudiated this role feel contemptuous and superior in relation to those women who have not. Sexism leads women to devalue parenting work while inflating the value of jobs and careers. Acceptance of sexist ideology is indicated when women teach children that there are only two possible behavior patterns: the role of dominant or submissive being. Sexism teaches women woman-hating, and both consciously and unconsciously we act out this hatred in our daily contact with one another.

Although contemporary feminist activists, especially radical feminists, called attention to women's absorption in sexist ideology, ways that women who are advocates of patriarchy, as well as women who uncritically accept sexist assumptions, could unlearn that socialization were not stressed. It was often assumed that to support feminism was synonymous with

---

*The first task being honest critique and evaluation of one's social status, values, political beliefs, etc.

repudiation of sexism in all its forms. Taking on the label "feminist" was accepted as a sign of personal transformation; as a consequence, the process by which values were altered was either ignored or could not be spelled out because no fundamental change had occurred. Sometimes consciousness-raising groups provided space for women to explore their sexism. This examination of attitudes towards themselves and other women was often a catalyst for transformation. Describing the function of rap groups in *The Politics of Women's Liberation*, Jo Freeman explains:

Women came together in small groups to share personal experiences, problems, and feelings. From this public sharing comes the realization that what was thought to be individual is in fact common: that what was thought to be a personal problem has a social cause and a political solution. The rap group attacks the effects of psychological oppression and helps women to put it into a feminist context. Women learn to see how social structures and attitudes have molded them from birth and limited their opportunities. They ascertain the extent to which women have been denigrated in this society and how they have developed prejudices against themselves and other women. They learn to develop self-esteem and to appreciate the value of group solidarity.

As consciousness-raising groups lost their popularity new groups were not formed to fulfill similar functions. Women produced a large quantity of feminist writing but placed little emphasis on ways to unlearn sexism.

Since we live in a society that promotes fadism and temporary superficial adaptation of different values, we are easily convinced that changes have occurred in arenas where there has been little or no change. Women's sexist attitudes towards one another are one such arena. All over the United States, women spend hours of their time daily verbally abusing other women, usually through malicious gossip (not to be confused with gossip as positive communication). Television soap operas and nighttime dramas continually portray woman-to-woman relationships as characterized by aggression, contempt, and competitiveness. In feminist circles sexism towards women is expressed by abusive trashing, total disregard and lack of concern or interest in women who have not joined feminist movement. This is especially evident at university campuses where feminist studies is often seen as a discipline or program having no relationship to feminist movement. In her commencement address at Barnard College in May, 1979, black woman writer Toni Morrison told her audience:

I want not to ask you but to tell you not to participate in the oppression of your sisters. Mothers who abuse their children are women, and another woman, not an agency, has to be willing to stay their hands. Mothers who set fire to school buses are women, and another woman, not an agency, has to tell them to stay their hands. Women who stop the promotion of other women in careers are women, and another woman must come to the victim's aid. Social and welfare workers who humiliate their clients may be women, and other women colleagues have to deflect their anger.

I am alarmed by the violence that women do to each other: professional violence, competitive violence, emotional violence. I am alarmed by the willingness of women to enslave other women. I am alarmed by a growing absence of decency on the killing floor of professional women's worlds.

To build a politicized, mass-based feminist movement, women must work harder to overcome the alienation from one another that exists when sexist socialization has not been unlearned, e.g., homophobia, judging by appearance, conflicts between women with diverse sexual practices. So far, feminist movement has not transformed woman-to-woman relationships, especially between women who are strangers to one another or from different backgrounds, even though it has been the occasion for bonding between individuals and groups of women. We must renew our efforts to help women unlearn sexism if we are to develop affirming personal relationships as well as political unity.

Racism is another barrier to solidarity between women. The ideology of Sisterhood as expressed by contemporary feminist activists indicated no acknowledgement that racist discrimination, exploitation, and oppression of multi-ethnic women by white women had made it impossible for the two groups to feel they shared common interests or political concerns. Also, the existence of totally different cultural backgrounds can make communication difficult. This has been especially true of black and white female relationships. Historically, many black women experienced white women as the white supremacist group who most directly exercised power over them, often in a manner far more brutal and dehumanizing than that of racist white men. Today, despite predominant rule by white supremacist patriarchs, black women often work in situations where the immediate supervisor, boss, or authority figure is a white woman. Conscious of the privileges white men as well as white women gain as a consequence of racial domination, black women were quick to react to the feminist call for Sisterhood by pointing to the contradiction—that we should join with women who exploit us to help liberate them. The call for Sisterhood was heard by many black women as a plea for help and support for a movement that did not address us. As Toni Morrison explains in her article "What the Black Woman Thinks About Women's Lib," many black women do not respect bourgeois white women and could not imagine supporting a cause that would be for their benefit.

Black women have been able to envy white women (their looks, their easy life, the attention they seem to get from their men); they could fear them (for the economic control they have had over black women's lives); and even love them (as mammies and domes-

tic workers can); but black women have found it impossible to respect white women . . . Black women have no abiding admiration of white women as competent, complete people, whether vying with them for the few professional slots available to women in general, or moving their dirt from one place to another, they regarded them as willful children, pretty children, mean children, but never as real adults capable of handling the real problems of the world.

White women were ignorant of the facts of life—perhaps by choice, perhaps with the assistance of men, but ignorant anyway. They were totally dependent on marriage or male support (emotionally and economically). They confronted their sexuality with furtiveness, complete abandon, or repression. Those who could afford it gave over the management of the house and the rearing of children to others. (It is a source of amusement even now to black women to listen to feminist talk of liberation while somebody's nice black grandmother shoulders the daily responsibility of child rearing and floor mopping, and the liberated one comes home to examine the housekeeping, correct it, and be entertained by the children.) If Women's Lib needs those grandmothers to thrive, it has a serious flaw.

Many perceived that women's liberation movement as outlined by bourgeois white women would serve their interests at the expense of poor and working class women, many of whom are black. Certainly this was not a basis for Sisterhood and black women would have been politically naive had we joined such a movement. However, given the struggles of black women's participation historically and currently in political organizing, the emphasis could have been on the development and clarification of the nature of political solidarity.

White females discriminate against and exploit black women while simultaneously being envious and competitive in their interactions with them. Neither process of interaction creates conditions wherein trust and mutually reciprocal relationships can develop. After constructing feminist theory and praxis in such a way as to omit focus on racism, white women shifted the responsibility for calling attention to race onto others. They did not have to take the initiative in discussions of racism or race privilege but could listen and respond to non-white women discussing racism without changing in any way the structure of feminist movement, without losing their hegemonic hold. They could then show their concern with having more women of color in feminist organizations by encouraging greater participation. They were not confronting racism. In more recent years, racism has become an accepted topic in feminist discussions not as a result of black women calling attention to it (this was done at the very onset of the movement), but as a result of white female input validating such discussions, a process which is indicative of how racism works. Commenting on this tendency in her essay "The Incompatible Menage À Trois: Marxism, Feminism, and Racism," Gloria Joseph states:

To date feminists have not concretely demonstrated the potential or capacity to become involved in fighting racism on an equal footing with sexism. Adrienne Rich's article on feminism and racism is an exemplary one on this topic. She reiterates much that has been voiced by black female writers, but the acclaim given her article shows again that it takes whiteness to give even Blackness validity.

Focus on racism in feminist circles is usually directed at legitimating the "as is" structure of feminist theory and praxis. Like other affirmative action agendas in white supremacist capitalist patriarchy, lengthy discussions of racism or lip-service to its importance tend to call attention to the "political correctness" of current feminist movement; they are not directed at an overall struggle to resist racist oppression in our society (not just racism in feminist movement). Discussions of racism have been implicitly sexist because of the focus on guilt and personal behavior. Racism is not an issue simply because white women activists are individually racist. They represent a small

percentage of women in this society. They could have all been anti-racist from the outset but eliminating racism would still need to be a central feminist issue. Racism is fundamentally a feminist issue because it is so inter-connected with sexist oppression. In the West, the philosophical foundations of racist and sexist ideology are similar. Although ethnocentric white values have led feminist theorists to argue the priority of sexism over racism, they do so in the context of attempting to create an evolutionary notion of culture, which in no way corresponds to our lived experience. In the United States, maintaining white supremacy has always been as great if not a greater priority than maintaining strict sex role divisions. It is no mere coincidence that interest in white women's rights is kindled whenever there is mass-based anti-racist protest. Even the most politically naive person can comprehend that a white supremacist state, asked to respond to the needs of oppressed black people and/or the needs of white women (particularly those from the bourgeois classes), will find it in its interest to respond to whites. Radical movement to end racism (a struggle that many have died to advance) is far more threatening than a women's movement shaped to meet the class needs of upwardly mobile white women.

It does not in any way diminish the value of or the need for feminist movement to recognize the significance of anti-racist struggle. Feminist theory would have much to offer if it showed women ways in which racism and sexism are immutably connected rather than pitting one struggle against the other or blatantly dismissing racism. A central issue for feminist activists has been the struggle to obtain for women the right to control their bodies. The very concept of white supremacy relies on the perpetuation of a white race. It is in the interest of continued white racist domination of the planet for white patriarchy to maintain control over all women's bodies. Any white female activist who works daily to help women gain control over their bodies and is racist negates and undermines her own effort. When white women attack white supremacy they are simultaneously participating in the struggle to end sexist oppression. This is just one example of the intersecting, complementary nature of racist and sexist oppression. There are many others that need to be examined by feminist theorists.

Racism allows white women to construct feminist theory and praxis in such a way that it is far removed from anything resembling radical struggle. Racist socialization teaches bourgeois white women to think they are necessarily more capable of leading masses of women than other groups of women. Time and time again, they have shown that they do not want to be part of feminist movement—they want to lead it. Even though bourgeois white women liberationists probably know less about grassroots organizing than many poor and working class women, they were certain of their leadership ability, as well as confident that theirs should be the dominant role in shaping theory and praxis. Racism teaches an inflated sense of importance and value, especially when coupled with class privilege. Most poor and working class women or even individual bourgeois non-white women would not have assumed that they could launch a feminist movement without first having the support and participation of diverse groups of women. Elizabeth Spelman stresses this impact of racism in her essay, "Theories of Race and Gender: The Erasure of Black Women":

... this is a racist society, and part of what this means is that, generally, the self-esteem of white people is deeply influenced by their difference from and supposed superiority to black people. White people may not think of themselves as racists, because they do not own slaves or hate blacks, but that does not mean that much of what props up white people's sense of self-esteem is not based on the racism which unfairly distributes benefits and burdens to whites and blacks.

One reason white women active in feminist movement were unwilling to confront racism was their arrogant assumption that their call for Sisterhood was a non-racist gesture. Many white women have said to me, "we wanted black women and other non-white women to join the movement," totally unaware of their perception that they somehow "own" the movement, that they are the "hosts" inviting us as "guests."

Despite current focus on eliminating racism in feminist movement, there has been little change in the direction of theory and praxis. While white feminist activists now include writings by women of color on course outlines, or hire one woman of color to teach a class about her ethnic group, or make sure one or more women of color are represented in feminist organizations, (even though this contribution of women of color is needed and valuable) more often than not they are attempting to cover up the fact that they are totally unwilling to surrender their hegemonic dominance of theory and praxis, a dominance which they would not have established were this not a white supremacist, capitalist state. Their attempts to manipulate women of color, a component of the process of dehumanization, do not always go unnoticed. In the July 1983 issue of *In These Times*, a letter written by Theresa Funiciello was published on the subject of poor women and the women's movement which shows the nature of racism within feminist movement:

Prior to a conference some time ago on the Urban Woman sponsored by the New York City chapter of NOW, I received a phone call from a NOW representative (whose name I have forgotten) asking for a welfare speaker with special qualifications. I was asked that she not be white—she might be "too articulate"—(i.e., not me), that she not be black, she might be "too angry." Perhaps she could be Puerto Rican? She should not say anything political or analytical but confine herself to the subject of "what the women's movement has done for me."

Funiciello responded to this situation by organizing a multiracial women's takeover of the conference. This type of action shows the spirit of Sisterhood.

Another response to racism has been the establishment of unlearning racism workshops, which are often led by white women. These workshops are important, yet they tend to focus primarily on cathartic individual psychological acknowledgement of personal prejudice without stressing the need for corresponding change in political commitment and action. A woman who attends an unlearning racism workshop and learns to acknowledge that she is racist is no less a threat than one who does not. Acknowledgement of racism is significant when it leads to transformation. More research, writing, and practical implementation of findings must be done on ways to unlearn racist socialization. Many white women who daily exercise race privilege lack awareness that they are doing so (which explains the emphasis on confession in unlearning racism workshops). They may not have conscious understanding of the ideology of white supremacy and the extent to which it shapes their behavior and attitudes towards women unlike themselves. Often, white women bond on the basis of shared racial identity without conscious awareness of the significance of their actions. This unconscious maintenance and perpetuation of white supremacy is dangerous because none of us can struggle to change racist attitudes if we do not recognize that they exist. For example, a group of white feminist activists who do not know one another may be present at a meeting to discuss feminist theory. They may feel they are bonded on the basis of shared womanhood, but the atmosphere will noticeably change when a woman of color enters the room. The white women will become tense, no longer relaxed, no longer celebratory. Unconsciously, they felt close to one another because they shared racial identity. The "whiteness" that bonds them together is a racial identity that is directly related

to the experience of non-white people as "other" and as a "threat." Often when I speak to white women about racial bonding, they deny that it exists; it is not unlike sexist men denying their sexism. Until white supremacy is understood and attacked by white women there can be no bonding between them and multi-ethnic groups of women.

Women will know that white feminist activists have begun to confront racism in a serious and revolutionary manner when they are not simply acknowledging racism in feminist movement or calling attention to personal prejudice, but are actively struggling to resist racist oppression in our society. Women will know they have made a political commitment to eliminating racism when they help change the direction of feminist movement, when they work to unlearn racist socialization prior to assuming positions of leadership or shaping theory or making contact with women of color so that they will not perpetuate and maintain racial oppression or, unconsciously or consciously, abuse and hurt non-white women. These are the truly radical gestures that create a foundation for the experience of political solidarity between white women and women of color.

White women are not the only group who must confront racism if Sisterhood is to emerge. Women of color must confront our absorption of white supremacist beliefs, "internalized racism," which may lead us to feel self-hate, to vent anger and rage at injustice at one another rather than at oppressive forces, to hurt and abuse one another, or to lead one ethnic group to make no effort to communicate with another. Often women of color from varied ethnic groups have learned to resent and hate one another, or to be competitive with one another. Often Asian, Latina, or Native American Indian groups find they can bond with whites by hating blacks. Black people respond to this by perpetuating racist stereotypes and images of these ethnic groups. It becomes a vicious cycle. Divisions between women of color will not be eliminated until we assume responsibility for uniting (not solely on the basis of resisting racism) to learn about our cultures, to share our knowledge and skills, and to gain strength from our diversity. We need to do more research and writing about the barriers that separate us and the ways we can overcome such separation. Often the men in our ethnic groups have greater contact with one another than we do. Women often assume so many job-related and domestic responsibilities that we lack the time or do not make the time to get to know women outside our group or community. Language differences often prevent us from communicating; we can change this by encouraging one another to learn to speak Spanish, English, Japanese, Chinese, etc.

One factor that makes interaction between multi-ethnic groups of women difficult and sometimes impossible is our failure to recognize that a behavior pattern in one culture may be unacceptable in another, that it may have different signification cross-culturally. Through repeated teaching of a course titled "Third World Women in the United States," I have learned the importance of learning what we called one another's cultural codes. An Asian-American student, of Japanese heritage, explained her reluctance to participate in feminist organizations by calling attention to the tendency among feminist activists to speak rapidly without pause, to be quick on the uptake, always ready with a response. She had been raised to pause and think before speaking, to consider the impact of one's words, a characteristic which she felt was particularly true of Asian-Americans. She expressed feelings of inadequacy on the various occasions she was present in feminist groups. In our class, we learned to allow pauses and appreciate them. By sharing this cultural code, we created an atmosphere in the classroom that allowed for different communication patterns. This particular class was peopled primarily by black women.

Several white women students complained that the atmosphere in the class was "too hostile." They cited the noise level and direct confrontations that took place in the room prior to class starting as an example of this hostility. Our response was to explain that what they perceived as hostility and aggression, we considered playful teasing and affectionate expressions of our pleasure at being together. Our tendency to talk loudly we saw as a consequence of being in a room with many people speaking as well as cultural background: many of us were raised in families where individuals speak loudly. In their upbringing as white, middle class females, the complaining students had been taught to identify loud and direct speech with anger. We explained that we did not identify loud or blunt speech in this way, and encouraged them to switch codes, to think of it as an affirming gesture. Once they switched codes, they not only began to have a more creative, joyful experience in the class, but they also learned that silence and quiet speech can in some cultures indicate hostility and aggression. By learning one another's cultural codes and respecting our differences, we felt a sense of community, of Sisterhood. Respecting diversity does not mean uniformity or sameness.

A crucial concern in these multi-racial classroom settings was recognition and acknowledgement of our differences and the extent to which they determine how we will be perceived by others. We had to continually remind one another to appreciate difference since many of us were raised to fear it. We talked about the need to acknowledge that we all suffer in some way but that we are not all oppressed nor equally oppressed. Many of us feared that our experiences were irrelevant because they were not as oppressive or as exploited as the experience of others. We discovered that we had a greater feeling of unity when people focused truthfully on their own experiences without comparing them with those of others in a competitive way. One student, Isabel Yrigoyei, wrote:

We are not equally oppressed. There is no joy in this. We must speak from within us, our own experiences, our own oppressions—taking someone else's oppression is nothing to feel proud of. We should never speak for that which we have not felt.

When we began our communication by focusing on individual experiences, we found them to be varied even among those of us who shared common ethnic backgrounds. We learned that these differences mean we have no monolithic experiences that we can identity as "Chicana experience," "Black experience," etc. A Chicana growing up in a rural environment in a Spanish-speaking home has a life experience that differs from that of a Chicana raised in an English-speaking family in a bourgeois, predominantly white New Jersey suburb. These two women will not automatically feel solidarity. Even though they are from the same ethnic group, they must work to develop Sisterhood. Seeing these types of differences, we also confronted our tendency to value some experiences over others. We might see the Spanish-speaking Chicana as being more "politically correct" than her English-speaking peer. By no longer passively accepting the learned tendency to compare and judge, we could see value in each experience. We could also see that our different experiences often meant that we had different needs, that there was no one strategy or formula for the development of political consciousness. By mapping out various strategies, we affirmed our diversity while working towards solidarity. Women must explore various ways to communicate with one another cross-culturally if we are to develop political solidarity. When women of color strive to learn with and about one another we take responsibility for building Sisterhood. We need not rely on white women to lead the way to solidarity; all too often opportunistic concerns point them in other directions. We can establish unity among ourselves with anti-racist women. We can stand together united in political solidarity,

in feminist movement. We can restore to the idea of Sisterhood its true meaning and value.

Cutting across racial lines, class is a serious political division between women. It was often suggested in early feminist literature that class would not be so important if more poor and working class women would join the movement. Such thinking was both a denial of the existence of class privilege gained through exploitation as well as a denial of class struggle. To build Sisterhood, women must criticize and repudiate class exploitation. The bourgeois woman who takes a less privileged "sister" to lunch or dinner at a fancy restaurant may be acknowledging class but she is not repudiating class privilege—she is exercising it. Wearing second hand clothing and living in low-cost housing in a poor neighborhood while buying stock is not a gesture of solidarity with those who are deprived or under-privileged. As in the case of racism in feminist movement, the emphasis on class has been focused on individual status and change. Until women accept the need for redistribution of wealth and resources in the United States and work towards the achievement of that end, there will be no bonding between women that transcends class.

It is terribly apparent that feminist movement so far has primarily served the class interests of bourgeois white women and men. The great majority of women from middle class situations who recently entered the labor force (an entry encouraged and promoted by feminist movement) helped strengthen the economy of the 1970s. In *The Two-Paycheck Marriage*, Caroline Bird emphasizes the extent to which these women (most of whom are white) helped bolster a waning economy:

Working wives helped families maintain that standard of living through inflation. The Bureau of Labor Statistics has concluded that between 1973 and 1974 the real purchasing power of single-earner families dropped 3 percent compared with only 1 percent for families in which the wife was working . . . Women especially will put themselves out to defend a standard of living they see threatened.

Women did more than maintain standards. Working women lifted millions of families into middle class life. Her pay meant the difference between an apartment and a house, or college for the children . . .

. . . Working wives were beginning to create a new kind of rich—and . . . a new kind of poor.

More than ten years later, it is evident that large numbers of individual white women (especially those from middle class backgrounds) have made economic strides in the wake of feminist movement support of careerism, and affirmative action programs in many professions. However, the masses of women are as poor as ever, or poorer. To the bourgeois "feminist," the million dollar salary granted newscaster Barbara Walters represents a victory for women. To working class women who make less than the minimum wage and receive few if any benefits, it means continued class exploitation.

Leah Fritz's *Dreamers and Dealers* is a fine example of the liberal woman's attempt to gloss over the fact that class privilege is based on exploitation, that rich women support and condone that exploitation, that the people who suffer most are poor, under-privileged women and children. Fritz attempts to evoke sympathy for all upper class women by stressing their psychological suffering, their victimization at the hands of men. She concludes her chapter "Rich Women" with the statement:

Feminism belongs as much to the rich woman as to the poor woman. It can help her to understand that her own interests are linked with the advancement of all womankind; that comfort in dependency is a trap; that the golden cage has bars, too; and that, rich and poor, we are all wounded in the service of the patriarchy, although our scars are different. The inner turmoil that sends her to a psychoanalyst can generate energy for the movement which alone may heal her, by setting her free.

Fritz conveniently ignores that domination and exploitation are necessary if there are to be rich women who may experience sexist discrimination or exploitation. She conveniently ignores class struggle.

Women from lower class groups had no difficulty recognizing that the social equality women's liberationists talked about equated careerism and class mobility with liberation. They also knew who would be exploited in the service of this liberation. Daily confronting class exploitation, they cannot conveniently ignore class struggle. In the anthology *Women of Crisis*, Helen, a working class white woman, who works as a maid in the home of a bourgeois white "feminist" expresses her understanding of the contradiction between feminist rhetoric and practice:

I think the missus is right: everyone should be equal. She keeps on saying that. But then she has me working away in her house, and I'm not equal with her—and she doesn't want to be equal with me: and I don't blame her, because if I was her I'd hold on to my money just like she does. Maybe that's what the men are doing—they're holding on to their money. And it's a big fight, like it always is about money. She should know. She doesn't go throwing big fat pay checks at her "help." She's fair; she keeps on reminding us—but she's not going to "liberate" us, any more than the men are going to "liberate" their wives or their secretaries or the other women working in their companies.

Women's liberationists not only equated psychological pain with material deprivation to de-emphasize class privilege; they often suggested it was the more severe problem. They managed to overlook the fact that many women suffer both psychologically and materially and for that reason alone changing their social status merited greater attention than careerism. Certainly the bourgeois woman who is suffering psychically is more likely to find help than the woman who is suffering material deprivation as well as emotional pain. One of the basic differences in perspective between the bourgeois woman and the working class or poor woman is that the latter know that being discriminated against or exploited because one is female may be painful and dehumanizing, but it may not necessarily be as painful, dehumanizing, or threatening as being without food or shelter, as starvation, as being deathly ill but unable to obtain medical care. Had poor women set the agenda for feminist movement, they might have decided that class struggle would be a central feminist issue; that poor and privileged women would work to understand class structure and the way it pits women against one another.

Outspoken socialist feminists, most of whom are white women, have emphasized class but they have not been effective in changing attitudes towards class in feminist movement. Despite their support of socialism, their values, behaviors, and lifestyles continue to be shaped by privilege. They have not developed collective strategies to convince bourgeois women who have no radical political perspective that eliminating class oppression is crucial to efforts to end sexist oppression. They have not worked hard to organize with poor and working class women who may not identify as socialists but do identify with the need for redistribution of wealth in the United States. They have not worked to raise the consciousness of women collectively. Much of their energy has been spent addressing the white male left, discussing the connections between marxism and feminism, or explaining to other feminist activists that socialist feminism is the best strategy for revolution. Emphasis on class struggle is often incorrectly deemed the sole domain of socialist feminists. Although I call attention to directions and strategies they have not employed, I wish to emphasize that these issues should be addressed by all activists in feminist movement. When women face the reality of classism and make political commitments to eliminating it, we will no longer experience the class conflicts that have been so apparent in feminist movement. Until we focus on class divisions between

women, we will be unable to build political solidarity.

Sexism, racism, and classism divide women from one another. Within feminist movement, divisions and disagreements about strategy and emphasis led to the formation of a number of groups with varied political positions. Splintering into different political factions and special interest groups has erected unnecessary barriers to Sisterhood that could easily be eliminated. Special interest groups lead women to believe that only socialist feminists should be concerned about class; that only lesbian feminists should be concerned about the oppression of lesbians and gay men; that only black women or other women of color should be concerned about racism. Every woman can stand in political opposition to sexist, racist, heterosexist, and classist oppression. While she may choose to focus her work on a given political issue or a particular cause, if she is firmly opposed to all forms of group oppression, this broad perspective will be manifest in all her work irrespective of its particularity. When feminist activists are anti-racist and against class exploitation, it will not matter if women of color are present or poor women, etc. These issues will be deemed important and will be addressed, although the women most personally affected by particular exploitations will necessarily continue in the forefront of those struggles. Women must learn to accept responsibility for fighting oppressions that may not directly affect us as individuals. Feminist movement, like other radical movements in our society, suffers when individual concerns and priorities are the only reason for participation. When we show our concern for the collective, we strengthen our solidarity.

Solidarity was a word seldom used in contemporary feminist movement. Much greater emphasis was placed on the idea of "support." Support can mean upholding or defending a position one believes is right. It can also mean serving as a prop or a foundation for a weak structure. This latter meaning had greater significance in feminist circles. Its value emerged from the emphasis on shared victimization. Identifying as "victims," women were acknowledging a helplessness and powerlessness as well as a need for support, in this case the support of fellow feminist activists, "sisters." It was closely related to the shallow notion of Sisterhood. Commenting on its usage among feminist activists in her essay "With All Due Respect," Jane Rule explains:

Support is a much used word in the women's movement. For too many people it means giving and receiving unqualified approval. Some women are awfully good at withdrawing it at crucial moments. Too many are convinced they can't function without it. It's a false concept which has produced barriers to understanding and done real emotional damage. Suspension of critical judgement is not necessary for offering real support, which has to do instead with self-respect and respect for other people even at moments of serious disagreement.

Women's legacy of woman-hating which includes fierce, brutal, verbal tearing apart of one another has to be eliminated if women are to make critiques and engage in disagreements and arguments that are constructive and caring, with the intention of enriching rather than diminishing. Woman-to-woman negative, aggressive behavior is not unlearned when all critical judgement is suspended. It is unlearned when women accept that we are different, that we will necessarily disagree, but that we can disagree and argue with one another without acting as if we are fighting for our lives, without feeling that we stand to lose all self-esteem by verbally trashing someone else. Verbal disagreements are often the setting where women can demonstrate their engagement with the win-or-lose competitiveness that is most often associated with male interactions, especially in the arena of sports. Women, like men, must learn how to dialogue with one another without competition. Jane Rule suggests that women can disagree without trashing if they

realize they do not stand to lose value or self-worth if they are criticized: "No one can discredit my life if it is in my own hands, and therefore I do not have to make anyone carry the false burden of my frightened hostility."

Women need to come together in situations where there will be ideological disagreement and work to change that interaction so communication occurs. This means that when women come together, rather than pretend union, we would acknowledge that we are divided and must develop strategies to overcome fears, prejudices, resentments, competitiveness, etc. The fierce negative disagreements that have taken place in feminist circles have led many feminist activists to shun group or individual interaction where there is likely to be disagreement which leads to confrontation. Safety and support have been redefined to mean hanging out in groups where the participants are alike and share similar values. While no woman wants to enter a situation in which she will be psychically annihilated, women can face one another in hostile confrontation and struggle and move beyond the hostility to understanding. Expression of hostility as an end in itself is a useless activity, but when it is the catalyst pushing us on to greater clarity and understanding, it serves a meaningful function.

Women need to have the experience of working through hostility to arrive at understanding and solidarity if only to free ourselves from the sexist socialization that tells us to avoid confrontation because we will be victimized or destroyed. Time and time again, I have had the experience of making statements at talks that anger a listener and lead to assertive and sometimes hostile verbal confrontation. The situation feels uncomfortable, negative, and unproductive because there are angry voices, tears, etc. and yet I may find later that the experience has led to greater clarity and growth on my part and on the part of the listener. On one occasion, I was invited by a black woman sociologist, a very soft-spoken individual, to speak in a class she was teaching. A young Chicana woman who could pass for white was a student in the class. We had a heated exchange when I made the point that the ability to pass for white gave her a perspective on race totally different from that of someone who is dark-skinned and can never pass. I pointed out that any person meeting her with no knowledge of her ethnic background probably assumes that she is white and relates to her accordingly. At the time the suggestion angered her. She became quite angry and finally stormed out of the class in tears. The teacher and fellow students definitely saw me as the "bad guy" who had failed to support a fellow sister and instead reduced her to tears. They were annoyed that our get-together had not been totally pleasurable, unemotional, dispassionate. I certainly felt miserable in the situation. The student, however, contacted me weeks later to share her feelings that she had gained new insights and awareness as a result of our encounter which aided her personal growth. Incidents like this one, which initially appear to be solely negative because of tension or hostility, can lead to positive growth. If women always seek to avoid confrontation, to always be "safe," we may never experience any revolutionary change, any transformation, individually or collectively.

When women actively struggle in a truly supportive way to understand our differences, to change misguided, distorted perspectives, we lay the foundation for the experience of political solidarity. Solidarity is not the same as support. To experience solidarity, we must have a community of interests, shared beliefs and goals around which to unite, to build Sisterhood. Support can be occasional. It can be given and just as easily withdrawn. Solidarity requires sustained, ongoing commitment. In feminist movement, there is need for diversity, disagreement, and difference if we are to grow. As Grace Lee Boggs and James Boggs emphasize in *Revolution and Evolution in the Twentieth Century:*

The same appreciation of the reality of contradiction underlies the concept of criticism and self-criticism. Criticism and self-criticism is the way in which individuals united by common goals can consciously utilize their differences and limitations, i.e., the negative, in order to accelerate their positive advance. The popular formulation for this process is "changing a bad thing into a good thing. . . ."

Women do not need to eradicate difference to feel solidarity. We do not need to share common oppression to fight equally to end oppression. We do not need anti-male sentiments to bond us together, so great is the wealth of experience, culture, and ideas we have to share with one another. We can be sisters united by shared interests and beliefs, united in our appreciation for diversity, united in our struggle to end sexist oppression, united in political solidarity.

Toward Gender-Inclusive Feminism: Men's Responses to Feminism

Among the misconceptions that some members of the general public have about any and all schools of feminist thought is that in order to be a true feminist someone has to be (1) minimally, a woman and (2) ideally, a woman who dislikes, distrusts, or even hates men, viewing them as "the enemy." Although it is true that some feminists believe that in order to overthrow patriarchal society women must abandon that society either by abstaining from heterosexual relations and/or by eschewing all relationships with men in the public as well as the personal realm, this has always been the minority view within feminism and appears to be further on the wane. *Gender* Studies curricula are replacing or supplementing *Feminist* Studies and *Women's* Studies curricula, and mixed groups of men and women are springing up everywhere as many of the all-women consciousness-raising groups of the past disband. Not men, women are assured, but a particular kind of society—patriarchy—is the problem, and it is a problem for the men as well as the women trapped within it.

A society is patriarchal to the degree that it is male-dominated, male-identified, and male-centered. To say that a society is male-dominated is to say that in such a society there are huge power differentials between men and women that result in men claiming larger shares of economic wealth and in wielding more political and cultural authority than women. To say that a society is male-identified is to stress that core cultural ideas about what is considered good, desirable, preferable, or normal are associated with men and masculinity. Men are selves; women are the other. Men are strong; women are weak. Men are rational, women are emotional. Finally, to say that a society is male-centered is to say that in such a society the focus of attention is primarily on men and what men do: namely, engage in sports activities, wage war, invest in the stock market, and so on.

To be sure, some women have done exceedingly well in patriarchal society, but such women are the exception not the rule. What's more, whether a man celebrates the patriarchal status quo or not, patriarchy will still confer certain benefits on him simply because he is a man. The question, then, becomes this: should men who recognize that patriarchy is an unjust social system join with each other and/or with dissatisfied women (feminists) to overthrow or reform it? Should these men of conscience try to persuade their disbelieving brothers that they are sexists and therefore need to change their attitudes and behavior? Or should these men of conscience simply focus on how they are part of the problem, seeking to improve their own relationships with women? As difficult as it is for men of goodwill to know what to do, one thing is certain: It is not easy to be honest about how one is a beneficiary of an unjust state of affairs. For this reason some men prefer to explore their sexism only with other men, finding themselves unable, as some of their brothers are, to be candid about their feelings in a mixed group.

Harry Brod is among those opponents of sexism who think that the best way for men to begin to fight sexism is to join together in all-male consciousness-raising groups. He maintains that "fraternity," by which he means a healthy sort of confessional male-bonding, precedes equality and liberty. In "Fraternity, Equality, Liberty," Brod asks feminists not to dismiss such gatherings of men as yet another version of the "old boys' club." Men are not inherently evil or flawed creatures, insists Brod. Rather they and their masculine traits are the distorted products of the same repressive system of patriarchy that has harmed women. Because men can work to effect the *political* changes in society that feminists propose, men can be feminists even though they lack the *personal* experiences women have. A man can work to reform laws that limit women's reproductive freedom, even though he cannot experience the trauma of an unwanted foetus growing and developing within his body.

In contrast to Brod, Jack Kammer and Robert Bly are critical of feminism. In " 'Male' Is Not a Four-Letter Word," Kammer accuses feminists of engaging in excessive "male-bashing" (p. 510). He claims that things have gotten so bad for men that no matter what a man does, he is told that it was the wrong thing for him to do. If a man works long hours, it's because he's overly competitive and slighting his duties to his wife and children. But, if he scales back his hours at the workplace, it's because he's lazy and relying on his wife to pick up the slack by working a so-called double day. Men, says Kammer, are tired of being portrayed as beasts, as rapists, child molesters, women-batterers, and sexual harassers. Nevertheless, men dare not protest this unjust portrayal of their sex for fear they will be labeled "whiners," says Kammer. As a result, women are encouraged to

demand even more from men. Not only must the rapist be severely punished, so too must the sexual harasser, pornographer, and pimp be severely punished. For that matter, so must any man who even dares to look at a woman with desire in his eyes. All men are guilty of crimes against women; few, if any, can be found innocent of offense. Women's great virtue must be protected from men's utter viciousness.

Angry about how badly men have it, Kammer observes that our society seems unconcerned that men commit suicide five times more often than women, that men die seven to eight years earlier than women, that 90 percent of all homeless people are men, and that men must fight the wars (p. 515). Worse, says Kammer, our society has little respect for its fathers and husbands. An increasing number of men are refusing to commit themselves to family life on the grounds that it makes no sense for them to try to be good husbands and fathers if no one is going to appreciate their efforts. Kammer predicts that unless women, and especially feminists, start treating men fairly, they will further worsen male-female relationships. Men will eventually rebel and stand up to women, and the confrontation will be far from pleasant.

In "The Pillow and the Key," Robert Bly provides a "mythopoetic" interpretation of men's fundamental being. Bly claims that, largely as the result of the feminist movement, men are getting "softer" and women are getting "harder." As a result, women's spirits are at an all-time high, while men are falling into ever-deeper states of depression and despair. The savage, John Wayne, macho man of the '50s has been replaced by the sensitive and sentimental man of the '60s and '70s—a very kind and gentle man, an entirely nice man, but a man incapable of exhibiting the kind of leadership and resolve that only a *real* man can exhibit. Such a man is idealized in the myth of Iron John who supposedly resides deep within each man. He is the Hairy Man, the Wild Man, the animal, universal man that seeks expression in the spirit, body, and mind of the particular human men in which he resides. This Wild Man is neither the savage man of the '50s nor the sensitive and sentimental man of the '60s and '70s. The former as well as the latter is a socially constructed, distorted image of man as he really is. The savage man mistook *meanness* for true strength, while the sensitive man mistook *softness* for authentic goodness. Nevertheless, women especially feminists, proclaimed the sensitive man superior to the savage man, only to discover that as bad as an abusive man is, a "wimp" is not necessarily an easier burden to bear.

Bly proclaims that the only way men can find the true Wild Man within themselves is by joining together to discover and experience what is best about "masculinity." Ideally, fathers and sons in particular should spend time together doing "guy things," totally removed from the taming influence of womenfolk. Men need to understand manhood from a male standpoint rather than from a female standpoint,

especially if that female standpoint is the kind of "male-bashing" standpoint Kammer previously identified. Bly writes:

If the son learns feeling primarily from the mother, then he will probably see his own masculinity from the feminine point of view as well. He may be fascinated with it, but he will be afraid of it. He may pity it and want to reform it, or he may be suspicious of it and want to kill it. He may admire it, but he will never feel at home with it (p. 530).

Bly wants sons to esteem their own and their fathers' Wild Man, for only wild men have the energy to live full lives. Moreover, Bly says he wants much the same for mothers and their daughters. Whether Bly is sincere about this *et tu* nod in the direction of women is, of course, a point feminists should consider. Will Wild Woman really find a soul mate in Wild Man, or will she find instead the embodiment of everything the term "feminist backlash" connotes?

The Profeminist Men's Movement: Fraternity, Equality, Liberty

Harry Brod

"Fraternity, Equality, Liberty." Those familiar with European history will recognize this as an inversion of the slogan of the French Revolution: "Liberty, Equality, Fraternity." The ordering of these principles by the ideologists of the revolution was not coincidental, but rather reflected a certain conceptual scheme. To their minds, the first order of business was to secure liberty, by which they meant freedom from restrictions imposed upon them by others. Having won this liberty, they would then proceed to establish a society of equality. Subsequently, once men were living in this new society, feelings of fraternity for the brotherhood of man would emerge among all men. From our contemporary vantage point, we recognize that this fraternity excluded women in principle, and in practice excluded or limited the participation of a great number of men who were not of the prescribed class, race, national origin, etc.

What would happen if we were to reverse this progression? Specifically, what would happen if we were to proceed by focusing first on real fraternity, that is, real commonality of interest *as men*? Could such an approach possibly lead to equality between and among men and women, and to real liberty for all?

At first glance this approach would seem to have little hope for success. Would not any identifiable interests men have *as men* be precisely those interests which separate them from

and pit them against women? How then could furthering these interests lead to any kind of universal equality and liberty? I believe, however, that these objections pose a false dichotomy. The interests men have in banding together in a fraternal way are interests in overcoming the limitations of the male sex role. And it is precisely this same male sex role which sets women and men at odds. I believe men's interests *as men* lie in overcoming sexism. I believe men have needs for separate strategies and tactics against sexism because we are coming to the project of eliminating sexism with different backgrounds, issues, and perspectives than women, but not ultimately different goals.

If one believes that men have common fraternal interests in ending sexism—a sexism that offers very real material rewards to men, but at too high a personal cost—then one has a *positive* basis upon which to work with other men. I, for example, do not regard men as "the enemy," nor do I believe I am opposing another man or violating his individual rights in moving against his sexism. When I intervene against a man's sexism I am doing him—and myself—a favor, because trapped inside destructive and self-destructive behavior is an individual who would be relieved to be rid of this mode of being if he had a free choice. If one shares my starting assumption that nurturing, intimacy, and support are real human needs, then it follows that it is essential that men establish *real* friendships with each other. Not the implicit, contract of traditional male camaraderie, in which we mutually agree to keep our defenses up but not to mind it, and to keep our prejudices intact while validating each other's masculinity; rather, a shared intimacy in which feelings, including fears and joys, flow freely. Otherwise, men will continue to turn to women to fulfill these needs. And while women's abilities to nurture are clearly admirable, the necessity that they do so is equally clearly oppressive. Furthermore, such friendships with men are essential for supporting men in making and sustaining the needed longterm changes.

I would like to take the idea of finding a positive approach to working with men against sexism a significant step further. I suggest that we stop looking for the "original sin" on the basis of which men can be said to have erected partiarchy. Many aspects of male psychology are put forth as candidates for "original sin" status. We are said to have innate aggressive instincts, to have dominating sex drives, to have obessive desires for immortality so that we force women to have our children, to have a need to create a despised "Other" in order to establish our own identities, to have a need to compensate for our "womb envy" of women's creative and regenerative powers, to either love or fear each other so much, depending on the theory, that we have institutionalized oppressive heterosexuality, and so on.[1] I propose that we stop looking for the fatal flaw in male psychology which is responsible for sexism. Instead, I will make the seemingly preposterous suggestion that sexist attitudes can be understood as stemming from inherently positive aspects of male psychology, aspects which are, however, distorted by an oppressive social order.

Let me explain how I reached this position, and then go on to specify exactly what I have in mind.[2] As a general rule of social analysis, I try to give people, men specifically included, credibility for integrity and insight. Thus, when I observe a group of people acting in what seem to me irrational ways, the question I pose is not "What's wrong with them?" but rather "What

are the distorted and distorting features of their situation which make these actions appear rational to them?" Until I have satisfied myself that, if I were in their shoes, their seemingly outrageous or inexplicable actions would also appear as legitimate options to me, I consider myself not to have succeeded in understanding or explaining anything. Applying this methodology to male sexist attitudes, I have obtained the following results. I believe that as we are growing up, in our early childhood years of attitude formation, we are socialized with a crucially important belief, namely the belief that in our society people get what they deserve. While this belief, in its usual interpretations, as applied to material success or social prestige, for example, is blatantly false and can be seen to be so upon reflection, it is nonetheless a principle of justice deeply inculcated in children as they are being raised. Children are also very observant. Specifically, they will observe and note that women are universally treated as less than fully human, in contrast to men. The conjunction of this principle and this observation can be expressed as a logical syllogism:

People get what they deserve.
Women are treated inhumanly.
Women are less than fully human.

I offer the above not as a historical account of the genesis of sexist attitudes and beliefs, but rather as a phenomenological description of the development of sexist beliefs and attitudes in contemporary consciousness. In this light, sexist beliefs and attitudes can be seen to result from an attempt to preserve a belief that the world is justly ordered in the face of observing the existence of gross inequality. Children are faced with a choice: either women really are less deserving than men in some fundamental way, or a basic structuring principle of their world is false, and their world loses coherence and credibility. Everything around them, as well as their own insecurities, impel children to affirm the former, sexist beliefs.

But precisely therein, I would argue, lies the hope for change. If my proposed reconstruction of the genesis of sexist consciousness is correct, then, paradoxically enough, sexist attitudes may be said to be rooted in the child's sense of justice. But as adults, we can now take the bad news that the world is indeed unjust and not reasonably ordered. That same sense of justice, the belief that people should be treated as they deserve, coupled with the belief that people really should have equal rights and freedoms regardless of such factors as the shape or color of their skin, can now be called upon to mobilize men to rectify sexist injustices.

Listen to sexist men defend their attitudes today, listen with a comprehending ear, and you will hear the pleas of someone trying to make sense of a world they never made: "There *must* be *some* reason why the world is this way." "That's just how it is." "It's always been like this, hasn't it." "You just can't change some things." This is the voice of confusion and fear, not a dominating will to power. I propose, then, that we not focus our attention on the search for an ultimate cause for sexism in the nature of the male psyche or body, but rather that we work with men in the here and now to undo the damage sexism does to all of us. While there is some need for a general explanatory theory of patriarchy so that we can properly direct our efforts for change and not pursue the wrong targets, I believe the search for such a theory is, for most of us, a misplaced emphasis.

I think we need to emphasize moving on from here, and worry less about how we got here. This is not simply a pragmatic retreat made because we happen not to have a fully satisfactory theory about the origins of patriarchy or what a future non-patriarchal utopia would look like. The search for such a blueprint for the future is misguided, an all too typically masculine attempt to impose a rigidly constructed plan upon the world. Rather, let us do the more intimately involved work of nurturing that new world to growth with our given materials. If it is true that fundamental change must be positively self-motivated and not merely reactive, then the priority must be to seek positive approaches which will enable men to make revolutionary feminist changes. The direction of these changes, as they emerge, will clearly enough show us what our new society is to look like. This is how I envisage fraternity developing. It is not simply a means to some pre-fabricated goal. To adopt a slogan from the peace movement: there is no way to fraternity, fraternity is the way.

Which brings me to the next of the three guiding concepts, equality. I believe all men are equal. Let me make that more directly relevant by making a statement that I expect some will find terribly false, and others will find trivially true. I hope to show that it is very significantly true. The statement is this: no group of men in our society is any more or less sexist than any other group of men. Gay or straight, black or white, rich or poor, we are all equal in this regard.

Let me proceed by articulating the point of view I take myself to be arguing against. It is fashionable in some circles to characterize our society as one dominated by white males. Fashionable, but inadequate, as many feminists are aware. Socialist feminists, for example, would insist that we are plagued not only by sexism and racism, but also by capitalism.[3] So the description of the dominating group has to be widened to ruling class white males. But why stop there? Our society also systematically discriminates against the old and the young, so one would need to specify the age bracket of the ruling group, and so on. By the time one was finished, one would have constructed a description which fits at most a relative handful of men, who, according to this theory, are somehow oppressing all the rest of us, usually in multiple ways. I regard such a result as untenable for a coherent social theory and practice. It is a mistake, and a serious one, to attempt to reduce the multiple systems of oppression which characterize our society into one matrix.

Let me give a personal example. Some people have attempted to commiserate with my wife, who is Greek, about how sexist Greek or Mediterranean men are. They thought they were practicing international feminist solidarity. What they were really practicing was Anglo-Saxon cultural imperialism. Mediterranean patriarchy is qualitatively different from Anglo-Saxon patriarchy. Each has distinctive features, which are more or less taken for granted within each culture and look more or less objectionable to others. To try to assess these qualitative differences on the same quantitative scale is, as the old saying has it, like trying to mix apples and oranges.

It makes more sense to say that we live in a patriarchy, and under patriarchy men oppress women. Period. We also live under captialism. Under capitalism, the ruling class, men and women, oppresses the working class. Period. And so on with regard to racism, etc. I am aware that the situation is in reality more complex than this. Patriarchy also orders men into hierarchies and capitalism divides the genders. However, the fundamental point I wish to make is that just as, for example, ruling class women's gender does not excuse them from accountability for their class privileges, so too their lack of class privileges does not excuse working class men from accountability for the exercise of their male privileges. These, and all other forms of oppression, are overlapping and interrelated but distinct systems. While it is true that, because they suffer from other forms of oppression, men from oppressed groups do not reap the material rewards of patriarchy to as great an extent as men from dominant groups, one should not therefore conclude that men from oppressed groups are to be held less accountable for their sexism.

I propose therefore that we abandon all discussions and debate about whether gay men, or working class men, or Hispanic men, or any other group of men, are more or less sexist or patriarchal than any other group. I propose instead that we realize that all sexism is simply wrong and unsupportable, and that to attempt to establish some sort of graduated scale is at best meaningless and at worst oppressive in some other form. And I propose further that men go back to their respective communities and get on with the task of instituting the specific and specifically different kinds of fraternities within each community which will enable us to move towards equality and liberty for all people.

Which brings me to the concept of liberty, the last of the triumvirate. Liberty is the most expressly political of the three concepts. I believe it is essential for men to retain a perspective which is self-consciously political, and not merely personal or psychological, regarding the tasks of overcoming male role restrictions. Correspondingly, we must also expressly link our efforts to the feminist movement. Personal freedom, of whatever kind, requires the securing of political liberty.

Let me give one example, drawn specifically from an aspect of the male role many are struggling with. Many men are trying to undo the damage done them by male role restrictions against showing their emotions. In these struggles, they are often joined and offered assistance by women, partly out of sympathy and partly—and this is the point I wish to stress—because women suffer from this aspect of the male role, not merely sympathetically, but in their own right as well. Our male dominated society confers real power on those who are skilled at withholding their emotions in many ways. Again, let us look not to flawed individual psyches but to broader social realities to understand male sexist behaviors and attitudes. Patriarchy draws to itself those who will seek its powers. No matter how much we raise men's consciousness about the value of expressing emotion, as long as patriarchy remains intact it impels men to adopt those emotional masks which give them power. Men's and women's roles cannot be simply conceptualized as complementary and equally restrictive roles, as some men's rights advocates would have us believe. Men's roles do carry real power with them. Any attempt to give up male role restrictions on an individual or apolitical basis is doomed to failure because existing power structures simply reproduce these roles, and exert enormous pressure on individuals to reassume them. The male sex role maintains itself not becuase men are either evil or stupid, but because it confers benefits and maintains men's distance from those who bear the brunt of the system: women. That is to say, men who are competing to be less emotional are competing to be less womanlike. I believe the same sort of analysis applies not only to emotional expressiveness but to all the other aspects of the male sex role. Male problems are the other side of the coin and are inseparable from male privileges. Hence men aware of the personal drawbacks of the male role should also be drawn to a feminist political identity for themselves.

I think it is important that men claim title to be considered feminist for several reasons. I say this knowing that many men and women whom I would count among my allies on the relevant political questions would disagree. Many men and women sincerely committed to the fight against sexism insist that the label "feminist" can only be applied to women.[4] To refer to feminism as a movement consisting exclusively of women is, I believe, not a sign of radicalism but of misplaced liberalism. It relegates men to a position of sincere support, but from a distance, of women "doing their thing." One of the obstacles all liberation movements have faced is the liberal spirit of abstract tolerance from afar—e.g., it's good that women or blacks are now moving on and I wish them well, but of course this doesn't directly involve me. All too often the ideology of support by granting "autonomy" ends up being a kind of "benign neglect" where real critical thinking

and support are withheld for fear of treading where one does not belong. Men should by no means dominate in women's activities of a political or personal nature, but too often a "hands off" kind of support, whose intent may be to create unity and support, may end up creating fragmentation and feelings of abandonment.

I respect the autonomy of the women's movement, but I take this stand as a feminist. My support for women's autonomy is based on a feminist political analysis which demonstrates that this autonomy is neccessary, rather than basing it on a desire for a lesser degree of involvement with the movement. Perhaps an analogy from Marxist theory will be helpful here. One can be a Marxist without being a member of the proletariat, despite the fact that Marxism assigns the key role in revolutionary struggles to the proletariat. For example, being a Marxist and a member of the middle class would simply mean that I have a theory and practice of social change in which I recognize that the struggles of my own group will not play the determining role in bringing about the new society. It means that when organizing within my own group—an important task despite force in revolutionary activity—I orient some of my efforts towards support for more key sectors. As a Marxist, I would also see the necessity for there being a working class party in which members of my class should not hold leadership positions. What I want to stress here is that I would be taking these positions *as a Marxist*—my politics is determined by how I act in my social position, not simply by seeing what class I belong to. The latter view is an example of the most crudely reductionist, determinist sort of analysis.

The relevance of this analogy to the question of men as feminists should be clear. As a male feminist, I see that my activities as a man will not be the determining ones in the struggle for a nonsexist society, and I see the need for an autonomous women's movement of which

I would not be a part. But I take these positions *as a feminist.*

Why is this important? In the first place, it affirms the character of the feminist movement as essential for a qualitatively better society, and not just as the concern of a particular interest group (women) within this society. Secondly, it helps to keep in mind the difference between one's life-style and one's politics. All of us are deeply indebted to the women's movement for bringing to popular consciousness the idea that "the personal is political," but the radical importance of this slogan is trivialized and lost if it is taken to mean that everything I do in my life *is* in politics. Politics must be more than life-style, it must involve public, organized political action, and insistence that one need not be a woman to be a feminist restores this dimension to the movement. While I cannot live a woman's life or feelings, being a man, I can however live her politics.

Perhaps most importantly, any stand other than the insistence that men can be feminists betrays the most radical potential of the movement. Under the slogan "Biology is not Destiny," the feminist movement challenged the regressive idea that one's biological make-up should have a role in determining one's social/political/economic role. The stance that men cannot be feminists is a regression back to a standpoint which feminism has surpassed.

Furthermore, part of the oppressive ideology of society is the myth that the divisions between groups have been total and absolute, that there has been allout warfare between women and men, blacks and whites, Jews and Gentiles, etc. While acknowledging the overwhelming reality of oppression, it must nonetheless be said that this is a falsification of our history and a denial of our strengths. The support which the early feminists received from their husbands and male friends *is* part of the history of feminism. The fact that approximately one third of the signatories to the 1848 Seneca Falls Declaration of the Rights of Women were

men is as important a part of the history of feminism as the exploits of John Brown are part of the history of Abolitionism in the same century.

I have no doubt that the process of building male-female feminist alliances will be difficult. At times, men will more or less unconsciously continue to play out old patterns of domination and step on the toes of the women they are attempting to assist. When this occurs, I hope and trust it will be corrected. But how many opportunities to support feminist growth will be lost if we do not make efforts to establish such alliances?

I believe a male feminist theory and practice which can have any hope of success in mobilizing men in a politically effective way behind the clear moral imperatives supporting feminism must always remain simultaneously focused on both aspects of the personal/political dialectic. Men as a group benefit from the social powers which correlate with the male sex role. They reap the material rewards the society has to offer. But men individually pay too high a price for these benefits, and it is in their real personal interest to overthrow the system which creates and grants these privileges. The male sex role is both unsatisfying and dangerous. The combination of breadwinner pressures, which make us neurotic, isolated competitors, and the restrictions on male emotional release for these pressures which are also part of the male role is a prescription for the earlier deaths and higher rates of tension-related health problems—heart attacks, ulcers, high blood pressure, suicides—we daily see men suffering from. Though not all men are aware of the source of their difficulties, I believe all men suffer from sexism. These are the disadvantages of the advantages men receive from a sexist system.

In these ways, the call for "Fraternity, Equality, and Liberty" presents us with the beginnings of a positive political analysis of and for changing men. I hope this becomes part of ongoing discussions of how to further feminist brotherhood.

NOTES

1. These hypotheses are among many popular in feminist theory, and one finds them in such frequently used women's studies texts as *Feminist Frameworks*, ed. Alison M. Jaggar and Paula S. Rothenberg (2nd edition McGraw-Hill, 1984) and *The Longest War*, by Carol Tavris and Carole Wade (2nd edition, Harcourt Brace Jovanovich, 1984). See also the articles by Azizah at-Hibri, Eva Feder Kittay, Iris Marion Young, Pauline Bart, and Ann Ferguson in *Mothering: Essays in Feminist*

Theory, ed. Joyce Trebilcot (Rowman & Allanheld, 1984).

2. Though he might well reject the analysis in this section, it is inspired by Albert Memmi's analysis of racism. See, for example, the section on "Racism and Oppression" in *Dominated Man*, Beacon, 1968.

3. See *Capitalist Partriarchy and the Case for Socialist Feminism*, ed. Zillah R. Eisenstein (Monthly Review Press, 1979).

4. See Jon Snodgrass, *For Men Against Sexism: A Book of Readings*, Times Change Press, 1977, p. 9.

The Men's Rights Movement: "Male" is Not a Four-Letter Word

Jack Kammer

ITEM: For months after six men raped a woman in Big Dan's Tavern in New Bedford, Rhode Island, in 1983 the media reported that a barroom full of male patrons had cheered the crime. As University of Dayton English professor Eugene August observes, the news stories included "righteous denunciations of the average man as secret admirer and blood brother of the gang rapist." In a March 5, 1984, story on the rapists' trial, however, *Time* magazine quietly reported that "aside from the six defendants and the victim, only three people were in the bar, and that the bartender and a customer sought to call the police, but were prevented from doing so by one of the six." Professor

From *Wingspan, Inside The Men's Movement*, © 1992 by Christopher Harding. Reprinted by permission of St. Martin's Press, Incorporated.

August is left to wonder "why the media engaged in such an orgy of sexist caricaturing."

ITEM: Writing in a 1988 edition of *Spectator*, Fredric Hayward, director of Men's Rights, Inc., reports that in a sample of 1,000 advertisements, he found that men were 100 percent of:

- Jerks in male-female relationships
- Those who were ignorant
- Incompetents
- Those who smelled bad
- Those who were put down without retribution
- The objects of rejection
- The losers of competitions
- The targets of anger
- The victims of violence

ITEM: Warren Farrell devotes a chapter of his successful 1986 book *Why Men Are the Way They Are* to "The New Sexism." He analyzes dozens of anti-male cartoons, books, magazine articles, and advertisements, and, by reversing the gender assignments in his examples, helps readers see clearly the bigotry they embody. "In the past quarter century," Farrell writes, "we exposed biases against other races and called it racism, and we exposed biases against women and called it sexism. Biases against men we call humor."

ITEM: In 1991, before the National Coalition of Free Men succeeds in having Hallmark mend its ways, the greeting card company manufactures a product that shows on its cover a stylish young woman saying, "Men are scum." Since the card is from Hallmark, America's premier purveyor of sentiment and warmth, the incredulous shopper expects to open the card and read something like "S for sweet, C for cute, U for understanding, and M for magnificent." Instead the inside panel says, "Excuse me. For a second there, I was feeling generous." In announcing its decision to pull the card from distribution, Hallmark acknowledges that the product was one of its best-sellers.

This is male bashing—the mean-spirited mockery and categorical denunciation of American men. Sincere criticism it is not.

John Gordon, Ph.D., professor of English at Connecticut College and author of *The Myth of the Monstrous Male and Other Feminist Fables*, tells us that male bashing is hardly a new phenomenon. In Dr. Francis Baumli's anthology *Men Freeing Men*, Gordon asserts that "the ongoing flood of anti-male hate literature" is "a continuation of an old campaign. Men are the main targets these days because they always have been." He cites *The Feminization of American Culture* by Ann Douglas, which "documents the history of two of the most popular and influential *genres* of the nineteenth and early twentieth centuries, the anti-male novel and the anti-male tract. These works—thousands of them—were part of a campaign," Gordon says, "to represent men as barbarians whose urges had to be leashed in by the forces

of decency—meaning women—if civilization were to survive."

But clearly male bashing is more common and ferocious today than it was, say, 30 years ago. Why is it happening so prominently now? Obviously, feminism unleashed a torrent of simple, crude, unenlightened animosity toward men. Rather than suggesting an evenhanded redistribution of power between men and women, feminists chose instead to frame sexism unilaterally according to the by-now familiar victim-perpetrator model. Only men had power. Only men were using it selfishly. Only men required self-improvement. Only men were wrong.

Another interesting way to conceive of the current abuses of men is to accept the feminist allegation that men have treated women as children. Now that women are asserting their independence many of them are having what could be called a difficult adolescence, a still-immature stage which is often accompanied by a know-it-all attitude and haughty disrespect for former authority figures.

Farrell suggests that male bashing, the New Sexism, is at least in part some modern women's reaction to their failure to achieve their primary (and sexist) fantasy—being taken care of by a man who makes even more money than they. As women's earnings have increased recently, Farrell points out, it is inevitable that fewer and fewer men will be able to fulfill that fantasy, and more and more women will feel angry, frustrated, and resentful toward men, whom they see now only in terms of their shortcomings. Furthermore, focusing on men's imperfections allows women to avoid the painful task of attending to their own.

This suggests yet another way to understand male bashing. Since male bashing is nothing if not offensive, and since, as the old adage goes, The best defense is a strong offense, we might ask, Are some women and their male protectors feeling a heightened need to defend something, trying to avoid an egalitarian sharing of some female domain or prerogative which men have begun to claim equally for themselves?

If in the early 1960s, when women were knocking on the door of corporate and academic America, seeking access to jobs, educations, and careers, men had mounted a scurrilous campaign about women's shortcomings, foibles, and imperfections, fair-minded people surely would have seen it for what it was. If, for example, a prominent male business executive had written, "The majority of women who compete with talented young men for careers and entrepreneurial opportunities are air-headed bimbos who have refused to study diligently, save their capital, work hard and devote themselves to the important and noble task of making money, who only want to file their nails, and who pose a serious threat to our hallowed American economy," no one could have failed to see that his real agenda was the exclusion of women from a male domain.

Perhaps, then, we can discern a clear payoff for women in male bashing, a classic example of which is found on the book jacket of Phyllis Chesler's *Mothers on Trial*: "Dr. Chesler shows that the majority of fathers who challenge nurturing mothers for custody are absent or psychologically damaging parents who have refused to pay child support and have kidnapped, brainwashed, economically intimidated and physically and sexually abused both their children and their wives." (For those readers who are unaware of her reputation we should mention that Dr. Chesler is considered a serious, sophisticated, and credible philosopher—not a ludicrous crackpot—of feminism.)

One of the most recurring and underlying themes of male bashing is indeed the unfitness of men to care for children. Certainly we cannot entrust our little babies to people who are sexually depraved, clumsy, selfish, hormonally inclined to violence, helpless, emotionally crippled, and generally morally inferior. We must leave that important work—"demeaned and devalued" as it may be—to women.

Since many men today are expressing an interest in being as involved with their children as women have been, it is understandable—as distinguished from acceptable—that some women will feel threatened. *The Motherhood Report*, published in 1987 by researchers Louis Genevie, Ph.D., and Eva Margolies, lends credence to this analysis. Genevie and Margolies found that 1) only about one mother in four thought that fathers should play a fifty-fifty role in raising the children; 2) mothers want fathers to help more with the children, but not to overshadow their role as primary parent; 3) two out of three mothers seemed threatened by the idea of a father's equal participation in child rearing; and 4) mothers themselves may be subtly putting a damper on men's involvement with their children because they are so possessive of their role as primary nurturer. Male bashing in this light can be seen as a not-so-subtle damper on men's involvement with their children, especially when divorce, separation, or simple jealousy force the designation of one parent as primary and the other as second class.

Moreover, even the most amateur politician knows that the party who defines the terms of the discussion will win the debate. As long as feminists keep sexual politics focused on men's failings, they will enjoy total immunity from scrutiny or calls to make changes other than the ones they have found to be in their immediate self-interest.

Keeping attention focused on men's shortcomings requires that men's shortcomings be found—or fabricated—at every turn. Writing in the *Liberator*, Frank Zepezauer marvels at the resourcefulness and flexibility of the process. He describes how three sociologists working with three different types of raw material all delivered the same fuel for male bashing. The first commented on the fact that men still put in longer work weeks than women by saying that "men are trying even harder to maintain their superiority." The second sociologist saw a picture of Native American women grinding corn while the men stood watch. Her interpretation: "The men were as usual leaving all the work to the women." The third, after examining the many ways in which males, like the Indian men standing guard, took risks to protect women and children, concluded that this was another way that males maintained dominance, their own version of a "protection racket." As Zepezauer detected, the process is really quite simple. "Whatever a guy does, you find a sneaky, self-serving reason. He holds a door open for you? He's asserting dominance. He doesn't hold the door open. He's insulting your dignity."

Farrell has seen the same process in different terms. "*The Hite Report*," he writes, "found that *men* prefer intercourse more than women; the *American Couples* survey by Schwartz and Blumstein found that *women* prefer intercourse more than men. Hite interpreted her findings to mean that men preferred intercourse because intercourse is male-centered, focused on penis pleasure, an outgrowth of male dominance and ego gratification." But Schwartz and Blumstein, Farrell notes, interpreted their findings in the opposite way: "We think women prefer it because intercourse requires the *equal* participation of both partners more than any sexual act. Neither partner only 'gives' or only 'receives.' Hence, women feel a shared *intimacy* during intercourse . . . ." Farrell concludes that "the findings are diametrically opposed, yet both interpretations could only consider the possibility that women favor intimacy and equality, and men favor ego gratification and dominance. This is distortion to fit a preconceived image— or, when it is applied to men, the new sexism."

Speaking as he often does of men in terms of father figures, Robert Bly comments on the same problem. In *Iron John* he writes "that something in the culture wants us to be unfair to our father's masculine side, find self-serving reasons for his generous words, assume he is a monster, as some people say all men are."

Blaming men for each and every male-female problem, as John Gordon suggested earlier, is not new. Shakespeare confirmed it in *As You Like It*: "O, that woman that cannot make her fault her husband's occasion, let her never nurse her child herself, for she will breed it like a fool!"

Indeed, sometimes male bashing seems to be nothing more than some feminists' celebration of their ability to make men wrong, an out-of-control demonstration of their skill in framing issues just the way they wish, to make men and only men say, "Oh, yes, I'm so sorry. I can see now that I must confront and take responsibility for my attitudes and actions. Forgive me please and assuage my guilt!" Sometimes it seems male bashers must be laughing incredulously to themselves, shaking their heads and saying, "When are these chumps going to wake up?"

It almost goes without saying that along with its power to defend women from scrutiny and from encroachments on their domain, the strong offense constituted by male bashing can have aggressive applications as well. Male bashing can be like carpet bombing, softening up men's determination to defend themselves, destroying male morale, and inclining men to surrender at the first sign of hostilities, paving the way for dictators, tyrants, and aggressors of all sorts.

The offensive uses of male bashing can be broad indeed. The more widely one can assert the idea of male beastliness and comparative female virtuousness, the more one can justify whatever special treatment of women one seeks, the more likely one is to find ready acceptance of even the weakest accusations—whether they be of employment discrimination, parental unfitness, sexual harassment, rape, child sexual abuse, date rape, domestic violence, or simple social or marital impropriety, to name but a few possibilities. On the topic of domestic violence, for example, R. L. McNeely suggests in the November-December 1987 issue of *Social Work* that the popular and aggressively asserted misconception that only men commit spousal abuse may be contributing to "men's social and legal defenselessness."

Why do men not protest more vigorously against male bashing? The answer seems to be that we have been made to think we deserve it. We are, after all, male. We are, on the ladder of life, at least a rung or two below women, closer to the worms while women consort with the angels. It's not our *fault* really. It's just, you know, that nasty testosterone. We begin early on to learn what Dr. Roy Schenk has called the Shame of Maleness. We learned that we are not sugar, not spice, not anything nice. In the 1990s, little boys are learning only a slight variation on that theme: they are "rotten, made out of cotton"; girls, on the other hand, are "dandy, made out of candy." While young boys are learning to devalue themselves as males, the only defense with which our supposedly male-dominated culture equips them is a feeble response: "Oh, yeah? Well, you've got cooties!" It is easy to see the difference between boys' allegations of what the girls *have*, and the female allegations of what the boys *are*. Males—inherently—are inferior. We deserve what we get.

The idea that we deserve what females dish out carries through to adulthood. As Bly observes, "A contemporary man often assumes that a woman knows more about a relationship than he does, allows a woman's moods to run the house, assumes that when she attacks him, she is doing it 'for his own good.'"

Apparently we even think we deserve bashing in a physical sense. In his book *Wife Beating: The Silent Crisis*, Roger Langley includes a chapter on battered men. He says that "the response most often heard—-from both men and women—to a story of a man beaten by his wife is: 'Good for her.'"

Is male bashing really all that harmful or are men's objections to it—as they have been characterized—simply "whining"? That's a fair question to which there is a fair answer. Male

bashing wounds men; it injures boys; it harms everyone who lives with or near them; it hurts everyone who seeks to have a relationship with them. In short, it is detrimental to everyone. It further rends our already tattered social fabric.

If we can agree that the American family is in serious decline, we might observe that the weakest element of the family is its male component. Male bashing only tramples fatherhood and husbandhood more thoroughly. In *Iron John*, Robert Bly, without referring specifically to male bashing, explains how it can damage marriages. "Conscious fighting," he wrote, "is a great help in relationships between men and women.... A good fight gets things clear, and I think women long to fight and be with men who know how to fight well." A man who has been bashed and browbeaten into guilt, shame, and submission, of course, knows not how to fight at all.

Male bashing also damages the young men families try to raise. In 1938, a social scientist named Tannenbaum articulated a theory of "labeling" that is still cited in the professional literature on juvenile delinquency:

There is a gradual shift from the definition of the specific acts as evil to a definition of the individual as evil, and that all his acts come to be looked upon with suspicion.... From the individual's point of view there has taken place a similar change. He has gone slowly from a sense of grievance and injustice, of being unduly mistreated and punished, to a recognition that the definition of him as a human being is different from that of other boys in his neighborhood, his school, street, community. The young delinquent becomes bad because he is defined as bad.

The process of making the criminal, therefore, is a process of tagging, defining, identifying, segregating, describing, emphasizing, making conscious and self-conscious. The person becomes the thing he is described as being.

Though Tannenbaum here refers to a boy being stigmatized in relation to other boys, we can perhaps see that male bashing stigmatizes all boys in relation to the rest of the human race. Researchers Myra and David Sadker found that "boys are more likely to be scolded and reprimanded in classrooms, even when the observed conduct and behavior of boys and girls does not differ." The effect of treating boys as if they are evil is to encourage and direct them toward evil.

Bly explains another deleterious effect of male bashing when he describes how undue harshness toward men saps our society of its vigor. "All the great cultures except ours preserve and have lived with images of . . . positive male energy. . . . Zeus energy has been steadily disintegrating decade after decade in the United States. Popular culture has been determined to destroy respect for it, beginning with the 'Maggie and Jiggs' and 'Blondie and Dagwood' comics of the 1920s and 1930s, in which the man is always weak and foolish."

Perhaps the most severe manifestation of male bashing may be found in the fact that for decades if not centuries the suicide rate for young men has exceeded the rate for young women, and that in recent years the gap has widened dramatically to a ratio of about four to one. In 1985, Edward S. Gold's doctoral dissertation at the Virginia Consortium of Professional Psychology investigated the "personal need systems" of a group of college students who had demonstrated suicidal or near-suicidal behavior. Among the males he found a common denominator: "lowered ego strength." "It is entirely possible," Dr. Gold said, "that the women's movement has had a lot to do with that. There has been a constant barrage of finger-pointing, a tremendous amount of criticism of men on nearly every front." Keep in mind that a whole spectrum of suffering exists between happiness and the extreme of suicide. Male bashing, simply put, can make men miserable.

Just as women started asking why the "glass ceiling" is all men, we must start asking why the "glass cellars" are all men.

Death Professions 94% of all people killed in the workplace are men.

Draft Draft registration is a male-only club. In the 20th century, over 99% of people killed in wars have been men. It is only men who enter the service who are required to serve in combat if needed. Why are women getting combat options but not sharing in combat obligations?

Suicide Why do men commit suicide 5 times more often than women?

Hostages Why does no one call it sexist when Saddam Hussein releases only women and children? Why does no one object to making hostages an all-male club?

Homeless The street homeless are approximately 90% men.

Assassinations Nearly 100% of political assassinations have been of men.

Prisoners Approximately 92% of all prisoners are men.

Executions Over 99% of the executed are men.

Early Deaths In 1920, men died only one year sooner than women; in the 1990s men died seven to eight years sooner. Why?

Disease Men die sooner than women from all of the ten most lethal diseases.

—Warren Farrell

But now let's turn to the optimistic part of this essay. What can we do about male bashing? A story from Bly in *Iron John* poses the question nicely:

A friend told me [that] at about thirty-five, he began to wonder who his father really was. He hadn't seen his father in about ten years. He flew out to Seattle, where his father was living, knocked on the door, and when his father opened the door, said, "I want you to understand one thing. I don't accept my mother's view of you any longer."

"What happened?" I asked.

"My father broke into tears, and said, 'Now I can die.'"

Fathers wait. What else can they do?

What we can do is stop waiting and get on our own offensive, an offensive in which the best masculine values constitute both the medium and the message. Calmly, patiently, fiercely, resolutely, lovingly, we can isolate, identify, and demand the cessation of that which damages us unfairly—especially the pervasive notion of the inferiority of masculinity—and replace it with a balanced analysis of the wounded relationship between woman and man, including a proper recognition of the strengths and weaknesses of both genders.

As a kid growing up I "knew" that male-female problems among my parents' friends were always the man's fault. Only the women would talk about them, and I therefore heard only the woman's side of the story. Nora Ephron candidly admitted that one of the reasons she wrote *Heartburn*, the story of her failed marriage to Watergate sleuth Carl Bernstein, was to control the version of the story that was told. Unlike my father and his male friends, and unlike the strong-but-silent Bernstein, we can begin to speak our truth, to confront the falsehoods and half-truths about us and resolve never to let our sons say what Bly

reports hundreds of men have said to him: "My father never stood up to my mother, and I'm still angry about that."

We should not only assert our truth to our female companions and partners, but also hold it out for our brothers to acknowledge, embrace, support, and share. All of us doing men's work know the power and the strength that arises from a man who says, "I'm glad you listened. I'm glad you understand. I thought I had a 'personal' problem. I thought I was the only one who felt this way."

Good, strong women will want to join our campaign once they see that good, strong men are at long last taking action. They should be invited and welcomed. In some circles, against some offenders, they can in fact lead our effort.

Finally, as we rise to our feet and signal "Enough!" we can take pride in knowing that it is precisely because we are good and always trying to be better that we have listened so long to the allegations that we are bad.

The Mythopoetic Men's Movement: The Pillow and the Key

Robert Bly

We talk a great deal about "the American man," as if there were some constant quality that remained stable over decades, or even within a single decade.

The men who live today have veered far away from the Saturnian, old-man-minded farmer, proud of his introversion, who arrived in New England in 1630, willing to sit through three services in an unheated church. In the South, an expansive, motherbound cavalier developed, and neither of these two "American men" resembled the greedy railroad entrepreneur that later developed in the Northeast, nor the reckless I-will-do-without culture settlers of the West.

Even in our own era the agreed-on model has changed dramatically. During the fifties, for example, an American character appeared with some consistency that became a model of manhood adopted by many men: the Fifties male.

He got to work early, labored responsibly, supported his wife and children, and admired discipline. Reagan is a sort of mummified version of this dogged type. This sort of man didn't see women's souls well, but he appreciated their bodies; and his view of culture and America's part in it was boyish and optimistic. Many of his qualities were strong and positive, but underneath the charm and bluff there was, and there remains, much isolation, deprivation, and passivity. Unless he has an enemy, he isn't sure that he is alive.

The Fifties man was supposed to like football, be aggressive, stick up for the United States, never cry, and always provide. But receptive space or intimate space was missing in this image of a man. The personality lacked some sense of flow. The psyche lacked compassion in a way that encouraged the unbalanced pursuit of the Vietnam war, just as, later, the lack of what we might call "garden" space inside Reagan's head led to his callousness and brutality toward the powerless in El Salvador, toward old people here, the unemployed, schoolchildren, and poor people in general.

The Fifties male had a clear vision of what a man was, and what male responsibilities were, but the isolation and one-sidedness of his vision were dangerous.

During the sixties, another sort of man appeared. The waste and violence of the Vietnam war made men question whether they knew what an adult male really was. If manhood meant Vietnam, did they want any part of it? Meanwhile, the feminist movement encouraged men to actually look at women; forcing them to become conscious of concerns and sufferings

that the Fifties male labored to avoid. As men began to examine women's history and women's sensibility, some men began to notice what was called their *feminine* side and pay attention to it. This process continues to this day, and I would say that most contemporary men are involved in it in some way.

There's something wonderful about this development—I mean the practice of men welcoming their own "feminine" consciousness and nurturing it—this is important—and yet I have the sense that there is something wrong. The male in the past twenty years has become more thoughtful, more gentle. But by this process he has not become more free. He's a nice boy who pleases not only his mother but also the young woman he is living with.

In the seventies I began to see all over the country a phenomenon that we might call the "soft male." Sometimes even today when I look out at an audience, perhaps half the young males are what I'd call soft. They're lovely, valuable people—I like them—they're not interested in harming the earth or starting wars. There's a gentle attitude toward life in their whole being and style of living.

But many of these men are not happy. You quickly notice the lack of energy in them. They are life-preserving but not exactly life-giving. Ironically, you often see these men with strong women who positively radiate energy.

Here we have a finely tuned young man, ecologically superior to his father, sympathetic to the whole harmony of the universe, yet he himself has little vitality to offer.

The strong or life-giving women who graduated from the sixties, so to speak, or who have inherited an older spirit, played an important part in producing this life-preserving, but not life-giving, man.

I remember a bumper sticker during the sixties that read "WOMEN SAY YES TO MEN WHO SAY NO." We recognize that it took a lot of courage to resist the draft, go to jail, or move to Canada, just as it took courage to accept the draft and go to Vietnam. But the women of twenty years ago were definitely saying that they preferred the softer receptive male.

So the development of men was affected a little in this preference. Nonreceptive maleness was equated with violence, and receptive maleness was rewarded.

Some energetic women, at that time and now in the nineties, chose and still choose soft men to be their lovers and, in a way, perhaps, to be their sons. The new distribution of "yang" energy among couples didn't happen by accident. Young men for various reasons wanted their harder women, and women began to desire softer men. It seemed like a nice arrangement for a while, but we've lived with it long enough now to see that it isn't working out.

I first learned about the anguish of "soft" men when they told their stories in early men's gatherings. In 1980, the Lama Community in New Mexico asked me to teach a conference for men only, their first, in which about forty men participated. Each day we concentrated on one Greek god and one old story, and then late in the afternoons we gathered to talk. When the younger men spoke it was not uncommon for them to be weeping within five minutes. The amount of grief and anguish in these younger men was astounding to me.

Part of their grief rose out of remoteness from their fathers, which they felt keenly, but partly, too, grief flowed from trouble in their marriages or relationships. They had learned to be receptive, but receptivity wasn't enough to carry their marriages through troubled times. In every relationship something *fierce* is needed once in a while: both the man and the woman need to have it. But at the point when it was needed, often the young man came up short. He was nurturing, but something else was required—for his relationship, and for his life.

The "soft" male was able to say, "I can feel your pain, and I consider your life as important as mine, and I will take care of you and com-

fort you." But he could not say what he wanted, and stick by it. *Resolve* of that kind was a different matter.

In *The Odyssey*, Hermes instructs Odysseus that when he approaches Circe, who stands for a certain kind of matriarchal energy, he is to lift or show his sword. In these early sessions it was difficult for many of the younger men to distinguish between showing the sword and hurting someone. One man, a kind of incarnation of certain spiritual attitudes of the sixties, a man who had actually lived in a tree for a year outside Santa Cruz, found himself unable to extend his arm when it held a sword. He had learned so well not to hurt anyone that he couldn't lift the steel, even to catch the light of the sun on it. But showing a sword doesn't necessarily mean fighting. It can also suggest a joyful decisiveness.

The journey many American men have taken into softness, or receptivity, or "development of the feminine side," has been an immensely valuable journey, but more travel lies ahead. No stage is the final stop.

FINDING IRON JOHN

One of the fairy tales that speak of a third possibility for men, a third mode, is a story called "Iron John" or "Iron Hans." Though it was first set down by the Grimm brothers around 1820, this story could be ten or twenty thousand years old.

As the story starts, we find out that something strange has been happening in a remote area of the forest near the king's castle. When hunters go into this area, they disappear and never come back. Twenty others go after the first group and do not come back. In time, people begin to get the feeling that there's something weird in that part of the forest, and they "don't go there anymore."

One day an unknown hunter shows up at the castle and says, "What can I do? Anything dangerous to do around here?"

The King says: "Well, I could mention the forest, but there's a problem. The people who go out there don't come back. The return rate is not good."

"That's just the sort of thing I like," the young man says. So he goes into the forest and, interestingly, he goes there *alone*, taking only his dog. The young man and his dog wander about in the forest and they go past a pond. Suddenly a hand reaches up from the water, grabs the dog, and pulls it down.

The young man doesn't respond by becoming hysterical. He merely says, "This must be the place."

Fond as he is of his dog and reluctant as he is to abandon him, the hunter goes back to the castle, rounds up three more men with buckets, and then comes back to the pond to bucket out the water. Anyone who's ever tried it will quickly note that such bucketing is very slow work.

In time, what they find, lying on the bottom of the pond, is a large man covered with hair from head to foot. The hair is reddish—it looks a little like rusty iron. They take the man back to the castle, and imprison him. The King puts him in an iron cage in the courtyard, calls him "Iron John," and gives the key into the keeping of the Queen.

Let's stop the story here for a second.

When a contemporary man looks down into his psyche, he may, if conditions are right, find under the water of his soul, lying in an area no one has visited for a long time, an ancient hairy man.

The mythological systems associate hair with the instinctive and the sexual and the primitive. What I'm suggesting, then, is that every modern male has, lying at the bottom of his psyche, a large, primitive being covered with hair down to his feet. Making contact with this Wild Man is the step the Eighties male or the Nineties male has yet to take. That bucketing-out process has yet to begin in our contemporary culture.

As the story suggests very delicately, there's more than a little fear around this hairy man, as there is around all change. When a man begins to develop the receptive side of himself and gets over his initial skittishness, he usually finds the experience to be wonderful. He gets to write poetry and go out and sit by the ocean, he doesn't have to be on top all the time in sex anymore, he becomes empathetic—it's a new, humming, surprising world.

But going down through water to touch the Wild Man at the bottom of the pond is quite a different matter. The being who stands up is frightening, and seems even more so now, when the corporations do so much work to produce the sanitized, hairless, shallow man. When a man welcomes his responsiveness, or what we sometimes call his internal woman, he often feels warmer, more companionable, more alive. But when he approaches what I'll call the "deep male," he feels risk. Welcoming the Hairy Man *is* scary and risky, and it requires a different sort of courage. Contact with Iron John requires a willingness to descend into the male psyche and accept what's dark down there, including the *nourishing* dark.

For generations now, the industrial community has warned young businessmen to keep away from Iron John, and the Christian church is not too fond of him either.

Freud, Jung, and Wilhelm Reich are three investigators who had the courage to go down into the pond and to accept what they found there. The job of contemporary men is to follow them down.

Some men have already done this work, and the Hairy Man has been brought up from the pond in their psyches, and lives in the courtyard. "In the courtyard" suggests that the individual or the culture has brought him into a sunlit place where all can see him. That is itself some advance over keeping the Hairy Man in a cellar, where many elements in every culture want him to be. But, of course, in either place, he's still in a cage.

THE LOSS OF THE GOLDEN BALL

Now back to the story.

One day the King's eight-year-old son is playing in the courtyard with the golden ball he loves, and it rolls into the Wild Man's cage. If the young boy wants the ball back, he's going to have to approach the Hairy Man and ask him for it. But this is going to be a problem.

The golden ball reminds us of that unity of personality we had as children—a kind of radiance, or wholeness, before we split into male and female, rich and poor, bad and good. The ball is golden, as the sun is, and round. Like the sun, it gives off a radiant energy from the inside.

We notice that the boy is eight. All of us, whether boys or girls, lose something around the age of eight. If we still have the golden ball in kindergarten, we lose it in grade school. Whatever is still left we lose in high school. In "The Frog Prince," the princess's ball fell into a well. Whether we are male or female, once the golden ball is gone, we spend the rest of our lives trying to get it back.

The first stage in retrieving the ball, I think, is to accept—firmly, definitely—that the ball has been lost. Freud said: "What a distressing contrast there is between the radiant intelligence of the child and the feeble mentality of the average adult."

So where is the golden ball? Speaking metaphorically, we could say that the sixties culture told men they would find their golden ball in sensitivity, receptivity, cooperation, and nonaggressiveness. But many men gave up all aggressiveness and still did not find the golden ball.

The Iron John story says that a man can't expect to find the golden ball in the feminine realm, because that's not where the ball is. A bridegroom secretly asks his wife to give him back the golden ball. I think she'd give it to him if she could, because most women in my experience do not try to block men's growth.

But she can't give it to him, because she doesn't have it. What's more, she's lost her own golden ball and can't find that either.

Oversimplifying, we could say that the Fifties male always wants a woman to return his golden ball. The Sixties and Seventies man, with equal lack of success, asks his interior feminine to return it.

The Iron John story proposes that the golden ball lies within the magnetic field of the Wild Man, which is a very hard concept for us to grasp. We have to accept the possibility that the true radiant energy in the male does not hide in, reside in, or wait for us in the feminine realm, nor in the macho/John Wayne realm, but in the magnetic field of the deep masculine. It is protected by the *instinctive* one who's underwater and who has been there we don't know how long.

In "The Frog Prince" it's the frog, the un-nice one, the one that everyone says "Ick!" to, who brings the golden ball back. And in the Grimm brothers version the frog himself turns into the prince only when a hand throws him against the wall.

Most men want some nice person to bring the ball back, but the story hints that we won't find the golden ball in the force field of an Asian guru or even the force field of gentle Jesus. Our story is not anti-Christian but pre-Christian by a thousand years or so, and its message is still true—getting the golden ball back is incompatible with certain kinds of conventional tameness and niceness.

The kind of wildness, or un-niceness, implied by the Wild Man image is not the same as macho energy, which men already know enough about. Wild Man energy, by contrast, leads to forceful action undertaken, not with cruelty, but with resolve.

The Wild Man is not opposed to civilization, but he's not completely contained by it either. The ethical superstructure of popular Christianity does not support the Wild Man, though there is some suggestion that Christ himself did. At the beginning of his ministry, a hairy John, after all, baptized him.

When it comes time for a young male to talk with the Wild Man he will find the conversation quite distinct from a talk with a minister, a rabbi, or a guru. Conversing with the Wild Man is not talking about bliss or mind or spirit or "higher consciousness," but about something wet, dark, and low—what James Hillman would call "soul."

The first step amounts to approaching the cage and asking for the golden ball back. Some men are ready to take that step, while others haven't yet bucketed the water out of the pond—they haven't left the collective male identity and gone out into the unknown area alone, or gone with only their dog.

The story says that after the dog "goes down" one has to start to work with buckets. No giant is going to come along and suck out all the water for you: that magic stuff is not going to help. And a weekend at Esalen won't do it. Acid or cocaine won't do it. The man has to do it bucket by bucket. This resembles the slow discipline of art: it's the work that Rembrandt did, that Picasso and Yeats and Rilke and Bach did. Bucket work implies much more discipline than most men realize.

The Wild Man, as the writer Keith Thompson mentioned to me, is not simply going to hand over the golden ball either. What kind of story would it be if the Wild Man said: "Well, okay, here's your ball"?

Jung remarked that all successful requests to the psyche involve deals. The psyche likes to make deals. If part of you, for example, is immensely lazy and doesn't want to do any work, a flat-out New Year's resolution won't do any good. The whole thing will go better if you say to the lazy part: "You let me work for an hour, then I'll let you be a slob for an hour—deal?" So in "Iron John," a deal is made: the Wild Man agrees to give the golden ball back if the boy opens the cage.

The boy, apparently frightened, runs off. He doesn't even answer. Isn't that what happens? We have been told so often by parents, ministers, grade-school teachers, and high-school principals that we should have nothing to do with the Wild Man that when he says "I'll return the ball if you let me out of the cage," we don't even reply.

Maybe ten years pass now. On "the second day" the man could be twenty-five. He goes back to the Wild Man and says, "Could I have my ball back?" The Wild Man says, "Yes, if you let me out of the cage."

Actually, just returning to the Wild Man a second time is a marvelous thing; some men never come back at all. The twenty-five-year-old man hears the sentence all right, but by now he has two Toyotas and a mortgage, maybe a wife and a child. How can he let the Wild Man out of the cage? A man usually walks away the second time also without saying a word.

Now ten more years pass. Let's say the man is now thirty-five . . . have you ever seen the look of dismay on the face of a thirty-five-year-old man? Feeling overworked, alienated, empty, he asks the Wild Man with full heart this time: "Could I have my golden ball back?"

"Yes," the Wild Man says, "If you let me out of my cage."

Now something marvelous happens in the story. The boy speaks to the Wild Man, and continues the conversation. He says, "Even if I wanted to let you out, I couldn't, because I don't know where the key is."

That's so good. By the time we are thirty-five we don't know where the key is. It isn't exactly that we have forgotten—we never knew where it was in the first place.

The story says that when the King locked up the Wild Man, "he gave the key into the keeping of the Queen," but we were only about seven then, and in any case our father never told us what he had done with it. So where is the key?

I've heard audiences try to answer that one: "It's around the boy's neck."

No.

"It's hidden in Iron John's cage."

No.

"It's inside the golden ball."

No.

"It's inside the castle . . . on a hook inside the Treasure Room."

No.

"It's in the Tower. It's on a hook high up on the wall!"

No.

The Wild Man replies, "The key is under your mother's pillow."

The key is not inside the ball, nor in the golden chest, nor in the safe . . . the key is under our mother's pillow—just where Freud said it would be.

Getting the key back from under the mother's pillow is a troublesome task. Freud, taking advice from a Greek play, says that a man should not skip over the mutual attraction between himself and his mother if he wants a long life. The mother's pillow, after all, lies in the bed near where she makes love to your father. Moreover, there's another implication attached to the pillow.

Michael Meade, the myth teller, once remarked to me that the pillow is also the place where the mother stores all her expectations for you. She dreams: "My son the doctor." "My son the Jungian analyst." "My son the Wall Street genius." But very few mothers dream: "My son the Wild Man."

On the son's side, he isn't sure he wants to take the key. Simply transferring the key from the mother's to a guru's pillow won't help. Forgetting that the mother possesses it is a bad mistake. A mother's job is, after all, to civilize the boy, and so it is natural for her to keep the key. All families behave alike: on this planet, "The King gives the key into the keeping of the Queen."

Attacking the mother, confronting her, shouting at her, which some Freudians are prone to urge on us, probably does not accomplish much—she may just smile and talk to you with her elbow on the pillow. Oedipus'

conversations with Jocasta never did much good, nor did Hamlet's shouting.

A friend mentioned that it's wise to steal the key some day when your mother and father are gone. "My father and mother are away today" implies a day when the head is free of parental inhibitions. That's the day to steal the key. Gioia Timpanelli, the writer and storyteller, remarked that, mythologically, the theft of the key belongs to the world of Hermes.

And the key has to be *stolen*. I recall talking to an audience of men and women once about this problem of stealing the key. A young man, obviously well trained in New Age modes of operation, said, "Robert, I'm disturbed by this idea of stealing the key. Stealing isn't right. Couldn't a group of us just go to the mother and say, 'Mom, could I have the key back?'?"

His model was probably consensus, the way the staff at the health food store settles things. I felt the souls of all the women in the room rise up in the air to kill him. Men like that are as dangerous to women as they are to men.

No mother worth her salt would give the key anyway. If a son can't steal it, he doesn't deserve it.

"I want to let the Wild Man out!"

"Come over and give Mommy a kiss."

Mothers are intuitively aware of what would happen if he got the key: they would lose their boys. The possessiveness that mothers typically exercise on sons—not to mention the possessiveness that fathers typically exercise on daughters—can never be underestimated.

The means of getting the key back varies with each man, but suffice it to say that democratic or nonlinear approaches will not carry the day.

One rather stiff young man danced one night for about six hours, vigorously, and in the morning remarked, "I got some of the key back last night."

Another man regained the key when he acted like a whole-hearted Trickster for the first time in his life, remaining fully conscious of the tricksterism. Another man stole the key when he confronted his family and refused to carry any longer the shame for the whole family.

We could spend days talking of how to steal the key in a practical way. The story itself leaves everything open, and simply says, "One day he stole the key, brought it to the Wild Man's cage, and opened the lock. As he did so, he pinched one of his fingers." (That detail will become important in the next part of the story.) The Wild Man is then free at last, and it's clear that he will go back to his own forest, far from "the castle."

WHAT DOES THE BOY DO?

At this point a number of things could happen. If the Wild Man returns to his forest while the boy remains in the castle, the fundamental historical split in the psyche between primitive man and the civilized man would reestablish itself in the boy. The boy, on his side, could mourn the loss of the Wild Man forever. Or he could replace the key under the pillow before his parents got home, then say he knows nothing about the Wild Man's escape. After that subterfuge, he could become a corporate executive, a fundamentalist minister, a tenured professor, someone his parents could be proud of, who "has never seen the Wild Man."

We've all replaced the key many times and lied about it. Then the solitary hunter inside us has to enter into the woods once more with his body dog accompanying him, and then the dog gets pulled down again. We lose a lot of "dogs" that way.

We could also imagine a different scenario. The boy convinces, or imagines he could convince, the Wild Man to stay in the courtyard. If that happened, he and the Wild Man could carry on civilized conversations with each other in the tea garden, and this conversation would go on for years. But the story suggests that Iron John and the boy cannot be united—that is, cannot experience their initial union—in the castle courtyard. It's probably too close to the mother's pillow and the father's book of rules.

We recall that the boy in our story, when he spoke to the Wild Man, told him he didn't know where the key was. That's brave. Some men never address a sentence to the Wild Man.

When the boy opened the cage, the Wild Man started back to his forest. The boy in our story, or the thirty-five-year-old man in our mind—however you want to look at it—now does something marvelous. He speaks to the Wild Man once more and says, "Wait a minute! If my parents come home and find you gone, they will beat me." That sentence makes the heart sink, particularly if we know something about child-rearing practices that have prevailed for a long time in northern Europe.

As Alice Miller reminds us in her book *For Your Own Good*,[1] child psychologists in nineteenth-century Germany warned parents especially about *exuberance*. Exuberance in a child is bad, and at the first sign of it, parents should be severe. Exuberance implies that the wild boy or girl is no longer locked up. Puritan parents in New England often punished children severely if they acted in a restless way during the long church services.

"If they come home and find you gone, they will beat me."

The Wild Man says, in effect, "That's good thinking. You'd better come with me."

So the Wild Man lifts the boy up on his shoulders and together they go off into the woods. That's decisive. We should all be so lucky.

As the boy leaves for the forest, he has to overcome, at least for the moment, his fear of wildness, irrationality, hairiness, intuition, emotion, the body, and nature. Iron John is not as primitive as the boy imagines, but the boy—or the mind—doesn't know that yet.

Still, the clean break with the mother and father, which the old initiators call for, now has taken place. Iron John says to the boy, "You'll never see your mother and father again. But I have treasures, more than you'll ever need." So that is that.

GOING OFF ON THE WILD MAN'S SHOULDERS

The moment the boy leaves with Iron John is the moment in ancient Greek life when the priest of Dionysus accepted a young man as a student, or the moment in Eskimo life today when the shaman, sometimes entirely covered with the fur of wild animals, and wearing wolverine claws and snake vertebrae around his neck, and a bear-head cap, appears in the village and takes a boy away for spirit instruction.

In our culture there is no such moment. The boys in our culture have a continuing need for initiation into male spirit, but old men in general don't offer it. The priest sometimes tries, but he is too much a part of the corporate village these days.

Among the Hopis and other native Americans of the Southwest, the old men take the boy away at the age of twelve and bring him *down* into the all-male area of the kiva. He stays *down* there for six weeks, and does not see his mother again for a year and a half.

The fault of the nuclear family today isn't so much that it's crazy and full of double binds (that's true in communes and corporate offices too—in fact, in any group). The fault is that the old men outside the nuclear family no longer offer an effective way for the son to break his link with his parents without doing harm to himself.

The ancient societies believed that a boy becomes a man only through ritual and effort—only through the "active intervention of the older men."

It's becoming clear to us that manhood doesn't happen by itself; it doesn't happen just because we eat Wheaties. The active intervention of the older men means that older men welcome the younger man into the ancient, mythologized, instinctive male world.

One of the best stories I've heard about this kind of welcoming is one that takes place each year among the Kikuyu in Africa. When a boy is old enough for initiation, he is taken away from his mother and brought to a special place the men have set up some distance from the village. He fasts for three days. The third night he finds himself sitting in a circle around the fire with the older men. He is hungry, thirsty, alert, and terrified. One of the older men takes up a knife, opens a vein in his own arm, and lets a little of his blood flow into a gourd or bowl. Each older man in the circle opens his arm with the same knife, as the bowl goes around, and lets some blood flow in. When the bowl arrives at the young man, he is invited to take nourishment from it.

In this ritual the boy learns a number of things. He learns that nourishment does not come only from his mother, but also from men. And he learns that the knife can be used for many purposes besides wounding others. Can he have any doubt now that he is welcome among the other males?

Once that welcoming has been done, the older men teach him the myths, stories, and songs that embody distinctively male values: I mean not competitive values only, but spiritual values. Once these "moistening" myths are learned, the myths themselves lead the young male far beyond his personal father and into the moistness of the swampy fathers who stretch back century after century.

In the absence of old men's labor consciously done, what happens? Initiation of Western men has continued for some time in an altered form even after fanatics destroyed the Greek initiatory schools. During the nineteenth century, grandfathers and uncles lived in the house, and older men mingled a great deal. Through hunting parties, in work that men did together in farms and cottages, and through local sports, older men spent much time with younger men and brought knowledge of male spirit and soul to them.

Wordsworth, in the beginning of "The Excursion,"[2] describes the old man who sat day after day under a tree and befriended Wordsworth when he was a boy:

He loved me; from a swarm of rosy boys
Singled me out, as he in sport would say,
For my grave looks, too thoughtful for my years.
As I grew up, it was my best delight
To be his chosen comrade. Many a time
On holidays, we wandered through the woods . . .

Much of that chance or incidental mingling has ended. Men's clubs and societies have steadily disappeared. Grandfathers live in Phoenix or the old people's home, and many boys experience only the companionship of other boys their age who, from the point of view of the old initiators, know nothing at all.

During the sixties, some young men drew strength from women who in turn had received some of their strength from the women's movement. One could say that many young men in the sixties tried to accept initiation from women. But only men can initiate men, as only women can initiate women. Women can change the embryo to a boy, but only men can change the boy to a man. Initiators say that boys need a second birth, this time a birth from men.

Keith Thompson, in one of his essays, described himself at twenty as a typical young man "initiated" by women. His parents divorced when Keith was about twelve, and he lived with his mother while his father moved into an apartment nearby.

Throughout high school Keith was closer to women than to other men, and that situation continued into college years, when his main friends were feminists whom he described as marvelous, knowledgeable, and generous, and from whom he learned an enormous amount. He then took a job in Ohio state politics, working with women and alert to the concerns of women.

About that time he had a dream. He and a clan of she-wolves were running in the forest. Wolves suggested to him primarily independence and vigor. The clan of wolves moved fast through the forest, in formation, and eventually they all arrived at a riverbank. Each she-wolf looked into the water and saw her own face there. But when Keith looked in the water, he saw no face at all.

Dreams are subtle and complicated, and it is reckless to draw any rapid conclusion. The last image, however, suggests a disturbing idea. When women, even women with the best intentions, bring up a boy alone, he may in some way have no male face, or he may have no face at all.

The old men initiators, by contrast, conveyed to boys some assurance that is invisible and nonverbal; it helped the boys to see their genuine face or being.

So what can be done? Thousands and thousands of women, being single parents, are raising boys with no adult man in the house. The difficulties inherent in that situation came up one day in Evanston when I was giving a talk on initiation of men to a group made up mostly of women.

Women who were raising sons alone were extremely alert to the dangers of no male model. One woman declared that she realized about the time her son got to high-school age that he needed more hardness than she could naturally give. But, she said, if she made herself harder to meet that need, she would lose touch with her own femininity. I mentioned the classic solution in many traditional cultures, which is to send the boy to his father when he is twelve. Several women said flatly, "No, men aren't nurturing; they wouldn't take care of him." Many men, however—and I am one of them—have found inside an ability to nurture that didn't appear until it was called for.

Even when a father is living in the house there still may be a strong covert bond between mother and son to evict the father, which amounts to a conspiracy, and conspiracies are difficult to break. One woman with two sons had enjoyed going each year to a convention in San Francisco with her husband, the boys being left at home. But one spring, having just returned from a women's retreat, she felt like being private and said to her husband: "Why don't you take the boys this year?" So the father did.

The boys, around ten and twelve, had never, as it turned out, experienced their father's company without the mother's presence. After that experience, they asked for more time with their dad.

When the convention time rolled around the following spring, the mother once more decided on privacy, and the boys once more went off with their father. The moment they arrived back home, the mother happened to be standing in the kitchen with her back to the door, and the older of the two boys walked over and put his arms around her from the back. Without even intending it, her body reacted explosively, and the boy flew across the room and bounced off the wall. When he picked himself up, she said, their relationship had changed. Something irrevocable had happened. She was glad about the change, and the boy seemed surprised and a little relieved that he apparently wasn't needed by her in the old way.

This story suggests that the work of separation can be done even if the old man initiators do not create the break. The mother can make the break herself. We see that it requires a great deal of intensity, and we notice that it was the woman's body somehow, not her mind, that accomplished the labor.

Another woman told a story in which the mother-son conspiracy was broken from the boy's side. She was the single parent of a son and two daughters, and the girls were doing well but the boy was not. At fourteen, the boy went to live with his father, but he stayed only a month or so and then came back. When he returned, the mother realized that three women in the house amounted to an overbalance of feminine energy for the son, but what could she do? A week or two went by. One night she said to her son, "John, it's time to come to dinner." She touched him on the arm and *he* exploded and *she* flew against the wall—the same sort of explosion as in the earlier story. We notice no intent of abuse either time, and no evidence that the event was repeated. In each case the psyche or body knew what the mind didn't. When the mother picked herself off the floor, she said, "It's time for you to go back to your father," and the boy said, "You're right."

The traditional initiation break clearly is preferable, and side-steps the violence. But all over the country now one sees hulking sons acting ugly in the kitchen and talking rudely to their mothers, and I think it's an attempt to make themselves unattractive. If the old men haven't done their work to interrupt the mother-son unity, what else can the boys do to extricate themselves but to talk ugly? It's quite unconscious and there's no elegance in it at all.

A clean break from the mother is crucial, but it's simply not happening. This doesn't mean that the women are doing something wrong: I think the problem is more that the older men are not really doing their job.

The traditional way of raising sons, which lasted for thousands and thousands of years, amounted to fathers and sons living in close—murderously close—proximity, while the father taught the son a trade: perhaps farming or carpentry or blacksmithing or tailoring. As I've suggested elsewhere, the love unit most damaged by the Industrial Revolution has been the father-son bond.

There's no sense in idealizing preindustrial culture, yet we know that today many fathers now work thirty or fifty miles from the house, and by the time they return at night the children are often in bed, and they themselves are too tired to do active fathering.

The Industrial Revolution, in its need for office and factory workers, pulled fathers away

Men need to make a parallel connection with the harsh Dionysus energy that the Hindus call Kala. Our story says that the first step is to find the Wild Man lying at the bottom of the pond. Some men are able to descend to that place through accumulated grief. However, connecting with this Kala energy will have the effect also of meeting that same energy in women. If men don't do that, they won't survive.

Men are suffering right now—young men especially. Now that so many men have gotten in touch with their grief, their longing for father and mentor connections, we are more ready to start seeing the Wild Man and to look again at initiation. But I feel very hopeful.

At this point, many things can happen.

NOTES

1. Alice Miller, *For Your Own Good* (New York: Farrar, Straus & Giroux, 1983).

2. William Wordsworth, *The Excursion*, lines 60–65.

3. D. H. Lawrence, *The Portable D. H. Lawrence*, ed. Diana Trilling (New York: Viking Penguin, 1955), p. 623.

4. D. H. Lawrence, *Sons and Lovers* (New York: Viking Penguin, 1958).

5. "Finding the Father," from Robert Bly, *Selected Poems* (New York: Harper & Row, 1986), p. 132.

6. Alexander Mitscherlich, *Society Without the Father* (London: Tavistock, 1969).

7. "A Meditation on Philosophy," from Bly, *Selected Poems*, p. 162.